Management of Child Development Centers

8

EDITION

Management of Child Development Centers

Patricia F. Hearron
Appalachian State University

Verna Hildebrand
Emerita, Michigan State University

Boston   Columbus   Indianapolis   New York   San Francisco   Upper Saddle River
Amsterdam   Cape Town   Dubai   London   Madrid   Milan   Munich   Paris   Montreal   Toronto
Delhi   Mexico City   São Paulo   Sydney   Hong Kong   Seoul   Singapore   Taipei   Tokyo

Vice President and Editorial Director: Jeffery W. Johnston
Senior Acquisitions Editor: Julie Peters
Editorial Assistant: Andrea Hall
Vice President, Director of Marketing: Margaret Waples
Senior Marketing Manager: Krista Clark
Production Project Manager: Jennifer Gessner
Procurement Specialist: Michelle Klein
Senior Art Director: Jayne Conte
Cover Designer: Suzanne Behnke

Cover Photo: © Rob Hainer, Shutterstock
Media Project Manager: Noelle Chun
Full-Service Project Management:
  Peggy Kellar, Aptara®, Inc.
Composition: Aptara®, Inc.
Printer/Binder: LSC Communications
Cover Printer: LSC Communications
Text Font: Palatino

Credits and acknowledgments for material borrowed from other sources and reproduced, with permission, in this textbook appear on the appropriate page within the text.

Every effort has been made to provide accurate and current Internet information in this book. However, the Internet and information posted on it are constantly changing, so it is inevitable that some of the Internet addresses listed in this textbook will change.

Library of Congress Cataloging-in-Publication Data
Hearron, Patricia F.,
  Management of child development centers / Patricia F. Hearron,
Appalachian State University, Verna Hildebrand, emerita, Michigan State
University.—Eighth edition.
    pages cm
  Includes bibliographical references and index.
  ISBN 978-0-13-357118-9—ISBN 0-13-357118-1 1. Nursery
schools—United States—Administration. 2. Day care centers—United
States—Administration. 3. Early childhood education—United States.
I. Hildebrand, Verna.   II. Title.
LB2822.7.H55 2015
372.21—dc23   2014000892

10

ISBN 13: 978-0-13-357118-9
ISBN 10:   0-13-357118-1

DEDICATION

We dedicate Management of Child Development Centers *to all the young children who share our small spaceship Earth, to the families and caregivers who nurture them, and to the managers of child development centers whose commitment to high-quality programs helps make that nurturing possible.*

PREFACE

This edition of *Management of Child Development Centers*, like those that preceded it, is based on the premise that high-quality programs for young children are an essential support for families—they are part of the family ecosystem. Managers of those programs must understand that ecosystem and realize that neither the family nor the child development program is an island: Each affects and is affected by the other, as well as by countless forces within the community and society at large.

Part 1 of this textbook provides an overview of the demographic and theoretical context within which child development programs operate. Chapters 4 through 15 (Part 2 of the text) address core competencies. Each chapter in Part 2 focuses on one of the 12 core competencies that are derived from a review of current literature in the field and are aligned with National Association for the Education of Young Children (NAEYC) accreditation criteria: personal and professional self-awareness; organizational, fiscal, and personnel management; human relations; facilities management; health and safety; food service; educational programming; family support; marketing and public relations; assessment and evaluation.

NEW TO THIS EDITION

The most obvious change to this edition of *Management of Child Development Centers* is the fact that it is now available as an eText—an innovation that makes possible other new features, including:

- Links to short **video clips** to illustrate or reinforce concepts presented within the text.
- Pop-up **glossary** definitions for key terms in each chapter.
- An **interactive** version of the **budget spreadsheet** in Chapter 6, which allows students to see what happens when they manipulate various components.

In addition to updated research throughout, other changes include:

- Clearly stated **learning outcomes** at the beginning of each chapter, which are aligned with questions for review at the end to help focus the student's reading.
- A new **Leadership Lens** feature in each chapter, integrating the concept of leadership throughout the text rather than addressing it in a separate chapter.
- A new feature, **Decisions, Decisions . . . ? Using an Ethical Framework,** in each of the chapters in Part 2 prompts students to apply concepts from the NAEYC Code of Ethical Conduct to determine a manager's best course of action.
- A new section on the use of **social media** for marketing in Chapter 14.

WHAT HAS NOT CHANGED

The text continues to present a synthesis of current information in clear, reader-friendly language. Concepts and terminology are illustrated with examples drawn from the authors' experience, as well as charts, graphs, and photographs. In addition, the text includes a variety of practical tools, such as menu planning and evaluation forms and links to relevant websites. Each chapter contains the following elements to facilitate the instructor's class planning and student learning:

- *Decisions, Decisions . . . ?* features ask the students to reflect on topics discussed in the chapters and apply the information to real-life situations.

- *Professional Portfolio* assignments help students create products that can be included in a portfolio to demonstrate their mastery of the core competencies. At least one portfolio assignment in each chapter incorporates the use of technology (e.g., internet-based research, desktop publishing software), thus supporting the integration of these skills within the core competencies.

- *Resources for Further Study* provide students and instructors with a convenient list of up-to-date resources, in print as well as online, for a deeper investigation of the topics discussed in each chapter.

- A *Technology Toolkit* in each chapter in Part 2 provides specific suggestions for using computers, digital photography, and Internet resources to help students achieve NAEYC Competency 10 (Technology) as they address other core competencies.

- Useful forms and tools include self-assessments for students, online versions of a needs assessment and board survey, a list of commercially available management software, personnel forms, a playground maintenance checklist and classroom floor plans, emergency medical form, staff and program evaluation forms, and lists of published instruments for assessing children and evaluating programs.

- Tables, charts, and illustrations clarify key concepts, for example, start-up versus ongoing expenses in Chapter 6, and assessment/evaluation cycle and concept of authentic assessment in Chapter 15.

- Engaging chapter-opening vignettes bring key concepts to life.

SUPPLEMENTS

This book is accompanied by an Instructor's Resource Manual, Test Bank, PowerPoint® Slides, and TestGen. Instructors can download instructor resources by going to www.pearsonhighered.com/educator. After registering, enter the author, title, or ISBN and select this textbook. Click on the "Resources" tab to view and download instructor resources.

AUDIENCE FOR THIS TEXT

This text is suitable for use in a variety of settings: in formal classes in 2- or 4-year college programs, in child development associate (CDA) training or in-service programs for practicing early childhood professionals, and as an independent study tool by individuals contemplating a move from classroom teacher or caregiver to center manager.

    Management of Child Development Centers, Eighth Edition, is the product of the authors' combined experience over decades of working with children and their families, with young people anticipating a career in the early childhood profession, and with practicing professionals at many levels. Previous editions have been field-tested in university classrooms, and the present edition incorporates much of what has been learned during that process. Managers who apply this information will be well positioned to meet the growing demand for high-quality programs that are capable of serving all children.

ACKNOWLEDGMENTS

We are indebted to the pioneering work of the late Dr. Beatrice Paolucci in the area of management and decision making, and to the students (many of whom are now our colleagues) whose questions and insights provided inspiration for our work. We are grateful to the early childhood educators who have welcomed us into their centers and classrooms over the years, to the children in those classrooms, and to their families. Special thanks are due to Andrea Anderson, director; Dr. Cindy McGaha, curriculum coordinator; and the staff members, children, and families at Lucy Brock Child Development Laboratory of Appalachian State University, who collaborated in the creation of many of the video clips used in this text.

We appreciate the guidance of our forward thinking editor, Julie Peters, who has encouraged and shepherded the book's adaptation to the needs of 21st-century learners. We gratefully acknowledge the skillful assistance of Peggy Kellar, project manager and Marianne L'Abbate, copy editor. We are indebted to Teri M. Brannum, North Central State College; Candace L. Lindemer, Lakeland Community College; Tenisha Powell, Winthrop University; Leanne Snider, University of Tennessee at Martin; and Carol Willis, Mount Olive College, for the many helpful suggestions in their thoughtful reviews of the previous edition.

BRIEF CONTENTS

CONTENTS

Management of Child Development Centers

PART

1

INTRODUCTION

CHAPTER

Managing Children's Centers in the 21st Century

LEARNING OUTCOMES

After studying this chapter you should be able to

- Define key terms, including *program administrator*, *leadership*, *management*, *advocacy*, *fertility rates*, and *child development center*.
- List and explain the core competencies required for directors of child development programs.
- Identify and describe the stages of professional development for early childhood program administrators or leaders.
- Discuss population trends that influence the field of early care and education.

Tanya felt a pleasant sense of anticipation when she turned off the alarm on Monday morning. She was looking forward to her first day on the job as assistant director at Rainbow Place, the child development program where she had worked for the past several years as a teacher in a classroom for 3- to 5-year-olds. She had learned a lot about how young children learn and develop from her on-the-job experience, and she had added to that knowledge by taking courses to complete her degree in early childhood education. She applied for the assistant director position because she felt ready for a new challenge. She knew that directing a program required knowledge and skill in another field—management. She looked forward to learning these things under the mentorship of Rainbow Center's director, Jeralyn Davis, and dreamed of becoming a director herself one day.

Have you always dreamed of owning and managing a school for young children? What do you need to know to perform the manager's role adequately and efficiently? Will your experience as a successful teacher make a difference in your ability to manage a center? If you have a master's of business administration (MBA) degree yet have never been a teacher, could you manage a group of classrooms in a school or center? Is experience as a teacher or child-care provider adequate preparation to take on the role of program manager? Many would argue that such experience is necessary but not sufficient, that managers need another type of specialized knowledge as well. This belief is not uniformly reflected in state licensing requirements, however. As of 2007, all but 8 states required program directors to have training in early childhood education prior to taking the job, while only 11 required preservice training in administration. Some states required in-service rather than preservice training, and a mere 3 required both.

DEFINING TERMS

This text focuses on management as applied in child development centers. Agreeing on definitions of key terms and concepts is essential. The National Association for the Education of Young Children (NAEYC) defines a **program administrator** as "the individual responsible for planning, implementing, and evaluating a child care, preschool or kindergarten program," a role that encompasses both leadership and management functions (2007a).

Although **leadership** is sometimes considered synonymous with management, NAEYC defines it as relating "to the broad plan of helping an organization clarify and affirm values, set [broad] goals, articulate a vision, and chart a course of action to achieve that mission." **Management**, then, refers to the day-to-day work required to fulfill that mission and make the vision a reality. It involves the processes of (a) setting specific goals, (b) allocating human and material resources judiciously for achieving the goals, (c) carrying out the work or action required to achieve the goals, (d) monitoring the outcome or product of the work or action based on established standards, and (e) making necessary adjustments or improvements to ensure that performance reaches or exceeds goals. Leadership focuses on influencing and inspiring people to achieve, to make a difference for the better, while management focuses on making sure the job gets done according to standards. **Advocacy** is another term

The program administrator is responsible for planning, implementing, and evaluating the child development program.

that has much in common with leadership. An advocate is someone who speaks or acts on behalf of someone or some cause. Figure 1.1 illustrates the interrelated nature of the three roles: manager, leader, and advocate.

A **child development center** is a facility that provides out-of-home education and care for young children in groups, a service that supplements the education and care parents give their child. The term encompasses programs that are full- or part-day and profit or nonprofit, and programs known as preschools, child-care centers, kindergartens, prekindergartens, cooperatives, Head Start, or variations of any of these.

Though the main focus of this text is on center- or school-based programs, many of the principles discussed are applicable to home-based family child-care providers. The definition of child development centers incorporates the concepts of education and care and asserts that the two are inextricably linked. A growing body of research, corroborated by the experience of parents and early childhood professionals, indicates that young children learn

FIGURE 1.1 Interrelated roles: manager, leader, advocate.

best in the context of a secure environment. Thus, the caregiving that creates that secure environment—regardless of whether that environment is in a family child-care home or large public school building—is the foundation on which efforts to educate young children must be based.

Management is a science; some individuals spend their careers perfecting this science. Management has a background of theory, research, experience, applications, and knowledge that must be brought together by any individual who assumes the managerial role in an enterprise. Management of a center is complex—more complex than operating a single entity such as a home or a classroom. Although many individuals are likely to have a stake in the outcome of a decision or action, the manager has the final responsibility for making decisions.

CORE COMPETENCIES FOR DIRECTORS

Historically, managers of child development programs have been promoted from the ranks of teachers, with little attention paid to the specific knowledge and competencies needed in their new role. Although the knowledge of developmentally appropriate practices is certainly essential to running a program for children, managers must know much more if they are to be successful. State requirements have been slow to recognize this, however. While 28 states issue director or administrator credentials, for most it is a voluntary process. Only four states (Delaware, Indiana, New Jersey, and Pennsylvania) require a college degree, and only five (California, Colorado, Florida, New Hampshire, and Texas) require coursework in business or administration (McCormick Center for Early Childhood Leadership, 2012; Bloom, Jackson, Talan, & Kelton, 2013).

Child development programs are support systems for families, providing peace of mind for working parents and emotional security for children.

Various authors have tackled the job of enumerating and categorizing the skills and knowledge required by competent directors, and although each list varies slightly from the others, they all agree on certain basics or core competencies. Statements of those core competencies have been fine-tuned and elaborated on over the years. An early example, put forward by Travis and Perreault in 1981, included organizational management, program planning and implementation (including curriculum, recruitment, nutrition, family services, and parent involvement), personnel management and staff development, community and public relations, financial management, evaluation, and advocacy. The list was refined over the next decades by Bonnie and Roger Neugebauer (1998), Paula Jorde Bloom (1999), and Gwen Morgan (2000). The most recent list, put forward by the National Association for the Education of Young Children (2007b), includes all of these areas and adds several within two broad categories: management (adding personal and professional self-awareness, oral and written communication, and technology) and early childhood (adding child observation and assessment, children with special needs, and professionalism).

This text addresses the knowledge and skill required to manage all aspects of a program, beginning with self-awareness, and including the nuts and bolts of maintaining a building, obtaining a license, and paying the bills. Also included are the people-oriented skills involved in working with staff, families, and communities; implementing curriculum; and exercising leadership. If you are reading this text as part of a degree program in child development or early education at a 2- or 4-year college, some chapters will serve as a review, or perhaps as a taste of things to come. You will probably study topics such as developmental theories, curriculum, assessment, nutrition, and partnering with families in much greater depth than what is possible in a single chapter. If you are studying independently, we hope that you will take advantage of the many resources for further study offered throughout the text to broaden your knowledge. Managing a child development program is a complex endeavor, and even the most seasoned directors must continually hone their knowledge and skills to manage such a program effectively. As you watch this video, notice the way the director touches base with teachers and parents at the beginning of her day. How do you think this helps her manage her program effectively?

? DECISIONS, DECISIONS . . .

What skills and knowledge do you think are necessary for being an effective manager? Draw up your own list and compare it with those of your classmates.

The authors of this text propose the following slate:

1. *Reflective management based on personal and professional self-awareness* Effective managers strive to know their own strengths and acknowledge their weaknesses so that they can capitalize on the former and compensate for the latter. They have a strong commitment to ethical practice, and they are informed about issues that influence the early childhood profession as a whole. They continually reflect on what they learn through experience, as well as through formal study, and integrate both types of knowledge in their practice.

2. *Organizational management* Child development programs are complex systems of interrelated parts. The manager's role is to make the parts work together smoothly. Child development programs are, in turn, part of the larger social system. Managers guide their programs' interactions with that system. They are not

lawyers, but they must have a working knowledge of the many regulatory systems governing the operation of early childhood facilities: State licensing regulations, federal food program requirements, fire safety and sanitation codes, and laws governing fair employment practices are just a few examples. Perhaps more important, managers must have a sense of the reasons for the regulations and the ability to operate programs within those constraints.

3. *Fiscal management*   No program can survive unless its manager uses its financial resources wisely. This includes creating a realistic budget, monitoring expenses to align with the budget, and knowing when to make appropriate adjustments. Fiscal management also includes finding ways to increase resources, perhaps through fund-raising or grant writing. The other side of the coin, of course, is finding ways, such as buying supplies in bulk, to economize without sacrificing quality.

4. *Personnel management*   Child development facilities are labor-intensive operations. Personnel costs comprise the bulk of the expenditures, and it is important that these dollars be invested wisely. This means that managers must learn how to recruit and hire employees with the greatest potential. But their job doesn't end there. Retaining those employees is a constant challenge in a profession with an annual turnover rate of about 40 percent. In addition to attracting and keeping good employees, managers must monitor their performance, provide feedback as needed, terminate when necessary, and create a staff development plan to build on the talents those employees bring to the job.

5. *Human relations*   An essential component of the manager's role is establishing and maintaining productive relationships with a variety of stakeholders: Governing board members, families of enrolled children, employees, and representatives of businesses or community agencies are only a few examples. In addition to the personnel functions described previously, managers must find ways to encourage teamwork and motivate their staff members. This work requires a basic knowledge of group dynamics, communication styles, and conflict resolution techniques.

6. *Facilities management*   In addition to putting together a smoothly functioning team of teachers and support staff, the manager is responsible for creating the spaces that support the day-to-day work of that team. This means designing spaces that meet regulatory requirements as well as professional standards—spaces that incorporate sound principles of child development and environmental psychology. It means implementing those designs by selecting the best equipment a program can afford and arranging it appropriately.

7. *Managing health and safety issues*   Keeping children safe and healthy is a fundamental requirement of any child development facility. The manager's job is to establish policies and procedures that accomplish this goal and then to see that they are carried out. Examples include establishing policies requiring each child entering the program to be fully immunized against communicable disease and teaching staff to follow safe diapering procedures. State and local regulations provide a framework for this task.

8. *Managing food service*   Meeting children's nutritional needs is another fundamental requirement. State licensing authorities provide basic guidelines, and the U.S. Department of Agriculture spells out requirements for programs receiving federal food subsidies. Managers must make sure that menus comply with these standards and that food is handled in a safe and sanitary manner from the point of purchase to when it is served to the children. They must also think about how their program's meals reflect the cultures of the families they serve and what those meals contribute to the program's curriculum.

9. *Educational programming*   Because many managers arrive at their positions after working as teachers in child development programs, this may be the area that feels most familiar and therefore comfortable for them. Nevertheless, managing a facility's educational program requires a broader perspective than that of a classroom teacher. It's one thing to carry out a particular curriculum yourself, and another to create conditions that support others in doing that job. Managers need a working knowledge of the various curriculum models so that they can select and implement an appropriate choice. Developmentally appropriate assessment strategies are crucial, particularly in light of the current emphasis on accountability reflected in legislation (the No Child Left Behind Act) and a growing movement to establish state standards for early childhood educational outcomes. The inclusion of children with disabilities and increasing numbers of English-language learners are both issues that concern managers.

10. *Family engagement*   A high-quality program for young children reflects the understanding that children do not exist in a vacuum. Serving children means serving families, and this requires an understanding of how family systems work and an appreciation for diverse parenting styles. It means establishing the type of open communication that helps the center form partnerships with parents. It means knowing enough about the community to help families access the resources needed to promote family wellness.

11. *Marketing and public relations*   No matter how high the quality of a particular program, it will not survive without continually enrolling new families. The manager develops a pool of potential clients by making sure that the community is aware of the program and, just as important, that it appreciates the program's high quality. (This may require educating the public about what constitutes high quality in children's programs.) Merely attracting potential clients is not sufficient, however. The program must offer services that meet the specific needs of its clients, and it is the manager's job to fine-tune this match.

12. *Assessment and evaluation*   The next step in the management process is to determine how well an organization has met its objectives. Then, of course, the cycle begins again, adjusting practices to meet objectives more effectively or setting new (perhaps higher) goals for the organization.

LEADERSHIP LENS

You don't have to be in a managerial position to be a leader or an advocate. In fact, you may have already served in one of these roles in other areas of your life—as an officer of a school club, perhaps, or a summer camp counselor. Perhaps you've emailed your state legislator to oppose an increase in college tuition, or tried to persuade your church to open a child-care center. If so, you've had a taste of advocacy. We hope that you will be inspired to continue (or assume) the roles of advocate and leader from the beginning of your early childhood career. We recognize that, as a new director, you will undoubtedly need time to master the rudiments of management, but we hope you keep a larger purpose in mind as you handle the day-to-day tasks. Ultimately your competence as a manager will enhance—and be enhanced by—your effectiveness as a leader and advocate.

Think about the leaders you followed as a child, as a student, and as an adult. What characteristics did they possess? Why were those leaders important in your life? Now look at yourself as a potential leader. What talents do you bring to the leader's role in a child development program? If you have managed a classroom, you certainly have had some experience planning, organizing, and monitoring. The classroom represents a microcosm of the entire program, and many of the skills you honed there can be applied to the director's role. We invite you to view each of the management functions or competencies discussed in the following chapters through a "leadership lens," looking for ways to see beyond keeping your program in operation toward a vision of what it might become, to make a difference in the world beyond your center.

13. *Leadership and advocacy*   Managers functioning at the highest level of professional development can see beyond the day-to-day concerns of keeping their facility afloat. They have a vision of where they want their organization to go and the ability to marshal all the resources at their command to attain that vision. They strive to influence spheres beyond their own organization, the profession at large, and the well-being of children in general.

Would you like being a manager? How will you know? Can someone else tell you whether you would like being a manager? What experience have you had that could make you a good manager? How many managers have you worked for? Were these "good" managers? What makes a manager good? What tasks performed by a manager are especially enjoyable? What tasks are difficult? Perhaps you have a dream of opening your own child development center someday. Figure 1.2 gives an overview of the steps involved in making that dream a reality. Each step draws on the knowledge and skills that you can begin to build in your study of this text.

Checklist for Starting a New Child-Care Center

_____ Determine the need for child care in your community. (Are there too few available slots or is there an available niche: e.g., existing programs are not high-quality or do not serve particular ages or at particular hours?)

_____ Become thoroughly familiar with licensing regulations and procedures for obtaining a license. (Attend an orientation session offered by your licensing agency or local child care resource and referral agency.)

_____ Define your vision; create initial draft of program philosophy and policy handbooks.

_____ Develop preliminary budget to determine financing needed.

    _____ Determine size of facility needed based on potential enrollment suggested by needs assessment.

    _____ Check with local authorities regarding zoning and building codes.

    _____ Locate property, meet with architect, and have plans approved by licensing, fire, sanitation authorities before beginning construction.   **OR**   _____ Locate a suitable facility, apply for licensure, and arrange for needed inspections (fire, sanitation, etc.).

    _____ Depending on size of proposed center, hire director and/or teacher to assist with planning environment and equipment lists.

    _____ Design outdoor environment with plan for landscaping and construction needed prior to opening as well as improvements to be phased in each year as funds permit.

    _____ Develop list of equipment and materials to be purchased prior to opening as well as what will be added each year as program becomes established.

_____ Construct or renovate building and outdoor play area to meet codes; arrange for any necessary re-inspections.

_____ Arrange for insurance coverage.

_____ Revise budget as needed to reflect actual costs.

_____ Finalize draft policies, parent handbook, employee handbook.

_____ Establish projected opening date; begin advertising and accepting enrollments.

_____ Arrange for utilities hook-up by opening date.

_____ Recruit and hire essential staff to assist with final planning and preparation.

_____ Order essential equipment and materials (with staff input if feasible).

_____ Recruit and hire any needed additional staff.

_____ Hold open house for families and staff to get acquainted.

FIGURE 1.2   Checklist for starting a new child-care center.

? DECISIONS, DECISIONS . . .

What is your image of what a manager of a child development program does? What parts of the job do you think you would enjoy? What parts do you think you would find difficult? Does it take a certain type of personality to do well in the manager's role?

STAGES OF PROFESSIONAL DEVELOPMENT

Where are you on your timeline of professional development? Management of a school or center can give your professional life new challenges after you have had a number of years of successful experiences in teaching. Or you may feel that you need more teaching experience before taking on a managerial role. As you can see in Figure 1.3, VanderVen (1999, pp. 196–197) identifies five stages in the development of early childhood administrators or leaders:

1. *Awareness*   As a newcomer to the profession, you might be so focused on the immediate concerns of your day-to-day interactions with children and families that you take little notice of the managerial work that makes it possible for you to do your job. Ironically, this is particularly true if you are fortunate enough to work with an effective manager. If that is not the case, you will most likely become aware of managerial tasks when they are not done or are done poorly and you experience the results. According to VanderVen, this managerial work is "ego alien" for you at this phase of your career: It just does not fit in with your image of yourself and your role.

2. *Induction*   As noted previously, your own dissatisfaction with the way things are done in your organization might be the catalyst that sparks a desire in you to change things. Whatever the reason, you are now ready to learn more about a new role.

3. *Competency*   Perhaps you are thrust into your new role as a consequence of the high rate of employee turnover in the field. Perhaps a promotion to management level is part of a carefully orchestrated staff development plan. Regardless of the route taken, as a new manager, you have a lot to learn—through classes or independent study, supervised practice, and the inevitable trial and error that come with on-the-job experience. Eventually, your hard work will pay off in a rewarding feeling of competency, a deep-seated knowledge that you can do this job.

4. *Proficiency*   Do you remember learning to ride a bicycle? You probably gripped the handlebars with all your might as you wobbled down the sidewalk. Eventually, you got the feel of it and finally reached a stage where you could hop on your bicycle and take off with your mind on where you wanted to go instead of worrying about how or whether you would get there. Perhaps you even tried more complex maneuvers with your bike, riding "no hands," for example. You had reached the stage of proficiency in bicycle navigation. Seasoned child development administrators experience a similar transition. They find it takes less conscious effort to accomplish tasks that were originally very challenging (e.g., recruiting and hiring a new staff member) and they move on to more complex tasks (e.g., developing a long-range staff development plan to help retain the most qualified staff).

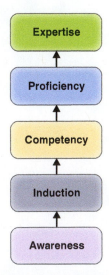

FIGURE 1.3 Stages in the development of an early childhood administrator or leader.

5. *Expertise*   You have arrived at this level and become an "expert" in your field when you can add creativity and innovation to all earlier accomplishments. At this point, you may be ready to move beyond managing one early childhood organization and assume a leadership role in your chosen profession.

> **? DECISIONS, DECISIONS . . .**
>
> Imagine yourself 5 or 10 years from now. Where would you like to be working? What would you like to be doing? Where do you think you will be in VanderVen's sequence of administrative development? What steps can you take now to achieve those dreams?

Some people are pressed into the management role with little or no preparation when a manager leaves suddenly and they must look for quick management courses and advice. Whether you are already a manager, expect to become a manager soon, or have management as a future goal, learning about the intricacies of child development center management can add a new dimension to your professional career. Knowledge of managerial principles can make you more appreciative and supportive of managers with whom you work, even when you are happy that the buck still stops at their desk.

CHILD CARE IN CONTEXT

Families throughout the world have the primary responsibility for nurturing children. Nurturing may be done by the natural or adoptive parent or parents, extended family systems, or institutions. Families often decide to supplement the care and education they can give with assistance from institutions outside the family. Historical, cultural, political, and economic factors within each society affect their decisions, but one thing is clear: More children around the world are spending time in out-of-home care than ever before. At the same time, neuroscience research is confirming that children need loving relationships and safe, secure, stimulating environments if they are to reach their potential. Taken together, these two facts suggest an increasing responsibility for societies to support families in caring for their children and to ensure that high-quality services are available when that care occurs outside the home.

Understanding the context within which families in today's world are living and rearing their children is essential if we are to effectively manage or administer services such as child development centers or any social service for families. Knowing the current situation and trends in one's field of business is part of effective management. The development of the Internet has made this task much easier. As just one example, the U.S. Census Bureau maintains an extensive website, www.census.gov, where you can obtain information about patterns of childbearing, employment, education, child-care arrangements, and a host of other topics for the nation as a whole, as well as for your particular state and county. Information on local employment trends is needed in addition to data showing a need for children's services. Your local community library, child-care resource and referral agency, or chamber of commerce can help you locate the best source of local and state statistics.

Demand for Child Care

On one hand, the overall U.S. birthrate among women ages 15 to 44 declined by 6 percent between 2007 and 2010, and it reached the lowest point ever recorded in 2011 (63.2

births per 1,000 women), with the largest decline seen in Mexican immigrant women. This decline is attributed to the effects of the economic recession that occurred in 2008 (Livingston & Cohn, 2012). On the other hand, the numbers of children, and the numbers of children in child care, are increasing such that the U.S. Department of Labor predicts a 20 percent to 28 percent increase in job openings for administrators of preschool and child-care programs over the next 10 years (Bureau of Labor Statistics, 2012b).

Between 2000 and 2010, the number of children under 5 in the United States grew by more than 1 million, to a total of 20,201,362 (Howden & Meyer, 2011). Furthermore, the percentage of mothers of children under 6 in the labor force has steadily increased since 1975, when about 40 percent of mothers with children under 6 worked outside the home. In 2011, that number rose to more than 60 percent for mothers with children under 6 as well as those with children under 3 (U.S. Department of Labor, 2012). The percentage of mothers of infants with jobs is only slightly lower (56 percent in 2010) (U.S. Department of Labor, 2011).

Multiple factors probably contributed to women's increased participation in the workforce. On the one hand, married mothers who might have stayed home with their children in an earlier era may have felt pressured to seek paid employment because of a rising cost of living or an economic downturn that eliminated their husbands' jobs. An increasing number of single mothers, divorced or otherwise, have had to work to support themselves and their children. In addition to expanded career opportunities for women, there has been a shift in public attitudes over the past 30 years. When asked in 1977 whether they agreed that men should earn the living while women tended the home, 52 percent of women agreed; in 2008, that percentage had declined to 39 percent. Among men, the change was even more striking: from 74 percent to 42 percent (Galinsky, Aumann, & Bond, 2008, p. 9). As mothers become part of the workforce, they have to find alternate forms of care for their children: relatives, neighbors, or more formal arrangements.

In 2011, organized facilities (i.e., child-care centers, nursery schools, and Head Start programs as opposed to care by relatives or in family child-care homes) provided care for 24 percent of children under 5 years of age, a figure that has held steady for over 10 years. Figure 1.4 compares the distribution of children of working mothers among various forms of child care in selected years from 1985 to 2011. Children of working parents are not the only ones receiving services, however. Nearly half (43 percent) of children whose parents are neither working nor in school are in some form of regular child care. This suggests that families expect programs to provide education and enrichment experiences beyond basic caregiving.

Income, race or ethnicity, and the mother's education level all make a difference in the type of child-care arrangements that families select. Families enrolled in various government antipoverty programs are more likely to rely on relatives, while more affluent families are more likely to use centers or family child-care homes (Adams, Tout, & Zaslow, 2007). A study following more than 10,000 children born in the United States in 2001 found that, at 9 months of age, African American children were more likely to be in nonparental care than White, Hispanic, or Asian children. They were also more likely to be in center-based care (Kreader, Ferguson, & Lawrence, 2005). This pattern was also evident among children ages 3 to 5 in 2005. Children whose mothers hold a bachelor's degree or higher are more than twice as likely to be in center-based care than those whose mothers have less than a high school education (U.S. Department of Education, 2007). Most children whose mothers work full time spend 35 or more hours in care, and many spend time in more than one arrangement each week (U.S. Census Bureau, 2013).

Historically, full-time child care was used primarily by poor families and was considered a last resort for mothers who could not stay home with their children

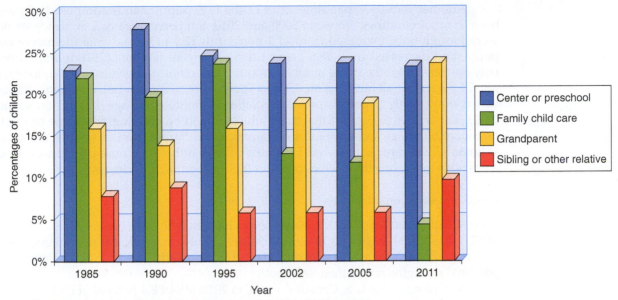

FIGURE 1.4 Types of child care for children under 5, from 1985 to 2011.
Source: U.S. Census Bureau (2005), Who's minding the kids? Child care arrangements: Spring 2005; U.S. Census Bureau (2013), Who's minding the kids? Child care arrangements: Spring 2011; http://www.census.gov/prod/2013pubs/p70-135.pdf

because their income was needed for basic survival. Affluent families sent their children to nursery school for a few hours a week to provide socialization experiences or intellectual enrichment. However, as more educated and moderate- to upper-income mothers entered the workforce, they began seeking full-day child care, expecting the high-quality education associated with nursery schools. This shift has thus contributed not only to an increased market for child care, but also to a demand for improved quality of that care.

Minority and Immigrant Populations

According to the U.S. Census Bureau, July 1, 2011, marked a dramatic shift in the makeup of our nation's population: the first time that minorities comprised more than half (50.4 percent) of all children younger than age 1, an increase of about 1 percent from the previous year. A closer look at birthrate data reveals a trend that suggests this number will continue to grow. In 2010, overall **fertility rates** (the number of children an average woman is predicted to have in her lifetime) for Hispanic women were significantly higher than those for non-Hispanic White women: 2.4 versus 1.8 (Passel, Livingston, & Cohn, 2012).

A rapidly expanding sector of the U.S. population is composed of people born in other countries.

Another rapidly expanding sector of the U.S. population is composed of people born in other countries. Between 2000 and 2010, the percentage of U.S. residents who were foreign-born increased from 11.1 percent to 12.9 percent, while the native-born population decreased from 88.9 percent to 87.1 percent (Patten, 2012). Immigration is only one reason for the rising numbers of racial and ethnic minorities. In 2011, for example, 23 percent of all births in the United States were to foreign-born women, although they comprise only 17 percent of the population of childbearing age (Livingston & Cohn, 2012). These figures suggest that many children will be entering programs where the dominant language and customs are dramatically different from those they experience at home. Child-care facilities will face the challenge of helping those children learn new ways without cutting themselves off from their rich cultural heritages.

Children with Disabilities

Federal legislation supports the inclusion of children who have (or are at risk for developing) disabilities in programs for all children. This means that center managers are challenged to find ways to accommodate diverse needs and to view differences as potential strengths rather than deficits.

According to the U.S. Census Bureau, in 2010, about 8.4 percent of children under the age of 15 had some sort of disability, with half of those being classified as severe. Percentages were lower for children under 3 (2.3 percent) and for children between 3 and 5 (3.6 percent), for whom disability was defined as developmental delay or difficulty moving about. For school-age children, for whom disability includes a wider range of impairments ranging from severe physical impairment to attention deficit hyperactivity disorder (ADHD) and difficulty doing schoolwork, the rate was 12.2 percent. These percentages vary across racial and ethnic groups, with higher rates among African American and Hispanic populations (Brault, 2012). Some disabling conditions, such as Down syndrome, blindness, or cerebral palsy, can be identified at birth or in early infancy, whereas others appear somewhat later. Children with autism or pervasive developmental disorder, for example, may appear to be developing typically until about 18 months, when they begin to withdraw and engage in repetitive behavior (Greenspan & Wieder, 1998, p. 7).

Still other conditions, such as delayed cognitive development or emotional impairment, may emerge as the result of environmental factors such as malnutrition, poverty, or abuse. Thus, when speaking of very young children, it is necessary to consider not only those with disabilities, but also those considered at risk for developmental delays or disabilities, a group estimated to comprise 5 to 15 percent of all infants born in the United States. The mother's health and nutritional status, her behaviors during pregnancy, prenatal care, the child's birth weight and gestational age, and the family's socioeconomic status are all factors that influence the level of risk. Experts and national policy makers recognize that appropriate and timely intervention can help prevent a child considered at risk from actually developing a disability or lessen the severity of a disability resulting from a particular condition (National Early Childhood Technical Assistance Center, 2011).

Poverty and Homelessness

The effects of poverty on children's development have been well documented for decades. Recently, however, neuroscientists at the University of California, Berkeley, have demonstrated those effects in a dramatic way, showing differences in the brain function of low-income children comparable to those found in stroke patients (Sanders, 2008). It makes sense that high-quality child care is one way to prevent, or at least reduce, those effects.

In 2010, more than one in five children in the United States lived in poverty, defined as an income of $22,050 per year for a family of four. This represented an increase of more than 1 million since the previous year and was the highest rate recorded since 2001. For black and Hispanic children, the numbers were more than 50 percent higher (Macartney, 2011). The 1996 Congress passed legislation to reform welfare, putting strict limits on the amount of time any family could receive government financial assistance through a program called Temporary Assistance for Needy Families (TANF). In 2011, the maximum monthly benefits paid for a family of 3 ranged from a low of 11 percent of the poverty guideline in Mississippi to a high of nearly 50 percent in Alaska and New York (Falk, 2013). Although the American Recovery and Reinvestment Act (ARRA) of 2009 increased funding available for TANF as well as several other programs designed to benefit poor families, accessing these programs is a challenge for many families because of factors such as lack of transportation. Consequently, fewer than half the number of eligible families participates in them (Boots, 2010).

The National Center on Family Homelessness reports that 1 of every 45 American children experiences homelessness each year, with the highest incidence occurring in the southern states; 42 percent of homeless children are under the age of 6 (2011). The economic downturn spurred the rate of mortgage foreclosures, and the costs for rental housing outpace earnings. Across the United States, the monthly fair market rent for a two-bedroom apartment is more than twice what a minimum-wage job pays (Children's Defense Fund, 2012, p. 20). In some cities, child-care facilities have been established to provide some measure of stability for young children in this stressful situation.

Conclusion

The task of managing a child development center is complex and evolving. Child development programs must continually grow and change because families are defining and redefining what they need for their children. As a manager, you are on the front line of decision making that can be supportive of families. You can exercise leadership among your staff members, among parents, and within your community and create a high-quality service that meets the needs of children in appropriate ways and helps them grow toward becoming strong, skilled, and healthy citizens of the future.

This chapter has identified the competencies required of effective program directors and the stages of professional development along the path toward achieving that competence. We have discussed population trends, such as family size and women's participation in the labor force, and government policies that affect child development services. In the coming chapters, we will review theories that affect your work as a manager and explore each of the core competencies you will need to succeed in the administrative role.

Questions for Review

1. Define *leadership*. Give one or more examples of leaders in the early childhood field that you have come to know through your own experience or in your reading.

2. Define *management*. How does it differ from *leadership*?

3. Define *child development center*. Give examples from your own community.

4. Based on your own experience or that of your classmates, try to cite examples of how directors in your community have demonstrated each of the 13 required competencies.

5. Describe the stages of professional development for child development administrators. At what stage would you place your own development right now? Explain.

6. Review the information about immigration, poverty, and homelessness presented in this chapter. How do you think these trends might affect a child development program that you direct?

Professional Portfolio

Begin creating a professional portfolio to document your progress toward achieving the skills and knowledge you will need as an administrator of children's programs. In a large looseleaf notebook, label one divider for each of the competencies addressed in Chapters 4 through 15 of this text.

Alternatively, your instructor may suggest different headings for each section of your portfolio, or you may live in a state where the licensing agency has established specific categories of portfolio assignments as requirements for a director's credential. As you complete the assignments associated with each chapter, select those that you feel best demonstrate your mastery of a particular competency (no matter which competencies you have chosen), and place them in the appropriate section. Create a cover sheet for each assignment that explains why you have included it and what you think it shows about your managerial abilities.

Resources for Further Study

PRINT

Boulton, P. (2008). The child care director: Not just anyone can do this job. *Exchange, 179,* 16–19.

Goffin, S. G., & Washington, V. (2007). *Ready or not: Leadership choices in early care and education.* New York, NY: Teachers College Press.

Sullivan, D. R. (2009). *Learning to lead: Effective leadership skills for teachers of young children* (2nd ed). St. Paul, MN: Redleaf Press.

Websites

FEDERAL INTERAGENCY FORUM

http://www.childstats.gov

The Federal Interagency Forum on Child and Family Statistics produces the annual federal monitoring report, *America's Children: Key National Indicators of Well-Being*.

KIDS COUNT

aecf.org

Kids Count is a project of the Annie E. Casey Foundation, which gathers information on several measures of child well-being at the local, state, and national levels in an annual census, available in hard copy and PDF format. Findings are also presented in searchable online databases as well as in tailored summaries addressing specific ethnic or demographic populations (e.g., newborns, teen parents, Southwest border residents).

NATIONAL CHILD CARE INFORMATION CENTER

http://nccic.acf.hhs.gov

National Child Care Information and Technical Assistance Center is a service of the Child Care Bureau, which describes itself as a "national clearinghouse and technical assistance center that links parents, providers, policy-makers, researchers, and the public to early care and education information." Click on "popular topics" to access organizations, resources, and publications (many in PDF format) on topics such as child-care arrangements, child care as a business, federal policy, licensing regulations, and tiered quality strategies.

2

CHAPTER

Types of Child Development Programs

LEARNING OUTCOMES

After studying this chapter you should be able to

- Identify and explain the primary focus of five types of child-care programs.
- Discuss the advantages and disadvantages of three ways to finance child development programs.
- Describe a systems approach to providing child-care services.

Rainbow Place is a medium-size child-care center. It enrolls 100 children, ages 6 weeks through 5 years, and is open year-round, Monday through Friday, from 7:00 a.m. to 6:00 p.m. Tanya worked the early morning shift as a teacher and is glad that one of her duties in her new position as assistant director is to open the center. She enjoys greeting the children and their parents as they arrive and sharing a few moments of conversation before the parents have to rush off to their jobs. Many have told her how comforting it is to know their children are safe and happy while they work. Others have wanted to know more about what their children were learning at the center, or to ask advice about child-rearing concerns. Tanya has come to realize that Rainbow Place is more than just a service for hire; it is many things to the families it serves, and she takes deep satisfaction and pride in being part of it.

The previous chapter discussed the broad context within which the field of early care and education is growing and changing. You read about trends within society that will shape your career as a manager of child development programs. This chapter narrows the focus just a little to examine the universe of child development programs.

This universe is complex. No matter what classification scheme is used (e.g., age of children served, length of day, or institutional affiliation), few programs fit neatly into a single category. Infant–toddler, preschool, and school-age programs often exist under a single roof, as do programs offering part-day, full-day, or after-school care. We have chosen to categorize child development programs in two ways. We use the term *type* to capture a program's central mission, often a direct outgrowth of its historical roots. The term **spon-sorship** refers to financial resources and the governance structure associated with that revenue. As you will see, there is a great deal of overlap between these categories.

FIVE TYPES OF CHILD DEVELOPMENT PROGRAMS

Child development centers serve young children outside their homes less than 24 hours a day. They are part of the public social service system, the education system, the philanthropic system, and the business system. The breadth and depth of service varies considerably among the centers, and such philosophical differences guide management decisions. Nevertheless, the principles of managing the centers remain substantially the same. Parents selecting a program for their child may find five basic **program types** available. Depending on their primary needs, interests, and available resources, parents may choose one rather than others. The five basic program types are as follows:

1. Consumer service
2. Supplement to the care and education provided by families
3. Remedial or compensatory service
4. Investment in human capital
5. Facility for research or teacher preparation

As noted earlier, the distinctions among program types represent a different concept than program sponsorship, although the two ideas are often intertwined. Sponsorship refers to the funding source and governance of organizations, while program type refers to the central mission or purpose of the organization. Each type of program described here can be funded in a variety of ways, and a program funded in any particular manner can function in ways that could place it in more than one of these categories. For example, programs to supplement care provided by families are funded through parent fees, state or federal government subsidies, corporate sponsorship, or (most likely) some combination of these and other resources. These types do not represent hard and fast labels, but rather a way of teasing out some of the elements that make up the phenomenon of child care. A single program, such as a family child-care home, might originate as a supplement to family care (type 2), aiming simply to keep children safe and happy while their parents work. The same family child-care provider might collaborate with a local agency serving children with disabilities to enroll one or more children whose placement in inclusive care is part of their individualized family service plan (IFSP). The family child-care home thus blends aspects of a type 3 program as well (offering remedial or compensatory service). Of course, any facility that provides a developmentally appropriate program is fulfilling the function of investing in human capital (type 4).

In an ideal world, these program types would merge into a single concept of developmentally appropriate practices that apply to all programs; however, the reality is that the way program managers and staff members envision their mission and families' perception of the program create distinctions that affect the level and quality of services provided. Staff members who view their job as "just babysitting" are likely to feel less professional and to interact differently with children than are staff members who see themselves as partnering with parents to foster a child's optimum development. Families who pay for nursery school as a consumer service may expect—and be willing to pay for—more "frills" than families who purchase 8 or 10 hours of supplemental care each day while the parents are at work. Families in subsidized programs, whose children are deemed at risk for school failure, are probably more likely to accept testing and evaluation of their children as part of the package than are families who have elected to pay either for an enriching nursery school program or full-day child care while they pursue careers.

Type 1: Consumer Service

The word **consumer** is an economic term referring to an individual or organization that acquires goods or services, usually in return for payment. Because it is often purchased by families, child care is sometimes perceived (by families, by providers, and by the public at large) as a consumer service. Although many full-day programs can fall into this category, the most basic example might be a drop-in facility at a shopping mall or other retail establishment where children are kept safe and entertained while their parents shop. This view is problematic for many reasons, but mostly because it oversimplifies a very complex phenomenon. Who is the consumer, for example? The parent who pays, or the child who receives care? What exactly is purchased? Is it merely a certain number of hours of freedom from the responsibilities of tending to a child's safety and well-being? Certainly that may be what some providers intend to deliver and what some families hope to purchase, but child care involves much more, and high-quality child care yields much more. Thus, we would argue that even child care viewed as a consumer service is likely to be an investment in human capital and a supplement to the care provided by families.

A program that defines itself solely as a consumer good is unlikely to strive for, or achieve, high levels of quality. In contrast to other services that may be purchased for a fee, child care works best when it is based on warm, reciprocal relationships among parent, provider, and child. Parents who believe they are simply purchasing a service (such as a carwash) may view their child's caregiver as anonymous and interchangeable, perhaps like a hotel maid. Caregivers who share such a perspective are probably less likely to view themselves as professionals or to know and use best practices. Some leaders in the field of early childhood have argued that the persistent view of child care as a privately purchased consumer good, distinct from education, which is recognized as a social good, is one of the barriers to creating a system of child care that is high quality, affordable, and widely accessible (e.g., Brauner, Gordic, & Zigler, 2004).

Type 2: Supplement to Care and Education Provided by Families

Supplemental care extends the strengths and talents that parents have for caring for and educating their children. As indicated in Chapter 1, the need for supplemental care for children has grown with the increasing participation of women in the workforce over the past several decades. Supplemental care arrangements support parents by nurturing and educating their children in the hours during the day when they must be at work or school or when they are otherwise unable to provide such care themselves. If child-care providers truly understand that they simply provide the nurturing that parents would provide for their children if the parents were available, they will make every effort to serve as a support for each family system. This means they must highly value parent–child bonding and attachment and work to strengthen, never to undermine, these crucial emotional relationships. In addition to filling in during parents' absence, sensitive child-care providers can offer information, guidance, and emotional support to enhance parents' ability to fulfill their role. Supplemental care must never become a substitute for parental nurturing and educating.

Child-care centers developed in the United States and Europe during the early 1800s to protect children while their mothers and siblings worked in factories. These were primarily custodial situations limited to physical care, distinct from programs with educational goals. Although this distinction persists in many minds, it has begun to fade as programs make concerted efforts to provide both care and education. Many factors have contributed to this development, including media attention to recent research findings on brain development in the early years; rising expectations of families, particularly educated professionals, who rely on child care; and state licensing regulations designed to improve the quality of all care. Certainly children who spend up to 10 hours a day, 300 days a year, in child care need enriching and educational experiences as much as or more than their counterparts in partial-day programs.

As a supplemental service to families, child-care centers continually evolve ways to respond to families' needs, including extended hours of operation to accommodate second- and third-shift workers; drop-in, irregular, or half-day enrollment for families that don't need full-day care; and after-school, summer, and backup (e.g., snow-day) care for school-age children. Accommodating families' needs for care when their children are mildly ill is another example of such efforts.

CARE FOR MILDLY ILL CHILDREN   According to the National Association for Sick Child Daycare (2009), more than 350,000 children under 14 stay home from school or child care every day, which means that working mothers miss up to 29 days of work and employers lose up to $12 billion each year. In the typical half-day nursery school of many years ago, a child with even a minor illness was routinely required to stay home. Full-day programs adopted the same policies, even though this meant financial hardship and a threat to the livelihood of parents who had to stay home from work when their children were sick. In the 1980s, this pressure created a demand for child development centers to establish facilities for the care of mildly ill children. Some communities created entire centers for this specific purpose. The American Public Health Association (APHA) and the American Academy of Pediatrics (AAP) have established standards for this type of care (American Academy of Pediatrics, American Public Health Association, National Resource Center for Health and Safety in Child Care and Early Education, 2011).

FAMILY CHILD-CARE HOMES   Family child care is another form of supplemental care popular with parents. Often, the family child-care home is in the neighborhood where the family lives, making it a convenient option. Some parents prefer family child care because it is provided in a smaller, more homelike setting and offers a closer match to the culture, values, and caregiving style experienced by the child at home.

Family child-care providers as a group are working toward a more professional status through affiliation with organizations such as the National Association for Family Child Care, which strives to promote adequate professional development, compensation, and resources for family child-care providers (2007). Frequently, people who begin by providing child care in their homes move on to become managers of centers as their business grows. Some center managers work out cooperative arrangements with nearby family child-care providers to pool resources and purchase supplies in bulk or refer families to another member of the group when needed services are beyond the scope of a particular provider. For example, a center that is licensed to care for children ages 2½ to 5 might develop a pool of nearby family child-care providers to care for younger siblings. Or the center might make an arrangement for certain family providers to accept those mildly ill children whose parents are unable to keep them at home. Such cooperation makes maximum use of resources for the benefit of all concerned.

Type 3: Remedial or Compensatory Service

Some programs enroll children to remediate or compensate for particular difficulties experienced by the child. These programs have their historical roots in the special schools for blind, deaf, or physically handicapped children that originated in the 19th century (Bailey & Wolery, 1992) and in the programs for economically disadvantaged children that grew out of the War on Poverty in the 1960s. A more recent trend is toward the inclusion of children with disabilities in programs for children who are developing typically. This trend is an outgrowth of several federal laws, which are summarized in Figure 2.1.

Progression of Public Laws Addressing Services for Children with Disabilities

- **1968:** PL 90–538 of 1968 establishes the Early Education Program for Children with Disabilities; provides funding for model programs to expand knowledge about serving young children with disabilities and their families.
- **1974:** PL 93–644 reserves 10 percent of available spaces in Head Start programs for children with disabilities.
- **1975:** PL 94–142, the Education for All Handicapped Children Act, establishes the right to a free public education for children with disabilities from ages 3 to 21 and mandates the use of an Individualized Education Program (IEP).
- **1983:** PL 98–199 provides funding to support state plans for extending the scope of services to include children from birth to age 5.
- **1986:** PL 99–457 institutes the Individualized Family Service Plan (IFSP) for infants and toddlers with or at risk of developing disabilities, and offers states incentives to provide services for them.
- **1990:** PL 101–576, the Individuals with Disabilities Education Act (IDEA), reauthorizes PL 94–142 and further extends services by adding autism and traumatic brain injury to the list of recognized disabilities.
- **2004:** PL 108–466, the Individuals with Disabilities Education Improvement Act of 2004, extends services to homeless children and their families as well as children who are wards of the state. Other changes include provisions requiring states to ensure that service providers are appropriately qualified and that intervention methods are based on peer-reviewed scientific research.

FIGURE 2.1 Progression of public laws addressing services for children with disabilities.

As a result of this legislation, children with typical as well as atypical patterns of development are being served together in the same child development programs, with distinct advantages resulting for both. The child with a disability acquires a group of peers to emulate and the satisfaction of play and friendship as rewards for progress. The children without disabilities learn social skills and compassion. As the movement toward inclusion gains momentum, many centers formerly reserved for children with disabilities actively recruit children without disabilities to be included in those settings. Problems with funding arise, however, because priorities in this country mean that subsidies for early education are designated only for those children with specific disabilities or those determined to be at risk for developmental delays.

Type 4: Investment in Human Capital

Skills, talents, knowledge, and abilities are a person's **human capital**. Parents who enroll a child in a child development center expect that enhancing the child's abilities or human capital will pay off later in terms of better performance in school and better job performance beyond school. Investments in human capital occur at a broader level in the form of publicly funded programs for young children that benefit society in at least two ways: (1) by increasing the pool of individuals capable of contributing to their communities and (2) by reducing the costs associated with school failure and its consequences. President Obama has repeatedly affirmed his support for investment in early

High-quality child development programs serve all children—those with and those without disabilities.

education as compatible with—in fact essential to—the country's economic well-being. An analysis of studies conducted over time has found that low-income children with preprimary school experience were less likely than children from similar backgrounds with no early education to be held back a grade, be placed in special education, become pregnant as teenagers, or become involved in the criminal justice system (Kilburn & Karoly, 2008, pp. 12–15; Dickens & Baschnagel, 2009).

PROJECT HEAD START   Project Head Start, which was initiated by the U.S. government in 1965, is an example of such an investment in children's human capital. Head Start was designed for disadvantaged children as part of President Lyndon Johnson's War on Poverty. The emphasis on giving young children a "head start" arose when it was observed that children of the poor had more difficulties with later school performance than did children with more advantages. The argument for Project Head Start was that an earlier start in preprimary school with more educationally oriented programs would decrease the number of later school dropouts and also decrease the number of children entering special education.

Head Start provides comprehensive, high-quality early care and education and support services, including access to health screenings, referrals and follow-up support, parenting resources, and social services. Originally targeting 3- and 4-year-old children, Head Start has evolved to include services for infants and toddlers (Early Head Start), as well as full-day programs and care for children of working parents. In 2010, the program served 908,016 preschool-age children and another 908,016 children under age 3 in Early Head Start (Children's Defense Fund, 2012). Throughout the program's history, limited funding has meant that the numbers of children enrolled in Head Start and Early Head Start have comprised only a fraction of those children whose family income would make them eligible for services. Unfortunately, those numbers are being further reduced by the automatic, across-the-board federal budget cuts required by the Budget Control Act of 2011 (National Women's Law Center, 2013).

UNIVERSAL PreK   Universal PreK refers to an initiative aimed at making publicly funded preschool services available to all 3- and 4-year-olds on a voluntary basis. Georgia led the nation in this movement in 1995, followed by Oklahoma in 1998. Florida and West Virginia have laws requiring that all 4-year-olds be provided with high-quality preschool education (National Institute for Early Education Research, 2009). Since 2002, the percentage of all 4-year-olds enrolled in preschool has doubled (from 14 percent to 28 percent), while the percentage of 3-year-olds has remained relatively flat (from 3 percent to 4 percent). In 2012, 40 states provided programs for 4-year-olds; 26 of those also provided programs for 3-year-olds (Barnett, Carolan, Fitzgerald & Squires, 2013). Many state-funded programs have eligibility requirements based on income or other risk factors. Many are part-day and do not fulfill the needs for child care when parents are working. Some require the parents to pay tuition. Other revenue streams come from the federal government's Head Start program and the Individuals with Disabilities Education Act (IDEA) or Title I of the Elementary and Secondary Education Act, a program for children at risk for school failure caused by poverty.

EARLY LEARNING INITIATIVE   In his State of the Union address in 2013, President Obama laid out a plan to expand on these investments in young children's learning and development by establishing a continuum of high-quality early education beginning at birth and continuing until age 5. The plan calls for federal–state partnerships to extend preschool to all children whose families' incomes are at or below 200 percent of the poverty level, with additional incentives for states to offer services for families above that level, perhaps using a sliding fee scale. The preschools would have to meet a number of quality standards, including appropriately trained and adequately compensated teachers. The plan would also expand services for infants, toddlers, and 3-year-olds through the existing Head Start program and home-visiting initiatives for at-risk families.

EARLY LEARNING STANDARDS   As more states invest dollars in early education, there has been a corresponding movement for states to establish standards for what young children are expected to know or be able to do after participating in early childhood programs. Having such standards in place was a requirement for states hoping to qualify for funding through the Race to the Top Early Learning Challenge in 2012. While many states have attempted to align their early learning standards with Common Core standards for kindergarten through grade 12, early learning standards are generally broader in scope, addressing all domains of development as well as academic content areas.

Type 5: Research and Teacher Preparation

Some centers are specifically organized to provide a group or groups of children for research in child development, child psychology, and early childhood education. One early example is a nursery school opened by the Institute of Child Welfare at the University of California, Berkeley, in 1928 (Harms & Tracy, 2006, p. 89). At times, these centers are also combined with teacher preparation programs to give university or community college students an opportunity to learn the various skills necessary to interact with young children. Some receive additional funding through a program of the U.S. Department of Education, Child Care Access Means Parents in School, which is designed to promote higher education for low-income parents.

A 1995 survey of 314 campus-based centers found that the majority defined their function as a combination of lab school and child-care service, 37 percent identified themselves as a child-care service only, and 11 percent as a laboratory school only (National Coalition for Campus Children's Centers, 2008). The lab school identity can have several implications, creating both advantages and disadvantages for families served (McBride & Hicks, 1999). For example, programs designed to support research might not admit children on a first-come, first-served basis, but rather establish enrollment criteria to ensure equal numbers of boys and girls. Families served by programs whose primary aim is teacher preparation benefit from the level of quality created as these programs strive to model best practices for their teachers-in-training. At the same time, many of the staff members in these programs are student teachers who possess varying degrees of skill and who come and go with each semester. In addition to these staff fluctuations, families must often accept the inconvenience of locating alternate care when the programs close during

University lab programs provide opportunities for young men and women to gain experience working with children.

breaks in the academic schedule. As funding sources tighten or university objectives change, these centers often face challenges to their continued existence (Freeman & Brown, 1999). In such an atmosphere, it is especially important to recognize the vital functions that these schools fulfill in developing innovative practices and preparing future leaders for the early childhood profession (Harms & Tracy, 2006).

> ### ? DECISIONS, DECISIONS . . .
>
> Based on the information provided in the vignette at the beginning of this chapter, what program type seems to apply to Rainbow Place? Why? Which type, or combination of types, seems most ideal to you? Why?

THREE WAYS OF FINANCING CHILD DEVELOPMENT PROGRAMS

You have read how child development programs can be classified as one or more of five distinct types, based on their central purpose or objectives. Now, we turn our attention to the ways that programs are funded. Whatever a program's purpose, it cannot be accomplished without financial resources to pay for staff, rent, utilities, equipment, and supplies. The source of those dollars influences not only how well a program is able to fulfill its mission, but often the nature of that mission as well. Basically, child development services can be funded in three ways, each of which spreads the cost over a successively wider base: (1) The narrowest base of support occurs when the cost is shouldered entirely by the individual families who are direct consumers of the services; (2) the base of support widens somewhat when costs are shared by social agencies that sponsor programs for philanthropic reasons or by corporations with vested interests in doing so; and (3) costs are spread across society as a whole when tax-supported initiatives at local, state, and federal levels fund programs. This last scenario is analogous to the system of funding public education for children over 5 years of age. Everyone who pays taxes helps pay for public schools, not just the parents with children in those schools, because everyone in a democratic society benefits from having a well-educated population.

In reality, many programs are funded by a combination of methods. Centers relying on parent fees for the bulk of their budget might supplement those fees by applying for grants from private foundations or by participating in the government-sponsored Child Care Food Program.

Lally (2005) argues that the various funding methods reflect distinct views of society's responsibility and children's rights. He uses the term economic rationalism to characterize the view that parents bear sole responsibility for their children and thus for providing substitute care when they are unavailable. Another view, instrumentalism, holds that a society acts in its own best interest when it funds child-care programs to counter the likelihood that abused or poor children will grow up to become burdens on society. According to Lally, neither approach recognizes children as citizens with rights in the present: "the right to be, the right to become, the right to enjoy, and the right to choose" (p. 45). This view, which Lally terms a social enrichment perspective, underlies the generous child-care policies in Europe, Australia, and New Zealand. As you read the following sections, consider the issues of funding and quality through a leadership lens, thinking about ways you can advocate on behalf of children and families to make high-quality care affordable and accessible.

LEADERSHIP LENS

Advocacy, defined as "the act of pleading or arguing in favor of something, such as a cause, idea, or policy" (*American Heritage Dictionary of the English Language*, 2011), is a natural outgrowth of leadership and professionalism. As a member of the early childhood profession, you are in a pivotal position to advocate for children. You have seen many families firsthand. You are in touch with them and are aware of their needs and concerns. You have credibility and expertise because your center is an important support service for families in your community.

Advocacy efforts vary in scope, from addressing the needs of a single individual (e.g., helping a family obtain needed service for a child with disabilities) to serving all children (e.g., encouraging the expansion of state subsidies for child care for low-income families). Between these extremes, you might work toward some benefit for your own center, perhaps a change in zoning regulations to allow expansion of your building. At the next level, you would work for something that would benefit the larger community, perhaps a new park or children's library. Publicly funded pre-K programs or changes in licensing regulations are state-level causes, while obtaining the federal dollars to support those initiatives requires advocacy at the national level. Figure 2.2 illustrates the gradually widening scope of potential advocacy efforts. Effective advocates understand the ways in which the ripple effect works: When you change one factor in the system, it affects and changes other factors.

Advocacy leadership (Blank, 1998) requires that you become committed to joining discussions and actions that support a cause that you think needs community attention. You learn about it, work for it, and persuade others to join you. Advocacy leaders have a strong belief that something can be done about most things if enough ideas and energy are brought to bear. As they advocate for an individual child, a group of children, or all of the children in our global village, they hold the optimistic view that, with effort, a better future is possible. Most important, they keep in mind that using the talents and ideas of everyone leads to more progress.

The process begins by establishing a common ground with your audience about what *should be*. Then you must show them how reality deviates from that shared ideal and explain why that deviation is important. Most people agree that all children deserve to be safe, healthy, and loved. If you can show how many, or how often, children in your community are deprived of these basic rights, and if you can explain what this situation means in the long run—for the children and for your community—your audience will be prepared to take the next step: thinking about how they can help turn what *should be* into what *is*.

Family Payments for Child Care

It may seem logical that child development programs derive their financial support by charging families a fee for the service, just as any other business charges its customers. A restaurant, for example, sets its prices for meals by calculating the costs of the food; salaries for kitchen and waitstaff; and overhead such as rent, utilities, laundry, and cleaning costs. If there is a deficit, the restaurant either raises the prices for its meals or lowers expenses, perhaps cutting corners on laundry costs by substituting paper napkins for table linens. Either option risks driving away customers, whether those who object to higher prices or those who prefer their filet mignon served on fine china and damask tablecloths. In the end, though, the restaurant's income must exceed its expenses or the business will founder.

Making ends meet in a child development center can be more difficult. One reason is that child care is a labor-intensive operation, meaning that staff salaries

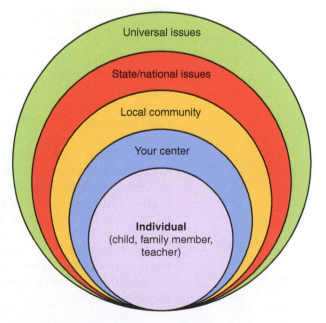

FIGURE 2.2   Scope of advocacy efforts.

make up the bulk of any program's expenses. Although a restaurant might economize by finding a less expensive source of vegetables, for example, a child development program can hardly cut down on staffing costs when salaries for many are already below the federal poverty level ($17,600 per year for a family of three). In 2008, the average salary for child-care workers was $9.43 per hour, or $19,605 per year (National Association of Child Care Resource and Referral Agencies, 2009b).

Child care is expensive, and although many families are already devoting substantial portions of their annual income to it, the burden is substantially greater for families with earnings below the poverty level. According to the latest available U.S. Census figures, employed mothers paid an average of $127 per week, or 7.7 percent of their family's annual income, for child care in 2011. While the average weekly fee paid by poor mothers was much lower, at $63.00, this amount represented a far greater proportion of their annual income (19.6 percent) (Macartney & Laughlin, 2011).

In 27 states, the cost of center-based care for a 4-year-old child is higher than the cost of in-state tuition at a public university (Children's Defense Fund, 2012, p. 34). It must be noted, however, that tuition and fees account for less than one-fourth of the total cost of college. State tax dollars, grants, endowments, and other sources comprise the bulk of revenue for public higher education. In contrast, fees paid by families comprise nearly two-thirds of the revenue stream for early care and education nationwide (Child Care Action Campaign, 2001). In this video, Kristin Rowe-Finkbeiner, founder and executive director of the organization Momsrising, describes the impact that this situation has on women in particular and calls for investment in children as a way of promoting gender equality in the workforce and a stronger economy overall.

? DECISIONS, DECISIONS . . .

What do you think child-care personnel should earn? Why? How much do they earn in your community? How much do you think families should pay for child care? As a manager of a child development center, how might you balance these two factors?

Thus, it is nearly impossible for child development programs to charge fees high enough to support living wages for their staff members. This situation is called the child-care trilemma. Programs struggle to meet three equally desirable, complex, interrelated, but competing or mutually exclusive, goals: program quality, fair compensation, and affordability. If they charge fees that parents can afford, they are unable to pay adequate salaries. If they keep salaries low, they are unable to attract highly qualified employees—or keep those they do attract—and program quality suffers. Yet raising rates to reflect the true cost of high quality services places those high-quality services outside the reach of most families. Even programs that rely on parent fees for the bulk of their income are likely to supplement that revenue with various fund-raising activities. The unspoken truth is that their underpaid employees are subsidizing the program with their own labor. Many early childhood professionals and child advocates have concluded that high-quality child care will be impossible to achieve unless the costs are spread beyond families to a wider segment of society.

Sponsored Programs

Because they recognize a need for services for young children, and the fact that families—particularly poor families—are unable to shoulder the full cost of such services, religious and civic organizations have a long history of either providing or underwriting the costs of programs (Rose, 1999). In fact, since the 1830s, charitable institutions have provided most of the center-based child care in the United States (Neugebauer, 2000b, p. 6). Although these organizations may have had philanthropic motives, business organizations have also found reasons to sponsor programs for children. Maria Montessori, a renowned innovator in early childhood education, began her work in Rome in 1907 when a group of Roman entrepreneurs hired her to keep children from vandalizing the housing developments they were attempting to renovate. Her Casa dei Bambini (Children's House) eventually became the model for the thousands of schools around the world that bear her name today (Goffin & Wilson, 2001, pp. 38–45). Enlightened corporations have continued to recognize that sponsoring child-care initiatives has benefits for the corporation, as well as for the children and families served.

CHURCH-SPONSORED OR FAITH-BASED PROGRAMS   Between 1992 and 2008, increases in the number of child-care programs housed in religious settings ranged from 47.7 percent for Jewish programs to 76.4 percent for Protestant programs; Catholic programs increased 52.6 percent. Some of these programs serve only members of their particular denomination, whereas others are open to all. In spite of these gains, many are feeling a pinch due to the growth of state-funded pre-K programs (Neugebauer, 2008).

Results of a recent examination of the relationship between quality of care and type of sponsorship suggest that, although nonprofit centers in general demonstrated higher quality in several areas (positive caregiving, caregiver wages, education, and professionalism), this does not hold true for religiously affiliated nonprofits, whose quality was closer to that of the for-profit programs. The authors warn, however, that the findings were not consistent across every indicator or age group and should be interpreted with caution (Sosinsky, Lord, & Zigler, 2007).

Although exempted from licensing regulations by some states, religiously affiliated programs are encouraged to become licensed voluntarily in order to demonstrate their adherence to the external standards, to reassure parents, and to access higher reimbursement rates (Child Care Bureau, n.d.). Recent federal initiatives have given churches and religious organizations new access to government resources. In January 2001, President George W. Bush established a White House Office of Faith-Based and Community Initiatives to expand and encourage such programs. The Center for Faith-Based and Community Initiatives within the U.S. Department of Health and Human Services, whose goals have been endorsed by President Obama, states that its mission is to "create an environment within HHS that welcomes the participation of faith-based and community-based organizations as valued and essential partners with the Department in assisting Americans in need" (www.acf.hhs.gov).

EMPLOYER SUPPORT FOR CHILD CARE   Employer-supported child care is not a new phenomenon. An early venture into industry-connected child care occurred during World War II when a federal law, the Lanham Act, financed centers to provide child care for children of women needed in the war industries. These were known by many as the Lanham Act Nursery Schools. Advisers to the government for these schools were people prominent in the field. Many centers had state-of-the-art facilities, equipment, and programs. After the war, most of these centers were abandoned, though their influence continues to be felt. In a survey conducted to mark the turn of the century, prominent leaders in early childhood education noted that the creation of these centers marked society's new acceptance of women working outside the home. The training materials they produced are still used in some centers.

Employer-supported child-care initiatives blossomed again in the 1970s and 1980s when women born during the baby boom years entered the workforce in great numbers. Many programs were the result of collaboration between employee unions and employers, including those in the private sector (e.g., the automobile and garment industries), as well as public-sector employers at local, state, and federal levels (Hildebrand, 1993, pp. 221–224). These accomplishments signaled an emerging trend toward the acknowledgment of child care as a core concern of employers as well as employees. Child care joined other issues on the bargaining table when stakeholders realized that the invention of constructive solutions can be beneficial to management as well as labor, assisting employers to recruit and retain a stable and productive workforce, while aiding unions to be responsive to their needs.

Employer support for families' child-care needs can include contracting with existing programs to purchase child-care slots for employees, providing or contracting for child-care referral services, and offering options such as flexible scheduling or job sharing. Most common, and least costly for the employer, is the flexible spending account, which allows employees to set aside pretax dollars to cover child-care expenses. (This is classified more properly as a combination of family payment and public support. On the one hand, families are spending their own dollars to pay for care; on the other, they are enjoying a tax savings, the true cost of which is actually spread among all taxpayers.)

Child-care resource and referral services help parents locate and evaluate the quality of child-care facilities. A 2012 study by the Work Family Institute found that 61 percent of employers with 1,000 or more employees provided resource and referral services versus 29 percent for those with 50 to 99 employees. At a deeper level of involvement, employers provided child-care assistance in one of three ways: (1) They provided child care at or near the worksite; (2) they provided vouchers or subsidies to pay for the cost of child care; or (3) they offered dependent care assistance plans that allow employees to pay for child care with pretax dollars. In each of these categories, the percentage of large employers far exceeded that of small employers. Not surprisingly, those most likely to provide child- and elder-care assistance were larger, nonprofit organizations that had more women in their workforces as well as in top positions (Matos & Galinsky, 2012). (See Figure 2.3.)

According to the Bureau of Labor Statistics, which has been tracking the numbers since 1990, employers providing these types of support are a distinct minority. Just as with resource and referral services, employees in larger establishments are more likely to have access to these benefits than those in smaller organizations. Although the expansion of employer-supported child-care programs has tapered off considerably as a result of the economic downturn, CEOs of the largest providers in North America predict that the long-term demand for such services will grow, fueled by growing numbers of women entering the workforce (Neugebauer, 2010).

Even though such programs are few in number, their high visibility and connections to the influential world of business mean that their potential impact on the field as a whole is substantial. Hill-Scott, for example, sees these programs as an important factor in the movement toward establishing a credential for administrator (2000, pp. 208–209). Thus,

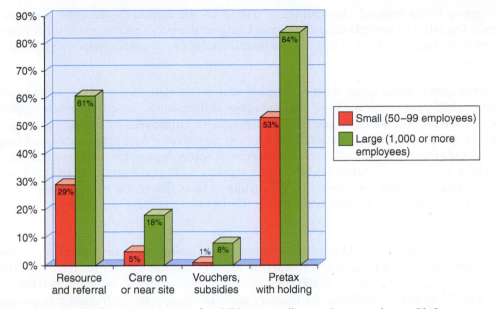

FIGURE 2.3   Types of employer support for child care: small versus large employers, 2012

Based on: Matos, K. & Galinsky, E. (2012). 2012 National Study of Employers. Families and Work Institute. Retrieved June 18, 2013 from http://familiesandwork.org/site/research/reports/NSE_2012_.pdf

whether or not you find yourself working in a corporate-sponsored program, you will want to keep an eye on this phenomenon, which will surely influence your management career.

Why, some might ask, should employers become involved in child care? There are several reasons. First, if employers want to attract the widest possible pool of highly qualified potential applicants, they must attract women as well as men. One-third of the "100 best companies to work for," cited by *Fortune Magazine* in 2012, provided on-site child care. Although child care is still largely viewed as a woman's issue, attitudes are changing, and today's workforce increasingly expects management to show more concern for family life by providing flexible scheduling, child care, and other supports. In addition to a recruiting edge, employers receive several benefits from providing programs and policies addressing the personal and family needs of their employees, including retention of highly valued employees, enhanced public image, lower absenteeism and turnover rates, and improved employee morale and productivity (Matos & Galinsky, 2012).

In the short term, the stress of worrying about unsatisfactory child-care arrangements or searching for replacements siphons parents' energy and attention from the workplace. In the long term, the children who languish in poor-quality care are far less likely to develop the emotional and cognitive qualities that will make them desirable employees in the future. In other words, employers are acting in their own interest when they help their employees access high-quality child care.

COLLEGE- AND UNIVERSITY-SPONSORED CHILD CARE   Community and four-year colleges, technical schools, and universities are in the child-care business to varying degrees. Most serve both students' and employees' children and have a sliding fee scale to adjust for income differences. Some of the programs are especially designed to help maintain student enrollments. Some are used by state social service programs to provide care for children of parents who are receiving state assistance to participate in training programs that will help the parents become financially independent. The programs range from full-day child care to drop-in care during the daytime or evening while the student parents attend a class. Many of the programs operate with grants from the college for the building and its maintenance. Other grants help with subsidies for low-income students.

HOSPITAL-SPONSORED CHILD CARE   Hospital and medical school complexes typically have a child-care center for their staff members and students. Hospital centers in some localities have responded to the flextime options for employees by extending the permitted hours a child can remain in child care. Some have instituted sick-child care, which taps their medical and nursing expertise. Another type of program is a playroom or child life program maintained by medical facilities to serve children and their siblings while they await treatment or the results of tests. There are more than 400 such programs in the United States and Canada (Child Life Council, Committee on Hospital Care, 2006).

MILITARY CHILD CARE   The U.S. military has become a major component of the employer-sponsored child-care field, with on-site care at bases around the world. These facilities serve about 200,000 children at 800 child development centers on military installations around the world. In addition, the military seeks to collaborate with child-care providers in the civilian community to meet the needs of the many military families who live off base. With an emphasis on quality as well as accessibility, 97 percent of military child development centers are accredited, compared with 10 percent or fewer of their civilian counterparts (Miles, 2008). One initiative contributing to this accomplishment is the caregiver personnel pay plan, which offers military child-care employees salary increases as they obtain additional training and demonstrate competence. In other words, they are treated more like other military workers and are less dependent on what parents can afford to pay for their compensation. Not surprisingly, these efforts have greatly reduced staff turnover at the centers (Bellm, Gnezda, Whitebook, & Breunig, 1994).

Government Support for Child Care

As mentioned earlier, tax credits for working families represent one way that the government subsidizes the cost of child care, in this case by foregoing a certain amount of revenue. More direct forms of government financial backing for child development programs come through the Child Care and Development Fund (CCDF). The Child Care and Development Block Grant of 1990 authorized $750 million for this purpose in fiscal year (FY) 1991. This amount has increased over the years, reaching $7 billion (including $2 billion through the American Recovery and Reinvestment Act) in FY 2009, and a plan proposed by President Obama in 2013 will substantially increase our investment in services for children. States receive a share of these funds according to a formula that takes into account the number of children under age 5, the number of children receiving free or reduced-price lunches, and the state per capita income. A portion of this money requires state matching funds, and the federal dollars must augment, not replace, the state and local monies already designated for child development programs. States must spend 4 percent on quality enhancement initiatives and consumer education (Center for Law and Social Policy, 2009).

TEMPORARY ASSISTANCE FOR NEEDY FAMILIES BLOCK GRANT   In 1996, Congress enacted a welfare reform law, Temporary Assistance for Needy Families (TANF) with the overall goal of ending adult dependence on public assistance as well as preventing such dependence in future generations. TANF was reauthorized in 2006. To receive TANF funds, states had to ensure that welfare recipients met minimum work requirements. At the same time, states were given considerable leeway in using TANF funds as long as the programs they set up were compatible with four purposes:

Purpose One: Provide assistance to needy families so that children may be cared for in their homes or in the homes of relatives.

Purpose Two: End the dependence of needy parents on government benefits by promoting job preparation, work, and marriage.

Purpose Three: Prevent and reduce the incidence of out-of-wedlock pregnancies and establish annual numerical goals for preventing and reducing the incidence of these pregnancies.

Purpose Four: Encourage the formation and maintenance of two-parent families (U.S. Department of Health and Human Services, 2008).

Thus, in addition to providing temporary, direct financial assistance to needy families, states have the option of creating or expanding programs to support the overall healthy growth and development of children. They might use TANF dollars to establish home-visiting programs to enhance parenting skills and prevent child abuse, alternative education programs to help teen parents complete high school or obtain a general educational development (GED) diploma, or programs aimed at building self-esteem in young men and women. Probably of greatest interest to you as a manager of a child development program is the fact that many states use TANF funds to create or expand before- and after-school child care, Head Start, and Early Head Start programs. TANF dollars also support initiatives such as Teacher Education and Compensation Helps (TEACH), which provides scholarships and salary increases for professional development by child development staff (National Governors' Association for Best Practices, n.d., pp. 4–10).

? DECISIONS, DECISIONS . . .

What do you see as outcomes if Universal PreK becomes a reality? Will it mean a loss of clientele (and revenue) for programs in the private sector? Will it mean more or fewer job opportunities for you as a manager of early childhood programs?

COLLABORATION: A SYSTEMS APPROACH

The foregoing discussion gives you a picture of the range of child development programs and their funding sources. It also points to a new era in early childhood care and education, one that you will want to follow closely. For many years, several institutions in the United States have worked independently to provide some early education and care for children in various sectors of the population. The differences in philosophies, services, and funding that parents confront are often confusing.

Ideally, the many varieties of early childhood services would collaborate to reduce duplication and maximize returns on society's investments. Zigler and Lang (1991) propose such a collaborative model in their "School of the 21st Century," centering on the public school districts across the country. This arrangement is attrac-

By collaborating across institutions and agencies, child development programs are often able to provide individualized attention that would not otherwise be possible.

tive, economical, and efficient. These schools already pay an installed administrative hierarchy and need only leadership from a qualified educator to set up high-quality early childhood education of the type needed for all families in the district. In addition, the districts often have space that can be made available. The proposal suggests that tuition from parents could help finance the endeavor, at least at the beginning. With this coordinated effort, early education and care could be provided for all children who need it (pp. 190–214).

The first School of the 21st Century was established in Independence, Missouri, in 1988. Since then, more than 1,300 programs nationwide have followed suit, and at least three states (Arkansas, Connecticut, and Kentucky) have launched statewide initiatives modeled on the concept. Yale University's Bush Center in Child Development and Social Policy continues to spearhead the movement, providing consultation, training, and evaluation for programs (Bishop-Josef, 2005). Universal PreK, discussed earlier in this chapter, is another initiative supported by the center.

As of 2010, 45 states had established coordinating councils for early care and education. The goals of these councils are to reduce wasteful duplication while expanding services to more children and families. An expected outgrowth of the expanded services for all children was the elimination of segregated programs for children who are poor or have disabilities (National Governors' Association, Center for Best Practices, n.d.). The goal of greater coordination has also received support at the federal level. The Head Start reauthorization bill of 2007 requires states to designate or establish a State Advisory Council on Early Childhood Education and Care for children from birth to school entry. The councils help states build a more coordinated system of services for young children and may also serve to generate awareness support among legislators and the general public. Another force for coordination and collaboration is the National Association of State Boards of Education, which launched the Early Childhood Network in 2006. This program provides grants and consultation to help states "advance the quality and coherence of their early learning initiatives" (Haynes, 2009, p. 5). The first phase of the project focused on improving the quality of early childhood programs to enhance outcomes and better prepare children for school. The second phase addresses better alignment of preschool with kindergarten and the primary grades, including smoother transitions across systems through so-called ready schools, in recognition of the fact that academic success is not solely a function of a child's readiness for school. In North Carolina, for example, a ready school is defined as one that "provides an inviting atmosphere, values and respects all children and their families, and is a place where children succeed. . . . It prepares children for success in work and life in the 21st century." Key elements or "pathways" include connections across early care and education programs, kindergarten, and primary grades; partnerships with families and communities; culturally and linguistically appropriate curriculum; and appropriate assessment (www.ncreadyschools.org).

Conclusion

This chapter has outlined several types of child development centers, including investment in human capital, supplemental care, remedial or compensatory research and teacher preparation, and consumer service. Individual programs often represent a combination of two or more of these types. Funding models for child development programs range from complete reliance on parent fees to varying degrees of government or corporate subsidization. Although the United States tends to lag behind most of the developed world, having ignored the needs of families for many years, managers of child development programs should certainly feel encouraged to see the momentum of support for child care as it is developing in this country. A number of factors, aspects of the human ecological system that will be discussed in the next chapter, suggest that society is on the verge of moving toward a higher status for child development services. Managers of child development programs are in a unique position to help make this happen.

Questions for Review

1. Name and describe five types of child development centers that you might manage. Explain how each serves a particular need for children, families, or society.

2. Describe the various ways in which child development programs are funded.

3. Explain how collaboration among agencies can improve the quality of care and services for young children. Give examples.

Professional Portfolio

Collaborate with your classmates to compile a list of potential funding sources for child-care programs in your community. Write a brief summary of each resource, including appropriate contact information, and enter this list in the Fiscal Management section of your administrative portfolio. Remember to add a cover sheet explaining what the list documents about your administrative competence.

Resources for Further Study

PRINT

Campbell, N. D., Appelbaum, J. C., Martinson, K., & Martin, E. (2000, April). *Be all that we can be: Lessons from the military for improving our nation's child care system.* Washington, DC: National Women's Law Center.

Zigler, E. F., Marsland, K., & Lord, H. (2009). *The tragedy of child care in America.* New Haven, CT: Yale University Press.

Websites

EARLY CHILDHOOD DEVELOPMENT

www.acf.hhs.gov/programs/ecd/early-learning-initiative

An office of the Administration for Children and Families within the U.S. Department of Health and Human Services; includes the link for the Early Learning Initiative with information about home visiting, child care, and early education components.

FAMILIES AND WORK INSTITUTE

www.familiesandwork.org

The Families and Work Institute is a nonprofit organization, founded in 1989, whose research on trends in family, work, and community life is aimed at encouraging the development of equitable, flexible, family-friendly policies in the workplace. The 2008 National Study of the Changing

Workforce can be downloaded at no cost; the full report as well as the data files allowing comparison among findings for 1992, 1997, and 2002 may be purchased.

FLORIDA CHILDREN'S FORUM

http://www.centraldirectory.org/uploads/inclusion.pdf

Understanding Inclusion and the Americans with Disabilities Act (ADA), an online publication of the Florida Children's Forum, answers questions frequently asked by child-care providers and provides an overview of the team approach to caring for children with disabilities. It includes a list of resources, definitions of terms, and information about specific disabilities.

NATIONAL INSTITUTE FOR EARLY EDUCATION RESEARCH

www.nieer.org

The National Institute for Early Education Research, originated at Rutgers University's Graduate School of Education and funded through a variety of private and governmental sources, collects and disseminates research on a variety of topics, such as teacher qualifications and interpretation of test results. The site includes a link to a comprehensive report in PDF format, *The State of Preschool: 2012 State Preschool Yearbook*, which provides state-by-state snapshots summarizing spending, accessibility, and quality of state-funded programs for 4-year-old children.

CHAPTER

Applying Theories in Managing a Child Development Center

LEARNING OUTCOMES

After studying this chapter you should be able to

- Define theory and explain why theories are important.
- Identify characteristics of four different types of child development theories.
- Describe key concepts associated with the major theories and give examples of how they are applied by child-care managers.
- Describe the ways that organization and management theories have changed over time and give examples.
- List and explain the five management processes.
- Describe the components of the ecological systems framework and give an example of how it can be applied by a manager of a child-care center.

It had been a challenge for Tanya to juggle her full-time job at Rainbow Center with taking college classes, but it had also been rewarding. One of the things she enjoyed most was being able to share real-life examples of abstract ideas with her classmates. When a professor spoke about a theorist named Lev Vygotsky and his concept of private speech, she thought of 4-year-old Darius, who loved watering the plants in his classroom every morning before the rest of the children arrived. With the greatest care, he poured water into each pot, all the while whispering to himself, "Watch out. It's going to spill. Be careful. Stop!" It was exciting for Tanya to realize that what she had formerly seen as just a cute mannerism was actually vivid evidence of Darius's thought processes at work. She became convinced that theory was not just a dry academic topic, but rather a way of seeing more in her daily experience with children and thinking more deeply about what she saw.

You may feel that theory is something outside the practical concerns of the manager of children's programs, any time you make a decision based on predicting the consequences of your actions, you are operating on a theory, whether consciously or not. Theories help human beings make sense of all the fragmented bits of information that confront them. They are frameworks that help answer the question of why one course of action might be preferable to another, why it might work better to accomplish your aims.

In formal terms, a **theory** is an organized set of related ideas, concepts, and principles that describes and attempts to explain a particular phenomenon. A good theory is carefully defined in writing and disseminated in the public domain so other scholars can evaluate it carefully. A theory is useful for organizing knowledge, drawing connections between observations, and making predictions. When you read about theories, you should realize that people are still testing and polishing them. New theories are proposed as information accumulates. You can assist in the work of theory development by thinking about and testing theories in your day-to-day work. Certainly, you can question a theory or ask whether it makes sense in light of your experience and values and those of the families you serve. When you do this in a thoughtful, rigorous way, you are engaging in evidence-based practice, part of a growing movement in the early childhood field (Buysse, Wesley, Snyder, & Winton, 2006).

THEORIES FROM MULTIPLE AREAS OF KNOWLEDGE

Managers of child development centers must coordinate information—and theories—from several areas of knowledge. First, they must think about how children grow and develop and how environments and activities help or hinder that development. Then directors must think about the best ways of managing complex organizations, such as child development centers, in order to achieve their goals for children and families. Finally, they need to remember that children do not exist in a vacuum; each child comes to the center with a complex history and set of relationships with his or her family and community. Center directors should therefore consider how families relate to the center and how both relate to other systems within the larger community. Experts in each of these broad areas of knowledge have developed a number of theoretical frameworks to organize ideas and create a rational basis for predicting outcomes.

DEVELOPMENTAL THEORY

Our ideas about developmentally appropriate practice incorporate the work of many scholars who tried to explain one or more aspects of human development. Jean Piaget, Lev Vygotsky, Howard Gardner, Benjamin Bloom, and B. F. Skinner focused primarily on cognitive, or intellectual, development. Erik Erikson studied social–emotional development. Arnold Gesell explored connections between cognitive and perceptual-motor development. Urie Bronfenbrenner examined the links between human development and its larger social contexts. Today's programs for young children reflect the thinking of all these and many other people, although some programs may operate without being aware of their theoretical bases. Because they are working with human beings and complex interactions, early childhood professionals cannot slavishly adhere to a single theory. They constantly refine their understanding and adjust their practice as they attempt to provide the best for each child in their care.

The document *Developmentally Appropriate Practice in Early Childhood Programs Serving Children from Birth through Age 8* (Copple & Bredekamp, 2009) is a case in point. Originally published in 1987 by the National Association for the Education of Young

Children (NAEYC), this work by a commission of professionals spelled out how developmental theory could be applied to the operation of early childhood programs. Based on research showing the step-by-step development of children, it described in practical terms the state of the art of applied child development at the time it was published. It was widely discussed and extremely influential in shaping programs for children in all types of child development centers, as well as public school settings. Other researchers applied the concept to early childhood special education (Fox, Hanline, Vail, & Gallant, 1994) and to standards for school-age child-care programs (Albrecht & Plantz, 1991). Some early childhood specialists criticized the document, however, because it seemed to present only one "right way" of doing things and appeared to favor White, middle-class patterns of child rearing. They argued that the practices defined in the document did not apply as easily to children from minority cultures or to children with disabilities (e.g., Mallory & New, 1994). NAEYC leaders listened to these concerns, and the revised edition (Bredekamp & Copple, 1997) addressed them by presenting a range of options for the early childhood practitioner to consider when making decisions. The third edition, responding to changing demographics and factors such as an increasing emphasis on standards and accountability, expands and clarifies the importance of the teacher's role and the urgent need to address the continuing achievement gap between poor children of color and their more advantaged peers (Copple & Bredekamp, 2009).

TYPES OF THEORIES OF HUMAN DEVELOPMENT

Theories of human development can be broadly classified as falling into four basic types. Maturationist theories emphasize that growth and development come largely from within the child and follow a predictable timetable. Environmentalist or behaviorist theories focus on the ways that growth and development can be influenced from the outside. Interactionist theories explore the ways that internal and external forces interact to propel development, suggesting that children with different backgrounds experience the same environment in very different ways. Ecological theories consider the individual within the context of all the systems that make up his or her environment. Table 3.1 summarizes some of the distinguishing characteristics of these four types of child development theories.

A maturationist, for example, when confronted with a 4-year-old who cannot (or will not) repeat a simple rhyme, might suggest simply waiting until the child has time to mature and develop greater language skills. An environmentalist might try using drill-and-practice sessions with rewards, such as stickers, for successful performance. An interactionist might consider internal factors, such as the child's previous language experience and interest in the project, as well as external factors, such as the manner in which the activity was presented. An ecologist might look at family and social contexts for this particular ability, such as the cultural relevance of the particular rhyme or the value placed on this type of language in general.

B. F. Skinner is known for his work on the behaviorist theory and its emphasis on reinforcement. People who have never even heard of Skinner are following one of his premises when they use rewards to encourage repetition of desirable behaviors. What has also been explained by the behaviorists is that, to eliminate a behavior (i.e., extinguish it), the behavior must never be rewarded. Intermittent rewards, even when spaced far apart in time, are still reinforcing. Benjamin Bloom, another behaviorist theorist, contributed to the concept of behavioral objectives in education, which he based on the belief that children achieve greater success if all tasks are broken down into manageable steps. Bloom's early research led him to state quite strongly the importance of the early years for later development, arguing that the most significant learning takes place during the first 5 years of life. Although scholars have disagreed with

TABLE 3.1   Characteristics of four types of child development theories.

	Maturationist	Behaviorist or Environmentalist	Interactionist	Ecological
Major Theorists	G. Stanley Hall Arnold Gesell	J. B. Watson B. F. Skinner	Jean Piaget Erik Erikson	Urie Bronfenbrenner Lev Vygotsky
Primary Interest	Predictable patterns of growth and development	Relating external events to observable changes in behavior	Mental or psychological constructions resulting from individual's interaction with physical or social environment	Relationships between and among individual and multiple environments
Emphasis	*Nature*	*Nurture*	*Interaction* of nature and nurture	*Interaction* of nature and nurture within *social and cultural context*
View of Human Development	Genetically determined process; unfolds over time if needs are met; cannot be rushed	Tabula rasa or blank slate: responses to environmental stimuli are either reinforced or extinguished depending on consequences	New experiences are either assimilated into existing mental frameworks or provoke creation of new ones (accommodation)	Widening sphere of understanding and control acquired through caring relationships with more experienced individual; shaped by culture and society
Role of Adult	Meet basic needs; support as child moves through predictable stages	Break learning goals into progressively more challenging steps; reinforce successful mastery of each	Provide opportunities for exploration and discovery in a supportive environment	Provide opportunities for exploration and discovery in a supportive environment; transmit cultural knowledge and values

the emphasis Bloom placed on the early years, the concept of critical periods in development and the crucial importance of the early years has received new attention as the result of recent research on brain development (National Research Council and Institute of Medicine, 2000).

POSTMODERN CRITIQUES OF CHILD DEVELOPMENT THEORY

A discussion of developmental theory should also acknowledge that a number of writers are critical of the fact that child development theories have been so influential in shaping our professional practices and our view of children. They argue that the theories are not based on objective knowledge, but are instead embedded in—and perpetuate—particular social systems. This postmodern perspective asserts that theorists cannot discover "reality" or "truth" because there is no such thing apart from our beliefs and perceptions. Those beliefs and perceptions are dominated by those in power at particular times and places. Postmodernism, as the term suggests, grows out of a critical reaction to a worldview characterized as modernism.

Child psychologist David Elkind (1994) summarizes the modernist view as resting on three basic beliefs: (a) that social progress is possible and tied to increasing scientific knowledge, (b) that nature is governed by universal principles that can be discovered and explained, and (c) that natural phenomena are regular and predictable. He says that postmodernism questions the ability of science and reason to solve all human problems because scientific objectivity is not possible (pp. 17–21).

Postmodern critics of child development theories indicate that those theories are rooted in the Western, middle-class experience and are not necessarily applicable to other groups (Dahlberg, Moss, & Pence, 1999). They also argue that too often theories are flawed because they purport to explain or predict aspects of groups or individuals without considering the ideas and perceptions of the people being studied. This is particularly likely to occur when the scientific establishment studies less powerful segments of society, such as children, poor people, or individuals with disabilities (e.g., Pugach, 2001). A modernist might try to explain, for example, how child care differs from preschool and define the particular skills needed by caregivers as distinguished from teachers. A postmodernist, on the other hand, would argue that the idea of child care and the idea of early education are just that: ideas. Each emerged to serve certain social purposes at particular times in history (e.g., Zigler & Lang, 1991). You will encounter the concept of postmodernism again when we look at theories of management later in this chapter.

Examples of Developmental Theories

PIAGET Piaget's theory represents a particular type of interactionist theory, often referred to as *constructivist,* because it holds that children must construct knowledge for themselves as they experience the environment. The idea is that children are not blank slates or empty containers to be filled with information. Instead, they are like scientists with their own hypotheses about the world, which they constantly test and refine as they move about in that world. For example, Piaget demonstrated that very young children (in what he called the preoperational stage) did not realize that an amount of water stays the same when poured from a tall, narrow container into a short, wide one. Nor, he argued, can adults teach them that this is so. Each child must discover this through countless experiences with pouring. Piaget's concepts help early childhood professionals understand children's thinking more clearly. Managers can use the theory to help teachers and parents appreciate the intelligence that goes into what appear to be "wrong" ideas.

VYGOTSKY The work of Lev Vygotsky, a Russian psychologist, has recently come into prominence, in part because of its application in the preschools of Reggio Emilia, Italy, which gained worldwide fame through the traveling exhibit "The Hundred Languages of Children." Vygotsky adds to Piaget's idea of the child constructing knowledge by suggesting that when more advanced learners—adults and older children in the culture—communicate with a child who is learning, they aid the child's thinking and learning. This concept is called the **social construction of knowledge**. To be effective, efforts to aid a child's thinking and learning must be calibrated to the child's **zone of proximal development (ZPD)**, that is, the cutting edge of child's cognitive development, or those concepts or skills beyond the child's current ability but which the child can tackle with help. Providing just the right amount of help for a child to accomplish a task or understand a concept is known as **scaffolding**. Notice how the teacher in this **video** provides just the amount of help that the child needs to complete the puzzle by calling his attention to shapes or colors without actually putting the pieces into place for him.

Also of interest to Vygotsky is private speech, in which a child may be observed audibly talking through a problem-solving situation, such as, "I'll put the big block here to keep this roof up." The private speech may be addressed to no one in particular, but it is an important link in the child's progression from merely reacting to external forces to acting with intentionality. Watch this **video** for a quick explanation of the similarities and differences between the theories of Piaget and Vygotsky.

Self-regulation is a term for this ability that has come into increasing prominence in recent years because it has been shown to be more predictive of school success than cognitive ability or family factors. Its biological basis is in the development of the pre-frontal cortex of the brain, though it is shaped by experiences and interactions with others. Its earliest manifestation is the infant's ability to settle back into sleep; later examples include inhibiting particular behaviors and purposefully focusing attention on a task. The ability to follow rules when someone is watching (to be regulated by oth-ers) is a rudimentary step toward self-regulation; however, true self-regulation emerges only when children experience regulating the behavior of their peers and regulating their own behavior when no one is watching. One of the most important ways children gain these experiences is through pretend play, where they voluntarily adapt their own language and behavior to the demands of particular roles and make sure that their playmates do likewise (Bodrova & Leong, 2008).

ERIKSON   Erik Erikson, another theorist in the interactionist category, turns our atten-tion from the realm of the intellect to social–emotional development. Erikson's theory of the Eight Stages of Man conceives of development as the individual's navigation through a series of stages, each of which is defined by two opposing outcomes. The task is to achieve an appropriate balance between the two: trust versus mistrust in infancy, autonomy versus shame and doubt in toddlerhood, initiative versus guilt in the preschool years, and so on, through the life span. Erikson worked to refine his theory throughout his life, adding a ninth stage describing the conflict and resolution culminating in old age when he himself was 86 years old. Thus, teachers in infant pro-grams are borrowing from Erikson when they talk about responding promptly to babies' cries so that the infants feel secure and gain a sense of trust. When we notice toddlers' insistence on feeding themselves, or their fondness for the word no, we are confirming observations that Erikson made years ago about the origins of autonomy. The practice of offering 3- and 4-year-old children large blocks of time for free (or self-initiated) play reflects Erikson's belief that children of this age are working on building a sense of initiative.

IMPORTANCE OF SOCIAL–EMOTIONAL DEVELOPMENT   In spite of Erikson's strong influence on what we know as developmentally appropriate practice, child development profes-sionals worry that too many contemporary programs for young children have shoved aside concerns for social–emotional development in response to demands that they pre-pare children for academic success (e.g., Elkind, 2008). Ironically, an emerging body of research and theory suggests that neglecting social–emotional issues in the push for academic excellence is actually counterproductive. Mental health experts tell us that "children who do not begin kindergarten socially and emotionally competent are often not successful in the early years of school—and can be plagued by behavioral, emo-tional, academic, and social development problems that follow them into adulthood" (Child Mental Health Foundations and Agencies Network, 2000). The brains of chil-dren, we have learned, are still under construction in the first few years of life. They need a rich variety of experiences to create new neural connections (in other words, to learn), but they also need to feel secure and connected to their caregiver in order to absorb those new experiences. When young children experience chronic stress, their bodies produce more of the chemicals that inhibit connections between neurons. Coping with fear and anxiety reduces a child's capacity for memory and learning because it taps the same areas of the developing brain (Levitt, 2009).

GOLEMAN   Psychologist Daniel Goleman argues that **emotional intelligence** is more important than IQ for success in life, that adults who are unable to recognize, express, and manage their feelings are more likely to fail at both relationships and careers. He says that children acquire emotional intelligence in "the crucible of the family," where parents model as well as teach these important abilities, but only if they themselves have achieved a level of understanding and mastery of their own feelings.

GREENSPAN   Stanley Greenspan, a prominent child psychiatrist, takes issue with Goleman's separation between intellectual and emotional intelligence. He theorizes that the two are inextricably intertwined, that the roots of cognitive development are embedded in emotional attachments. Greenspan describes six levels of the mind's development. In the first stage, the infant struggles to organize myriad physical sensations to achieve what Greenspan calls "global aliveness." At the next stage, "the related self," infants begin to form a connection with another person and develop a sense of shared humanity. In the next two stages, the infant's actions become more intentional, and in the last two stages, the child acquires the ability to think symbolically.

GARDNER   Howard Gardner's (2006) theory of multiple intelligences can be seen as another example of interactionist theory in its assertion that particular characteristics of individuals cause them to perceive and interact with their environment in different ways. His theory also challenges the customary distinction among cognitive, social–emotional, and perceptual–motor development. Gardner argues that humans are capable of at least seven ways of knowing the world: language, logical–mathematical analysis, spatial representation, musical thinking, the use of the body to solve problems or to make things, an understanding of other individuals, and an understanding of themselves. Each individual has a particular "profile of intelligences" resulting from his or her unique pattern of strengths and weaknesses across the seven areas. In Gardner's view, traditional concepts of intelligence have focused too narrowly on language and logical–mathematical thinking, with the result that our educational system has not supported the development of individuals with strengths in other areas.

In reviewing these theories of development, you might notice that it is extremely difficult to "slice up" the various domains of development. The traditional categories of physical, cognitive, social, and emotional development seem to overlap and blend into each other within every individual. To make matters even more interesting (you might say complicated), it also can be argued that individual development cannot be examined apart from its social context. Erik Erikson, for example, addressed the interaction between stages of an individual's development and the larger social forces at work during the individual's lifetime.

BRONFENBRENNER   Urie Bronfenbrenner (1997) takes a closer look at these interactions. His ecological model of human development depicts the infant as nested within a series of concentric systems, beginning with the family (the microsystem) and culminating with the society at large (the macrosystem). The theory takes into account the importance of subjective experience and perception as well as measurable, objective factors that influence development, and it emphasizes the importance of understanding individuals within the context of real life as opposed to isolated experimental situations. Development consists of the child's growing competence within, and understanding of, ever-widening spheres of environment. It occurs when children regularly participate in increasingly complex activities with people who care about them and to whom they are emotionally attached. The interaction between humans and their environments is two-way: They shape their environment as they are shaped by it. Babies, for example, rely on parents to provide what they need to develop, but parents also develop as parents through the experience of caring for their babies.

Bronfenbrenner sees his theory as evolving or developing since its first articulation in the 1970s and is concerned about "growing chaos in the lives of children, youth, families, schools, the world of work, and the ever-greater commuting in between" (Bronfenbrenner, 2005, pp. 13–14). He argues that the future of the human species depends on the willingness of societies to apply the findings of developmental science.

A recent report by the Committee on Integrating the Science of Early Childhood Development, pulling together the most recent information about development from a broad spectrum of sources, is a good example of human ecological theory applied. The committee concluded that healthy child development depends on factors at every level of the family ecosystem, from the physical and emotional nurturing that occurs within the family microsystem to the social policies and programs or macrosystem supporting that nurturing. The committee argued that the nation should support healthy development of all children both because it is the right thing to do and because it is an investment in the human capital that sustains democracy (Shonkoff & Phillips, 2000).

The Challenge of Applying Theories of Development

Because they reflect the complex nature of the human beings involved, child development programs rarely embody a single theory in its pure form. The NAEYC's Developmentally Appropriate Practice, noted earlier, incorporates ideas from all four types of theorists, with a particular emphasis on constructivism, a specific form of interactionist theory (Copple & Bredekamp, 2009).

Further complicating matters is the fact that members of other professions working with young children have been trained according to different theoretical frameworks, and these frameworks have evolved, just as they have in the field of early childhood education. Bruce Mallory, for example, describes the theoretical models that shape early childhood special education as developmental–interactionist, functional (or behaviorist), and biogenetic, and he argues that a "triangulated" approach, using ideas and methods based on all three, is necessary to serve children most effectively (Mallory, 1994). Now imagine the even greater challenge created by this variety of perspectives when a child with a disability is included in a program based on constructivist views of typical child development. All of the professionals involved must work together to develop a common vocabulary and function effectively as a team.

How Managers Apply Theories of Development

As noted earlier, theory is always in a state of flux until it becomes accepted as fact, but solid facts are seldom found in the arena of human development and behavior. If you feel that these complicating factors and continual changes make the study of theory too confusing and time-consuming, we offer three compelling reasons for you to reconsider. First, the theory (or theories) that underlie your program influence the ways you see children and families and all of the decisions you make as you interact with those children and families.

Second, even though theory is often difficult for beginning teachers and caregivers to apply to their work, one of the manager's tasks is to encourage staff members to become more reflective as they gain experience, to think about what and how children are learning. Each of the developmental theories can serve as a lens, a way of bringing particular aspects of what is observed into sharper focus, of seeing more clearly.

Third, as Tanya found in the chapter-opening vignette, studying theory will make your own work with children and families more exciting when you see examples of what the theorists mean in the behaviors before your eyes, or when you find possible explanations for things that have puzzled you. As a future manager of child development programs you will, no doubt, be taking additional courses in early childhood curriculum where you will learn more about these and other theorists. Some additional resources are listed at the end of this chapter, or you can consult your library to find others.

To apply any developmental theory, start with a general knowledge about the way children grow and develop to plan environments and activities for them. If you know your center will enroll children from 6 weeks through 8 years of age, organize an environment for each age range (infant, toddler, etc.) according to what research and experience says children are like at that age. Then look at the particular individuals in your group and adjust your generic planning to fit the developmental needs of these children. That may mean making sure teachers have access to materials to support children's emerging fascination with insects or fire trucks, for example, or providing adaptive equipment for children with particular disabilities. Finally, take into account the families and communities in which your particular group of children grow and develop so that your program incorporates and respects their particular patterns of child rearing. At each step of this process, your theoretical orientation will influence your decisions and actions.

? DECISIONS, DECISIONS . . .

Review the brief description of child development theories in Table 3.1. Which theory seems closest to your own beliefs about how young children learn and develop? Explain your answer. Was it difficult to decide on just one theory? Discuss your ideas with your classmates.

MANAGEMENT THEORY

As individuals, we all live and work within families, agencies, and groups. All of these entities have goals for their existence, use resources, and serve the needs and desires of the individuals within the society. All groups need an activity or process that coordinates individual efforts toward achieving goals, allocates resources effectively, and serves needs. That activity is called management.

Management is needed in every effective group to attain the desired goals with the least expenditure of time, energy, and money. Whether the operation is an agency, school, business, or family, whether it is operated for profit or on a nonprofit basis, management is needed. A manager is the person who applies management theory and uses management techniques. A manager may also be called administrator, executive, chief executive officer (CEO), supervisor, director, or boss.

A management theory is an organized set of related ideas, concepts, and principles that attempt to describe the process of managing an organization. An organization is a group of people intentionally coordinated to achieve a common goal. A crowd at a baseball game is not an organization, but the teams competing and the leagues to which they belong are. A child development center is an organization. Management, as we have seen in Chapter 1, is the process of ensuring that the goals of the organization are met as efficiently as possible. Therefore, management theory grows out of organization theory.

Although management is widely recognized as a science, some would argue that it is an art because it encompasses creativity and requires new approaches and new ways of looking at old procedures. However, even the most creative manager must use management science as a basis for action. Just as you have seen in the case of child development theory, there have been a number of management or organization theories and volumes of studies designed to test those theories. Different theories appear to apply better to one type of organization than to another. Just as with child development theory, total agreement does not exist on the most desirable management theory to use. Most managers probably incorporate concepts and principles from several theories as they approach their jobs.

Historical Evolution of Organization Theory

Understanding how organizations function and why they thrive or fail has fascinated scholars for centuries. A review of the evolution of organization theory reveals four successive stages, each influenced by concepts drawn from many disciplines, and each with a different view of the manager's role (Hatch, 1997, pp. 5–55):

- *Organization as machine*   The first half of the twentieth century was dominated by the view that organizations are like machines, designed to accomplish specific purposes, and managers are like engineers, who create and operate the machines. This view drew heavily on the fields of economics, engineering, and sociology, particularly the ideas of Adam Smith, Karl Marx, Emile Durkheim, and Max Weber.

- *Organization as organism*   Beginning around 1950, the emerging disciplines of political science, ecology, industrial sociology, and social anthropology helped shape the image of the organization as an organism, a living system adapting to its environment as needed. The manager, in this view, is one of the components of the system, interdependent with all the others. The writings of Talcott Parsons, Alfred Gouldner, and Ludwig von Bertalanffy informed this view.

- *Organization as concept*   During the 1980s, Erving Goffman, Roland Barthes, and Kenneth Burke, as well as other scholars of cultural anthropology, folklore, semiotics, and linguistics, put forward the idea that an organization is a concept, like culture, created by human thought with no objective existence, though it is treated as real by the mutual consent of society. By extension, then, the manager is also a social construct, perhaps a symbol for the organization.

- *Organization as theory*   The postmodern perspective emerged on several fronts, including architecture, literary theory, and culture studies, in the 1990s. As you saw in the discussion of child development theory, postmodern theory focuses more on how knowledge is created than on the content of that knowledge, and it is often critical of that process. Ideas drawn from the writings of Michel Foucault, Jacques Derrida, Mikhail Bakhtin, and others contributed to the idea that an organization is like a collage (or a theory), combining bits of past knowledge to create new ways of viewing things. The manager, then, is akin to the artist (or theorist).

Theoretical Paradigms

Lemak (2004) argues that this chronological approach fails to capture the essential distinctions among a rapidly growing array of theories. Instead of focusing on when they emerged, he examines theories for their underlying assumptions about people and organizations. Every theory rests on assumptions, or ideas accepted as given. In his review of management literature, Lemak found six key assumptions that can be characterized as implicit answers to the following questions: Should one study individual workers, groups, or systems to understand how organizations work? What motivates workers? Are people basically rational, or are they controlled by emotions? Should managers be concerned with what workers do, or with what they think and feel? What is the goal of the organization, and what function does the manager fulfill in accomplishing that goal? Lemak found that three distinct clusters of theories emerged, each representing a particular paradigm or conceptual model:

- The classical paradigm views the individual worker as the unit of analysis and assumes that monetary rewards are effective motivators because those workers are rational beings. With efficiency as the main goal, the manager's job is to lay out the steps of production and then supervise workers to make sure they follow procedures.

- The behavioral paradigm focuses on the group rather than the individual and views social connections and the resulting job satisfaction as more powerful than economic motivators. Social change rather than profit is seen as the goal, and the manager's role is team building. (Note that the descriptor, *behavioral*, is a term used within the field of organizational management and not to be confused with *behaviorist*, which applies to psychological theories discussed earlier in this chapter.)

- The systems paradigm stems from the concept of cybernetics (i.e., automatic control systems), developed during World War II. The idea is that any system, whether animal, machine, or organization, must continuously adapt in response to feedback from its environment. The unit of analysis in this paradigm is the system as a whole, which must maintain equilibrium or balance within a constantly shifting environment in order to survive. The goal is to transform inputs into outputs as efficiently as possible, and the manager serves the dual function of taking in and interpreting feedback while helping to coordinate the system's responses to that feedback.

While acknowledging that each model developed within a particular historical context, Lemak asserts that ideas from one period often have roots in earlier eras or may be echoed in the writings of theorists who ostensibly belong to a later school of thought. Thus, the chief proponents of the classical paradigm emerged during the second half of the nineteenth century and drew ideas from engineering and physical science. The behavioral paradigm is frequently presented as a later development, most closely associated with the Great Depression of the 1930s, although its tenets can be traced to writings that appeared a half century earlier criticizing social ills brought on by the Industrial Revolution.

? DECISIONS, DECISIONS . . .

Think about your basic assumptions about people and organizations. Do you think people are more strongly motivated by money or by feelings that they contribute to a team effort? Do they generally think things through and behave logically, or are they more governed by their emotions? What is the best way for a manager to relate to employees? Divide your class into pairs and discuss these questions.

APPLYING MANAGEMENT THEORIES

Just as no individual program is likely to be a "pure" example of one type of child development theory, management approaches often reflect elements of more than one paradigm. This text is no exception. It is organized around a framework of managerial processes that are derived from the classical paradigm, while incorporating concepts about family systems (which we discuss later in this chapter) that share much in common with Lemak's third paradigm. You, too, are likely to find ideas from many types of management theories useful in your work, depending on the particular situation. Lemak (2004) suggests that the three paradigms be considered analogous to management styles and that individual managers gravitate toward theorists whose assumptions about human nature, and the like, most closely resemble their own (p. 15).

TOTAL QUALITY MANAGEMENT

One approach to management that has gained increasing popularity in the United States recently is total quality management, which is based on the belief that organizations must strive for continuous improvement in order to survive (Rampersad, 2001). This approach is based on the ideas of two Westerners, W. Edwards Deming and Joseph Juran, who developed it in Japan more than 50 years ago when U.S. industries were entrenched in the opposite, top-down approach to management. Japan's achievements in gaining a large share of the world market for automobiles and electronic equipment prompted U.S. manufacturers to take a closer look at Deming's theories.

Total quality management contrasts with traditional management methods in several ways:

1. Power is shared. Ideas flow upward from the people actually doing the work and downward from the organization's leaders.
2. Responsibility is shared. Everyone is expected to understand and be committed to the organization's mission, spot problems, propose solutions, and take appropriate action to solve the problems.
3. Customer satisfaction is the central focus.
4. Quality is achieved by doing even the small things right the first time. When products or outcomes are faulty, the process is examined and altered as needed.
5. Successful businesses do not rest on their laurels but strive for continuous improvement.

According to Dorothy Hewes (1994), who studied the history of educational management systems, total quality management may have seemed revolutionary to U.S. industry when it came into vogue in the 1980s, but it should sound very familiar to those of us in the field of early childhood education, where prominent leaders have been espousing self-government and bottom-up management for over a century. In fact, the accreditation process of the National Association for the Education of Young Children begins with a detailed self-study by all of the people involved in a child development center, followed by self-initiated movements toward greater quality. This process is discussed in greater detail in the next chapter.

MANAGEMENT PROCESSES

All managers use five basic processes regardless of what enterprise they manage. These five basic managerial processes are examined in greater detail in later chapters. In the following brief overview, we relate each to the role of a child development center manager.

Planning

Planning can be defined as creating a mental image of what you want to accomplish and how you will go about doing so, a road map of where you want to go and how you will get there. Andrew DuBrin defines three levels of planning. Strategic planning is the organization's "overall master plan that shapes its destiny." Tactical planning breaks that master plan down into specific goals, assigning them to various parts of the organization. Operational planning spells out the specific procedures or steps needed to meet the goals (DuBrin, 2000, p. 95). When designing and building a house, for example, the strategic plan is represented by the architect's drawings. Tactical planning occurs when a contractor hires the electricians, plumbers, carpenters, masons, and

It may look like child's play, but all of the managerial process are required for assembling the time, materials, and adult support that make positive interactions possible.

other professionals needed to work on the many interdependent components of the house. Each of these professionals engages in operational planning as they figure out how to lay the foundation, build the walls, or install the wiring and plumbing.

Organizing

Organizing is defined as arranging elements (e.g., people, supplies, and equipment) and coordinating joint activities so that all of the interdependent parts contribute effectively to the desired goal. This critical process begins after planning and requires assembling the people, physical space, equipment, and materials in an orderly process to accomplish the center's goals. Some people are very good at suggesting ideas or even writing plans, but they fall short when the time for implementation arrives. If you see this occurring, you may need to step in and guide them. It is through organizing that the dreams begin to materialize and the hard work of the center gets done.

In the organizing process, the manager delegates and organizes units to facilitate conducting the programs stipulated in the goals. An internal logic and consistency should be applied to the delegation of duties. Also, the manager assembles and uses space, facilities, materials, and equipment effectively to accomplish the work of the center.

Staffing

People make the major difference in any service institution. The importance of people is indicated by the statistic that salaries for the personnel of a center often consume over 70 percent of the operating budget. Staffing is a process of recruiting, developing, and deploying the human resources (human capital) required to perform the functions of the center.

The staffing process begins with recruiting and selecting the individuals most qualified to carry out the center's goals efficiently. High standards begin with high-quality staff members. Once staff members have been hired, it is the manager's job to orient them to the center's policies and procedures and to ensure that they are thoroughly informed about their specific duties as well as the standards for performance of those duties.

Staff members agree to their job description, which serves as the basis for the evaluation. Careful evaluations during a staff member's probationary period, and at least annually thereafter, help the individual make corrections in practices and are a wise investment of a manager's time. Because there is so much to learn about this vital field of service that deals with vulnerable human beings, a dynamic and ongoing plan for building human capital through staff development is another wise investment.

Leading

Leading is a process of directing and influencing others through example, talent, information, and personal interaction skills. A leader anticipates developments based on broad knowledge of the field at the national as well as the local level and communicates those possibilities to all members of the organization. The leader inspires enthusiasm and helps individuals maintain a holistic and dynamic picture of their responsibilities, thus minimizing problems of burnout. A leader makes decisions, takes actions, and assigns responsibilities necessary to transform possibilities into realities. A leader reaches out beyond the center and assumes responsibility for professional activities at the community, state, and national levels.

Monitoring and Controlling for Quality

Monitoring and controlling are defined as the evaluation and action functions of maintaining high quality in the promised services. In other words, after a plan of action has been developed and put into action, the manager must check regularly to ensure that the plan is actually being carried out and meeting its intended aims.

Standards are the measuring sticks used to determine how well the center is accomplishing its aims. A good manager establishes personal standards based on professional knowledge and individual experience, as well as the standards provided by one or more outside sources. All centers must adhere to licensing standards, which are minimum requirements established by the state for the protection of children when they are not in their parents' care.

In addition to licensing standards, some centers are required to meet standards established by their funding bodies. Many states, for example, fund programs for 4-year-old children in public schools; to qualify for these grants, school districts must

---

LEADERSHIP LENS

Wise managers understand that licensing rules are minimum standards and that they are the result of a collaborative effort of many people just like themselves. They ensure that their centers adhere to the rules and do not try to "get around" them. A manager who aspires to leadership might work with staff members to meet additional standards designed to establish a benchmark of quality beyond the minimum welfare and safety considerations of licensing regulations. Accreditation is a distinction awarded to early childhood schools and child-care centers that have met the standards established by the National Academy of Early Childhood Programs, a division of the National Association for the Education of Young Children (NAEYC). These standards were agreed to by early childhood professionals and parents from across the nation before they were accepted by the NAEYC board.

Looking beyond their own centers, leaders understand that they can have a voice in improving rules that need to be changed as new needs arise or new information develops. In other words, the manager of a child development center works in partnership with the licensing agency and accreditation body to maintain a baseline of quality; a leader takes a broader perspective and works with regulatory systems to raise the bar for all children.

comply with specific guidelines. Federally funded Head Start programs have another set of detailed guidelines to follow. In each case, these regulations are above and beyond minimum licensing standards and must be followed consistently in order for the center to maintain its funding.

ECOLOGICAL SYSTEM FRAMEWORK

We turn our attention now from theories about child development and organizational management to a framework for understanding the ecosystem in which both families and child development programs operate. As noted at the beginning of this chapter, managers of a child development centers have to understand children and families as well as program operation, and they must integrate this knowledge with the demands of society. A useful approach to help achieve such goals is to find a framework for analysis— that is, a theory for examining the various parts and the whole. You encountered the topic of systems in our discussion of management theory. In this section we will look at how systems theory can be applied to families and child development programs.

Systems theory is based on the idea that every phenomenon comprises interrelated parts within itself at the same time that it makes up part of some larger system. The human brain, for example, is a complex arrangement of cerebellum, cerebral cortex, and other specialized parts, each comprised of cells, which are in turn made up of atoms. The brain is also part of the larger central nervous system, which governs all bodily functions. In the social realm, the various departments of a large corporation are all examples of systems in that they are smaller units or individuals who must work together to function effectively, and together they make up the larger system, the corporation. Ecology is a branch of science concerned with the interconnections of organisms and their environments. Thus, an ecosystem framework looks at the connections between systems and the contexts in which they operate.

The biological sciences use an ecological system framework to explain the interdependence between biological organisms and the encompassing environment. The phenomenon of global warming is an example of such interdependence among humans, other living organisms, and the environment that has received a great deal of media attention. Carbon dioxide and other gases act like the glass in a greenhouse to trap heat from the sun. Without this greenhouse effect, temperatures on earth would not be warm enough to make life possible. However, scientists have determined that human use of fossil fuels such as coal and oil to produce energy over the past century has resulted in the buildup of greenhouse gases and a consequent rise in the earth's temperature, with negative effects on water, energy, agriculture, and health (U.S. Global Change Research Program, 2009).

The ecosystem framework is useful for understanding social systems, such as families or child development centers, as well as biological systems (Nickols, 2003). Both require energy and use feedback from the environment to achieve equilibrium. Bubolz and Sontag (1993) proposed a family ecosystem framework that examines interactions within and across three environments:

1. The physical–biological environment refers to the environment formed by nature, such as soil, climate, and natural resources.

2. The human-built environment is what human beings have constructed or altered to fit their needs, such as factories, roads, farms, and pollution.

3. The social–cultural environment includes other people as well as the more abstract results of interactions between people, such as cultural values and institutions.

The child development program is part of—or interacts with—each of these.

Child development programs can help children appreciate and care for the physical–biological environment.

The Physical–Biological Environment

The **physical–biological environment** comprises the natural world, including soil, climate, animals, vegetation, mineral resources. It affects the operation of a child development center in many ways, both obvious and subtle. For example, centers located in extremely cold or hot climates spend more on heating and air conditioning, respectively; a Head Start program located in a rural area must budget for higher transportation costs because of the distances between children's homes; and all centers should plan for coping with natural emergencies such as tornadoes. Natural resources also relate directly to the wealth of the community and individuals within the community. The presence of many natural resources provides productive jobs for the parents of children, increases the amount of income they receive, and stimulates their desire for early childhood education for their children. On the other hand, an absence of natural resources is likely to be correlated with unemployment or low-paying jobs for parents and an inability to pay for high-quality service.

The Human-Built Environment

Natural resources become more valuable economic resources as they move through factories, businesses, and farming enterprises and into retail consumer markets. All of these examples are aspects of the **human-built environment**, that is, constructions or alterations to the natural world to fit human needs, such as factories, roads, farms, and pollution. Jobs for citizens result from such enterprises. Some of the holders of these jobs are the parents of the children in our child development centers.

Although the human-built environment depends on the physical–biological environment, it transforms that environment in many ways. Some transformations are purposeful, while others may be accidental by-products of human actions. The results of such transformations might be beneficial, apparently neutral, or at times harmful. The child-care center itself is a part of the human-built environment: a physical structure built to serve specific human purposes. Good roads and efficient public transportation systems make it easier for parents to get their children to the center and themselves to work.

Some changes wrought by humans are less benevolent, as in the case of air or water pollution. These might seem like issues far removed from your role as manager of a child development center, but people in a child development program breathe the same air and drink the same water as people elsewhere in the community. High concentrations of automobile exhaust in a city can result in pollution levels that keep everyone indoors for several days. An emergency resulting from the bacterial contamination of a city's water supply can mean that a center must purchase bottled water, spend extra energy boiling a supply of drinking water, or perhaps suspend services until the situation is brought under control.

The Social–Cultural Environment

The **social–cultural environment** is the product of people interacting with one another and with elements of their environments, forming relationships and creating cultural patterns and social and economic institutions. Expectations regarding roles and norms of behavior are also part of the social–cultural environment. The extended family and neighborhood network of friends are two examples of social–cultural environments. The teachers, caregivers, cooks, and custodians at child development centers interact with children and parents to create another social–cultural environment. Just as in the human-built environment, interactions within the cultural environment require energy: emotional and intellectual energy, as well as physical energy.

EQUILIBRIUM AND ENERGY IN THE ECOSYSTEM

Striving for an equilibrium or balance is an important characteristic of the human ecological system. Families create an internal family ecosystem and also interact with environments outside the family; they attempt to maintain equilibrium between themselves and the other systems. A child development center interacts with numerous systems, and it too must seek equilibrium.

In a child development center, nonhuman resources, such as fossil-fuel energy, natural raw materials, and solar energy, are used in the structure and to heat and cool it. Nonhuman resources are organized and activated by human energy—the energy people derive from food. Human energy, represented by skill and know-how, is needed in every aspect of the child development center operation. Much of the knowledge and skills present in staff members result from energy expended in other systems—their homes, schools, and colleges. This point illustrates how an investment in the human being (in human capital) at one time often pays off at another time.

A human service, such as a child development center, can be called energy intensive, requiring high-energy inputs from many people. The child development service supplements parental energy. The children's energy is channeled into exploring their own learning activity and helping with some of the center's work. For example, children learn to pick up after themselves and take care of their own needs, reducing the demand on teachers for energy inputs. The quality of human-energy inputs is represented by costs to the community and the family. One can readily hypothesize that the quality of programs for children is related to the available energy of teachers and caregivers for each child. Energy includes the knowledge, skills, and stamina to carry on the work.

APPLYING THE ECOSYSTEMS MODEL

The human ecological systems model is useful in planning and coping with problems that arise. Locating the source of the problem within one of the three environments is a first step toward a solution. Suppose, for example, a manager notices that a great deal of

LEADERSHIP LENS

Advocacy leadership requires an understanding of the human ecological system framework and the ways in which the ripple effect works: When you change one factor in the system, it affects and changes other factors. Think about the impact of a child development program in your community, for example, perhaps one where you are currently employed. Consider how it contributes to the local economy—not only by employing the people on its staff, but by making employment or pursuit of education possible for all the parents it serves. How might you disseminate this information and help others see these connections?

Problem:
Children are not eating food prepared for them.

Physical–Biological Environment:
Is food of high quality, fresh, and flavorful?

Human–Built Environment :
Does the center have equipment and supplies
to store food safely and maintain freshness? Is food
served at proper temperatures to be safe and appetizing?

Social–Cultural Environment:
Do staff consider cultural preferences
when planning menus? Do they measure ingredients
and adjust recipes accurately? Are serving sizes appropriate?

FIGURE 3.1 Using the human ecological systems model to locate the source of a problem.

food is being wasted because children are not eating the meals prepared for them. Figure 3.1 illustrates a way to approach the problem by considering possible causes within each of the three environments. Once the manager determines the source of the problem, corrective solutions can be selected. Note that in the example provided, none of the possible sources of the problem can be addressed by doing anything with or to the children. In general, solutions dealing with things rather than people are more easily implemented and should be tried first.

?   **DECISIONS, DECISIONS . . .**

Consider another problem from the human ecological systems perspective: Suppose that nap time in the center where you work is chaotic, with children crying and fussing instead of resting peacefully. List the elements you might check in the physical–biological environment, the human-built environment, and the social–cultural environment in order to make nap time more peaceful.

Conclusion

Management of a child development center requires an integration of theories and principles from child development, organizational management, and human ecology. A **theory** is an organized set of related ideas, concepts, and principles that describe a particular area of knowledge. A theory must be stated as clearly as possible, published in the public domain, and tested by independent scholars, who also publish their results in the public domain. A theory provides explanations for *why* a course of action might be desirable. Individuals may find particular theories more convincing or compatible with their own assumptions, but no one theory can be said to explain everything. Managers who understand a range of theories can choose the one that best fits a particular situation.

All managers use five basic processes regardless of what enterprise they manage: planning, organizing, staffing, leading, and monitoring and controlling for quality.

Questions for Review

1. Define *theory* and state requirements of a good theory. Tell how theory differs from fact.
2. Tell how the four types of child development theories differ from each other.
3. Compare and contrast the three major types of management theory.

4. Give an example of how a child development program director uses each of the five management processes.
5. Give examples of how each of the three environments in the ecosystems model is involved in operating a child development center.

Professional Portfolio

Consult the website for the National Association for the Education of Young Children (http://www.naeyc.org/academy/pursuing/overview), to learn the steps involved in accreditation. Develop a plan that a center could follow to accomplish each step and achieve accreditation. For each step, describe what must be done, who will be responsible, when it should be completed, and what resources might be helpful. Include this plan in your administration portfolio in the section labeled Assessment and Evaluation. Be sure to add a cover sheet describing what the plan shows about your competency as a manager of programs for young children.

Resources for Further Study

PRINT

Colley, J. L., & Doyle, J. L. (2007). *Principles of general management: The art and science of getting results across organizational boundaries.* New Haven, CT: Yale University.

Edwards, C. P. (2002, Spring). Three approaches from Europe: Waldorf, Montessori, and Reggio Emilia. *Early Childhood Research and Practice*, 4(1). Online at http://ecrp.uiuc.edu/

National Scientific Council on the Developing Child. (2007). *The science of early childhood development.* Online at http://developingchild.harvard.edu/initiatives/council/

Websites

NAEYC OFFICE OF APPLIED RESEARCH

http://www.naeyc.org/resources/research

A service of the National Association for the Education of Young Children, this office provides information on accessing, evaluating, and using early childhood research, and sources of data.

NATIONAL SCIENTIFIC COUNCIL ON THE DEVELOPING CHILD

http://developingchild.harvard.edu/initiatives/council/

Housed at the Center on the Developing Child at Harvard University, the council is a nonpartisan collaboration among scholars in neuroscience, early childhood development, pediatrics, and economics. Its mission is to provide policy makers with access to scientific knowledge to help them make informed decisions for investing public funds to promote successful learning, adaptive behavior, and sound physical and mental health for all young children. The site includes links to publications and working papers on several aspects of early development.

PART
2

CORE COMPETENCIES

4

Reflective Management: Personal and Professional Self-Awareness

LEARNING OUTCOMES

After studying this chapter you should be able to

- Explain the importance of reflective practice for effective management.
- Describe several management and leadership styles.
- Discuss the role of emotional intelligence in management.
- Identify several types of decisions and give examples.
- List the steps involved in the decision process.
- Use a system of prioritizing tasks as a time management strategy.

Ever since coming to work at Rainbow Center, Tanya had admired the grace and efficiency with which Jeralyn handled the myriad demands of the director's job. She always seemed to have time for a smile and a bit of friendly conversation with staff or family members, even on days when a major report was due and the 3-year-olds clogged the sink in their classroom trying to wash all the sand-table toys. When Tanya wondered aloud whether she would be able to do the same, Jeralyn shared one of the things she had learned at a stress management workshop sponsored by the local resource and referral agency. "It's a matter of figuring out what's really important," she said, "and not letting all the little things distract you from that. For me, people matter more than paperwork and plumbing. My relationships with staff and families are what make this work worthwhile for me. I try to block out time for those interactions every day, as well as some protected time to handle the report. And," she laughed, "I make sure I have the phone number of a good plumber on speed dial!"

As you learned in the previous chapter, administrators of children's programs draw on a complex, continually evolving body of knowledge in at least three areas: child development, family ecosystems, and management. A solid understanding of current thinking in each of these areas is a necessary, but not sufficient, element of your preparation for the manager's role. Effective management is not a question of learning a few "right" techniques and simply applying them. As you have seen, there is no agreed-upon right answer. Managing always involves human interactions, whether the facility managed produces computer parts or a human service such as the care and education of young children. This makes managing a complex undertaking, requiring professional judgment and the ability to think on one's feet.

REFLECTIVE PRACTICE

Personal and professional self-awareness is listed as the first of 10 management competencies needed by program administrators in programs seeking accreditation from the National Association for the Education of Young Children (NAEYC). Components include understanding principles of adult development, self-knowledge regarding beliefs and values, ability to apply a code of ethics, and "the ability to be a reflective practitioner and apply a repertoire of techniques to improve the level of personal fulfillment and professional job satisfaction" (National Association for the Education of Young Children, 2007a). Personal and professional self-awareness can be compared to what Peter Senge, a prominent authority on organizational management, calls "personal mastery," people's ability to keep clearly in mind and continually refine what is most important to them, combined with an accurate assessment of where they are in relation to that vision. He adds:

Managers, like children, need time to pause and reflect about what they are doing.

> But personal mastery is not something you possess. It is a process. It is a lifelong discipline. People with a high level of personal mastery are acutely aware of their ignorance, their incompetence, their growth areas. And they are deeply self-confident. Paradoxical? Only for those who do not see that "the journey is the reward." (Senge, 2006, pp. 131–133)

Managers must absorb a great deal of information from the "experts" as well as from the situation at hand, and they must be able to select and apply that information in the way that makes most sense to them at the time. They observe what happens, and what they learn from experience becomes part of their knowledge base for future decisions. This entire process of looking back and making sense of your experience is called reflection. Another term for reflection is *critical thinking*. It is an activity essential to any type of learning beyond simple rote memorization. In the Decisions, Decisions segments that appear in each chapter, this text asks you to engage in reflection—to think about what you are reading in the context of your own experience and to apply your thinking to some new situation.

Seibert and Daudelin (1999) traced the history of reflection in education back to the Greek philosopher Socrates and argued for its application to management theory and practice. They distinguished between two types of reflection, believing that successful managers must use both types, and offered suggestions for enhancing each. Active reflection occurs in the situation, "on the fly in the midst of challenging experiences." All managers engage in active reflection—that is, they ask themselves questions about what is happening, what they should do, and what might happen as a result. They answer their own questions by interpreting what they observe. Managers can enhance this active reflection process by becoming more aware of it. They can listen to themselves and try to generate more probing questions, always remembering that their interpretations of situations are not necessarily final. They should find ways to capture the ideas that occur to them in the heat of the action and use spare moments throughout the day to mull over current problems (pp. 206–207).

In proactive reflection, managers take time away to reflect on their experience, often after completing a particular task or project. They review what happened, compare it to their other experiences, formulate explanations, and make plans for what they might do differently another time (p. 148). Community reflection is a particular type of proactive reflection in which a group of managers approaches similar questions under the guidance of a facilitator. Some managers report that they not only learn more through this collaborative approach, they also develop feelings of greater closeness with their colleagues (p. 205).

KNOWING YOURSELF

Seibert and Daudelin (1999, p. 18) pointed out that the Latin root of the word *reflection* is *reflectere*, which means "to bend back." And, as you read in the preceding section, managers do "bend back" in their thinking as they review what has happened and formulate new ideas. Another, perhaps more common, association with the word *reflection* is the image that looks back at you from mirrors or other shiny surfaces. Managers look into metaphorical mirrors to acquire self-reflective knowledge, which is an understanding of one's purpose or mission and of one's strengths and weaknesses in relation to that purpose. Brown and Manning (2000, pp. 84–85) considered self-reflective knowledge one of four types of core knowledge for directors of children's programs. Common sense tells you that you must have a strong sense of who you are and what you believe, as well as the humility to acknowledge what you do not know, if you are to be credible and effective in a leadership role. The "mirrors" that managers of child development programs use are self-assessment tools; feedback from colleagues, employees, and families; and self-reflection within a context of professional knowledge. See Figure 4.1 for a survey you can use to examine your own personal and professional self-awareness.

WHAT WILL BE YOUR MANAGEMENT STYLE?

The previous chapter presented an overview of three paradigms, or conceptual models of management. If you have some work experience, you have probably already witnessed the application of at least one of these models. Managers applying the classical model use concepts of cost and increased efficiency. They analyze jobs and figure out the "best way" for the job to be done and expect that the job should be done that way. In the behavioral approach, the manager recognizes that the way workers feel about their jobs, both individually and as a group, has profound effects on job outcome. This type of manager gives employees more independence and helps them take more responsibility and develop maturity in their jobs. In the third approach, based on a systems theory of organizations, a manager strives to understand the "big picture" and help all the parts work together so that the organization as a whole can adapt to changing situations within the larger environment.

Examining My Personal and Professional Self-Awareness

1. My beliefs (select one):
   - I generally follow instructions and don't ask questions.
   - I have given thought to what I do and the reasons for my actions, including my personal values.
   - I base my beliefs and actions on what I have learned about human development as well as on my personal values.
   - I have created a written statement of my philosophy as an early childhood professional.

2. My understanding of others (select one):
   - I am aware that there is a variety of personality types and learning styles.
   - I can recognize characteristics of personality types or learning styles in others.
   - I try to take individual differences into account when interacting with others.
   - I am generally able to maintain positive, supportive relationships with any personality type.
   - I can mentor (facilitate the professional development) of others.

3. My ethical and moral practice (select one):
   - I am unfamiliar with a professional code of ethics. I generally follow instructions and don't ask questions.

   - I am familiar with the NAEYC Code of Ethical Conduct (or know where to find it).
   - I have affirmed the Statement of Commitment to uphold the Code in my work with children.
   - I have used the Code to resolve an ethical dilemma.
   - In addition to the above, I am familiar with the Supplement for Administrators.
   - In addition to the above, I have used the Supplement to resolve an ethical dilemma.

4. My reflective skills (check all that apply):
   - I have a clear picture of my strengths (or potential strengths) as well as areas that I need to work on as a program administrator.
   - I know where to get help with the areas that need improvement.
   - I am generally comfortable receiving feedback from others, including constructive criticism.
   - I manage my emotions effectively, expressing feelings clearly and appropriate in a given situation.
   - I am usually able to manage my time effectively and complete important tasks on schedule.
   - I know and use several strategies to reduce or cope with stress in my personal and professional life.

FIGURE 4.1   Self-examination of personal and professional self-awareness.

In addition to reflecting your ideas about organizations and human nature, your management style will be influenced by aspects of your personality, such as power orientation, ways of dealing with conflict, reaction to stress, and psychological type (Benfari, 1999).

Power and Conflict

You might think of power, for example, as based on fear of punishment or a desire for reward. You might see it as based on respect for either the position itself or the expertise of the individual holding that position. Or you might see power as something based on subordinates' personal admiration and affection for the person in authority (Zeece, 1998). Your basic approach when confronted with conflict can range from avoiding a fight by capitulating or pretending the issue doesn't exist to defending your position at all costs. Between these two extremes, you might seek a solution in which both parties settle for something less than they wanted or, ideally, collaborate to find a solution that satisfies everyone and may even be better than what either had imagined.

Stress

Your reaction to stress can vary from time to time, just as it varies from that of other individuals. One manager may need predictability and stability, while another thrives on the challenges of opening new programs and juggling special fund-raising activities, all while handling the day-to-day operations of a center. The second manager, in fact, may become bored without the added stimulation, yet an illness or family crisis could change that picture quite suddenly. In other words, stress can be viewed as an interaction among external conditions or events, your perceptions of those conditions, and your inner reserves for dealing with them. Chronic stress overload leads to burnout or the inability to function—in work or in life in general. In this video, you will hear a director explain her approach to managing the stress that comes with her job.

Emotional labor is a term coined by sociologist Arlie Russell Hochschild (1983) to describe the psychological effort involved in controlling the expression of one's emotions on the job. Waiters, for example, are generally expected to display a friendly attitude toward customers; nurses are expected to show caring and concern. Displaying the desired emotion regardless of how one really feels is called surface acting, in contrast to deep acting, which is attempting to alter one's genuine feelings to match the expectations of the job. Consistent demands for either type of acting can be draining and stressful. However, a third type of emotional labor, expressing one's naturally felt emotions, can have a positive effect if the emotions displayed are consistent with one's identity and core values.

It is easy to see that emotional labor is obviously a significant factor in work with young children. Caregivers are expected to display patience, affection, and enthusiasm toward children. When they actually feel these things, their work is joyful and fulfilling. If they are only going through the motions (surface acting) or struggling to feel what they don't (deep acting), exhaustion and burnout can result (Cox, 2009). Emotional labor is also performed by managers who use it to influence the feelings of employees, expressing pleasure in a job well done or disapproval and firmness when needed. "Leading with emotional labor" (Humphrey, Pollack, & Hawver, 2008) has the same potential for either exhaustion or fulfillment. Putting on a front, particularly surface acting, takes a toll, whereas skillful use of deep acting and expression of genuine emotion can increase feelings of satisfaction and enjoyment for both managers and employees.

One cautionary note reflects the fact that managers, more than their subordinates, are likely to identify so strongly with their role that the emotional labor involved with expressing genuine feelings begins to consume all their energy (Humphrey et al., p. 153). The key is to recognize signs of overstress in yourself and take action before burnout sets in. Your goal is to thrive, not merely survive. To do that, you will need to distinguish between the essential and the trivial and to let go of the expectation that you can be all things to all people (Bloom, 2008). Although it may seem contradictory, delving more deeply into your work can be as effective at preventing burnout as letting go. Linda Yaven, who teaches in the Graduate Design Program at California College of the Arts in San Francisco, was inspired by documentation she witnessed in the preschools and infant–toddler centers of Reggio Emilia and began applying the concept to her own work with adults. Over the next four years she taught—and learned along with her students—how to use photographs, drawings, and written records to make their learning visible. She writes, "The fact that I looked forward to coming to class each day did not go unnoticed by me. There are teachers in Reggio who have been teaching there for decades without burnout. I had glimmers while there what that might be about" (Yaven, 2005, p. 10).

In addition to reducing and managing your own stress, you will want to help your staff members do the same. Burnout due to stress is one of the factors contributing to high rates of turnover among child-care personnel (Hale-Jinks, Knopf, & Kemple, 2006). Figure 4.2 lists symptoms of burnout and offers suggestions for reducing and/or dealing with stress.

Symptoms of Stress

Physical

- Loss of appetite
- Frequent indigestion
- Fatigue
- Difficulty sleeping
- Sweating, faintness, nausea (without apparent cause)
- Frequent colds

Emotional

- Feeling inadequate, incompetent
- Sense of hopelessness
- Overreacting (crying or extreme irritation)
- Loss of interest in pleasurable activities
- Inability to let go of problems and relax at end of workday

Strategies for Coping

Eliminate or Reduce Causes

- Regular physical exams to discover and treat health problems that can add to stress
- Pare down or postpone commitments at work and/or at home
- Delegate tasks where possible
- Set realistic goals and timeframes for achieving them
- Distinguish between what you can change and what you cannot; focus on the former and let go of the latter

Strengthen Inner Reserves

- Exercise vigorously several times a week
- Choose a healthy diet
- Meditate or practice yoga
- Cultivate a relaxing hobby
- Spend time with family and friends
- Establish a relaxing bedtime ritual
- Begin to eliminate unhealthy habits (smoking, junk food)
- Seek professional help from a counselor or physician

FIGURE 4.2   Recognizing and coping with stress.

Source: Based on *Professional Life Stress Scale*, by David Fontana. Retrieved July 4, 2005, from http://honolulu.hawaii.edu/intranet/committees/FacDevCom/guidebk/teachtip/stress-t.htm; and *How to Fight and Conquer Stress* by Rose Medical Center, Denver. Retrieved July 4, 2005, from http://www.rosemed.com/healthcontent.asp?page=/hic/stress/index.

? DECISIONS, DECISIONS . . .

Look at the list of symptoms of stress in Figure 4.2. Do any of them describe your own feelings and attitudes toward your job or schoolwork? If so, think about which of the suggestions for reducing stress you might be able to apply. Choose two or more suggestions from the list of suggestions for strengthening your ability to deal with stress and make a plan to put them into practice.

Psychological Type

Psychological type refers to a concept introduced by Carl Jung in the 1920s that attempted to explain variations in human personality based on the way individuals preferred to use their perception and judgment. This theory became the basis for a widely used instrument developed by Isabel Briggs Myers in the 1940s. The Myers-Briggs Type Indicator (MBTI) seeks to determine an individual's basic preferences in four areas, each identified by a particular letter: (E) *extraversion* or focus on the outer world versus (I) *introversion*; (S) *sensing* or focus on information versus (N) *intuition* or focus on interpretation; (T) *thinking* versus (F) *feeling*; and (J) *judging* or decisiveness versus (P) *perceiving* or postponing judgment. These preferences interact to create 16 possible combinations or personality types, each designated by a four-letter code. Individuals characterized as INTJ, for example, lean toward the inner world, interpret rather than accept information at face value, rely on thought and logic, and would rather settle on a solution than keep matters open (Myers & Briggs Foundation website, http://www.myersbriggs.org).

No single type is superior to another, and in fact it is desirable to have many types represented within an organization because the strengths of each will complement the others. Even though you are likely to feel most in tune with those most like yourself when interviewing candidates for a job opening, it is probably wiser to look for the person who can provide balance. Beyond the hiring phase, understanding variations in personality types can help you think about adjusting the ways you interact with individuals in your organization. For example, although you may prefer a logical approach, your well-articulated arguments are likely to be ineffective if addressed to someone who focuses more on feelings (Khanagov, 2007).

LEADERSHIP STYLES

Management is defined as the process that coordinates individual efforts toward achieving goals, allocates resources effectively, and serves needs. Leadership is one of the five functions of management, defined by DuBrin (2000, p. 232) as "the ability to inspire confidence and support among the people who are needed to achieve organizational goals." In other words, leadership is the human element of management. When people refer to someone's style of *management*, they are often thinking about that person's *leadership* style.

DuBrin identified three leadership styles (2000, pp. 244–245). His categories may be familiar if you have read about parenting styles in your child development classes. Autocratic leaders hold most of the authority in their organizations and focus on getting the job done rather than on people's feelings. At the opposite extreme, the free-rein leader relinquishes authority to the group, expecting its members to figure out the best way to accomplish a given task. Steering a middle course between these two styles, participative leaders involve group members in decision making; however, not all such leaders involve group members to the same degree. At the level of least group involvement, consultative leaders merely seek the group's opinions before making the final decision themselves. Consensus leaders facilitate discussion to arrive at some level of agreement or consensus among all group members and base decisions on that. Democratic leaders listen to everyone's ideas and let the group vote on the final decision. Note that in a consensus decision, discussion continues until everyone can agree on an issue, at least to some extent. In democratic decisions, everyone listens to the discussion, but in the end, the majority rules. Xavier (2005) characterizes effective managers as those who can navigate a path between these extremes, tapping the resources and expertise of all their staff members but always accepting responsibility for making the hard decisions needed to keep the organization going.

Participative leaders seek input from others when making decisions.

EMOTIONAL INTELLIGENCE

Xavier (2005) argues further that successful managers not only adapt well to change and avoid crucial errors, but also exercise high degrees of emotional intelligence, a concept that has been popularized by Daniel Goleman (1995) and a prerequisite for effectively performing the emotional labor discussed earlier in this chapter. Emotional intelligence includes four areas of competence: self-awareness, self-management, social awareness, and relationship management.

Self-Awareness

In essence, self-aware individuals know themselves. Their confidence in their abilities stems from realistic notions of their strengths and weaknesses. They recognize their feelings and understand how those feelings might color their perceptions and judgments.

As a manager of a child development program, you need to realize that you don't have all the answers, that human development is complex, and that our understanding is in a constant state of flux. This is partly because new discoveries mean there is more to learn, and partly because the more we learn, the more we realize that what appeared simple and straightforward is actually subtle and complicated. Knowing you are fallible and do not have all of the answers should not paralyze or discourage you, however; instead, it should motivate you to study and challenge your ideas about what is best for children.

As you struggle with a shoestring budget and the mundane daily realities of lost mittens or clogged toilets, you may at times feel overwhelmed by feelings of discouragement and frustration. Self-awareness means recognizing these emotions as temporary states rather than objective assessments of the situation. Today's catastrophe may well become the kernel of a hilarious story in weeks to come.

Self-Management

Recognizing your feelings is a foundation for the next component of emotional intelligence, which is to manage those feelings. This means keeping things in perspective rather than indulging in emotional extremes in reaction to circumstances. It also means being able to rise above one's personal feelings for the good of a common goal rather than venting frustrations on those around you. You need patience, or emotional self-control, to encourage children, families, and staff members to strive to learn when you are tempted to provide ready-made, but perhaps inadequate, solutions to problems. If you have patience, you do not expect instant results from children, families, staff members, or yourself.

Managing your feelings means maintaining a positive outlook in the face of adversity and summoning the energy to tackle a job even though you are tired. It means standing up for what you believe rather than taking the path of least resistance. You can accommodate families' needs, for example, without allowing yourself or your program to be taken advantage of. Clearly formulated policies, discussed with each family on enrollment, help you avoid unwanted situations: for example, parents who decide to do a few errands on their way to pick up their children and arrive late, causing tired staff members to be even later than usual in getting home to their own children. Setting fees at a level that allows you to pay staff members a living wage requires no apology—although it may require some effort to help families who cannot afford the rates locate financial assistance. These are simply examples of healthy assertiveness, without which you are less able to fulfill your mission of service.

Managing your emotions will be easier if you remember that your own energy requires replenishment from time to time. A healthy diet, exercise, time with family and friends, hobbies, and outside interests all help you give your best. The trick is to give your best when you are at work and then leave that work behind at the end of each day. Remember that, although your work is important, it is not the only important thing in your life.

Social Awareness

In addition to understanding and managing their own feelings, effective managers understand and care about the feelings of others. They derive satisfaction from helping others, and they are sensitive to the complex nature of human relationships.

People who work in child development centers are entrusted with the task of helping parents nurture and educate their children. They are expected to love and care for these children as though they were their own beloved offspring. As manager, you are expected to care about each individual; work to allay conflict; and maintain an atmosphere of peace, love, security, trust, and respect. To accomplish this enormous task, you need the professional dedication to view your work as more than "just a job."

Socially aware managers recognize that institutions should serve people—never use them. Their ultimate goal is to strengthen children and their families. Their role is to supplement, never supplant, the care that families give their children. Because families are often in desperate need of child care, they can be vulnerable to programs that assume unwarranted power over them. Professional ethics demand that you avoid this possibility. Following are examples of how a program takes advantage of its power over people who need its services:

- Demanding that children arrive by 9:00 a.m. or be turned away even though a parent must take another child to school several blocks away and cannot get back to the center before 9:30.

- Requiring attendance at parent meetings as a condition of enrollment but failing to take parents' work schedules into account when arranging meetings.

- Expecting all of the children at the center to participate in a holiday-themed celebration when not all of the families celebrate that particular holiday.

Parents, already pressured by their multiple roles, scarcely need the extra pressure of unrealistic demands from the child development center.

Relationship Management

This aspect of emotional intelligence includes what are commonly called "people skills": inspiring, motivating, and convincing others; bringing out the best in people; getting them to work together; and helping them work through disagreements.

Given the sheer number of people and the myriad complex relationships involved in a child development program, it's easy to see how crucial this aspect of emotional intelligence is to a manager's success. It is the manager who communicates the program's vision to families and staff and who works out strategies for attaining that vision. These strategies can include planning dynamic professional development activities for staff or helping families understand and accept rate increases needed to prevent staff turnover. When inevitable conflicts or disagreements arise—with families or among staff members—the manager must help the parties hear one another and arrive

Daniel Goleman (2000), who pioneered the concept of emotional intelligence, identified six leadership styles, each of which represented a different configuration of traits. He found that each style had a different effect on an organization's climate or working environment. The effect on climate was also reflected in the organization's overall productivity and ultimately in its bottom line.

To understand the concept of organizational climate, think of how its elements might be manifested in a child development center: Are teachers expected to follow a script, or is creativity encouraged? Is everyone expected to help the center achieve accreditation or just to do enough to meet minimal licensing standards? Does everyone have a clear understanding of the center's mission and values? Do they feel a sense of responsibility and shared commitment to that mission? Now think about leadership styles:

- An *authoritative* leader, with high levels of self-confidence and empathy, inspires others with her vision and is an effective catalyst for change.
- An *affiliative* leader promotes organizational harmony, excelling at empathy, communication, and building relationships.
- A *democratic* leader, whose strengths include communication, collaboration, and team leadership, strives for consensus.
- A *coaching* leader, strong in empathy, self-awareness, and mentoring others, focuses on bringing out employees' long-term potential.
- A *coercive* leader, characterized by a drive to achieve, initiative, and self-control, expects employees to follow orders.
- A *pacesetting* leader shares some traits with the coercive (conscientiousness, drive to achieve, initiative), sets high standards, and expects employees to follow through, but models rather than simply gives orders (pp. 82–83).

Goleman found that the first four styles had a positive effect on organizational climate, with the authoritative style ranking highest. The last two styles had negative effects on climate. Goleman's point is not that one style is "right" and another "wrong," but rather that different styles fit different situations. Although authoritative leaders are most successful overall, Goleman acknowledged that there may be times when a coercive style is needed to deal with a crisis or a particularly uncooperative employee. Because each of the styles taps different aspects of emotional intelligence, leaders who cultivate a wide range of emotional competencies are more likely to possess such a repertoire and have the skill to use it. The most effective leaders are able to select the most appropriate style for a given situation from that repertoire almost without thinking.

at satisfactory solutions. All this may seem to require superhuman qualities, but relationship management also involves reaching out for help from policy and advisory boards, staff members, outside consultants, families, community members, and the children themselves, recognizing that all of them are potential sources of new ideas and creative solutions to challenges.

DECISION MAKING

Decision making is the central activity of the manager of any organization. It is a mental activity that may require hours of sitting at your desk reading relevant materials, making calculations or drawings, and developing draft copies of plans until the best possible plans have finally evolved. In some ways, decision making is a lonely activity. It certainly requires time. To some of your staff members, who are busy getting things done, it may seem like loafing—after all, you are just sitting there at your desk with a pencil in your hand. When the right decision is made and the right direction is taken, things look rosy. On the other hand, conditions may be gloomy if the wrong decision is made and the wrong direction taken. Dissonance frequently occurs as decisions are made. Your task is to reduce dissonance to a minimum and guide it toward constructive change. Each of the basic functions of management—planning, organizing, staffing, leading, and monitoring and controlling—requires decision making.

Interrelated Decisions

Decisions are often interrelated in complex ways.

Rational decision making requires considering information from many sources and being open to other points of view.

CHAIN PATTERN   One pattern of decision making is called a **chain pattern**, characterized by a straight line, each decision being dependent on the preceding choice (Paolucci, Hall, & Axinn, 1977, pp. 108–109). The chain can stop and recommence at any point. An example of chain-pattern decisions in a child development center might be as follows:

- *Decision 1:*   The policy board decides to organize a child-care center.
- *Decision 2:*   The board members decide the first year to enroll only 3- and 4-year-old children.
- *Decision 3:*   They decide to establish a 4- and 5-year-old group the next year from the previous year's enrollees and continue the first classroom by enrolling 2½- and 3-year-olds.
- *Decision 4:*   The following year, they decide to add a new group for kindergarten children who need a place to go before or after their half-day of regular school.

Each decision in the list above is based on the experience gained from the preceding decision.

CENTRAL–SATELLITE PATTERN   In the **central–satellite** type of decision making, a central decision is followed by several satellite decisions that are dependent on the central decision (Paolucci et al., 1977, pp. 106–108). For example, in a center, a board policy decision to start an infant care unit is a central decision. Then numerous satellite decisions follow, such as decisions about housing, equipping, staffing, and organizing the unit. If the central decision is different, the satellite decisions likewise change.

One might conceptualize several central decisions as being strung together in a chain, with all decisions being related to the overall goals of the center. The satellite decisions for each central decision may relate only minimally to those of the other central decisions. For example, is providing only one type of service more cost-effective or efficient than providing several services? Also, are the expanded services consistent with the central goal of the center?

Decision Types

DuBrin (2000, p. 114) describes two types of decisions. **Programmed decisions** are those that are made so frequently that they become routine and involve simply following prescribed procedures. For example, managers of those programs with established admission policies need not agonize over which family on the waiting list should be offered the next opening; they simply apply the procedures in place. In contrast, **nonprogrammed decisions** are made when new or more complicated situations arise. What should a manager do, for instance, when a highly competent teacher, with a long history of excellent performance, suddenly begins missing work or treating children inappropriately? Before answering this question, the manager needs more information about the reasons for the sudden change. The manager also must know what options might realistically be considered available in a climate of acute teacher shortage. And, perhaps most important, the manager may have to use creative or original thinking to make this nonprogrammed decision.

The more programmed decisions you face, the easier is your job as manager. You can increase the proportion of programmed decisions by establishing ground rules or general principles that apply in all similar cases. Recall the discussion of reflection and use proactive reflection to generate the ground rules or principles. Take some time to look back on an experience and learn from it what can be applied to future situations.

Consider the following problem confronting the director of a small, two-classroom center. Although she had hired a sufficient number of staff members to maintain appropriate adult–child ratios, as well as extra help to cover for absences, the system was stretched beyond its limits when several people happened to be out at the same time. In addition to unplanned absences because of illness or family emergencies, the director had to plan for coverage when staff members took well-deserved vacation days. Approving the requests for vacation time case by case was a nonprogrammed decision. The director had to think through every request and consider all other planned or unplanned absences that might occur on the requested days, what might happen to staff morale if requests were denied, and issues of fairness in deciding whose request took priority. After several experiences of active reflection (while coping with days when both lead teachers were on vacation and a substitute called in sick), the director stepped back to think and to use proactive reflection. In fact, she and the teachers used community reflection to arrive at a general principle that shifted the decision of approving or denying requests for time off from the nonprogrammed to the programmed realm. They decided that the two lead teachers could not take the same days off, nor could the lead and the associate teachers in one classroom take the same day. Following this decision, the staff members simply had to consult one another before requesting approval for time off, and the director no longer had to spend undue time trying to decide whether to grant the approval.

Perhaps you are thinking that this sounds like a lot of trouble to go through for an apparently simple problem. You might think the director could have simply decreed the policy from the beginning. In the realm of human relations, however, nothing is as simple as it might seem. One of your challenges as a manager is to know which decisions can be programmed or routine and which should be nonprogrammed or handled creatively. In the interest of saving your time—and your sanity—handle as many decisions as possible with established procedures. However, an organization can become rigid, stifling creativity and growth, with too many established procedures. The refrain "But we always do it this way" has killed countless good ideas in the brainstorming stage and discouraged budding innovators who may have had a better way in mind. To make matters trickier, new developments can occur in an issue that seems routine and has always been treated as a programmed decision. Suppose, for instance, that the lead teachers in the previous example found themselves in conflict because both, for very good reasons, wanted the same day off. All of a sudden, the director's nice, neat procedure no longer works, and the group is confronted with a nonprogrammed decision. More community reflection at this point might lead to a new, more encompassing guiding principle. Instead of asking teachers to coordinate their vacation days, the teachers and director could decide that teachers must come up with the way to resolve conflicts over scheduling. This principle might then become applicable to other conflicts between staff members, further reducing pressures on the director.

> **?   DECISIONS, DECISIONS . . .**
>
> A parent of a child in your center has just lost her job and cannot make the required monthly fee payment. As manager of the center, you explain that you can allow a one-week grace period before discontinuing care. Is this a programmed or nonprogrammed decision? Can it be classified as either? Is it preferable to treat it as one type or the other?

Ethical Decisions

An ethical decision is one that navigates questions of what is right or wrong according to the accepted principles of a profession. The National Association for the Education of Young Children (NAEYC) developed a code of ethics to help guide early childhood professionals in their interactions with children and families. Recognizing that the manager's responsibilities encompass more people and relationships than those of the classroom teacher, a working group developed a supplement to the NAEYC Code of Ethical Conduct for administrators (National Association for the Education of Young Children, 2006). Both the original code and the supplement are available online at http://www.naeyc.org/positionstatements. Each consists of a set of basic ideals and principles regarding responsibilities to children, families, colleagues, and society.

Some situations are relatively easy to resolve because they represent ethical responsibilities that are clearly mandated within the code; others are more complex and pose an ethical dilemma or conflict between two or more basic principles. Not all ethical problems are ethical dilemmas. An ethical problem is one for which a clear answer is readily determined. For example, a parent might demand that a caregiver use spanking to control a child's behavior. This might be a problem for a caregiver who wants to honor a parent's preferences, but it is not a dilemma because the code clearly states that early childhood educators should "create and maintain safe and healthy settings that foster children's social, emotional, cognitive, and physical development and that respect their dignity and their contributions" (Code of Ethical Conduct, Ideal I-1.5). The center follows a fundamental principle of using positive guidance techniques with children; furthermore, it must comply with state licensing regulations that prohibit all forms of corporal punishment.

Suppose, however, that instead of asking you to spank the child, the parent insists that every day at pickup time you provide her with a detailed report of every incident of the child's "misbehavior" that has occurred that day. She says that she wants to follow up with her own discipline at home that evening. While making such reports would not actually be harmful for the child (unless you have reason to believe the discipline administered at home would be abusive), it does contradict your policy, as explained in your center handbook, which is to handle misbehavior when it occurs. In the event that typical positive guidance techniques prove ineffective and the child's behavior escalates, you would request a private meeting with the parents rather than discuss the issue in front of the child or other parents.

This situation, then, constitutes an ethical dilemma. As noted earlier, you have an ethical responsibility to "create and maintain safe and healthy settings that foster children's social, emotional, cognitive, and physical development and that respect their dignity and their contributions" (Code of Ethical Conduct, Ideal I-1.5). On the other hand, you also have a responsibility to acknowledge families' child-rearing values and their right to make decisions for their child (Ideal I-2.6). Ethical dilemmas seldom have one right solution and can be resolved only by careful reflection and discussion that involves all parties. Ideally, the parties find a way to sustain the spirit of both principles; if not, they have to decide which takes precedence.

In the example given, the parents might lack information about other, more effective, methods of getting their child to "behave." They might view the center's positive guidance techniques as spoiling the child. In an honest and open discussion, you may be able to explain that your goal is for the reunion between children and their parents to be a joyful time, not an occasion for recriminations or fear of reprisal. You can also explain that consequences for "misbehavior" meted out hours after the infraction has occurred are likely to be ineffective because young children live in the here and now.

If there were an easy answer, however, this would not be a dilemma, defined as a problem for which there seem to be two or more equally unsatisfactory solutions, a catch-22. When faced with such predicaments, people sometimes speak of choosing the lesser of two evils. In this example, if you and the parents cannot come to some agreement, it may be necessary to "agree to disagree," and the family may decide to withdraw the child. Whatever the final outcome, the thoughtful manager realizes that ethical decisions like this are complex, requiring the consideration of several competing ideals and principles.

?   ## DECISIONS, DECISIONS . . .

Using an Ethical Framework

Use the NAEYC Code of Ethical Conduct and the Supplement for Early Childhood Program Administrators to think through two possible alternatives for the dilemma described: rejecting or complying with the parent's request for a daily report of the child's misbehavior. What core values are involved? What ideals and principles regarding responsibilities to children, families, and employees apply? What course of action seems most right?

THE DECISION PROCESS

Five steps make up the decision process:

1. Identifying the problem
2. Developing alternatives

3. Analyzing alternatives
4. Making the final decision
5. Implementing the decision and following up to determine effectiveness

Identifying the Problem

Just as decisions can be categorized by type, so too can problems be categorized as to when they arise. Type 1, routine problems, arise because of a breakdown in something that should be regular or routine. Type 2, nonroutine problems, arise when things are less structured and thus less predictable. When a problem arises, you can quickly determine whether it is a type 1 or type 2. With the routine type, such as staff members spending too much time searching for supplies in a disorganized storage closet, the problem might arise repeatedly, perhaps every day. Immediate attention to the sequence of events leading up to the problem heads off trouble. At times, stopgap measures must be taken, but routine is desired and is the goal. In the example given, a short-term solution would be to recruit one or two volunteers to straighten and organize the storage closet. A more sustainable long-term solution would involve the entire staff in forging an agreement to maintain the organization system by routinely putting things back in their proper place and notifying the office when supplies of any particular item run low.

The nonroutine problems often have elements that can be programmed or made routine in advance. For example, a power outage caused by a severe storm one morning makes serving the planned hot lunch impossible. This problem can be foreseen to some extent by maintaining a backup supply of foods that do not require cooking. Serving this alternate menu would make the solution somewhat routine, though stress producing nonetheless.

Developing Alternatives

Possible alternative solutions can be determined by stimulating the creative thinking of everyone involved. Staff members can be very helpful with generating alternatives if a climate of trust exists such that their creativity can emerge. One way is to brainstorm among the staff members for alternatives—even seemingly impossible alternatives are recorded and valued as a contribution. Any idea may have usable elements or stimulate thinking that leads to better ideas. Avoid premature evaluation. As manager, you can offer several alternatives, showing that you trust the process.

Information is essential to developing alternatives. Your staff members have information accumulated through years of experience. Various readily available publications have relevant information. Sometimes you may wish to bring in consultants or contact a consultant for specific information. For example, information on children's diets can come from a dietitian. You can obtain information about employee insurance by getting bids from a number of companies and by questioning other child development center managers regarding their solutions to the problem. Information gathering generally has a cost, in time or money, that the organization must bear if the best possible decision is to be made.

Analyzing Alternatives

In a group discussion, allow each staff member to state the pros and cons of the various alternatives. By consensus, you can begin to erase some from the list that are not right for your situation at this time. Listen carefully to staff members and value each one's contribution. The goal is to be as rational or objective as possible. One common method of analyzing alternatives, referred to by the acronym SWOT, is to list four elements:

Strengths: resources available or readily accessible to carry out the proposed alternative

Weaknesses: resources required to carry out the alternative but that your program lacks

Opportunities: what your program stands to gain if the alternative is implemented

Threats: potential costs or roadblocks associated with the alternative

This method should help you compare alternatives based on whether the potential benefits of each outweigh the potential costs.

Making the Final Decision

Soon, only a few alternatives remain, and these can be voted on or decided by consensus. Improved decisions result when staff members have a voice, particularly in person-centered organizations such as child development centers. Normally, a problem has many aspects, and talking things over helps the manager gain perspective on the problem. Obviously, there is very little substance to the decision-making process if only a single alternative is considered.

Implementing the Decision

A decision is not truly made until it is put into practice. Only by actually implementing your decision will you be able to receive the feedback you need to evaluate its quality and the effectiveness of your decision-making process.

> ### ? DECISIONS, DECISIONS . . .
>
> Sunshine Child Development Center serves children ages 2½ through 6 years. Several of the children enrolled have siblings younger than 2½. A group of parents has approached the director, requesting that the center expand its service to younger children. They argue that it is impractical to have children in two different centers and that, if they have to find another center for their younger children, they will be reluctant to change when the children are old enough to attend Sunshine Center. Use the SWOT chart in Figure 4.3 to brainstorm the pros and cons of this proposal. Add your own ideas to each segment of the chart and then discuss with your classmates to make a decision about what the center should do.

TIME MANAGEMENT

Time is a valuable, nonrenewable resource. Managing this resource carefully is essential if you are to achieve the goals set forth in your plans. If you are moving up in the ranks from a teaching position, you may have difficulty delegating some of the responsibility and may tend to do things that your teachers or other staff members can do for themselves. You must learn to let others do their share of the work and to leave your time for the managerial and leadership functions that are now your responsibility. Effective time management is one of the most important tools for giving you a sense of control and thus reducing stress.

Sunshine Child Development Center serves children ages 2½ through 6 years. Several of the children enrolled have siblings younger than 2½. A group of parents of these children has approached the director, requesting that the center expand its service to younger children.

	Pro	Con
Internal Factors	**Strengths:** resources available or readily accessible to carry out the proposed alternative • There is a market for the service—parents are asking for it • Center reputation for quality • Administrative structure in place • ? • ?	**Weaknesses:** resources required to carry out the alternative but that the program lacks • Space (will need to reconfigure current classroom arrangements) • May need additional staff or reassign current staff (who may not be pleased) • Equipment (cribs, diapering facilities) • ? • ?
External Factors	• **Opportunities:** what the program stands to gain if the alternative is implemented • Families enrolling infants likely to remain; unlikely to switch from other center • Shortage of infant–toddler care • Positive public relations • ? • ?	• **Threats:** potential costs or roadblocks associated with the alternative • Licensing requirements (lower group size and adult–child ratios for infants and toddlers) • Cost (for extra staff, new equipment) • Raising fees might lead to loss of enrollment or dissatisfied families • ? • ?

FIGURE 4.3   Example of SWOT analysis.

Prioritizing Tasks

Management expert Stephen Covey (1989) said that the essence of time management is to "organize and execute around priorities." He suggests that managers determine priorities using the criteria of importance and urgency:

1. Activities that are both important and urgent
2. Activities that are important but not urgent
3. Activities that are urgent but not important
4. Activities that are neither urgent nor important (p. 101)

As a center manager, you may find yourself constantly dealing with crises of minor importance unless you manage to allocate significant amounts of your time to activities that, in Covey's language, belong to the "second quadrant"—that is, they are important but not urgent. Planning your center's public relations

Effective managers use a variety of time management tools to plan ahead and avoid crises.

strategy, for example, may seem insignificant compared to a broken water pipe, but neglecting the planning may lead to larger problems, such as declining enrollment. Watch this video for a more detailed explanation of the types of activities that belong in each category.

Using these criteria, you might decide to take the time to recruit and train a volunteer to do routine tasks such as sorting mail, knowing that your investment will pay off in many hours saved later on. Even tasks that qualify as both important and urgent can be delegated if you have selected your staff members wisely and explained the task carefully. A staff member, for example, can keep children's time records and generate invoices or send reminders to parents, freeing you to work on a feasibility study for a new infant–toddler component. Activities that may seem unimportant, such as having lunch with key board members or individual staff members, can promote valuable relationships and help your organization develop a clear, unified vision. Knowing your priorities helps you decide which activities to tackle, which to delegate, and which to put off for another time as you face your weekly or daily to-do list.

Managing Distractions

Following such a system is easier said than done. There will be interruptions and distractions as you attempt to concentrate on your high-priority tasks. Inevitably, some interruptions will come from outside—perhaps a staff member requesting your immediate assistance with a crisis. Delegating specific responsibilities to key staff members will help minimize those external distractions if you make it clear that you have confidence in their ability to handle the job. Often, however, distractions come from within yourself as worries about how much you have to do, or ideas about how you will do it, crowd your mind. You may have set aside a precious hour to write a grant proposal, but find yourself fretting about a licensing visit next week or filled with creative ideas for a staff development activity—all admittedly important concerns. As your mind races from one to the other, though, the hour slips by with no progress on any front. One method for gaining control of such internal distractions is to jot down intruding thoughts when they occur in the middle of an important task and set them aside. Knowing that you've captured an idea for consideration at a later time can free your mind to work on the task at hand. Accomplishing what you set out to do instead of spinning your wheels will go a long way toward reducing your stress.

Finally, put a picture of your family or other reminder of your life outside work on your desk so that you remember to get things accomplished efficiently in order to have time for them. To be fresh and inspirational as a manager requires that you spend some time in a pursuit that revitalizes your psychic energy. Time is a precious, nonrenewable resource. Use it wisely and guard it appropriately.

Technology Toolkit

Technology has made it possible to streamline the task of maintaining your to-do list with electronic systems for tracking appointments. One is probably included with your computer's software programs, and you can find several online by entering the term *digital calendar* into a search engine. You may have to create an account to use the feature, but there is no charge. Regularly recurring appointments or due dates for reports are filled in with a click of the mouse; you can view appointments and reminders for the day, week, or month; and you can select your desired time frame for receiving reminders via email or pop-up announcements. Exporting your appointment calendar to a mobile phone or personal digital assistant (PDA, also called a handheld computer) will allow you to keep track of your appointments and task list from any location.

Conclusion

This chapter described the role of reflection in your personal and professional development as an early childhood administrator. Active and proactive reflection is the means by which managers learn from experience. Self-reflective knowledge, an awareness of one's strengths and weaknesses, is essential when managing groups of people. Management style reflects both your basic beliefs about people and organizations and personal factors, such as psychological type and emotional intelligence. Management styles vary in their emphasis on accomplishing tasks versus motivating people and in the degree to which subordinates are involved in decision making. Bronfenbrenner's ecological model of human development and the ecosystems theory are useful for conceptualizing the professional development of early childhood managers as their awareness and influence expand beyond the classroom to society at large. This chapter outlined the steps of the decision-making process, a central activity of management, with special attention to ethical decisions. The material focused on the core competency of personal and professional self-awareness as the foundation for all of the other competencies required for effective management. You now turn your attention outside yourself to the management of the human and nonhuman resources that comprise the child development program.

Questions for Review

1. Explain the importance of reflective practice for effective management.

2. Describe several management and leadership styles. Which seems the best fit for you? Why?

3. Discuss the role of emotional intelligence in management.

4. Identify several types of decisions and give examples.

5. List the steps in the decision-making process and give an example using all the steps.

6. Divide a sheet of paper into four sections. Label the top left section "urgent/important," label the top right section "not urgent/important," label the bottom left section "urgent/not important," and label the bottom right section "not urgent/not important." Think back over your activities during the past 24 hours and write each in the appropriate section. What conclusions can you draw about your time management effectiveness?

Professional Portfolio

1. Select a tool to use to assess your strengths and weaknesses as a manager or potential manager of an early childhood program. (Your instructor may give you some suggestions, or you can consult the Resources for Further Study at the end of this chapter.) After completing your self-assessment, develop a plan for capitalizing on one or more of your strengths and a plan for addressing at least one of your weaknesses. Include the specific strategies you will use and develop a timeline for completion. For example, if you have a weakness in the area of budgeting and finances, you might attend a workshop on financial management by a specific date. If relating to families is a strength for you, you might capitalize on this skill by looking for ways to involve families at a deeper level in your program. Your strategy might be to conduct a focus group seeking families' input on the issue.

2. Make a list of several time management strategies and describe how you will use each in your role as an early childhood administrator. Examples might include creating a daily to-do list, prioritizing tasks and using your peak energy times to focus on the most important tasks, or using a computer program (e.g., Google Calendar) to track appointments and tasks.

Resources for Further Study

PRINT

Bruno, H. E. (2011). *What you need to lead: An early childhood program—emotional intelligence in practice*. Washington, DC: National Association for the Education of Young Children.

Carter, M., & Curtis, D. (1998). *The visionary director: A handbook for dreaming, organizing, and improvising your center*. St. Paul, MN: Redleaf Press.

Websites

MYERS & BRIGGS FOUNDATION

http://www.myersbriggs.org

Website of the Myers & Briggs Foundation; provides extensive information about the purpose, development, and uses of the Myers-Briggs Type Indicator, with explicit cautions that the instrument must be administered and interpreted by a qualified professional in order to obtain valid results.

6 SECONDS

http://6seconds.org

Website of a nonprofit California corporation founded in 1997 to promote the role of emotional intelligence in schools and organizations; contains more than 175 articles as well as links to other resources regarding emotional intelligence.

SOCIETY FOR ORGANIZATIONAL LEARNING

http://www.solonline.org

Website of the Center for Organizational Learning, founded at the Massachusetts of Technology (MIT) in 1991 by Peter Senge with a mission of fostering collaboration among members (individuals and institutions) to create organizations worthy of the commitment of their employees and communities. Includes detailed description of "five disciplines of organizational learning" as well as links to articles and interviews with Peter Senge.

CHAPTER

Organizational Management

LEARNING OUTCOMES

After studying this chapter you should be able to

- Define the terms *organizational management* and *stakeholder* as they relate to operating a child development center.
- Describe the roles of the policy board and the advisory board.
- Explain the differences among policies, procedures, and rules.
- List and explain the regulatory and legal requirements governing the operation of child development programs.
- Give examples of the types of planning that managers use.
- List steps in the planning process and give examples.

At the last meeting of the board of directors, center director Jeralyn had presented the idea of seeking a five-star (highest) rating, explaining that the center already maintained compliance with licensing regulations as required by state law and that meeting the more stringent requirements of the rated license was voluntary. The board concurred that meeting the highest standards was in agreement with the center's mission of providing high-quality care but wanted to know more about the process, the requirements, and the resources that would be needed to accomplish that goal. Jeralyn delegated the task of investigating the process and requirements to Tanya, not only to reduce her own workload, but to help Tanya learn more about working within the state's regulatory system. After Tanya found that information, Jeralyn would identify resources that might be needed and develop a possible timeline for completing the process. She decided to ask Tanya to accompany her when she presented their report at the next board meeting to give her practice in another important aspect of the manager's role, communicating with stakeholders.

In this chapter, our attention shifts from *knowledge of self* to *knowledge of others*—in particular, to knowledge of the stakeholders involved in early childhood programs (Brown & Manning, 2000). A **stakeholder** is defined as a person or group who stands to benefit (or suffer) in some way as a result of an organization's success or failure.

Planning and organization are required to make sure that lunch for these toddlers is nutritious, on time, and served in an attractive setting that supports their independence and enjoyment of the meal.

Children and families are, of course, the primary stakeholders in a child development program. If you recall what you learned about the human ecosystems perspective in Chapter 3, it should come as no surprise to learn that the stakeholders in child development programs extend far beyond the children and families directly served by the program. Teachers, legislators, corporate sponsors, and members of society in general all have a stake in how well a child development program functions. We have chosen the term *organizational management* to encompass all of the activities involved with aligning a program with the interests of these broadly defined stakeholders. This chapter focuses on stakeholders beyond the immediate program participants. The relationships with staff members and families as stakeholders are discussed in later chapters. Organizational management competency includes (1) a working knowledge of the many regulatory systems governing program operation, (2) an understanding of the reasons for the regulations, and (3) the ability to manage the program within those constraints.

Organizational management requires the ability to think on one's feet, to see things from more than one perspective, and to tap intuitive as well as rational and technical knowledge. According to organizational management experts Lee Bolman and Terrence Deal (2008), it is possible to view any organization through four different frames or perspectives: structural, human resource, political, or symbolic. Viewed through the structural frame, organizations are factories where efficiency and technology are prized. Through the human resource frame, they are families where relationships are paramount. From a political perspective, organizations operate like jungles rife with competition and power struggle. Finally, within the symbolic frame, organizations are cultural entities embodying rituals, stories, and heroes. None of these perspectives represents reality, but rather ways of perceiving reality. Although different managers (or management experts) might prefer one over the others, Bolman and Deal argue that a single frame can yield only a partial understanding of any situation and that such inflexibility or tunnel vision causes the downfall of many otherwise astute managers (Bolman & Deal, 2008, pp. 10–21).

How might the concept of frames apply to your work as manager of a child development center? It may seem as though the human resources frame provides the best fit; child care is in many ways an extension of the family, and human relations—between and among staff members, children, and families—are at the heart of the enterprise. Ignoring that aspect while striving for efficiency or power will certainly cause problems. Nonetheless, there are situations within the center's operation (e.g., food service, purchasing supplies) that can benefit from the more technical, efficiency-oriented perspective of the structural frame. A political frame may help in understanding competition among staff members, shed light on dealing with a board, or suggest strategies for approaching funders and lawmakers. Finally, the symbolic frame illuminates the culture of the center, its "set of expectations, language, routines, and ways of being together that shape the group's identity" (Carter, 2008b).

THE POLICY BOARD

The policy board is usually the ultimate authority in an organization that makes plans for services, hires the individuals to carry out the plans, and monitors the provision of the services. If you direct a child development program that is part of a public school system, an elected board of education fulfills these functions. In other child development centers, the board may derive its authority from private or public sources. Community people usually make up boards of this sort, and sometimes the funding agency mandates that specific groups be represented on the board.

When you are hired to manage an existing center, the policy board is already in place—it made the decision to hire you. If you are hired to direct one of many centers owned by a large corporation, you may have few or no dealings with the policy board. If, however, you are fortunate enough to participate in the establishment of a new policy board, you must be aware of the political strategy to use when encouraging people to run for or be appointed to the board. The strategy of getting many groups involved, informed, and supportive of the child development services necessitates that people from the community's groups should serve on the board. That is, people from the community's labor unions, businesses, or other organizations reflect the needs and views of these groups. Having professionals from child development and health organizations as members will facilitate some of the board's technical planning. Of course, parents, as consumers of the service, should be represented, including parents of children with disabilities and ethnic or cultural minorities. The board should reflect the diversity of the population served by the center so that there is a good fit between the center's policies and the needs of its clientele.

Whether you have a voice in creating a policy board or are hired by an existing board, your job as manager is to carry out decisions made by the board. You can help the board make the best decisions by providing your expertise in child development, as well as information about the center's operations. You are an intermediary between the policy board and the center's staff members, children, and families. This means that you have to develop your communication skills to a high degree, cooperating when possible and being assertive enough to stand up for what you believe to be right when necessary.

? DECISIONS, DECISIONS . . .

A member of your policy board has suggested that your child development center begin using a popular commercial phonics instruction program with the 3-year-olds. The issue has been placed on the agenda for the next board meeting. What will you do to prepare for the discussion? What will you say at the meeting?

Although it is important that you and the board have clearly stated expectations of each other from the beginning so that you do not waste energy trying to do each other's jobs, in some cases responsibilities are shared. A treasurer or finance committee generally prepares a budget and monitors income and expenses; the director implements the board's directives and accounts for any deviations resulting from unforeseen events. A committee might be in charge of raising funds or in-kind contributions and might secure board approval for grant applications developed by the director or other staff members. A personnel committee establishes policies, approves and revises job descriptions and salaries, and hires and evaluates the director. The director hires and evaluates all other staff members following the policies established by the board (Ratekin & Bess, 1998).

Because board members serve limited terms, the manager often serves to provide continuity as the group composition changes over time. You may also have to educate board members who have little knowledge of best practices in early child education or in business. This makes clear, effective communication doubly important. Plan to provide an orientation for new board members where they can learn exactly what is expected of them. Collaborate with the board president to make sure board members have the information they need well before scheduled board meetings, including an agenda that ensures the best use of their time. Soliciting their feedback after meetings can provide valuable guidance for future planning. Figure 5.1 is an example of a brief

Exit this survey	Evaluation of July 15 Board Meeting
	1. Default Section

1. Did you receive the materials you needed well enough in advance of the meeting to be an informed participant?
- ○ *I received all necessary materials one week (or more) before the board meeting*
- ○ *I received all necessary materials, but less than one week prior to the meeting*
- ○ *I did not receive all the materials I needed. (Please explain)*

Comments

2. Was the meeting well organized? (Choose all that apply.)
- ○ *I received an agenda in advance.*
- ○ *The agenda included all necessary items of business.*
- ○ *The agenda omitted important items. (Please explain below.)*
- ○ *The agenda allocated sufficient time for each.*
- ○ *The chairperson adhered to the agenda.*
- ○ *The meeting began and ended on time.*

Comments

3. Appropriate action was taken on each agenda item.
- ○ *Yes*
- ○ *No (Please explain.)*

No. (Please explain.)

4. I left the meeting with a clear understanding of what I and/or other board members were expected to do next. (If not, please explain.)
- ○ *Yes*
- ○ *No*

Other (please specify)

5. Was the atmosphere of the meeting conducive to full participation of all board members?
- ○ *I felt comfortable expressing my thoughts and felt I was heard. If not, please explain.*
- ○ *Participation of all members was encouraged. If not, please explain.*
- ○ *The chair guided the discussion so that no single person monopolized it. If not, please explain.*

Other (please specify)

6. What suggestions do you have for the next board meeting (e.g., agenda items, procedures)?

FIGURE 5.1   Sample board survey.

survey for obtaining such feedback. Using an online survey tool will simplify both distribution and responding, thus encouraging a higher response rate. Consider teaming with other child development centers to provide group training and orientation so that board members can learn from their counterparts throughout the community (Gadzikowski & Lipton, 2004).

Bylaws

The primary functions of the policy board are to write the bylaws and set broad policies for the center, leaving the day-to-day details to the manager. Bylaws are rules adopted by the organization to spell out how the board is established and maintained, how decisions are made, and how changes can be made. Figure 5.2 is an example of bylaws that

---

BYLAWS

Rainbow Place

Article I. Name
The corporate name of the center is Rainbow Place, located at 123 Rightway, Shady Grove, North Carolina 28237.

Article II. Purpose
The purpose of the center is to provide high-quality, accessible, affordable care and education for the children of the Shady Grove community.

Article III. Policy Board
3.1 The corporate powers of the center are vested in the Policy Board.

3.2 The Policy Board shall consist of a minimum of five (5) and a maximum of nine (9) members.

3.3 One Policy Board member shall be selected from each of the following community groups: business, labor, parents, community services, and early childhood education. Four at-large board members may be appointed by the Policy Board.

3.4 The Policy Board shall meet a minimum of eight (8) times a year.

3.5 The Policy Board, by resolution adopted by a majority of the members, may delegate to the Executive Committee the management of the affairs of Rainbow Place.

3.6 A quorum of over one half of the duly constituted Policy Board shall be able to transact business.

Article IV. Officers
4.1 The Policy Board shall elect annually from their number a President, First Vice President, Second Vice President, Secretary, and Treasurer who shall constitute the Executive Committee.

    4.1.1 The offices of President, Second Vice President, and Treasurer shall be filled by election in odd-numbered years. These officers shall serve for two years.

    4.1.2 The offices of First Vice President and Secretary shall be filled by election in even-numbered years. These officers shall serve for two years.

    4.1.3 Each officer may serve only two consecutive terms in an office.

4.2 The President shall preside at all meetings of the Policy Board and of the Executive Board.

4.3 The First Vice President shall preside and perform the duties of the President in the President's absence.

4.4 The Second Vice President shall preside and perform the duties of the President in the absence of both the President and First Vice President.

4.5 The Secretary shall record and preserve the minutes of all meetings of the Policy Board and of the Executive Committee.

FIGURE 5.2 Sample bylaws.

4.6 The Treasurer shall keep the Policy Board informed of the financial status of the center. The Treasurer shall countersign checks in excess of an amount designated by the Policy Board. The Treasurer shall be a member of the Finance Committee. Auditing shall be done yearly.

Article V. Staff

5.1 The Policy Board shall appoint the manager of Rainbow Place.

5.2 The manager shall employ such staff as required to carry out the purposes and objectives of Rainbow Place in accordance with policies established by the Policy Board.

> 5.2.1 The manager shall keep the Policy Board fully informed of all aspects of the program of Rainbow Place.

> 5.2.2 The manager shall keep a record of all information of value to Rainbow Place and shall be the intermediary between all units of Rainbow Place and the Policy Board.

Article VI. Organization

6.1 The work of the Rainbow Place shall be organized under the standing committees named in Article VII of these Bylaws and under such other committees as shall be authorized by the Policy Board.

6.2 The members of all committees, excluding the Executive Committee, shall be appointed by the President.

Article VII. Standing Committees

7.1 *Committee on Personnel.* This committee shall be headed by the Second Vice President.

> 7.1.1 This Committee shall be responsible for hiring, negotiating terms of employment, and monitoring the performance of the manager of Rainbow Place.

> 7.1.2 This Committee shall establish personnel policies in accordance with applicable laws and needs of the center, approve and revise job descriptions and set salary levels in consultation with the manager.

7.2 *Committee on House and Grounds.* This committee shall be headed by the First Vice President.

> 7.2.1 This Committee shall handle problems related to equipping and maintaining the facility of Rainbow Place.

> 7.2.2 This Committee shall make recommendations for any improvements, expansions, or renovations.

7.3 *Committee on Finance.* This Committee shall be headed by the Treasurer.

> 7.3.1 This Committee shall prepare the budget with the manager.

> 7.3.2 This Committee shall monitor the center's financial operations and review for prior approval any expenditures in excess of budgeted amounts.

> 7.3.3 This Committee shall assist in obtaining the funds necessary for the operation of the center.

7.4 *Committee on Programs.* This Committee shall handle problems dealing with the child-care services program.

7.5 *Committee on Nominations.* This Committee shall be headed by the President.

> 7.5.1 This Committee shall prepare the slate of officers to fill any vacant positions or list those rotating up for election.

> 7.5.2 New board members shall take office at the January board meeting.

Article VIII. Amendments

8.1 Amendments to these Bylaws may be proposed at any regular meeting of the Policy Board having a quorum present. The vote on the proposed amendment shall be taken at the next meeting of the Policy Board and requires a two-thirds majority to pass.

Adopted _____ (date)

FIGURE 5.2   Sample bylaws. (*Continued*)

may be adapted to fit the particular circumstances of any child development center. The bylaw amendment procedures should be somewhat complex to help maintain the organization's stability. Items that may change periodically, such as enrollment figures and tuition fees, are not included in the bylaws—such decisions are made by the policy board at its meetings.

THE ADVISORY BOARD

If a policy board's function is to create policy, it follows that an advisory board exists to give advice. It may be formally or informally organized. You can simply select a few people representing different areas of expertise to be your eyes and ears in the community, to provide feedback on innovations you are considering, or to provide insight on problems. This type of group can be very useful in your somewhat lonely authority role of manager.

As a manager of any enterprise, you need a method of keeping in touch with people in other organizations who might have connections with families or children's services. Try to identify people in city government, civic organizations such as the League of Women Voters or chamber of commerce, the school board, health or mental health providers, the media, labor unions, churches, or a cooperative extension service. Choices might include parents of formerly enrolled children. An advisory board composed of members of such groups gives you a different and larger perspective from that of the parents and teachers you see daily. It also widens your circle of influence in the community, with each member becoming an ambassador for your center within his or her own sphere.

Start with a small group that you can afford to invite to a simple dinner to get acquainted. Keep meetings short with planned agendas to avoid infringing heavily on people's schedules. If you want to keep things informal, you may keep dated notes on your organization's activities, participants, and accomplishments rather than a set of bylaws. Once you become acquainted with these individuals, you can call them for advice as particular situations arise.

❓ DECISIONS, DECISIONS . . .

Your center's policy board, in an effort to accommodate the needs of working parents, has decided to offer an additional service that would allow mildly ill children to continue coming to the center rather than exclude them, as has been the practice. How will you tap the expertise of your advisory board to help you carry out this plan?

POLICIES, PROCEDURES, AND RULES

Policies are "general guidelines to follow in making decisions and taking action" (DuBrin, 2000, p. 110). Generally, the policies in a child development facility are established by the policy board after careful, thoughtful deliberation. Policies should be stated in general terms to allow the flexibility necessary to deal with specific situations. They should be stated in writing and given to board members, staff members, and parents. Once established, policies must be followed consistently. If they prove unworkable or if evolving circumstances warrant it, changes may be made by formal board action. Finally, policies should be as complete as possible, covering all relevant categories: services to be provided; administration; and dealings with staff members, children, and families. Many states, for example, require that centers provide families with written policies, such as those governing admission and withdrawal, food service, and discipline.

Your center must also have the procedures and rules necessary to implement each policy. **Procedures** specify how to handle certain tasks. For example, a child development program may have a policy stating that staff members who take college classes will receive partial reimbursement for tuition. The center would also have an accompanying procedure outlining how to apply for the reimbursement. **Rules** state in particular detail how a procedure is carried out. In the example just mentioned, the rules might state which specific courses at what sort of institutions would qualify for reimbursement, what documentation must be provided, and what minimum grade must be earned. States that have policies requiring all providers of child care to be licensed also have procedures detailing how such licenses are to be issued; monitored; and if necessary, revoked. Once the policies and procedures are in place, specific rules are created to establish minimum standards for things like adult–child ratio, space, equipment, and staff qualifications. The rules can be changed without changing the policy or procedures.

To take another example, suppose that you are the manager of the ABC Center. The center's mission is to "provide high-quality, developmentally appropriate care and education for children 18 months to 6 years of age on a full-time, year-round schedule." Because your goal is to provide high-quality, developmentally appropriate care and education, and research has established a link between staff training and the quality of care (e.g., Bowman, Donovan, & Burns, 2001), you and your board establish the policy that the center will hire only those individuals whose education, experience, and personal characteristics equip them to work with young children. To apply this policy, a manager has to determine what specific education, experience, and personal qualities are needed for each particular job. A candidate whose temperament and skills are ideally suited for an infant classroom may not be successful in an after-school program, for example. Although your policy might specify formal course work or degrees, you must still exercise your independent judgment because a degree in "early childhood education" may or may not include specific training pertaining to the developmental needs of specific age groups.

The procedure for implementing your staffing policy might state: "For each teacher opening, a job specification must be developed that sets forth the requirement that a candidate must hold a valid early childhood certificate or an endorsement with course work and/or experience pertinent to the job requirements. Job specifications will be circulated to the placement centers in colleges and universities that offer early childhood teacher preparation programs and to those state associations where experienced teachers are likely to see the notice."

Any search for new employees invokes another policy regarding nondiscriminatory hiring practices—not only because it is the right thing to do, but because it is required by law. The center's policy in this area might state that "Center XYZ does not discriminate on the basis of race, color, creed, gender, age, ethnicity, sexual orientation, or disability." A more proactive nondiscriminatory policy might add, "Center XYZ actively seeks to increase the diversity of its staff." The procedures for implementing such a policy must require that application forms ask only for information directly related to the job and stipulate that job openings be posted where they are most likely to reach a diverse pool of candidates.

The following rule spells out in detail how the manager is to ensure compliance with the center's stated policy and procedure regarding teaching staff: "The manager personally reviews each candidate's college transcripts and teaching license, checks employment references to verify the person's qualifications, and determines whether the candidate fits the job requirements."

Written policies, procedures, and rules encourage consistent and timely decision making, while discouraging those decisions made without sufficient information. They constitute the blueprint for achieving the established goals of the center.

? DECISIONS, DECISIONS . . .

Using an Ethical Framework

Suppose you are the director of a center with a policy that it "accepts all children, families, and employees on a nondiscriminatory basis without regard to race, color, creed, gender, ethnicity, sexual orientation, or disability." You have recently hired Denzel, a new graduate of your local university's child development program, to work in the toddler room. He is doing an excellent job and the children seem to love him, but you have heard rumblings from several family members that they don't think he should change diapers or help children with toileting. Should you tell Denzel to leave all diapering and toileting duties to his co-teacher, Yolanda? Using the National Association for the Education of Young Children (NAEYC) code, try to determine what core values are involved. What ideals and principles regarding responsibilities to children, families and employees apply? What course of action seems most right?

WORKING WITH THE REGULATORY AND LEGAL SYSTEMS

Licensing

One of the first legal systems you encounter as a program director is licensing. You may be tempted to view licensing rules as a bothersome list of petty details. Perhaps you feel a certain amount of anxiety when the licensing agent comes to inspect your program and breathe a sigh of relief when you pass inspection for another year. If you think about it a little more deeply, though, you may begin to see things differently.

Licensing is the mechanism by which the state acts on behalf of its citizens to protect their interests when it is impossible for individuals to do so for themselves. With licensing, a state prohibits a particular activity or enterprise and then selectively lifts that prohibition for individuals or organizations who meet specific requirements. In the case of child-care licensing, the state assumes responsibility for safeguarding the health and welfare of children whose parents are not present. Although most states make exceptions for small numbers of children or particular circumstances, such as limited time in care or care provided by religious organizations, they essentially declare that no one may care for groups of other people's children unless specific requirements are met. The requirements, which are established by state agencies concerned with health and welfare issues, set forth minimal levels of safety and protection for children. They are mandatory, meaning that they have the force of law, and the state empowers its licensing agency to enforce the regulations by imposing penalties when providers violate the rules.

Unfortunately, the "minimal level" of licensing regulations is just that in most states. The National Association of Child Care Resource and Referral Agencies has established benchmarks for assessing the effectiveness of states' regulations as well as the systems in place for enforcing those regulations. Benchmarks for regulations include ratios and group sizes aligned with NAEYC standards, education and training requirements for staff members, and requirements for program components in six developmental domains. Benchmarks for oversight specify frequency of inspection, educational qualifications and workload of licensing staff, and parent access to inspection and complaint reports on the internet. No state meets all recommended standards for ensuring the safety and well-being of children (National Association of Child Care Resource and Referral Agencies, 2009c). Recently, however, some states have used funds from the Child Care and Development Fund to encourage programs to exceed the minimum licensing standards and to acknowledge those that do by establishing a Quality Rating Improvement System (QRIS). As of 2012, 41 states had such a system in place (Mitchell, 2012). You can find out whether your state has a system in place at the website of the QRIS National Learning Center, included in the resources for further study at the end of this chapter. All QRISs are composed of five common elements:

1. *Standards:*   QRIS standards are built on the foundation of child-care licensing requirements and add multiple steps between licensing and higher quality standards, such as those associated with accreditation.

2. *Accountability measures:*   Accountability and monitoring processes are used to determine how well programs meet QRIS standards and to assign ratings.

3. *Program and practitioner outreach and support:*   Support for providers, such as training, mentoring, and technical assistance, are included to promote participation and help programs achieve higher levels of quality.

4. *Financial incentives:*   Financial incentives, such as tiered subsidy reimbursement (which pays a higher reimbursement rate to providers who care for children from families who receive subsidies and meet standards beyond minimum licensing), are awarded to programs when quality levels are achieved.

5. *Parent/consumer education efforts:*   Most QRISs award easily recognizable symbols, such as stars, to programs to indicate the levels of quality and to inform and educate parents.

Who are the stakeholders represented by licensing or quality rating systems? Certainly, parents want to know their children are kept safe in their absence. The legislators who enact the laws requiring that programs be licensed and the licensing agencies who enforce those laws have an interest. In a broader sense, every element of society is a stakeholder in the regulation of child care because when children are harmed, society bears the cost. Short-term costs include lost time at work or lowered productivity for parents, additional strain on families, and extra burdens on healthcare systems, as well as—perhaps most important—the stress and unhappiness experienced by children in poor-quality care. Long-term costs include the loss of human capital when children are prevented from growing up to be healthy, functioning, productive adults.

You, too, are a stakeholder in the licensing system, both as director of a single program and as a member of the early childhood profession. From the administrator's perspective, licensing regulations help level the playing field by requiring all programs to meet at least minimum standards for health, safety, staff training, adult–child ratios, nutrition, and the like. This reduces the possibility that unscrupulous program operators are able to gain an unfair advantage—for example, offering reduced prices because they have cut corners on these basic elements. Your status as a member of the early childhood profession means that, in addition to a concern for your own program's survival in the marketplace, you care about (i.e., have a stake in) the well-being of all children. Therefore, you want to support strong licensing systems to protect that well-being.

Other Governmental Regulations

A number of other governmental regulations govern your program's physical facility and your interactions with employees and the children and families you serve:

- *Zoning laws* in many communities determine where a business may be located and may dictate how much parking space you must provide or the type of fencing you may install around your playground. Some communities exempt family child care from zoning regulations; others are working on inclusionary zoning ordinances promoting the creation of child-care facilities as well as affordable housing (Warner, Anderson, & Haddow, 2007, p. 17).

- *Building codes* address issues such as fire safety and sanitation. If you are the manager of a program that is building a new facility, you will want to work closely with those inspection agencies during the planning phases. It is far easier to install an adequate number of exits in the proper location initially than it is to revise these features once the mortar is set. If you inherit an existing facility when you take on the manager's role, your concern is to ensure that the building remains in compliance with codes. Buildings deteriorate, occupants become careless (e.g., obstructing exits or propping open doors that are intended to prevent fires from spreading), and codes change. Sometimes modifications to a building or changes in the way a building is used trigger additional requirements.

- *The Americans with Disabilities Act* requires child-care facilities to make reasonable accommodations, based on a case-by-case assessment of individual needs, to allow children with disabilities to be included in the program. These accommodations include nondiscriminatory admission policies; changes in policies, practices, or procedures (unless this would fundamentally alter the nature of the program); and communication assistance and removal of physical barriers (unless this would place an undue burden or expense on the program). Accommodations include features such as ramps in addition to stairs and wider bathroom doors with levers instead of knobs.

LABOR LAWS   In addition to laws and regulations governing the physical plant and program operations, managers must be familiar with numerous labor laws. Those addressing hiring and compensating staff members are discussed in a later chapter. Other laws govern payroll deductions and safe work environments:

- The Occupational Safety and Health Act of 1970 requires that employers furnish employees a safe place to work.

- Federal income tax laws require employers to collect employees' income tax and deposit it in a federal depository. The failure to comply is a criminal offense.

- The Social Security Act of 1935 and Federal Insurance Contributions Act provide retirement, disability, burial, and survivor benefits to eligible employees and self-employed individuals.

- The Federal Wage Garnishment Law sets restrictions on the amount of an employee's earnings that may be deducted in any one week through garnishment proceedings. It also regulates terminating employment because of garnishment.

RIGHTS OF CHILDREN AND FAMILIES   Your role as manager also requires familiarity with laws that address the rights of children and families.

- The *Individuals with Disabilities Education Act (IDEA)* of 1991, as amended in 1997 and reauthorized in 2004, affirms the right of children with disabilities to an appropriate education, and the rights of families to participate in developing plans for that education. IDEA Part C addresses the needs of infants and toddlers from birth through 2 years, whereas Part B governs special education and related services for children and youth ages 3 to 21. The individualized family service plan (IFSP) for infants and toddlers addresses all domains of the child's development as well as family concerns, resources, and priorities, while the individualized education plan (IEP) for children age 3 and older focuses more narrowly on the child's educational performance. You will encounter these plans again in subsequent chapters.

• *Family Educational Rights and Privacy Act (FERPA)*, passed in 1974, prohibits releasing information about a child to any person or agency without the consent of a parent. An exception to the confidentiality requirements exists when a child development professional has reason to suspect that a child is being abused.

• *Child Abuse Prevention and Treatment Act*, passed in 1974 and reauthorized in 2003 as the *Keeping Children and Families Safe Act*, defines child abuse and neglect as any recent act or failure to act on the part of a parent or caretaker that results in death, serious physical or emotional harm, sexual abuse or exploitation; or an act or failure to act that presents an imminent risk of serious harm. Individual states are responsible for establishing their own definitions and legal penalties for maltreatment of children. All 50 states have laws that require certain professionals (including teachers and child-care providers) to report suspected abuse or neglect. The laws also protect those who make such reports from any liability stemming from the report.

Because state and local laws vary considerably, managers should seek information through their legal advisers, accountants, and licensing agency to ensure that they are aware of and in compliance with the laws that relate to their center. Discussions with other center managers may help clarify certain regulations and the appeal procedures available.

BUSINESS CONCERNS   Keeping abreast of, and complying with, regulations regarding taxation and insurance are crucial elements of organizational management.

• *Tax-Exempt Status*   The corporate status of a child development facility has several implications for you as the manager. Some organizations are granted 501(c)3 tax-exempt status by the Internal Revenue Service, meaning that charitable contributions they receive are tax deductible for the donors. Applying for tax-exempt status can be complicated and expensive, but it may enable the center to tap into particular funding sources such as grants or charitable foundations. Nonprofits are more likely to involve a board of directors composed of representatives from several sectors. As a manager of a nonprofit program, you will need grant-writing skills, as well as the skill to relate well to many "bosses." As the owner-manager of a small for-profit center, your life may be somewhat simpler because you are able to make decisions without consulting a board. It is also riskier, however, because responsibility for the success or failure of the center rests largely on your shoulders. Larger for-profit programs are often operated as part of multisite franchises or have contracts with corporations to provide child care for employees. In either case, the director functions more as a middle manager, answerable to the corporate chain of command. Obviously, a goal of the for-profit program is to make a profit, but even nonprofit centers must pay attention to the bottom line; consequently, directors of either type must have financial-management skills.

- *Insurance*   Whether you manage a for-profit or nonprofit program, you must purchase several types of insurance to protect the organization's assets. Property insurance is necessary to cover losses caused by theft, fire, or other disaster. If the program provides transportation, it must have vehicle insurance. Liability insurance protects the organization, as well as you and your employees, from claims that result from accidents or injuries. Some states mandate the types and amounts of insurance required for child-care centers but not for family day-care homes. Family child-care providers operating out of their homes should be aware that their homeowner's policy does not cover their business and they, too, need liability insurance. Purchasing insurance is not the time to look for the cheapest price; make sure you are dealing with a reputable company. Get your policy in writing and study it to understand exactly what it covers or excludes. Remember to update your coverage as you acquire new equipment or take on new responsibilities (e.g., transporting children) that might invalidate a policy.

THE PLANNING PROCESS

The owner of a winning baseball team once said, "Luck is the residue of design." In other words, success does not occur by accident. It results from careful planning. Planning charts a course by which goals can be reached most effectively. While planning overall is your responsibility as manager, you will not accomplish it alone. Rather, you will delegate some of this responsibility to employees in each unit (e.g., teachers, food service, clerical, transportation). Do not assume, however, that employees will automatically be able to fulfill this function. Depending on their level of experience and training, they may require very specific assistance. Providing this assistance is a worthwhile investment of your time for several reasons:

- Staff members who participate in planning are more likely to have a clear understanding of those plans and their relationship to the organization's goals.

- Staff members who see that their ideas are valued as part of the planning process are more likely to feel that they are part of a team with a joint obligation to the organization's goals.

- With a clear understanding of plans and a commitment to goals, staff members are more likely to follow through and carry out plans.

- The esprit de corps developed as staff members work together on plans is likely to spill over into many other aspects of the program's operation, including more conscientious job performance, increased satisfaction, and lower turnover rates.

As a teacher, you have made daily plans, monthly plans, yearly plans, lesson plans, and children's plans. If you have taught in a small center, you may also have experience doing some of the managerial tasks described in Chapter 3. When you become a manager, you will move beyond planning for a single group to planning a

Planning together helps develop an esprit de corps—a common sense of purpose—so that staff members are more motivated to work toward fulfillment of plans.

LEADERSHIP LENS

Bloom (1998) suggested that managers move through a hierarchy of competencies as they grow into leaders: technical, staff relations, educational programming, public relations, and symbolic. *Technical competency* involves handling budgets, developing policies, and meeting regulatory requirements—in essence, organizational management. *Staff relations competency,* the ability to get staff members to work together to accomplish program goals, is grounded in effective communication skills.

Neither the technical competency nor the staff relations competency requires specialized knowledge about children and families or about early education and care. These skills can be acquired through general management training or business experience. Yet both are fundamental to the operation of a child development program and must be in place before the manager can progress to the higher-level competencies: *educational programming, public relations,* and *symbolic.* Administrators who have risen from the ranks of teacher already have some expertise in educational programming and must now learn to promote this competency in others. Once they have accomplished this, they can begin carrying their message to the world outside their center (public relations competency). Finally, at the highest level, those directors with symbolic competency "serve as a symbol for the collective identity of the group by articulating a vision, clarifying and affirming values, promoting reflection and introspection, and creating and sustaining a culture built on norms of continuous improvement and ethical conduct" (Bloom, 1998, p. 36). At this level, the director moves from competence to excellence, from manager to leader.

center operation with a number of classrooms, a greater number of children and families, a larger staff, a bigger budget, and perhaps more varied services. You will also be responsible for monitoring and helping your staff members accomplish the planning required for their jobs.

You may recall that earlier we defined planning as creating a mental image of what you want to accomplish and how you will go about doing so, a road map of where you want to go and how you will get there. We also identified three levels of planning: strategic planning or the organization's "overall master plan that shapes its destiny"; tactical planning, which means breaking that master plan down into specific goals and assigning them to various parts of the organization; and operational planning, which spells out the specific procedures or steps that it takes to meet the goals (DuBrin, 2000, p. 95). In other words, a plan describes what should be done and how it is to be done. Because plans, particularly strategic plans, are most effective when developed in collaboration with stakeholders, we view the management process of planning as most closely aligned with the competency area of organizational management.

Strategic Plan and Central Concept

Initially, a strategic plan requires clear agreement on the statement that sets forth the center's central concept. This statement (which may also be called a vision or mission statement) describes the program's ultimate goal in general terms. A center may have a central concept statement when the manager is hired, or one may have to be developed as the work proceeds. Working to ensure that this statement reflects the highest values and best knowledge of the early childhood profession is an important way that managers exercise leadership. The wise manager collaborates with all of those who hold a stake in the center's operations when developing this statement: members of the policy board, parents, and staff members. Involving parents helps the center better understand and serve the needs of its customers; involving staff members helps ensure that they are committed to the center's ultimate goals. The central concept may be a simple statement such as "The ABC Center will provide high-quality, developmentally appropriate care and education for children 18 months to 6 years of age on a full-time, year-round schedule."

Another part of your job as manager is to interpret, with input from your stakeholders, the meaning of this policy. You might, for example, define "high-quality" as achieving a certain numerical score on an instrument such as The Early Childhood Environmental Rating Scale (Harms, Clifford, & Cryer, 2005). Or you could determine that "developmentally appropriate" means meeting the accreditation standards of the National Association for the Education of Young Children (2007a). A "full-time, year-round schedule" could mean operating round-the-clock to accommodate several work shifts, or it could mean remaining open from 7:30 a.m. to 5:30 p.m. and closing for two weeks each summer.

Often the central concept includes additional elements. An early childhood laboratory program on a college campus provides developmentally appropriate care and education, but its major focus typically is to provide experience with children for college students preparing to enter the field of early childhood education. An employer-sponsored child-care center in a hospital also provides developmentally appropriate care and education, but its major focus is often to provide a convenient service that helps the hospital attract and retain skilled medical staff. Yet another child development center might be operated as a franchise of a large corporation with at least part of its purpose being to make a profit for stockholders. Ideally, the central concept statement is reviewed by all stakeholders at least every five years, and the strategic plan for fulfilling that central concept is reviewed annually. Documenting these reviews in writing, perhaps with minutes of relevant meetings, is part of the manager's responsibility (Talan & Bloom, 2004, pp. 38–39).

Tactical and Operational Plans

As the strategic plan is translated into tactical and operational plans, the administrator must apply licensing and professional standards to the services proposed and ensure that staff members understand the standards and follow them. Licensing standards vary from state to state, so it is important to have accurate information about the specific standards that apply in your state. For example, some states allow as many as 12 toddlers or 20 4-year-olds per caregiver. Regulations in other states come closer to the NAEYC recommendations of no more than four infants and toddlers, or ten children ages 3 through 5, per caregiver. You can learn the specific licensing requirements for your state by visiting the website for the National Resource Center for Health and Safety in Child Care, listed under Resources for Further Study at the end of this chapter.

Management by Objectives

Planning involves developing goals and objectives for the center that are both appropriate and realistic. **Goals** are general statements of what a program hopes to achieve in the long term; **objectives** are more specific statements outlining the strategies or steps the program will take to reach the stated goals. For example, the goal of having happy, well-adjusted children might imply objectives addressing staff retention because children who are able to form secure long-lasting relationships with their caregivers are more likely to be happy and well adjusted. **Management by objectives (MBO)** is a system designed to increase employee involvement and motivation by involving them in setting clearly defined objectives and measuring performance according to those objectives. It consists of the following sequence of steps:

- Step 1: The policy board or top administrators establish broad goals and map out each unit's responsibilities necessary to meet the overall goals.
- Step 2: Mid- and lower-level managers translate the organization's general goals into specific goal-oriented objectives for their respective units. The objectives spell out what is to be accomplished in concrete, measurable terms, with specified timelines

for completion. Ideally, they are established with team input. The objectives are realistic enough that competent workers can meet them, but they are sufficiently challenging to inspire workers to aim a little higher than usual.

- Step 3: Individuals set their own objectives and propose methods for meeting the goals assigned to their units.
- Step 4: Managers either accept the plans submitted by team members or negotiate workable compromises.
- Step 5: Once they reach an agreement, the participants develop the action plans necessary to achieve their objectives.
- Step 6: Performance reviews are conducted at specific intervals (e.g., every 6 or 12 months) to determine whether an individual has met most of the established objectives and to examine possible causes for any that are not achieved. New objectives are set then because the end of one review period marks the beginning of the next, and the cycle is repeated.

? DECISIONS, DECISIONS . . .

Suppose you are the manager of the ABC Child Development Center whose vision or strategic plan is "to provide high-quality, developmentally appropriate care and education to children 18 months to 6 years of age on a full-time, year-round schedule." In consultation with your board, you have translated this into a tactical operational plan to achieve NAEYC accreditation within the coming year. Review the four steps to accreditation at www.naeyc.org and develop a series of goals and objectives for carrying out this plan.

Innovative Planning

Innovative planning is a technique that gathers concerned people together to brainstorm possibilities for a new service or a new direction. Innovative planning can be used for retrenchment, as well as for an expansion into new programs. The manager or board president generally sets the stage for brainstorming by providing information about forthcoming possibilities. Getting small discussion groups involved in making extensive lists of creative ideas, without regard to the reality of present restraints or structures, leads to ideas triggering other ideas. One way to evaluate alternatives that emerge during brainstorming is to conduct a SWOT (strengths, weaknesses, opportunities, and threats) analysis of each idea, as described in a previous chapter.

Following these brainstorming sessions, a committee may group the ideas into categories. Additional discussion sessions may follow. Perhaps one committee has met to devise a sample needs

Getting small groups involved in brainstorming often results in one suggestion triggering other creative ideas.

survey, and another committee has met to explore the costs, locations, services, human skills, and so on, needed for some of the proposed major categories. Openness is desirable at all stages. People who are involved feel more committed to the final outcome. When planning child development services, professionals should involve parents who represent the user–consumer perspective. Eventually, tentative and specific proposals can be developed by representative committees or task forces. If funding does become available, the reports on the work already accomplished provide a basis for a final proposal to develop a new program or revise an existing one. Writing proposals for funding will be addressed in greater detail in a subsequent chapter.

Time, Scope, and Cycling of Plans

Plans may be short-range or long-range; they may be put in place to deal with routine, recurring events or to handle emergency situations. Figure 5.3 provides examples of these dimensions of plans. In some centers, a long-range plan covers only one year; in another, it might cover five years. Some plans that are called short-range may cover a year or less. A comprehensive plan may cover the entire childcare center or elementary school, while another may be more narrow in scope, covering only one classroom or one service. The level of the planning also influences the plan's scope. Classroom teachers develop plans that are implemented only in their classrooms, while the manager develops plans covering all of the center's classrooms. If several centers function within one organization, a superplan may be made to cover them all.

Repetitiveness is also a feature of plans. A skeleton plan may cover a center's regular routine, with teachers filling in details on a weekly and monthly basis. Cycle menus and curriculum cycles are examples of planning for repetitive tasks. Contingency plans for emergencies can be repeated and should be made to streamline decision making. For example, during inclement weather, the playground may be unusable; a general plan for sharing an indoor space for a large motor activity avoids confusion for both adults and children because necessary changes in a routine are known in advance. A contingency plan for coping when illness strikes staff members is essential. Evacuation plans, used in the event of fire, hurricane, or tornado, are required, often by law.

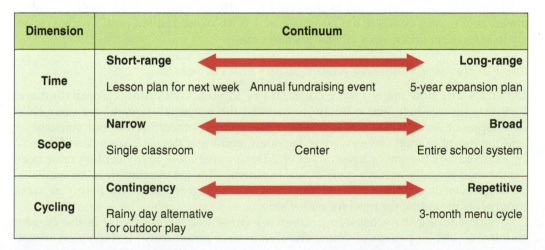

Dimension	Continuum		
Time	**Short-range** Lesson plan for next week	Annual fundraising event	**Long-range** 5-year expansion plan
Scope	**Narrow** Single classroom	Center	**Broad** Entire school system
Cycling	**Contingency** Rainy day alternative for outdoor play		**Repetitive** 3-month menu cycle

FIGURE 5.3   Time, scope, and cycling of plans.

Time for Planning

Planning is very time consuming, and time set aside for planning is often eaten away by what seem like more pressing concerns. The wise manager, however, recognizes that planning is an investment that saves future time and energy. Effective planning is closely related to high-quality outcomes. This is true for all staff members, not just the manager. Planning time must be protected from interruptions and paid for as part of the job.

Finding time for planning—and the dollars to pay for it—in a busy child development center requires careful management. Because planning is so essential to the achievement of goals in high-quality programs, one of your first tasks is to create time for planning. Once scheduled, it is essential that the time is actually used for planning. This may mean an evening meeting or a weekend retreat at center expense for center-wide planning. It can mean simply 2 or 3 hours of designated time each week for teachers to make classroom plans while someone else manages the children. Of course, such arrangements are costly in terms of time and dollars, but unplanned programs are also costly because they are far less likely to deliver the quality of services promised to the children and their families. According to a national study, teachers in state-sponsored early childhood programs report an average of 4.1 planning hours per week, ranging from 1.6 to 7.9 hours (Gilliam & Marchesseault, 2005, p. 13). In this video, the director and teachers find time to discuss their observations and make curriculum plans over lunch while other staff members supervise children at nap.

STEPS IN THE PLANNING PROCESS

Step 1: Define the Central Concept of Your Child Development Center

What services will your center provide to society? How will your center create those services? Will your center have some distinctive services or methods of creating services? The policy board and the manager take this step together. For example, you can state, "The ABC Center will provide high-quality, developmentally appropriate care and education for children 18 months to 6 years of age on a full-time, year-round schedule."

Step 2: Establish the Goal(s) That Your Center Will Pursue

Your goals are based on the central concept statement. Goals must first state clearly what service the organization is chartered to perform. Based on the central concept stated above, your goal is to operate a licensed, NAEYC-accredited center with a capacity to serve 40 children, ages 18 months to 6 years.

Step 3: Develop Planning Assumptions and Forecasts

Do you know how many young children live in your community? Population and birthrate figures help you estimate or forecast the potential demand for your child development services. Do you know how many centers there are in your community and the extent of their services, costs, locations, and other details? Are industries and/or labor unions becoming involved in children's care? How many centers have been established recently or have gone out of business? This information may be available through licensing officials or a resource and referral agency and will help you make judgments regarding the need for a new service.

Considering the ecosystem framework presented earlier, what is the current number of jobs for parents of young children in your community? Is the region attracting new businesses? If so, where are they locating, and what is the potential job market forecast? Is there an educational institution where parents are enrolling young children who need child care? What is the community knowledge base regarding early childhood programming? Do families prefer one program or philosophy over another? How much can parents afford to pay? These questions are important to planning whether your center is a profit or nonprofit institution.

The public schools generally carry out a school census each year to enable them to forecast the need for classrooms and teachers for each age. You can access data about your community's population through the U.S. Census Bureau. You can get more specific information about the child-care needs of that population by conducting your own research using a survey or needs assessment, a systematic process for acquiring an accurate picture of the potential demand for child care in your community. By using a form similar to Figure 5.4 and questioning neighborhood residents, you can discover the number, ages, and present care and education arrangements of the community's children. Accurate forecasting based on reasonable assumptions is indispensable to the planning process. For example, when predicting enrollment for a new center, it is

---

Exit this survey

Child Care Needs Assessment
2. Default Section

1. Please indicate by age the number of children not yet in school for whom you need or would like a childcare or education program:

    ○ under 12 months   ○ 12–24 months   ○ 25–35 months   ○ 3 year old   ○ 4 year old   ○ 5 year old

2. Indicate the days that you would need or prefer this service:

    ○ Monday through Friday

    Other (please specify)

    [   ]

3. Indicate the hours that you would need or prefer this service:

    ○ 7:30 a.m. to 6:00 p.m.

    ○ Other (please specify)

    [   ]

4. Please indicate by age the number of school-age children for whom you need or would like a child-care or education program:

    ○ 5 years
    ○ 6 years
    ○ 7 years
    ○ 8 years
    ○ 9 years
    ○ 10 years

5. Indicate the days and hours that you would need or prefer this service:

    ○ Before and after school on regular school days   ○ Full day during school vacations, on snow days, school
      (beginning 7:30 a.m.; ending 6:00 p.m.)   holidays and /or teacher work days (circle all that apply)

    Other (please specify)

    [   ]

6. Please provide the information below if you would like to be informed of the results of this survey or be contacted in the event that a new program for children is developed.

    Name: [   ]
    Address: [   ]
    Address 2:   [   ]
    City/Town: [   ]
    State: [-- select state --]
    ZIP/Postal Code: [   ]
    Email Address: [   ]
    Phone Number: [   ]

    [Prev] [Done]

FIGURE 5.4 Sample needs survey.

important to remember that it takes time for the reputation of a center to become known and for parents to begin using it. Overly optimistic projections that ignore this reality are bound to result in disappointment.

Step 4: Evaluate Resources

Resource types include financial, managerial, personnel, building and yard space, and equipment. Based on your evaluation, some programs or expansions may be more or less feasible. What financing or credit is available to you? What is the real estate situation in your community? Is there a shortage of available buildings, meaning that prices will be higher should you purchase or rent? Are there vacant spaces in churches or public schools that you might access? Is there a pool of qualified personnel in your community? If one type of resource is absent, the project faces added difficulties.

Step 5: Outline Objectives or Steps toward Meeting Your Goal

Figure 1.1 in Chapter 1 listed the steps you would have to take in order to open a new child-care facility. Depending on what you learned in Step 4 about available resources, your specific objectives might be to locate a building to rent, secure financing, carry out any renovations needed to meet licensing requirements, and purchase equipment. Other objectives would include drafting your program philosophy and family handbook; recruiting, hiring, and training staff; advertising your services; and enrolling and orienting families.

Step 6: Implement the Plan

Implementing the plan is the action stage and the exciting one. You will work toward accomplishing each objective, organizing material resources, staffing the project with qualified people, and providing leadership as the plan moves ahead.

Step 7: Evaluate the Plan

Checking every step as the plan is being implemented is the evaluative or controlling function of a manager. It is essential to see that the plan is carried out and to check for quality—whether it is the quality of a floor covering or of a human relationship. Evaluations and corrective actions are essential in every enterprise. The world changes, people change, needs change, and therefore plans must change. Conduct periodic reevaluations to ensure that all aspects of the plan fit today's conditions and can be readily changed to fit tomorrow's. Managers must be at the forefront of change and must be looking ahead to be ready.

THE MANAGER'S JOB: A JUGGLING ACT

In a previous chapter, you learned about five management processes used by all managers: planning, organizing, staffing, leading, and monitoring and controlling for quality. You may find it tempting to view these as an orderly sequence of activities: The leader of a student group, for example, draws up a plan to build a float for the homecoming parade. The leader then organizes the resources needed to fulfill that plan—perhaps a truck bed, chicken wire, tissue paper, paint, and so on. Next, the leader finds people to carry out the plan and leads them through the construction process. While the plan is underway, the leader continually checks the group's progress and makes adjustments as needed so that the finished product matches the planned objective. The reality of managing a child development program—or any complex human enterprise—is somewhat less tidy. First, you are juggling more than one of these processes at any given time as you attend to the many components of your job. Second, within each component, you move through the five processes in a cyclical, rather than a linear, manner.

Competency Areas and Management Processes

Let's explain the cyclical nature of the five management processes. The 13 competency areas that were discussed at the beginning of this text represent the components of the manager's job (and comprise the major headings for your professional portfolio). Think about which of the five management processes are involved in just the first area, personal and professional self-awareness. To be even more specific, think about what you might do to complete a self-assessment. Your initial *planning* might consist of checking with your instructor or online to learn about some of the self-assessment tools available. (One example of such a tool is found in Figure 5.5.) You would then *organize* your time and energy to locate the selected tool and complete it. Because you are the only person involved in this task, neither *staffing* nor *leading* play much of a role. On the other hand, the entire task of self-assessment can be seen as part of *monitoring* and *controlling for quality* because it requires that you identify some of your strengths and weaknesses, and make concrete plans to enhance the former and remedy the latter. In other words, you will have to revisit the planning and organizing processes and begin the cycle again.

As you proceed through the remainder of this text, you will see that each of the competency areas involves most, if not all, of the five management processes, although specific competencies might emphasize one process more than the others. Your job as a center director does not afford you the luxury of choosing which competency to exercise. Certainly, the manager who "loves people" and "hates numbers" cannot spend all available time on staff development and ignore the budget. From time to time, however, the demands of one area might pull your attention from others. When you are trying to meet a deadline for preparing next year's budget, for example, you are less able to find time for reflection and self-assessment. In other words, fiscal management crowds out personal and professional self-awareness for the time being. If this happens consistently, however, and you continually neglect one or more areas, your program will suffer. So you can see that the manager's job is a juggling act. Think of a circus performer keeping 13 plates spinning atop 13 poles. The juggler propels each plate with a vigorous shove and moves on to the next. Any plate that loses

---

Assessing My Organizational Management Skills

---

1. Regulatory systems (select one):
   - I am not familiar with my state's licensing requirements and don't know where to find them.
   - I am familiar with my state's licensing requirements and know where to find any additional information I need.
   - I am familiar with the process by which licensing requirements are established.
   - I have participated in the process of establishing or revising licensing requirements (attended hearings, written letters, etc.).

2. Legal systems: I am familiar with the requirements of (or know where to find information about (check all that apply):
   - Zoning and building codes
   - Americans with Disabilities Act
   - Individuals with Disabilities Act
   - Child Abuse and Prevention Act
   - 501(c)(3) Tax Exempt Status

3. Planning (select one):
   - I generally do my job and handle tasks as they arise.
   - I understand how my tasks fit into the bigger picture (a center's mission and goals).
   - I can (or do) participate in developing plans for a single unit (e.g., classroom).
   - I can (or do) participate in developing plans for all units of an entire center (classrooms, food service, accounting, transportation, etc.).
   - I can (or do) delegate planning responsibility to others and follow up to ensure that it is carried out.

4. Working with a board of directors (select one):
   - I am unclear about the role of a board of directors and how it relates to that of the center director.
   - I can explain the role of a board of directors and how it relates to that of the center director.
   - I can communicate effectively and am comfortable collaborating with a board of directors

FIGURE 5.5   Self-assessment of organizational management skills.

momentum falls unless the juggler comes back to give it another spin; therefore, the performer must move along the row quickly and continually. Now, imagine that you are that juggler and that each pole is one of the manager's competency areas. The spinning plates represent your movement through the cycle of the management processes—from planning to monitoring and controlling for quality. If you don't keep all of your "plates" spinning (i.e., recycling through these processes), they will fall.

Conclusion

Child development programs do not operate in a vacuum. They are part of the larger social system. To function effectively, a manager must understand how that system governs the operation of the facility. The term *organizational*

management refers to all of the activities a manager uses to align a program with the interests of the stakeholders representing the larger system. We view this broad understanding of where a program fits in the bigger picture as a requirement of effective planning, which is a primary task of managers. Depending on a program's corporate structure, plans start with a policy board, a business partnership, or an individual entrepreneur—the center's central concept is established, money is allocated, and a manager is hired. The manager has the overall responsibility for planning, organizing, and delegating responsibilities to other staff members. Staff members participate in planning, especially for their own units. The manager, knowing

that monitoring and controlling for quality are integral parts of management, fits a control function into all plans to help ascertain when a plan has been carried out effectively. The manager may periodically report on the center's progress to the policy board. This chapter has reviewed types of plans and steps in the planning process. The concept of planning as it relates to other aspects of the manager's job, such as fiscal or personnel management, is discussed in later chapters.

Questions for Review

1. Define the terms *organizational management* and *stakeholder* as they relate to operating a child development center.
2. Tell how the role of the policy board differs from that of the advisory board.
3. Explain the difference among policies, procedures, and rules; give an example of each.

4. List and explain the regulatory and legal requirements governing the operation of child development programs.
5. Identify the types of planning that managers use and give examples.
6. List steps in the planning process and give examples.

Professional Portfolio

1. Write a strategic planning statement for a child development program. Remember that a strategic plan is an organization's "overall master plan that shapes its destiny."

2. Write three policies translating your strategic plan into operational terms. Write out the procedures that must be followed to implement one of your stated policies.

Resources for Further Study

PRINT

Bloom, P. J. (2000). *Circle of influence: Implementing shared decision making and participative management*. Redmond, WA: Exchange Press.

Wischnowski, M. W. (2008). Getting the board on board: Helping board members understand early childhood programs. *Young Exceptional Children, 12*(1), 20–30.

Websites

AN ADMINISTRATOR'S GUIDE TO PRESCHOOL INCLUSION

http://www.fpg.unc.edu/node/784

Authors Ruth Wolery and Sam Odom provide in-depth coverage of all aspects of managing programs for young children with and without disabilities.

BOARDSOURCE

http://www.boardsource.org/

A nonprofit organization providing information and consultation to promote excellence in nonprofit boards and help train future leaders. Includes links to research papers and answers to questions on topics such as job descriptions for board officers or how to become a nonprofit organization.

NATIONAL RESOURCE CENTER FOR HEALTH AND SAFETY IN CHILD CARE AND EARLY EDUCATION

http://nrckids.org/states/states.htm

This website for the National Resource Center for Health and Safety in Child Care and Early Education provides links to child-care licensure regulations and changes for each state, as well as contact information for licensing agencies and other child-care contacts within your selected state.

QRIS NATIONAL LEARNING NETWORK

http://www.qrisnetwork.org/

Information clearinghouse created by a coalition of states and organizations to provide resources and information for states that have a QRIS or that are interested in developing one. Includes links to state contacts.

U.S. DEPARTMENT OF JUSTICE: COMMONLY ASKED QUESTIONS ABOUT CHILD CARE CENTERS AND THE AMERICAN WITH DISABILITIES ACT (ADA)

http://www.ada.gov/childq&a.htm

6

CHAPTER

Fiscal Management

LEARNING OUTCOMES

After studying this chapter you should be able to

- List resources needed to start and maintain a child development program.
- Discuss sources of funding for child development programs.
- Explain the relationship among parent fees, staff salaries, and quality of care.
- Calculate costs for staff salaries.
- Construct a budget.
- Identify strategies for managing center finances.

One of the aspects of the director's job that Tanya felt least confident about was managing the program's finances. Even though Rainbow Place was a relatively small center, the amount of money needed to run it seemed astronomical to Tanya. Besides, she told Jeralyn, she had always considered herself more a "people person" than a "numbers person." Jeralyn laughed and confessed that the prospect had seemed daunting to her as well when she first became a director, but with patience and perseverance, she had gradually mastered the tasks. "And," she added, "I learned that you can't do much good as a 'people person' or turn your plans into reality if you can't make the numbers come out right."

A child development program, just like any business or, for that matter, any family, cannot survive unless the manager makes wise use of its financial resources. This includes creating a realistic budget, monitoring expenses to align them with the budget, and knowing when to make appropriate adjustments. Fiscal management includes finding ways to increase resources and to economize without sacrificing quality. Managing monetary resources requires all of the managerial functions: planning, organizing, staffing, leading, and monitoring and controlling. To keep your center on firm financial ground, you must balance a tough head for understanding, monitoring, and controlling the budget with a tender heart for meeting the needs of children, their families, and your staff members.

Whether a program is for-profit or nonprofit, its financial practices are subject to scrutiny by several sources, including the Internal Revenue Service and auditors that might be required by funding sources. Accreditation criteria of the National Association for the Education of Young Children (2007a) require that a child development center be fiscally sound in order to serve the needs of children and families effectively and efficiently and that the manager be included in all aspects of financial planning and review (p. 76). Sound budget planning and accounting practices are also addressed in the Program Administration Scale (Talan & Bloom, 2004), a tool designed to complement widely used classroom rating scales.

RESOURCES REQUIRED FOR A CHILD DEVELOPMENT CENTER

A **resource** is a means—a person or thing—through or by which an end or goal is attained. Money is the medium of exchange for purchasing the resources needed to provide child development center services—the end or goal desired. Resources are dormant until human ideas and human energy organize and use them to achieve goals. Resources required for a child development center can be grouped in four categories: materials, equipment, space, and human energy, abbreviated as **MESH**. Your task as manager is to mesh or synchronize these resources to meet your program goals. The MESH categories may be expanded as follows:

- *Materials* include all of the physical items and information materials used in the center.
- *Equipment* includes all toys (large and small), kitchen and office equipment, furnishings, and transportation.
- *Space* includes buildings, playgrounds, and interior arrangements, and the organization, decoration, and utilization of the space. Insurance expenses also fit in this category.
- *Human energy* (or human capital) includes the knowledge, skills, and abilities of all adults involved in developing and delivering the service, as well as that of the children, families, and volunteers.

Figure 6.1 illustrates how the MESH formula can be used to generate a detailed list of the resources required to operate a child development program. Obviously a greater investment of resources will be needed to start a center than to maintain an existing enterprise.

Money is required to obtain most resources—materials, equipment, space, and the human capital of teachers, cooks, custodians, and others. Human capital includes the energy of children and their parents as well as that of program staff. When the children's energy is directed toward hanging up coats, tidying up rooms, and serving and feeding themselves, less adult energy has to be expended on those tasks. More important, children are learning significant skills. One of the main objectives of early childhood education is the channeling and directing of the children's energy into developing skills, talents, and independent behavior, including self-care.

Start-up costs for a new child development program includes major investments in equipment, such as these large hollow blocks.

		Start-Up Costs	**Operating Costs**
M	Materials	• Teaching materials (toys, games, art supplies, books, dramatic play props, etc.) • Child care supplies (bedding, paper products—bathroom and facial tissue, paper towels • Food service supplies (cookware, tableware, groceries) • Clerical supplies (paper, pens, pencils, staplers, postage)	• Replenish consumable supplies (food, paper products, postage, etc.) • Repair or replace worn toys, books, props • Upgrade: add new toys, books, and props
E	Equipment	• Classroom furnishings: cots or cribs, tables, chairs, shelves and cubbies • Indoor and outdoor play equipment • Technological equipment (computers, phones, sound and video systems) • Office furniture and equipment • Kitchen equipment • Furniture for teacher workroom and/or lounge • Furniture for parent resource area	• Repairs • Refurbishing as needed • Replacement as needed • Purchase additional equipment and furniture for upgrade or expansion
S	Space	• Capital costs for land, design, construction, landscaping or renovation of existing space • Connection fees and deposits for utilities • Incorporation fees • Taxes	• Rent or mortgage • Property taxes • Insurance (fire, liability, accident, property) • Repair and maintenance of building and grounds
H	Human Energy	• Planning services (needs survey, location study, etc.) • Legal services (corporate structure, tax status, contracts) • Accounting services • Marketing and public relations • Advertising and recruiting (families and staff)	• Salaries (administrator, caregivers, teachers, clerical, food service and maintenance staff, substitutes) • Consulting fees (e.g., health, parent educator, social services) • Benefits (Social Security, worker's compensation, health and unemployment insurance, medical and personal leave, holidays, retirement, child care) • Staff development (consultant for in-service training, professional dues and publications, support for conference attendance) • Marketing and public relations

FIGURE 6.1 Using the MESH formula to identify the resources required to establish and maintain a child development center.

Parents contribute their time and energy when they help with field trips or special projects or when they volunteer for particular tasks such as building a playhouse for outdoor play, tilling a plot of land for the children's garden, or setting up a parent email listserv or center website. In one center, the parents organized themselves to give teachers a "gift of time" in lieu of the more typical items usually purchased for staff at holidays. Each teacher received a handsome certificate indicating that a particular parent would serve as a classroom substitute for a 4-hour period on a mutually agreeable date.

FUNDING SOURCES

Recall that child development centers are funded in a variety of ways:

- Families shoulder the entire cost through tuition and fees.
- Social agencies or corporations subsidize programs or families.
- Society as a whole provides support through the use of tax dollars.

Most programs need a combination of all these funding sources to survive and, in many instances, there may be differences between a center's expended costs (cash outlays) and the full cost of providing child development programs. The difference is made up through the use of volunteer labor or in-kind donations such as free or reduced rent for the use of facilities provided by churches, schools, or community agencies.

Fees Charged to Families

Establishing fees for the services provided by your center requires a constant balancing between what it costs you to provide the care and what price the market in your community will bear. As you will learn in the next section, the largest component of a center's operating costs is labor. Factors influencing your labor costs include the types of services you provide, the level of quality you hope to maintain, and the current job market for teachers in your community.

Infant–toddler programs are more expensive to operate because they require one teacher for every three or four babies, while programs for older children can meet National Association for the Education of Young Children (NAEYC) standards with one teacher for as many as ten 3-, 4-, or 5-year-olds. Because you aspire to offer a high-quality program, you want to hire teachers with appropriate education and experience, and they expect higher salaries than employees without such qualifications. Competition from other child development programs (or from jobs outside the field entirely) may raise this figure even higher.

Average fees vary from one community to another and rates are higher in the Northeast and in urban areas. In 2011, the annual cost of full-time care ranged from the low in Mississippi ($4,591 for infants, $3,911 for 4-year-olds, and $1,954 for school-age children) to the highest in Massachusetts ($14,980 and $11,669); New York had highest rate for school age care ($10,962) (Child Care Aware of America, 2012, pp. 36–37). (See Figure 6.2.)

To learn the average prices for child care in your state, consult the National Association of Child Care Resource and Referral Agencies (NACCRRA) website at www.naccrra/org. The best way to determine the fee level that the market in your community will bear is to find out what other programs in your area charge for various types of services. Your local child-care resource and referral agency may be able to provide this information. You should gather information about several programs to make sure you are not comparing apples and oranges in your final analysis (e.g., do not compare infant–toddler rates in one program with rates for older children in another).

Another method of establishing a ballpark figure for your fees is to check with your local department of social services, or whatever agency handles subsidy payments for child care, and ask about the maximum allowable fees established for each category of care: full- and part-day, infant, toddler, preschool, school-age. Note that both of these methods might lead you to underestimate the

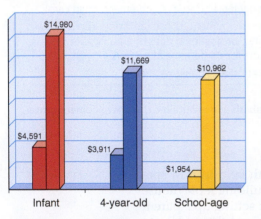

FIGURE 6.2 Average annual costs of full-time child care reported by states (lowest and highest).

Source: Based on Child Care Aware® of America (2012). Parents and the high cost of child care: 2012 report. Retrieved June 28, 2013, from http://www.usa. childcareaware.org/publications/naccrra-publications/2012/8/parents-and-the-high-cost-of-child-care-2012-report

actual cost of providing care by a substantial margin. Local subsidy rates are usually based on the "market rate" that is calculated annually by surveying providers to learn what they are charging. If providers in a given community maintain unrealistically low rates, whether out of sympathy for parents or out of a fear of competition, the market rate reflects these unrealistic figures rather than the true cost of service, and the problem is perpetuated.

FEES AND QUALITY   Artificially depressed rates can impact the *quantity,* as well as the *quality*, of the services. Take rates for infant–toddler care, for example. As you have learned, the staffing requirements for this age group are more than twice as high as the requirements for older groups. The logical implication is that fees for infant–toddler care should be more than double those for older children. Logical or not, this difference would price many, if not most, families out of the market for infant–toddler care. Consequently, center operators choose to charge less than the true cost of infant–toddler care. Some providers simply absorb the loss; others structure their fees so that programs for older children actually subsidize the infant–toddler components, an option that will become less available as more 4-year-olds are absorbed by state-funded prekindergarten programs. The unintended consequence is that many providers simply opt out of the unprofitable business of caring for babies, and the shortage of care for this age group is perpetuated.

Government Subsidies

Many child advocates believe that families are already paying as much as they can for child care. They argue that government has a responsibility to help families shoulder the burden because a good beginning for every child is in society's best interest. Government subsidies, however, whether direct or indirect, are subject to shifts in the country's fortunes and political mood, and many hard-fought gains for children stand to be lost in economic downturns or calls for cost reduction through welfare reform.

Supplementing the funds from family payments, the federal government contributes 19 percent of the total cost of child care through some 90 programs within 11 agencies. Examples of these programs include Head Start, the Child and Adult Care Food Program, and the Child Care and Development Block Grant. State governments must often match these federal contributions, and many states allocate additional funds for their own initiatives such as public school prekindergartens. These forms of public support target specific groups (i.e., children in poverty, with disabilities, or considered at risk for school failure) rather than applying to all children (Barnett, Brown, & Shore, 2004). You can find out what agency handles child-care subsidies in your state by visiting the website of the Office of Child Care, a division of the Administration for Children and Families in the Department of Health and Human Services, at http://www.acf.hhs.gov/programs/occ/resource/ccdf-grantee-state-and-territory-contacts.

Fund-Raising

As you have no doubt concluded already, locating and maintaining funding for a center requires a good deal of your attention, unless you direct a program funded entirely by state or federal dollars. Even in that case, your challenge is to cope with fluctuating allocations and the possibility of budget cuts from year to year. If you manage a program with a policy board, the responsibility for raising money might fall to a finance committee. In fact, board members are sometimes selected because of their connections to a funding source. In this **video**, a director shares some of the ideas her program has considered to help generate additional income.

Your fund-raising objectives might include capital investment dollars, ongoing operating expenses, or a one-time special purchase (e.g., revamping the outdoor play area). Small amounts of money may be raised with the support of parents and the community. Possibilities include sponsoring bake sales, rummage sales, or concerts. In addition to raising funds, such events can rally the support of parents and the community, as well as generate valuable media attention.

IN-KIND DONATIONS   In the quest for funds, directors should not overlook the possibility of in-kind donations. The difference between property rental market rates and the amount charged by the church where Rainbow Place is housed is an in-kind donation. Other examples might include businesses publicizing a center as part of their community outreach, donating used computer hardware or office furniture when they upgrade or redecorate, or contributing regularly discarded materials (e.g., wood scraps from a lumberyard) that can be used in a variety of ways. A civic club may provide a number of hours of its members' labor if the center becomes its cause to support. Use the combined imaginations of your board and staff members to generate creative possibilities for new resources as well as uses.

GRANT PROPOSALS   Seeking funds may be as simple as writing a letter to a civic club requesting scholarship funds for a child or two. Such a request can be an unsolicited proposal—just a shot in the dark—or you might develop a more systematic approach by actively searching for funding opportunities offered by government agencies, philanthropic organizations, or corporations. These entities regularly issue **requests for proposals (RFPs)**, or announcements outlining specific goals and inviting applications for funding from individuals or agencies whose projects align with those goals. A directory of foundations in your state, usually available at libraries, is a good source of information about the foundations' particular interest areas and currently available RFPs. When you locate one or more with interests that seem to match your own, you can consult the foundation's website for eligibility requirements, deadlines, and the application process.

When you locate an RFP that seems to match your needs, you and your board can decide whether you have the time and talent to develop a proposal and, if it should be funded, whether you have the appropriate staff to carry out the proposal. **Proposals** are documented requests that show your expertise and ability to fulfill the proposed project and your timetable, budget, and procedures. It is essential to follow directions and meet the deadlines set by the funding agency. Proposals can be simple or complex depending on the dollar size of the request, the funding agency, and the accounting requirements. Writing your first proposal is the hardest because you are collecting many materials for the first time. However, if you are careful to save the various components in digital format, you will have the information readily available to use in future proposal writing. If the funding agency has a specific proposal format, as many do, be sure to follow it as exactly as possible and proofread carefully to eliminate errors. Your attention to these details is one measure of your ability to execute your plan successfully. Figure 6.3 outlines components of a typical proposal's contents.

The review process your proposal undergoes may explain some of the requirements regarding format and deadlines. Funding agencies often establish panels of reviewers to read the proposals and rank each one according to established criteria. These reviewers may include recognized experts, practitioners from the field, potential consumers of the service, or other stakeholders. (You may be invited to serve on such a review panel some day.) Agency staff members are the gatekeepers of the review process. They screen proposals that have arrived by the announced deadline and distribute only those that meet requirements to the reviewers. Thus, attention to seemingly small details can be the difference that gets your proposal the consideration it deserves. All of

Title Page. Project title, organization's name, applicant's name, related addresses, agency to which it is submitted, total budget, appropriate signatures, and date submitted.

Executive Summary. Imagine that you have been granted a 15-minute interview with a busy executive during which you want to convince her that your project is worthwhile and that you can deliver the proposed solution. Address four points in one page:

1. **Problem.** A paragraph or two stating the problem
2. **Solution.** What will happen? Where and how? Who will do it? Who and how many will benefit? How long will it take?
3. **Funding Requirements.** How much money is needed? Do you plan to obtain any part of the funding from sources other than the granting agency? Is this a one-time expense, or do you anticipate needing continued funding? If so, where will that come from?
4. **"Fit."** Why is your program uniquely suited to do what you propose? What is your history, purpose, track record?

Rationale. In no more than two pages, spell out why the problem matters, both to society and to the funding agency. Support your arguments with relevant facts and statistics from experts as well as from your own experience, but avoid "padding" or overstating the problem so that it seems insoluble. Use logical, persuasive arguments. *Example: If you are requesting funds so your center can add an after-school component for elementary school children, state the problem in terms of the hardship for families, employers, and communities caused by lack of such care. Then show how your program will alleviate those hardships.*

Project Description. Three pages detailing what you hope to accomplish and how, what personnel are needed, how you will measure success, and whether the project will continue after the grant period. Include:

1. **Objectives.** Concrete and measurable outcomes. *Example: Rather than "increase the supply of high-quality infant care in X community," say "to increase the licensed capacity of XYZ center by providing six additional infant spaces, maintaining a rating of at least 6.0 on the Infant-Toddler Environmental Rating Scale."*
2. **Methods.** Tell how and when you will carry out objectives. *Example: Give a timeline for acquiring the space you hope to use, ordering equipment and supplies, hiring and training staff, and enrolling children.*
3. **Personnel.** How many staff members will be needed? What qualifications are required and why? How will they be selected? *Example: Because you propose to maintain high standards of quality, you will probably want to specify certain levels of education and experience for your teachers. You will need to explain this because the persons reading your application may hold the misconception that "anyone" can take care of children.* Remember to include details about who will administer the program—most likely, you—and documentation of your credentials to do so.
4. **Evaluation.** How will you determine whether you have met your objectives and to whom you will report these findings?
5. **Potential.** How will your project impact extend beyond the grant period? *Example: How will you continue after-school care when the grant ends?*

Budget. May be limited to an outline of proposed expenses, or may need an additional section detailing proposed revenue and a narrative explaining each line item. Group categories of expenses: for example, personnel costs include subcategories for salaries and benefits as well as outside services; nonpersonnel costs include all materials, space, and equipment.

Organization Profile. Two-page summary giving more details about your program's history, mission, and make-up; include information about the qualifications of staff, board members, and volunteers as well as the role that each plays.

Wrap-Up. In one or two paragraphs, make your best case for why your proposal should be funded.

FIGURE 6.3 Components of a typical proposal.

Source: Based on information provided in the Foundation Center's online *Proposal Writing Short Course.* Retrieved July 6, 2005, from http://fdncenter.org/learn/shortcourse/prop1.html

your hard work creating the proposal is wasted if it is eliminated before the review process because you used the wrong format, submitted too few copies, or mailed it at the last minute and missed the deadline. Following the prescribed format also helps the individual reviewers who are looking for specific elements in your proposal.

The procedure of applying for grants takes time and energy, and the wait for an answer may be long, but the rewards are worth it. A funded proposal not only extends the resources of your center, but also may bring recognition for your center and staff members in the local, state, or national child development center arena. Even the process of writing a proposal that does not get funded can stimulate you, your advisory board, and your staff members to work harder or in new directions.

? DECISIONS, DECISIONS . . .

Using an Ethical Framework

Suppose a teacher in the preschool classroom in your center has been studying the Reggio Emilia approach to early education and comes to you with a request for a light table and several new types of art material for her classroom. You want to support her desire to try new things and you think the children will benefit from these ideas, but there is currently no room in the budget for these purchases. A board member brings you a brochure from a company that promises you an easy, pain-free method of raising funds by selling candy or gift-wrap paper. The idea is to ask families in your center to buy the product themselves as well as sell it to their friends and neighbors. The company provides the product at a set price and the center earns a percentage on each sale. You know that comparable or even better candy and gift wrap are available in local stores at lower prices. You also know that, even though many of the families you serve are having a hard time making ends meet without such extraneous purchases, some will feel obligated to participate. How will you decide what to do? Using the NAEYC code, try to determine what core values are involved. What ideals and principles regarding responsibilities to children, families, and employees apply? What course of action seems most right?

HOW FUNDS ARE SPENT

Put yourself in Jeralyn's shoes, as the manager of Rainbow Place, a medium-size child development program that serves 100 children, ages 6 weeks through 5 years. The program operates year-round from 7:00 a.m. to 6:00 p.m. To keep our example simple, let's also assume that you have obtained 501(c)3 tax-exempt status, and your program is housed in a church that charges less than the market rate for rent and utilities. In addition to that amount, you must pay for staff salaries, cleaning and other services, food, and all other equipment or supplies out of the fees you take in each month, or you must find other sources of revenue to make up any shortfall.

Calculating Staff Costs

Salaries in child care are very low, a fact confirmed by comparisons to salaries for parking lot attendants, animal caretakers, and other occupations. (See Figure 6.4.) Nevertheless, your biggest expense will be labor. As far back as the late 1970s, the National Day Care Study (Ruopp, Travers, Glantz, & Coelen, 1979) indicated that 69 percent of an average child-care program's budget went for personnel. That figure is substantially greater today, as you will see in the case of Rainbow Place, where salaries and benefits comprise a little over 90 percent of the total budget. Before we began to calculate personnel costs, we must make some decisions about how many staff members are needed and when they are needed. We set the following guidelines:

1. The program must meet or exceed the NAEYC standards for group size and adult–child ratios for each age group as well as those established by the American Academy of Pediatrics for your youngest infants.

2. During the first and last hour of each day, when attendance is low, children from two classrooms within each range will be grouped together.

3. Teachers will have at least an hour's paid planning time daily.

4. All staff members will have appropriate breaks.

5. One teaching assistant in each classroom will be paid for a half-hour's work after the center closes to tidy the room and ready it for the following morning.

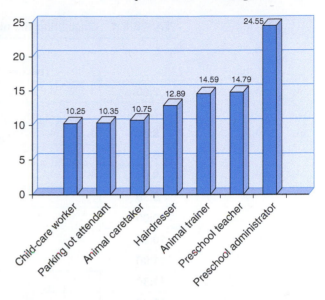

FIGURE 6.4 Average hourly wage for child-care workers compared to employees in other occupations.

Source: Bureau of Labor Statistics (2012a). May 2012 national employment and wage estimates, United States. Retrieved June 29, 2013, from http://www.bls.gov/oes/current/oes_nat.htm#00-0000

Table 6.1 illustrates one way of calculating the number of staff hours needed for a single classroom, using the listed guidelines. We multiplied those figures by the number of classrooms to come up with a total for the center. Because Rainbow Place has eight classrooms, we needed eight full-time teachers, eight full-time assistants, and eight part-time (¾-time) assistants. To determine salaries, we took job responsibilities and staff qualifications into account. Note that staff benefits add roughly 30 percent to our salary figures. Calculating total salary costs becomes complicated when deciding

when or if the director and assistant director are figured into the adult–child ratio. Your state licensing standards will help you make these decisions.

For the purposes of our example, we based salaries for teachers, assistant teachers, and the director on 2011 average hourly wages reported by the U.S. Department of Labor, Bureau of Labor Statistics ($14.80 per hour for teachers, $10.25 per hour for assistants, $25.00 for the director). We are keenly aware that these are far from the ideal put forward by NAEYC more than two decades ago: that compensation of early childhood professionals should include salaries and benefits commensurate with those of other professionals with comparable training, experience, and responsibilities and not be dependent on the type of setting or age of children served (Willer, 1990).

Child care is a labor-intensive enterprise, meaning that personnel costs are the greatest expense for any child care program.

	Teacher	Assistant (Full-Time)	Assistant (¾-Time)	Number of Staff
TABLE 6.1 Calculating the number of staff hours needed per classroom.				
7:00				1
7:30				1
8:00				2
8:30				2
9:00				2
9:30				2
10:00				2
10:30				2
11:00				2
11:30				2
12:00		Break		2
12:30				3
1:00	Break			2
1:30				2
2:00	Planning time			2
2:30				2
3:00			Break	2
3:30				2
4:00				2
4:30				2
5:00				1
5:30				1
6:00			Cleaning	1
Number of hours	8 hrs + 1 hr break (includes 1 hr planning time)	6 hrs + ½-hr break	8 hrs + ½-hr break	

Unless the center serves a very wealthy clientele, it will be impossible to achieve this goal if the only source of revenue is parent fees. In many communities, however, subsidies are available in the form of programs such as the TEACH Early Childhood Scholarship project, which provides stipends for individuals who complete educational requirements and commit to staying in the field, as well as for the programs that employ them (Child Care Services Association, 2012). In addition, some states partner with private providers as part of a move toward "Universal PreK," providing funding to hire licensed teachers and meet public school preschool standards. To learn what initiatives are available in your state or local community, consult the 2008 report compiled by the Center for the Child Care Workforce, *Compensation Initiatives for the Early Care and Education Workforce* (available online at www.ccw.org.).

BUDGET PLANNING

Once you have a rough idea of how much money is available, where it is coming from, and where it has to go, it is time to begin putting the details on paper—part of the manager's planning process. A budget is a plan, expressed in dollar amounts, for how your program will use its resources to meet its goals. Thus, creating a budget is part of the planning process discussed in Chapter 5. Following a budget and making adjustments when needed is part of another process, monitoring and controlling.

Types of Budgets

Different types of budgets are needed at different points in the organization's life cycle. A start-up budget is just what the name implies: a plan for starting a new program from scratch, for translating a concept into reality. Operational budgets plan for the upcoming year. Some organizations might budget for longer cycles. A narrative budget (often required as part of grant proposals) is a written explanation of what is included in each category and why.

Establishing Priorities

The first important thing to remember is that *the budget is a tool for achieving goals, not an end in itself.* It is a plan, not a straitjacket. It is based on predictions of what the program's income and expenses will be, and it is subject to change when those predictions do not develop. Of course, the more complete the information is that supports your predictions, the more accurate they are likely to be, so it is essential to do your homework. Start with your strategic plan, determine what you need in order to achieve it, and then allocate dollars accordingly. For example, if your strategic plan is to provide high-quality care and you know that staff education and stability are key components of that quality, you want a salary and benefits package that attracts highly qualified candidates, as well as a system of promotions and raises that encourages them to stay with your program. With this in mind, you may, for example, choose to add money to your salary budget rather than purchasing an expensive packaged curriculum.

No program enjoys unlimited income, however, and the available dollars may not stretch to cover all of your goals at the level you would like. Thus, you have to prioritize those goals or establish a time frame for accomplishing them gradually. In the previous example, we suggested that salaries were given a much higher priority than purchasing a packaged curriculum. You may even give salaries a higher priority than something as worthy as new, high-quality playground equipment. But even after prioritizing, you might discover you cannot immediately pay the salaries you would like. Instead, you have to establish a long-term plan for reaching that goal over a number of years, perhaps by raising fees for the next budget cycle or initiating an ongoing fund-raising activity.

In our hypothetical small center, Rainbow Place, the manager is the person responsible for gathering the information and preparing the budget. Should you manage a larger organization, you may have help from a financial manager or assistant director. In corporate franchises or public school programs, your job may be to carry out budget decisions made by a central office. We used a spreadsheet computer program to begin constructing an actual budget for Rainbow Place. (You can do the same thing with pencil, paper, and a handheld calculator, but you cannot make changes as easily as you can with the computer.) If you are not familiar with using spreadsheets, this **video** provides a quick introduction to the basics.

INCOME   First, under the heading Income, list all sources of expected revenue for the period covered by your budget. Figure 6.5 demonstrates one way to organize and display your calculations.

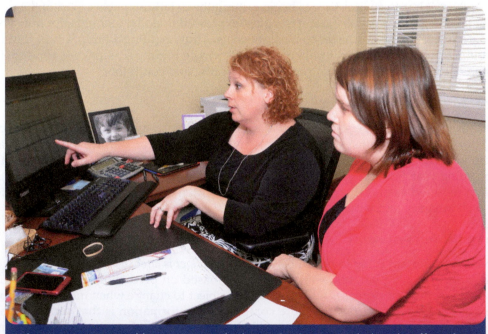

Using a computer spreadsheet to create a budget makes it easy to calculate the effect of changes (such as raising fees or staff salaries) on the bottom line.

Sample Budget for Rainbow Place*

INCOME				
Tuition	Number	Week	Annual	
Infants ($210/week)	12	$2,520.00	$128,520.00	
Toddlers (195/week)	16	$3,120.00	$159,120.00	
Preschool ($175/week)	72	$12,600.00	$642,600.00	
Total Tuition Income				$930,240.00
Other Income				
Initial enrollment fee ($120.00)	25*	$3,000.00		
USDA food subsidy		$6,000.00		
Interest		$600.00		
Grants		$1,200.00		
Fund-raising Activities		$6,000.00		
Total Other Income			$16,800.00	
Estimated 1% vacancy rate			$(9,302.40)	
TOTAL INCOME				$937,737.60
EXPENSES				
Salaries				
Director			$52,000.00	
Assistant director			$38,000.00	
Lead teachers (8 at $30,784 each)			$246,272.00	
Full-time assistant teachers (8 at $21,320 each)			$170,560.00	
Part-time assistant teachers (8 at $16,000 each)			$128,000.00	
Substitute(s)			$10,000.00	
Cook (3/4 time at $10.00/hr)			$15,600.00	
Total Salaries			$660,432.00	
Benefits (estimated at 30%)			$198,129.60	
Total Personnel Cost			$858,561.60	
Other Expenses				
Rent and utilities			$24,000.00	
Food			$24,000.00	
Equipment			$10,000.00	
Supplies			$11,176.00	
Insurance			$5,000.00	
Custodial service			$5,000.00	
Total Other Expenses			$79,176.00	
TOTAL EXPENSES				$937,737.60
BALANCE				$—

*Example assumes 25 new enrollees per year as current children leave program

FIGURE 6.5 Sample budget for Rainbow Place.

Some budgets, such as those you might submit with a grant application, include in-kind resources and list those in a separate column from cash income. For the sake of simplicity, we will consider only cash income for this example. In this **monthly budget PopUp 6.1** for Rainbow Place, income sources include tuition fees, enrollment fees, government subsidies, interest on bank accounts, grant awards, and money obtained through fund-raising activities. If you place your cursor over any cell, you will see that some contain simple numbers (for example, cells B4, B5, and B6) that appear as such at the top of the spreadsheet. Others contain formulas that also appear at the top of the spread sheet. For example, if you place your cursor on cell C4, the formula "=B4*210" appears at the top of the spreadsheet. This means that the amount shown in cell C4 represents the number of children indicated in B4 multiplied by the amount of weekly tuition specified in cell A4. Place your cursor over cell D4 to see the formula "=C4*51," meaning that the weekly total in C4 is multiplied by 51 to arrive at an annual total. Although there are 52 weeks in the year, we used 51 intentionally to allow for the fact that enrollment might dip at times throughout the year as families move away or withdraw for other reasons. Note that if you make a change in the formula for one cell (raising or lowering the number of children in a particular age group, for example), it will percolate throughout the spreadsheet and change the bottom line.

IMPORTANCE OF ACCURATE PROJECTIONS Recall that the accuracy of our budget predictions depends on the degree to which they reflect complete information, so we must also include an item in our income category to reflect a potential loss of income. It is highly unlikely that Rainbow Place will operate at its capacity of 100 children for 12 months a year. Families move or withdraw their children for other reasons, and even with an extensive waiting list, it may be impossible to fill the vacancies immediately. The center may suffer some losses when families fall behind in payments and leave owing money. Insert a row in your spreadsheet and enter a formula to total each type of income, as well as another row and formula that totals all of the income. Be sure to enter the dollar amount for expected vacancies as a negative number.

EXPENSES Next, create a category for expenses and enter all of the expense types that your program will incur. Personnel costs include salaries for each staffing category, as well as an amount for Social Security deductions, workers' compensation, unemployment compensation, and any benefits (e.g., health insurance) that you will provide. For the sake of simplicity in this example, we estimated benefits at 30 percent of total salaries. Other expenses include occupancy costs (rent or mortgage, utilities, telephone), food, equipment, supplies, and fees for services such as cleaning or bookkeeping. In addition to insurance covering your building and equipment in the event of theft, fire, or other damage, you will need liability insurance to protect against lawsuits resulting from accidental injuries that can occur no matter how vigilant you and your staff members are. Of course, you will need vehicle insurance if you provide transportation, but you will also need liability protection if you contract with an outside agency or use public transportation or parent volunteers for field trips. Your state licensing regulations may specify minimum amounts of coverage.

Again, insert a row on your spreadsheet and enter a formula to total each subcategory of these two categories (Personnel and Other Expenses), and another to add those two totals together. Compare that number to the sum total of your projected income. If the two numbers match, you have a "balanced budget." If, as is more likely, your anticipated expenses exceed your anticipated income, revise the budget, finding ways either to raise revenue or to lower expenses.

Take a moment to study the sample budget for Rainbow Place in Figure 6.5 and consider the factors that went into the projections. The vision guiding our planning is, of course, a commitment to the highest possible quality of care. In keeping with this overall goal, our group sizes and staff ratios meet or exceed NAEYC standards, and we based our salaries on data from national surveys, as discussed earlier.

Balancing Act

When balancing our budget, however, we had to face the fact that we cannot offer our teachers salaries that are competitive with what they might earn elsewhere, for example, in public schools. Even to meet these modest salaries, however, we had to set our annual fees at $10,710 for infants, $9,945 for toddlers, and $8,925 for preschool-age children—well above the minimum levels depicted in Figure 6.2. Achieving a balance between a fair wage for staff members and affordable fees for families is one of the director's most challenging tasks. (See Figure 6.6.)

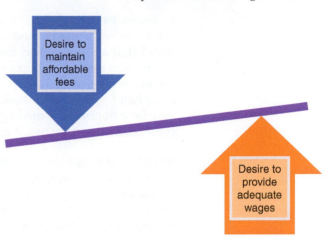

FIGURE 6.6   Balancing adequate wages with affordable fees.

In determining other income, we made conservative assumptions about the number of new children we would enroll each year as other children leave the program. On the other hand, we also assumed that we would be able to fill vacancies rapidly (as a consequence of our high-quality services). Note that this is an operating budget for an established center. If we were drafting a start-up budget for a new facility, we would have based our calculations on a much higher vacancy rate, with a corresponding reduction in anticipated staffing costs until the program reached full enrollment. Obviously, our projected equipment expenses would also have been considerably higher.

We had to make several other sacrifices to balance our budget. We decided that we could not afford even a part-time secretary or custodian and opted instead to contract with a cleaning service for a few hours a week. This means that the director and assistant director must handle the secretarial duties and that the teachers have to pitch in by serving the afternoon snack and doing some day-to-day cleaning. You will note that the budgeted amounts for supplies and equipment are minimal—again assuming that the director and teachers will take up the slack by locating and using free or inexpensive materials and assisting with fund-raisers or applying for grants to cover major purchases.

? DECISIONS, DECISIONS . . .

Examine the budget in Figure 6.5. What changes would you suggest? For each change, note what other changes are required in order to balance the budget. Use the digital version of the spreadsheet so that you can see the way your proposed changes alter other aspects of the budget.

Control of Funds and Expenses

Once you have the budget in place, move from the planning process to organizing its implementation. The monitoring and controlling process involves comparing actual performance with projections and making necessary adjustments. You are also expected to report to the board periodically—quarterly or yearly.

FINANCIAL DECISIONS   Each process requires you to make decisions. Financial decisions can be either programmed or nonprogrammed, as discussed in a previous chapter. Recall that a programmed decision is one that is routine, handled the same way from one time to the next. For example, the formula for calculating an employee's withholding tax is the same and does not require new procedures each time it is done. On the other hand, when a parent cannot pay the tuition and asks for an extension, your answer may be a nonprogrammed decision that necessitates procedures for weighing various considerations and arriving at the best decision for that individual and your center.

WRITTEN POLICIES AND PROCEDURES   In financial matters, as in other areas, written policies and procedures simplify your decision making and help maintain consistency and fairness within the operation. Will your center offer different rates for full- or part-time enrollment? What about discounts for families with more than one child enrolled, or a sliding fee scale based on family income? Under what circumstances will you make tuition refunds? Will your program pay for employee health insurance? If so, will you cover all of the cost or only a portion? Will part-time employees be eligible? How much sick leave will an employee earn each month? What circumstances qualify for the use of sick leave?

Once the policies are determined, procedures must be established to facilitate speedy and consistent decision making. For example, once the amount per child is decided, you must decide whether tuition payments are to be collected weekly, monthly, or quarterly. This decision may depend on whether many of the parents are paid weekly, biweekly, or monthly. As you and your policy board formulate the policies regarding fees, you must also consider the following questions:

1. Will payment be required in advance or after services are rendered? Payment in advance, obviously, lessens the chance that the center will be "stuck" with a large outstanding balance if a family withdraws its child. For many families, however, advance payment is not a realistic expectation. Furthermore, government agencies do not usually allow centers to bill for services until after they are rendered.

2. Will parents be required to pay only for the actual days their child is in the center's care? Or will they be expected to pay for an agreed-on number of hours per week, whether or not the child actually attends those hours? On the one hand, parents usually balk at paying for a service they feel they have not received; but on the other hand, centers must schedule and pay staff regardless of whether a particular child is out ill or a family goes on vacation one week. Some centers handle these fluctuations in attendance by sending employees home when few children are present, but this approach hardly seems fair to employees who must be able to count on their salaries each week.

3. Will families be required to pay additional fees if they arrive late to pick up their child? Certainly, this occurrence is a problem for staff members who are eager to get home to their own children, but sometimes the costs in public relations exceeds the gain to be had by charging the extra few dollars. Is there a way to offer a "grace period" or to consider the number of times a parent has been late before imposing the penalty?

RECORD KEEPING

Keeping business records, like teaching, is a professional skill. Whether your program is for-profit or nonprofit, you or the person to whom you delegate this task will need special training to do an adequate job of keeping the books. Consulting an accountant or tax adviser is essential. Many centers contract with a regular accounting service to prepare records that are clear and accurate each month. These records are used to prepare quarterly and annual reports for the policy board and for reporting income taxes.

Cash-Flow Analysis

Whereas your budget is your plan for the year, a cash-flow analysis is a tool that tracks the rate at which money is coming in and going out. It shows how much cash your program has on hand and compares your expected receipts and expenses with the actual figures for each month. Using a computer spreadsheet program simplifies the preparation of this document. Figure 6.7 is a sample cash-flow analysis.

Begin by looking at the totals for items in your annual budget and break those numbers down into the amounts you expect to receive or spend each month. For example, Rainbow Place's $24,000 annual fee for rent and utilities is recorded as $2,000 under Projected Expenses for each month, and the same amount is listed under Actual Expenses each month because rent typically does not vary from month to month. Should the church raise the rent midyear, the new figure would be recorded under Actual Expenses, indicating a variation from the projected figure. Because some other expenses, such as insurance or bulk orders for classroom supplies, occur only once or twice a year, they do not appear every month. Receipts can be expected to vary as well. For example, Rainbow Place's Expected Receipts from tuition payments are listed in the

Cash Flow Analysis for Rainbow Place				
	January, Projected	January, Actual	February, Projected	February, Actual
Opening Cash Balance	950	950	655	655
RECEIPTS				
Tuition	69,768	71,360	69,768	69,768
Enrollment fees	100	100	100	300
USDA food subsidy	416	550	416	550
Interest	50	58	50	58
Grants	0	0	0	0
Fund-raising activities	0	0	500	750
TOTAL RECEIPTS	71,284	73,018	71,489	72,081
EXPENDITURES				
Salaries	49,164	49,164	49,164	49,164
Benefits	14,749	14,749	14,749	14,749
Rent and utilities	2,000	2,000	2,000	2,000
Food	2,000	2,200	2,000	1,850
Equipment	4,000	0	0	1,500
Supplies	1,500	1,200	1,200	1,200
Insurance	2,500	2,500	0	0
Custodial service	500	550	500	450
TOTAL EXPENDITURES	76,413	72,363	69,613	70,913
Closing Cash Balance	−5,129	655	1,876	1,168

FIGURE 6.7 Cash flow analysis for Rainbow Place.

Many early childhood program managers feel proficient with word-processing applications, but they are much less familiar with spreadsheet applications or database management programs. If this description fits you, you might want to invest in a commercial software program specifically designed for child-care center record keeping. Some of these programs are a one-time purchase; others require a monthly subscription fee to access an online system. Before adopting any software package, make sure it does what you need it to do; is user-friendly, affordable, and compatible with your computer; and is backed by technical support as well as a warranty (Walker & Donohue, 2005). As an alternative, you (perhaps with the help of someone with more expertise) could use generic software to set up your own system for managing center finances. A spreadsheet like the example in Figure 6.5 enables you to calculate quickly and easily the effect a particular pay increase for all your teachers would have on your bottom line and what adjustments in your fee schedule would be necessary to cover it. A database is a useful tool for recording details like child immunization records and generating periodic reports showing which children are due for boosters. An online payment system to accept credit card payments is a convenience for families and may help avoid cash flow problems for you.

budget as $930,240 per year (calculated at 51 weeks per year to allow for vacations). Deducting 1 percent from that figure for an anticipated vacancy rate yields $69,768 per month. Should the vacancy rate exceed 1 percent, receipts will fall below projections. During months when Rainbow Place enjoys full enrollment, actual receipts will exceed projections. Another potential discrepancy between projected and actual receipts will occur if the center receives state-subsidized payments for any of the children enrolled because the payment for the care of those children in any given month is actually received sometime during the following month.

In both the Expected and Actual columns, the total expenses for a given month are subtracted from the total receipts, yielding a cash balance for that month. This is a negative number in those months in which expenses exceed income. The cash balance for the month is added to the opening cash balance (the amount on hand at the beginning of the month) to arrive at the new cash balance to be carried forward to the following month.

? DECISIONS, DECISIONS . . .

Figure 6.7 shows an anticipated negative cash balance for January. What factors account for the fact that the center actually ended the month with a positive balance of $655? What action would be needed if the shortfall did occur?

? DECISIONS, DECISIONS . . .

Explore and evaluate two or more management software programs using the questions above as a guide. (See the list of companies with their web addresses in the Resources for Further Study at the end of this chapter.) Which seems to offer the best value in terms of usefulness, ease of application, and cost?

INTERNAL CONTROLS

Any cash income, including parents' checks, should be deposited promptly. Some centers keep a petty cash fund for small items and give staff members specific guidelines for its use. A specific record must be kept when petty cash payments are made. Drawbacks to petty cash include the potential for pilfering as well as the danger of impulsive spending rather than planning ahead for more economical bulk purchases.

Keep Track

New purchases must be added to the inventory. Packages should be checked immediately on delivery to verify the condition of the contents. You should develop or purchase a software system that allows you to add and delete items from the inventory.

Avoid Waste

Judicious use of all resources (energy, money, food, supplies, and time) is another aspect of the control process, requiring the help of your entire staff. Control utility costs by installing energy-efficient light fixtures and keeping thermostats at reasonable levels. Monitor leftover foods to determine which recipes should be adjusted to eliminate leftovers and avoid contamination, waste, or improper use by employees. Be sure you and the center's cook know the rules governing the use of leftover foods.

Allocate a given quantity of supplies to each classroom so the teachers can take responsibility for using it wisely. Encourage them to avoid overfilling dispensers with paper products, such as napkins, towels, and tissues, and enlist children as well as staff members in efforts to conserve resources and protect the environment. Instead of filling cups with paint that must be discarded when muddied, use pump bottles and show children how to take only the amount of the paint color they need. Return the savings to teachers by allowing them to buy extras for their classrooms rather than expecting them to use their own money for such purchases.

Compare Prices

It is important to ensure that you are getting a fair price for the resources you purchase. For large items, ask several companies to make bids. For smaller items, check vendors' websites or call for prices and make comparisons.

Consider Hidden Costs

Determine, for example, whether disposable tableware, which must be continually replenished, is actually less expensive than a one-time investment in multiuse tableware and a commercial dishwasher. Remember to include any costs incurred for trash disposal with the former alternative and the cost of staff time to load, operate, and empty the dishwasher in the latter.

Think Big

As the term *giant economy size* suggests, a product such as laundry detergent generally (though not always) costs less per ounce when purchased in the gallon jug instead of the 6-ounce container. Unit prices posted in grocery stores reveal whether or not this is true, and you can use the information to your advantage in several ways.

BUY IN BULK WHEN FEASIBLE   Paper goods, for example, can be purchased in quantity at considerable savings if you have secure, fireproof storage facilities. Buying groceries in quantity can also save money, but certain foods require appropriate storage to avoid spoilage and may in fact be more costly if the excess contents of large containers is wasted.

Some of the best materials cost little or nothing. "Beautiful stuff" collected by the children and displayed in organized, attractive ways encourages creativity while stretching budget dollars. *Beautiful Stuff* (Topal & Gandini, 1999) is the title of a book about collecting materials as a classroom project.

PLAN AHEAD   Create menus for 3 or 4 weeks and repeat the cycle to make purchasing more efficient and reduce the likelihood of packaged foods being stored for too long. Cycle menus also help to manage the labor costs because cooks develop time-saving techniques with repeated preparation of the recipes.

JOIN FORCES   Band together with other centers in your community to increase your bargaining power by purchasing supplies in greater quantities than would be possible for any single center Take advantage of group plans for insurance or other benefits offered through professional organizations such as NAEYC.

BE PROACTIVE TO SURVIVE AND THRIVE IN HARD TIMES
The early childhood field has a long history of making do. Homemade materials such as play dough, fingerpaint, and paint extenders are certainly less expensive and sometimes superior to their commercial counterparts. Anyone who has watched children spend more time playing with the cardboard box than with the toy it contained knows that recycling found materials can stimulate untold depths of creativity. Programs inspired by the preschools of Reggio Emilia, Italy, have learned that this is especially true when those found materials are presented to children in an organized, aesthetically pleasing display.

Child Care Exchange, a magazine for directors, challenged visitors to its website during the last recession (www.ccie.com) to confront bad news about the national economy by creating a child-care "stimulus package." Some innovative responses included bartering (e.g., allowing families to provide services for the center in lieu of payment when they lost their jobs). Some mentioned capitalizing on a center garden to provide not only an interesting educational activity, but relaxation for children and adults, a connection with the community, and a supply of fresh produce to brighten menus and lower food bills.

Conclusion

It takes a tough head to plan the budget, organize its implementation, and monitor and control the balance sheet—all the while maintaining a tender heart for giving the children the loving care and education a high-quality program requires. Your assertive leadership and vision are essential to marshal the funds needed to operate such a program. You must spend a great deal of your time securing funding and then actively monitoring and controlling so that those funds yield the best possible program for children.

NAEYC accreditation standards require that centers maintain a sound fiscal policy in order to meet their obligations to children and families. Written policies and procedures are required to keep decision making consistent and fair. Managers must MESH, or coordinate all materials, equipment, space, and human energy, to achieve program goals. They must develop a careful procedure for budgeting, purchasing, record keeping, and controlling expenditures.

This chapter provided an overview of the financial aspects of an early childhood administrator's job. You should enlist the advice and assistance of business and accounting experts when you assume the manager's role. You should also continue your own study of this topic. You can begin by consulting some of the Resources for Further Study listed at the end of this chapter, and you can take courses in business management at your university or community college.

Questions for Review

1. Use the MESH formula to list resources needed to start and maintain a child development program. What items would you add to the suggestions in Figure 6.1?

2. Identify source(s) of funding for each item you listed in response to question 1.

3. Explain the relationship among parent fees, staff salaries, and quality of care.

4. Using the sample budget given in the chapter, calculate the adjustments that would be needed if enrollment were reduced by 25 percent. How many staff would be needed? Would fees have to be raised?

5. Using the sample budget given in the chapter, calculate changes in parent fees and/or enrollment numbers that would be needed to raise staff salaries by 5 percent.

6. Explain how a budget differs from a cash-flow analysis.

7. Either interview the director of a child development program or reflect on your own experience to give examples of at least five ways of controlling waste, expenses, and funds.

Professional Portfolio

1. Begin constructing a business plan for a program you hope to manage some day. At this point, you should be able to write the mission and goals statements, as well as the financial plan. As you complete subsequent chapters, you can add the organizational and marketing sections. Write the executive summary after you have completed the entire plan.

2. Develop an annual budget for your hypothetical program. Add a narrative component explaining how your budget reflects your program goals and objectives.

3. Develop short- and long-range fund-raising options to support your goals; evaluate the cost effectiveness and appropriateness of each.

4. At your public library, your local child-care resource and referred agency, or on the Internet, locate an actual RFP that applies to child development programs. Write a grant proposal for your hypothetical center or for a real center in your community.

Resources for Further Study

PRINT

Greenman, Jim. (1998). *Places for childhoods: Making quality happen in the real world*. Redmond, WA: Exchange Press.

Jack, Gail. (2005). *The business of child care: Management and financial strategies*. Clifton Park, NY: Delmar.

Schoenberg, D. (2008, July/August). Using technology to improve fee collection. *Exchange, 182,* 28–31.

Villarosa, C., & Villarosa, A. (2009). *Down to business: The first 10 steps to entrepreneurship for women*. New York: Avery.

Websites

CHILD-CARE MANAGEMENT SOFTWARE SOURCES

Child Care Manager
http://www.childcaremanager.com/

Childplus Software
www.childplus.com

CMSC, Ltd.—Maggey Software
www.maggey.com

Emerging Technologies
www.etwebsite.com

EZ-Care2—SofterWare
www.softerware.com

ICare Software
www.orgamation.com

Jackrabbit Class
http://www.jackrabbitclass.com/

The Preschool Partner by on-Q Software, Inc.
www.on-qsoftware.com

Procare Software
www.procaresoftware.com

SchoolLeader—Kressa Software
www.SchoolLeader.com

THE CHILD-CARE SOFTWARE STORE

http://www.childcaresoftwarestore.com

Provides reviews and video demonstrations of several different programs.

PROVIDER RESOURCES

http://www.acf.hhs.gov/programs/ccb/providers/index.htm#funding

Provider Resources from the Administration for Children and Families, U.S. Department of Health and Human Services. Includes documents such as What Providers Should Know about Child Care Assistance for Families (English and Spanish versions) and links to several resources for funding to start or improve a child-care program.

SMALL BUSINESS PLANNER

http://www.sba.gov/smallbusinessplanner/index.html

Tool provided by the U.S. Small Business Administration; includes information and resources to help with every stage of the business life cycle: planning, start-up, managing, and closing.

CHAPTER

Personnel Management

LEARNING OUTCOMES

After studying this chapter you should be able to

- Describe the steps in the job design process and create an example of each.
- Discuss the role of organizational structure, authority, and span of control in coordinating the jobs in a child development center.
- Give an overview of the steps involved in the staffing process.

Tanya's promotion to assistant director created a vacancy for a teacher at Rainbow Child Development Center. One of Tanya's tasks in her new role was to serve on the hiring committee to find her replacement. She was able to help update the job description based on her experience, and she assisted with reviewing applications, selecting the most promising candidates, interviewing, and making the final decision. She then had the pleasant task of contacting Derek to offer him the job, and she will be responsible for his orientation during his first few days on the job. She had been very motivated to find just the right person to take over "her" children, and she feels confident that the committee made a sound choice. Now that she has a full appreciation of how much work goes into hiring a new employee, she wants to make doubly sure that Derek feels welcome and comfortable in his new position.

You've done the planning and have the program's broad goals outlined, along with ideas about how to implement those goals. You have created a budget—a plan, expressed in dollar amounts, that governs how your program will use its resources to meet its goals. It's time to begin the tasks of organizing and staffing and come one step closer to bringing those plans on paper to life. Thus, we turn our attention to **personnel management**, an administrative competency that taps into both the organizing and staffing processes. *Organizing* involves deciding what jobs must be done, what skills or training are required, and how those jobs relate to one another. Once those decisions are made, *staffing* consists of developing procedures for recruiting, selecting, and retaining employees to do the various jobs. After those employees are hired, your human relations competency is necessary to fully use and enhance the resources they bring. The next chapter will explore the human competency aspect of personnel management.

JOB DESIGN

Consider the following example: A child development specialist was given the task of organizing services at a camp for orphans in the war-ravaged African country of Rwanda. Jacqueline Hayden arrived at the camp with no supplies, no assistance, and no office space. Within 12 weeks, she had organized children into mixed-age, family-style groups with an adult refugee assigned as "tent mother"; found "foster families" for the youngest and most traumatized orphaned children; and enlisted groups of children and adults to take care of cooking, laundry, foraging for supplies, making storybooks, and making culottes to clothe the other children (Hayden, 1995). She did not use magic to create order out of chaos. She recognized the potential human resources available in the midst of overwhelming need and broke a huge task into manageable components to make effective use of those resources.

You may never work in a refugee camp, but wherever you start a new program, your first organizational task is to determine what jobs must be done. **Job design** is "the process of laying out job responsibilities and duties and describing how they are to be performed" (DuBrin, 2000, p. 162). Job design is needed when setting up a new business and deciding what jobs will be needed. In a small dressmaking factory, for example, some employees cut out the patterns, others stitch the pieces together, and others add the buttons or other trimmings. Other jobs include creating the designs, buying the fabric and other supplies, distributing the materials to the workstations, checking the finished product, selling the dresses, shipping them to buyers, and so on. If the factory is large enough, the jobs might be even more specialized, with different workers assigned to sew each part of the garment. The factory owner may strive to make each job as automated as possible in order to meet the goal of maximum production at minimum cost.

> **?**   **DECISIONS, DECISIONS . . .**
>
> With your classmates, create a list of all of the jobs required in a child development program. Discuss how much specialization or automation is possible or desirable in each.

Job Analysis

While job design occurs in the planning stages, before a position exists, **job analysis** can occur either during the planning stages or at some point later as the job is being performed. For example, you may be hired to manage an existing program, perhaps one that grew from a very small operation where everyone "just knew" what had to be done and did it without much planning or discussion. To put this program on a more businesslike footing, you should complete a job analysis for each individual. A job analysis identifies the specific tasks associated with an existing job, the competencies (knowledge, skills, and abilities) directly related to performing those tasks, and the factors that are important for evaluating candidates for the position. You can conduct this analysis by observing the person who is doing the job or by having that person help. Begin by listing the primary duties of the job and all the tasks required to fulfill those duties. (What does the worker do? How? Why? What output is produced? What tools, procedures, and aids are involved? How much time does it take to do the task? How often does the worker perform the task in a day, week, month, or year?) After careful analysis, you might decide to reallocate some of the tasks assigned to that staff member.

Next, identify the competencies required to perform those tasks. Examples of competencies are oral communication, flexibility, customer service, teamwork, and leadership. They should be stated in objective, measurable terms for each category:

1. Knowledge required (subject matter; specific facts and principles; level, degree, and breadth needed)
2. Skills required (activities requiring ease and precision; manual operation of equipment or tools)
3. Abilities required (e.g., written and oral language; math proficiency; problem solving; level of instructions needed; interpersonal, supervisory, or managerial qualities; physical strength; coordination; visual acuity)

Once you have determined the competencies needed, you can list them on a worksheet like the one in Figure 7.1 and make judgments about their relative importance for determining the best candidate for a position. Does the person need the knowledge, skill, or ability even to begin the job? Or is it something that can be learned on the job? Which competencies are needed for exceptional job performance?

Next, consider the frequency and degree to which activities such as pulling, pushing, throwing, carrying, kneeling, sitting, running, crawling, reaching, and climbing are required and conditions of the work environment such as ventilation, noise, or crowding. Consider the extent to which the job typically entails any of the following:

1. Situations involving the interpretation of feelings, ideas, or facts in terms of personal viewpoint.
2. Influencing people in their opinions, attitudes, or judgments about ideas or things.
3. Working with people beyond giving and receiving instructions.
4. Performing repetitive work.
5. Performing under stress when confronted with emergency, critical, unusual, or dangerous situations; or in situations in which work speed and sustained attention are make-and-break aspects of the job.
6. Performing a variety of duties, often changing from one task to another of a different nature without a loss of efficiency or composure.

Finally, consider whether the job would appeal to someone with a preference for dealing with objects, data, or people; for routine or mechanical as opposed to abstract or creative work; for tangible evidence of accomplishment or psychological rewards. Figure 7.2 is an example of a completed job analysis for the position of cook in a child development program.

Job Classification

Once you have completed the job analysis, you can determine where that job fits in the overall picture of your organization. How does it compare with other jobs in degree of difficulty, responsibility, required preparation, and need for supervision? The resulting job classification assigns a specific level to the job. Salary can then be based on the level of the job in the classification. Figure 7.3 illustrates a job classification scheme for teaching staff.

Job Specification

After completing all these steps, you are ready to devise a job specification to be used in advertising the open position. This document is based on the job analysis. It specifies the type and level of education and previous experience required. It lists essential personal characteristics such as judgment; initiative; physical effort; physical skills; communication skills; emotional characteristics; and the necessary sensory demand such as seeing,

Job Analysis Worksheet for Competencies

Competency	Source	Importance	Need at Entry	Distinguishing Value
[List required competencies here; add additional lines as needed]	e.g., licensing regulations	see below	see below	see below

Importance Scale	Need at Entry Scale	Distinguishing Value Scale
How important is this competency for effective job performance?	When is this competency needed for effective job performance?	How valuable is this competency for distinguishing superior from barely acceptable job performance?
1 = Not Important	1 = Needed the first day • Essential; won't acquire through training or experience • Desirable; those who possess it develop competence more readily • Not needed because acquired through training or experience	1 = Not Valuable
2 = Somewhat Important	2 = Must be acquired within the first 3 months	2 = Somewhat Valuable
3 = Important	3 = Must be acquired within the first 4–6 months	3 = Valuable
4 = Very Important	4 = Must be acquired after the first 6 months	4 = Very Valuable
5 = Extremely Important		5 = Extremely Valuable

FIGURE 7.1   Job analysis worksheet for competencies.

Source: U.S. Office of Personnel Management (2007). *Delegated examining operations handbook: A guide for the federal agency examining offices.* Retrieved July 8, 2009, from http://www.opm.gov/deu/Handbook_2007/DEO_Handbook.pdf.

hearing, and smelling. The position's responsibilities are clearly stated. It includes information regarding compensation, the procedure for applying, a deadline, and contact information. Figure 7.4 is an example of the job specification for a child development center teacher. The job specification is the basis for advertising the vacancy.

Job Description

The job description should be available when you hire an individual. It is a written statement describing the duties, hours, and specific responsibilities associated with the

Identifying Information
Name of Incumbent: Mary Jones
Organization: XYZ Child Development Center
Title: Food Service Employee: Cook
Date: [Today's date]
Interviewer: Janie Bolls

Brief Summary of Job

The cook plans menus; prepares breakfast, lunch, and midmorning and midafternoon snacks for children and staff in the center; assists with serving breakfast and lunch; prepares market orders; and keeps kitchen, dining areas, and food storage areas clean and sanitary.

Job Tasks

Cook's Duties: Daily (8 hours, 5 days weekly; 6:30 a.m. to 2:30 p.m.)

1. Prepares breakfast and helps serve to center's young children and staff.
2. Prepares lunch and helps serve to center's young children and staff.
3. Prepares snacks for children and break beverages for staff.
4. Operates commercial dishwasher for tableware; washes cookware by hand as needed.
5. Maintains cleanliness of food preparation area (countertops, appliance tops, floors).
6. Maintains compliance with licensing and sanitation regulations regarding food service.

Occasional Duties

1. Prepares 3-week cycle menus for manager's approval.
2. Places food orders as directed by manager.
3. Checks deliveries for accuracy and ensures that food supplies are stored appropriately.
4. Maintains inventory of food and paper supplies.
5. Monitors condition of kitchen appliances and reports problems.
6. Assists with classroom projects as directed by manager (ordering food, preparing play dough, cookie dough, etc.).
7. Attends in-service workshops or meetings.
8. Makes year-end inventory of food and supplies in June.
9. Recommends maintenance or replacement of appliances or painting of surfaces in the unit.

10. Attends staff meetings as applicable.
11. Prepares (with help) food for special occasions such as parents' meeting, directors' meeting, staff meeting.

Knowledge, Skills, and Abilities Required

1. Knowledge required:
   a. Knowledge of appropriate cooking techniques for the typical foods served in the center
   b. Knowledge of the nutritional requirements for children
   c. Knowledge of the characteristic food habits of children
   d. Knowledge of sanitation principles related to food and food service
2. Skills required:
   a. Food preparation and cooking techniques
   b. Organization to acquire, assemble, and prepare several foods to meet the serving schedules of the center
   c. Mechanical skill to operate and maintain kitchen appliances
3. Abilities required:
   a. Ability to read recipes, regulations, written memos
   b. Ability to write shopping lists, memos, etc.
   c. Ability to calculate quantities for recipes and food costs using simple arithmetic
   d. Ability to explain or demonstrate to an assistant or volunteer how to do an activity such as prepare a food or set up the dining room
   e. Ability to relate to children, parents, staff members, and vendors in a positive manner
   f. Ability and stamina to work while standing, to lift or move 25–50 pounds of food or equipment

Physical Activities

Include walking around the kitchen, storeroom, and dining room for most of the 8 hours and lifting up to 50 pounds.

Environmental Conditions

Environment is kitchen, storerooms, and dining room. Generally pleasant, may be extra warm when ovens are used. A variety of interpersonal relationships with staff, children, and parents. Generally a moderately quiet place except for happy sounds of children playing.

FIGURE 7.2 Job analysis for a child care center cook.
Source: Based on U.S. Civil Service Guidelines.

Typical Work Incidents

1. Conferring with manager regarding menus, inventories, purchase orders (generally Fridays).
2. Cooking is routine activity, not repetitive because different menus are used daily in 3-week cycles. Challenge is to get a large number of meals on the table at a set time.
3. Routine cleaning tasks are generally minimal because they are done daily.
4. Emergencies may arise if orders do not arrive or appliances do not work; thus, ingenuity is required to keep the service at a high-quality level.

5. Other staff, children, and parents are a pleasant group to work with, generally caring about individuals and their interests.

Work Interest Areas

1. Involves work for the good of others
2. Involves work satisfaction when meals are served on time, taste good, are attractive and nutritious, and are enjoyed
3. Involves variety, yet some routine

FIGURE 7.2 (*Continued*)

position. It should be written in terms that allow it to serve as the basis for periodically monitoring or evaluating the staff member's work. Figure 7.5 is an example of a job description for a teacher. Notice that the description includes a space for both the manager and the employee to sign and date it. The staff member should read this document carefully and agree to the tasks. Later, the manager and staff member should confer before reassigning or adding tasks. This document serves as an agreement and acknowledgment that the job description will be used as the basis for periodic evaluations of the individual's performance.

	Assistant	Teacher	Curriculum Coordinator
Qualifications: • **Education** • **Experience** • **Other**	Associate degree in early education/child development 2 years experience. Physical/TB test. Child abuse and criminal clearance.	Bachelors degree in early education/child development. Teacher licensure. 3 years experience. Child abuse and criminal clearance.	Masters degree in early education/child development. Teacher licensure. 5 years experience. Child abuse and criminal clearance.
Duties	Assist with basic caregiving. Interact with children. Assist in monitoring environment for safety.	Plan, implement, and evaluate daily activities. Establish and maintain relationships with families. Write progress reports. Administer assessments.	Consult with teachers to plan, implement, and evaluate daily activities. Coordinate long-range plans with teachers and families. Provide training and resources for improving curriculum.
Problem Solving	Complete required tasks according to established procedures and under supervision.	Understand and apply policies and procedures, adapting as needed. Collect and interpret information to solve problems. Advice and input available from coordinator.	Understand, interpret, and apply policies and procedures. Take lead in collection of and interpretation of information to develop unique solutions to problems.
Supervisory Duties	May supervise student employees or volunteers.	Supervise assistant teacher.	Supervise teachers in curriculum development.

FIGURE 7.3 Example of a job classification scheme for teaching staff.

Job Title

Child development center teacher

Position Available: September 1, 2014

Qualifications

BA or BS degree in early childhood education, child development or related field; state teaching license in early childhood education preferred; clear criminal records background check, proof of medical exam and negative TB test.

Experience

At least one semester supervised student teaching with young children (ages birth through 5).

Responsibilities

- Plan and implement a developmentally appropriate program for children (in collaboration with assistant or coteacher and curriculum coordinator).
- Organize and maintain environment to support program goals.
- Establish and maintain relationships with families through group meetings, home visits, and conferences.
- Participate in professional development activities.
- Maintain records and write reports.

Hours: 8:00 a.m. to 5:00 p.m., with one-hour lunch break and one-hour planning period, Monday through Friday.

Compensation: Commensurate with education and experience. Benefits include health insurance, paid holidays, and vacation days.

Contact

Mary Right, Manager
Child's Life Child Development Center
444 Adams Street
Baker, TX 67777
214-555-4567
Email: childslifecdc@aol.com

Procedure

Send resume and contact information for three professional references to address above.

Closing Date

July 1, 2014

An equal opportunity employer

FIGURE 7.4   Sample job specification.

Child development centers are dynamic rather than static, meaning that they must grow and develop to meet changing community needs. Job descriptions must be current and reflect any changes that occur when staff members are reassigned or given additional duties as a result of this growth. Figure 7.6 provides an overview of each of the tools described in this section.

Job Title: Child development center teacher

Description: The teacher plans, implements, and documents a developmentally appropriate program for children (in collaboration with assistant or coteacher and curriculum coordinator) and works in partnership with parents to promote each child's development.

Hours: 8:00 a.m. to 5:00 p.m. with one-hour lunch break and one-hour planning period, Monday through Friday.

Responsibilities

- Collaborate with colleagues to plan, implement, and document curriculum.
- Collaborate with colleagues to organize and maintain environment to support program goals.
- Establish and maintain relationships with families through group meetings, home visits, and conferences.
- Maintain records and write reports.
- Participate in professional development activities.

Signed _____ Date _____
Employee

_____ Date _____
Manager, XYZ Child Development Center

FIGURE 7.5   Sample job description.

	Job Design	**Job Analysis**	**Job Classification**	**Job Specification**	**Job Description**
Function	Lays out responsibilities and duties for a proposed job and describes how they are to be performed.	Identifies specific tasks associated with an existing job, the competencies (knowledge, skills, and abilities) directly related to performing those tasks, and the factors that are important for evaluating candidates for the position.	Compares jobs within an organization; assigns specific level to each based on the following: • degree of difficulty • responsibility • preparation required • amount of supervision necessary	Uses job analysis findings to spell out requirements for a job: • type and level of education and experience • essential personal characteristics and skills • responsibilities of the position • compensation • application procedure • deadline and contact information	Describes the duties, hours, and specific responsibilities associated with a particular position.
Timing	When jobs are being created for a new organization, or a new job within an existing organization.	Either during planning stages for new position or when clarification of an existing job is desired.	During planning stages for new position.	When a new position is created or an existing position becomes vacant.	Written copy provided at point of hiring, signed by employee and supervisor.
Purpose	To plan personnel needs.	To clarify responsibilities and qualifications.	To provide objective data for setting pay scale.	To provide the basis for advertising a position.	To ensure that both parties clearly understand expectations for the job.

FIGURE 7.6 Elements in the job design process.

JOB COORDINATION

Now that you have analyzed, or carved into specific jobs, the work necessary to accomplish your goals, you have to figure out how to put all of those parts together. This requires decisions about organizational structure, authority and responsibility, and span of control. Your job is to keep the broad picture in mind.

Organizational Structure

Plan A in Figure 7.7 shows the teacher as the clear, top authority figure, with the assistant teacher responsible to the teacher and the aide responsible to both the teacher and the assistant teacher. Some center managers prefer Plan B in Figure 7.7—that is, to hire teachers of equal qualifications and give them co-teaching responsibilities. In either case, the aide is responsible to both teachers. Particularly in child-care operations exceeding an 8-hour day, having coteachers with staggered times of arrival and departure makes considerable sense.

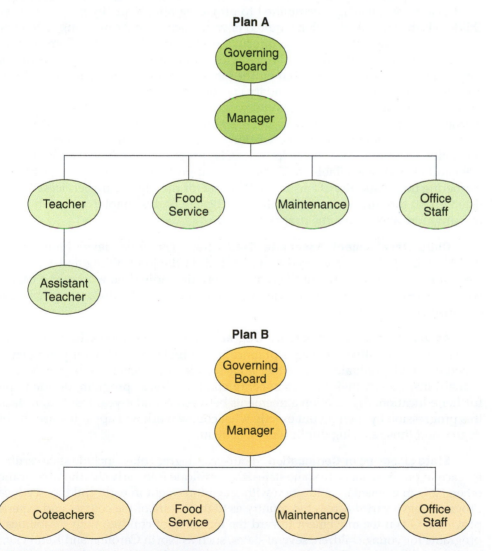

FIGURE 7.7   Examples of organizational charts.

TEACHING STAFF   Decisions you have made about educational and experience requirements for your teachers will have a bearing on the organizational structure that best suits your program. Many centers expect to hire certified teachers to lead each group of children and hire somewhat less-educated people to serve as aides or assistants. Other centers expect to hire one certified program director who works with all caregivers to plan the center's educational program. The National Association for the Education of Young Children (NAEYC) accreditation criteria require that all teachers have at least an associate's degree or equivalent, with at least 75 percent having a baccalaureate or equivalent in an early childhood specialty area. All staff members who implement the program under direct supervision must have a high school diploma or general educational development (GED) diploma; 50 percent must have a child development associate (CDA) credential or equivalent, with all others enrolled in a program leading to that goal (National Association for the Education of Young Children, 2007a, pp. 53, 96).

Although questioned by some researchers (e.g., Early, Maxwell, & Burchinal, 2007), the consensus among numerous studies has demonstrated the connection between staff training and program quality (Cassidy, Lower, & Kintner, 2008). One of your major policy decisions as a manager committed to providing a high-quality program for young children is the level of education required of your teaching and caregiving staff members.

A wide range of formal and informal preparation is possible. Some employees may enter as aides with no formal training or experience and develop the skills necessary to work with young children on the job. Others may come with formal training acquired in a variety of ways. Secondary vocational schools and community colleges, as well as 4-year institutions, offer several programs that prepare caregivers and assistant teachers. Such programs generally include child development and practicum courses that give the student experience working with children in a center. The Teacher Education and Compensation Helps (TEACH) program is a national effort, initiated in 1990 and currently available in 22 states, to support early childhood practitioners in furthering their education. Consult the Web site for the Child Care Services Association listed under Resources for Further Study at the end of this chapter, or watch this video to learn more about what the program offers.

Child Development Associate Credential   The child development associate (CDA) credential can be viewed as a blend of on-the-job training and formal study. Assessments are conducted in the center where the individual works, and candidates work individually or with other candidates to enhance and document their skills in specified competency areas.

Associate and Baccalaureate Degrees   Early childhood education programs offered by 2- and 4-year colleges prepare individuals to work with young children. When finished, graduates hold either an associate or a bachelor's degree. Many individuals, inspired by their success in completing the 2-year program, decide to pursue further education. Articulation agreements between 2- and 4-year institutions facilitate this progression by spelling out exactly what course work will apply toward the higher degree and thus reducing duplication of content.

State Licensure or Certification   Four-year degrees often include state certification to teach in public schools. In some states, the certificate is in early childhood education; in others, it is in elementary education with an endorsement in early childhood education. Programs have varied across the country as to the nature of the courses and experiences provided. Given the movement toward the inclusion of children with disabilities in all programs for young children, several states, such as North Carolina and Kentucky, offer an early childhood certificate that combines course work and practical experience in child development, early childhood education, and early childhood special education.

Some states have defined from three to six levels of competency for early childhood personnel. In New Jersey, for example, the levels are (1) aide or paraprofessional, (2) assistant teacher with CDA, (3) associate teacher with a 2-year degree or formal course work in early childhood education, (4) classroom teacher with 4-year degree or state endorsement, (5) master teacher with master's degree and at least 3 years' teaching experience, and (6) leadership with a master's degree and extensive experience working with young children as well as in adult supervision (Center for the Study of Child Care Employment, 2008).

SUPERVISORY STAFF   An employee called a **curriculum coordinator**, or assistant to the manager, may be assigned to help plan the children's programs and advise the teachers about curriculum choices and children's behaviors. This position may be staffed when a manager has several building sites and cannot be available to oversee the details of each classroom or in centers where less than highly qualified teachers are hired to operate the classrooms. This supervision may be required by licensing regulations. In this case, joint planning is required, which means that the supervisor and teachers need a time and place to go over the plans and get their ideas coordinated before the teachers carry them out. Plans must be understood, match each teacher's ability, and fit the characteristics of the children in the group. The details of this coordination effort should be included in the job description of each teacher and the supervisor.

Another way to look at this position has been developed in the world-renowned early childhood programs of Reggio Emilia, Italy. There, a **pedagogista** works collaboratively with teachers from several centers "to analyze and interpret the rights and needs of each child and family, and then use this knowledge in [their] work with children" (Filippini, 1994, p. 116). The *pedagogista* also facilitates parent–teacher relations and organizes meetings where they can discuss and extend the children's curriculum projects. There is no exact translation for the job title in English, but some programs in the United States are finding it useful to have such a facilitator to help the teachers reflect on their observations and interactions with children and families as they plan where to go next in their curricula.

SUPPORT SERVICES   The work in a child development program includes much more than the day-to-day interactions between children and teachers. There are several behind-the-scenes jobs that support those interactions.

Office Services   Child development centers are businesses and require systems for record keeping as well as for interacting and communicating with parents and the public. Records are essential to document compliance with regulations and to track financial matters such as fees, bills, rents, and taxes. Centers must have up-to-date lists of family names with home addresses and phone numbers, work addresses and phone numbers, and other pertinent data, as well as contact information for vendors; health, fire, and social services; and professional organizations. Someone must collect the fees from the parents, write receipts, pay bills, and deposit money in the bank. The office support unit is responsible for the timely

As a business, a child development center must have systems for maintaining records.

and accurate payments of salaries, benefits, withholding and Social Security taxes, bills, and rents.

Efficiently organizing and storing the center's various forms (e.g., admissions, health, and financial) and office supplies from the outset facilitates handling routine matters. A larger center usually hires an office assistant or secretary at least part-time. An accounting system must be established with the aid of a qualified accountant. Routine accounting services may be obtained through a contract if the center cannot afford to hire one. Smaller centers may attempt to handle day-to-day secretarial chores with volunteer help, perhaps from a parent. It is shortsighted for qualified managers to spend much of their time typing, sorting mail, filing, and answering the phone when someone to do these tasks can usually be hired at a relatively small cost to the center. As noted in the previous chapter, all these tasks can be streamlined by developing spreadsheets and databases or adopting commercially available software. The manager's time should be spent more productively writing grant applications, for example, or conferring with teachers or parents.

Food Services   Both licensing regulations and accreditation criteria follow the food service standards of the U.S. Department of Agriculture. A qualified cook is capable of planning the meals and all of the activities of the kitchen and dining room. As manager, you may have to plan the meals for a less-qualified cook, or you may contract with a registered dietitian for this service. Procuring the food and other supplies may be the responsibility of the manager, the cook, or an employee assigned to handle all purchases. The person assigned this task must purchase and organize the supplies and control the inventory carefully to minimize expense and avoid the risks of loss, waste, theft, and food spoilage.

Planning for links between the classrooms and the food service unit saves time and dollars. Foods used as part of various learning experiences can readily be purchased in large lots with other foods and then incorporated into the regular menus. For example, a teacher might plan to make fresh-squeezed orange juice with the children as a science activity exploring simple machines. The juice can be served as a snack beverage. This requires that the cook purchase an orange for each child and make a corresponding adjustment in the total quantity of snack beverages purchased that week. A number of food items used in learning activities are not eaten; for example, play dough requires flour and salt.

Because the organization chart does not show all of the tasks included in the list of the cook's duties, a job analysis and a job description are needed. It is important, for example, to indicate who asks the cook to provide oranges for the science activity or the flour and salt for play dough. Do teachers ask the cook directly, or should they go through the manager's office? If such purchases are specified in the cook's job description, they can become a simple routine activity. If not, the cook may feel burdened by the request.

Maintenance and Cleaning Services   These services apply to the entire center, covering the classrooms, service areas, and outdoor play areas. Cleanliness and safety are essential and very dependent on adequate attention to maintenance details on a daily, even hourly, basis. A custodial-maintenance person may provide the most effective arrangement, with the center manager helping with overall goals and timetables. In small centers, one individual may have complete responsibility. In the organization's plan, the procedures to acquire maintenance tools, cleaning tools and supplies, and services are needed. Duties include light and heavy cleaning; trash and garbage removal; storage and repair of equipment; painting and general upkeep; disinfecting the kitchen, food service areas, and rest rooms; and maintaining the outdoor play area. Teachers and children should share responsibility for maintaining a clean, orderly environment. Parent volunteers can help with specific projects from time to time. The more everyone pitches in, the more they will feel ownership and pride in the center.

Transportation Services   Transportation services are important benefits to some center customers. Clearly, licensing standards for the qualification of drivers, seat belts for children, and extra adults are all essential. Although having a center bus or van makes field trips easy, transportation is a costly item, and finances must be calculated carefully, including adequate insurance coverage.

The job specifications for each of these positions should be carefully drawn, always keeping human factors clearly in mind. One of the hallmarks of excellence in high-quality programs is the family atmosphere that is engendered when the support staff interact with the children regularly, becoming rich resources along with the teachers. Even though your management techniques must be professional and business-like, your center provides high-quality care to the extent that it resembles a home more than a business. In addition to the obvious skills required of a secretary, cook, janitor, or bus driver, it is wise to include the ability to relate well to children as part of the job description. Programs are enriched immeasurably when children get to know these important people in their lives. In one center, for example, the cook worked with a small group of children to design and create a "wedding cake" as part of a month-long curriculum project. Another group of children invited the center's housekeeper to lunch, giving careful thought to which day's menu might be most appealing and corresponding with her via messages taped to her vacuum cleaner.

Support staff can be teachers too, so managers should look for candidates with some of the same qualities they seek in teachers. Here center's cook is encouraging a child to help distribute breakfast to classrooms.

Authority and Responsibility

A clear definition of responsibility is essential when assigning teachers or other staff members the authority to manage their duties and workspaces. For example, although you might expect teachers to arrange space, organize storage, set up learning centers, and make appropriate adaptations for individuals and situations in their classrooms, you might not expect them to handle business matters such as collecting and recording fee payments.

Giving teachers the authority to manage their own classrooms is an example of **decentralizing authority**. This decentralization generally makes for a responsive, creative, and adaptive organization, highly desirable qualities in any people-centered operation. Remember that a central tenet of quality management is the empowerment of all staff members so that each one has the maximum feasible authority to carry out the assigned responsibilities. Teachers who have the authority to manage their classrooms invest more creativity and energy than those who simply have the responsibility to carry out the manager's plans.

Some employees might be granted the authority to direct the work of other employees. The program's organizational chart is a visual representation of these lines of authority. In the Plan A organization (see Figure 7.7), the teacher directs the assistant teacher, reflecting the difference in training and experience required for each job. In the Plan B organization, coteachers share authority. This type of organization is used when job specifications call for teachers of equal training and experience. It symbolizes the expectation that the work and the responsibilities are shared equally.

Clear lines of authority are necessary because they help employees know where to turn for solutions to their problems. They also let the parents and even the children know who can make a final decision. Unless your center is very small, it is a good idea to put these lines of authority down on paper in the form of a flowchart or graph that clearly shows the chain of command. This visual representation can be supplemented with written policies that inform parents and staff members where to go with particular concerns.

COMPENSATION AND TIME FOR ADDITIONAL RESPONSIBILITY Delegating managerial functions to teachers requires an organizational system that allows paid time for their accomplishment. The Center for the Child Care Workforce (1998) recommends a minimum of 2 hours of paid planning time per week, plus closing the program at least 1 day per year for long-range planning and renewing the physical environment. To achieve high quality, the standards are 5 hours per week and 2 days per year.

LINKS BETWEEN CLASSROOMS AND OTHER UNITS Links between the classrooms and the program's maintenance, food service, and business units are essential. In a decentralized plan, a system for obtaining materials, supplies, and equipment is especially critical for preventing duplication and waste. Each teacher might be assigned a budget for classroom use. Teachers could make appropriate inventories and place requests for supplies, which can then be ordered collectively. In a centralized plan, the manager assumes more responsibility for ordering, allocating, and distributing supplies.

? DECISIONS, DECISIONS . . .

A local club has just raised $1,000 for your center to purchase some new play equipment. Because your philosophy is to delegate as much authority as possible to the teachers, you ask them to decide how to spend the money. How can you do this yet ensure that the money is spent wisely—that is, on materials of high quality? How will you organize the task to accomplish both goals?

Span of Control

Span of control generally refers to the number of subordinates reporting to a manager. In child development centers, the span of control refers to the number of children and families within the group assigned to a particular teacher. Thus, span of control incorporates concepts of teacher–child ratio as well as group size. These concepts are of particular significance when close supervision is required to provide the individual attention and analysis that are the hallmarks of high-quality service. How many people can one or two teachers comfortably and effectively influence through their caring and teaching?

GROUP SIZE Although many consider low adult–child ratios to be indicators of quality, even a one-to-one adult–child ratio does not ensure a high-quality experience for children if the manager does not also consider the number of children to be cared for in one group or classroom. Imagine a room full of 20 crying babies! More than a quarter century ago, the National Day Care Study made a distinction between human ratio and mathematical ratio:

> In a group of 14 children with two caregivers the mathematical ratio is 1:7, just as the mathematical ratio for 28 children and four caregivers is 1:7. The human ratio is, for the caregivers involved, twice as much in the second case as the first. *Each* caregiver has 28, not 14, children's names and needs to know. (Ruopp, Travers, Glantz, & Coelen, 1979, pp. xxvi–xxvii)

TABLE 7.1 Recommended adult-child ratios and maximum group sizes.

Maximum Number of Children per Caregiver				Maximum Group Size			
NAEYC		APHA/AAP		NAEYC		APHA/AAP	
Birth to 15 months	4	Birth to 12 months	3	Birth to 15 months	8	Birth to 12 months	6
12–28 months	4	13–30 months	4	12–28 months	12	13–30 months	8
21–36 months	6	31–35 months	5	21–36 months	12	31–35 months	10
30–48 months	9	3-year-olds	7	30–48 months	18	3-year-olds	14
4-year-olds	10	4-year-olds	8	4-year-olds	20	4-year-olds	16
5-year-olds	10	5-year-olds	8	5-year-olds	20	5-year-olds	16
Kindergarten	12	6- to 8-year-olds	10	Kindergarten	24	6- to 8-year-olds	20

Source: National Association for the Education of Young Children, Early Childhood Program Standards and Accreditation Criteria (2007a), and American Academy of Pediatrics, American Public Health Association, National Resource Center for Health and Safety in Child Care and Early Education (2011).

Managers who want to achieve the highest quality when organizing classrooms must look beyond their state's licensing regulations. Although the minimum standards for adult–child ratios are included in each state's licensing regulations, they vary widely from state to state. In spite of its importance, only 38 states regulate group size for infants and toddlers, while even fewer (34) do so for 3- and 4-year-old children (National Association for Regulatory Administration, 2010, p. 69).

At least two other sets of standards do address this issue. The National Association for the Education of Young Children makes recommendations but does not include group size as a required criterion for accreditation. It notes, however, that exceeding the recommended limits will have a negative impact on a program's ability to meet standards and achieve accreditation (2007a, p. 83). The recommendations of the American Academy of Pediatrics and the American Public Health Association (2011) support those of the NAEYC. Table 7.1 shows the adult–child ratios and maximum group sizes recommended by each organization for children of various ages.

Public school policy makers are also paying attention to group size, with several states establishing goals for reduced class sizes. Full-day kindergartens can also have a positive impact. Recall the concept of human ratio (as distinct from mathematical ratio) discussed earlier. Although a kindergarten teacher with 20 children in the morning and another 20 in the afternoon is dealing with a *mathematical ratio* of 1:20, the *human ratio* for the teacher is 1:40 because that is the number of names, personalities, and families to

A manageable group size means that each child is able to get the teacher's attention at least some of the time.

know. With only one group of 20 and the extended time period, a teacher can get to know each child and each family far better than with two groups of 20.

AGE RANGES Organizing also applies to the group composition within classrooms. There are many arguments for single-age groups and for multiage groups, with strengths and weaknesses on each side. Multiage groups are thought to be more family-like, providing older children opportunities to be helpful to younger ones. On the other hand, some argue that activities in a single-age group can be more challenging. Teachers in multiage groups might avoid difficult or complex projects because they think the younger children will be frustrated—either by trying to do things beyond their capacity or by being excluded from an activity that might be too hard or dangerous for them. An alternative to mixed-age grouping is a strategy popularly known as looping, meaning that a teacher stays with a group of children for more than 1 year, either moving with the group to the next classroom or modifying the original classroom as the children's developmental needs change. The concept of human ratio provides an argument in support of either mixed-age groups or looping. When each child stays with the same teacher over several years, the teacher deals with fewer new families in any given year. The teacher, child, and family are spared learning about each other anew every year and are able to develop deeper relationships.

> **? DECISIONS, DECISIONS . . .**
>
> Divide your class into two teams. Let one team brainstorm a list of the pros and cons of mixed-age groupings, while the second does the same for looping. Discuss your lists. Which set of arguments do you personally find most persuasive?

THE STAFFING PROCESS

Merely defining the jobs necessary to accomplish your program's goals is, of course, not enough. You have to find the right people to do those jobs. A child development center is a labor-intensive operation. That is, lots of human energy or labor is essential for the center to reach its goals. No mechanical robots can perform the services. People's knowledge, skills, abilities, stamina, enthusiasm, and love are aspects of their human energy. Such attributes are called human capital. The importance of human capital is underscored by the statistic that the salaries for a center's personnel often consume the bulk of the operating budget. Staffing is the process of recruiting and dealing with the human resources (human capital) required to perform the center's functions.

Some managers take the perspective that recruiting is a perpetual process. They constantly keep an eye out for potential candidates so they are never in a position of starting a search in a last-minute panic (Vicars, 2007). Whether or not you have adopted that strategy, when a staff vacancy occurs, you have an opportunity to reanalyze that position and consider various alternative organizational structures. You might reorganize your groups or promote a staff member. You may try to hire someone with more experience or education in the hope that such an individual will prove a better fit and thus derive more satisfaction from the job, ultimately leading to less staff turnover. Depending on the size of your operation, you might hire a person to work as a part-time teacher and a part-time librarian or as a part-time parent educator. Or two people might be hired to share one position. In other words, the vacancy gives you an opportunity to think about new ways to structure the work assignments.

As you sort through these possibilities, you may consult your policy and advisory boards. Your center may already have established policies concerning promotion from within or the qualifications for specific jobs. If these options seem unworkable, you have to work with your board to change them before proceeding.

Organizing the Search

Once a decision is made to hire, a committee should be formed to conduct the search. Unless your board is very small, it is wise to include only selected representatives on the hiring committee. Other potential members of the hiring committee include parents of children enrolled in the center and staff members who will be working with the new teacher. Each of these groups can bring a valuable perspective to your deliberations. Parents consider whether they feel comfortable leaving their child with a particular candidate or sharing their own concerns with that person. Staff members are likely to wonder whether the candidate will pitch in and do a fair share of the work or be fun to work with.

Make it clear at the beginning who has the authority for the final decision. Will it be a democratic process? Or will the committee provide recommendations, with the final authority resting with the manager? Each method has advantages, so you want to weigh your decision carefully.

? DECISIONS, DECISIONS . . .

Using an Ethical Framework

As the director of ABC Child Development Center, you are committed to a democratic style of leadership. You include two staff members along with two family representatives and two board members on the hiring committee for a teacher vacancy. You and the board members favor candidate A, whose background includes a 4-year degree in early childhood education and who has some field experience in programs serving children with disabilities. The family members and teachers on the committee favor candidate B, who has worked at the center for two years and recently completed an associate's degree in early childhood education. Using the NAEYC code, try to determine what core values are involved. What ideals and principles regarding responsibilities to children, families, and employees apply? What course of action seems most right?

Legal Aspects of Staffing

A number of laws and regulations govern the operation of a child development program, including those specifically related to staffing. It is important for managers to be familiar with these requirements, but it is equally important to seek the advice of legal experts because interpretations, as well as the laws themselves, can change over time and vary with locale.

Recall that the Civil Rights Act of 1964 prohibits all discrimination on the basis of race, sex, religion, color, or national origin. This is the law that addresses the issue of sexual harassment. An earlier law, the Equal Pay Act of 1963, mandates that employers give women and men equal pay for equal work. The Civil Rights Act of 1991 gives victims of discrimination the right to sue for compensatory and punitive damages, in amounts up to $300,000, depending on the size of the employer. Because some laws protecting workers' rights apply only to employers above a certain size, a small child development program may be legally (if not morally or ethically) exempt.

- The Fair Labor Standards Act (FLSA) prescribes standards for wages and overtime pay, which affect most private and public employment. The act requires employers to pay covered employees who are not otherwise exempt at least the federal minimum wage and overtime pay of one-and-one-half times the regular rate of pay. The Wage and Hour Division also enforces the labor standards provisions of the Immigration and Nationality Act (INA) that apply to aliens authorized to work in the United States under certain nonimmigrant visa programs (H-1B, H-1B1, H-1C, H2A).

- The Americans with Disabilities Act of 1990 prohibits employers of 15 or more employees from discriminating against individuals on the basis of disability or chronic illness unless their condition prevents them from performing the job functions or the employer would suffer "undue hardship" by accommodating them.

- The Age Discrimination in Employment Act of 1967 applies only to organizations with 25 or more employees and prohibits discrimination (including mandatory retirement based on age) against individuals 40 and older.

- Employers with more than 21 employees may not discriminate against pregnant women as long as they are able to do their jobs, according to the Pregnancy Discrimination Act of 1978.

- Under the Family and Medical Leave Act of 1993, employers of 50 or more must provide up to 12 weeks of unpaid, job-protected leave for employees during any 12-month period to care for newborn, newly adopted, or seriously ill children or a spouse or parent.

- Under the Affordable Care Act of 2010, employers with more than 50 full-time equivalent staff are required to offer health insurance coverage that meets minimum standards to full-time employees (and their dependents).

Listing the Job

After your job specification is prepared, you must use a number of avenues to put it before the public so possible candidates can see it. You can duplicate it and hand it out to possible candidates at a meeting, or you can post a flyer, with tear-off tags listing the program's phone number, where potential employees might see it. You can list your job opening with the U.S. Department of Labor and state employment offices serving your community, and advertise in a local newspaper. Placement services operated by unions, professional organizations, and colleges are other possibilities.

The internet is one way to publicize openings to the widest possible audience. You can ask your local child care resource and referral agency to post the announcement on their website or you can tap into a much larger pool by posting your announcement on the websites that reach a national audience, such as the Career Forum of the National Association for the Education of Young Children (www.naeyc.org) or the Child Care Information Exchange (www.childcareexchange.com). Personal contacts in agencies or among your professional colleagues across the country can be excellent sources of referrals. Finally, you may encourage particular individuals to apply for positions rather than simply waiting to see who responds to a published job specification.

LEADERSHIP LENS

Every time there is a vacancy to fill on your staff, you have an opportunity to take a leadership role in enriching the diversity of the child-care workforce. By giving your job specifications as much visibility as possible, you will reach a larger pool of potential candidates. Men have always been underrepresented in the early childhood workforce, and with the increasing population of English language learners (ELLs) in early childhood programs, bilingual staff are sorely needed. Make it your goal to proactively seek out these valuable additions to your staff each time you undertake a search for applicants.

The first step is to make sure that your advertising methods do not inadvertently exclude any particular group. If you are posting your advertisements in English only, you are less likely to reach members of the Hispanic or Asian communities. Try posting translated versions in churches, community centers, or other agencies serving those populations. To reach more male candidates, you might consider advertising under a heading like "recreation supervisor" in addition to child care or early education. Make the priority you place on diversity clear in your handbook and on your website. Spread the word among the families of children in your center and your own network of community contacts.

Be creative and open to indirect ways of accomplishing your goal. A Spanish-speaking parent who volunteers to lead stories and songs a few hours a week might need only a little encouragement from you to apply for a job as secretary or cook at the center and then take the coursework that would warrant a move into a teaching position. Perhaps your center has a young man working part-time as a bus driver or custodian. Could you offer him the opportunity of full-time employment by adding hours as a classroom assistant with the expectation that he take part in professional development activities with teachers? In either case, you might have set someone on the path toward a new career in early childhood, enhanced the lives of children in your center, and made a difference in your community.

Job Application

You should develop a standard job application form that provides the information your screening committee needs (see Figure 7.8). For professional jobs, a curriculum vitae or résumé and a letter of application may be preferred. Some managers ask for a letter from applicants to help gauge the quality of the candidate's writing and language usage. The job specification announcement should state where applications are available and, if desired, where letters and résumés should be sent. An application form should include name, address, phone, educational background with credits or degrees, work experience, most recent position and a reference from that position, a list of previous employers and references, and general character references. In accordance with antidiscrimination laws, you may not ask applicants questions regarding race, religion, gender, pregnancy, number or ages of children, marital status, child-care plans, height or weight, disabilities, age, criminal record, union affiliation, medical problems, or

Managers must ensure that advertising methods do not inadvertently exclude any particular group. Men, for example, are underrepresented in early childhood programs.

Name _____

Address _____ Telephone _____

_____ Email _____

EDUCATION

School or College	Dates Attended	Degree or Certificate
_____	_____	_____
_____	_____	_____
_____	_____	_____

WORK EXPERIENCE (beginning with most recent)

Employer _____

Position _____ Dates of employment: From _____ to _____

Supervisor _____ Phone _____ email _____

Employer _____

Position _____ Dates of employment: From _____ to _____

Supervisor _____ Phone _____ email _____

Employer _____

Position _____ Dates of employment: From _____ to _____

Supervisor _____ Phone _____ email _____

REFERENCES

Name	Phone	Email
_____	_____	_____
_____	_____	_____
_____	_____	_____

I certify that the information above is accurate and complete.

Signature _____ Date _____

_____

FIGURE 7.8 Sample application form.

workers' compensation claims on previous jobs, *unless the area in question is job related* (DuBrin, 2000, p. 216). Thus, child development programs may ask—and are usually required to do so by state licensing regulations—for information about a candidate's health and criminal history. Some centers require the potential employee to sign a declaration similar to that in Figure 7.9.

I hereby certify in good faith that a case of abuse or neglect has not been substantiated against me nor have I been named in any proceeding for abuse or neglect that is pending in any court. I also certify that I have not been convicted of any crime (excluding minor traffic offenses) nor are there felony charges pending against me. I understand that the falsification of this or any part of my application is grounds for my discharge from employment.

_____   _____

Date   Signature

_____

FIGURE 7.9 Sample employee statement.

Most states now require that all child-care workers be screened for serious criminal convictions and histories of the abuse or neglect of children or adults. The two types of screening should not be confused: Screening for criminal convictions does not reveal a history of child abuse unless the person has been convicted in criminal court. In many states, instances of child abuse are handled in family or probate court and do not result in criminal convictions. Some states require this screening for the director only, while others require it for each employee. Some states require it at initial licensure only, and some require it annually. Some states allow employees a provisional period during which they may work until clearances are obtained; others require clearances to be on file before an employee starts work. Ask your licensing consultant for the correct procedure in your particular state.

Completing the necessary screenings does not mean, however, that you have, in fact, eliminated all applicants with such histories. Police records are incomplete in some instances, and perpetrators of abuse can assume false identities to conceal their records. Experts on child sexual abuse contacted during a federal study of child-care employee screening practices concluded that the best safeguards were "(a) education and alertness of parents, staff, and children; (b) careful listening and observation by parents and staff; (c) child care participation and monitoring by parents; and (d) parent networks within programs" (Staley, Ranck, Perrault, & Neugebauer, 1986, p. 23). Figure 7.10 is an example of written procedures for screening applicants.

Checking References

Before the interview, you should check the references provided by the applicant. Contact each reference by telephone rather than relying on written statements an applicant might submit. In addition to verifying the authenticity of the written statements, you can follow up on areas where you have questions, and you can listen for subtle cues or hesitations that suggest the person's recommendation for a particular candidate is less than wholehearted. References are not foolproof, however. First, these are names provided by the applicant, and they probably can be expected to give a positive view. One way to surmount this difficulty is to ask the applicant for permission to contact "nonindicated" references (i.e., persons not listed with the application). With that permission, you can then ask the reference to give you the name of another person or two who is acquainted with the applicant's job performance. By calling those people, you may be able to get a more balanced picture. Of course, you would have to respect the wishes of an applicant who may refuse such permission, or request that you not contact specific individuals (e.g., a current employer). Another challenge when contacting references stems from the fact that many employers, out of a fear of lawsuits, are reluctant to provide any information except to confirm an individual's dates of employment. Thus, you have to rely on the information you can glean during your contacts with the candidate.

The Interview

After the closing date for receiving applications is passed, the applications are organized in individual folders with all relevant attachments—letters of reference, transcripts, personal letters from the candidate, and any notes you may have made during contacts. The next steps are to rank the applicants in order of apparent desirability based on how well they meet requirements listed in the job specification, to schedule appointments with the most promising candidates, and to conduct interviews. These tasks are carried out by the selection committee.

The primary objective during the interview is to get the applicant to talk about experiences; knowledge of the job; and, for teachers, knowledge of the philosophy of disciplining children and organizing classrooms. Of course, knowledge is one thing

RAINBOW CHILD DEVELOPMENT CENTER

All employees (full or part time) and volunteers shall submit the following no later than five business days after beginning work:

1. a certified criminal history check from the Clerk of Superior Court's office in the county where the individual resides;

2. a signed Authority for Release of Information using the form provided by the [State] Division of Child Care Licensing;

3. a fingerprint card using the form provided by the State Police (If the employee has lived in [the state] for less than five consecutive years immediately preceding the date the fingerprint card is completed, a national check shall be completed); and

4. a signed statement declaring under penalty of perjury whether he or she has been convicted of a crime other than a minor traffic violation.

If the employee or volunteer has been convicted, has pending charges or indictments, is under deferred prosecution, or is on probation for a crime, the employee shall acknowledge on the statement that he or she is aware that the employment is conditional pending approval by the Division. He or she may submit to the Division additional information concerning the conviction or charges that could be used by the Division in making the determination of the provider's qualification for employment. The Division may consider the following in making a decision:

• length of time since conviction;
• nature of the crime;
• circumstances surrounding the commission of the offense or offenses;
• evidence of rehabilitation;
• number and type of prior offenses; and
• age of the individual at the time of occurrence.

Rainbow Child Development Center will submit the documents to the [State] Division of Child Care Licensing no later than three business days after receipt. A copy of each along with the employee's declaration statement shall be maintained in the center's personnel file until the notice of qualification is received, at which time the submitted information and the declaration statement may be discarded. The notice of qualification shall be maintained in the center's personnel file, and shall be available for review by a representative of the Division.

The employee or volunteer shall be on probationary status pending the determination of qualification or disqualification by the Division.

FIGURE 7.10   Sample screening procedure.

and attitudes are quite another. Some people believe that they can teach appropriate methods to a person who has an open and caring attitude toward children and a genuine enthusiasm for learning much more easily than they can change a negative attitude in a person who knows all of the theories and "right answers."

When interviewing a job candidate, you may ask only job-related questions. Here is where all your hard work creating a program philosophy and job specification pays off. You can use these documents to help formulate appropriate questions and stay on track during the interview. Questions should be clear and concise, giving the candidate the chance to demonstrate the abilities needed from day one (as determined in your job analysis) rather than looking for things that will be learned on the job. Of course, you want to avoid unlawful or unfair questions that serve only to discriminate against certain groups and are not relevant to the person's ability to do the job. For example, you may ask what languages an applicant speaks fluently because that has a direct bearing on the job of a teacher in a center where children come from several ethnic backgrounds. However, you may not ask about an applicant's ancestry or nationality. Because most

Do *Not* Ask	Ask or State Instead
Are you a U.S. citizen? Where were you (or your parents) born?	Are you authorized to work in the United States?
What is your native tongue?	What languages do you speak/read/write fluently? (Ask only if relevant to the job)
How old are you? When did you graduate? What is your date of birth?	Are you over the age of 18?
Are you married? Do you live with someone? How many children do you have? Do you plan to have a family? What are (or will be) your child-care arrangements?	Are you able and willing to work the hours that the center is in operation? (Must be asked of all applicants—male and female)
Do you have any disabilities? Have you had any recent or past illnesses or operations? How is your family's health?	Are you able to perform the essential functions of this job as described in job specification (e.g., lifting babies, sitting on floor)? Can you demonstrate how you would perform these job-related functions?
When was your last physical exam?	As part of the hiring process, if a job is offered to you, a physical exam will be required.
Have you ever been arrested?	Have you ever been convicted of a crime? Have you ever been found guilty of abuse or neglect of children? As part of the hiring process, if a job is offered to you, a criminal background check and clearance regarding abuse and/or neglect will be required.
What clubs or organizations do you belong to?	List any memberships in professional organizations that you consider relevant to your ability to do this job.
If you were in the military, were you honorably discharged?	In what branch of the armed forces did you serve (if any)? What type of training or education did you receive?

FIGURE 7.11 Examples of questions to avoid and possible alternatives.

states regulate the minimum age at which a staff member can be counted in the adult–child ratio, you may ask a question such as, "Are you 18 years old or older?" You should not ask, "How old are you?" or "What is your date of birth?" Do *not* inquire about personal matters, such as marital or parental status, national origin, religious or other affiliation, or type of discharge from military service. Questions about criminal record or disability may be asked only in connection with job requirements. For example, while you may not ask about prior arrests, licensing rules require disclosure of criminal convictions and history of abuse or neglect of children. You may inquire about current, but not prior, use of illegal drugs. You may describe the duties of the job (e.g., lifting children, getting down on the floor, or moving quickly to keep up with children) and ask whether the applicant can perform them with or without reasonable accommodation. Your state's department of civil rights can provide more detailed guidance about fair hiring practices. See Figure 7.11.

The hiring committee may use a structured form, as shown in Figure 7.12, to review each application for completeness and make careful records of the responses from each candidate's references. A form such as the one shown in Figure 7.13 will help ensure that each candidate is treated equally and fairly. Because follow-up questions have the potential to introduce bias so you should take particular care to state them in neutral terms such as "Can you give an example?" or "Would you explain what you mean by . . . ?" The hiring committee should discuss its findings only after each member

(to be completed individually by each member of hiring committee)

Position: _____

Name of Applicant: _____

Review of Application Materials:

• Applicant _____ meets _____ exceeds minimal experience specifications. Comment(s):

_____

_____

• References Contacted:

1. Name: _____ Position: _____

   Comment(s):

2. Name: _____ Position: _____

   Comment(s):

3. Name: _____ Position: _____

   Comment(s):

FIGURE 7.12 Sample application review form.

has recorded his or her individual impressions, and all the interview records should be saved as documentation of fair hiring practice.

Try to establish a comfortable environment for the interview so that candidates can relax and show their best abilities. Let them know in advance that there will be several people asking questions and how long you anticipate the process to take. As part of the

(to be completed individually by each member of hiring committee)

Position: _____

Name of Applicant: _____

Interview Questions (developed in advance by hiring committee; examples included below):

1. [After committee chair reviews job specification] What interests you about this position?

2. Describe the strengths you could bring to the position based on your prior experience and/or education.

3. What aspects of your work have given you the most satisfaction? Why?

4. What situations have you found most challenging? Why? How did you approach those challenges?

5. What would you do if . . . [hypothetical situation]

Classroom Observation (if applicable):

Recommendation:

Signed: _____

Title: _____ Date: _____

(Retain in center's personnel files.)

FIGURE 7.13 Sample interview record.

> **Four-year-old Johnny comes to school with a holster holding a toy gun attached to his belt. What would you do?**
> How do the candidate's ideas about toy weapons fit with center policy on this controversial issue? Can the candidate enforce policy, yet respect the feelings of the children and parents?
>
> **Three-year-old Jennie picks a dandelion in the yard and shows it to you. What would you do?**
> Does the candidate's response reflect a sensitivity toward the child and an awareness of the curriculum possibilities contained within this simple encounter?
>
> **A business offers your center a thousand multicolored handbills printed on one side but unusable because they contain the wrong information. Your center is short of funds for supplies, and you appreciate the donation. What would you do with the handbills?**
> Is the candidate able to think creatively and generate several possible uses for this potential resource?

FIGURE 7.14 Hypothetical situations for teacher candidates.

interview, you may wish to pose hypothetical questions about situations appropriate to the job the person is seeking.

See Figure 7.14 for examples related to a teaching position. Using this interviewing technique requires planning to avoid leading, or giving the applicants your answers. Rather than simply posing hypothetical situations, some programs ask teacher candidates to spend time in a classroom in order to observe their interactions with children and other staff members. Again, if this is part of your process, let candidates know in advance so they know what to expect and can dress appropriately. Notice how the director in this video sets the candidate at ease and how, later in the video, she uses open-ended questions and nods attentively to encourage the candidate to express her ideas about working with children.

Keep in mind that all of the parts must fit together: Your job description reflects your center's basic philosophy, and performance evaluations are based on the job description. Therefore, your interview questions should tap the qualities that you will be evaluating later.

From the Candidate's View

Wise candidates do their homework and know a lot about your center before arriving for the interview. They want to check out information they have heard or read, so allow ample time for them to ask you questions. A tour of the facility and an opportunity to meet staff members will help applicants get a feel for the working conditions and be more ready to respond should you make an offer.

Highly qualified professionals may interview for several positions simultaneously and have several offers from which to choose. Thus, your screening process must be short enough to encourage candidates to stay with you throughout. If your application process is too slow, they may select another position. Continued communication with them and prompt action are essential. Although you want to be very careful and hire the right

Wise managers seek to hire the most well-qualified teachers—those whose education, experience and dispositions enable them to respond to children with a playful spirit.

individual, you must realize that the applicant also has criteria for selecting a position. If another organization fulfills most of those criteria, the applicant may decide to accept that organization's offer, leaving you back where you started.

The Offer

Hiring staff is a lengthy, costly process that you do not want to repeat frequently. Your goal is to hire excellent people and keep them, making openings infrequent. After reflecting on what was learned through the interview process, the committee ranks the applicants and decides which one(s) should receive an offer of employment. The manager may ask the committee for permission to proceed down the prioritized listing should the first-choice candidate drop out of the running. Generally, an offer can be made by phone, with a follow-up letter sent immediately after. The salary, working hours, and assignment should be provided by phone and in the letter. The benefits that the job carries should also be stated. Presumably the applicant has received a job description (see Figure 7.5), but a copy should be attached to the letter and reflect any modifications that may have been negotiated. For example, if the applicant's child received admission to the center as part of the offer, then that agreement should be put in writing. You and the candidate also have to agree on the starting date for the position. Generally, there is a probationary period for new employees, and this point should be stated clearly, both orally and in writing.

In some instances, a physical examination is required; thus, the job offer is tentative until the examination is completed. If the applicant is to bear the expense of this exam, this requirement should be clearly stated from the beginning.

Some centers prefer a contract that is signed by the candidate, manager, and head of the policy board. Whether a contract or letter is used, copies of all hiring documents should be sent to all parties and filed. Once you have signed documents from a candidate, communicate that information to your staff members. Common courtesy requires that you inform the other applicants that a decision has been reached as soon as possible after your offer of employment is accepted and the papers are finalized.

Orientation

Finally, the new employee arrives. There are payroll, Social Security, and income tax withholding documents to sign. Keys are issued at this time, and any printed information prepared for new employees is provided (see Figure 7.15). Be careful, however, not to overwhelm the new employee with paperwork and policies. Your goal is to set the stage for a long-lasting relationship; imagine welcoming a new family member or neighbor. Carter (2008b) recommends reserving the first week on the job for guided observation and study with no direct responsibility for children. Although this may seem costly, it can save money in the long run if it contributes to a more long-lasting, satisfying relationship and ultimately to higher-quality care and lower turnover.

The manager or a designee should take responsibility for orienting the new employee, assigning a more experienced employee, or mentor, to help alleviate early anxiety for beginners. The concept of mentoring is discussed in further detail in the next chapter. A warm welcome from all employees sets a positive tone from the outset and is especially important when a new employee is somewhat different from current staff members. "Different" may mean a male in an all-female staff, a person of color in an all-white staff, a younger person in an older staff, and so on. The focus should be on the skills and talents the person brings to the job rather than any differences. During the orientation with a new employee, clearly state how you evaluate

Employee Name: _____

Position: _____ Date of Hire: _____

Note: The purpose of this checklist is to ensure that you have been adequately oriented to Rainbow Child Development Center and to the policies for which you will be responsible. Please initial and date the items listed below as they are accomplished. When all are completed, please sign the form and return it to the office for the manager's signature and date.

- **Explanation of orientation process**

Hiring conference

Hiring conference
- Discussed and signed job description
- Signed contract
- Provided center policy handbook and state licensing rules
- Provided timetable for introductory phase
- Discussed probationary period
- Set date for first day of work

Routine procedures and policies
- Set daily schedule
- Completed paperwork (payroll_____, W-4_____, health certificate_____, child abuse form_____)
- Clarified call-in procedures
- Discussed pay dates

Professional responsibilities (see handbook)
- Dress and appearance
- Code of conduct
- Discipline policies
- Supplies

Orientation to the school
- Received tour of facilities and designated personal space
- Issued keys and supplies
- Introduced to staff members
- Introduced to children and parents
- Explained coworker relationship
- Explained emergency procedures

Probationary conference
- Discussed center policy handbook and licensing rules
- Results of initial observation of skills shared
- Clarified expectation for ongoing professional development
- Had opportunity for your questions

Comments:
_____
_____
_____
_____

Employee's Signature: _____ Date: _____

Manager's Signature: _____ Date: _____

FIGURE 7.15 New employee orientation checklist.

on-the-job performance and other activities. State how often you monitor the performance—monthly, quarterly, yearly—with the proviso that you will make efforts to become familiar with the new employee's work by dropping in frequently and getting acquainted. Strategies for conducting a performance appraisal and providing feedback are discussed in the following chapter.

You and the staff should remember that, during the candidate's probationary period, the candidate is not the only one being evaluated. The center is also being evaluated by the candidate. After devoting so much time to the hiring process, you should make every effort to make the new employee comfortable and successful.

Conclusion

Details about organizing and staffing your program flow from the goals developed during the planning process. You must determine the specific jobs necessary to achieve those goals and define an organizational structure that coordinates all of the individual jobs into a coherent whole. Human capital (knowledge, skills, and abilities) and nonhuman resources are required to produce the center's services. Many steps are required for hiring staff members, orienting them to their new job, and setting the stage for evaluating their performance. This chapter has addressed the mechanics of organizing and staffing your program. In the next chapter, we turn our attention to the human relations involved in retaining staff and developing their potential.

Questions for Review

1. Define job analysis. Observe a staff member at a child development program and write a job analysis of that person's function.

2. If you have had experience working in a child-care center, diagram its organizational structure and discuss the pros and cons associated with it. What type of authority was in place? What was the span of control assigned to each teacher? If you have not had experience in a child-care center yourself, try to interview someone who can answer these questions.

3. Imagine you are the director of a child-care center looking for a new teacher for a classroom of 3-year-olds. Use the job specification in Figure 7.4 to brainstorm a list of questions you will ask applicants for the position.

Professional Portfolio

1. Write a job description, job specification, and job classification for a position in a child development center.

2. Create (or locate and copy of) a staff evaluation instrument that reflects the qualities addressed in your job description and classification. Describe how you would use it.

3. Develop a career ladder and salary scale for your program that takes into account the individual employee's education, experience, and job performance.

Resources for Further Study

PRINT

Gordon, J. (2006, May/June). Eight interview questions to help you know who you're hiring. *Exchange, 169*, 6–8.

Harvard Business Review. (2011). *On managing people: HBR's 10 must-reads.* Boston, MA: Harvard Business School Publishing Corporation.

Websites

CHILD CARE SERVICES ASSOCIATION

www.childcareservices.org

A nationally recognized nonprofit organization that provides free referral services to families seeking child care, technical assistance to child-care businesses, and educational scholarships and salary supplements to child-care professionals through the T.E.A.C.H. Early Childhood® and Child Care Wage$® projects. Publishes a fact sheet summarizing requirements of the Affordable Care Act for employers.

MENTEACH

http://www.menteach.org

MenTeach is a national nonprofit organization that publishes a free online newsletter. The organization serves as a clearinghouse for research, education, and advocacy with a commitment to increase the number of men teaching young children in early and elementary education.

U.S. SMALL BUSINESS ADMINISTRATION

http://www.sba.gov/smallbusinessplanner/index.html

Information from the U.S. Small Business Administration covering all phases of business operation from planning to closure. Click on "Manage Employees" under the column "Manage Your Business" for detailed advice about writing job descriptions, interviewing, and applicable laws.

CHAPTER

Human Relations

LEARNING OUTCOMES

After studying this chapter you should be able to

- Explain the importance of understanding staff members' needs, desires, and motivation.
- Apply techniques for fostering effective communication with and among staff members.
- Give examples of strategies for supporting professional development of staff members.
- Describe the elements of a performance appraisal system.

Rainbow Center director Jeralyn decided to try something new at a staff meeting. Instead of inviting an outside expert to talk about emergent curriculum planning, she showed some short video segments of interesting things she had observed children doing in the center's classrooms and invited staff members to share their reactions. The discussion that ensued was lively as the teachers bounced ideas off each other. It seemed that the more they talked, the more they began to see—about the power of children's thinking and about the ways adults could support them. The time flew by, and afterward the teachers told Jeralyn how meaningful and enjoyable the meeting had been for them. The idea of following children's interests made more sense when viewed in connection with real children in their own classrooms. They said that Jeralyn's confidence in their ability to think deeply about their practice made them feel respected and appreciated.

HUMAN RELATIONS AND MANAGEMENT

People are the resources that hold the key to meeting the goals of a service organization such as a child development center. Of course, many nonhuman resources (e.g., facilities, equipment, and supplies) are needed, but these resources stand idle or are ineffectively used without skilled people to put them into appropriate operation.

A child development center is a labor-intensive operation. That is, lots of human energy or labor is essential for the center to reach its goals. No mechanical robot can perform the staff functions. As you learned in the previous chapter, people's knowledge, skills, abilities, stamina, enthusiasm, and love are all aspects of human capital. Your job as manager is to invest that capital wisely—put it to its best use—so that it grows. Your ability to do that depends on your human relations competency. No matter how much you know about finances and the legal aspects of staffing your program, achieving the center's goals is possible only if you understand and relate well to people.

The day-to-day work of creating a supportive environment and helping staff members enhance their skills is your primary responsibility. Although the responsibility for these tasks rests with you, you have help from a variety of sources, including your staff members, if you are wise enough to tap that resource. Accomplishing these tasks hinges on the relationships you are able to cultivate with and among the staff members. Relationships do not happen overnight; they grow from the countless interactions that occur minute-by-minute and day-by-day in any human enterprise. As manager, you have to create some opportunities for interactions. Most interactions are informal, almost automatic, but even these informal interactions can be made more productive if you make a conscious effort to improve your communication skills. Both the formal and informal interactions with staff members are enhanced if you have a basic understanding of human motivation.

Understanding Staff Members' Needs and Desires

Why would people want to work in your child development center? Why do people work at all? The research of psychologist Abraham H. Maslow (1954) has had a major impact on management education and practice. To help explain people's motivation, Maslow proposed a hierarchy of needs, symbolized by a ladder or pyramid representing the different levels of needs that people have (see Figure 8.1).

Physiological needs—food, clothing, and shelter—form the foundation of the pyramid because they are the most basic. Maslow's theory is that, once the basic needs are reasonably satisfied, a person becomes concerned about the needs at the next level—safety and security. Once the first two levels are met, the next level comes into prominence, and so on.

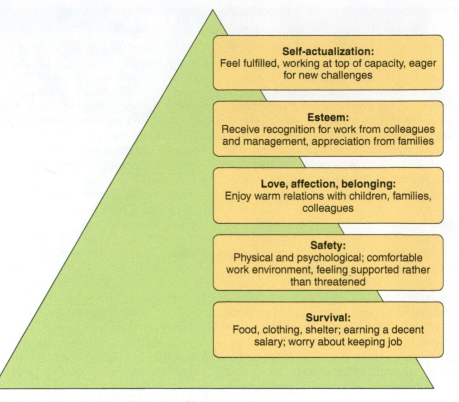

Self-actualization:
Feel fulfilled, working at top of capacity, eager for new challenges

Esteem:
Receive recognition for work from colleagues and management, appreciation from families

Love, affection, belonging:
Enjoy warm relations with children, families, colleagues

Safety:
Physical and psychological; comfortable work environment, feeling supported rather than threatened

Survival:
Food, clothing, shelter; earning a decent salary; worry about keeping job

FIGURE 8.1   Abraham Maslow's hierarchy of human needs.
Source: Based on Maslow, A. H. (1954) *Motivation and personality.* New York: Harper & Row.

Maslow also suggested that people have two basic desires: the desire to know (i.e., to be aware of reality, get the facts, and satisfy curiosity), and the desire to understand (i.e., to systematize and look for relations and meanings). Understanding where your individual staff members may be with regard to Maslow's hierarchy is part of respecting and valuing diversity.

Consider these examples: At the most basic level, the theory suggests that staff members with salaries too low to provide their families with adequate food, clothing, and shelter are unlikely to get much out of a staff training session. Similarly, staff members who suffer from spousal abuse or live and work in violent neighborhoods are unlikely to benefit from efforts to address the higher level needs unless their physiological and safety needs are met. Understanding these basic needs means that you will strive to adhere to established standards regarding wages, benefits, health and safety, and physical setting. You might also advocate for adequate salaries, offer

Staff members who feel supported and encouraged will be more likely to support and encourage children.

resources for counseling, or take part with your staff in neighborhood committees to combat violence.

Within the child development center, a manager's role in relation to these basic needs is to provide a supportive environment, in the physical as well as psychological sense. Staff members have a basic right to a safe, healthy work environment, where their needs as adults are addressed along with those of the children. Programs create a supportive physical environment by providing a place away from the children where staff members can relax or work on planning using adult-size chairs and by providing on-the-job amenities such as child-size steps up to the diapering area to save employees' backs from the stress of lifting heavy toddlers. A supportive psychological environment minimizes stress-inducing demands, such as responsibility for too many children at a time or expecting staff members to accomplish cleaning and clerical tasks on top of caring for children (Whitebook et al., 2009).

The need for love, affection, and belonging is supported when group size is small enough to allow teachers to interact warmly with each child, when they have time to get to know families, and time to enjoy a meal or conversation with their colleagues. You can help staff members meet esteem needs by providing constructive feedback about their performance and calling attention to their successes when appropriate. You can encourage your staff members to become all that they are capable of becoming by guiding them toward formal and informal opportunities for professional development and by challenging them with tasks that tap their new skills.

It is important to remember that the progression through Maslow's hierarchy is not a simple one-way process. People who typically function at the highest level, self-actualization, might revert to an earlier level in the face of a personal or family crisis. An effective manager has the ability to recognize where on the hierarchy a particular staff member might be at any given time.

? DECISIONS, DECISIONS . . .

Think about your own development in relation to Maslow's hierarchy of human needs. At which level are you functioning in relation to various aspects of your life—school, work, family, friendships? Have you noticed any changes over the past few years? What factors do you think account for the changes?

Employee Motivation

An important consideration for the manager concerned with staff members' needs and desires is the distinction between intrinsic and extrinsic motivation. Intrinsic motivation has to do with satisfaction in accomplishment or doing something for its own sake, while extrinsic motivation implies doing something simply for the sake of getting something else. Research has shown that "rewards cause people to lose interest in whatever they were rewarded for doing" (Kohn, 1994). Other research has suggested that teachers who enter the profession for extrinsic motives (e.g., using it as a stopgap until they get the job they really want) are most likely to leave the profession (Curtis, 1995). These findings did not imply that extrinsic rewards, such as adequate salaries, are not important; rather, they suggested that rewards are necessary but not sufficient. Satisfying work and a living wage are both necessary to keep our best professionals in the field.

> ### ❓ DECISIONS, DECISIONS . . .
>
> You have noticed that the bulletin board displays in your center's classrooms are becoming yellow and frayed with age. Someone suggests that you offer coupons for free pizza to the teachers as an incentive for changing the displays more often. Is this an intrinsic or extrinsic reward? What are the likely results? What happens when you run out of coupons? What alternatives can you imagine?

Increasing responsibility can be a motivating force and can result in greater satisfaction for employees. The concept of job enrichment is applicable here. According to DuBrin (2000, p. 185), job enrichment is "an approach to making jobs involve more challenge and responsibility, so they will be more appealing to most employees." DuBrin identifies eight characteristics of an enriched job (pp. 165–166). Applied to the early childhood teacher's position, these characteristics are:

1. *Direct feedback*—either from a supervisor or from the successful completion of a particular task (e.g., helping an anxious child settle down for a nap without tears for the first time).

2. *Client relationships*—interacting with and serving children and families instead of just working for a boss.

3. *New learning*—either on the job or through more formal staff development opportunities.

4. *Control over scheduling*—being able to decide when to do which tasks (e.g., schedule snack or group time) or even setting working hours to the extent possible within the framework of the program's goals and resources.

5. *Unique experience*—a key aspect of working with young children whose ideas and behavior are a continual source of delight and challenge for teachers.

6. *Control over resources*—opportunities to make decisions such as how to spend the classroom's equipment budget, how to use particular materials, or how to allocate the duties of classroom aides or volunteers.

7. *Direct communication authority*—being able to speak directly with the children and families who benefit from or use one's services, a feature usually built into client relationships.

8. *Personal accountability*—responsibility for outcomes whether positive (e.g., when a group of children and parents return from a field trip excited and happy) or negative (e.g., when a poorly planned field trip leads to tearful children and cranky parents).

The concept of job enrichment as a motivating factor corresponds with the earlier discussion of Maslow's theory of basic needs and desires: After meeting their basic needs, people seek achievement and self-fulfillment.

Surely one way to promote staff members' feelings of esteem is to work toward the recognition that comes with National Association for the Education of Young Children (NAEYC) accreditation. Aside from low pay, a reason that child development professionals leave the field is the low status that comes from a public perception that they are "just babysitting." NAEYC center accreditation is a nationally recognized hallmark of excellence, and the self-study process that it entails can help raise staff members' consciousness about the value of their work.

Fostering Teamwork and Collaboration

One of the most effective means of motivating staff members is to build a sense of belonging to a team, of contributing to something larger than oneself. Without this feeling, individuals work at cross purposes, wasting energy that could have contributed to translating an organization's vision into reality. In contrast, when a group of people function as a whole, they share a vision and understand how to align their efforts with one another to achieve it (Senge, 2006, pp. 217–219). If you accomplish this, you have enlisted the help of all staff members in motivating each other.

Some team-building efforts take place outside regular work hours and involve playful simulations of challenging situations. For example, teams might try to build the tallest possible structure from a collection of odds and ends or help each other navigate a makeshift pathway across an imaginary pond without falling in. In the process, members get to know and trust each other a little more and gain new (or renewed) appreciation of the power of collaboration.

Teamwork and collaboration can be fostered on the job as well if managers make a conscious effort to do so. Neugebauer (1998a, pp. 250–254) developed a list of five steps to effective team building. Note that his steps correspond closely to the planning, organizing, staffing, leading, and monitoring management functions:

1. Set goals acceptable to all team members, goals that are neither too ambitious to be realistic nor too modest to inspire commitment and effort. Translate goals into measurable objectives and establish time frames for their achievement.

2. Break each goal down into the tasks necessary to reach it, and then assign specific team members to each task. Make sure that people performing the behind-the-scenes tasks get attention—this encourages group spirit and draws out the less assertive members.

3. Foster supportive relationships between team members by identifying the strengths of individual members that can be tapped by the others, as well as teaching the art of giving constructive feedback to each other. Provide opportunities for the open communication of each member's perceptions and feelings. In Senge's terms, distinguish between dialogue and discussion, recognizing that both are needed. In dialogue, ideas are put forward to see things in a new light, seeking a new understanding rather than agreement without judgment; in discussion, participants actively defend their points of view and seek to convince others (Senge, 2006, pp. 221–232).

4. Ensure that the group reaps the full benefit of what each member has to offer. Encourage everyone to contribute: Raise interesting problems to solve, provide opportunities for learning new ideas and approaches, and allow individuals to pursue their own interests. Show your interest in each team's progress and hold off criticism of creative ideas that may seem unworkable at first. When a team gets stuck, offer help, but be judicious about how much and how soon.

5. The manager and the team members monitor the team's effectiveness. Are the goals being accomplished? If not, is there at least some measurable progress toward goals? More important, is the group functioning more smoothly as a team?

COMMUNICATION

Some managers are so aloof and unapproachable that employees quake at the thought of entering their offices. Other managers try the "pal" approach and downplay their authority. Which style works best for a child development center? Probably, some position in the middle is best. Managers, like all other people, have unique qualities that must be used advantageously. They should be approachable, yet they must also be authoritative.

Communication Among Staff Members

Teachers see many children and parents each day—they must have time to share their own lives and concerns with colleagues. Ironically, some early education and care programs profess a belief in person-to-person communication, yet they set little time aside for personal communication between staff members. Staff members are often scheduled to arrive at staggered times to cover the entire time the children are present and to limit each person's workday to 8 hours. When teachers are on duty, they must pay close attention to the children and not be chatting with one another about personal matters. Usually, teachers are also responsible for the children during lunch and at break time; one teacher takes charge of the children with the support of an aide and the other teacher is out of the room. Thus the teachers have no time together to learn about one another. This example is typical of the situations that interfere with personal communication.

Without planned outlets, staff members may resort to talking about personal concerns when they should be listening to and talking to the children. Other symptoms that staff members have too little time to talk with one another include instances when a staff member has an emergency at home with a child, spouse, or aged parent, and other staff members do not even know, or when misunderstandings arise over little things that might have been worked out in a friendly fashion if people had been talking together.

What can you, as a manager, do? You can plan evening or weekend events that bring the teachers together to socialize freely. Apart from time for socializing, paid planning time outside the center's usual hours of operation can help promote communication because, even though the focus is on professional matters, the atmosphere is likely to be more relaxed. You might consider paying the teachers for a few hours one evening or one Saturday each month to do planning. Joint planning sessions boost the esprit de corps, and the money invested in providing this time pays off in high-quality programs.

You can also facilitate communication among staff members more directly. When a staff member comes to you with a concern, determine whether the concern is a personal matter or whether it involves several people. Sometimes the most effective approach is to bring all parties involved to the table together. In one center, for example, teachers had frequent complaints about the cook not preparing sufficient food, not having it set out on time, or not making modified meals available for a child with cerebral palsy who had difficulty swallowing. The director believed that simply repeating these criticisms to the cook would engender defensiveness and resentment, so instead she invited the teachers and the cook to sit down together and discuss the problems. It turned out that there had been several misunderstandings about the expectations that the teachers and the cook had for one another. Each walked away from the meeting with a new understanding of the challenges faced by the others and a concrete plan for correcting the problem.

Communication Between Manager and Staff

Just as you devise strategies for facilitating communication and collaboration among staff members, you need to plan consciously for effective communication between you and staff members. An informal technique for opening channels of communication with your staff is termed managing by walking around (Albrecht, 1998). Applied to a child development center, this approach involves the manager walking around; dropping into classrooms, playgrounds, and lounges; and mingling with staff members and children as they are involved in their activities. The manager becomes familiar and is seen as relaxed and approachable, giving staff members a feeling that their work is known and appreciated. Using this style, a manager can give a word of encouragement or a suggestion personally and quietly, or make note of material shortages or needed repairs that had not been reported.

In addition to these informal encounters, managers need to schedule regular opportunities to meet with individual staff members to help them reflect on their experiences, thoughts, and feelings in a safe, supportive setting. The manager's role in this exchange is not to solve problems for the staff member or make judgments, but rather to listen carefully, offer support, and collaborate when needed in generating alternative perspectives on situations, thus helping the staff member develop new insights. This reflective supervision supports the mental health and well-being of staff members and contributes to their ability to maintain healthy relationships with families (National Center on Parent, Family, and Community Engagement, n.d.). Additional structured opportunities for communication with staff members include regularly scheduled evaluation reviews, meetings (with the entire staff or with particular subgroups), and individual appointments when concerns arise. Whatever the context for your communication, active listening and conflict resolution skills will help.

Active Listening

Active listening as an approach to communicating among individuals is a concept recommended by parenting educator Thomas Gordon (1970, pp. 41–94). Gordon adapted the method for use by teachers and managers as well (Gordon, 1974). Active listening means more than just keeping quiet while the person talks; it means showing with your body language that you are giving the speaker your full attention and letting that person know that you have heard and understood what was said by restating it in your own words. Active listening focuses on the feeling expressed, not on the content of a person's complaint, and restating that feeling in a nonjudgmental manner so that the person can either confirm or correct your impression. The responsibility for the feeling expressed and finding a solution rests with the person who owns the problem. Consider the following examples of how you might respond when Sherri, a teacher in the classroom for 2-year-olds, storms into your office one morning with a complaint:

Scenario I

SHERRI: I've had it. Either Deanna (her coteacher) goes or I do! I just can't work with her any more.

MANAGER: There, there, now. Try to simmer down. I'm sure you can work things out.

SHERRI: Believe me, I've tried. But she is constantly undermining me with the children. When I try to ignore Molly's temper tantrums, Deanna rushes over and picks her up.

MANAGER: It can't be that bad. You two just have different styles.

SHERRI: That's not the point. All that attention is just making the problem with Molly worse.

MANAGER: Well, I don't know what you expect me to do about it. You're just going to have to work something out.

Scenario II

SHERRI: I've had it. Either Deanna (her coteacher) goes or I do! I just can't work with her any more.

MANAGER: I can hear that you are frustrated. Can you tell me more about what the problem is?

SHERRI:	Well, for one thing, she constantly undermines me with the children.
MANAGER:	You feel as though you are working at cross purposes.
SHERRI:	Yes. Yesterday, Molly had another one of her temper tantrums. I tried to let her cry it out, but Deanna ran right over to pick her up and made a big fuss. I think that makes Molly think tantrums are a good way to get attention.
MANAGER:	You feel that your coteacher is making matters worse instead of supporting you.
SHERRI:	Yes. I'm afraid some of the other children might get the idea that they should have tantrums, too.
MANAGER:	You're worried that the problem will spread if you and Deanna can't agree about how to deal with tantrums. What would you think about the three of us sitting down during nap to see if we can generate some solutions together?

How would you feel as the teacher in each of these scenarios? Which response from a manager would make you feel that your concerns had been taken seriously? Which would make you more willing to think about constructive solutions to the problem?

Conflict Mediation

While constant conflict is probably a sign of deeper problems, occasional conflict is a part of life and it occurs even in well-managed organizations. If you are like many people, you may feel uncomfortable with conflict and prefer to avoid it all together. You may be tempted to keep things moving smoothly by rushing in to solve conflicts between staff members. A more productive approach is to learn the multistep procedure described below and model it for your staff members so that it becomes ingrained in the culture of your program. The process, based on the work of Evans (2009) and Kostelnik, Gregory, Soderman, and Whiren (2012), was developed to provide teachers with a method to help children resolve a dispute, but the steps are equally applicable in adult situations:

Step 1:   Acknowledge that there is a problem and decide to address it. In the situation described earlier, the manager might say to Sherri and Deanna, "I understand that you disagree on the best way to handle Molly's temper tantrums. The inconsistency is not helping her with the problem, and I'm sure it is frustrating to both of you. Let's sit down together during nap and see if we can come to some understanding."

Step 2:   Listen carefully to both sides, gathering the facts as well as understanding the feelings involved. Sherri believes that tantrums are typical behavior for a 2-year-old, so the tantrums should be ignored as long as Molly is not in danger of hurting herself or the other children. Deanna is concerned about the other children being frightened by Molly's screams and thrashing about, so she thinks Molly should be picked up and soothed. Each teacher feels resentful that the other does not seem to respect her point of view.

Step 3:   Recap. Summarize each person's point of view as you understand it. This not only helps the individuals feel that they have been heard, but it gives them another chance to hear the other person's perspective. "Both of you are feeling stressed because of this issue. Sherri thinks the tantrums will go away if the behavior is not reinforced with attention. Deanna finds it hard to ignore behavior that is so disruptive to the group. The problem is that Molly is confused by the different responses she gets and, in fact, that may prolong the problem. Each of you feels irritated when your teaching partner seems unsupportive, and this is damaging your ability to function as a team. We need to find a solution you can both live with."

Step 4:   Brainstorm several possible ways of resolving the issue. As one party offers a suggestion, the other should be given a chance to react frankly and constructively. If neither can develop potential solutions, the manager might make some tentative suggestions or suggest some resources that the teachers could consult for ideas.

Step 5:   Help the parties arrive at consensus about a solution that each can live with. No one should leave the conversation feeling coerced into an unacceptable solution. In this situation, the teachers might agree that they will neither ignore nor fuss over Molly's tantrums. Instead one of them will move her to a safe part of the room away from other children and stay nearby, calmly reassuring Molly that she is safe and that the strong feelings will pass.

Step 6:   Acknowledge the work that each individual contributed to the problem-solving process. The manager thanks both Sherri and Deanna for listening to each other and for persevering to map out a solution.

Step 7:   Follow up by checking in with the teachers a few days later to see if they have implemented their plan and ask how they think it is working. Be prepared to go back to the planning table in the event that the solution has proven unworkable.

Some programs have found it useful to underscore the value they place on openly addressing and resolving inevitable conflicts by putting procedures similar to these in writing and asking staff members to sign a statement indicating that they will follow them (Carter & Curtis, 1998, pp. 243–245).

STAFF MEETINGS

Staff meetings are an important avenue of communication. Managers should be sure that staff meetings serve the communication goals of three different groups: manager to staff, staff to manager, and staff member to staff member.

Paid Staff Meetings

The Model Work Standards (Center for the Child Care Workforce, 1998) require at least one paid staff meeting per month. Although it is a challenge to carve out the time, it is simply not fair to expect teachers, whose salaries are already too low, to put in extra unpaid hours at meetings. Some centers solve this problem by scheduling meetings during nap times. Others either pay teachers for attending evening meetings or give them equivalent amounts of compensatory time off during the regular school day. Of course, providing compensatory time off has a price tag: either paying for a substitute teacher or using your time to fill in for the absent teacher.

Full Staff versus Team Meetings

Meetings with the entire staff are desirable for some purposes. At the beginning of a new school year, or at any time when there has been an influx of new staff members, full-staff meetings help build solidarity—everyone has a chance to get to know one another. Or you may want to boost staff morale and commitment by scheduling a full-staff meeting to reflect on and perhaps revise the program's mission statement. For other purposes, such as accomplishing a specific task, meetings involving only a small team may be more productive. Issues that concern only a single staff member should be dealt with individually.

Agenda

Make the most of your precious meeting time by establishing clear goals in advance. Except in dire emergencies, announce meetings and distribute an agenda at least a week in advance. Identify which items on the agenda will require action, which are for discussion, and which are merely for information, and allocate the relevant amount of time for each. Participants will need to be familiar with past discussions to deal with action items, they may need to read or consult some outside sources to contribute to discussion items, and particular individuals should be assigned responsibility for preparing reports or other items of information. Start the meeting with a few moments for announcements, and give staff members who wish to speak time to do so. Items of special interest raised by the speakers can become agenda items for future meetings, if desired. Time is precious, and following an agenda helps to keep meetings at a reasonable length. Move the meeting along by sticking to the agenda topics. Setting time limits for each item prevent one item from consuming the entire agenda while other items are neglected.

Trying to force closure on issues by calling for a vote and letting the majority rule may save time, but it could be a false economy. People who do not feel ownership of a decision are not likely to support it wholeheartedly. If it is not possible to arrive at a solution that reflects everyone's priorities during the time allowed during a meeting, table the issue until the next meeting. If the issue is one that cannot wait, you can make a temporary decision that reflects the group's best effort at reaching a consensus, with a clear understanding that the topic will be revisited at the next staff meeting.

Minutes

Assign someone to record meeting minutes or the agreements reached at the meeting. This task is simplified by opening a digital copy of the agenda on a laptop computer and using it as an outline for organizing the minutes. Include a list of individuals present at the meeting, and circulate the minutes within the next few days. Save a copy (paper or digital) as a record for future reference.

Managing Group Dynamics

Complex interactions occur when groups come together. It is up to you to ensure that everyone's voice is heard and that everyone participates actively. If employees get the idea that meetings are just a formality—you listen to their opinions and then go ahead with your own plans—they may become cynical and disengage themselves from discussions. For that reason, it is important to make it clear from the outset which decisions belong to the group and which rest with you or the board of directors. For example, do not let the employees think that it is their decision whether or not to pursue NAEYC accreditation if the board has already mandated that course of action. They can decide, however, how to go about the process: which components to tackle first, which individuals are responsible for particular tasks.

Personal characteristics also influence group dynamics. Shy staff members may be tempted to sit quietly while the discussion whirls around them. Those who are more assertive might dominate the discussion, causing others to feel left out. Your job is to find ways to engage the former and rein in the latter without embarrassing either. One technique is to ask participants to discuss an issue in pairs or threes and have each small group report their opinion to the whole group. Tactfully arrange the groups so that dominant personalities are together with others who can hold their own in the conversation. This gives the quieter individuals a chance to blossom in a group of their counterparts.

An employee with a personal grudge can derail your best-laid plans by picking at everything. If you allow yourself to be drawn into a verbal duel with such an individual, the rest of the participants might withdraw in embarrassment. Try to remain calm and acknowledge the validity of the person's opinion to the extent possible. Ask the others for their opinions about the statements, and put the ball back in the complainer's court by asking him or her to suggest possible solutions to the problem—preferably in writing. This lets the person know you take the issue seriously and encourages constructive thinking as an alternative to complaining.

Some negative attitudes and behaviors displayed by staff members may have nothing to do with you; rather, they grow out of childhood experiences. Consistently practicing the conflict mediation strategy discussed earlier can help build your staff members' trust and perhaps reduce negative feelings. Sometimes what you experience as resistance to your ideas stems from different life experiences and cultural perspectives. Being sensitive to this possibility is another example of respecting and valuing diversity. For example, consider the reaction of this hypothetical trainee attending a session on appropriate diapering techniques:

> I don't want to be told how to change diapers. I feel like I've been cleaning up poop all my life, and now somebody wants me to pretend I like doing it. As a woman of color, I feel like I have to clean up the poop of the world and I'm really sick of it. (Shareef & Gonzalez-Mena, 1997, pp. 7–8)

Be careful not to see every disagreement as a problem or a challenge to your authority. If all of your meetings run smoothly with everyone agreeing on every issue, you may be experiencing groupthink—conformity for conformity's sake. Honest disagreements, openly discussed, can stimulate creative new solutions.

? DECISIONS, DECISIONS . . .

An Ethical Decision

Your program has a tradition of celebrating the end of the school year with fairly elaborate "graduation" parties. Families seem to enjoy and expect the parties and always participate in large numbers. At the April staff meeting, you ask for volunteers to organize this year's celebration. Several staff members raise objections—the preparation and the cleanup afterward are too much work, often in the form of unpaid overtime. Others chime in that they have been reading articles that suggest that such parties are developmentally inappropriate. Using the NAEYC code, try to determine what core values are involved. What ideals and principles regarding responsibilities to children, families, and employees apply? What course of action seems most right?

STAFF MEMBERS' PROFESSIONAL DEVELOPMENT

Lack of adequate preparation can be one reason for high turnover rates in child care. Staff members without a solid understanding of developmentally appropriate practice, for example, are more likely to set unrealistic expectations for children. They become frustrated when children fail to do what is asked, and these staff members are thus more prone to quitting. They can also add to the stress and frustration felt by more qualified staff members who work alongside them. More experienced staff may experience feelings of stagnation on the job, leading to dissatisfaction and turnover as they look for more interesting challenges elsewhere. A sustained, thoughtful approach to professional development can increase the job satisfaction—and employee loyalty—of both neophytes and veterans.

We deliberately use the term *professional development* instead of *staff training* because we believe it more accurately conveys the complexity of the process as well as the participation of staff members in their own growth and learning. In our view, staff training implies a more passive role for the individuals being trained and suggests that providing high-quality care and education is simply a matter of mastering the "right" techniques and applying them across the board.

Your job specification and job description should clearly state that each staff member is expected to participate in ongoing professional development. Clearly stating this expectation during the hiring process avoids later complaints. Stated more positively, professional development is a "right of each individual teacher *and of all teachers within the school*" (emphasis in original) (Rinaldi, 1994, p. 55). Professional development keeps every staff member—including you—alive and growing year by year.

Stages of Professional Development

Lilian Katz, a prominent teacher educator, has suggested that there are four developmental stages for early childhood teachers (Katz, 1984). These stages and the associated needs are illustrated in Figure 8.2. Because the teacher's job is not the same as the

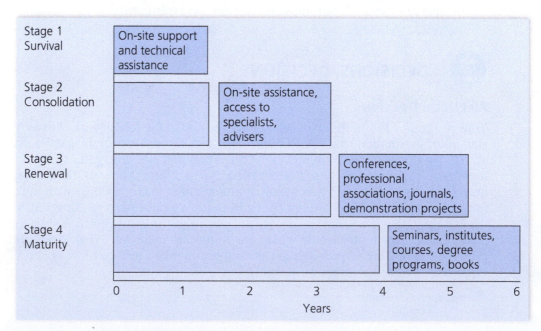

FIGURE 8.2 Teachers' development stages and in-service needs.

Source: Based on Katz, L. G. Developmental stages of preschool teachers. In M. Kaplan-Sanoff & R. Yablans-Magrid (Eds.), *Exploring early childhood* (Upper Saddle River, NJ: Prentice Hall, 1984), pp. 478–482.

manager's job, you will note that these are somewhat different from the stages of professional development for program directors that you encountered in an earlier chapter.

Stage 1:   *Survival* lasts for about the first 2 years. Teachers at the survival stage may, at times, feel overwhelmed at having the full responsibility for a group of immature and vigorous young children. These are the teachers you see at a conference eagerly harvesting ideas to take back to their classrooms on Monday morning. Katz said, "During this period the teacher needs support, understanding, encouragement, reassurance, comfort, and guidance."

Stage 2:   *Consolidation* covers the period from approximately 18 months to 3 years. By this stage, the teacher has decided she can survive and is ready to consolidate her gains. According to Katz, this teacher requires on-site assistance, access to specialists, colleague advice, consultants, and advisers.

Stage 3:   *Renewal* comes between the third and fifth years. Now, the teacher has become tired of the routine and wants to learn about new developments. The teacher finds it rewarding to meet colleagues from various programs at conferences and to compare notes with them. At this time, teachers become objective about looking at their classrooms, according to Katz.

Stage 4:   *Maturity* is reached between the fourth and fifth years. The person has come to terms with being a teacher and is ready to look at deeper and more abstract questions. Conferences, institutes, or advanced-degree programs are needed to stimulate this person.

? DECISIONS, DECISIONS . . .

Where are you in your professional development? What connections do you see between Maslow's hierarchy of human needs and Katz's stages of professional development? Again, if you are comfortable sharing any examples, discuss them with your classmates.

Supporting Professional Development at All Stages

Centers support professional development when they provide paid registration and time off for staff members to attend workshops and conferences. They also promote professional development when they provide ongoing, knowledgeable feedback and arrange paid time for teachers to collaborate on projects, to observe each other's classrooms, and to reflect on their teaching practices (Rous, 2004). Professional development can be viewed as an ongoing process that is fostered whenever teachers observe children closely, reflect on those observations, and share their ideas with parents or other staff members. Margie Carter (2008a), who has worked extensively in the area of professional development in early childhood programs, has found that by focusing on their observations of children's play, early childhood professionals are able to gain insight and develop new knowledge without the stress and defensive feelings usually incurred when focusing on staff behaviors or externally imposed standards. Helping staff members learn to enjoy play themselves is a crucial component of professional development. Unless they have experienced the joyful satisfaction of combining materials and ideas in creative ways, adults will be hard pressed to see and understand what children are doing in their play (Bush, Nell, & Drew, 2013).

Sharing observations and documentation of children's experiences after visiting one another's classrooms is an effective means of professional development for teachers.

Professional development can be stimulated through interactions with individuals or small groups from the same job category or the entire staff. As noted earlier, such interactions can occur at the center or in conferences elsewhere. Depending on the topic and your knowledge of the staff members' individual learning styles, you might distribute a handout for all staff members to read and discuss. Or you might, with permission, visit a classroom to observe, reflect, or model some technique; suggest that teachers visit one another's classrooms; or bring in an outside consultant. Whatever mode or location is selected, professional development activities cost time and money and must become a budget item.

Sometimes what seems like just another responsibility can become a vehicle for rewarding professional growth. For example, the teacher at stage 3 or 4 who is asked to take responsibility for helping a new employee can be challenged to rethink his or her own practice in the process, with the result that both teachers learn and grow. Similarly, employees who participate in discussions about the center's mission and policies are engaging in the type of reflection that fosters their professional growth.

Mentoring

A **mentor** is someone who provides information, guidance, and emotional support for a person with less experience. With the help of a mentor, new staff members learn how to fit in with your organization's "culture," its particular way of doing things based on shared beliefs (Hatch, 1997, pp. 202–206).

Mentors can be an important professional development component at any stage of one's career. You may have enjoyed the support of several mentors in your life's journey thus far. Perhaps a teacher helped you think about career options and decide which college program to enter. A supervisor may have encouraged you to apply for a promotion and suggested the skills you needed to hone in order to qualify for it. Now, as manager, it is your job to mentor your staff members.

As noted earlier, assigning an experienced staff member to take a new employee under her wing is one way to multiply the benefits of mentoring. Pairing two staff members and clearly stating your intent that the more experienced help guide the less experienced can facilitate cooperation. The new employee may feel more at home and less anxious working alongside another employee. Staff members assigned to mentor newcomers take pride and satisfaction in this recognition of their talents, and they are less likely to feel they are in competition with new staff members for your approval. More important, mentoring another individual stimulates one to think a little more deeply—to reflect—about the reasons for the procedures being demonstrated or explained. This is a surefire strategy for professional growth. In other words, you mentor the experienced employee when you ask him to mentor someone else.

The value of mentoring extends beyond the new employee. Assigning a mentor can help a long-term employee move to the next level of competence. Taking on the mentoring role can rejuvenate a staff member's enthusiasm and prevent burnout. Although people routinely and informally seek advice from those with more experience, the concept of mentoring implies a particular, more formal type of relationship. The key ingredients of the mentoring relationship, according to Fenichel (1992, p. 9), are reflection, collaboration, and regularity. Mentor and protégé must both think about the reasons for their actions and decisions. They should view themselves as partners, respecting the valuable resources and life experiences that each brings to the task, and they must be clear about what they hope to accomplish.

A mentor is someone who provides information, guidance, and emotional support for a person with less experience.

Last, they must have regularly scheduled, protected periods of time to meet with each other.

Another way to provide mentoring relationships for your staff members is to partner with other programs in the community. Each teacher visits the other's classroom on alternating weeks, and the teacher pairs meet with a facilitator once every two weeks to process what they have learned. An important part of this facilitator meeting is to help participants discuss and resolve conflicts and disagreements openly so that everyone grows from the experience (Poelle, 1993).

Professional Development Activities

Planning professional development for your staff members is much like planning curriculum for children; that is, start where individuals are and use their interests as guides. NAEYC accreditation criteria stipulate that individual professional development plans should be linked to staff evaluations and updated at least once a year. In addition to on-site activities such as mentoring and coaching, staff members should be encouraged to upgrade their credentials through credit-bearing course work. Topics addressed should include ethical issues, program policies and procedures, early childhood curriculum, relationship and team-building skills, and building partnerships with families and communities (National Association for the Education of Young Children, 2007a, p. 81).

Resources for Planning for Professional Development

Figure 8.3 lists several suggestions for professional development activities. You can get additional ideas from publications such as *Child Care Exchange* (www.childcareexchange.com), a bimonthly journal tailored to child development program directors that features a section called Beginnings Workshop in every issue. It focuses on a particular topic, such as environments, and is chock full of information, as well as ideas for sparking staff discussions. *Texas Child Care* (http://www.childcarequarterly.com), a

1. Invite teachers to complete a self-assessment and create a plan for their own professional development. Set an example by doing the same thing yourself. Examples of self-assessment and planning tools can be found at http://www.ncchildcare.org.

2. Set up a teacher resource area equipped with books, journals, CDs and DVDs, and a computer with Internet access. Include time in the workday for teachers to search for information about topics of interest to them, with the stipulation that they share their findings with others. Let the teachers know when you add items related to their interests.

3. Encourage teachers to visit one another's classrooms and share their observations and questions afterward. When a particularly significant project takes place in one class, be sure other teachers, and sometimes the children, get a chance to visit that classroom and see the results (e.g., children's block structures, dramatic play props, paintings).

4. Suggest that teachers expand their horizons by subscribing to an electronic discussion group on the Internet and read the postings at least once a week. The Early Childhood and Parenting Collaborative (http://ecap.crc.uiuc.edu), affiliated with the University of Illinois, hosts several on a number of topics of interest to early childhood professionals (e.g., the Reggio Emilia Approach and the Project Approach). Use postings as discussion starters or encourage teachers to post their own responses to topics raised.

5. Show (or learn along with) teachers how to use documentation panels to capture the excitement and insights that characterize children's thinking. Documentation panels, an idea drawn from the renowned early childhood programs of Reggio Emilia, are visual displays that include photographs, drawings and diagrams by the children and teachers, printed transcripts of recorded conversations, and teachers' reflections on what the children are thinking and learning. (See Forman, G., & Pufal, E., *Mindsets to Avoid and Seek When Making Documentation Panels,* available from www.videatives.com.)

6. Encourage teachers to make presentations at local, state, or national conferences and to practice giving their presentations to center staff beforehand so they can get suggestions for improvement and build confidence.

7. Form a partnership with another center, ideally one where families and staff members differ in some way from those in your center so that the exchange is enriched by diversity. Arrange joint staff meetings to share perspectives on issues or solutions to challenges. Invite individual teachers to form pairs with counterparts from the other center for ongoing exchange of ideas and support.

8. Tap into the expertise within your pool of families and ask them to share it with an individual staff member, a small group, or a meeting of the entire staff. Parents, grandparents, aunts, uncles, and even older brothers or sisters may have skills to share. A nurse, doctor, or emergency medical technician may be able to offer first-aid or CPR training. An artist or craftsperson might provide information about the possibilities inherent in fibers or clay. Members of various cultural groups can share information, stories, songs, and customs that can become part of the curriculum, as well as sensitize everyone to individual differences.

FIGURE 8.3 ● Suggestions for professional development activities.

quarterly journal for early childhood personnel, includes a self-study guide in each issue that challenges readers to ponder and apply the ideas contained in the articles. Some publishers and organizations offer materials—videos with discussion guides or slide presentations that can be downloaded from the internet. Other resources are listed at the end of this chapter.

Another possibility is to collaborate with schools and centers in your locality for in-service events. In some communities, several child development organizations (e.g., a Head Start agency, the school district, and corporate child-care chains) have pooled their resources to establish a consortium for professional development. This approach enables them to bring in several outside speakers throughout the year, and they all benefit from a wider array of activities than any one of them could afford.

Technology Toolkit

- *Use video to learn about children:*   With the teacher's and parents' permission, video-record one or more children doing something interesting in each classroom. Review the video clip with the individual teacher, with a focus on what the children might be thinking or learning. (See examples at www.videatives.com.) Again with permission, show examples at a staff meeting to stimulate a discussion on a particular topic (e.g., supporting children's play or helping them resolve conflict).
- *Use video as a tool for self-reflection:*   If a teacher is comfortable and gives permission, video-record a teacher–child interaction and review the clip with the teacher. Ask how the teacher felt about the episode. What was the thinking behind the teacher's actions? What was satisfying, and what might he or she like to have done differently? Why? The idea is not to evaluate or correct the teacher, but to encourage a habit of reflective practice.

VOLUNTEERS

Everything you have read about understanding people's needs, desires, and motivation and about communication and conflict mediation can apply to volunteers as well as paid staff members. Volunteers are valuable assets who contribute considerable amounts of human capital to child development centers each year. Some volunteer for an hour or two a month; others volunteer many hours each week. Following the same steps with volunteers as you do with paid staff members will help make the best use of this valuable resource. That is, you have to locate people whose skills and attitudes make them suitable for work in a child development center, acquaint them with your center's organization and policies, provide any necessary training, assign them worthwhile tasks, monitor and guide them in the performance of those tasks, let them know how they are doing, and give appropriate recognition for a job well done.

Families of enrolled children, churches, civic clubs, high schools, and colleges are all potential sources of volunteers. Contacting schools and youth clubs is a way for managers to begin. In addition, some high schools and colleges offer courses in child development or early childhood education. A high-quality child development center where students can learn appropriate practices can serve as a laboratory for those students, reaping the benefit of their youthful enthusiasm, energy, and fresh ideas in the process. Senior citizens are often available to volunteer regularly in schools and centers, providing warm laps, skillful storytelling, and one-to-one attention. You may be more successful recruiting people you know rather than approaching senior citizen groups or civic groups. After a few volunteers find they enjoy helping, word will spread, and others are likely to follow suit.

Volunteers can be very well educated and experienced; however, untrained volunteers must be trained, supported, and rewarded if they are really to be of help and to stay on over a period of time. Guiding volunteers takes time—both the

In addition to providing valuable services, volunteers receive satisfaction from the positive relationships they build with children.

manager's time and the classroom teachers' time—but the efforts have many payoffs. The more you treat your volunteers like professionals, the more professionally they will behave. Remember to include volunteers in the professional development opportunities made available for staff members. Guard against always giving them the dirty work or the cold side of the play yard while paid staff members take the more pleasant tasks or stay indoors where it is warm.

In addition to giving from their storehouse of human capital, volunteers receive satisfaction from the positive and pleasurable relationships they build with the children and staff members. The work experience added to the volunteer's résumé is potentially a more tangible benefit; all volunteers should be encouraged to keep records of their volunteer time. Perhaps most important, volunteers usually become more knowledgeable and more committed to serving children and their families. They are marvelous allies to have in a community. With their connections to many groups, they can rally political support should that become necessary.

PERFORMANCE APPRAISAL SYSTEM

Inadequate pay is a serious concern, but teachers report that many other factors contribute to their job dissatisfaction, including unrealistic or ill-defined workloads, unfair or disrespectful treatment, and lack of basic support (e.g., having to pay for supplies out-of-pocket or arrange for one's own substitute when sick) (Whitebook & Bellm, 1999, p. 40). New employees want to start the job with a clear understanding of what is expected of them and how they will be evaluated. They want to know that if they perform well, they will have fair chances for promotion, and that if their performance does not live up to expectations, they will be given a chance to improve rather than being summarily fired. They want to know what to expect from one day to the next and to have a voice, or at least a warning, when changes in work assignment or center policies are needed. This means that you need a well-thought-out performance appraisal system in place.

As you design and implement your appraisal system, it is important to remember that early childhood professionals vary widely, as all people do, in their modes of interacting and preferred learning styles. Recall from our discussion of personality type that some people are naturally more extroverted than others; they enjoy dealing with the public and feel comfortable speaking up about their ideas and feelings. Others are more reserved and prefer to watch from the sidelines, think things over, and interact with one or a few people at a time. Some people find it easiest to gain new ideas and information by reading or listening to lectures. Others have to try things for themselves and learn best by doing. Having a set of detailed rules for every operation makes some people feel secure, while it might be stifling for someone with a very playful disposition and a high tolerance for risk taking. Some of these characteristics and preferences are related to cultural background; however, there is likely as much difference between individuals within a given culture as there is between cultures. Respecting and valuing diversity means being proactive and setting a tone that encourages employees to reflect on their own and others' heritage and to think about ways that their differences complement one another.

Setting the Stage

You lay the groundwork for a positive relationship with each employee before his or her first day on the job by providing a clear job description. Recall Maslow's concept that people need a sense of belonging and contributing to a higher purpose; you want to ensure that the new employee knows the program's mission and overall goals as well as the way his job fits into that plan. This can be part of the orientation process discussed in the previous chapter. The beginning of any relationship is full of potential—for positive or negative outcomes. The time and energy you devote to getting off on the right foot with a new employee is an investment that will be repaid many times over. During the orientation with a new employee, clearly state how you evaluate on-the-job performance and other activities. Indicate how often you monitor performance—monthly, quarterly, yearly—and that you will become familiar with employees' work by dropping in frequently and getting acquainted. This information should be available in writing in a staff handbook.

Following Through on Expectations

One purpose of these regular appraisals is to provide an early indication that an employee has trouble meeting the expectations for the job. An opportunity to discuss progress should be provided every week or two at first, then less frequently as the employee adjusts. Supportive and positive feedback is always essential, but especially during the early weeks. Remember that the job description is your agreement between you and the employee about what is expected, so your appraisal instrument should reflect those expectations and spell out components of each. Figure 8.4 is an example of a performance appraisal for a child development teacher based on the job description provided in the previous chapter.

After the probationary period, continue to use the appraisal instrument as a basis for evaluation conferences with each staff member at least once each year. Invite staff members to give their own appraisal of their performance in each area. The discussion should focus on an evaluation of past performance as well as projections for the future, including specific suggestions or plans for growth and improvement. Your task is to acknowledge success and discuss problems in a straightforward manner, seeking the employee's input about reasons for the difficulties as well as possible solutions.

A written summary of the points discussed, with space for the employee's comments, should be signed by the manager and the employee, with copies provided to each. It is important to date your observations and evaluation forms and to keep copies of each in the employee's personnel file.

As you strive to handle performance appraisals in a professional and systematic manner, remember that they are also an important means of building a trusting relationship with individual staff members. You are trying to find out what is going well or not so well with an employee, and also something about that person's goals and the ways that you can help them be fulfilled (Kilbourne, 2007). In addition to maintaining all the required information about tuberculosis tests, college credits, and police clearances, connect on a more personal level by encouraging teachers to document their own growth and development with images or reflective writing (Carter, 2008b).

Dismissing Staff Members

Sometimes, an employee simply does not work out satisfactorily and has to be dismissed. This step should not be taken lightly. Individuals have a right to due process, which means receiving prompt feedback as part of an evaluation process, with a clear statement of expectations for improvement and the consequences for the failure to do so. You might bring in an objective outside observer if you wonder whether a personality conflict, rather than the quality of the work, is the cause of

Name _____ Period Covered _____ to _____

Circle response that most accurately describes performance during current evaluation period.
(Key: **N** = Never or Seldom; **O** = Occasionally; **F** = Frequently; **C** = Consistently)

Plan, implement, and document developmentally appropriate curriculum (in collaboration with colleagues)

• Bases plans on observations of children's interests	N	O	F	C
• Fosters emotional, social, physical, and intellectual growth	N	O	F	C
• Incorporates children's prior knowledge, skills, etc.	N	O	F	C
• Promotes growth and development for ALL children	N	O	F	C
• Assesses each child's needs and progress regularly	N	O	F	C
• Materials and activities reflect and respect diversity	N	O	F	C
• Balances small/large group; teacher/child initiated	N	O	F	C
• Supports children effectively as they play and learn	N	O	F	C
• Uses effective communication techniques with children	N	O	F	C
• Documents children's experiences with variety of tools/techniques	N	O	F	C

Comments:

Organize and maintain environment to support program goals

• Arranges room to support children's play and self-regulation	N	O	F	C
• Prepares and maintains organized display of materials	N	O	F	C
• Engages children in maintaining orderly environment	N	O	F	C
• Adheres to all health and safety requirements	N	O	F	C

Comments:

Establish and maintain relationships with families through group meetings, home visits, and conferences

• Treats families with respect and warmth	N	O	F	C
• Shares information about child or program informally	N	O	F	C
• Shares results of formal assessments appropriately	N	O	F	C
• Uses planned contacts (home visits, progress notes, telephone calls, conferences) effectively	N	O	F	C
• Contributes meaningful material for center newsletter	N	O	F	C
• Contributes to documentation panels and displays	N	O	F	C
• Encourages family participation in program in variety of ways	N	O	F	C
• Helps plan and participates in meetings or other family events	N	O	F	C

Comments:

Maintain records and write reports

• Maintains required records accurately (e.g., attendance)	N	O	F	C
• Records observations of children and compiles progress reports	N	O	F	C
• Keeps records of contacts regarding individual children (e.g., parent concerns, therapists' suggestions, etc.)	N	O	F	C
• Respects and maintains confidentiality	N	O	F	C

Comments:

FIGURE 8.4   Sample performance appraisal for a child development center teacher.

Participate in professional development activities

	N	O	F	C
• Works with a mentor to develop and implement individual plan	N	O	F	C
• Helps to plan and attends staff meetings and retreats	N	O	F	C
• Attends workshops and/or professional conferences	N	O	F	C
• Maintains membership in professional organization(s)	N	O	F	C
• Reads professional journals, books, etc.	N	O	F	C

Comments:

_____   _____
Signature of Employee   Date   Signature of Evaluator   Date

FIGURE 8.4 (*Continued*)

the problem. If, after efforts are made to get the performance on track, the employee has not responded, you have no choice but to terminate employment. Copies of evaluation forms, dated observation notes, and a written record of any conferences, including dates and actions taken, are necessary to support your decision to dismiss the individual.

You, as manager, may have to say, "We have a problem. Somehow this job is not right for you." A humane attitude lets the person know that you care about him or her as an individual, but that you must act when performance is not up to par because so much depends on each staff member doing his or her job well. Generally, an employee is surprised to find warmth and is grateful for the opportunity to depart gracefully, and will leave in a short time. In the meantime, you have an obligation to limit the person's duties to those where children will not be harmed in any way. Such a humanistic procedure does less harm to the morale of the remaining staff members than outright firing. Obviously, such an approach cannot be used in cases of suspected abuse of the children because your obligation to protect the children takes precedence over other concerns. In these cases, licensing and law enforcement authorities become involved; if the abuse is substantiated, immediate dismissal is warranted.

Exit Interview

Of course, not every staff member who leaves your program has been fired. People quit for a variety of reasons. By conducting an exit interview with employees who resign, you gain valuable information that can be used to improve aspects of the program such as staff turnover, morale, and training procedures. In addition to obvious questions about the person's reason for leaving, you could ask that the employee

- identify aspects of the job that were particularly satisfying or dissatisfying (and why)
- discuss whether the center's orientation process and ongoing supervision conveyed clear expectations and support for meeting them
- identify training or information that could have enhanced the employee's performance

Exit interviews can take place face-to-face before an employee leaves, or you can follow up a few weeks later via a telephone interview or an online survey.

Conclusion

Human relations are the heart and soul of any human service organization, and child development programs are no exception—particularly in view of the acute staffing shortage in this field. Successful managers understand human needs and motivation, and communicate effectively with individuals and groups during their day-to-day interactions, as well as in more formally structured encounters. The manager's relationship with staff members begins prior to hiring and continues until (and often after) an employee leaves the program. The manager's job is to make the best use of each employee's store of human capital and to help each employee develop that capital to the fullest extent possible. Encouraging mentoring, fostering teamwork, and providing clear feedback are all part of the human relations aspects of the manager's role.

Questions for Review

1. Give examples of what it would take to satisfy each level of needs in Maslow's hierarchy.

2. What do active listening, management by walking around, and the seven-step conflict mediation process have in common?

3. How is planning professional development activities similar to planning curriculum for children?

4. What are the advantages, for managers and for staff members, of having a well-thought-out performance appraisal system?

Professional Portfolio

1. Locate an instrument used to evaluate staff members at a child development program in your community, or develop one that you might use in a center that you manage. Describe how you would use the instrument: Who is evaluated? Who completes the instrument? When and how often are staff members evaluated? When and how is the staff member informed of the results? What happens afterward?

2. Access the website sponsored by the National Early Childhood Technical Assistance System (NEC*TAS) at http://www.nectac.org. Describe the information provided and explain how you could use this internet resource as part of a staff development plan in a program that you manage.

3. Outline a professional development plan for staff members in a child development program and address the following components: the goals for each individual or staff level, the resources available for meeting each goal, the strategies a program might use to facilitate or support the pursuit of the goals, and reward completion.

Resources for Further Study

PRINT

Bloom, P. J. (1997). *A great place to work: Improving conditions for staff in young children's programs* (rev. ed.). Washington, DC: National Association for the Education of Young Children.

Bloom, P. J. (2005). *Blueprint for action: Achieving center-based change through staff development* (2nd ed.). Lake Forest, IL: New Horizons.

Carter, M. (2007, May/June). Staff development resources right under your nose. *Exchange, 175,* 28–31.

Neugebauer, B., & Neugebauer, R. (2005). *Staff challenges: Practical ideas for recruiting, training and supervising early childhood employees.* Redmond, WA: Exchange Press.

Websites

NATURAL RESOURCES LISTSERV

subscribe-natural_resources2@listserv.unc.edu

Provides weekly email announcements of free or low-cost professional development resources in a variety of formats and on topics related to early childhood and early intervention, along with "tips for trainers." Send an email to listserv@unc.edu. Leave the subject line blank, and type the following in the body of the message: subscribe naturalresources2.

NORTH CAROLINA INSTITUTE FOR EARLY CHILDHOOD PROFESSIONAL DEVELOPMENT

http://ncicdp.org/

Website for the North Carolina Institute for Early Childhood Professional Development. Just one example of a state initiative to support professional development, the North Carolina website provides online workbooks for teachers and administrators to develop a personal and professional plan of action, as well as a planning checklist for communities wishing to support professional development as a means of increasing child-care quality.

RESOURCES ON E-LEARNING FOR EDUCATORS

http://www.naeyc.org/yc/pastissues/2004/may

List of resources from the May 2004 issue of *Beyond the Journal*, an online supplement to *Young Children*, the journal of the National Association for the Education of Young Children. It includes links to a wide variety of online resources for professional development.

TEAMPEDIA TOOLS FOR TEAMS

http://www.teampedia.net/

A collaborative encyclopedia of free team-building activities, icebreakers, and tools for use by managers, teachers, and other team leaders. Activities are categorized by type (e.g., icebreakers, rhythm games, breaking down stereotypes) as well as suggested group size. Directions include materials needed, setup, possible modifications, and suggestions for debriefing.

Facilities Management

LEARNING OUTCOMES

After studying this chapter you should be able to

- Compare the regulations and professional standards that apply when planning the physical environment of a child development center.
- Discuss ways that space is organized to meet children's basic environmental needs.
- Explain how factors such as intended use and traffic flow influence the layout of a building or classroom.
- Create or evaluate classrooms floor plans for infants, toddlers, and preschool-age children.
- Describe ways to adapt the physical environment for children with disabilities.
- Describe elements of a high-quality outdoor environment for play and learning.

Derek had been on the job a few weeks when he asked Tanya to meet with him during his afternoon planning time. He said that he had been inspired by a session on outdoor play that he attended at the last state conference for early childhood educators and that he hoped to try out some of the ideas at Rainbow Center. As he spoke, Tanya realized that the topic had been prominently featured in nearly every professional journal to cross her desk in recent months, and she had to admit that Rainbow's playground looked a little barren. Together, she and Derek laid out a short-term plan to hang a bird feeder outside Derek's classroom window, plant a sunflower forest in one corner of the yard, and carve out another small corner for digging in the dirt. They resolved to approach their director, Jeralyn, with the idea of involving the children, their families, and the other staff members in creating a long-term plan for upgrading Rainbow Center's outdoor environment. Realizing they would need guidance from someone with expertise in outdoor design, Derek agreed to check with the county extension office and the horticulture department of the local community college for potential advisers while Tanya investigated possibilities for grant funding from the state's child-care quality enhancement initiative and local civic organizations.

The physical facility that houses a child development program supports (or impedes) all of the human interactions therein. Managers must consider the activities and needs of both children and adults and exercise all management functions as they procure, renovate, allocate, arrange, furnish, and maintain living space for their programs. We call the competency required to create and maintain space that supports human interactions **facilities management**.

MANAGING INDOOR AND OUTDOOR LEARNING SPACES: AN ECOSYSTEMS PERSPECTIVE

A center's physical facilities are part of the human-built environment of the human eco-logical system. In other words, like schools, shopping centers, and office buildings, they are physical structures constructed to serve human needs. As part of the human-built environment, the center exists within and has many connections with the natural, phys-ical-biological environment discussed earlier. The land on which the building rests, the surrounding terrain, the play yard's size and landscaping, the fresh air and sunshine, and the drainage and wind protection all have an impact on the quality of life. The sun, which gives the center light and heat inside and makes playgrounds usable even on cold days, is part of the natural environment, as are the fuels used for heating and cool-ing the building. Within the natural, physical–biological environment, the center com-prises a complex social–cultural environment where humans interact for the purpose of nurturing and educating young children. The current emphasis on sustainability in almost every facet of life is an example of the interface between the physical–biological and social–cultural environments. Concern for the planet and the well-being of future generations has led people at all levels of society to seek ways to use resources more efficiently and to minimize harmful consequences for humans or the environment. Certainly child-care facilities, with their focus on the children who will inherit the planet, should strive to be models of **sustainability**, "the art and science of leaving for future generations opportunities equal to or better than those left us" (Durrett & Torelli, 2009, p. 20). This requires attention to all aspects of the physical environment: from ini-tial decisions about building construction materials, insulation, and climate control sys-tems to day-to-day choices about using resources such as food, water, and classroom or office supplies.

Interactions within the center reflect its social and cultural context, as well as the moment-to-moment personal contacts of the individuals involved. For example, child development centers in the United States place a higher priority on teaching children to talk through their conflicts than do centers in Japan (Tobin, Hsueh, & Karasawa, 2009). Individual children and adults bring different temperaments, learning styles, abilities, cultures, and experiences to their relationships with one another, as well as with the tangible environment. Some people feel constricted by an overly neat environment, while others crave visual order and symmetry. What seems like a pleasant hive, hum-ming with activity, to one person can seem like noisy chaos to another. Ideally, the physical environment (both natural and human-built) promotes emotional as well as physical health as it supports relationships between and among the center's children, staff members, and families, as well as connections between the center and the world surrounding it (Ceppi & Zini, 1998).

REGULATIONS AND PROFESSIONAL STANDARDS

Local building codes and state licensing regulations set minimum standards for the location and configuration of child-care facilities. Some cities, for example, prohibit the location of infant or toddler classrooms on a second floor. Fire codes mandate the num-ber of required exits and specify that they must be easily pushed open from the inside even when locked to entry from the outside. Lighting, fresh air circulation, hot water temperature, and the number and location of sinks and toilets are the province of sanita-tion codes. Parent organizations or sponsoring agencies may require new construction or renovation projects to be certified through the Leadership in Energy and Environmental Design (LEED) Green Building Rating System, documenting compliance with sustainable practice. LEED for Schools recognizes "high-performance schools that are healthy for students, comfortable for teachers, and cost-effective," addressing issues such as classroom acoustics, lighting, and mold prevention (U.S. Green Building Council, 2007). It may seem confusing to coordinate the requirements of so many sets of regulations, but your state licensing representative can help you sort things out. If you are involved in planning a new facility or in renovating an existing one, it is a good idea (and usually a requirement) to draw up plans and submit them to the various authorities for review before beginning construction. Correcting the direction of a door swing or the location of a handwashing sink is much easier, and less costly, on paper than after it is set in bricks and mortar.

The National Association for the Education of Young Children (NAEYC) accreditation criteria call for 35 square feet of indoor space per child and 75 square feet of outdoor space. The latter can be calculated on the basis of the number of children using the play yard at a given time (National Association for the Education of Young Children, 2007a). Some argue that 40 or 50 square feet of indoor space per child comes closer to ideal (Olds, 2001). Earlier recommendations regarding minimum square footage were based on observing children's behavior (Ruopp. Travers, Glantz, & Coelen, 1979). Recent advances in methodology, however, have made it possible to measure the physiological effects of overcrowding, concluding that at least 54 square feet of space per child is needed to prevent elevated stress levels (Legendre, 2003). Licensing regulations, on the other hand, specify the minimum amount of space required for each child. If you are fortunate enough to be involved in the planning and building of a facility, you may have an opportunity to argue for the ideal space allowance. Most managers must work with existing facilities, however, and they are usually pressed to stretch available space as far as licensing regulations allow.

Even then, additional considerations must go into calculating the capacity of a given space. Imagine an empty warehouse with 35,000 square feet. Using the standard of 35 square feet per child, some might conclude that this space could accommodate 1,000 children. But licensing regulations regarding the number of toilets and

LEADERSHIP LENS

As a good manager, you must make sure that your center meets or even exceeds the minimum space requirements set by your state's licensing standards. As a leader, you might take a broader view and advocate for raising those standards on behalf of all children. In other words you can decide to take a stand on an issue that is important and try to influence others to take action.

The first step in advocacy is to do your homework so you can provide information essential to wise decision making. You should be comfortable with this role, especially when it involves facts about children's development and the early childhood profession. You know about available information sources and where to look for them. One place to start is the article "The Great 35 Square Foot Myth" (White & Stoecklin, 2003), which can be found online at http://www.whitehutchinson.com/children/articles/35footmyth.shtml.

Share what you learn with others. Give a short presentation for your colleagues in a directors' support group, at a parent meeting for the families of children you serve, or at the monthly breakfast meeting of a community organization (such as the Kiwanis) that has an interest in children's issues. Learn which legislators in your state sit on the committee concerned with regulating child care and write them a letter. Find out when and how child-care rules are revised in your state and attend meetings where public feedback is invited. You may not see immediate success for your efforts, but you can take satisfaction in the fact that you raised people's awareness of the issue and laid the groundwork for possible future change.

washbasins, the amount of equipment, and the number of required staff members add constraints to your total capacity. And if you are striving for a quality above and beyond the minimum regulations, you must be concerned, of course, with maximum group sizes. When all of these details are taken into consideration, your 35,000-square-foot warehouse—with the addition of toilets and washbasins—may house no more than 20 children, and those 20 children will be too overwhelmed by the openness of the space to have a high-quality experience. Adding walls and additional bathrooms can increase the capacity, but you have to plan carefully so that all of the new rooms have proper exits and ventilation. In short, managing spatial resources is a complex matter and deserves careful thought.

CHILDREN'S BASIC ENVIRONMENTAL NEEDS

Anita Olds was a visionary leader in the design of child-care facilities based on principles of human development and psychology. She founded and directed the Child Care Institute, an annual seminar cosponsored by Tufts University and the Harvard Graduate School of Design, where she guided child development and design professionals to explore the ways in which the human-built environment supports and enhances life. Olds believed that every child is a "miracle" and that a child development program designed with that belief in mind differs radically from one designed simply to meet minimum standards. According to Olds, children have four basic needs that must be supported by the environment: movement, comfort, competence, and a sense of control. Olds believed that planners must take all four needs into account, adjusting the emphasis on each to achieve a balance. If, for example, you are going to ask children to sit still for group time or meals, you will be more successful if you provide interesting things to do or look at, comfortable places to sit, and a view that imparts a sense of control over the space (Olds, 2001, pp. 8–12). An understanding of each of these needs will help guide the design and maintenance of a child development center's physical environment.

An Environment That Encourages Movement

The first function of any physical environment is to meet physical needs, and children's first physical need is to move. Asking them to sit or stand still for long periods, in addition to being an impossible task, inhibits their healthy growth and leads to inevitable frustration for both children and teachers. If the environment does not provide legitimate and safe opportunities to run, climb, jump, and crawl, children create their own—sometimes dangerous—challenges. Planning to accommodate these natural drives with safe opportunities for movement in the classroom supports the children's growth and makes life easier for teachers.

Children's need for movement is supported by the provision of an active zone where movement is permitted and encouraged. Texture and sound can help convey the possibilities within a given space. The same room can signal when it's time for active play or napping simply by adjusting the light and adding or removing soft background music. A low-pile area rug on a hardwood or vinyl floor creates a well-defined boundary for block building, and the exposed perimeter floor suggests a "road" that steers riding toys away from block structures. Given boundaries and cues such as these, the children easily learn the appropriate behavior for each space.

An Environment That Supports Comfort

Comfort, in the psychological sense, requires an environment with just the right amount of stimulation or variety. Too much stimulation is overwhelming, while too little is

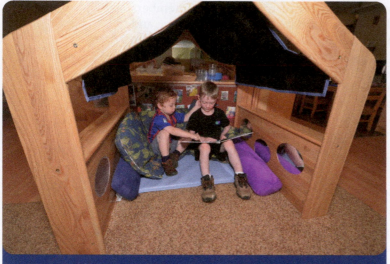
A cozy covered alcove provides a comfortable place for children to enjoy a respite from the stimulation of the classroom.

deadening. Olds suggested that designers take inspiration from nature's rhythmic fluctuations to counter the sterile sameness of many institutional settings. She contrasted babbling brooks, soft breezes, and the play of light and shadow when sunlight is filtered through leaves with echoes bouncing off hard tile floors in long corridors and rectangular classrooms flooded with harsh fluorescent light. Comfortable settings provide "difference in sameness" by introducing variations in scale, floor and ceiling height, and the texture of interior finishes and furnishings. Such settings carve out spaces for being alone or with companions, for quiet or active pursuits.

The typical child development center is full of sensory stimulation for children. It might be the sound of their playmates laughing in the block corner, the sight of a piñata being constructed in the art area, or the smell of cookies baking in the kitchen. Stimulation for its own sake is not necessarily desirable, however. Constant bombardment with visual or auditory stimulation can lead to children—and adults—tuning out their environments. Too many early childhood classrooms are visually chaotic—walls are crammed from floor to ceiling with dozens of commercial "decorations" and multiple versions of every craft project from the beginning of the year. Many people in such an environment simply shut out the excess stimulation and stop seeing their surroundings. Because some children may not be able to exclude the excess stimulation, they can have difficulty focusing on any one aspect of the environment. If you want children to take in information, provide some blank space around the pictures and symbols displayed on the walls. The same principle applies to sound. Some teachers feel that they are creating an appreciation for music by using it as a "background" for play. Does the Muzak in the shopping mall or elevator stimulate an appreciation in adults, or do adults simply tune it out?

In addition to managing the sensory load of an environment, attention to its aesthetic quality is an important way to support comfort. The impact of this quality on human interactions and perceptions is illustrated by a study that Abraham Maslow and Norbett Mintz conducted in the 1950s. They arranged three separate rooms: a "beautiful" room with comfortable furnishings, natural lighting, and tasteful decorations; an "ugly" room with "bare light bulbs, grey walls, and torn shades," and an "average" room that was clean and neat but nondescript. Then they asked volunteers to sit in each room, examine photographs of people, and decide which showed evidence of "energy" and "well-being." The volunteers, as well as two of the three research assistants who interviewed them, were unaware of the actual purpose of the study, which was to see whether people reacted differently while in the three environments.

The findings were striking. Not only did the volunteers find the same pictures more full of "energy" and "well-being" when they viewed them while in the "beautiful" room, but the research assistants also spent less time on the interviews in the "ugly" room and had more negative feelings toward their work there, including "monotony, fatigue, headache, sleepiness, discontent, irritability, hostility, and avoidance." The findings for the "average" room were more like those for the "ugly" room than for the "beautiful" room (Hiss, 1987).

The point is that children and staff members deserve—and will function more healthily and happily—in an environment that is beautiful. Many centers today are using more muted and subtle tones rather than the garish mixture of primary colors so often associated with children's spaces. Think of what you would like in your own home instead of limiting yourself to stereotypical images of what children are thought to like.

An Environment That Fosters Competence

Well-designed spaces are adapted to the children's size and abilities so that they can move about freely and accomplish their aims without constant adult help. Any group of children displays a wide range of abilities and tastes, and any

When the materials within each area are organized and accessible, children can concentrate and carry out their plans.

child's preferences vary from day to day. Offering a wide variety of activities ensures that each child is able to find something to do that is just challenging enough to be interesting. When the room arrangement creates several defined spaces, children are less overwhelmed and can see the choices available to them. Their perception of their own competence is enhanced when they can easily get to play areas and toileting facilities (Maxwell, 2007). When the materials within each area are organized and accessible, children can concentrate and carry out their plans. Low chairs and tables, child-height bulletin boards and easels, and accessible equipment stored on open shelves invite children to get their own learning materials and to put them away when they are finished.

While it is important to provide novelty by introducing new materials or rearranging a space, it is also important for the room arrangement to remain stable, especially for younger children or children with some types of disabilities, to promote feelings of security and competence that come from knowing where things are. Any major changes should be introduced one at a time, perhaps after consulting the children. Indoors, a few lightweight room dividers or hollow blocks often encourage the children's spatial creativity—they might build an office, a hideout, or an airport. For the older children, who have been in school for a period of time and feel very secure, a reorganization of space often stimulates new ways to play. For example, if the music area is moved near the blocks, the sight of blocks may stimulate the children to build a stage for an impromptu performance. Moving the blocks near the housekeeping corner may stimulate them to combine the blocks and the dolls or to add to the housekeeping area by using the blocks to build a room. Older children can participate in the decisions about the changes and learn a great deal in the process as they discuss the merits of various possibilities or draw proposed floor plans.

An Environment That Encourages a Sense of Control

Spaces designed to meet this need allow children to experience the sensation of privacy without foregoing the need for adult supervision. Child-height barriers, cubbyholes, and small alcoves offer possibilities for retreat and momentary solitude. Child-size equipment and low door latches facilitate children's control of the environment. Child-high

In this example of a prepared environment, each child has a tray to define a space for painting and an attractive set of small cups holding different hues of food coloring for experimenting.

lavatories, toilets, and drinking fountains help children gain control of their own personal care sooner. Handrails on stairs make it easier to go up and down independently. Children also benefit from predictability in their environment, from knowing how to get in and out of a room, as well as what is on the other side of the door or wall. A loft, or similar structure, that affords an overview of the entire space helps meet this need. Children (like adults) feel more control in protected spaces, with walls at their backs, than exposed in the middle of large open spaces.

A principle called **prepared environment**, applied in the Montessori schools, requires that each material be limited to its own special space for use. The child is taught where to use the material and to return it to its rightful place on the shelf when finished. The items to be used in a particular activity are often color-coded to help with organization: Two small blue pitchers with a blue sponge on a small blue tray, for example, comprise a pouring activity complete with the tool needed for cleanup. The materials are also arranged on the shelves in a sequential order of difficulty so a child knows that something from the top left, for example, is easier than something from the bottom right. Small mats are provided for children to spread on the floor and demarcate their workspace. These aspects of Montessori's approach to managing spatial resources have been adopted by many teachers in other types of centers to help children work independently and without interference from others.

The concepts of personal space and territoriality are relevant to the sense of control.

All individuals, including young children, need some **personal space** that is theirs to claim and defend, according to Pastalan (1971), who argued that "possession of a tangible piece of space seems almost essential for one's identity." In the child development center, this is usually the cubby holding the children's personal belongings—their coats, boots, and items they accumulate at school such as paintings. A cot set up in a certain spot each day is personal space. According to Pastalan, it should be arranged so that it is very difficult for others to infringe on the individual's personal space. With this point in mind, the center that has no cubbies for children's belongings, or a teacher who removes a 5-year-old's toy from his locker and places it on a high shelf, must be violating children's sense of personal space and contributing to their insecurity.

Territoriality refers to people's use of space to communicate ownership of areas they are occupying. In a child-care center, it means a child's specific claim to a place in the learning environment—the place at the easel, in the sandbox, or on the carpet in the block room. Territoriality also refers to the amount of space you need between you and others to feel comfortable in a social interaction, a characteristic highly influenced by culture. Some North Americans, for example, have experienced discomfort traveling in other countries where people stand much closer together when commuting on crowded buses or push against one another to get served at train stations or post offices. If they judge these behaviors by their own cultural standards, they might become offended at what they perceive as rudeness when, in fact, their distancing behavior might seem insulting to members of the other culture.

Further complicating these cultural differences are the differences that exist between individuals because of temperament or other personality factors. Some people simply do not like to be touched as much as others. All of these factors influence the behavior of even very young children as well as the adults in the center.

> **? DECISIONS, DECISIONS . . .**
>
> During your observations of child development centers, have you witnessed any conflicts that seemed to be caused by territoriality? Describe what you saw and provide suggestions on how a director might manage the space to alleviate the problem.

Managing Density

Density, or the number and size of the people who use a space, affects the degree to which each of the environmental needs is met. Clearly an overcrowded classroom impedes opportunities for movement either because children bump into one another or because teachers try to limit movement in order to prevent such bumps. Increased density relates to comfort because more people produce more noise and movement, with the possible result that children suffer from sensory overload. As children get a little older, they may be able to cope with more people and larger spaces, but even adults can be susceptible to the negative effects of overload. Feelings of competence and control are also affected.

The National Day Care Study compared groups of 12 children and groups of 24 children and found that the small groups fostered positive behaviors, such as cooperation, reflection, and innovation, in the children. Compared to the children in the larger groups, those in the small groups were more verbal, more involved in tasks, and less frequently seen wandering aimlessly (Ruopp et al., 1979). NAEYC accreditation criteria stipulate a group size of 6 or 8 for infants, 6 to 12 for toddlers and 2-year-olds, 12 to 18 for 3-year-olds, and 16 to 20 for 4- and 5-year-olds (National Association for the Education of Young Children, 2007a). Of course, each of these groups must have a minimum of two adults present at all times.

Density applies not only to the total space for the whole group, but also to the ways children use that space. Dividing the room into learning or interest centers so that children work and play in small groups facilitates positive behaviors. There must be a sufficient number of centers, however, and they must be interesting and appealing to children. To foster children's sense of competence and control, they should be allowed to move from one area to another as they finish what they were doing.

The number of children in each area can be flexible and still be limited for safety reasons. Older children in particular can take part in deciding how to control the traffic flow. To avoid overcrowding and prevent conflict, some teachers post "tickets" or signs with stick figures that show the number of children the area can accommodate, for example, four in the painting area or six building with blocks. The children are expected to learn to read the numbers or count the stick figures, count the children already in the space, and wait their turn if there is no space available. Teachers who use this method argue that it teaches children one-to-one correspondence, counting skills, and the ability to delay gratification. The system has drawbacks, however. For it to work, it must be enforced consistently. Children who have difficulty remembering to count themselves in the total or waiting their turn are often evicted from an area only to slip back in when teachers are not looking, undermining all prior "learning" of the rule. In some centers, the teachers seem to give as many reminders at the end of the school year as they did at the beginning—a good sign that the rule is not being learned and perhaps that it is inappropriate.

Some teachers question whether they should invest so much time and energy in the role of enforcer and whether children should be taught blind obedience to arbitrary rules. They prefer to manage spatial density more subtly, and more efficiently, through the use of indirect guidance techniques (Hearron & Hildebrand, 2013). That is, they arrange the environment to give concrete cues that tell the children something about how many can play in a given area, as well as something about why that is so. For example, two pairs of safety goggles are in the woodworking area, and there is a rule that safety goggles must be worn in order to protect the eyes.

Besides ensuring that enough interesting activities are available at any one time, it is important to offer popular activities often enough for the children to get their fill. A sign with four stick figures will not succeed in limiting the number of children crowded around the play-dough table if the dough is rarely available and all of the other materials in the room have been there since the day the center opened. When there is an especially popular center, children are often content to wait if they can put their names on a sign-up sheet and be assured that they will get a turn. Rather than imposing their own arbitrary time limits on play in a particular area (e.g., with a cooking timer), teachers can ask the children in the area to tell the next child on the sign-up sheet when they are finished. When given the right to decide for themselves, children often surprise us by relinquishing the spot much sooner than the arbitrary timer would have dictated, and while in the learning center, they focus more on their play and less on their impending eviction.

Whether teachers choose the direct or indirect way of limiting group size, there are at least two good reasons for doing so. First, children in groups of four or fewer are more likely to participate more fully in the group's activity. Second, because group unity decreases as the size of a group increases, larger groups require more outside control. Thus, the freedom and self-control desired in a high-quality child development center is facilitated by small groups.

ORGANIZING SPACE

Building Layout

When designing the overall layout of a child development center, it is important to consider several factors: safety, function, and traffic flow.

SAFETY Heat sources, such as furnaces and water heaters, must be separated from children's areas by fire-retardant walls. Pathways to exits must be clear, and although doors may be locked to entry from the outside, they have to be unlocked and easily opened from the inside. All rooms should be equipped with smoke detectors and fire extinguishers. Sufficient security to prevent theft and vandalism requires locks on windows, doors, storage sheds, and gates, as well as careful control over the center's keys.

Ease of supervision is an aspect of safety. Learning centers set off by child-high shelves or dividers not only encourage children to select an activity and settle down to concentrate on that activity, but they also enable adults to observe the entire room at a glance so they can notice behavior that might become dangerous and move quickly to provide closer supervision or take care of an emergency. Adequate supervision contributes to the children's safety and to the protection of the center's reputation. More than one center has found itself mired in an investigation of possible sexual abuse because staff failed to notice curious children exploring each other's bodies in a hidden corner of a classroom or playground.

Based on a study of sexual abuse in child-care centers, experts recommended that doors and stalls in bathrooms be eliminated along with any other place where a young child could be isolated (Finkelhor, Williams, Kalinowski, & Burns, 1988). This precaution serves to protect staff members from unwarranted accusations, as well as to protect the children from harm. A wise manager ensures that staff members are not put in the position of being alone with the children.

Public space in the center should be located near the entrance, allowing traffic patterns to flow from there to progressively more private spaces.

FUNCTION In addition to these safety issues, building layout must take into consideration the activities or functions that will occur. What separate spaces for infants, toddlers, and older children are necessary? What spaces will staff members need for planning or rest breaks? Will the program offer hot meals and need a kitchen? Where can parents linger with the children or meet with teachers? Which activities should be located near each other, and which should be apart? Which activities or functions will be assigned to the most convenient or attractive spaces? When you have to make a choice, who gets the sunniest room? Who gets the rooms with easiest access to the outdoor play area? It seems logical to give infants and toddlers priority on these spaces because older children can usually get outside easier and stay longer periods once they are out there (Olds, 2001, pp. 110–113).

TRAFFIC FLOW Movement patterns between the separate spaces influence decisions about where to locate doors and windows and where to establish inside common areas. Olds called the common area the "center of gravity of social life" in a children's center and recommended that it be placed at the heart of the building, centrally located, but protected from through traffic. The *piazza* of the Diana School in Reggio Emilia, Italy, is a prime example of such a space, echoing both the form and function of the town's central plaza. Olds distinguished this public space from the more private spaces such as children's classrooms, bathrooms, offices, or kitchen. She recommended that public spaces be located near the building's entrance, allowing traffic patterns to flow from there to progressively more private spaces, much as they would in a private home (Olds, 2001, pp. 116–121). In this **video**, a director explains the value of locating cubbies outside the classroom so that children have a few moments with family members before entering the group.

Room Layout

When designing the layout of an individual room, begin by considering the activities planned for that room—the space's functional requirements. Every age group requires, in varying degrees, space for four activity types: (1) caregiving, (2) movement and active play, (3) quiet play, and (4) messy play. Programs with infants also need space for the babies to sleep. The first activity type, caregiving, takes place throughout the room, while the other three (movement and active play, quiet play, messy play) require separate zones. The decision about where to place each of these

The gate separates infants, protecting them from the more mobile toddlers in this classroom, while allowing them to view and interact with each other.

zones is influenced by the room's fixed features, the parts that are built in and cannot be changed. Door locations determine the entry and exit points and convey a feeling of exposure, while corners lend a sense of protection. The room arrangement must respect these qualities in order to work.

REGIONS AND ZONES   The room's fixed features help divide it into two regions: a wet region comprising the entry zone and the messy zone, and a dry region comprising the quiet and active play zones (Olds, 2001, pp. 137–141). The room's water source dictates the location of the wet region, which should have waterproof, easy-to-clean flooring. Carpeting can demarcate the dry region.

Well-defined zones within each of these regions and arrangements that reduce or control traffic through the zones make it possible for children to play without undue interference and conflicts. Children begin to know what the appropriate behavior or activity is in each area. For example, furniture arrangements that eliminate long open pathways make it less likely that children will run about and collide with each other or the furniture. Painting takes place in the wet region/messy zone because the washable floor surface means that spills do not matter. Blocks are located in the dry region/active zone on carpeted areas where sounds are deadened, and out of traffic lanes, so that cherished building constructions are less likely to be knocked down accidentally.

Other activities appropriate for the messy zone include water and sand play, woodworking, arts and crafts, cooking, eating, and science and nature study. This is also the place to locate bathrooms, changing tables, water fountains, and separate sinks for handwashing and for the children's activities, as well as the cupboards and closets needed to store all of the necessary materials for these activities.

In addition to the blocks, the active zone supports climbing and other types of large muscle play, dramatic play, music and movement, and fantasy play with puppets or other miniature figures. The quiet zone provides space for reading, writing, listening, playing with manipulatives (e.g., puzzles or small construction materials), resting or relaxing, and group meetings. The line between the carpet and the washable floor surface marks the boundary between wet and dry regions. This boundary, as well as the boundaries between the various zones, can be emphasized by lighting variations or by ceiling and floor height. A strategically placed tall structure, such as a loft, helps create a buffer between zones (Olds, 2001, pp. 144–152).

?   DECISIONS, DECISIONS . . .

Sketch the floor plan of a child development classroom you have visited or worked in. Think about the considerations discussed in this section and decide what, if any, changes you would recommend. Discuss with your classmates.

CLASSROOM DESIGN

Figure 9.1 is a sample floor plan for a room intended to accommodate a mixed-age group of eight infants and toddlers. It has direct access to the outdoor play area via a low covered deck. The room is carpeted except for the section in the middle, which houses all water-related functions and has vinyl flooring. A food preparation area opens toward the children's eating area. The bathroom is separated from the kitchen by a full-length wall and is surrounded on the three other sides by half-walls so that teachers can easily keep an eye on the entire room while diapering children or helping them with toileting. Teachers can also see over the shelf that defines their workspace, which has two long work surfaces with room for files and storage beneath. Adult-size seating in the infant area and in the greeting and departing area provides a comfortable place for teachers to hold and read to children and encourages family members to linger with their children. A low shelf nearby contains parent information, and the wall below provides a place to display images of the children or their artwork. A large, open, carpeted area is easily reconfigured with movable shelves and risers.

The sample classroom for 3- to 5-year-olds in Figure 9.2 shows the use of shelves, furnishings, or dividers to help define the activity expected to take place and provide nearby storage for necessary equipment and supplies. The dramatic play area includes the area below the loft, which expands possibilities for a variety of play themes, and it is furnished with a child-size stove, sink, table, refrigerator, and other props. Blocks located outside the traffic areas, on the carpeted area of the room, allow children to

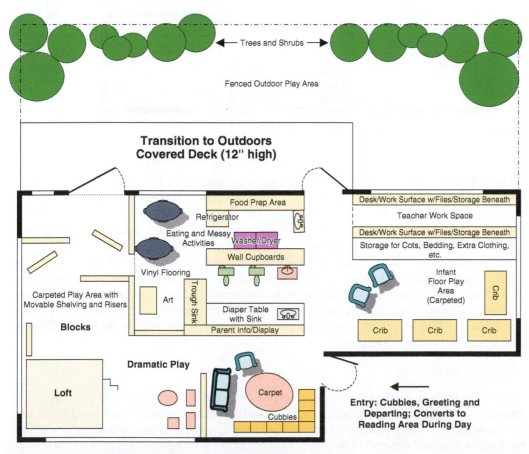

FIGURE 9.1 Sample layout for an infant-toddler room.

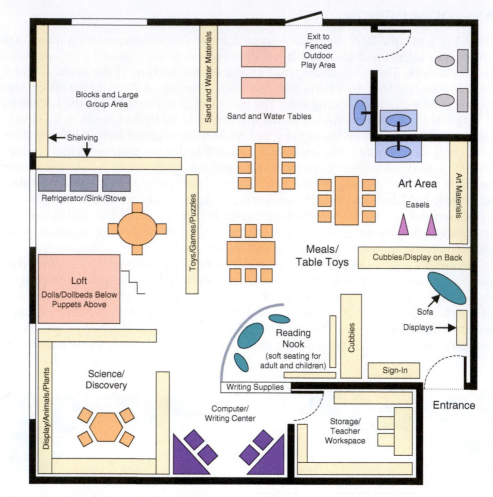

FIGURE 9.2 Sample classroom layout for children ages 3 to 5.

build with a minimum of interference from other children. When the blocks are put away, this area also serves as a place to hold large-group activities. Placing tables and chairs, easels, and two low sinks on the side of the room with tile flooring allows for activities requiring water. Snacks or meals are served in this area, too, so that inevitable spills are easily cleaned. A separate sink is available inside the bathroom to promote good sanitation practices. Adequate shelving enables the teachers to rearrange most areas in numerous ways to stimulate interest in the various activities. Cubbies and a sign-in area are conveniently close to the door where children enter; a small sofa in that area invites family members to linger a few moments before leaving for work. The room has a direct exit to an enclosed outdoor play area, and large windows on two walls provide abundant natural lighting.

Learning Areas

The theory or theories that you choose as your program's foundation will provide guidance in the selection of materials to include in the various areas. Additional ideas are available in most early childhood curriculum books, as well as in some of the resources for further study at the end of this chapter. Following are suggestions to start your own brainstorming process.

WRITING/COMMUNICATIONS AREA

- Table with seats for about four children
- Working typewriter or computer and printer
- Paper in a variety of sizes, weights, and colors
- Envelopes
- Pencils, markers, and pens
- Receptacles labeled with each child's name for receiving messages
- Stick-on letters
- Divided trays for sorting letters cut from newspapers
- Old greeting cards
- Stamps, stickers, and reply envelopes from junk mail
- Old checkbooks or check registers
- Blank books

LITERACY AREA

- Book display rack
- Appropriate books (including some made by the teachers and children) representing diverse ages, cultures, and abilities
- Comfortable seating (e.g., cushions, soft chairs)
- Adequate lighting
- Compact disc player and headphones
- Audio recordings of familiar stories (commercial or teacher-made)
- Storybook props (e.g., puppets, flannel boards, and figures)

SCIENCE AREA

- Table or cupboard with a working surface
- Magnets and objects to pick up
- Magnifying glasses
- Prisms
- Scales
- Thermometer
- Dry-cell batteries with hookups for lights and bells
- Bulletin board and display area with interesting items (e.g., photos, insects, acorns, bones, and rocks) arranged to encourage the children to look at them on their own
- Cages, food, and water for animals if the appropriate facilities and care are available
- Field guides to birds, minerals, plants, and so forth
- Notebooks and pencils for recording observations
- Various containers for sorting and organizing collections

BLOCK AREA

- Unit blocks
- Other blocks of interest

- Block accessories—plastic or rubber figures of people and animals, small vehicles, markers and tagboard for signs, pipe cleaners and other materials for child-made accessories
- Hollow wooden blocks

Some teachers prefer reinforced cardboard blocks instead of the hollow wooden blocks for younger children because they are easier to stack and less likely to cause injury if they fall on a child. Others simply consider them more economical and are disappointed to find that they deteriorate rapidly when older children stand or walk on them.

ART AREA

- Table and chairs sufficient for about six children
- Two easels
- Supplies—18-inch × 24-inch easel paper (newsprint roll ends often obtainable from newspaper shops), manila drawing paper, construction paper, pastel mimeograph paper, fingerpainting paper, wrapping paper, powdered tempera in many colors including white, wheat paste for mixing fingerpaint, liquid soap for extender, pastel chalk, large crayons, felt markers, scissors for both the left and the right hand, white glue (buy a dozen small bottles and fill them from a gallon jug of glue using a plastic squeeze bottle with a pointed tip like a mustard bottle), paste brushes, easel brushes, collage materials (usually found materials), stapler, masking tape, and handheld paper punch

TABLE GAMES

- Table and chairs sufficient for about six children
- Shelves and puzzle racks
- Wooden puzzles from simple to complex designs
- Lotto games
- Sorting games of various shapes, sizes, and colors
- Perceptual matching toys
- Parquetry block set
- Dominoes with both numbers and pictures
- Nested toys
- Tinker toys and other connector toys
- Beads and strings
- Candy Land and other commercial, teacher-made, or child-made games (see Kamii, 1982)

CARPENTRY AREA

- Worktable
- Hammers (adult quality; lightweight)
- Saws (variety of types)
- Vises
- Nails (variety of sizes and types)
- White glue
- Soft wood scraps (usually available at cabinet shops)

- Safety goggles
- Peg board with space delineated for hanging each tool

MUSIC/RHYTHM AREA

- Simple compact disc player that children can operate
- Variety of recorded music (folk, classical, jazz, etc., in addition to "children's" music)
- Illustrated music books
- Rhythm instruments (e.g., drums, maracas)
- Xylophone

WATER/SAND PLAY TABLE

- Child-height table with waterproof liners, permitting water or sand play for about six children (separate tables for sand and water are ideal)
- Unbreakable containers for pouring, measuring, or comparing amounts of water or sand
- Pipes, pulleys, and pendulums
- Sifters and waterwheels
- Small animal figures and vehicles

DRAMATIC PLAY AREA It is ideal to provide two areas: one for representing home life and another that children can modify to re-create other types of settings. Each area should include the following;

- Child-size stove, sink, and refrigerator
- Table and two chairs
- Doll high chair
- Bed, sturdy enough for a child to lie in
- Blankets, tablecloth
- Cooking utensils, tableware, and dishes
- Grocery items stored in cupboards and refrigerator
- Dolls, male and female, with various ethnic characteristics
- Dress-up clothing representing both genders and variety of adult roles
- Several phones
- Full-length mirrors
- Literacy items typically found in homes (e.g., newspapers, magazines, telephone books, paper and pencils for grocery lists)
- Letters, stamps, and so forth, to play post office
- Menus, trays, and pizza pan to play restaurant
- Rollers, play razor, and combs to play hairdresser/barber shop
- Tent and suitcases for camping out
- Keyboard, paper, and phones for office play

In addition to these activity areas, the center should provide the following spaces: nap facilities and an isolation space,

NAP FACILITIES

- Either in a separate room where the cots can remain set out or in a safe storage area away from the children's play
- Enough cots for each child to have one labeled with her name, or cots equal to the number of children who will be napping on any given day (cots should be sanitized between uses)
- A blanket for each child, labeled with the owner's name and stored apart from all of the others to avoid cross contamination

Some centers find that bath towels serve the purpose well and are less bulky to store. If the cots are used by the same children each day, the blankets can simply be stored on the individual cots, unless they will come in contact with any part of another cot.

ISOLATION SPACE

A small space equipped to make an ill child comfortable while waiting for a parent to come is necessary. Often, a protected space in the center office is used for this purpose, enabling the manager or office staff to keep an eye on the child while attending to other duties. If a separate room is used, a staff member must be present, perhaps completing some paperwork task while the child sleeps. Never leave a child unsupervised. This space should include the following items:

- Child's cot, sheet, blanket, and pillow
- Child's chair near the cot
- Adult chair, perhaps a rocker
- A child's book or two
- Soft, washable, cuddly toy

Family Resource Area

The objective is to provide an inviting place for a parent to wait for a child, visit another parent, or select reading material. This room could also serve as a conference room or the policy boardroom. If the table is large, it can accommodate staff members while they assemble booklets, advertising, and so on. The following items should be included in this space:

- Table and chairs
- Bookcase with books to lend
- Bulletin board with educational exhibits
- Wastebasket
- Coffee-making supplies

ADAPTATIONS FOR CHILDREN WITH DISABILITIES

Child-care centers, like all public facilities, must meet the requirements of the Americans with Disabilities Act (ADA) by removing barriers that limit participation of children (or their family members) unless those modifications impose an undue burden on the center. For answers to commonly asked questions about the law, visit the U.S. Department of Justice website at www.ada.gov/. To begin with, a center that accommodates children with walkers and wheelchairs needs more space: 50 square feet per child is recommended by the Easter Seals Child Development Center Network (2003).

One major concern when considering space for meeting special needs is accessibility. The center itself and all of the activities in the center must be accessible to all children. If you are planning a new center or renovating an old one, local building codes may require that you install ramps, wider doorways, larger restrooms, and handrails. Advocates for **universal design** hold that "products and environments should be usable by all people, to the greatest extent possible, without the need for adaptation or specialized design" (Center for Universal Design, 1997). Child development centers adhere to this principle insofar as they already have materials on low shelves, hand-washing sinks at children's height, and several other features that make things more accessible to all children. Are these same shelves and drinking fountains accessible to children using wheelchairs or walkers? What about the blocks—are they accessible to children who cannot get down on the floor? Or can an elevated platform be installed that allows everyone to build?

Another important concern is safety. For the sake of all the children, eliminate sharp corners on furniture and obstacles that might trip people; these precautions become doubly important when you enroll a child with vision impairment. The fire drill signal you have always used may not alert a child with a hearing impairment. Is there room on your bus for wheelchairs? Do you have a place to store adaptive equipment? Hearing aids, for example, often need replacement batteries, and these must be stored and disposed of safely. Children with severe physical disabilities might have a variety of standers for different positions, and those that are not in use must be stored out of the way so that classrooms are not cluttered.

Space must be managed to provide the additional services that children with disabilities might need. Sometimes, this means providing a separate, quiet room where speech therapy can take place away from distractions. Many therapists, however, are moving toward more integrated ways of delivering services to children. Instead of singling out the child with a disability, they might stay right in the classroom and work individually with the child or with a small group that includes children who are developing in typical as well as atypical patterns. Some therapists adopt a consultative model—they discuss the child's needs with the teacher or caregiver and offer suggestions for modifying everyday classroom routines and activities to accomplish therapeutic aims. Typical center classrooms and offices can probably meet the spatial needs of these approaches without much alteration.

Some types of disabilities require that children wear diapers or receive more help with toilet functions than their age mates. Thus, diapering surfaces may have to be enlarged and made sturdier to accommodate the larger bodies. The diapering surface may have to be lowered to reduce the strain on the caregivers' backs, or it may have to be relocated to provide privacy for those older children whose mental and emotional maturity exceeds their physical capability.

Although organizing space to meet the needs of children with disabilities may seem daunting to some managers and caregivers, it will help put the challenge into perspective if you consider that child development centers have been accommodating special needs as long as they have been in existence. After all, child-size toilets, or sippy cups, or wooden puzzles with large knobs on the pieces are adaptations to the special needs of individuals who are smaller in stature or less physically coordinated than others. The essence of developmentally appropriate practice is that programs and services for children be individually appropriate, as well as age-appropriate—they begin with a general knowledge of what children are like at various ages, but tailor this knowledge to the unique needs of each individual. Accommodating the needs of children with disabilities may take a little extra effort, but it is really a matter of extending the concept of developmental appropriateness to all children.

Center managers can take comfort in the fact that they are not alone as they try to meet the special needs of a particular child with a disability. Recall that children with disabilities must be provided with an individualized education plan (IEP) or an individualized family service plan (IFSP), depending on whether they are over or under 3 years of age. These plans are the product of collaboration on the part of parents, teachers, therapists, or other specialists. If the child is enrolled in the center as part of a previously formulated plan, the manager and caregivers will certainly want to study the plan and perhaps have a role in subsequent revisions. Sometimes, the planning process results when center staff members observe signs of developmental delays and make an appropriate referral for screening. In that case, child development staff members may be included in the team from the beginning. The challenge is not for any one member of this team to meet all the child's needs, but rather for the team to develop the communication and cooperation needed to make the best use of each individual member's expertise.

The plan might include providing special types of equipment for the child with a disability. Standers or other positioning devices can help a child stand or sit to play with peers. Electronic switches allow a child with limited use of hand muscles to control movement or sound in electronic toys. Some types of communication devices can be programmed to play brief statements when tapped, so that a child with language impairment can communicate a message such as "I want to play" or "I'm all done." Many communities have resource centers where such adaptive equipment can be borrowed. Usually the specialists on the child's IFSP or IEP team can help locate these resources, as well as funding if needed. All adaptive equipment need not be high-tech, however. Everyday items can often be modified relatively easily to meet special needs. One inventive teacher found that by simply twisting the handle on an ordinary teaspoon, she made it possible for a child with cerebral palsy to maneuver food into his mouth. Haugen (n.d.) suggests seven strategies for adapting materials so that all children can use them:

1. Add something to make the item easier to use (e.g., foam wrap on paintbrush handles or fluffers between book pages).

2. Hold the item steady so the child can use it (Velcro on blocks, a dab of clay on the bottom of a toy pan to keep it from sliding while the child stirs).

3. Make things easier (fewer materials to choose from, puzzles with fewer pieces, lower basketball hoop).

4. Provide boundaries (raised edges on tables to prevent spills, enclosed space for reading alone).

5. Appeal to many senses (colored blocks, textured or musical balls, scented play dough).

6. Expand the choices (stack beanbags instead of blocks, provide recorded stories as well as books).

7. Involve other children (to catch and retrieve balls or follow a parade led by child in a wheelchair).

Whatever the challenge, the center manager can find help from a number of sources. For example, the child's family has already found ways to make an ordinary house meet new and changing needs. For example, you can ask what they have done to make it possible for their child to get up close to the dinner table and adapt their ideas to make tables in the classroom more accessible.

? DECISIONS, DECISIONS . . .

Think about a child development facility you have visited or worked in. What modifications to the environment might be necessary to accommodate a child with severe vision impairment? What about a child who uses a wheelchair or walker? Discuss with your classmates.

THE OUTDOOR LEARNING ENVIRONMENT

The outdoor learning environment has the potential to support children's development in all domains—emotional, social, and intellectual as well as physical (Frost, Brown, Sutterby, & Thornton, 2004). A growing body of research indicates that outdoor play, especially in rich natural environments, promotes creativity, problem solving, and focus while helping to alleviate stress, aggression, and symptoms of attention deficit disorder (e.g., Burdette & Whitaker, 2005; Taylor & Kuo, 2009). Other research tells us that children today spend much less time outdoors than children born a generation ago, and what time they have outdoors is more likely to be occupied by organized sports than exploration of nature (Clements, 2004), leading to what Richard Louv (2006) has described as nature deficit disorder. Many factors contribute to this phenomenon: the competing attraction of electronic entertainment, fears for children's safety, shrinking availability of neighborhood fields or woodlots, and the hectic schedules of modern families that leave no time for play.

Child-care centers, where so many children spend the majority of their waking hours from birth until they enter school, are in a unique position to counter this trend, but only if they devote the same level of planning and thought to their outdoor environment as they invest in their indoor spaces. Involving children in this planning makes the entire process an enjoyable and intellectually challenging experience. Children can draw images of what they'd like to see and they can create miniature three-dimensional versions of their ideas using sand, twigs, or other found materials. As you watch this video, listen to what children say about what they would like in their outdoor play area and how they feel about participating in its design.

In too many child-care facilities, the outdoor play area seems tacked on as an afterthought, a place where children are expected to run around and let off steam while staff members relax on the sidelines. The amount of running around they do is significantly lower than conventional wisdom suggests, though it varies a great deal from program to program (Pate, Pfeiffer, Trost, Ziegler, & Dowda, 2004). Children who have been in child care are significantly more likely to be obese when they enter kindergarten than their peers who have not been in care (Maher, Li, Carter, & Johnson, 2008). Factors that influence children's level of exertion outdoors include adult enthusiasm and participation and the availability of interesting activities (Brown, Googe, McIver, & Rathel, 2009).

Investing your time and energy in planning and maintaining the outdoor learning environment can produce dividends for your staff members as well as for children. Adults also experience relief from stress in beautiful natural settings. They benefit from the healthful effects—and pleasure—of physical exertion. And they are likely to enjoy their jobs more because it is easier to supervise children who are happily engaged in play, who come indoors with healthy appetites for lunch, and who are pleasantly tired at nap time.

Using an Ethical Framework

Teachers and children at your center love to gather "treasures" from nature and bring them inside for use in art, science and other activities. The classrooms are filled with collections of rocks, seashells, seeds, twigs, leaves and other items—all carefully sorted and artfully displayed. A sanitation inspection is required as part of your license renewal and the person conducting the inspection has been on the job only a few weeks. He tells you that the materials are unsanitary and will have to be discarded. This was never mentioned by previous inspectors, and you are not sure it is actually a part of your county's sanitation code, but you worry that questioning his authority might jeopardize your working relationship with this new inspector. When you discuss the issue at the next staff meeting, the teachers protest that these collections are a vital part of their curriculum. They suggest that, because the license renewal inspections occur at the same general time each year, they simply remove the materials for a week or so and bring them back out after the inspection is completed. What should you do? Using the NAEYC code, try to determine what core values are involved. What ideals and principles regarding responsibilities to children, families, and employees apply? What course of action seems most right?

The Outdoor Landscape Sets the Stage

A covered deck creates a transition between the indoor and outdoor play areas and allows children to play outdoors when rain or muddy ground might have made that impractical. Wide-open spaces where children can run with abandon and develop locomotion skills should be arranged outdoors, but there should also be outdoor places for quiet play, such as the sandbox, tables for snacks or games, and easels (perhaps attached to fences) for painting. Children soon learn to play where their energy needs dictate when there are choices of quiet or active play.

Carefully selected shrubs and trees provide shade to protect children from harmful overexposure to sun and give a variety of foliage and blooms. Bushes can also serve the same purpose as low dividers inside the classroom—that is, they break up the space into smaller, more intimate areas and help control density without obstructing adults' ability to see what children are doing. Some shrubs can serve as windbreaks, making the yard usable for much of the year, even in colder climates. Quick growing willow trees can be planted in a circle and trained to form dome-like structures where children can play. Be sure to check with a local authority (e.g., cooperative extension agent, university agricultural science program) for which plants may be dangerous or toxic for children. Knolls and hills make the yard more interesting and help children gain experience running over uneven surfaces. To make tricycle riding safer and more organized, a

A garden adds a rich dimension to the outdoor play area.

continuous loop of pavement around a segment of the yard is useful.

It is desirable to leave some areas without grass so children can experience the joy of digging in the dirt as well as planting a garden when spring comes. A few flowers and vegetables with short growing seasons provide opportunities to learn about plants, dig in the soil, and find earthworms. Grass must be mowed when children are indoors or not at the center because of the danger of objects that may be sent flying by lawn mowers.

Water is an essential ingredient of the outdoor learning environment. In addition to gardening, children use it for moistening the sandbox, playing in mud, and washing the sidewalk or the tricycles. A shallow "creek" where a small trickle

Water in any form is a source of endless fascination for children.

of water runs downhill over a bed of rocks can be a source of endless fascination and science discovery for children. Both children and teachers need plenty of fresh water to drink, especially in hot weather. To avoid expensive plumbing repairs, keep the drinking fountains separate from the water sources used in the children's play so that there is no temptation to fill the drain with sand or leaves (McGinnis, 2000, pp. 60–61).

Safety

Safety is, of course, the primary concern, starting from the ground up:

- All trees, shrubs, vines, or other plants should be safe for children. A state university or agricultural extension agency such as the one listed in the Resources for Further Study section at the end of this chapter can provide lists of safe and hazardous plants as well as invasive species to be avoided for your geographic area.

- Tripping hazards, such as exposed tree roots, should be removed.

- An area extending at least 6 feet from all sides of any item of playground equipment where children climb or swing should be filled with cushioning material (either an approved commercial product or wood chips, chemical-free mulch, sand, or pea gravel). The amount or depth of cushioning required depends on the type of material used and the maximum height from which a child might fall.

- Minimize the likelihood of falls by ensuring that any elevated surface is enclosed by a guardrail at least 29 inches high (24 inches for toddlers; 38 inches for school-age children).

- Make sure that any opening large enough for a child's body to slip through is also large enough for his or her head (i.e., smaller than 3.5 inches or larger than 9 inches).

- Avoid metal surfaces (e.g., on slides) that absorb heat and can become hot enough to burn children.

- Remove or otherwise correct hardware where children might pinch their fingers in moving parts. Close S-hooks and shorten or cap protruding bolts that can snag clothing and perhaps cause strangulation (U.S. Consumer Product Safety Commission, 2008).

These slides nestled into a grassy hillside add interest and eliminate a falling hazard.

Public Playground Safety Handbook, published by the U.S. Consumer Product Safety Commission (2008), provides detailed guidelines for these and all other aspects of planning, equipping, and maintaining safe outdoor play areas.

Developmental Needs

The equipment must be suited to the children's sizes and level of development. That is, it should not be too small or too large, too easy or too difficult. This is important from the point of view of safety as well as overall development of children. Equipment that is too easy or too small often inspires children to increase the challenge by using it in unsafe ways, while equipment that is too large or too difficult poses risks that children lack the skills to manage.

The outdoor play area must be tailored to the needs of each age group. Infants benefit from a variety of textures to crawl over, shady areas to protect them from harsh sun, and ground surfaces that do not scrape their tender knees—all in a space where they are not trampled by more mobile children. Toddlers need the addition of more places to walk in or on, to climb over or crawl under, and items to carry about. Still more challenging opportunities should be added for 3- and 4-year-old children: pedal toys, swings, skates, ropes, climbing structures, balance beams, and seesaws. Children of all ages enjoy digging in sand or dirt, although care must be taken to prevent the youngest from putting it in their mouths.

The outdoor play area must also consider the needs of children with disabilities, providing multiple ways to access and ways to use various areas. Paths must be smooth enough and wide enough to accommodate wheelchairs or other devices for physical support. All children, not only those with visual impairments, benefit when the outdoor play area is rich with sensory appeal: varied textures underfoot, the scent of herbs or new-mown grass, the sounds of wind in trees or homemade chimes and percussion instruments. Some children, such as those with autism, may need protected areas where they can play alone sometimes.

Equipment

Large pieces of fixed equipment are expensive and may not provide as many potential play opportunities as loose parts and natural landscape features. If the center chooses to add fixed equipment and has the budget to do so, it essential that all safety guidelines be met. It is important to study all options carefully before making the investment. Items designed for backyard use by one or two children can become unstable and dangerous when subjected to the heavy use of a large group of children. Even sturdy, commercial equipment can take up too much space and quickly become boring. Children need open spaces to run, skip, and pull their wagons.

TABLE 9.1   Age-appropriate outdoor equipment.

Toddler: Under 2	Preschool: Ages 2–5	Grade School: Ages 5–12
• Climbing equipment under 32" high • Ramps • Single-file stepladders • Slides with gentle slope and 19" deep platform to allow child to sit before sliding • Spring rockers • Stairways • Swings with full bucket seats	• Climbers • Horizontal ladders no higher than 60" • Merry-go-rounds • Ramps • Rung ladders • Single-file stepladders • Slides with platform at least 14" deep; average incline no greater than 30° • Spring rockers • Stairways • Swings (belt, full bucket seats, rotating tire)	• Arch climbers • Chain or cable walks • Fulcrum seesaws • Ladders (horizontal, rung, and step) • Overhead rings • Merry-go-rounds • Ramps • Slides with platform at least 14" deep; average incline no greater than 30° • Stairways • Swings (belt and rotating tire) • Vertical sliding poles

Source: U.S. Consumer Product Safety Commission (2008). *Public playground safety handbook.* Bethesda, MD: Author. Available online at http://www.cpsc.gov/cpscpub/pubs/325.pdf

The requirement of sufficient individual play spaces for the number of children using the playground applies outdoors as well as indoors. If there are more than enough places, one can anticipate more harmony on the playground than if there is a shortage of equipment and related play spaces. Remember that it is not always necessary to spend a lot of money to provide an adequate number of play spaces. Children sometimes have the most fun and spend the most time with found or homemade items. An empty refrigerator carton can serve as a house, a hideout for the "bad guys," or a ship at sea from one day to the next and then be sent off to the recycling center when it finally falls apart. Some movable equipment stimulates children to create their own spaces—they may enclose an area with packing boxes or use long planks to wall off an area. Consider the following list when equipping an outdoor learning environment:

- Containers and shovels for use with sand and dirt
- Packing boxes of various sizes or sturdy wooden boxes (sanded smooth and coated with protective, nontoxic finish to prevent splinters)
- Planks or logs to create enclosures
- Wheel toys—tricycles and wagons
- Balls of various sizes
- Plastic bats and hoops
- Outdoor wooden blocks (large size)
- Garden tools—shovel, rake, and hoe
- Age-appropriate fixed equipment for gross motor activity (see Table 9.1)

Many of the activities that you plan for indoors can be carried on outside as well, meaning that equipment and materials can serve double duty. Children can help to choose which dress-up clothing, dramatic play props, art supplies, books, and games to take outside, and they can help gather them up when it's time to come inside.

SPACE FOR STAFF MEMBERS

Space should also be designed and furnished to meet adult needs, supporting them as they meet children's needs. Comfortable, adult-size seating in the classroom makes it easier for staff members to relax and cuddle children, promoting attachment and a sense of security. A retractable set of stairs leading up to the diapering table reduces the risk of back injury at the same time that it supports children's motor skill development and drive for independence.

In addition to the spaces they share with children, adults must have a secure place for their personal items such as handbags or wallets and clothing; conveniently located adult rest rooms; and a quiet, comfortable place with appropriate furniture and adequate storage where they can attend to paperwork tasks and prepare classroom materials. A washable counter with a sink where the children's paints can be mixed is highly desirable—the teachers should not have to mix paints in the children's bathroom. These materials must be kept orderly. Paper supplies present a fire hazard, as do the collections of fabric and paper scrap used for art projects.

Although the teachers usually do not have desks, they do need a cupboard where all of these materials can be organized and readily available. A workroom with adult tables is desirable for planning and preparation. Each teacher needs some office supplies to handle the business portions of the job. Lined tablets, scratch pads, memo pads with the center's letterhead and telephone number for notes to parents, stapler, staples, ruler, yardstick, masking tape, adhesive tape, glue, rubber cement, paper clips, scissors, pens, and pencils are necessary.

The manager should have a closed-off office space for working alone and holding one-to-one conferences with parents or staff members. Equipping the manager's space deserves high priority because the work accomplished there makes it possible for the entire facility to function smoothly. Here the manager attends to many details related to licensing and reporting requirements, confers with parents and staff members, and does the planning and organizing required so that all staff members can function effectively. A desk and chair of appropriate size and height and adequate lighting are essential. Additional seating is needed to accommodate conversations with visiting parents or staff members. Filing cabinets to organize and store paperwork and an adequate computer system are essential. This is likely where families will receive their first impression of your center when they come to enroll their child. Will that impression be one of sterility with no sign that children live and work here? Will it be cluttered and chaotic? Or will it be peaceful and businesslike, with displays of the children's art and photographs of center events to convey a sense of the program's spirit? Some centers display photographs of each staff member in this space so that the parents can recognize the people with whom they leave their child each day.

Separate storage facilities are needed for any bulk quantities of classroom supplies. Fire safety regulations require that storage rooms have fire-retardant walls and that the doors remain closed. You can further reduce the fire hazard by keeping these materials well organized and sorted into noncombustible containers. Only the amounts actually in use daily should be brought into the areas used by the children. Building and equipment maintenance requires a separate workroom and an array of supplies. Dangerous cleaning solvents and other similar materials must always be kept locked away from the children.

The kitchen and food service areas must meet state requirements. Work surfaces should be easy to keep spotless. Storage should be adequate for the required supplies and kept locked to prevent the children and others from entering. Of course, art and cleaning supplies are not stored in areas designated for food. A sanitary and safe place for garbage and waste disposal must be provided, along with frequent garbage removal. Employees are expected to keep the area clean and free of odors, insects, and rodents. A washer and dryer are considered a must by many managers for laundering clothing and bedding, as well as dress-up clothes, aprons, and soft toys.

Managers should encourage adults to be as creative and flexible as the children as they try new ways to organize the available space. If teachers often find themselves carrying certain equipment from place to place, they might question whether new storage for that equipment could be located nearer to its usual use area. Could carts or dollies be used to save the teacher's energy and give the children an experience with energy-saving equipment? Could duplicate items be purchased if the item is frequently needed in two locations? Creative solutions to spatial problems can often be found by questioning the customary usage and then developing alternatives to test. Children can help with this problem solving.

> **? DECISIONS, DECISIONS . . .**
>
> Consider the tasks to be performed by each of the following staff members: center manager, secretary, cook, and custodian. List the furnishings and supplies that should be made available in a workspace for each of them. Visit a child development center and compare your lists to the items you observe.

MAINTAINING THE FACILITY

The building and grounds of the center represent a huge investment of time and money. Although some depreciation in value is to be expected over time, it is important to protect that investment by planning ahead to maintain and monitor the condition of both the indoor and outdoor environments. Figure 9.3 is a checklist of items to consider in regularly scheduled inspections of the outdoor play area. Planning for maintenance yields both human and financial benefits. For example, adequate and conveniently located storage is a key element of space that is easily kept clean and organized, a feature that contributes to children's sense of mastery and lightens the burden on staff members. Inadequate or inconveniently located storage makes it more likely that staff members and children will leave materials lying around where they can be damaged or lost. Worse, it might tempt adults to save energy by not getting things out in the first place, meaning that money spent on the materials is essentially wasted and children are deprived of opportunities to use the material and to learn how to care for it.

Thinking ahead about how space will be used is another example of how planning contributes to maintenance. The creation of wet and dry zones discussed earlier eliminates problem areas where children might be admonished to "be careful" or be reprimanded if they spill something. Buffer zones between the indoor and outdoor play areas make it possible to clean dirt and sand from shoes before coming inside. Some centers require staff members and children to wear slippers or designated indoor shoes when entering the classroom in order to cut down on tracked-in dirt. Carpeting or other flooring material, as well as paint and counter surfaces, must all be selected with attention to durability and ease of cleaning. Professional carpet cleaning at regular intervals, in addition to daily vacuuming and regular steam cleaning, must be scheduled at least occasionally to keep carpeting sanitary and odor-free.

Adequate protective surfacing under and around equipment

    ____ Yes   ____ No (Install or replace)

Surfacing material free of foreign objects or debris

    ____ Yes   ____ No (Rake; remove debris)

Surfacing materials still in place under heavy use areas (slides, swings)

    ____ Yes   ____ No (Rake and fluff or replace)

Satisfactory drainage, especially in heavy use areas (slides, swings)

    ____ Yes   ____ No (Improve; fill depressions)

All equipment securely anchored

    ____ Yes   ____ No (Correct)

Equipment intact and in good repair (handrails, guardrails, protective barriers, steps, rungs)

    ____ Yes   ____ No (Repair or replace)

Equipment is free of rust, rot, cracks, splinters (especially where in contact with ground)

    ____ Yes   ____ No (Repair or replace)

Paint on equipment is lead-free and in good condition (not peeling, cracking, chipping, chalking)

    ____ Yes   ____ No (Correct)

Equipment is in original condition (no added strings, ropes, swings looped over top rails, etc.)

    ____ Yes   ____ No (Remove or correct)

Equipment is free of sharp points, corners, or edges

    ____ Yes   ____ No (Correct: e.g., remove, cover)

Protective caps or plugs in place and in good repair on all equipment

    ____ Yes   ____ No (Install or replace)

Equipment free of hazardous protrusions, open S-hooks, or protruding bolts

    ____ Yes   ____ No (Correct: remove, cover, replace)

Play area free of trip hazards (exposed footings on play equipment; rocks, roots, etc.)

    ____ Yes   ____ No (Remove, cover)

Equipment free of crush and shearing points on exposed moving parts

    ____ Yes   ____ No (Correct)

Equipment in good condition (no worn parts, loose fastening devices)

    ____ Yes   ____ No (Replace or correct)

Trash receptacle(s) available and emptied regularly

    ____ Yes   ____ No (Provide or replace receptacle; empty trash)

FIGURE 9.3 Playground maintenance checklist.
Source: U.S. Consumer Product Safety Commission (2008). *Public Playground Safety Handbook,* p. 41.

Technology Toolkit

Access one of the classroom planning tools provided at the following websites and experiment with creating your own design by manipulating the digital images.

- http://classroom.4teachers.org/
- http://www.eichild.com (Environments; click on "Environments Resources" and select "Planning Guides.")
- http://www.kaplanco.com/resources/floorPlannerIndex.asp (Kaplan Early Learning Company)
- http://www.lakeshorelearning.com (Lakeshore Learning Store; click on "classroom designer" under "resources.")
- http://www.communityplaythings.com/; click on "free resources," then select "Infant-Toddler Spaces" or "Pre-K Spaces."

Conclusion

Because a carefully planned environment supports growing children and their development and learning, managers and teachers must plan carefully to use indoor and outdoor space well. Four basic needs should guide the planning:

1. An environment to encourage movement
2. An environment to support comfort
3. An environment to foster competence
4. An environment to encourage a sense of control

When planning the use of spatial resources, managers must consider the needs of all children, including those with disabilities, and plan for accessibility, safety, special services, and privacy of older children. Suggestions were offered for organizing space to facilitate supervision and promote positive behavior as well as to meet adults' needs and support their work. All are part of the desired balance within the center's ecosystem.

Questions for Review

1. Given a class of 18 children, ages 3 through 5 years, calculate the required total square feet of indoor space and outdoor space using the NAEYC accreditation standards. How does this compare with licensing requirements in your state?

2. List the four basic environmental needs of young children. Give an example of how a child development center can meet each need.

3. Sketch the floor plan of a child development center you know. Does the arrangement of classrooms, office(s), and other spaces allow for smooth traffic flow? Are there spaces designated for staff members as well as children? Do children of all ages have ready access to outdoor play areas?

4. Using one of the tools listed in the Technology Toolkit, create a floor plan for an infant, toddler, or preschool classroom. Begin by determining where each region and zone will be located. Note traffic flow patterns.

5. Create a list of equipment needed for your room design and add any changes or adaptations that you would make if a child with a disability (e.g., cerebral palsy or blindness) were included in the class.

6. Observe an outdoor play area at a child development center in your community. List the natural elements and movable equipment present. What additions would you suggest?

Professional Portfolio

1. Observe and record the way children use one or more of the existing interest centers in a program where you work or where you have been assigned as a practicum student. With permission of your supervising teacher, make any changes necessary to increase the level of the children's participation and engagement. Be sure to take "before" and "after" photographs. Observe and record the children's behavior for several days after the changes are made. Write a description of what you did, including the rationale for your changes, and what happened afterward. Evaluate the effectiveness of your changes.

2. Draw a floor plan for a staff resource center in a child development program. List the furnishings and other items (including specific books, journals, video recordings, etc.) you would include and explain your rationale. If you have access and proficiency, use a software program such as AutoCad to create your design. Calculate the cost of creating such a center and list possible suggestions for obtaining the necessary funds.

Resources for Further Study

PRINT

Curtis, D., & Carter, M. (2003). *Designs for living and learning: Transforming early childhood environments*. St. Paul, MN: Redleaf Press.

Frost, J. L. (2004). *Playground checklist*. In J. L. Frost et al. (Eds.), *The developmental benefits of playgrounds*. Olney, MD: Association for Childhood Education International, pp. 227–231.

Isbell, R., & Exelby, B. (2001). *Early learning environments that work.* Beltsville, MD: Gryphon House.

Moyer, J. (Ed.). (1995). *Selecting educational equipment and materials for school and home.* Wheaton, MD: Association for Childhood Education International.

Websites

AGRICULTURE AND NATURAL RESOURCES, UNIVERSITY OF CALIFORNIA

www.ucanr.edu

Website of the University of California, Division of Agriculture and Natural Resources; includes link to section titled "Safe and Poisonous Garden Plants," with extensive lists of both toxic and safe plants by common and scientific name.

INFANT AND TODDLER SPACES: DESIGN FOR A QUALITY CLASSROOM

http://www.communityplaythings.com/resources/articles/RoomPlanning/Spaces/InfantToddlerSpaces.pdf

A planning guide providing principles and step-by-step directions for designing a classroom layout.

NATURAL LEARNING INITIATIVE

http://www.naturalearning.org/

Housed in the College of Design, North Carolina State University, the purpose of the Natural Learning Initiative is "to promote the importance of the natural environment in the daily experience of all children." Resources available on the website include a searchable database for identifying plants that will thrive in each region of the United States, guidelines for designing play environments that integrate manufactured play equipment with the living landscape, and directions for activities with children such as constructing a vine teepee or harvesting rainwater.

PLANET EARTH PLAYSCAPES

http://www.planetearthplayscapes.com

Website for Rusty Keeler, a designer and consultant who promotes creation of beautiful, meaningful outdoor environments for young children. Includes images depicting examples of Keeler's work on outdoor play areas for infants, toddlers, and preschool children in the United States and China; also provides a link to The Natural Play Environment Group, an international online discussion group of designers, child-care professionals, and others.

PreK SPACES: DESIGN FOR A QUALITY CLASSROOM

http://www.communityplaythings.com/resources/articles/RoomPlanning/Spaces/SpacesBooklet.pdf

Step-by-step guides to planning and equipping classrooms, created by Community Playthings in cooperation with California's WestEd Program for Infant Toddler Caregivers and other national experts. Other resources include sample room plans with itemized equipment lists and detailed guides for creating six interest areas (blocks, dramatic play, manipulative, reading/listening, science/sensory, and art). Available at no charge in hard copy or PDF format.

10

CHAPTER

Managing Health and Safety Issues

LEARNING OUTCOMES

After studying this chapter you should be able to

- Describe the policies and practices that child-care centers should have in place to protect and promote children's health.
- Give examples of risk management strategies for child-care centers.
- Discuss the health and safety aspects of meeting children's physiological needs.
- Explain how child development centers help meet children's mental health needs.
- Describe procedures to follow in caring for sick children.
- State the signs of child abuse and neglect, procedures for reporting, and ways to prevent its occurrence in the center.

Tanya kept thinking about a conversation she had recently while enrolling a new infant at the center. Akinobu's parents were worried about all the immunizations he would need within the next few months because they had heard rumors about other babies becoming very sick or even worse after getting their shots. The parents agreed to comply with the center's requirements because quitting their jobs was not an option and they needed child care. Still, Tanya realized her assurances did little to allay their concerns. She also recalled other recent conversations about health issues: One parent wondered why his child was sent home because of diarrhea when "he had caught it at the center in the first place." Another parent wondered why the center took the children outdoors on days that she considered too cold. When Tanya discussed these concerns with her supervisor, Jeralyn suggested that Tanya work on revising Rainbow Center's parent handbook, incorporating complete explanations of the reasons for their health policies and practices. She helped Tanya compile a list of resources she could draw on, and reminded her to ask the public health nurse, who served as the center's health consultant, for input.

Above all else, parents and society trust you to keep the children safe and healthy while they are in your care. It is a trust that you and your staff members must assume with a deep sense of responsibility. Fulfilling that trust will require careful planning, collaboration with families and health professionals, and the cooperation of everyone on staff.

PLANNING FOR A HEALTHY ENVIRONMENT

As we emphasized in previous chapters, plans for a child-care facility's structure, decor, layout, equipment, finishes, and furnishings must all begin with attention to the children's safety and include provisions for maintenance and upkeep. You have seen that plans for staffing must also begin with safety and health in mind as you establish the number of staff members you will need to supervise children and the skills you will expect them to have. Research suggests that the dispositions and habits acquired in high-quality early education programs lead to lifelong health benefits for children (see, for example, Reynolds et al., 2007). In this chapter we examine more closely the strategies you will need to promote children's physical and mental health, keep your center a safe and healthy place, and deal with accidents or illness when they occur.

POLICIES AND PRACTICES

A society's health-care system is part of the human-built environment. As a center manager, you contribute to the well-being of the families you serve, as well as to the survival of the program when you plan ahead and think through all of the ways in which your facility can protect the children from harm and keep them healthy. The health and safety of children are significant aspects of the accreditation criteria established by the National Association for the Education of Young Children (2007a). A careful reading of this chapter and a familiarity with the national guidelines will prepare you to meet the health and safety standards of the accreditation process.

Licensing Regulations

Licensing regulations are designed to ensure that child development facilities maintain children's health, prevent exposure to unhealthful conditions, and protect children from harm. They establish minimum standards for record keeping and reporting in cooperation with public health officials. The American Public Health Association and American Academy of Pediatrics have developed national health and safety guidelines for child-care programs (American Public Health Association, American Academy of Pediatrics, & National Resource Center for Health and Safety in Child Care and Early Education, 2011). These guidelines are published in print form as well as online at the website for the National Resource Center for Health and Safety in Child Care and Early Education, http://nrckids.org. The digital version is updated regularly as new information becomes available. Specific requirements vary from state to state, so it is imperative that you refer to the regulations for your own state. You can find your state's current regulations under "resources" at the website just mentioned. Examples of licensing requirements include the following:

1. Certification that all staff members are free of tuberculosis
2. Permission from parents for the center to seek emergency medical care for their child
3. Requirements for immunizations, medical checkups, and a physician's statement of good health for each child
4. Prior written permission from each parent to give prescription medication to a child
5. A policy requiring that a doctor's prescription for a child's special diet be on file
6. A plan for health-care services provided by the center
7. Individual records on children's health indicators

8. A plan for reporting child abuse, protections from abuse occurring within the center, and compliance with regulations prohibiting the hiring of staff members with records of child abuse

9. A plan for medical and safety emergencies

10. A plan for training staff members and communicating with parents on health and safety matters

Medical Advice and Referral

When planning the center's health-care services, the manager works closely with health professionals. The American Academy of Pediatrics recommends that every child-care facility have access to a child-care health consultant, a recommendation reflected in NAEYC accreditation criteria (National Association for the Education of Young Children, 2007a, p. 40). This medical professional, with specialized knowledge of pediatrics and developmentally appropriate practices for child-care settings, can help:

- Review and develop your policies and practices regarding health, safety, and nutrition practices
- Provide information on nutrition, feeding, and communicable diseases
- Train staff members
- Develop and implement plans to care for children with special health needs
- Create connections with community resources such as health screening or mental health programs

Staff members must be aware of the closest source of emergency medical treatment and the procedures for calling for help. Some centers establish contacts with the nearest hospital in anticipation of emergencies. In this way, they can be sure that the records they keep on file meet the hospital's requirements should a child require emergency treatment when a parent cannot be reached. Some hospitals require specific wording on permission forms, for example, or they might expect the center to provide health insurance information for the injured child. A manager who keeps these links open can serve the children better. Phone numbers for emergency medical service should be posted at each phone.

A Medical Home for Every Child

The American Academy of Pediatrics asserts that every child should have a medical home, a term that refers not to a place, but to a concept or an approach to providing health-care services that are "accessible, continuous, comprehensive, family centered, coordinated, compassionate, and culturally effective" (American Academy of Pediatrics, 2002a). For information about efforts to achieve this goal in your state, visit the website of the National Center of Medical Home Initiatives, a project of the American Academy of Pediatrics, at medicalhomeinfo.org. Although this is a worthy goal, the sad fact is that 1 in 10 children in the United States from birth to age 18 were uninsured in 2010. For children of color, the percentage of uninsured was much higher: 1 in 6 Hispanic and 1 in 9 Black children were without health insurance (Children's Defense Fund, 2012, p. 21). The picture is changing, however. Since Congress and President Obama reauthorized the Children's Health Insurance Program in 2009, at least 13 states have expanded their coverage to include more low-income families. Even in the face of declining tax revenues due to the economic downturn, states are increasing income eligibility levels, simplifying enrollment procedures, and extending coverage to legal immigrants and pregnant women (U.S. Department of Health and Human Services, 2011).

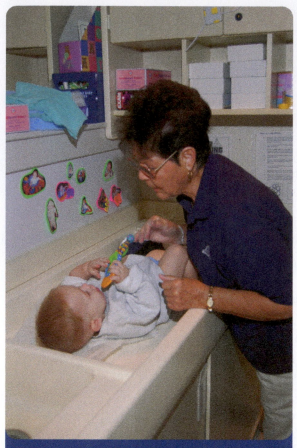

Assigning a primary caregiver to each child and limiting the number of children each primary caregiver is responsible for helps reduce risk of transmitting infection.

Child-care providers are in a unique position to partner with families, medical professionals, and community agencies to work toward the goal of a medical home for every child. In the process of obtaining required records of physical examination and immunization upon each child's enrollment, providers quickly learn whether families have access to health care. They can help families who do not by providing information and referrals to community resources. As teachers come to know a particular child over time, they become sensitized to changes in appearance or behavior that signal illness or potential problems. Because of their knowledge of child development and direct experience with many children, child-care providers are often able to notice cues that parents might miss. They can bring these to the parents' attention and suggest a medical evaluation. For example, teachers might be the first to notice subtle signs of unexplained hyperactivity or lethargy, either of which can be a symptom of elevated blood lead levels, a condition estimated to affect 535,000 U.S. children ages 1 to 5 years (Centers for Disease Control and Prevention, 2013). Observant, sensitive caregivers who keep careful records become valuable components of the child's medical home, cooperating with parents and medical professionals to safeguard health.

Primary Caregiver

It is clear from the preceding discussion that one reason child-care providers can play this important role in the child's medical home is because they get to know the child over time. Thus, consistency of care is an essential component of any health plan. This consistency of care is important for all young children, but doubly so for infants and toddlers, who are unable to tell you when they do not feel well. Assigning a primary caregiver responsibility for no more than four infants or toddlers provides a real opportunity for that caregiver to know those children well. This approach not only helps meet the mental health needs associated with emotional attachment, but also gives the caregiver plenty of opportunity to become familiar with the way a particular child looks and acts when she or he is healthy. Then any change in activity level or appearance can be investigated as a possible sign of illness. Another advantage to assigning primary caregivers is that the number of children any one caregiver contacts is reduced, thereby limiting the potential of spreading contagious diseases to all of the other children in the center.

Confidentiality

You and your staff members must use the families' personal information as is expected of any professional—in confidence and only for the benefit of the parent or child. You should not permit staff members to gossip about any confidential information. Right-to-privacy laws should be kept in mind as you make any records. Expect that the parents will eventually read your notes and records and refrain from writing down anything that you would not want them to see. Direct, dated observational notes are acceptable. These notes should remain without interpretation unless you are an expert.

Any information about the child should be available to the parents, especially if the parents ask.

During each family's orientation, ask that any family happening, event, or crisis that could cause a change in the child's behavior be reported to the teacher. It can be a happy occurrence, such as a visit from grandparents, or a sad situation, such as a divorce or death in the family. Whoever receives the information must relay it to the appropriate teachers or caregivers to help them determine the best way to interact with the child. All such information received from the child's parents must remain confidential.

Employees' Health

The **Patient Protection and Affordable Care Act** of 2010 affects child-care programs and their employees. Child-care workers, like most individuals, are required to maintain minimum health insurance coverage or pay a penalty. The law provides for exchanges, operated by individual states or the federal government, to help individuals compare coverage plans and simplify enrollment. It also establishes graduated levels of refundable tax credits based on family income and cost of coverage. Requirements for offering affordable coverage apply to businesses with more than 50 employees; small businesses with fewer than 25 employees will be eligible to receive up to 50 percent of the premium cost. Requirements pertaining to individuals, employers, and insurance providers are scheduled to be phased in over a period of years. Due to logistical challenges, enforcement of some requirements has been postponed. To be sure that you have the most up-to-date information about your responsibilities as an individual and as an employer, check the website www.healthcare.gov.

In addition to having an up-to-date tuberculosis test on file, each employee should otherwise be in good health and have the physical strength to do the necessary lifting and other required physical activities. A model health assessment form for child-care staff members has been developed by the American Academy of Pediatrics and American Public Health Association; it can be accessed online (as Appendix F) at http://nrckids.org/. It is desirable to provide paid sick leave to reduce the chance that an ill staff member who cannot afford to miss a day's pay will expose others.

Providing information about health and wellness and encouraging healthy lifestyle choices should be part of the center's professional development program for staff members. Adults who take care of themselves are less susceptible to stress or depression and better able to care for others. Those who are overweight and sedentary make poor role models and will be unlikely to promote the vigorous physical activity that children need each day. In one community, an innovative resource and referral agency partnered with the local health department to obtain a grant that funded gym memberships and nutrition counseling for child-care staff. Participants not only lost weight and improved their overall health, they carried their new habits into their classrooms, planning healthier snacks and more active play opportunities (Nicholson, 2009).

Implementing Policies

The center's health consultant makes recommendations regarding practices and policies for ensuring health promotion and preventing infection and injury. Once policies and procedures are established, the manager must organize a system to ensure that they are implemented consistently. A number of routine health forms may be developed and signed by the parents when a child is enrolled. Often, state licensing regulations mandate the completion of specific forms (e.g., permission to obtain emergency medical care or to administer medication to children). You will also need a system to ensure that children have the required immunizations for their age at the time of enrollment and that their immunizations are kept up to date in accordance

Providing child-high sinks and teaching children to wash hands frequently, especially after toileting and before meals, is part of a developmentally appropriate curriculum.

with the recommendations of the American Academy of Pediatrics (nrckids.org, Appendix G at the website). Forms to help you monitor this may be provided by your state or local health department as part of its monitoring system.

In addition to securing the necessary documents, meeting ongoing health needs requires routine application of standard (or universal) precautions outlined by the Centers for Disease Control and Prevention. All bodily fluids (such as blood, vomit, urine, and feces) should be thoroughly cleaned up with soap and water, and then the surface should be treated with a **disinfectant**, registered with the Environmental Protection Agency (EPA); the disinfectant must be applied according to directions. Child development centers can further reduce the transmission of germs by using the same disinfectant to sanitize faucets, door handles, and table surfaces frequently.

Toys that have been mouthed by children and thereby contaminated with saliva must be cleaned with soap and water and treated with a **sanitizer** registered with the EPA; the sanitizer must be applied according to directions. This precaution is of special concern in infant and toddler groups where mouthing is an expected behavior. One center has colorful plastic buckets suspended out of children's reach where a staff member can quickly put a toy that has been mouthed until it is put through the dishwasher and then sanitized. Such procedures reduce the spread of germs and increase the staff members' awareness of health conditions.

Probably the greatest line of defense against germs is proper handwashing (by children and adults) upon entering the classroom; after using the toilet; before eating or preparing food; and after coughing, sneezing, or using a tissue. Staff members should also wash their hands after helping children with diapering, toileting, or nose blowing. Proper handwashing means using soap and warm running water, lathering for at least 10 seconds, rinsing thoroughly, and drying with a disposable towel. This **video** explains why handwashing is required before meals and after toileting, messy play, or messy outdoor activity, and provides suggestions for teachers to build handwashing into the children's day without taking away from play time unnecessarily.

Monitoring Health and Safety Conditions

Monitoring and controlling for quality is a vital aspect of managing health and safety issues. Ongoing vigilance is necessary to ensure that all policies and procedures are being implemented as planned and to determine when those policies and procedures should be changed. To assess the health and safety performance of your center, make a list such as the one shown in Figure 10.1 and review it at least once a month. That way you can catch small problems before they turn into large ones. If you notice a pattern of problems in the same areas from month to month, you can bring it up at a staff meeting or perhaps enlist the assistance of your health consultant to achieve a more long-lasting correction.

✓	Check Each Item Observed	Comments or Corrections Needed
	Written health and safety policies reviewed with all staff upon hiring and at least annually thereafter	
	Health and safety policies included in handbook for families; reviewed before enrollment	
	Emergency procedures for fire, tornado, and accident or injury posted; parents informed	
	Emergency telephone numbers posted (fire, police, ambulance, poison control, child abuse, director)	
	Permission to seek emergency medical treatment on file for each child; current contact information	
	Medication administered only with written permission of parents; physician's instructions; documented	
	Written health and emergency plans in place for each child with disability or chronic illness	
	Compliance with fire regulations maintained (date inspected _____; corrections made)	
	Smoke detectors and fire extinguishers in place and maintained	
	Fire drills conducted monthly; staff trained in evacuation plans for tornado; chemical spill; other	
	Compliance with sanitation regulations maintained (date inspected _____; corrections made)	
	No indoor hazards (e.g., water temperature at outlets accessible to children 120° or less; electrical outlets covered)	
	Cleaning supplies, medications, staff belongings, other hazardous materials stored away from children	
	Cribs meet safety standards (slats at least $2^3/_8$ inches apart; fitted mattress; no protruding corner posts)	
	No choking hazards (e.g., toys less than 1 inch diameter; popcorn, peanuts, hotdogs, whole grapes)	
	Separate sinks for food preparation, handwashing, and other activities; sanitized regularly	
	Handwashing procedures posted; followed by staff and children before handling food, after contamination	
	Sanitation solution proper strength, mixed daily; used regularly on tables, counters, toys, etc.	
	Outdoor play area free of hazards: sharp edges, protrusions more than 1 inch, entrapment (openings smaller than $3^1/_2$ inches or larger than 9 inches)	
	Railings in place to prevent falls from climbing equipment; adequate cushioning in fall zone	

FIGURE 10.1 Monitoring health and safety conditions.

? DECISIONS, DECISIONS . . .

Using an Ethical Framework

Your local health department is offering the H1N1 flu vaccine to high-risk groups. Pregnant women, people who live with or care for infants younger than 6 months of age, and children 6 months and older are identified as high-risk. One of the infant teachers in your center has told her coteachers that she will not get the vaccine because she doesn't believe it is safe. You have heard the same concern from a few parents of toddlers and preschoolers. Using the NAEYC code, try to determine what core values are involved. What ideals and principles regarding responsibilities to children, families, and employees apply? What course of action seems most right?

RISK MANAGEMENT

When you accept responsibility for other people's children, you inevitably incur a certain degree of **risk** or exposure to the possibility of damage or loss. **Risk management** is the continuing process of identifying, analyzing, and evaluating that potential exposure and taking steps to reduce the effects. Accidents happen and risk cannot be eliminated; it can be reduced by adhering to good health and safety practices. Liability insurance does not protect the children's health and safety—only staff members following sound procedures can do that. Insurance simply protects the center's owners and operators from financial devastation. Most allegations of negligence come as a result of problems in the health and safety arena.

The child development center should have a system to ensure that only authorized individuals are allowed to enter. This can be accomplished through human vigilance or through the use of technology. Watch this **video** for examples of the safeguards used by one center. Once children are in the center, perhaps the most important factor in protecting their safety is adequate supervision. Children must be supervised at all times. Adult–child ratios are set by licensing authorities to ensure the children's safety. The level of supervision required depends on the children's ages. Infants and toddlers require close supervision; older children may do some things alone, although adults must still be completely aware of where they are and what they are doing.

Safe Arrival and Departure

Parents are usually responsible for the children as they are transported to and from the center. You can help protect the children by encouraging families to use seat belts and child restraint devices whenever they transport their children. The next step is to organize a safe procedure for parking. Children should not have to walk alone in parking lots. They are so short in stature that drivers may not see them. If there is no room to park

A sturdy fence with a locked gate protects children from traffic as well as intrusion by unauthorized individuals.

immediately adjacent to a safe sidewalk, establish a one-way traffic circle approaching the building's entrance in a counterclockwise direction so that the car's passenger side is closest to the door.

Your records must contain the names of any people to whom the center is authorized to release a child, and staff members should require photo identification if they do not know an individual on sight. Young children cannot be expected to know who is or is not allowed to pick them up, especially if the person is a familiar and now estranged parent or grandparent. Staff members should refuse to release a child without written authorization, and families must be informed of this policy upon enrollment. It is better to cope with the momentary anger of the person you turn away than to risk releasing a child to the wrong person.

> **? DECISIONS, DECISIONS . . .**
>
> One afternoon at your center, a woman you have never seen comes in, asking to pick up her niece. She shows you her driver's license, which indicates that she has the same last name as the 1-year-old girl. However, her name does not appear on the list of people authorized to pick up the child. What should you do?

Transporting Children

Some centers transport children to and from school each day. Others transport children only occasionally, on field trips, for example. In every case, transporting children requires special preparations and precautions, such as the following:

- Vehicles must be in safe operating condition and properly insured.
- Drivers must be well qualified and hold the license required for the type of vehicle used.
- There should never be more passengers (adults or children) than the vehicle is designed and equipped to hold.
- A sufficient number of adult assistants must be present to ensure that the children are under control and the driver can concentrate on driving.
- The driver as well as all passengers (children and/or adults) must use an approved restraint device that is properly installed and used in accordance with manufacturer's specifications. For young children, up to and including most 4-year-olds, this means a special car seat when riding in a private vehicle. The U.S. Department of Transportation's National Highway Traffic Safety Administration provides specific guidelines for the use of restraint devices; these guidelines are available online at http://www.nhtsa.gov/Safety/CPS.
- The driver should be provided with a list of the children names as well as emergency information for each child.

When children are taken home, drivers must be certain that they are received by authorized people and not left on a corner or allowed to walk unaccompanied into an empty house or other potentially unsafe situation. Careful accounting procedures are necessary to ensure that no child is left in an unattended vehicle. This is especially crucial when transporting infants or children with disabilities because they may not be able to make their presence known. More than one tragic news story has reported the death of a child left all day in a parked vehicle in stifling heat.

The same type of accounting is used to ensure that no child is left behind on field trips. When parent volunteers drive, make sure that each small group stays with the same car and driver going and returning. Licensing regulations (and common sense!) require that centers secure a parental release before taking children on supervised field trips. Before each trip, parents must be informed specifically when and where the children are going.

Emergency Procedures

Risk management is not limited to accident prevention—it also includes being prepared to deal with emergencies when they occur. A legible, up-to-date list with telephone numbers for fire, police, ambulance, poison control, licensing representative, and child abuse authority should be prominently posted near each telephone. Also include your home or cell telephone number because emergencies may occur in your absence. It is also a good idea to display the center's name, address, and telephone number prominently on the list because the stress of an emergency could cause even well-prepared staff members to experience a momentary memory block and thereby delay the arrival of help. In any emergency, it is useful to know where the electricity breakers, water valve, and gas valve are located so these can be turned off. Keep a flashlight handy to use in case the electricity goes off, and test it regularly to be sure the batteries work.

FIRE, TORNADO, OR OTHER DISASTERS   Smoke alarms should be tested regularly and located in each room and the exit corridor. They provide an early warning in case of fire. Post a fire emergency plan in each classroom showing the quickest route from the classroom to a designated meeting area outdoors. The plan should also indicate which staff member is responsible for certain duties: leading the children out, checking to make sure no child is left behind, bringing attendance records to the meeting place. Once the plan is created, it must be practiced. Frequent drills help ensure that each staff member and child knows what to do and can remain calm.

If a fire occurs, the children must be removed from the building immediately. Their safety is your number one priority. Adults must remain calm because the children's lives are depending on them. The children should be counted several times by different people and checked against attendance records to be sure no one is missing. Reporting the fire is second in importance. Each adult in the center should be aware of the location of the nearest fire alarm box.

REPORTING A SERIOUS ACCIDENT OR FIRE   Whenever a child is injured, an accident report must be completed immediately. It should indicate the time, place, and people present. In addition to the manager's office, the center's insurance company and the licensing agency require the reports. Fires resulting in the loss of life or property must be reported immediately to the appropriate state official—usually the fire marshal. Check your state's licensing regulations for the fire reporting procedures.

?   ## DECISIONS, DECISIONS . . .

You have been told that monthly fire drills are recommended to ensure that all staff members and children become thoroughly familiar with the routine. Four weeks have passed since your last drill and you want to have another, but it has been cold and snowing. What should you do and why?

A plan similar to the fire evacuation should be in place in case of a tornado or severe weather warning. You can get advice for your specific situation from local civil defense authorities. Generally, the rule is to go to a basement and get near inside walls, such as halls, and away from windows. Remember that if a tornado or other weather emergency occurs, the children's parents are likely miles away. They have to seek shelter where they are and depend on the center staff members to give their child the best possible protection. Parents should be aware of the emergency plans so that they know where to expect to find the children and teachers. Provide this information to the parents during their orientation.

ACCIDENT OR INJURY   Bumps and scrapes are an inevitable part of childhood, and their occurrence multiplies in settings where a large number of children spend their days. A special form for reporting to parents any minor blows and abrasions should be devised. The report, dated and signed, should include the day and time the mishap occurred. Keep a copy for your file. At an office supply outlet, you can purchase a ledger containing perforated, self-carbon forms sometimes used to record telephone messages. The teacher tears off the top sheet (about a quarter page in size) and sends it home; the second carbon sheet remains in the ledger.

Making written reports and keeping copies are essential procedures. Without them, staff members find it difficult to recall accurately the particulars of a minor incident after a long, busy day. Family members who are notified at pickup time that their child had some mishap may become upset, but their reaction is likely to be far stronger should they encounter an unexplained bruise or scrape when bathing their child later that night.

MEDICAL EMERGENCIES   Some injuries require more than simply writing a note to the family. Part of your procedure for handling more serious accidents or injuries begins at enrollment, when you secure the parents' permission to obtain medical treatment in the event of an emergency. State licensing regulations often prescribe specific forms for obtaining this permission as well as other emergency information. Figure 10.2 is an example of such a form. Handling emergencies involving children with disabilities requires more detailed information. The American Academy of Pediatrics has developed a sample form, which can be downloaded at http://www.aap.org/advocacy/ blankform.pdf. Obtaining the information is important, but it is just as crucial for teachers to know what is on the emergency forms, to know where they are kept, and to have access to them at all times.

BASIC FIRST AID TRAINING   All staff members should know how to treat minor injuries and to recognize when outside help is needed. This training is generally available from public health services or the American Red Cross.

CARDIOPULMONARY RESUSCITATION   It is essential to have at least one individual in the center at all times who can administer cardiopulmonary resuscitation (CPR). The most practical way to meet this standard is to give staff members the initial training and refresher classes in CPR and first aid as a matter of routine. Training for CPR is obtained from the American Heart Association and the American Red Cross.

KEEPING FOOD SAFE IN AN EMERGENCY   Flood, fire, national disaster, or the loss of power from high winds, snow, or ice could jeopardize the safety of food. If your center is in a location that could be affected by flood, make sure food is stored on shelves that will be safely out of the way of contaminated water. In the event of a power outage, keeping the refrigerator and freezer doors closed will keep food safely cold for about 4 hours; a

Dear Parent or Guardian:

This form is provided for you to leave with those responsible for your child in your absence. If your child needs emergency medical treatment during your absence, the completed form will be presented to the attending physician. Individual hospitals and medical personnel may require additional authorization. Please return this form to Rainbow Child Development Center. Report any changes to the center office.

Child's name _____ Birth date _____

Address _____ 1st date of attendance _____

Child lives with: ___one parent ___both parents ___other   Child's language _____

Parent/Guardian (1)

Name _____ School/employer _____

Language _____ Start and end hours _____

Home phone _____ Work phone _____

Parent/Guardian (2)

Name _____ School/employer _____

Language _____ Start and end hours _____

Phone: Home _____ Cell _____ Work _____

Other person(s) to whom child may be released in absence of parent/guardian

_____

(Note: parent may not be denied permission unless legal custody papers are on file)
Person(s) to contact in emergency if parent/guardian cannot be reached

Name _____ Phone _____

Name _____ Phone _____

List any allergies to food, insects, medication, or other

_____

Describe any special procedures required to care for child

_____

Describe any disability or condition that would limit child's participation in program activities

_____

Child's physician _____

Address _____ Telephone _____

List any medications the child is now taking

Date of most recent physical exam _____ Last tetanus shot _____ Blood type _____

Insurance/Medicaid name and number _____

AUTHORIZATION

I hereby authorize the treatment of my minor child _____ in the event of an emergency occurring in my absence. This authorization extends to any hospital and both physician and nursing personnel within the hospital. I authorize the hospital medical authorities and physicians to perform those medical procedures deemed necessary for my minor child. If I cannot be reached in case of an emergency, please allow [NAME OF CENTER] to act in my behalf.

_____   _____
Signature of Parent or Legal Guardian   Date

_____   _____
Witness   Date

FIGURE 10.2 Emergency medical treatment consent form.

full freezer will hold the temperature for approximately 48 hours (24 hours if it is half full). If you know the power will be out longer than that, have a plan to obtain dry or block ice: 50 pounds of dry ice for an 18-cubic-foot full freezer for 2 days. Keep an emergency supply of food that doesn't require refrigeration and can be eaten cold: for example, shelf-stable dry food, boxed or canned milk, water, canned goods, and ready-to-use baby formula for infants. Remember to use these items and replace them from time to time. Be sure to keep a handheld can opener for an emergency.

MEETING CHILDREN'S PHYSIOLOGICAL NEEDS

It is the center's responsibility to ensure that each child's basic physiological needs regarding nutrition, digestion, elimination, respiration, and circulation are met daily. All of these systems are interrelated and require an equilibrium or balance. For example, the body needs adequate and appropriate food to be well nourished. The timing, amount, and type of food; intake of fresh water or other beverages; and exercise all influence digestion and elimination. Exercise, fresh air, and rest are related to respiration and circulation.

Consistent routines for eating, resting, eliminating, and exercising help children develop habits that contribute to their overall physiological health and well-being. Research has demonstrated a positive correlation between healthy lifestyles in early childhood and higher quality of life in adolescence (Chen, Sekine, Hamanishi, Yamagami, & Kagamimori, 2005). Teachers quickly become aware of the individual differences in the children's physiological functioning and set the stage so that the children can take care of their own needs independently as soon as they are ready.

In addition to meeting children's needs, staff members should provide parents with the details of how that was accomplished throughout the day via a written record that indicates feeding times, bowel movement(s), and naps. This is especially helpful with infants and young toddlers, for whom the daily note also might report special milestones the child has reached (e.g., stood alone, spoke a new word, walked 10 feet). In some states, these and other written records are required by licensing regulations.

Activity and Rest

As discussed in the previous chapter, equipment, both indoors and outdoors, must be developmentally appropriate and challenging enough to encourage children to take healthy risks; the children should not be permitted to use inappropriate equipment in unsafe ways. If you find yourself constantly reminding the 4-year-olds to "go down the slide on your bottom," it could be that they are bored with the available toddler-size climber and are simply trying to create a more interesting challenge for themselves.

Allow plenty of time for outdoor play every day so that the children can breathe fresh air and exercise their lungs and muscles. Typically, programs remind the families to provide appropriate clothing for such play and set reasonable

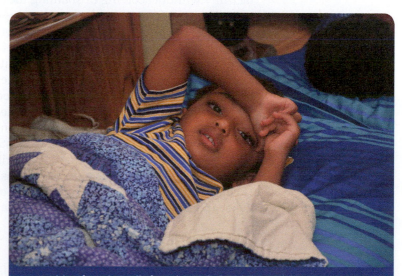

A cot with a favorite quilt from home helps children feel secure and makes nap time more pleasant for them and their teachers.

guidelines (e.g., wind-chill factor, not staff preference) for determining when to stay inside. A nutritious snack replenishes energy needs after a busy hour or two of play. To help children rest and recuperate after a period of active play, teachers might plan a restful activity such as story time. A high-quality program balances active, less active, and quiet play. Energy levels differ among children or even within a single child from day to day, however, so teachers' expectations should be flexible, allowing one child to engage in a restful activity, such as listening to CDs, while others enjoy more vigorous play. With such a plan, the children can choose the activity most suited to their current need.

In a half-day program, the need for rest is usually met by having a quiet snack, story time, or singing time. Making children lie down on mats is not recommended because the time spent getting them to comply is often less than restful. However, in a full-day program, a planned resting period is needed, and most children will sleep during this time. Many full-day children arrive early and are ready for a nap after lunch. To be refreshed and restored for another round of play and interaction, they need an hour or so of sleep about midday. Some centers put children who actually sleep in a supervised room apart from those children who only rest quietly. This practice applies particularly when older children are in attendance. Although all children need a quiet period to rest and recuperate from a busy morning, the amount of actual sleep required varies with the individual and often depends on how much sleep the child gets at home. For young children up to age 5, nap and nighttime sleep are both necessary. Children who nap well are usually less cranky and sleep better at night.

Usually, nap time follows immediately after lunch and toileting. Keeping a low-key atmosphere in a darkened room helps the children sense that quiet behavior is expected. By receiving quiet personal attention, each child is encouraged to get ready for a nap without dawdling. Teaching children to breathe deeply with their eyes closed and to think about what they will do after resting is usually all that is needed to get them to relax and fall asleep. Some caregivers sing a personalized song to the child as soon as she or he arrives on the cot—a positive reward for getting ready quickly. In other centers, caregivers gently rub the children's backs or softly stroke their heads to help them relax. Nap time should never become a battle of wills; rather, it should be a pleasant respite for children and staff members alike. If problems occur, the manager should make suggestions to help the situation. Bedwetting accidents should be handled tactfully without scolding or shaming the child.

The nap room must be equipped with a washable cot or crib and appropriate sheets and blankets for the exclusive use of each child. Sheets should be laundered each week or whenever they become wet or soiled. The opening between crib railings must be narrow enough to prevent entrapment of babies' heads, and they should be high enough that children cannot climb over them. To reduce the risk of sudden infant death syndrome (SIDS), infants should always be put to sleep on their backs, on a firm mattress that fits snugly against all sides of the crib.

Managers must give special attention to providing adequate supervision for napping children. There should be sufficient staff on duty to evacuate the sleeping children safely in case of a fire or tornado. All cribs and cots and other furnishings must be placed so that the fire exits are free. Rooms must be equipped with smoke detectors. At least one crib should be small and sturdy enough to be pushed out a door in case of an evacuation. Several sleeping infants can be easily moved this way.

Diapering Infants

When child development centers enroll infants, diapering procedures must be carefully planned and executed to prevent the spread of contamination by feces. The type of diapers to use in child development centers has come into question. Some argue that disposable diapers are costly and that depositing untreated feces in landfills is problematic. National health and safety guidelines state that either disposable diapers with an absorbent filling or cloth diapers with a waterproof covering are acceptable—if the cloth diaper and waterproof covering are removed together and neither part is used again before being sanitized. In other words, caregivers should not put the same pair of plastic pants back on the child after they change the diaper underneath (American Academy of Pediatrics, American Public Health Association, National Resource Center for Health and Safety in Child Care and Early Education, 2011, Standard 3.2.1.1). Therefore, center managers can take factors, such as cost or environmental concerns, into consideration when they decide between these two alternatives.

Always use a diapering table, not the carpet or any other surface, for changing babies. The table surface must be cleaned and disinfected after each use, whether or not a disposable paper cover was used. After changing the diaper, the caregiver's hands as well as the child's must be washed thoroughly and a paper towel used to turn the faucet off to avoid recontamination. Better yet, install a faucet that is motion activated or operated by a foot pedal. Soiled diapers must be placed in a sealed container (for laundry pickup or for disposal) immediately. Disposable gloves are not a substitute for handwashing and, if improperly used, may actually be a source of contamination. Some adults and children suffer serious allergic reactions to latex, a material often used in disposable gloves.

Ensure that staff members realize how important it is for primary caregivers to diaper their own children and to talk to the infants and respond to communication cues from the babies while they are doing so. This eye-to-eye contact provides an opportunity for the infant to develop a trust in the caregivers. It helps babies feel important to those caring for them and to practice communicating with others. Children are not machines, and assembly-line techniques, such as having one person diaper all the children, may seem efficient on the surface, but they are actually counterproductive. How much more efficient it is to meet a child's needs for intimacy, attachment, language stimulation, and cleanliness—all through the simple act of diapering. How inefficient it is to have to close a center because one child's shigella diarrhea has been spread to everyone, staff and children alike.

Toilet Training

The manager and staff members must confer with the parents of toddlers to reach agreement on when the toddlers are ready to be toilet trained and the techniques to be used. This coordination with the parents is absolutely essential so that the children face similar expectations and routines at home and at school. Even the words to be used for urinating and defecating have to be discussed.

Most professionals feel that if toilet training is started only after the muscle and nervous systems are sufficiently mature, a child can become responsible for independent toileting faster and more easily. Parents may push for toilet training before you feel it is developmentally appropriate. They may believe that it is an adult's responsibility to

Child-size bathroom fixtures and an easy-to-operate soap dispenser promote independence. In this center, diapers are conveniently stored on nearby shelves, while hooks higher on the wall hold bags with items to be sent home with children.

anticipate a child's need to urinate or defecate and to get the child on a potty chair in time. They may not realize that what is possible when caring for one child whom you have known since birth is more difficult when caring for four (or more) children with whom you are less familiar. You must be sensitive to parents' concerns as you try to reach a consensus about what is appropriate for their child.

Helping children accept and adjust to their changing bodies is a basic developmental task that continues from birth through life. Children are very interested in learning about their bodies and how to take care of themselves. Good health habits relating to urinating, defecating, washing hands, and eating must be established during the early years. During the course of teaching these routines, questions about the genitalia may arise. These questions should be accepted and answered at the child's level of understanding. No shame should be attached to a child's questions or explorations. Self-manipulation of genitalia is a common behavior among young children. It is also harmless; thus, the child should not be admonished for doing it. At times, there may be chapping or a rash in the genital area that needs a simple cleaning and baby lotion to heal. Staff members might require help understanding these issues because old myths and practices may have been part of their upbringing. Be sure they are not shaming the children.

? DECISIONS, DECISIONS . . .

A 4-year-old boy in your center has toilet accidents several times each week. The lead teacher in his room has started confining him to a time-out chair after each incident. What would you say to this teacher as the program manager? Discuss with your classmates.

MEETING CHILDREN'S MENTAL HEALTH NEEDS

A discussion of children's health needs is not complete without mentioning their mental health needs. Child-care professionals support children's mental health when they:

- Promote the development of relationships that foster security and attachment by arranging for children to stay with a consistent caregiver over time.
- Develop strong connections with families so children know that the important adults in their lives respect and care about each other.
- Provide warm, loving interactions that promote development of a positive self-concept.
- Provide plenty of time for children to do what they do best—that is, play—and provide appropriate challenges so that children develop strong feelings of self-efficacy.
- Recognize the importance of eating, toileting, and dressing as opportunities to meet both physical and mental health goals.
- Use positive guidance with the goal of promoting self-discipline and never punishment to control children's behavior.
- Help families see their children in a positive light by pointing out increasing abilities or sharing important accomplishments.
- Provide opportunities for families to learn more about child development behavior, from "experts" as well as from other families.

Helping Children Cope with Catastrophic Events

People were comforted by dozens of stories of individual courage and human compassion after the attacks on the World Trade Center and Pentagon on September 11, 2001. Along with firefighters, police, and emergency personnel, several early childhood professionals emerged as heroes on that dark day. Sue Shellenbarger (2001) reported in the *New York Times* that 14 teachers at the Children's Discovery Center (located in a building that later collapsed) evacuated 42 children safely. They followed the procedures they had practiced every month, even though they had to improvise once outside because their planned destination was inaccessible. The teachers, some barefoot as their paper booties shredded, commandeered shop-

When children learn to clean up their own spills, they help maintain a safe, healthy environment and develop their own feelings of self-efficacy.

ping carts to transport their charges more than a mile, and passersby donated their own shirts to protect the babies from flying debris. The children were resting peacefully in a hospital and a preschool by the time their parents arrived to get them. Meanwhile, at the Pentagon, 36 child-care staffers evacuated 136 children and kept them calm through five relocations, even as the director worried about her husband, a naval officer working in the path of Flight 77. He was safe, as it turned out, but three children in the program lost a parent that day.

These stories of heroic efforts in the face of disaster underscore the crucial importance of planning for health and safety. Well-thought-out emergency procedures that are practiced regularly can save lives and help both staff members and children remain calm during a disaster. Early childhood professionals have a responsibility for the children's psychological and emotional safety, not just their physical safety. Sometimes, as in the aftermath of the terrorist attacks of September 11, 2001, even children who have not directly experienced the traumatic event are deeply affected. Symptoms can include increased anxiety, exaggerated fears, acting-out behaviors such as tantrums or aggression, crying, clinging, whining, and physical aches and pains (Hogan & Graham, 2001, p. 3). Children with none of these obvious symptoms might reveal their fears or confusion during their play.

Adults who believe that children are unaware of frightening events may avoid the topic or try to distract children who ask questions. Most experts agree, however, that these efforts to protect children are misguided (Council for Professional Recognition, 2001; Hogan & Graham, 2001). Children are comforted by the knowledge that they can talk about their fears with at least one important person in their lives. Without overemphasizing the issue, adults can invite children to say or draw what they understand. They can listen without judging, and provide clarification and reassurance later. Adults must ensure that the children experience the stability of a predictable schedule at their child-care center and that they know the teachers will keep them safe. Perhaps, most important, adults can help put some fun back into the children's lives with special projects or activities.

Not all catastrophes are on the scale of 9/11 or Hurricane Katrina, but the effects of more personal crises may be just as devastating for individual children or class groups. More than 2 million children in the United States have had a parent deploy to

Afghanistan or Iraq. In the case of dual-military career families or single parents, this often means the child is left in the care of grandparents or other relatives. If the parents are members of the National Guard or military reserves, they do not live on military bases with access to support services. Children of deployed parents may exhibit a range of behaviors, from listlessness to hyperactivity, clinginess, tantrums, sleep problems, refusing to eat, and weight loss. Older children may regress to behavior that they have outgrown. These children are at risk for elevated stress levels both during and after deployment, and their families can face increased risk for domestic violence. As part of the support system for the nondeployed parent, the child development center plays a crucial role in supporting the well-being of children of military personnel. In addition to sharing the burden of caring for the child, the program can help strengthen the family by modeling child-sensitive interactions, teaching age-appropriate relaxation techniques, and providing an element of consistency in the child's life (Child Trends, 2013, July 22).

Sooner or later, all early childhood professionals are called on to respond to the children's feelings and questions about death. A family pet or the classroom guinea pig may die. One of the children enrolled in your center might lose a grandparent. Somehow, these losses seem part of the natural scheme of things, best handled by responding to children's comments and questions in a calm, reassuring manner. Be careful not to exaggerate or give more information than the children can comprehend. Helping children and families confront the death of a classmate or a member of a child's immediate family is likely to be much more challenging for you and your staff members. Be sure to confer with the family who has suffered the loss so you know what the child has been told. Then tell the other families what you are saying to the children so that they can give the same information at home if their child asks. Then they can provide the necessary factual information, reassurance, and comfort.

Preparation for coping with any catastrophe must begin long before one occurs. Such preparation should be built into your program's curriculum and professional development plans. A focus on building emotional competence in yourself, your staff members, and the children will help everyone withstand and bounce back from traumatic events. If they are going to model such competence and help children achieve it, adults need to recognize their own feelings and to distinguish them from those of the children, and to be aware of how their feelings influence their own behavior. They need the skill to put their own feelings into words and to help children do the same. They (and the children) can benefit from the ability to calm themselves with techniques like deep breathing and yoga. Building practice with these skills into professional development activities will help staff members bolster their own resilience as well as give them tools to carry back to their classrooms, thus enhancing everyone's ability to cope with all kinds of disasters (West & Albrecht, 2007). The U.S. Department of Veterans Affairs, Center for Posttraumatic Stress Disorder, has developed detailed suggestions for parents and caregivers to help infants, toddlers, and preschool and school-age children deal with the effects of disaster. The handout is available online at http://www.ptsd.va.gov/public/pages/terrorist-attacks-children.asp.

SICK CHILDREN

Because children are generally exposed to many groups and public places in addition to attending a child development center, the center cannot be held responsible for all of the children's illnesses. But the center is responsible for establishing and enforcing policies to eliminate, as much as possible, children's exposure to communicable illness. Parents are more likely to cooperate with you in this effort if you communicate clearly the reasons behind your policies and emphasize that you are trying to protect their child as well as all the others.

National health and safety guidelines specify that children should not be at the center when they are too sick to join in the activities; when caring for them makes it impossible to care for the other children adequately; or when any of the following conditions exist: fever over 101°F, indications of severe illness such as lethargy or wheezing, uncontrolled diarrhea, repeated vomiting, mouth sores with drooling, rash with fever or behavior change, conjunctivitis with discharge, scabies or head lice, tuberculosis, impetigo, strep infections, chickenpox, mumps, pertussis, or hepatitis A. Once the child has received treatment or the infectious period has passed, as confirmed by medical personnel, the child may be readmitted. Unless otherwise indicated by a health professional, children with common colds, runny noses, coughs, mild fevers without other symptoms, or rashes without fever and without behavior changes may all be allowed to remain at the center (American Academy of Pediatrics, American Public Health Association, National Resource Center for Health and Safety in Child Care and Early Education, 2011).

Center staff members must walk a fine line in deciding when to exclude children—protecting the other children from exposure to illness without needlessly overburdening parents. Even those who want to cooperate with center policies may be tempted, if their job hangs in the balance, to claim that a fever is caused by teething, for instance, or that the diarrhea is the result of too many blueberries the night before. Some health professionals argue that mildly ill children who are no longer contagious should be cared for in their regular center. They reason that the sick child has already infected others during the disease's incubation period and that excluding the child from the regular center only increases the chance that a desperate parent will simply take the child to another (unsuspecting) center and infect more children.

You can help prevent problems by making your exclusion policies clear at the time of enrollment and by providing ongoing opportunities for parents to learn more about health issues. In return for their cooperation, parents have a right to expect that you will ask them to pick up a sick child only when truly necessary. This means educating teachers to know the difference between a rash that signals infectious disease and noncontagious eczema. If your teachers are inexperienced, you may want to make it a policy that they check with you before calling a parent. Your center health consultant can help, perhaps by giving talks at parent or staff meetings or by providing information you can pass on to both groups. The National Resource Center for Health and Safety in Child Care and Early Education gives a detailed rationale for each of the recommended standards (available on line at www.ncrkids.org). Becoming familiar with this information will help you explain your policies to parents and bolster your confidence that you are acting in the best interest of children. You can also work with families at the time of enrollment to devise a plan for what they will do in case of the child's illness. In two-career families, the plan may involve sharing the responsibility of picking up their ill child. In other cases, the parent may be able to enroll the child in a service such as the network of family child-care providers or a hospital-based center. The Community Coordinated Child Care Association or a similar agency in your locale may be able to provide a variety of resources that you can share with parents.

WHEN CHILDREN BECOME ILL AT THE CENTER

In spite of your best efforts, you will eventually be faced with a child who becomes ill at the center. Your staff members must be trained to recognize the signs and symptoms of illness—fever, unexplained rashes, and/or lethargy. A 3-year-old might be able to tell you that she vomited last night, but an infant must rely on your power of perception. Your center's health consultant can help with ongoing training in these skills as required by the national health and safety guidelines. You should also maintain contact with local health authorities so you can tap their expertise when an outbreak of communicable disease occurs.

Children who become ill at the center should be separated from the other children until a parent arrives. They must be supervised while isolated, and they often need special attention from a staff member to help them feel secure at this time. In addition to a quiet, secluded place where the child can wait to be picked up, the center needs accurate information to reach a parent or another emergency contact person. It is important that parents understand the need to inform you of any changes in the location, schedule, or telephone number of their place of employment, as well as any changes in the emergency contact information. Obsolete information is as bad as no information at all. Just as bad is information locked in an office file cabinet and inaccessible to staff members who might be faced with a sick child when you are not there.

Readmission After Illness

Some conditions require a medical evaluation. Although some centers routinely require a physician's statement before they will readmit a child, this practice could place an undue burden on the time and finances of working parents. Your health consultant can help you decide exactly what is needed to readmit a child after various illnesses. Such discretionary decision making requires consultation with local health authorities as well as your licensing agency.

With some conditions, such as head lice, a child may be readmitted once appropriate treatment has been administered. Treatment includes thoroughly washing all linens, clothing, or toys that have come in contact with the infected child(ren)—at home and at the center. Items that cannot be washed can be sealed in airtight plastic bags for 2 weeks. As with an infectious disease, parents should be informed so that they can watch for symptoms in their own child. Center staff members should also monitor all children for signs of infestation and be especially vigilant about cleaning dress-up clothing.

Whether or not you allow mildly ill children to remain at your facility, if the illness becomes serious or a child is injured, you must have a plan to get the child to the nearest hospital or emergency facility. The plan must provide for a staff member to stay with the child until the parents arrive and provide for backup care for the children who remain at the center. Figure 10.2, the emergency medical care permission form, has space for emergency contact information.

In some communities centers have been established specifically to care for sick children—a response to working parents' needs. Because this type of care is beyond many teachers' professional expertise, it may require specialized personnel. Caring for sick children is an expensive service because of the special facilities and personnel required. Other communities are experimenting with a system in which family child-care providers are paid to reserve a certain number of spaces for sick children. Parents pay to enroll their children in the network, and families meet with providers in advance. When an illness arises, parents have the peace of mind that comes with knowing that there is a place for their child, and the children are not placed with a total stranger while feeling sick and vulnerable. Another option might be for a center manager to maintain a list of caregivers (perhaps a substitute list or applicants waiting for full-time openings at the center) who could be sent into the sick child's home to provide care.

DISABILITIES AND CHRONIC MEDICAL PROBLEMS

As a center manager, you are not only concerned with protecting the health and safety of the children in general, but you must also be prepared for the special health needs of children with disabilities, allergies, or chronic medical problems. The key to your successful response to this challenge is your ability to form a partnership with the parents and health professionals. You must educate yourself and your staff members and establish procedures to make the center a safe and healthy place for all children. Your greatest asset is knowing and trusting that others will help. The burden is not yours alone.

The National Resource Center for Health and Safety in Child Care and Early Education (www.nrckids.org) provides assistance with developing a service plan for children with special needs and coordinating services among the various components of the health, education, and social services systems involved. All children—and especially those with allergies—should be protected from dust mites, pesticides, and mold. Staff members should avoid perfumed soaps and lotions or air fresheners. Animals should not be brought into the center before checking with families.

Once the plan, the space, and the equipment are in place, staff members must acquire the knowledge and skills necessary to accommodate special feeding, toileting, or respiratory needs. Some disabilities involve difficulty swallowing, and staff members must be alert for choking. Other conditions might involve catheterization or suctioning, and staff members must be trained to carry out these procedures. Depending on the nature of the disabilities involved, staff members may have to know how to handle seizures (remaining calm and removing hazards from the child's vicinity) and when to call for medical help if the seizures become uncontrollable.

The percentage of children in the United States afflicted with chronic medical problems, particularly asthma, obesity, and behavior and learning problems, increased from 12.8 percent in 1994 to 26.6 percent in 2006 (Lowry, 2010). This suggests that the likelihood of your center caring for such children is very high. As manager, therefore, you must ensure that your staff members can recognize the signs of an asthma attack and that they know how to help a child calm down and regain control of her or his breathing. With a diabetic child, staff members must be alert for the symptoms of low blood sugar and be prepared to assist with sugar cubes, fruit juice, or hard candies and to call for medical help if the child does not respond to these interventions. Children with sickle cell anemia are subject to painful episodes triggered by exertion. When an attack occurs, teachers should comfort and quiet a child until parents can be summoned. Children with fragile immune systems due to cancer or heart problems may need extra rest or treatments with special equipment that must be stored appropriately.

The key to handling all of these situations lies in planning. Decide ahead who will be responsible for helping the child in crisis, who will go or call for help, and who will attend to the other children.

Because nearly 4 percent of pregnant women in the United States use drugs such as marijuana, cocaine, and ecstasy (March of Dimes, 2013), it is very possible that your center will care for a child suffering from exposure to such drugs. Like all children, they exhibit individual differences and do not conform to stereotyped preconceptions. Some infants have to be swaddled and held or rocked in special ways; some young children have a greater need for stability and predictability in their environment. Careful consultation with the families and medical professionals will help you and your staff members learn the most effective ways of assisting each child.

Acquired immune deficiency syndrome (AIDS) is another health problem that early childhood professionals confront, although intervention efforts nationwide have succeeded in dramatically reducing the incidence of AIDS in babies. According to the Centers for Disease Control and Prevention, in 2011, only 192 cases occurred in children under 13. Even if no child in your center is infected, however, you may encounter the disease in one of your caregivers or a child's family member. Hepatitis B is another virus, also transmitted via blood or infected bodily fluids, that is of growing concern to public health officials because of the increasing number of carriers, particularly children adopted from parts of the world where the virus is widespread.

Your role as manager is to seek accurate, up-to-date information to combat the fear and ignorance that surround these diseases. Train your staff members to practice the universal precautions described earlier in this chapter.

Staff members and families may worry about the risk that ill children pose to others at the center. Although the child with hepatitis B who bites other children does pose a health risk, it is actually the adults or children with human immunodeficiency virus (HIV) who require extra protection from exposure to normal childhood illnesses because of their depressed immune systems. If they are exposed to measles or chickenpox, for example, they should be immediately referred to their health-care provider for follow-up (www.nrckids.org Standard 7.3.6.2).

As a center manager, you are in a unique position to provide needed education and to model compassion and common sense for the entire community in the face of these challenges.

Prescription Medications

Ideally, all medication would be administered to children by their own family members while the child is at home. Sometimes, however, a condition requires medication during the time the child is in your care. For the protection of the child as well as that of your staff members, you will need a written policy stating clearly when, and under what conditions, your staff members will undertake this task. Because regulations vary from one state to another, you should work closely with your health consultant to develop your policy for administering medication. The following are basic questions to consider:

- Will you administer only prescription medication, or will you also administer over-the-counter treatments, such as diaper creams or cough syrups? (Note that sunscreen is also treated as a medication.) If the medication is an over-the-counter type, how will you ensure that it is, in fact, appropriate for the child in question?

- What written information and instructions will you require from parents? Again, states vary in the precise wording required, but certainly the parental permission must specify the name of the child, the name of the medication, the amount, and the method and time(s) for administering the medication.

- Does your state require special training for any individual administering medication? Identifying one person, with a backup in case of absence, to administer all medication can help prevent the possibility that a child will either miss a dose or be given too much medicine. What steps will you take to ensure that the parents' instructions are appropriate for the child, that is, that they comply with a physician's orders and match the instructions on the label?

Technology Toolkit

Log onto the following pages from the website for the Centers for Disease Control and Prevention to download and print a recommended immunization schedule for children (http://www.cdc.gov/vaccines/parents/downloads/parent-ver-sch-0-6yrs.pdf) and a handout on "Common Questions Parents Ask About Infant Immunizations," available in both English and Spanish (http://www.cdc.gov/vaccines/parents/parent-questions.html)

- Do you have a plan for storing medication safely (e.g., out of reach of children, under refrigeration if needed, and where it cannot accidentally contaminate food)?
- How will you document each dose, including the time and person administering it? How long will you keep this documentation on file?

The same precautions (written permission, careful labeling, etc.) apply to sunscreen and diaper ointments.

CHILD ABUSE AND NEGLECT

Child-care professionals are often the first to notice, and address, early signs of abuse or neglect when it does occur. **Child abuse** consists of an act or failure to act on the part of a parent or caretaker which results in death, serious physical or emotional harm, sexual abuse or exploitation of a child. **Neglect**, on the other hand, is defined as the failure of a parent, guardian, or other caregiver to provide for a child's basic needs. Neglect may be physical, medical, educational, or emotional. In most states, child-care providers, along with school personnel, social workers, health-care professionals, and law enforcement officers, are considered **mandatory reporters** of child abuse—that is, they are legally required to report to the appropriate authorities any evidence of a child's having been abused. Failure to do so can result in criminal as well as civil liability. You can learn the requirements for your state by visiting the website for the Child Welfare Information Gateway listed in the Resources for Further Study at the end of this chapter. One of your responsibilities as a manager will be to educate your staff members about the signs of abuse. Figure 10.3 gives a list of signs and symptoms that

---

🔍 LEADERSHIP LENS

Looking beyond their responsibilities as mandated reporters when child abuse or neglect is suspected, program directors and child-care staff members can assume leadership roles in preventing such occurrences. Research has identified several protective factors for reducing abuse and neglect:

- Parents' resilience in the face of stress
- Social connections
- Knowledge of parenting and child development
- Access to support in times of need

Child-care programs are uniquely situated to help build each of these protective factors. Not only do they reach large numbers of children, but they have the potential for establishing long-lasting relationships with families, and they can offer a sympathetic ear and words of encouragement when needed. They provide a place where families can connect with each other for mutual support, and where they can learn about child development and develop new parenting skills. The child development center can help families connect with community services for assistance in preventing or dealing with crises. All of these efforts enhance a family's ability to cope with the stresses and strains of life and make it less likely that family members will lash out at children.

In addition to these benefits for families, child development programs contribute to the social and emotional competence of children, reducing the types of behaviors that might trigger an outburst in an overstressed parent. A curriculum that fosters children's self-regulation and teaches them how to manage and express emotions appropriately is part of everyday appropriate practice, and its rewards extend beyond the walls of the center. As a leader dedicated to making a difference in the world, a program director can help staff members see, and be inspired by, these larger implications of their work.

Consider the possibility of **physical abuse**	
When the **child:**	When the **parent or other adult caregiver:**
• Has unexplained burns, bites, bruises, broken bones, or black eyes. • Has fading bruises or other marks noticeable after an absence from school. • Seems frightened of the parents and protests or cries when it is time to go home. • Shrinks at the approach of adults. • Reports injury by a parent or another adult caregiver.	• Offers conflicting, unconvincing, or no explanation for the child's injury. • Describes the child as "evil" or in some other very negative way. • Uses harsh physical discipline with the child. • Has a history of abuse as a child.
Consider the possibility of **neglect**	
When the **child:**	When the **parent or other adult caregiver:**
• Is frequently absent from school or child care. • Begs or steals food or money. • Lacks needed medical or dental care, immunizations, or glasses. • Is consistently dirty and has severe body odor. • Lacks sufficient clothing for the weather. • Abuses alcohol or other drugs. • States that there is no one at home to provide care.	• Appears to be indifferent to the child. • Seems apathetic or depressed. • Behaves irrationally or in a bizarre manner. • Is abusing alcohol or other drugs.

Note that these types of abuse are more typically found in combination than alone. A physically abused child, for example, is often emotionally abused as well, and a sexually abused child also may be neglected.

Consider the possibility of **sexual abuse**	
When the **child:**	When the **parent or other adult caregiver:**
• Has difficulty walking or sitting. • Suddenly refuses to change for gym or to participate in physical activities. • Reports nightmares or bedwetting. • Experiences a sudden change in appetite. • Demonstrates bizarre, sophisticated, or unusual sexual knowledge or behavior. • Contracts a venereal disease. • Runs away. • Reports sexual abuse by a parent or another adult caregiver.	• Is unduly protective of the child or severely limits the child's contact with other children, especially of the opposite sex. • Is secretive and isolated. • Is jealous or controlling with family members.

FIGURE 10.3   Recognizing signs of abuse or neglect.

Source: National Clearinghouse on Child Abuse and Neglect Information, U.S. Department of Health and Human Services.

might indicate a child is being abused or neglected. Most child abuse occurs in the home. Not every bump or bruise is caused by abuse, but a pattern of recurring bumps and bruises, without plausible explanations for their sources, may be sufficient to suspect abuse. Keeping a dated record each time you observe such marks on a child, as well as any explanation you are given, is the only way you will be aware if such a pattern develops. Some centers keep such a record in a spiral-bound notebook (pages cannot be inserted or rearranged) that serves as evidence should staff members be falsely accused of injuring a child.

Reporting Suspected Abuse

Your staff members will also need to know what procedures to follow should they suspect a child has been abused. If you are unsure of whom to contact, call the Childhelp USA National Child Abuse Hotline (1-800-4-A-CHILD) and make careful note of where and how to file a report in your community so you will have the information readily available should the need arise. The person who suspects the abuse should make the report to the appropriate agency. This is generally the child's caregiver; however, as manager you need to be kept informed when caregivers have reason to suspect a child is abused or neglected. Your responsibility would be to support the caregiver in making the decision to report and to document the fact that he or she did so. Although the identity of the individual making the report is confidential, families are very likely to suspect the center and may become very angry and take it out on the child's caregiver. You can help a caregiver prepare to remain calm in the event of confrontation, but you may also have to step in to defuse it. A family may even withdraw the child from care, and the staff members need to be prepared for the feelings that such action will evoke.

Children who have been abused may have a greater need for a relationship with a consistent caregiver and extra patience to help them reestablish their trust in adults. They may have trouble controlling their impulses and require continued, firm reminders of the center's limits. They may make caregivers uncomfortable as they work through their concerns in dramatic play. You may wish to secure the advice of mental health center personnel or other professionals if a child in your center has been abused. Some drop-in centers are specifically established to take in children whose parents are prone to child abuse and are in treatment. The parent may secure counseling nearby while the child plays in the center.

Preventing Abuse in the Center

Your first responsibility in preventing abuse from occurring in your child-care program is to hire staff members who are capable of proper conduct toward children. Highly publicized cases of child abuse in child-care facilities some years ago horrified the child-care community; however, a review of research in this area indicates that fewer instances of abuse occur in child-care programs than in homes or residential facilities (Fiene, 2002). Nevertheless, managers must take every precaution to ensure that such acts never occur in their centers. States have instituted clearance procedures for teachers, caregivers of young children, and family child-care operators in an effort to prevent convicted child abusers from entering child-care work. Your role is to know and follow the law carefully in this regard. Ask your licensing office for information if you do not know.

Child abuse can be **physical abuse**, **emotional abuse**, or **sexual abuse**. Research indicates that the most likely form of physical abuse is excessive discipline, which may be related to a caregiver's conflict with a particular child or a family's encouragement of the use of corporal punishment (Schumacher & Carlson, 1999). Of course, no high-quality center uses corporal punishment as a form of discipline. Nor should a center tolerate mental punishment in the form of teasing, scolding, or shaming a child as a means of controlling behavior. Any teacher or caregiver who cannot handle a group of children without resorting to physical or emotional punishment should be immediately discharged. You can prevent the likelihood of having to discharge an employee by minimizing stress levels for staff members; for example, provide appropriate staff–child ratios, frequent breaks, and effective staff development, and focus on developmentally appropriate practices and expectations (Daly & Dowd, 1992, cited in Fiene, 2002). You must also monitor your staff members to ensure that they interact appropriately with children. One advantage to having a probation period for a new employee is that it gives you an opportunity to determine whether the employee's temperament and methods of dealing with children are compatible with high standards. Many managers require that all interior doors remain open so that staff members can monitor one another. This policy also protects staff members from false accusations.

With regard to sex abuse, research indicates that 60 percent of the sexual abuse in child care is done by men, even though men represent only an estimated 5 percent of the staff. Perpetrators were caregivers, volunteers, janitors, bus drivers, staff family members, and outsiders. In two-thirds of all cases, the sexual abuse occurred in the facility's bathroom. Removing bathroom partitions and stalls that create private areas where children can be isolated and establishing control over who takes children into the toilet areas are two ways you can lower the risk of such abuse occurring in your center (Finkelhor, Williams, Kalinowski, & Burns, 1988, pp. 1–16).

Conclusion

Both parents and society trust you to keep children safe from harm. This chapter discussed the health of teachers and caregivers, the ways that child development centers can protect the health and safety of all children, and the ways teachers and caregivers can work with the families and other professionals to meet the needs of children with disabilities or chronic health problems. Policies and practices relating to immunizations, medical examinations, medications, observations and record keeping, and the exclusion and readmission of ill children have been suggested. Safety precautions during the transportation of the children, measures for preventing and reporting child abuse, and helping children and staff members recover from catastrophic experiences were outlined.

Questions for Review

1. What health and safety policies and practices are required for licensing a child development center?

2. What is a medical home? Why is it important?

3. Define risk management and give examples of how it applies in child care.

4. Explain how child-care centers promote health and safety when meeting children's physiological needs for activity, rest, and toileting.

5. What should a child-care provider do if a child becomes ill at the center?

6. Give examples of how the day-to-day best practices in a child-care center promote children's mental health.

7. Describe a situation in which a caregiver might suspect that a child has been abused. Explain what the caregiver should do.

Professional Portfolio

1. Learn your state's requirements for administering medication to children while in child care. Write a sample policy that meets those requirements and could be included in a parent handbook.

2. Use database software to create a checklist of the health forms a center must collect for each child enrolled. Some community health departments furnish child-care providers with such forms on disk, or you could write to commercial vendors of child-care data management programs and request a preview. Print out a sample report and add a cover sheet explaining how you would monitor the health records in a program that you manage. For example,

in addition to recording immunizations at the initial enrollment, how would you document that children had received subsequent immunizations according to the recommended schedule?

3. Download a copy of the publication *Strengthening Families: A Guidebook for Early Childhood Programs*, Revised Second Edition, from the website of the Center for the Study of Social Policy at www.cssp.org. Click on "publications," then select "Strengthening Families." Use one or more of the self-assessments as a guide for creating plans for a center you might manage, or to evaluate the practices of a center you know.

Resources for Further Study

PRINT

Aronson, S. S., & Shope, T. R. (Eds.) (2013). *Managing infectious diseases in child care and schools* (3rd ed.). Elk Grove Village, IL: American Academy of Pediatrics.

Bergen, S., & Robertson, R. (2012). *Healthy children, healthy lives: The wellness guide for early childhood programs*. St. Paul, MN: Redleaf Press.

Button, L. (2008). When is a child too sick? Devising a "sick child" policy for your center. *Exchange, 183,* 6–10.

Health and safety topics for early childhood educators. (2004, March) *Young Children, 59*(2), entire issue.

National Association of School Psychologists. (2003). *Helping children cope with loss, death, and grief: Tips for teachers and parents.* Available online at http://www. nasponline.org/resources/crisis_safety/griefwar.pdf

Websites

THE AFFORDABLE CARE ACT: WHAT IT MEANS FOR CHILDREN, FAMILIES, AND EARLY CHILDHOOD PROGRAMS

http://www.acf.hhs.gov/programs/ecd/the-affordable-care-act-what-it-means-for-children-families-and-ece

Web page provided by the U.S. Department of Health and Human Services, Administration for Children and Families. It includes information for obtaining health insurance for providers and their families, and about coverage for employees and tax credits.

CHILD WELFARE INFORMATION GATEWAY

http://www.childwelfare.gov/

A service of the Children's Bureau, Administration for Children and Families, U.S. Department of Health and Human Services. Includes links to documents defining abuse, identifying signs or symptoms of abuse, and a summary of individual state policies and statutes.

HEALTHY CHILD CARE AMERICA

healthychildcare.org

Website for the Healthy Child Care America campaign of the American Academy of Pediatrics. Includes sections for families, child-care providers, and health professionals and links to free materials on child health issues as well as contact information for the Healthy Child Care American representative in each state.

INFORMED GREEN SOLUTIONS, INC (IGS)

www.informedgreensolutions.org

Nonprofit organization created in 2009 to educate the general public on the benefits of environmentally preferable purchasing and the impacts our purchasing decisions have on human health and the environment. Resources include *Green Cleaning, Sanitizing and Disinfecting: A Toolkit for Early Care and Education Programs,* which presents practical information on using less hazardous products to keep environments safe while protecting children and staff members from infectious diseases.

IT PAYS TO PREPARE

http://nrc.uchsc.edu/RESOURCES/VAEmergencyPreparBro.pdf

It Pays to Prepare! An Emergency Preparedness Guide for Child Care Providers. This publication was developed by the Virginia Department of Health; it includes guidelines for evacuation plans, emergency kits and supplies, handling medical emergencies and communicable diseases, and staff responsibilities.

NATIONAL DISSEMINATION CENTER FOR CHILDREN WITH DISABILITIES

http://www.nichcy.org

The National Dissemination Center for Children with Disabilities is operated by the Academy for Professional Development and funded by U.S. Department of Education's Office of Special Education Programs. It provides information on specific disabilities, related legislation, and research-based practices. It is available in English and Spanish as well as via a BrowseAloud text reader.

NATIONAL RESOURCE CENTER FOR HEALTH AND SAFETY IN CHILD CARE AND EARLY EDUCATION

http://NRCKids.org/

The National Resource Center (NRC) for Health and Safety in Child Care and Early Education is a project of the University of Colorado Health Science Center and the Maternal and Child Health Bureau of the U.S. Department of Health and Human Services. The website provides links to online version of the latest edition of *Caring for Our Children* and the companion document, *Stepping Stones to Using Caring for Our Children;* current licensing and regulation information for each state; and other health and safety resources for child-care providers.

Managing Food Service

LEARNING OUTCOMES

After studying this chapter you should be able to

- Discuss ways to set up and maintain a safe, healthy food program.
- Apply basic guidelines to plan nutritious meals for children at each age level.
- Explain how the center's food program relates to curricular goals.

Sophie, the cook at Rainbow Center, is a vital part of the program. The children know her by name and often ask their parents to make their favorite dishes "like Sophie does." The center has a custom of inviting family members to dine with children on their birthdays. For toddlers, Sophie tries to include one of the child's favorite foods in the menu. Older children have the opportunity to consult with her on the menu. Sophie has prepared a collection of laminated pages, each featuring an image of a particular food, and she has organized these in categories in a loose-leaf binder. About a week before the big day, the birthday child looks through the binder with Sophie, selecting one item from the meat or meat substitute section, two from the fruits and vegetables category, and so on, to create a lunch menu that meets United States Department of Agriculture (USDA) requirements. Parents are often surprised at the healthy foods their children choose—and enjoy.

Ironically, in a country where millions of children live in poverty and go to bed hungry at least part of the time, millions are also either obese or somewhat overweight. Sometimes the two groups overlap. As a result of the economic downturn, increasing numbers of children experience food insecurity. At the lowest level, **food insecurity** means they live in household where families have resorted to lower-nutrient food choices in order to stretch their budget. At the most severe level, children go to bed hungry and suffer a lack of nutrition. Children who subsist on unhealthy low-cost foods are at risk for **obesity**, dental problems, and a host of associated health consequences. Children who experience hunger are more likely to suffer from anxiety, hyperactivity, behavioral problems, and impaired cognitive development—all contributing to poor school performance. The problem is widespread: In 2010, one in nine children lived in households struggling with food insecurity (Children's Defense Fund, 2012).

Whether you are dealing with homeless and hungry children or with children at risk for health problems because of obesity, as a center manager, you are well positioned to make a positive difference for the children you serve. Given the finding that children who have been in child care are significantly more likely to be obese when they enter kindergarten than their peers who have not been in care (Maher, Li, Carter, & Johnson, 2008), it is imperative that you devote considerable attention to providing the food that the children must have today and to fostering the healthy eating habits that they need for a lifetime.

A SAFE AND HEALTHY FOOD PROGRAM

The number of meals children consume at a child-care facility varies with the length of time they spend there: Those in short-day programs generally have a snack, whereas those in full-day programs have breakfast, lunch, and snacks in the morning and afternoon. Some centers require parents to send sack lunches or snacks with their children; some provide all the meals; and others fall somewhere in between, perhaps providing snacks and milk but requiring families to provide the lunch.

Regardless of who furnishes the food, providing young children with adequate nutrition for growth and body maintenance requires a great deal of planning. Proper nutrition is necessary for all areas of a child's development—physical, mental, social, and emotional. And proper sanitation is necessary to prevent illness. Parents and teachers generally have a number of goals for each child:

1. To eat a well-balanced nutritious meal
2. To enjoy mealtime with friendly people
3. To taste, and ultimately enjoy, a wide variety of foods
4. To learn to eat independently
5. To sit at the table and develop acceptable table manners
6. To develop an understanding that good food is related to growing and being strong and healthy
7. To see a connection between the foods eaten at home and those eaten at school

Of course, serving a highly nutritious menu does not guarantee that each child will eat a nutritious meal. Careful guidance helps children learn to eat, and eventually enjoy, a variety of foods. Eating a wide range of foods is considered an important factor in being well nourished throughout life.

? DECISIONS, DECISIONS . . .

Using an Ethical Framework

Suppose you are a manager of a child development program struggling to make ends meet financially. You have been unable to give staff members an increase in salaries for the past two years. Although you would like to do so, it would require raising fees, and you know that several families enrolled in your program would be unable to afford even a marginally higher rate. One of your board members suggests that you discontinue providing meals at the center and require families to send snacks and lunches for their children instead. Using the National Association for the Education of Young Children (NAEYC) code, try to determine what core values are involved. What ideals and principles regarding responsibilities to children, families, and employees apply? What course of action seems most right?

Meeting Regulations and Professional Standards

Because many factors must be considered when developing a good food service program, it is essential that adequate time be devoted to planning. The national health and safety guidelines (American Academy of Pediatrics, American Public Health Association, National Resource Center for Health and Safety in Child Care and Early Education, 2011), National Association for the Education of Young Children (NAEYC) accreditation criteria, and state licensing regulations all require that child-care facilities adhere to recommended standards regarding the types and amounts of foods to be served, the conditions under which food is prepared and stored, involvement of families, and plans for handling emergencies or special dietary requirements. Specific requirements for nutritional content of meals have been established by the U.S. Department of Agriculture (USDA) and the Child and Adult Care Food Program (CACFP).

Organizing Food Service Facilities

As manager, you may have the opportunity to plan an ideal kitchen and serving area. Or you may have to use the space and equipment that someone else planned or spend some time planning a renovation. Adequate equipment and space for food preparation and storage, dishwashing, and serving meals are essential for high-quality meal service.

Your state's minimum child-care licensing standards must be applied from the very beginning—you may be able to obtain technical assistance and consultation from your licensing agency as you make your plans. Institutional dishwashers and other equipment may be required by the licensing standards. It is a good idea to visit several other centers with food service programs to get advice about the latest and best arrangements or the best equipment to buy. Learning from others who have recently made similar decisions or who are involved with a food service program daily may eliminate some costly mistakes.

Always compare the information obtained informally from colleagues with the specific written standards for food service equipment. The National Sanitation Foundation (NSF International) is an independent, nonprofit organization that certifies the safety of products and equipment to protect public health. You can search for manufacturers of NSF-certified food equipment at http://www.nsf.org/Certified/Food/.

Even the most modern facilities for preparing and serving food are of little use if appropriate storage and the equipment and supplies necessary to keep the facilities clean are not available. Note the following minimum requirements:

- Floor and counter surfaces in the food preparation area must be easy to clean.
- Shelves where food items are stored should have hard-gloss finishes that are easy to clean. Crates or cans of food should never be stored on the floor.
- Refrigerators and freezers should be equipped with thermometers so that the temperatures can be monitored.
- The kitchen (as well as the entire center) should be well ventilated, with screens on any windows or doors that open.
- A separate sink for handwashing must be stocked with soap and paper towels.
- Disposable gloves must be worn when handling food.
- Food preparation surfaces must be cleaned and sanitized after each use; the floor should be mopped at least daily, more often if it is soiled.
- Trash cans must have covers and disposable liners and be emptied at least daily.
- Outside the center, garbage should be stored in a covered Dumpster or can and removed at least weekly.

Food Service Personnel

When initially planning the food service program, the manager and the board determine the staff members that they can afford to hire. A large child-care corporation or agency with many centers may hire a dietitian or nutritionist, while individual or small centers may use a dietitian on a consultative basis one or two days per month to help plan menus and give advice when problems arise. Or the manager may be able to fulfill the nutritionist's role, so only a cook is needed. Carefully writing a job analysis, job specification, and job description is necessary. Food service personnel are usually responsible for the following tasks:

1. Planning menus with proper nutritional content
2. Buying foods
3. Checking in food ordered and keeping track of inventories
4. Operating and maintaining the kitchen and dining rooms
5. Maintaining high sanitation standards for all food handling and preparation, dishwashing, and garbage disposal
6. Monitoring costs, reporting to the manager, and assisting with the USDA reports
7. Cooperating with the teaching staff to provide any food-product learning material, such as play dough, or foods used in learning projects in the classrooms
8. Preparing foods using methods that maintain the foods' nutritional quality
9. Getting to know the children, their individual needs, and the appropriate guidance methods for interacting with them—especially related to eating
10. Appreciating the families' needs and cultural differences that may affect meal service

The food service personnel who work in the kitchen are responsible for following the menus and organizing the food, equipment, and labor needed to get the meals to the table on time. Each task requires the ability to think through the steps to completion. Once items appear on the menus, the organizing begins. The food service director must consider the feasibility of each menu in terms of equipment, utensils, and available help. For example, a main dish and a dessert that both require the oven may not be feasible on the same day unless the dessert is cooked ahead of time.

Food service workers must know, or be willing to learn quickly, the proper methods of cooking to preserve nutrient qualities. A reputable quantity-cooking recipe book is essential. If staff members follow the suggested methods and temperatures, the products should remain nutritious. Vegetables, for example, generally cook quickly; prolonged cooking destroys the very vitamins the vegetables are expected to provide the children.

The food service staff must understand children—their development, nutritional needs, and typical behaviors related to food. Ideally, food service staff members are included in all professional development activities, and nutrition education for the entire staff should include information about how children develop healthy eating habits and appropriate guidance techniques. Staff should not admonish a child for not eating, cajole a child to entice him to eat, or talk across the child as though she were not present. For help with nutritional questions, managers might recruit a board member with a dietetic or family and consumer science background. Together, the manager and board member can help the teachers plan and integrate nutrition education within regular play activities.

Preventing Foodborne Illness

All staff members who handle food must be fully aware of their responsibility for preventing **foodborne illness**. In addition to the harm done to the individuals involved, a food-poisoning outbreak among the children or staff members can severely damage a center's reputation. According to the Centers for Disease Control and Prevention, about

40,000 cases of salmonella infection are reported each year, with the number of unreported incidences estimated at 30 or more times greater. It is most associated with meat, poultry, seafood, eggs, and dairy products, but it can also grow on fruits, vegetables, and sprouts and in orange juice if the right conditions exist. You cannot see, taste, or smell it. Symptoms, including diarrhea, cramps, fever, and sometimes chills, headache, and vomiting, appear between 8 and 72 hours after eating the contaminated food and last up to 7 days. Most victims recover without medical intervention, but effects can be severe or life-threatening in the very young or elderly.

Other food-poisoning bacteria cause similar symptoms; however, botulism can be fatal in very small doses. Therefore, home-canned foods or foods from damaged or unlabeled cans should never be used.

Safe food-handling practices prevent illness by keeping the bacteria from growing to high levels and by destroying the bacteria through thorough cooking. The USDA's Food Safety and Inspection Service (U.S. Department of Agriculture, Food Safety and Inspection Service, 2013) recommends four basic strategies for preventing food-borne illness:

1. *Cleanliness*   Wash hands thoroughly before handling food and after toileting, diapering, or touching pets; wash and sanitize dishes, cooking utensils, and work surfaces after each use; use nonporous cutting boards and disposable towels.

2. *Separation*   Keep raw meat, poultry, and seafood apart from other foods; use a different cutting board for each; don't put cooked food on a plate that has held raw meat, poultry, or seafood.

3. *Cooking*   Use a clean thermometer to make sure meats are cooked to at least 145°F for roasts and steaks, 160°F for ground beef, 170°F for poultry parts, and 180°F for whole poultry. Cook eggs until firm and fish until it is opaque and flakes easily. Cover, stir, and rotate food to avoid uneven cooking when using a microwave oven.

4. *Cooling*   Refrigerate all perishable food; always defrost frozen food in a refrigerator, under cold running water, or in a microwave; make sure air circulates in the refrigerator.

As a center manager, you are responsible for ensuring that staff members understand the importance of good hygiene practices. Posting signs over sinks and in lavatories may help remind some to wash their hands. Simple training exercises can be conducted at staff meetings to emphasize the importance of thorough handwashing practices.

Staff members should never work with food if they have symptoms of an illness, such as diarrhea or vomiting, or cuts or sores on their skin that cannot be covered with disposable gloves. Using disposable gloves must not lull staff members into laxness about washing their hands. Ideally, staff members responsible for changing diapers should not be responsible for preparing food. In smaller facilities, where such double duty might be unavoidable, staff members must be even more scrupulous about washing their hands with soap and running water each time they move from caregiving to food preparation.

One way to help you and your staff conceptualize the sanitation aspects of your center's food service is to ask yourselves whether you would feel comfortable eating in a restaurant with a kitchen that resembled yours. Sometimes, in their effort to create a homelike atmosphere, child-care providers forget that they are feeding a public clientele and must exercise every precaution to protect the health and safety of their "customers."

Considerations When Feeding Babies

The food requirements for infants are noted in Figure 11.1. Licensing standards also provide important details. Each baby's needs are likely to be very different from those of the baby in the next crib. The proper amount and kind of formula is essential to the infant's health and well-being. Some centers provide infant formula, and some rely on the parents to bring it. In either case, it must be handled properly. That means that each bottle must

	Birth Through 3 Months	4 Through 7 Months	8 Through 11 Months
Breakfast	4–6 fluid ounces of formula[1] or breast milk[2,3]	4–8 fluid ounces of formula[1] or breast milk[2,3]; 0–3 tablespoons of infant cereal[1,4]	6–8 fluid ounces of formula[1]; or breast milk[2,3]; 2–4 tablespoons of infant cereal[1]; and 1–4 tablespoons of fruit or vegetable or both
Lunch or Supper	4–6 fluid ounces of formula[1] or breast milk[2,3]	4–8 fluid ounces of formula[1] or breast milk[2,3]; 0–3 tablespoons of infant cereal[1,4]; and 0–3 tablespoons of fruit or vegetable or both[4]	6–8 fluid ounces of formula[1] or breast milk;[2,3] 2–4 tablespoons of infant cereal[1]; and/or 1–4 tablespoons of meat, fish, poultry, egg yolk, cooked dry beans or peas; or $\frac{1}{2}$–2 ounces of cheese; or 1–4 ounces (volume) of cottage cheese; or 1–4 ounces (weight) of cheese food or cheese spread; and 1–4 tablespoons of fruit or vegetable or both
Snack	4–6 fluid ounces of formula[1] breast milk[2,3]	4–6 fluid ounces of formula[1] or breast milk[2,3]	2–4 fluid ounces of formula[1] or breast milk[2,3], or fruit juice[5]; and $0-\frac{1}{2}$ bread[4,6]; or 0–2 crackers[4,6]

[1]Infant formula and dry infant cereal must be iron fortified.

[2]Breast milk or formula, or portions of both, may be served; however, it is recommended that breast milk be served in place of formula from birth through 11 months.

[3]For some breast-fed infants who regularly consume less than the minimum amount of breast milk per feeding, a serving of less than the minimum amount of breast milk may be offered, with additional breast milk offered if the infant is still hungry.

[4]A serving of this component is required when the infant is developmentally ready to accept it.

[5]Fruit juice must be full strength.

[6]A serving of this component must be made from whole-grain or enriched meal or flour.

FIGURE 11.1 Meal requirements for infants in child care.
Source: USDA Child Care Nutrition Resource System.

contain only enough for one feeding, be labeled with the child's name and date, and be stored in the refrigerator. Formula left in a bottle after a feeding must be discarded.

Infant caregivers should hold the baby warmly while giving the bottle. One reason for the recommended 3- or 4-to-1 infant–adult ratio is the babies' need to have one-to-one contact with the same caregiver. Security and trust are fostered in both infants and parents by this arrangement. In addition to meeting psychological needs, holding babies while feeding them avoids choking and ear infections. It also prevents dental caries that can result when babies are put to bed with bottles in their mouths.

Because of the special benefits that breast-fed infants receive, even for a few months, the center should assist mothers who desire to feed their infants this way. Encourage breast-feeding mothers to return to the center to feed their infants and provide a comfortable rocking chair in a quiet, private room or corner so mother and baby can enjoy a relaxing time together. Mothers who cannot come to the center during their workday can leave expressed breast milk in a bottle. If a mother is planning to do this, you might recommend that she try using the bottle at home a few times before you try it at the center. That way, the baby does not have to adapt to too many changes all at once. Of course, refrigerate breast milk as you do any milk. It can be stored in the refrigerator for up to 48 hours, in the freezer for 2 weeks. Frozen breast milk should be thawed in the refrigerator. Watch this **video** for specific steps to follow when using breast milk with babies.

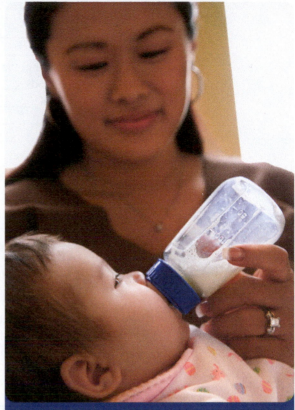
Babies who cannot hold a bottle on their own should be held while feeding.

Warm all baby bottles by putting them in pans of hot (not boiling) water for 5 minutes. Never use the microwave because it heats foods unevenly, and bottle contents that feel only lukewarm to the skin on your adult wrist can scald a baby's tender mouth.

Solid foods are started around the sixth month, always in consultation with the child's parents. Introduce foods one at a time and carefully observe the child for possible allergic reactions before introducing another food. Because babies have grown accustomed to using a different type of tongue movement for sucking, they may require some time to learn the finer points of taking and swallowing food from a spoon. Pushing food out of the mouth with the tongue may be part of this effort and not necessarily a sign of dislike. Be alert for possible choking.

All foods should be of high quality and unsalted, and kept covered and fresh. Never feed a child directly from a jar of baby food. The saliva on the spoon can carry bacteria back to the jar where it can multiply and cause illness the next time you use it. For each feeding (and for each baby if you are feeding more than one at a time), use a clean spoon to place a small amount of food in a clean dish. Replace the cover on the jar and refrigerate it immediately. Discard any food left in the dish at the end of the feeding.

At about 6 months of age, the infant begins self-feeding and will enjoy a graham cracker while sitting at the feeding table. It is the beginning of independence. Be careful that you do not provide foods that can cause choking: avoid grapes, pretzels, or popcorn. If you serve hotdogs, make sure the skin is not tough—slice them in half lengthwise and cut the strips into small chunks.

Your center is usually required to keep records on the individual infants, showing food intake, sleeping patterns, bowel movements, and developmental milestones. A copy

XYZ Child Development Center

Caregiver _____

Baby's Name _____ Date _____

Food: Times for bottle _____

         New foods _____

         Unusual _____

Sleeping: A.M. _____ P.M. _____

         Unusual _____

Bowel Movements _____

         Unusual _____

New Motor Skills _____

New Words

Other _____

Note: Parents, please feel free to discuss any item with your baby's caregiver.

FIGURE 11.2 Sample report to parents.

of the report should be sent home with the parents daily. Parents must also be encouraged to report to the center staff members any unusual changes in their baby's food intake, sleeping patterns, or bowel movements. A sample report form is shown in Figure 11.2.

Monitoring and Controlling Food Programs

Monitoring the menus, food shopping lists, supermarket specials, and the center's storage systems helps managers get the most food service for their food dollars. To prevent food service personnel from intentionally mixing up too much food, it is essential to have a policy prohibiting anyone from taking leftover food home. Keeping freezers and storerooms locked is advisable. A large inventory is costly when interest rates are high; thus, keeping an inventory larger than reasonable amounts for emergencies is a questionable practice. Check the contents of all food deliveries immediately to insure the quantities billed are correct.

Monitor the nutritional content of the meals and note any wasted food left on the plates after the children have finished their meal. Occasionally, the waste can be explained by its being a new food or a different recipe, but it is still wasted food. Plan to serve new food or a new recipe in smaller quantities until the children develop a taste for it through repeated exposure. Parents may give you helpful feedback through the questions they ask and the recipes they request after their children report to them about the foods they are eating at school.

In addition to keeping track of costs, nutritional quality, and waste, it is important to monitor the health and safety of the food program to insure that staff members are following through with proper food preparation and storage techniques, and practicing good hygiene themselves. Managers may use an evaluation form similar to that shown in Figure 11.3 to check the food system.

PLANNING NUTRITIOUS MENUS

The USDA has established guidelines, adopted by the American Public Health Association (APHA) and the American Academy of Pediatrics (AAP), that specify the amounts and types of foods that must be included in each meal or snack for each age group.

Figure 11.4 shows the nutritional standards for children ages 1 to 12 years.

Rating Scale: 4—Very Satisfactory 3—Satisfactory 2—Unsatisfactory 1—Very Unsatisfactory

Personnel

___ 1. Dietitian or home economist plans menus with adequate nutritional quality?

___ 2. Food service director takes adequate leadership to ensure high-quality service?

___ 3. Food service assistants are trained to do their jobs adequately?

___ 4. Food service personnel are appropriately clean, with hair nets and clean aprons, and hands washed with soap?

___ 5. Food service personnel are at work on time?

___ 6. Food service personnel have required health checks?

Facilities

___ 7. Is the food service space adequate in size?

___ 8. Is the food service equipment operating properly?

___ 9. Is the storage space adequate in the food service area?

___ 10. Is the refrigeration space adequate?

___ 11. Personnel keep the kitchen, appliances, and counter spotless?

___ 12. Children's chairs and tables are adequate in number and size?

___ 13. Dishes, utensils, and glasses are safe and adequate in number?

___ 14. Appropriate dishwashing procedures are used?

Menu Planning

___ 15. Menus for meals meet minimum USDA standards?

___ 16. Menus for snacks meet minimum USDA standards?

___ 17. Records for federal funding are kept daily (if applicable)?

___ 18. Are cycle menus being used appropriately?

___ 19. Are menus posted for parents and others to read?

___ 20. Are copies of menus made available to parents?

___ 21. Are records of the children's intake maintained?

___ 22. Are children's prescriptions for special diets posted where a substitute cook could easily find them?

Preparation and Service

___ 23. Do food service personnel know appropriate cooking methods for each type of food?

___ 24. Is food served in a very sanitary manner?

___ 25. Is food served on time?

___ 26. Is food service well organized with each worker knowing the required tasks and doing them well?

___ 27. Is food regularly served family-style?

___ 28. Is adequate attention given to individual children's needs?

___ 29. Does each teacher who sits with children have good rapport with the group of children?

___ 30. Does each teacher get enough to eat?

___ 31. Is a worker ready to take care of emergencies so the teacher does not have to leave the table?

___ 32. Are procedures known to children who have been in attendance for a while?

Interpersonal Climate

___ 33. Do children seem to be happy and enjoying the meals?

___ 34. Are voices quiet and pleasant?

___ 35. Do children seem adequately rested to facilitate eating?

___ 36. Are children regularly given a quiet restful period just before mealtime?

___ 37. Are parents invited to attend a meal periodically?

Nutrition Education

___ 38. Do teachers tell children about foods that are good for them?

___ 39. Do children demonstrate an interest in foods?

___ 40. Are food projects offered in the curriculum?

___ 41. Are parents informed about food projects?

Budgetary Matters

___ 42. Is cost consciousness adequate among food service staff?

___ 43. Is the amount of wasted food reasonable?

___ 44. Is leftover food appropriately stored and used?

___ 45. Does the food service staff plan adequately to avoid running out of commodities, calling for quick trips for supplies?

___ 46. Are orders placed and deliveries made on time?

___ 47. Are deliveries checked for correct quantities?

___ 48. Is petty cash disbursement monitored?

FIGURE 11.3 Food service monitoring guide.

Breakfast (3 components)

Food Components	Ages 1–2	Ages 3–5	Ages 6–12[1]
1 milk			
fluid milk	$\frac{1}{2}$ cup	$\frac{3}{4}$ cup	1 cup
1 fruit/vegetable			
juice[2], fruit and/or vegetable	$\frac{1}{4}$ cup	$\frac{1}{2}$ cup	$\frac{1}{2}$ cup
1 grain/bread[3]			
bread or	$\frac{1}{2}$ slice	$\frac{1}{2}$ slice	1 slice
cornbread or biscuit or roll or muffin or	$\frac{1}{2}$ serving	$\frac{1}{2}$ serving	1 serving
cold dry cereal or	$\frac{1}{4}$ cup	$\frac{1}{3}$ cup	$\frac{3}{4}$ cup
hot cooked cereal or	$\frac{1}{4}$ cup	$\frac{1}{4}$ cup	$\frac{1}{2}$ cup
pasta or noodles or grains	$\frac{1}{4}$ cup	$\frac{1}{4}$ cup	$\frac{1}{2}$ cup

Lunch or Supper (4 components)

Food Components	Ages 1–2	Ages 3–5	Ages 6–12[1]
1 milk			
fluid milk	$\frac{1}{2}$ cup	$\frac{3}{4}$ cup	1 cup
2 fruits/vegetables			
juice[2], fruit and/or vegetable	$\frac{1}{4}$ cup	$\frac{1}{2}$ cup	$\frac{3}{4}$ cup
1 grains/bread[3]			
bread or	$\frac{1}{2}$ slice	$\frac{1}{2}$ slice	1 slice
cornbread or biscuit or roll or muffin or	$\frac{1}{2}$ serving	$\frac{1}{2}$ serving	1 serving
cold dry cereal or	$\frac{1}{4}$ cup	$\frac{1}{3}$ cup	$\frac{3}{4}$ cup
hot cooked cereal or	$\frac{1}{4}$ cup	$\frac{1}{4}$ cup	$\frac{1}{2}$ cup
pasta or noodles or grains	$\frac{1}{4}$ cup	$\frac{1}{4}$ cup	$\frac{1}{2}$ cup
1 meat/meat alternate			
meat or poultry or fish[4] or	1 oz.	$1\frac{1}{2}$ oz.	2 oz.
alternate protein product or	1 oz.	$1\frac{1}{2}$ oz.	2 oz.
cheese or	1 oz.	$1\frac{1}{2}$ oz.	2 oz.
egg or	$\frac{1}{2}$	$\frac{3}{4}$	1
cooked dry beans or peas or	$\frac{1}{4}$ cup	$\frac{3}{8}$ cup	$\frac{1}{2}$ cup
peanut or other nut or seed butters or	2 tbsp.	3 tbsp.	4 tbsp.
nuts and/or seeds[5] or	$\frac{1}{2}$ oz.	$\frac{3}{4}$ oz.	1 oz.
yogurt[6]	4 oz.	6 oz.	8 oz.

FIGURE 11.4   Meal requirements for children ages 1 through 12 in child care programs.
Source: USDA Food and Nutrition Service. http://www.fns.usda.gov/sites/default/files/Child_Meals.pdf.

Snack *(2 Components)*

Food Components	Ages 1–2	Ages 3–5	Ages 6–12[1]
1 milk			
fluid milk	$\frac{1}{2}$ cup	$\frac{1}{2}$ cup	1 cup
1 fruit/vegetable			
juice[2], fruit and/or vegetable	$\frac{1}{2}$ cup	$\frac{1}{2}$ cup	$\frac{3}{4}$ cup
1 grains/bread[3]			
bread or	$\frac{1}{2}$ slice	$\frac{1}{2}$ slice	1 slice
cornbread or biscuit or roll or muffin or	$\frac{1}{2}$ serving	$\frac{1}{2}$ serving	1 serving
cold dry cereal or	$\frac{1}{4}$ cup	$\frac{1}{3}$ cup	$\frac{3}{4}$ cup
hot cooked cereal or	$\frac{1}{4}$ cup	$\frac{1}{4}$ cup	$\frac{1}{2}$ cup
pasta or noodles or grains	$\frac{1}{4}$ cup	$\frac{1}{4}$ cup	$\frac{1}{2}$ cup
1 meat/meat alternate			
meat or poultry or fish[4] or	$\frac{1}{2}$ oz.	$\frac{1}{2}$ oz.	1 oz.
alternate protein product or	$\frac{1}{2}$ oz.	$\frac{1}{2}$ oz.	1 oz.
cheese or	$\frac{1}{2}$ oz.	$\frac{1}{2}$ oz.	1 oz.
egg[5] or $\frac{1}{2}$	$\frac{1}{2}$	$\frac{1}{2}$	
cooked dry beans or peas or	$\frac{1}{8}$ cup	$\frac{1}{8}$ cup	$\frac{1}{4}$ cup
peanut or other nut or seed butters or	1 tbsp.	1 tbsp.	2 tbsp.
nuts and/or seeds or	$\frac{1}{2}$ oz.	$\frac{1}{2}$ oz.	1 oz.
yogurt[6]	2 oz.	2 oz.	4 oz.

[1]Children age 12 and older may be served larger portions based on their greater food needs. They may not be served less than the minimum quantities listed in this column.

[2]Fruit or vegetable juice must be full strength. Juice cannot be served when milk is the only other snack component.

[3]Breads and grains must be made from whole-grain or enriched meal or flour. Cereal must be whole grain or enriched or fortified.

[4]A serving consists of the edible portion of cooked lean meat or poultry or fish.

[5]One-half egg meets the required minimum amount (1 ounce or less) of meat alternate.

[6]Yogurt may be plain or flavored, unsweetened or sweetened.

FIGURE 11.4 *(Continued)*

Although you may remember "the four basic food groups" from your elementary school days, the USDA and the Department of Health and Human Services have recently updated the way we conceptualize a balanced diet (see Figure 11.5). The old Food Guide Pyramid has been replaced with Choose MyPlate to emphasize a more personalized approach to gradual improvement in healthy eating and physical activity. It takes into account the proportion, as well as the variety, of foods required for a healthy diet, but it recognizes that exact amounts will vary among individuals depending on many factors, including physical activity level. Each food group (grains, vegetables, fruits, oils, milk, and meat or beans) is represented by a section on the plate, with vegetables and grains occupying larger sections than those assigned to proteins and fruits. Individuals are encouraged to log onto the website www.myplate.gov to calculate

FIGURE 11.5 MyPlate. A guide to daily food choices.

Source: U.S. Department of Agriculture.

suggested daily amounts of each food group based on age, gender, and daily activity level.

Several considerations can guide food choices. In addition to meeting standards for nutrition and safety, meal and snack menus should include foods that are colorful and interesting in texture and flavor. The children's preferences should also guide menu planning. Though it is highly desirable to introduce children to new foods, it helps their transition from home to school to be served some familiar foods. Foods from various ethnic groups are often desirable for this reason. All children can learn to enjoy foods from a variety of ethnic groups.

Cycle menus provide a shortcut to menu planning. The cycles are often a 15- or 20-day sequence of menus repeated throughout a season with minimal changes. New cycles can be planned for a new season. Once checked by a dietitian, the combinations should not be changed without checking the nutritional content of the substitute food. To keep a balanced diet, it may be better to substitute an entire day's menu if you have a shortage of some crucial item. Sample menus for eight weeks are available online from the National Food Service Management Institute at www.nfsmi. org. Click on "Child and Adult Care Food Program" and look for menus under "Child Care Resources."

Figure 11.6 is a sample worksheet that you can use to plan a week's menu. The USDA publishes nutritional standards and other helpful meal planning information for centers and for families. These materials are available online from the Child Care Food Program, U.S. Department of Agriculture, at http://www.fns.usda.gov/cnd/care/; from your local cooperative extension service; or from the nutrition department of many universities. Commercial software programs available for programs participating in the Child and Adult Care Food Program can automate the process of preparing menu production records and calculating the number of free, reduced, or paid meals served. See, for example, Minute Menu Systems at http://www.minutemenu.com/.

Snacks

Snacks should be considered a nutrition break that restores the children's energy after a busy period of play. Sitting at the table for a short time also provides active children with a needed rest. Snack time is usually a social time of day, with conversations about activities and events at school or home. Only highly nutritious foods should be served. The emphasis should be on vegetables, fruits, cereal, and protein foods. Foods or beverages with high sugar content should be avoided. As you may note in Figure 11.3, the snack requirement calls for any two of four food categories: milk, juice or fruit or vegetable, meat or meat alternate, and bread or cereal. For example, milk and apples, juice and sandwiches, or carrots and cheese sticks all are adequate snacks.

Children need plenty of drinking water throughout the day. A small cup of water is preferred by younger children, and older children can usually manage a drinking fountain. Many do not like ice water.

Allergies and Special Diets

Centers must cooperate with families and medical personnel when children have allergies or other special dietary needs. Managers should develop a written policy defining the responsibilities of parents and center staff members in regard to special diets. Requiring parents to bring a physician's statement when special diets are requested protects the center as well as the child. Some parents who are highly conscious about dieting themselves are minimally informed about nutrition and could jeopardize their

	Week of:	Monday	Tuesday	Wednesday	Thursday	Friday
Breakfast	Fluid milk					
	Fruit, vegetable, or juice					
	Cereal or					
	Cereal/bread/alternative					
A.M. Snack	*Choose 2 (of 4)*					
	Fluid milk					
	Fruit, vegetable, or juice					
	Cereal/bread/alternative					
	Meat or alternative					
Lunch	Fluid milk					
	Meat or alternative					
	Vegetable or fruit					
	Vegetable or fruit					
	Bread or alternative					
	Other (e.g., condiments)					
P.M. Snack	*Choose 2 (of 4)*					
	Fluid milk					
	Fruit, vegetable, or juice					
	Cereal/bread/alternative					
	Meat or alternative					

FIGURE 11.6 Menu planning worksheet.

child's health with diet restrictions. Diet restrictions that may make sense for sedentary or weight-conscious adults do not generally make sense for active, growing children.

The physician's statement should identify the child's condition and specify foods to be avoided as well as acceptable substitutes. It should also indicate the symptoms associated with exposure to the allergen and instructions for what center staff members should do in the event of an allergic reaction. Posting a list of children's names and specific allergies in each area where food is prepared or served is essential to help staff members make sure that children never receive food that could be harmful for them.

Some families request special diets for their children because of religious or other personal preferences. Child-care facilities are challenged to balance their goal of being family friendly with their responsibility to ensure that children's needs are met. For example, some nutritionists are concerned about vegetarian diets because giving young children enough complete and tasty protein without using meat, poultry, or fish requires concerted attention. Centers enrolling children whose families espouse vegetarianism must give special attention to the children's need for protein to support their growth—building a mass of muscle tissue composed largely of protein. Milk, cheese, egg, whole-grain cereals, dry beans, soy products, and peanut butter are the protein foods that appear in vegetarian diets. A young child who is growing and highly active requires calories and nutrients for these activities that an unknowing parent may attempt to deny. This is another instance where your health consultant may be able to help you work with families so that you can be sensitive to their preferences while still upholding your professional obligation to protect children's health.

Some centers provide the special foods, for example, soy milk for children who are lactose intolerant or graham crackers made with vegetable shortening rather than lard for children whose culture prohibits consumption of pork. Others ask that families provide the necessary substitutions. Even in those cases, however, it is a child-care center's responsibility to ensure that every child receives all required food components and to supplement those that families may fail to provide.

Collaborating with Families about Food Matters

Whether food is provided by the center or brought from home, centers and families collaborate in a variety of ways. When families provide the food, the expectation for adequate nutrition must be clearly spelled out in the center's nutrition policy and included in the handbook families receive when they enroll their children. In the short term, the simple correction for occasional lapses is for the center to provide the missing food component when the meal from home falls short. When the meals from home are consistently inadequate, a more comprehensive approach is needed. Begin by discussing the issue with the family. They may need a reminder of your policy, or they may simply be unaware of what constitutes adequate nutrition and you can provide information. They may be experiencing financial hardship, in which case you can guide them to community resources for help. If the situation persists in spite of your efforts, you may need to report the family to the appropriate authorities as possibly neglecting the child.

When the center provides the meals, parents like to know what their children are eating at school so that they do not duplicate the menu at home in the evening. Accreditation criteria, as well as national health and safety guidelines, require that parents be informed of the type of food served at the center. Menus can be posted where the parents can see them as they drop off or pick up their child. Observing and recording what a child eats helps parents as well as the food service staff members plan wisely. Some schools report to the parents exactly what their child ate by using a daily checksheet. The USDA website MyPlate.gov, listed among the resources for further study at the end of this chapter, includes a link to a Daily Food Plan for Preschoolers, with a chart showing recommended daily servings of each food group and a method of tracking the individual child's intake. The visual record provides an easy way to see whether the child is getting too little or too much of any particular food group(s).

The center should encourage families to report any special problems their child has or might have as a result of some home experience. The report could include events such as a digestive upset during the night or having a relative in for a big supper the night before, which kept the child eating fancy food at all hours. Either episode may significantly affect the child's food intake the next day.

Another way to involve families in regard to food is to invite parents to eat with the children when convenient. For those children whose parents cannot come at lunchtime, extend the invitation to breakfast or snack time as well. Adults learn to appreciate their children's eating habits when they see them functioning with other children. They also gain additional respect for the teaching staff members when they realize how much effort and organization a simple meal requires. If you are encouraging the children to invite their parents for meals, remember that children with divorced parents may want to invite each parent on a different day. The child might also be encouraged to invite a grandparent, aunt, or special family friend. A child should be helped to feel included in a special event even if a parent cannot come.

Many families enjoy joining their children for lunch on birthdays, and they often want to bring a treat. Some local sanitarians take a strict interpretation of the AAP/AAPH guidelines on food from home (e.g., being labeled for the individual child and not shared) and prohibit the use of homemade birthday treats. If you do allow them, you should do so only for children ages 3 and over. Encourage parents to consider healthy alternatives prepared in individual servings, such as frozen yogurt popsicles or oatmeal cookies. An alternative would be to invite the birthday child's family to come in on the big day and help make cupcakes using the center's ingredients (which you know come from approved sources and have been safely stored).

Accreditation guidelines also recommend a nutrition education program for parents. Telling parents about the nutritional quality of a food (perhaps in a special "cook's corner" in your newsletter) may help them understand why you include it on the menu. If a child particularly likes a food, you might share the recipe with the parents. You can let families know what you are doing at the center to encourage healthy eating and exercise and share ideas for doing the same things at home. Be careful about preaching, however, because you don't want parents to feel pressured or blamed. Recall our earlier discussion about the limits of adult influence on children's eating behaviors and the fact that coaxing a child to eat or refrain from certain foods can actually have the opposite effect.

Culture and Food

It is necessary for managers to consider the cultural diversity of their families because culture influences people's beliefs about what foods are to be eaten and what behaviors regarding food are acceptable. Some groups have strong prohibitions against eating certain foods. For example, many Hindus do not eat beef, many Muslims and Jews do not eat pork, and some groups are vegetarian. Substitutes for meats must be available.

Some groups that do not typically serve a particular food in their homes do not object if their children learn to like that food at the center. For instance, Chinese typically do not serve raw vegetables, but their children can eat raw carrots, broccoli, or cauliflower at school if they like. People from Germany may consider corn a food only for pigs, but they often learn to enjoy corn when they come to the United States. Some groups use a lot of seasoning or eat fried foods, yet they can learn to taste foods that are bland or cooked without much fat. Such differences should be kept in mind as menus are planned and meals are served. Guiding children to try foods they have never seen at home takes patience and will likely be more successful if you start with small servings.

Western middle-class culture places a high value on independence, and many adults believe that, except for infants, who are not yet ready to feed themselves, a child should be encouraged to become self-sufficient. Other cultures place a higher priority on interdependence, however, and believe that children learn to be tender caregivers when they are helped with things that they could actually do for themselves (Gonzalez-Mena, 2005). If the conservation of precious food resources is a concern, adults might find it wasteful to let children smear food around their high-chair trays. It is important to recognize and respect cultural differences and arrive at mutually satisfying arrangements through open-minded discussions with the families.

Federal Subsidies for Food Programs

Child development centers and family child-care homes may qualify for federal reimbursement of the meal and snack costs if 25 percent of the children are needy. Although the USDA manages the food program, it is administered locally by state or regional agencies. In some states, for example, the Department of Education administers the Child Care Food Program. You can find out who administers the program in your state by checking the CACFP website at http://www.fns.usda.gov/cnd/Contacts/StateDirectory.htm.

For each child, the center must document the parents' income level and the family's size and report this information on the application. The center is reimbursed at a higher rate for the costs associated with feeding the lower-income children than the rate reimbursed for the moderate- and higher-income children. A center serving 30 children could receive reimbursements ranging from $200 to $2,500. The federal funds do not completely pay for the food service program, but they are enough that many centers find it worthwhile to participate in spite of the extra effort required.

The calculations for receiving the reimbursements are somewhat complex, and detailed records must be kept for each meal. Also available is some reimbursement of the costs associated with paying personnel to take the training, do the bookkeeping, and file the reports. Computer software companies that have developed child-care center record-keeping programs have created a program specifically designed to keep the records for USDA food reimbursements.

SUPPORTING DEVELOPMENT IN ALL DOMAINS

A high-quality food program serves many purposes beyond nourishing children's young bodies and providing the energy needed for play. Children can gain skill and confidence in feeding themselves, increase the variety of foods they enjoy, establish healthy eating habits, learn to behave in socially acceptable ways at the table, and much more—but only if great care and thoughtfulness goes into planning where and how you will serve the nutritious meals you have worked so hard to provide.

Serving and Seating Children

Large lunchrooms are overwhelming for young children and frustrating for the adults who accompany them. Small-table settings with an adult and five or six children are much more conducive to a pleasant dining experience. Planning the children's places at the meal tables means that children who need help can be located where an adult can reach them. Seating independent eaters among the less experienced allows children to learn from peer role models. Having a name card or a regular seat at the table assures each child that he has a place to sit.

Choosing where and with whom to sit can also be an interesting social activity for young children. Some programs, inspired by the preschools of Reggio Emilia, Italy, have developed the practice of forming small "committees" of children to help with table setting and seating assignments each day, providing rich opportunities for discussion, negotiation, and learning to consider other people's preferences and feelings.

Family-style serving bowls promote independence and mastery of self-help skills.

An adult should sit and eat with each small group of children so that the program can meet socialization goals without sacrificing sanitation. The teacher sitting with a small group serves the children family-style and grows accustomed to each child's likes and dislikes. In this video, early childhood teachers confess their initial apprehension at the thought of children serving themselves. What strategies did they use to help make it an enjoyable experience for everyone?

Volunteers, school-age children, and high school students can serve as helpers at meal times. Make the serving bowls small enough for the children to manipulate reduces the risk of contaminating large quantities of food should a child lick a serving spoon, for example, or handle all the toast on the plate. The adult gives each child a serving to get things started and then children can serve themselves seconds. They often eat more when they can serve themselves. Keep servings child-size so that children who are unfamiliar with a food, or think they don't like it, are not overwhelmed by an unappetizing mound on their plates. A small pitcher, holding just a cup of milk so that the children can pour it by themselves, will entice many of them to drink a second helping. Adults should remember that children like lukewarm food—not very hot or cold—so they should not be bothered when the soup gets cold and the ice cream gets mushy. That is the way most children like soup and ice cream!

If your goal is to support children's independent eating, remember that bite-size pieces of meat or other foods are easier for small fingers to grasp. As the children get a little older, they can manage small spoons and forks. Often the spoon is held in one hand while the child happily carries food to her mouth with the other. Once children have mastered eating utensils, they may be ready to use a stick of toast rather than their fingers to push food onto the spoon. Children should be taught to keep the food on their plate rather than strewing it around the table.

Observing other children independently serving themselves and eating encourages a more dependent child to assume the same responsibility. Parents who visit at lunchtime are often amazed at the maturity of their child who, they say, "acts like a baby at home!" Teachers and caregivers should never cajole or bribe a child to eat. If the child is too tired to eat, it may be helpful to schedule a resting time just before mealtime or to eat a little bit earlier.

Young children have quite a bit of concentrating to do as they eat, and after a busy morning they are usually hungry. However, as they become more adept at quelling their hunger pangs, their attention turns to conversations during meals. Children should never be told to "be quiet and eat" if a pleasant mealtime atmosphere is desired.

Brushing one's teeth after meals is part of a developmentally appropriate food service program.

They can talk about how they helped prepare the food, how milk makes their teeth strong, or the origins of the food they are eating. Caregivers can provide a good example by speaking quietly and only to the children at their table rather than to adults or children at another table. They should take care not to detract from the pleasure of the occasion in their zeal to make it a learning experience.

Children should be encouraged to sit at the table until they have finished eating, to carry their plate to a serving cart for their dessert, and to remove their dishes when finished. If a child wants to get up and down frequently, she may not be hungry and, with adult assistance, should be excused to go to the toilet and get ready for nap time. Because the teacher eating with the children should not leave them to tend to a child who is ready to leave early, another adult must be available to help. This is a good time for children to learn to brush their teeth after meals, another healthy habit to cultivate.

As you watch this **video**, notice how well the children manage pouring from the small pitcher, eating with real tableware, and cleaning up after themselves. What do you think the teachers did to help the children develop these competencies?

It can be tiring for teachers and aides who have worked all morning with the children to eat their lunch with them; however, the children really do better at eating and feeding themselves if these familiar people guide their mealtime. Managers and food service staff must be aware of the teachers' needs and ensure that they get adequate food as they supervise mealtimes. Having adequate support people at mealtime eliminates the need for the teacher to jump up and get items or tend to emergencies—interruptions that interfere with the teacher's resting and eating an adequate meal.

Influencing Children's Eating Behaviors

Adults have probably always worried about, and tried to influence, what and how much children eat, and this concern is exacerbated by recent concern regarding obesity rates in the United States. Between 1998 and 2010, the percentage of low-income children who were obese rose from just over 13 percent to nearly 15 percent, while the percentage of extremely obese children rose from 1.75 percent to 2.07 percent (Centers for Disease Control and Prevention, 2012). Although the trend appears to have slowed since 2003, the numbers remain alarming because obesity is associated with serious health problems, including diabetes, hypertension, and elevated cholesterol levels in children just as in adults. Furthermore, children who are overweight or obese are more likely to suffer low self-esteem, depression, and social withdrawal. How can child-care providers help counteract this trend? The answers may not be as simple as we would like.

First of all, obesity in children and adults is heavily influenced by our human-built and social–cultural environments, which include highly processed foods, hectic family schedules promoting dependence on fast foods, sedentary lifestyles, and the pervasive influence of advertising. Parents and other adults may try mightily to influence children's eating behaviors, but research shows that peers and advertising are much stronger influences (Lumeng, 2005).

Some research suggests that the more adult control exerted over a child's eating habits at age 5, the greater the likelihood of that child eating while not hungry at age 9 (Lumeng, 2005). Children who are allowed to follow their body's signals are able to adjust their intake of food to meet their caloric needs. Because energy needs vary from day to day and because adult interference reduces children's capacity to recognize their bodies' signals, adults should not be concerned or call attention to the fact that a child does or does not eat very much at any given meal. Research has shown that when children are given a wide variety of appropriate foods from which to choose, they eat a

Part of the appeal of the fresh green salad is being able to serve it oneself.

balanced diet. They may taste a new food as many as 10 times (without being forced or coaxed) before deciding they like it (Birch, Johnson, & Fisher, 1995, pp. 71–78).

One good reason for serving meals family-style is that children can ask for—or better still, help themselves to—second portions. This approach helps the children learn to make their own decisions. Research has demonstrated that children who receive a food as a reward for eating another food increase their preference for the "reward" food and learn to dislike the food they were supposedly being encouraged to eat (Birch et al., 1995, p. 74). Accordingly, child-care providers should never use food (including dessert) as a reward for a clean plate, withhold it as punishment, or use it as reinforcement in any way.

Although child-care programs might not be able to control what children eat at home, or even what they choose to eat at the center, they can make sure that while at the center the child has a healthy selection from which to choose. In addition to adhering to the USDA guidelines, centers can incorporate the following strategies, suggested by Carol Huettig and her colleagues (Huettig, Sanborn, DiMarco, Popejoy, & Rich, 2004, p. 51):

- Use low-fat milk for children over 2.
- Limit fruit juice consumption to 6 ounces per day. Use fresh fruits instead of juices to meet that meal component, and let children have water instead of second helpings of juice.
- Encourage children to drink plenty of water throughout the day, outdoors as well as indoors.
- Make healthy foods more attractive by involving children in their preparation (e.g., fruit smoothies, vegetable kabobs).

Food and Curriculum

Food provides more than just nourishment for the body. Because food involves so many sensory modalities and offers such immediate gratification, it is engaging for young children. It provides a rich source of topics to investigate because it is so much a part of daily life, culture, and commerce. Projects and investigations about food production, distribution, and preparation help the children become aware of all aspects of the human ecological system, providing what Katz and Chard called "horizontal relevance"—connections between school life and life in the everyday world outside (Katz & Chard, 2000).

As noted earlier, food is integrally bound up with culture, making it an excellent means of cultivating an appreciation for diversity. Breads and noodles, for example, are used in many forms by various cultures of the world, and the forms these items take are often associated with particular stories or beliefs. Young children could begin by thinking about all of the bread types they have eaten and eventually branch out into tasting the breads eaten by other cultures (Mitchell & David, 1992). Such a study has the additional advantage of avoiding a "tourist" approach—exposure only to the exotic aspects of other cultures.

Growing a vegetable garden may encourage children to try new foods.

DECISIONS, DECISIONS . . .

List the pros and cons of fingerpainting with chocolate pudding as an art activity for 2-year-olds. Is the list the same if you considered the activity for 4-year-olds?

When thinking about learning goals for young children in connection with food, teachers might consider the four categories suggested by Katz and Chard:

1. Knowledge (factual information, content)
2. Skills (actions that can be taught and practiced)
3. Dispositions (mental habits or tendencies such as curiosity and creativity)
4. Feelings (emotional states such as feeling of belonging or competence) (2000, pp. 25–26)

In the realm of knowledge, you might want the children to know things about various foods—their names, sources, or value for growing healthy bodies. Or you might want them to know general things—colors, shapes, size comparisons, or the meaning of printed labels. As they become progressively more mature, children are expected to develop certain skills, such as drinking from a cup; eating finger foods; using napkins, spoons, forks, and simple food preparation tools; chewing with their mouths closed; and observing the table manners appropriate to their culture. With assistance, the children eventually develop a disposition to eat healthy foods and to eat only as much as they need to satisfy their hunger. Finally, feelings of belonging to a culture, of competence at being able to meet one's own needs, and of friendliness toward meal companions should be nourished.

If you keep these goals in mind, together with what you know about the development of the children's cognitive abilities and food acceptance patterns, you can avoid using guidance techniques that work at cross purposes to your goals. For example, the lessons about "the four food groups," favored by so many teachers, are probably ineffective for two reasons. First, the concept of which foods go together is too abstract for young children to comprehend. They are much more likely to categorize food in ways that are personally meaningful: liked and disliked foods, for example, or foods at home and foods at restaurants.

One classification scheme to be avoided is "good" and "bad" foods. Most nutritionists counsel that there are no bad foods and that the important thing is a balance among all of the foods eaten. Second, the ultimate goal of such lessons lies more in the realm of disposition than of knowledge. After all, how many adults do you know who can recite all of the food pyramid's components but subsist on a diet of fast-food sandwiches and soft drinks?

DECISIONS, DECISIONS . . .

Keep a record of everything you eat for 1 week. Compare your findings with the recommendations listed at MyPlate.gov. Do you consume more or less than the recommended amounts of any food category?

As we noted earlier, research suggests that the best way to cultivate a disposition toward healthy eating habits and openness to new food experiences is by providing "children with a variety of healthful foods in a positive social environment and then allowing children the freedom to eat what they wish" (Birch et al., 1995, p. 78). Children also seem more disposed to eat foods that they have helped prepare, so wise managers include frequent opportunities for the children to help peel carrots for a snack or slice and assemble fruit kabobs. Children's participation in food preparation is even greater when they plant, tend, and harvest vegetables in their own garden.

Modeling is another factor: Children who think they do not like a food are often persuaded to try it when they see another child enjoying it. On the other hand, these adults who encourage children to take a bite of green beans, when they do not eat any themselves, usually meet with little success.

? DECISIONS, DECISIONS . . .

Is there a particular food that you eat too often? Is there one that you dislike intensely? Think about your childhood experiences with that food. Can you see any connection between those experiences and your attitude toward that food today? Discuss your conclusions with your classmates.

Field trips to the dairy, orchard, or grocery store are all concrete ways for children to learn about the food they eat. Teachers should prepare the children for such visits by encouraging them to think of questions they want to ask and, once there, give them plenty of time at the site to explore. It helps to prepare the people you are visiting so that they have an idea of what to tell the children. One group of 4-year-olds paid little attention as the orchard owner told their teacher and parents all about his modern farming methods, but they became very excited when told that a particular row of young trees and was 4 years old. "Just like us!" they exclaimed. The conversations at the snack table, as they enjoyed their apple slices the next day, contained many references to the 4-year-old trees.

Volunteers and visitors can help you meet many nutrition-related goals. Parents might make family or ethnic specialties for the children or, better yet, come in and make them with a small group of children. Older children can come in to help with meal service and to eat with the children so that more of them can have individual attention. Boy or Girl Scout groups, 4-H Clubs, and home economics classes are all potential sources of volunteers to share information or conduct food-related activities. A dentist or hygienist could demonstrate toothbrushing techniques. The possibilities are limited only by your own creativity.

Technology Toolkit

✓ Log onto the Food Safety Education section of the USDA Food Safety and Inspection Service website at http://www.fsis.usda.gov/Food_Safety_Education/index.asp. Select "Play a Food Safety Game" from the list under the heading, "I want to . . ." on the right side of the page and play the game to test your knowledge of safe food-handling practices. Click on "Ask a Food Safety Question" to locate information on specific topics.

✓ Access the website "ChooseMyPlate" at www.choosemyplate.gov to access a variety of resources (videos, posters, activities) for helping children develop healthy eating and exercise habits.

✓ Access the USDA website, "SuperTracker Home" (https://www.supertracker.usda.gov/default.aspx) to get a personalized nutrition and physical activity plan, track the nutritional value of foods you eat, and get tips and support to help make healthier choices.

Conclusion

Meeting the children's food needs requires all of the steps in the managerial process—planning, organizing, staffing, leading, and controlling. Meal service may consist of breakfast, lunch, and snack, or snack only. The careful monitoring of expense, waste, and leftovers is essential to get the most nutrition from the food dollar. Meals may be provided by the center, by the families, or by some combination thereof. Licensing and accreditation standards apply to food service, regardless of the source. Because of the integrated, holistic nature of young children's thinking and learning, food is viewed as part of the curriculum. Whether they are making a special snack as a science experience or enjoying a healthy lunch with their friends, the children are acquiring knowledge, skills, dispositions, and feelings related to healthy nutrition.

Questions for Review

1. Describe the basic requirements for setting up and maintaining a safe food preparation area.

2. Why should infants be held while being fed a bottle?

3. Would a platter of carrot and celery sticks with a dip of ranch dressing constitute an appropriate snack for a 9-month-old? For a 4-year-old? Why or why not?

4. How can a center demonstrate appreciation for cultural diversity in its food service program?

5. Give examples of how a center's food service program promotes the development of children's knowledge, skills, dispositions, and feelings about food.

Professional Portfolio

1. Write a job description for a food service manager in a child development facility. See the chapter on personnel management for an example.

2. Write 15-day cycle menus for breakfast, lunch, and an afternoon snack.

3. Using a desktop publishing program, create a brochure to distribute to families that provides information about children's nutritional needs and suggestions for making mealtimes at home pleasant for the entire family.

Resources for Further Study

PRINT

American Academy of Pediatrics, American Public Health Association, and National Resource Center for Health and Safety in Child Care and Early Education. (2010). *Preventing childhood obesity in early care and education: Selected standards from caring for our children: National health and safety performance standards; guidelines for early care and education programs*, 3rd Edition. http://nrckids.org/CFOC3/PDFVersion/preventing_obesity.pdf

Bergen, S., & Robertson, R. (2012). *Healthy children, healthy lives: The wellness guide for early childhood programs*. St. Paul, MN: Redleaf Press.

U.S. Department of Agriculture. (2000). *Building blocks for fun and healthy meals: A menu planner for the child and adult care food program*. Washington, DC: Author. Available online or in hard copy by request at http://www.fns.usda.gov/tn/Resources/buildingblocks.html

U.S. Department of Agriculture. (2013). *Nutrition & wellness tips for young children: Provider handbook for the child and adult care food program*. Washington, DC: Author. Available online or in hard copy by request at http://www.teamnutrition.usda.gov/Resources/nutritionandwellness.html

Websites

CACFP WELLNESS RESOURCES FOR CHILD CARE PROVIDERS

http://healthymeals.nal.usda.gov/cacfp-wellness-resources-child-care-providers

The Healthy, Hunger-Free Kids Act (HHFKA) of 2010 encourages child-care providers to promote health and wellness in child care through nutrition, physical activity, and limited electronic media use. This website is dedicated to helping CACFP providers find the resources they need to meet recommendations in these areas.

FOOD AND NUTRITION SERVICE

http://www.fns.usda.gov/cnd/care/

Child and Adult Care Food Program page on the U.S. Department of Agriculture's Food and Nutrition Service website; includes links to information about eligibility, reimbursement, and meal pattern requirements for the Child and Adult Care Food Program.

FOOD SAFETY AND INSPECTION SERVICE

http://www.fsis.usda.gov

Food Safety and Inspection Service of the U.S. Department of Agriculture; provides fact sheets on safe food handling, appliances, and foodborne illnesses, and links to other resources.

JAMIE OLIVER FOOD FOUNDATION

www.jamieoliver.com

Website of British chef and international television star, Jamie Oliver, whose goal is to lead a food revolution to combat obesity by changing US eating habits. Includes links to toolkits with information about school food, recipes for healthy dishes, and resources for building partnerships with other organizations.

MENUS FOR CHILD CARE

http://nfsmi-web01.nfsmi.olemiss.edu/documentLibrary Files/PDF/20080225095731.pdf

Publication of the National Food Service Management Institute at the University of Mississippi. Eight complete weekly menus, including breakfast, lunch or supper, and snack meeting the meal pattern requirements for 3- to 5-year-olds. Portion sizes can be adjusted for other age groups. The menus have been analyzed for major nutrients, and the analysis is provided. Crediting information appears in parentheses after each item on the menu.

TEAM NUTRITION

http://teamnutrition.usda.gov/

An initiative of the USDA food and nutrition service to support the child nutrition programs through training and technical assistance for food service, nutrition education for children and their caregivers, and school and community support for healthy eating and physical activity. Resources include nutrition and gardening curricula and a best practices sharing center.

CHAPTER

Educational Programming

LEARNING OUTCOMES

After studying this chapter you should be able to

- Discuss regulations and professional standards concerned with educational programming.
- Articulate the manager's responsibility for the educational program.
- Identify the basic requirements of a good educational program.
- Explain differences among curriculum models.
- Describe appropriate daily schedules and create weekly activity plans for 3- to 5-year-old children and for infants and toddlers.
- Give examples of ways to increase the meaningful involvement of families in the educational program.

A few months ago, the children in Derek's classroom seemed to have developed an obsession with robots. They painted pictures of robots; created miniature versions with Legos, clay, or wood; and transformed themselves into robots in the dramatic play and block areas.

One day at circle time, Derek asked them what they knew about robots and tried to capture their responses as they bubbled over with ideas. When the question of how robots could move arose, several announced with confidence that "they have batteries." Four-year-old Ellie, who had spent several mornings pretending to be a robot, blurted out, "I want to BE the battery!" When Derek reflected on this discussion with Tanya later that day, she suggested that a child could "be the battery" in a robot of sufficient size. They decided to offer the children some large cardboard boxes and invite them to work with each other to create robots on a larger scale.

The next day, a delighted Ellie marched around the circle wearing a box into which Derek had helped her cut holes for arms and eyes. Over the next several weeks, small groups of children collaborated during play time every day to create what they decided should be a "boys' robot" and a "girls' robot," often singing as they worked what sounded to Derek like an anthem: "We can do it." They solved conflicts about what color to paint a robot by opting for "rainbow-color." They experimented with solutions to problems such as getting paint to adhere to aluminum foil so they could have a "shiny" robot or replacing the front of the box with a piece of Plexiglas (which had to be measured and cut to size) so that the inner workings would be visible. The final creations were unveiled at the end-of-the-year family gathering—to the delight of all.

In this chapter, we focus on what happens in the facility's classrooms and outdoor spaces—what some call the curriculum. As you will learn, curriculum is much more than a sequence of prescribed activities for the children, and the manager's role requires more than merely purchasing a book of activities for staff members to follow. In our view, the manager is responsible for guiding the staff members and stakeholders (e.g., corporate sponsors, policy boards, parents) as they select—or invent—the desired curriculum. Then the manager's role is to do what is necessary to make it possible for the staff members to do their work—implement the chosen curriculum so that it supports the children's growth and development as fully as possible.

Your mission statement provides a starting point for developing an educational program. The decisions you make about the educational program both dictate and reflect the facility's design, the staff selection, and the implementation of systems to support the staff. In general terms, if the goals of your educational program are for children to explore, to challenge themselves, to form relationships with others, and to experience joy, you need indoor and outdoor play spaces designed and equipped to invite those behaviors. You also need staff members with the knowledge and disposition to recognize and appreciate them when they occur. Specific types of educational programs often imply more precise requirements. For example, adopting a Montessori approach calls for specially designed materials and room arrangements, and staff members with particular qualifications. All of these aspects are discussed in detail in chapters dealing with organizational, personnel, and facilities management.

As with all of the other aspects of your managerial role, educational programming requires planning, organizing, staffing, leading, monitoring, and controlling. As the educational leader of your center, you will take an active part in planning the overall shape of the educational program. Once your staff is in place, you may delegate the responsibility for organizing individual classrooms and planning the daily activities to the teachers. Then your management skills will be used to support and facilitate their work and to troubleshoot problems. You must monitor all aspects of the program to be certain that the goals and standards established during your planning sessions become realities.

REGULATIONS AND PROFESSIONAL STANDARDS

Planning and implementing an educational program requires familiarity with multiple levels of regulations and professional standards. Some are mandatory (e.g., licensing), while some are voluntary (e.g., accreditation). Others may be either mandatory or voluntary depending on the program's funding or organizational context. State-supported public school programs for 4-year-olds, for example, may be required to achieve a specific level on a tiered licensing system as a condition of continued funding. A governing board might establish a policy that its program will attain accreditation (through the National Association for the Education of Young Children [NAEYC] or the American Montessori Society, for example). Keeping your program's mission and goals clearly in mind will help you work your way through what can seem like an overwhelming array of requirements.

Licensing

Because state licensing regulations are designed to set minimum standards to protect the health and safety of children in out-of-home care, they typically address educational programming only in general terms. For example, they usually require that centers provide certain types of activities (e.g., construction, dramatic play, art, outdoor play) in order to promote development in all domains and that there be a sufficient supply of each type of material to accommodate the number of children in care. Knowing and complying with these requirements is essential, but it is only the first step toward creating a high-quality educational program.

> ### ? DECISIONS, DECISIONS . . .
>
> What aspects of the educational program are addressed by licensing regulations in your state? If you have not already done so, you can access the relevant documents and the responsible agency at the website for the National Resource Center for Health and Safety in Child Care, http://nrc.uchsc.edu/STATES/states.htm. Discuss with your classmates how a manager of a child development program would meet these requirements.

Accreditation

Accreditation gives early childhood professionals a goal to work toward after meeting the minimum licensing standards. It also gives parents some assurance that their child is receiving appropriate opportunities to develop cognitively, physically, socially, and emotionally. High-quality children's programs were largely unrecognized until 1984, when the NAEYC launched its center accreditation program. In 2007, NAEYC published an updated version of *Early Childhood Program Standards and Accreditation Criteria*. The new standards focus on four areas: children, teaching staff, partnerships with family and community, and leadership and administration. In the first focus area (children), educational programming is addressed in four standards:

- The program promotes positive relationships among all children and adults to encourage each child's sense of individual worth and belonging as part of a community, and to foster each child's ability to contribute as a responsible community member.

- The program implements a curriculum that is consistent with its goals for children and promotes learning and development in each of the following domains: aesthetic, cognitive, emotional, language, physical, and social.

- The program uses developmentally, culturally, and linguistically appropriate and effective teaching approaches that enhance each child's learning and development in the context of the program's curriculum goals.

- The program is informed by ongoing systematic, formal, and informal assessment approaches to provide information on children's learning and development. These assessments occur within the context of reciprocal communications with families and with sensitivity to the cultural contexts in which children develop. Assessment results are used to benefit children by informing sound decisions about children, teaching, and program improvement. (National Association for the Education of Young Children, 2007a, pp. 9–10)

Detailed performance criteria have been developed for each standard, and criteria are identified as applying to all early childhood programs ("universal") or to programs serving particular age groups (infant, toddler, preschool, or kindergarten). For example, in the category of curriculum, eight criteria spell out essential requirements for all programs (e.g., based on knowledge of child development, responsiveness to individual needs, reflecting families' values and beliefs). An additional criterion for programs serving infants and toddlers requires that materials and equipment "encourage exploration, experimentation, and discovery; sensory and motor learning; and developing physical skills through self-initiated motor learning" (Standard 2.Topic area A. Accreditation criterion 09). A curriculum for preschool or kindergarten children is expected to help "teachers plan for children's engagement in play (including dramatic play and blocks) that is integrated into classroom topics of study" (2.A.12).

The standards define curriculum as including "the goals for the knowledge and skills to be acquired by children and the plans for learning experiences through which such knowledge and skill will be achieved." To become accredited, programs must foster children's development and learning in four developmental domains: social–emotional, physical, language, and cognitive (including literacy, mathematics, science, technology, creative expression and appreciation for the arts, health and safety, and social studies).

Criteria for teaching approaches address scheduling, environments, handling routines, and interacting with children in ways that build on their strengths and support their intellectual development. Criteria for assessment specify areas to be addressed in the program's plan for assessment, characteristics of appropriate procedures, and communicating with families. They also delineate appropriate uses of assessment to identify children's interests and abilities, determine their progress toward program goals, and make needed adaptations.

Tiered or Rated Licensing

As mentioned in a previous chapter, some states have instituted a tiered licensing system to recognize and reward providers who exceed minimum standards, thus encouraging others to do the same. Several states have adopted the *Early Childhood Environmental Rating Scale* (Harms, Clifford, & Cryer, 2005) and companion scales for infant and toddler, school-age, or family home child care as a component of their rating system. Managers who strive to attain a higher-level license need to become familiar with indicators of quality defined by these instruments. In addition to requirements for space and furnishings, personal care routines, and provisions for parents and staff members, the scales address several aspects of educational programming:

1. The "language and reasoning" subscale contains four items pertaining to number and types of books and pictures, and the ways adults support children's communication and thinking skills throughout the day.

2. The "activities" subscale identifies types of activities to be included (e.g., fine motor, art) as well as materials to support those activities and the amount of time children should (or in the case of electronic media, should not) have access to those materials. The program's attention to diversity is also considered here.

3. The "interactions subscale" assesses the general tone of interactions among children and between staff members and children, as well as the ways staff members supervise play and guide behavior.

4. The "program structure" subscale assesses the balance and flow of the daily schedule, with specific attention to provisions for free play, group time, and children with disabilities.

Each item in each subscale is rated on a scale from 1 to 7, with 1 being inadequate and 7 being excellent. For example, in the "activities" subscale, a program would score a 1 if art activities were rarely available or never involved individual expression. It would score a 7 if, in addition to meeting criteria for the amount and accessibility of materials and providing plentiful opportunities for free expression, some art activities reflected other classroom experiences, children could occasionally carry a project over several days, and the program provided opportunities for using materials such as clay or wood (Harms et al., 2005, p. 28).

State Early Learning Standards

In response to the federal government's Good Start, Grow Smart initiative, requirements of the Child Care and Development Fund, and the proliferation of state-funded public school programs (sometimes referred to as the Universal PreK movement), your state may have established standards for children's learning and development before kindergarten in addition to requirements for licensing. While licensing and accreditation focus on what goes into the educational program, early learning standards focus on outcomes—on what young children should know or be able to do by the end of their participation in those programs.

As of 2012, 40 states had such standards in place (Barnett et al., 2013). In addition to standards for 3-, 4-, and 5-year-old children, 31 states have established similar standards for children from birth to age 3, although these are more generally referred to as early learning guidelines (Gebhard, 2010). Most of these standards address five domains defined by the National Education Goals Panel (physical–motor, social–emotional, approaches to learning, language, and cognition), although they vary in the degree to which particular domains are emphasized as well as in the overall level of specificity. Academic areas (language and cognition) are represented in state standards at about three times the rate for developmental areas (social–emotional, physical–motor, and approaches toward learning) (Scott-Little, Kagan, & Frelow, 2005).

Managers of child development programs that use state standards can help raise the level of quality of their educational programs, but only if those standards adhere to principles established by the National Association for the Education of Young Children and National Association of Early Childhood Specialists in State Departments of Education. They must address all domains of development and establish expectations that are meaningful, developmentally appropriate, and sensitive to cultural, linguistic, and ability differences among children (National Association for the Education of Young Children and National Association of Early Childhood Specialists in State Departments of Education, 2004). Ideally, state standards will not replace or drive educational programming but simply provide a gauge of whether your curriculum does, in fact, address what your state expects of young children. Given the fact that many states' standards place disproportionate emphasis on the domains of language and cognition, you should establish much broader and more comprehensive expectations for what children will gain from your educational program. Unfortunately, there is a danger that, in their zeal to focus on areas covered in the standards, some programs scale back their efforts to support development in all domains. NAEYC accreditation criteria (which affirm the importance of all domains) can help you guard against this pitfall if you happen to work in a state with narrowly defined standards. The goal should be a program that is developmentally appropriate *and* meets state standards, not either/or.

Early Intervention

The term early intervention refers to services for children from birth to age 3 with or at risk for developmental delays or disabilities. Services may include speech therapy, occupational therapy, and physical therapy; they may be provided in a specialist's office, in the child's home, or in a child-care facility. The services are provided under a federal grant program, Part C of the Individuals with Disabilities Education Act

(IDEA), in the hope that these services, provided early, will address any delays in development so that the child will not need services later. Children ages 3 through 5 are served under Part B of IDEA. Congress established this program in 1986 and reauthorized it in 2004. For a state to participate in the program, it must ensure that early intervention is available to every eligible child and his or her family. A lead agency in each state receives the grant and administers the program, and is advised by an interagency coordinating council (ICC) that includes parents of young children with disabilities.

Early intervention is a collaboration between families and professionals, including child-care providers. You or your teachers may be involved in team meetings to write or review and update service plans for children: individualized family service plans (IFSPs) for children under age 3 or individualized education plans (IEPs) for children ages 3 through 5. The service plan may include therapies administered by various therapists while the child is in care. Your involvement may be limited to providing an appropriate space and coordinating the classroom schedule with the timing of the visit (e.g., making sure the child has been fed and changed). Or your teachers may be expected to observe what the specialists do with the child and carry out their instructions so that therapies are integrated into the child's regular routines.

Early intervention addresses emotional or social issues as well as physical or cognitive problems. The finding that preschool children are three times more likely to be expelled from their school than are students in elementary or high school (Gilliam, 2005) highlighted an urgent need to enlist early childhood teachers as partners in a more holistic approach to intervention. An infant mental health approach focuses on building the child's social–emotional competencies within the context of relationships rather than treating isolated issues (Marsili & Hughes, 2009). It builds on the guidance that is an integral part of the educational program in any high-quality program: indirect guidance strategies that make it easier for children to regulate their own behavior (e.g., ample time for play, plenty of interesting choices, and environmental cues for behavior) as well as direct guidance strategies such as coaching, encouraging, redirecting, and implementing logical consequences (Hearron & Hildebrand, 2013). With effective guidance strategies in place to support positive behavior of all children, classrooms function more smoothly, and teachers are able to focus more closely on individual children with problems and collaborate with mental health professionals to obtain individualized services for those at highest risk.

? DECISIONS, DECISIONS . . .

Consult the website of the National Child Care Information and Technical Assistance Center at http://nieer.org/publications/state-preschool-2012 to find out whether your state has established early learning standards and, if so, for what age group. Are they mandatory or voluntary? If they are mandatory, which child development programs or types of programs must comply?

MANAGERS' RESPONSIBILITY FOR THE EDUCATIONAL PROGRAM

With the exception of very small centers or family child-care settings, the manager is not directly responsible for carrying out the educational program. Instead, the manager establishes the basic framework of that program, based on knowledge of development and familiarity with regulations and standards. Then the manager's primary responsibility is to support the teachers who are delegated the task of implementing high-quality programs. Managers must fulfill six essential requirements in order to accomplish this.

1. *Managers must know what constitutes high-quality and appropriate interaction.*

Managers cannot support high quality unless they know what it is. Even those who have been in the field for years must invest time and effort to stay abreast of the rapidly expanding knowledge base. Managers who are well informed have more resources to share as well as greater credibility with the professional teaching staff. Basic child development principles may have stayed the same for many years, but ideas about how those principles should be applied undergo constant transformation as new information becomes available.

Years ago, for example, early childhood teachers believed that reading and writing were matters for elementary school and bemoaned the pushed-down curriculum that brought workbooks into programs for young children. As more research about very young children's awareness of print became available, teachers began to think about ways to support this emergent literacy. Those who were stuck in their earlier (justified) resistance to workbooks did not want to hear about writing centers for young children, but those who kept abreast of new developments found that supporting literacy acquisition was very appropriate—and lots more exciting than teaching prereading skills. Unfortunately, in some programs the emphasis has moved from supporting emergent literacy to literacy instruction, which is so narrowly defined and repetitive that it is actually counterproductive (Neuman & Roskos, 2005; Schickedanz, 2008).

A similar tension exists between those who feel computers have no place in early childhood programs and those who believe that the program that does not offer this experience is failing to prepare its children for life in the 21st century. Certainly, television and computers have become fixtures in the lives of American children, and child development professionals worry that there has been insufficient research to understand the consequences fully (Anderson & Evans, 2001). The American Academy of Pediatrics recommends no media exposure for children under 2 and a limit of 2 hours per day with careful adult guidance for older children (American Academy of Pediatrics, 2002b). On the other hand, intervention specialists argue rightly that computers support many forms of assistive technology and adaptive equipment for children, including toddlers, with disabilities (Dunst, Trivette, Hamby, & Simkus, 2013).

Where older children are concerned, resolution of the debate may have more to do with how, rather than whether, computers or other devices are used. Whereas much of the software previously available for the general population of young children offered little more than an animated workbook exercise, recent offerings have expanded to include child-friendly cameras, drawing programs, and active games in addition to on-screen books and puzzles (Buckleitner, 2008). A good manager knows that even the most sophisticated computer will never replace paints, blocks, dramatic play, hands-on experiences with nature, or the other traditional early childhood activities that belong in all good programs. More important, even the most user-friendly computer cannot replace complex interactions with living, breathing human beings. Recognizing the computer's place alongside these time-tested elements of a high-quality program for 3- to 5-year-olds, NAEYC accreditation criteria include technology as one of the curriculum content areas for cognitive development, specifying that its use be limited to developmentally appropriate programming, that it be accessible to all children with adult help as needed, and that it be used to extend or enrich learning (National Association for the Education of Young Children, 2007a, p. 25).

Perhaps most important, well-informed managers are less likely to fall prey to misinterpretations of research that lead to unsound practices. Recent media attention about the importance of the early years for brain development is a case in point. Some individuals have concluded erroneously that babies benefit from intensive "lessons" designed to teach particular concepts when, in fact, such lessons may actually impede the infant's learning (Lally, 1999, p. 105).

2. *Managers must hire well-prepared staff members and work to ensure that they receive adequate compensation.*

The children's specific learning activities are primarily the responsibility of the center's teachers and caregivers. The manager's role begins with the employment of people who have the professional preparation and know-how necessary to plan a high-quality program. Caregivers' formal education and specialized training, as well as that of their supervisors, are all factors influencing program quality (Vu, Jeon, & Howes, 2008). Those who have more formal education and more specialized training pertaining to children (Howes, 1997; Phillipsen, Burchinal, Howes, & Cryer, 1997) offer care that is more stimulating, warm, and supportive. They are also more likely to organize materials and activities into more age-appropriate environments for children, as reflected in higher scores on scales such as the *Early Childhood Environment Rating Scale* and *Infant Toddler Environment Rating Scale* (Cost, Quality, & Child Outcomes Study Team, 1995). Writing job specifications and job descriptions that reflect these facts and hiring well-prepared people are very important steps toward developing a high-quality program. Providing adequate compensation so that highly qualified people can afford to remain in the field is essential (Russell & Rogers, 2005). While it may not be entirely in the manager's power to make this happen, making sure that decision makers and funding bodies realize the importance of adequate compensation is a step in the right direction.

3. *Managers must provide the conditions and resources that highly qualified teachers need in order to do their jobs: appropriate group sizes, sufficient support staff, and adequate supplies and materials.*

Teachers do not work in a vacuum; they need the support of many others, beginning with an administrator who sets group sizes and adult–child ratios at levels known to support quality. The manager also arranges for support staff members, some of whom are professionals who render specific services to the center's children and parents. A pediatrician might serve as the child-care health consultant to provide guidance and information regarding health issues. A psychologist might be consulted about a particular behavior problem, or a family-life educator might plan and chair a series of parent meetings on topics that interest parents. Volunteers can do a number of routine chores, extending the energies of the regular staff. All support personnel, paid or volunteer, require training to be really helpful, a responsibility that the manager must assume.

A good program is relationship-based. Children are cared for in small groups that stay together over time.

Children need equipment, games, books, and materials that support their desire to explore, discover, try out, talk about, think about, question, and expand their understanding and control of their world. Managers support teachers by making sure that the appropriate items are available in sufficient quantity and at the time and place needed.

4. *Managers must provide opportunities and support for teachers to plan the program.*

Careful planning and preparation for each day are hallmarks of high-quality programs. They help ensure rich experiences for children and increase each teacher's ability to be relaxed and responsive to children's needs and interests. When planning and preparation are adequate, the

Teachers need protected time to collaborate and plan an effective curriculum.

children are busy and productive in indoor and outdoor learning environments. A lack of planning can result in programs that are either chaotic or dull and repetitive.

Given the importance of planning, it follows that teachers should be paid for the time it takes. Far too many teachers in today's child-care centers must do what planning they can after working 8 hours with the children. Overworked teachers are forced to draw on ideas that have worked in the past, taking little time to develop new ideas or improved approaches. Many do not have much time to confer with their coworkers to share ideas and insights. This lack of paid planning time is a major impediment to high-quality educational programming.

Managers must find a way to provide teachers with a few hours away from the children each week so that they can think, read, organize, confer with colleagues, and develop challenging ideas. The less experienced the teacher, the more time and support for planning are needed. As a manager, you might consider the following alternatives:

- Hire a permanent substitute who can "float" among the classrooms and free each teacher for a block of planning time one or more days per week.
- Take over each classroom yourself for an hour or two each week to relieve each teacher to do planning. (This suggestion has important advantages: The manager practices professional skills, maintains credibility with the staff, becomes better acquainted with the children, and understands program problems and needs.)

After you have arranged the teachers' planning time, you may have to help some to use the time effectively by providing resources or guidance and feedback as they discuss options. Teachers may require help focusing on specific children and developing a program that fits their needs.

Another aspect of planning involves coordinating the various programs that might serve the same children. Children with disabilities, for example, might spend mornings in special educational or therapeutic settings and afternoons in a child development center. School-age children often move within the same building—from their regular classroom and teacher to another room with another adult for after-school programs. Too frequently, the staff members in one program have no idea what happened in the other—whether it is down the hall or across town. High quality demands that all of the adults in a child's life collaborate to provide the best possible program wherever it happens to occur.

In addition to regular planning, the teachers need to plan for times when they may be absent. Assigning coteachers or a teacher and assistant to each group of children makes it easier to carry on in the absence of one of them. As teachers develop more collegial relationships with the other teachers and assistants, planning becomes a shared process, and everyone in the center knows the daily routine as well as the current topics or projects under way. Thus, when a teacher is out ill, a substitute has many sources of information and support in addition to the written plans she has helped create. In some centers, the classroom assistant moves into the lead teacher's position during her absence, and the substitute fills the assistant role. As programs move toward a play-based program with large blocks of time for the children to initiate their own projects and activities, the need for adult direction decreases. One first-grade teacher reported with pride that, when she returned from a brief illness, the principal (who had substituted for her in her absence) remarked that the children did not seem to need him at all! They entered the room, marked their names on the attendance chart, put a token in the appropriate container to indicate whether they wanted to order a hot lunch, and went to work in the learning centers according to their individual weekly plans. Obviously, routines have to be established in advance in order for the children to function so efficiently.

5. *Managers must support teachers' continued growth with regular, positive feedback and opportunities for professional development.*

Your goal as a manager is to provide the kind of feedback that fosters teachers' feelings of confidence and competence, and encourages them to be self-motivated. Suppose, for example, that you and your staff members have decided to use displays of photographs and transcripts of the children's comments to convey information about the curriculum to parents. Instead of telling the teachers that they made a "great bulletin board," you might want to tell them that you are aware of the work that went into it and that you have seen several parents stop to look at the photographs and read the captions. This sort of feedback has been referred to as encouragement, as distinguished from praise (Hitz & Driscoll, 1994). Other ways to ensure that teachers receive positive feedback are to suggest that parents visit a classroom to see the work that a teacher has been doing with the children or to suggest that one teacher consult another because of some particular expertise the latter has to offer.

A potential for growth should be one criterion for employee selection. No job stands still, and everyone should be expected to learn and improve. That is why all job descriptions require that the candidate continue learning by participating in courses, workshops, and other professional development activities. Reference materials for early childhood curriculum should be available in your center to serve as guides and as inspiration for the teachers. As manager, you can make it a practice to maintain an up-to-date collection of professional literature for staff members. As a result of their professional growth, teachers are motivated to plan more meaningful learning experiences and more appropriate responses based on a greater understanding of children's behavior. As noted in a previous chapter, more-experienced teachers may be mentors for less-experienced teachers, with important benefits for each. Your efforts as manager should be diagnostic—observe where and what help is needed and look for ways to provide it. By observing teachers as they plan, you may learn where professional development efforts should be focused.

6. *Managers must interpret program practices for parents and other stakeholders and sometimes advocate on behalf of staff members when practices they know to be developmentally appropriate are questioned or criticized.*

LEADERSHIP LENS

Pedagogy is the science of teaching. **Pedagogical leadership** (Katz, 1994) requires a program manager not only to be a good teacher, but also to have the ability to explain the reasons for particular teaching practices to teachers, parents, and the public. Rather than slavishly adopting a particular curriculum, a pedagogical leader is knowledgeable about, and able to apply, current theories and research findings in early childhood education. Because the knowledge base continues to expand and public expectations change over time, the pedagogical leader's job is to select and apply the most promising information, interpreting pedagogical theory and research for staff members, families, and others who may not share the same depth of knowledge about young children.

A pedagogical leader applies knowledge and experience to help families enjoy their children and recognize the many ways they demonstrate their growing abilities. At every stage of life, children have some negative characteristics that may bother their parents, especially those who do not understand children's growth and development very well. Policy makers often impose unrealistic expectations for academic achievement because they do not understand the enormity of the children's accomplishments in other areas. Simply by sharing news of a child's achievements, you can inspire the parents and others to look more closely and notice things they may have taken for granted. Many centers have discovered the power of attractive displays that document the children's work with photographs, drawings, and samples of their conversations. Making learning visible in this way promotes respect for the children's thinking and the work that teachers and caregivers do.

Helping parents and other members of the public appreciate the experiences offered the children in your program should be high on your agenda. As you conduct enrollment interviews with families, you can inform them of what to expect and what they should appreciate about the type of program you offer. Many parents have little background on which to base an evaluation and may welcome reassurance from you. A parent may pressure a teacher to have children practice correct letter formation; a board member may complain that your teachers "just let children play" rather than preparing them for school. Your job is to articulate (and help your teachers articulate) the reasons behind educational program decisions.

? DECISIONS, DECISIONS . . .

Using an Ethical Framework

A parent of a child enrolled in your program complains that the "children don't do anything but play all day in this center." She says that she recently received a letter from the school where her child will attend kindergarten next year. The letter lists skills that the school expects all children to have when they arrive. These include printing their names with appropriate use of upper- and lowercase letters, reading simple words and sentences, accurately counting up to 20 objects, and recognizing numerals from 0 through 20. She says your program's main job is to prepare children to succeed in school and unless she sees evidence that you are doing this (in the form of worksheets, for example), she will send her child to another center.

You have visited the kindergarten class yourself and, while you share the goal that children succeed in school, you believe that much of what happens there is developmentally inappropriate. How will you respond to this parent? Using the NAEYC code, try to determine what core values are involved. What ideals and principles regarding responsibilities to children, families, and employees apply? What course of action seems most right?

GUIDES TO PROGRAM DEVELOPMENT

Table 12.1 summarizes and gives examples of basic principles of human development. Keeping these developmental principles in mind, you can provide an effective educational program for young children if the teachers have adequate training, sufficient protected and paid time to plan carefully, and the manager's support and encouragement. Teachers should make tentative, general plans for their assigned age

TABLE 12.1 Basic principles of human development.

Principle	Examples
The interplay of nature and nurture shape development.	All human development is based on a physiological foundation that is determined genetically at conception and nurtured during the prenatal period and thereafter. Later development builds on early development; that is, nurturing and education must build on this early genetic base and on each preceding stage of development.
Development unfolds in a predictable sequence.	Given the appropriate opportunities, children walk before they run, babble before they speak, and scribble before they draw faces.
Development proceeds according to each individual's unique timetable.	One child may walk at 8 months, another at 15 months; one gets the first tooth at 4 months, another at 12 months; one speaks a first sentence at 16 months, whereas another is twice that age—but all are within a normal range of development.
Development moves from simple, undifferentiated patterns to more specific and complex.	A child first grasps an object like a crayon in a fist, then uses fingers and thumbs together to pick up tiny objects, and finally masters a keyboard or violin. Each skill is increasingly complex, requiring integration with other skills. Similar examples can be given for development with respect to reasoning, speaking, or getting along with others.
Internal and external factors (and interactions between the two) influence development.	A child may be delayed in walking because of internal factors, such as neural or muscular disorders, or because of external factors, such as a lack of opportunity. A child who experiences both a physical disability and an unsupportive environment is likely to experience greater delays.
There are dynamic interrelations between areas of development.	With the increase in speech development comes an increased ability to play with other children (a connection between speech and social development). With increased motor control and the ability to hold a crayon, pencil, or paintbrush, the child can explore and express ideas through drawings and paintings (a connection between physical and cognitive development).
Critical periods are windows of opportunity and risk.	If certain conditions exist during those periods, a child can be prevented from proceeding to more advanced levels. Good nutrition, freedom from disease, and secure relationships are all essential for an infant's brain development. When children master rudimentary skills of running, jumping, and skipping by age 6, they are more likely to enjoy the physical and social benefits afforded by the games of school age and adolescence.
Individuals generally strive to reach maximum potential.	When deprivation, nutritional or otherwise, is severe, the body shows a strong drive to overcome the deficiency. When avenues for growth are blocked, many individuals find ways around those roadblocks. For example, a sightless child uses all of the other senses to compensate for the deficit.

group, then observe and seek additional information to understand the individual development of each child within the group. The following 10-point guide gives teachers and managers a framework for planning and evaluating their program:

1. A good program is planned for the whole child, with an emphasis on the child's strengths and potential, and holds high expectation for every child, regardless of ability, to reach his or her full potential.

2. A good program is inclusive. It proactively extends its services to children with disabilities or at risk of developing disabilities and treats all children with respect, regardless of race, gender, or ability. It collaborates with families and other professionals to accommodate children's special needs by removing physical or structural barriers and providing a variety of ways for children to learn (Delaney, 2001; Division for Early Childhood/National Association for the Education of Young Children, 2009). Adults teach the children to value who they are, to show empathy for those who are different from them, and to recognize and stand up against unfairness toward themselves or others.

3. A good program is relationship-based, providing **continuity of care** so that the children, particularly infants, can develop secure relationships with their primary caregivers. Children are cared for in small groups that stay together over time, forming relationships with each other as well as with their teacher. The program encourages teachers to cultivate reciprocal relationships with family members, welcoming and working closely with them, particularly as the child acclimates to the new environment (Raikes & Edwards, 2009).

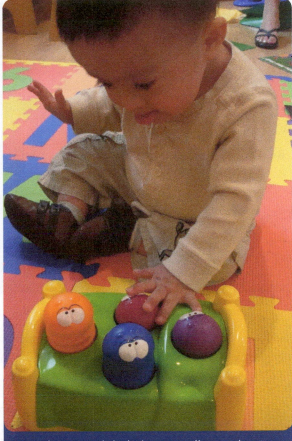

A good program is inclusive, extending services to children with disabilities, and treats all children with respect.

4. A good program begins where the children are in their development. Plans are based on observations made as the children engage in naturally occurring play and interactions, rather than on prescribed or scripted activities.

5. A good program provides balance. Children have opportunities for both active and quiet play. Teachers allow plenty of time for the children to initiate their own activities, and they also introduce their own ideas, or provocations, to stimulate the children's thinking. In large time blocks, the child has the freedom to select the type of activity preferred. The schedule balances the routines of physical care and learning experiences in a logical sequence of events. Recognizing that tension and fatigue interfere with learning, teachers avoid prolonged sitting as well as prolonged physical exertion.

6. A good program recognizes that children's emotional and social development is as important to school readiness as their cognitive and language development. A good program supports emotional and social development by promoting attachment, accepting and reflecting children's feelings. It offers materials and activities that invite children to play with one another, so that they learn through

A good program allows plenty of time for children to initiate their own activities and to choose whether to play alone or with others.

experience to share, to take turns, to choose friends, and to be chosen. At the same time, the program allows the children to be alone and regroup as needed, to grow in self-direction and independence within the context of appropriate limits on behavior, to learn to make choices that respect the rights of others, and to learn the reasons for rules.

7. A good program encourages thinking. It encourages children to reason, remember, experiment, and generalize. It engages the children's minds with topics and materials that are both attractive and meaningfully connected to the children's lives and the world they inhabit. It engages the teachers' minds as well so that they become learners with the children, discovering new ideas about a particular topic as well as about the children in their care. Teachers observe carefully and follow up on the children's interests as they plan experiences.

8. A good program encourages the children's verbal expressions. To learn words and sentence structure, all children must have an opportunity to use the language skills they have. Rather than viewing English language learners as deficient, a good program recognizes and values their accomplishments. It provides support for continued growth in their home language, ideally by hiring staff members who speak that language. If that is not possible, perhaps because children at the center come from many different language backgrounds, the center actively recruits volunteers among families or in the larger community who can interact with children in their languages. And all staff members make the effort to learn at least a few words in the language of each child in their care. In addition, a good program supports and encourages the children's use of many "languages" to explore and express their thoughts—graphic art, reading or telling stories, dramatic play, music, and movement are part of every day's activities.

9. A good program encourages the children to learn about and care for their bodies. It establishes a routine of handwashing, eating, resting, and eliminating, and it places priority on safety training, both to protect the children and to teach them to protect themselves. It is action packed with daily opportunities, indoors and outdoors, for vigorous activity. The classroom is frequently noisy compared to traditional upper-age classes. The reasons why action, noise, and talking are permitted may have to be explained to administrators and others so that the program is not curtailed unnecessarily.

10. A good program includes the parents in partnership with the teachers and children, recognizing the parents' primary importance to their children's growth and development. Communication is two-way, with the center actively soliciting and accepting the parents' opinions and ideas, as well as offering support, advice, and appropriate referrals as needed.

SELECTING A CURRICULUM MODEL OR APPROACH

When selecting a curriculum model or approach for your educational program, you should check with your state licensing agency or funding body to determine whether they have established specific criteria or identified particular approved examples. If the choice is entirely yours, look for a curriculum that is comprehensive (i.e., addresses all developmental domains rather than focusing on narrow academic skills) and accommodates diversity as well as individual differences. It should provide guidance for creating a welcoming, stimulating indoor and outdoor environment, for planning experiences that respond to children's interests and backgrounds, and for interacting with children and their families to promote children's attainment of challenging and achievable goals. Whether the choice is yours or is made for you, a high-quality child development center uses an adopted curriculum as a tool, not as a convenient "teacher-proof" solution to the educational program. You and your staff members need to bring your own knowledge of child development and early education to use as you put a curriculum model or approach into practice.

Some models prescribe particular practices based on a particular individual's beliefs about how children grow and develop rather than formal theory. For example, Maria Montessori, an Italian physician, began her career as an educator working with children with mental retardation and in 1907 established a school for poor children in a Rome tenement, where she continued to refine her ideas. Since her approach first gained recognition among educators in the United States in the 1960s, many of her innovations have become accepted practice in early childhood education. For example, the "prepared environment" consists of child-size furnishings and self-correcting materials, such as cylinders or blocks in graduated sizes, carefully displayed on low shelves so that children can select their own "work" and return the items when they have finished. The use of the term *work* for these activities conveys the sense of respect for the child that is further exemplified by the soft voices and serious demeanor of the adults as they interact with the children.

Other models attempt to apply the ideas of theorists whose own work may not have prescribed specific educational methods. For example, while Piaget himself did not offer pedagogical advice, Constance Kamii studied with him and has written several books suggesting ways in which his theory can be used to help children build their understanding of arithmetic in more appropriate and effective ways. The HighScope curriculum is also based on Piaget's theories and has been widely used by child development programs as well as public schools. Lilian Katz is a proponent of the project approach, which draws on the work of John Dewey and emphasizes the importance of fostering dispositions (such as curiosity and perseverance) as well as knowledge and skills by investigating topics that spark children's interest. Elena Bodrova and Deborah Leong apply Vygotsky's theories to develop early childhood practices that scaffold (i.e., support and enhance) children's pretend play as a primary vehicle for developing self-regulation and cognitive growth.

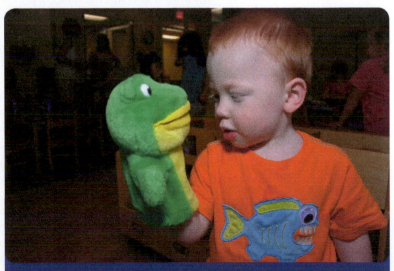

Pretend play is a primary vehicle for children to develop language and cognitive growth.

Research is inconclusive regarding the superiority of one curriculum model over another. Few programs offer "pure" examples of any single approach. Most blend many approaches, using what makes sense for their group, or groups, of children at any given time. Furthermore, popular and professional opinion about what is best for children shifts with time. In spite of differences in emphasis, many curriculum types can fit under the umbrella of developmentally appropriate practice as defined by the NAEYC. Certainly, all professionals want children to learn and to reach their highest human potential. The label on an early childhood program is not as important as whether the interactions support growth in all areas of development—physical, cognitive, social, and emotional. To help staff members and stakeholders make an informed choice about which curricular approach to use, the manager must have a firm grounding in the basic developmental principles outlined in Table 12.1.

Because many curriculum models incorporate elements of several theories, another way to conceptualize differences among them is to look at whether they focus on the individual child's specific skills, on the physical or social context for learning and development, or on the content to be learned. For each of the curriculum types discussed next, Figure 12.1 gives examples of published curricula for infants and toddlers and for children ages 3 to 6.

- Some curricula focus on eliciting or supporting the *individual child's specific skills* in each domain of development (e.g., fine and gross motor, cognitive, social, communication, and adaptive or self-help). Teachers assess the children to determine which skills or objectives they have mastered and then follow a prescribed sequence of progressively more challenging activities thought to support the next level of achievement. A target skill for a child who can stand without support, for example, is to take steps while holding on to an adult with two hands. Adults are directed to design particular activities to practice walking or to look for opportunities to embed the practice in the child's daily routines.

- Some curricula focus on establishing a *physical and social context* that supports learning and development. The emphasis can be on a *physical environment* that facilitates children's spontaneous play as the primary means of physical, social, emotional, and intellectual growth. Such a curriculum views the classroom as the textbook and the teacher as both the designer who enriches the textbook and the guide who helps the children get the most from it. The HighScope approach (based on Piaget's theory of cognitive development) emphasizes the *key experiences* that children should have as a consequence of their interaction with the environment, with their teachers, and with other children. The representation of one's ideas, communicating them to others, is one such key experience—for example, drawing a picture of one's block structure. Other key experiences include classification, language and literacy, and relating to adults and other children.

- Another approach focuses on *content* or *concepts* to be learned. The **thematic approach** suggests that teachers select a topic (such as farm animals or community helpers) and organize activities or infuse materials related to that topic throughout the classroom. The **project approach** (as illustrated in the chapter-opening vignette) differs from the thematic approach in that neither the topic for investigation nor the length of time devoted to its study is predetermined by the teacher. Once teachers have identified a topic, either because they have observed an interest during the children's play or because they have a hunch it will be exciting for the children, they help the children organize the investigation of that topic. They might begin with a discussion to elicit the children's current knowledge of the topic, as well as their questions and curiosity. They then follow up with field trips, special visitors, or other activities designed to gather

Focus: Individual Child's Specific Skills	
Examples for Infants and Toddlers	**Example for Children Ages 3 Through 5**
Bricker, D., & Waddell, M. (2002). *Volume 3: AEPS curriculum for three to six years.* Baltimore: Paul H. Brookes. Cryer, D., Harms, T., & Bourland, B. (1987). *Active learning for ones.* Reading, MA: Addison-Wesley.	Bricker, D., & Waddell, M. (2002). *Volume 4: AEPS curriculum for three to six years.* Baltimore: Paul H. Brookes. Powell, D. & Dunlap, G. (2009). *Evidence-based social-emotional curricula and intervention packages for children 0-5 years and their families. (Roadmap to Effective Intervention Practices).* Tampa: University of South Florida. Available online at http://www.challengingbehavior.org/

Focus: Physical or Social Context	
Examples for Infants and Toddlers	**Examples for Children Ages 3 through 5**
Dodge, D. T., Rudick, S., & Berke, K. (2006). *The creative curriculum for infants and toddlers and twos* (2nd ed.). Washington, DC: Teaching Strategies. Available in Spanish. Post, J., & Hohmann, M. (2000). *Tender care and early learning: Supporting infants and toddlers in child care settings.* Ypsilanti, MI: High/Scope Press.	Dodge, D. T., Coker, L. J., & Heroman, C. (2002). *The creative curriculum for preschool* (4th ed.). Washington, DC: Teaching Strategies. Available in Spanish. Hohmann, M., & Weikart, D. P. (2002). *Educating young children: Active learning practices for preschool and child care programs* (3rd ed.).Ypsilanti, MI: High/Scope Press.

Focus: Content or Concepts	
Examples for Infants and Toddlers	**Examples for Children Ages 3 through 5**
Maguire-Fong, M. J. (1999). *Investigations: A responsive approach to infant curriculum. Program for Infant Toddler Caregivers.* Available online at http://www.pitc.org/resources/macfonghnd.htm	Helm, J. H., & Katz, L. (2001). *Young investigators: The project approach in the early years.* New York: Teachers College Press. Mitchell, A. & David, J. (1992). Explorations with young children: A curriculum guide from the Bank Street College of Education. Lewisville, NC: Gryphon House.

FIGURE 12.1 Examples of curricula.

more information. Often, small groups of children collect particular bits of information and devise ways to communicate their findings to their classmates. The project culminates in some event or construction that pulls together all of the new understandings the children have acquired. (See the section called Families' Role in the Educational Program later in this chapter for a description of another project sparked by children's fascination with a particular phrase in a story read by their teacher.)

Some educators have begun to move beyond simply adopting a predefined curriculum model, arguing that rigid adherence to any particular model tends to cast teachers in the role of technicians rather than professionals and decision makers. Inspired by the early childhood programs of Reggio Emilia, Italy, they opt instead for an approach that views teachers as researchers, constantly creating and re-creating their own theories of teaching and learning as they observe and document the children's experiences (Goffin & Wilson, 2001). (See, e.g., Branscombe, Castle, Dorsey, Surbeck, & Taylor, 2003; Curtis & Carter, 1996, 2008; Scheinfeld, Haigh, & Scheinfeld, 2008.)

The Reggio Emilia approach is just that—an approach to early education that has been evolving in the town of that name since the end of World War II, although it did not come to the attention of U.S. educators until the 1980s (see, e.g., Gandini, 1984), when an exhibition featuring the work of the town's early childhood schools, The 100 Languages of Children, began touring the United States. It is not a curriculum or a method; one cannot attend training to become a certified "Reggio teacher," nor can a program become accredited as a "Reggio school," although several schools in the United States have established special relationships with the Italian programs over years of study and interaction. Early childhood professionals who have studied the approach speak of being inspired by it and work to adapt its core principles within their own contexts. These core principles, gleaned from writings and conference presentations by educators from Reggio Emilia and their colleagues in other countries, include the following:

- An image of the child as competent and capable, full of questions and theories and having rights as opposed to needs
- Teachers as researchers who partner with children and with parents and learn alongside them
- The environment as a coteacher, where every aspect reflects the values and history of the participants and supports the children and teachers as they explore and learn
- Parents as full participants in the life of the school and who contribute as well as learn in meaningful ways
- School as a place where life (not preparation for life) happens, where values and knowledge are constructed, not merely passed on
- Small-group work, collaboration, and many forms of expression (or "100 languages") as essential for learning
- Documentation as a process that involves observing children; collecting and analyzing data; reflecting in collaboration with children, colleagues, and families; and finally presenting results in ways that make the learning of all participants visible

The work produced in the Reggio schools is so compelling, and the Reggio educators are so passionate and eloquent in their articulation of the philosophy, that many early childhood professionals around the world are eager to study and adopt the approach. Although that idealistic yearning for excellence is to be applauded, some caution is also warranted. Educators who do not understand the complexity and depth of thought behind each of the principles can mistakenly assume that they will be "doing Reggio" if they purchase certain types of equipment or set up an *atelier* ("art studio"). They don't realize that adapting this approach takes years of study and reflection, that it is actually a never-ending process because the approach itself is continually evolving.

If you are a new administrator and the teachers you hire have minimal experience in early childhood education, it might make sense to take a more gradual approach. The curriculum resources described in this chapter are only a few examples that you might use to establish a foundation upon which you could build as you learn more about the Reggio approach.

Managers support curriculum when they provide appropriate equipment and encourage teachers to facilitate children's explorations.

For example, both the Creative Curriculum and the HighScope approaches provide basic guidelines for setting up an environment to facilitate play and exploration. Both offer specific suggestions for scheduling as well as ways teachers can interact with children, ask questions to provoke thought, and set up small- or large-group learning experiences. There are training opportunities associated with each, as well as systems for assessing children's progress toward educational goals.

Within this overall context, teachers can address particular IFSP or IEP goals by drawing on one of the individual, skills-based curricula. Given a rich environment and a consistent daily schedule that allows plenty of time for play in that environment, children will inevitably reveal their ideas and interests. Once they have become comfortable supporting and observing children's play, teachers can begin to notice emerging topics and help children pursue investigations of those topics, using either a thematic or a project approach. As you and your teachers collaborate to implement these approaches, to question and reflect on your practice, you can continue to study more about the Reggio approach, gradually moving toward an adaptation of its principles that is uniquely suited to your particular context.

PUTTING CURRICULUM INTO PRACTICE

Scheduling

Schedules help the teachers and the support staff members know what to expect as they work together. Schedules help the children gain a sense of security as they come to realize that the sequence of events is the same every day. When children know what to do without being told, they grow in self-direction and confidence.

A general schedule should be posted where parents can see it and have some idea of what their children are doing at particular times of the day. This does not mean, however, that the children's movements must be rigidly programmed minute-by-minute throughout the day. A time block plan, with generous periods set aside for particular types of activity, is more realistic and child-friendly. Figure 12.2 is a sample time block plan for 3- to 5-year-old children, with approximate times noted for each block. Short-day programs use time blocks II, III, and IV; full-day programs follow all of the blocks.

Time Block I 7:30–8:30 A.M.	**Arrival and Breakfast** Breakfast for those desiring it; self-selected activities (classroom groups may be combined until more children arrive); clean up.
Time Block II 8:30–8:45 or 9:00 A.M.	**Morning Meeting (Arrival for Short-Day Program)** Groups gather in individual classrooms to discuss plans for day; songs, fingerplays, stories (adjust length of time depending on ages and abilities of children; may begin with only 5 or 10 minutes and gradually lengthen as year progresses).
Time Block III 8:45 or 9:00–10:30 A.M.	**Self-Selected Activity (Indoors)** Small-group work on projects; free play in interest centers (table toys/games/math materials, art, music/movement, blocks, sand/water, dramatic play, science, writing, books); self-serve snack as an option until 10:00.
Time Block IV 10:30–11:45 A.M.	**Transition; Self-Selected Activity (Outdoors)** Clean up; toileting/handwashing; dress for outside; small groups move outdoors with an adult as they are ready; climbing, running, riding toys, balls, sand/water, swings, slides, books, art, dramatic play.
Time Block V 11:45–12:30 P.M.	**Transition to Lunch (Departure for Part-Day Program)** Toileting, handwashing, lunch served family-style, repeat toileting and handwashing; prepare for nap.
Time Block VI 12:30–2:30 P.M.	**Nap** Quiet music, individual or group story, backrubs; quiet play for children who do not sleep.
Time Block VII 2:30–6:00 P.M.	**Self-Selected Activity (Indoors or Outdoors)** Toileting and handwashing as children awaken; snack in small or large group; wash hands and move to interest areas; outdoor or indoor motor activity available as a choice; prepare to go home; combine classroom groups as numbers diminish; teachers set up for following day.

FIGURE 12.2   Time block plan for 3- to 5-year-old children.

Note that the period for self-selected indoor activity in this schedule lasts at least 90 minutes, followed by another hour for self-selected activity outdoors. For individuals without extensive experience with children's programs, this might seem like an overly long period of "just playing." Research has shown that play is crucial for the development of social skills, coping with stress, and building cognitive skills such as problem solving (Wenner, 2009). Longer play periods promote a greater complexity in the children's thinking, as well as in their social interactions (Christie & Wardle, 1992). The Early Childhood Environment Rating Scale (Harms et al., 2005), a widely accepted measure of quality, underscores this concept by requiring not only that programs make particular types of materials available to children, but also that those materials be accessible to children for a "substantial portion of the day" or at least "one-third of the time the children are in attendance" (p. 7).

Self-selected activity or free play does not mean that children are left to their own devices. Teachers are actively involved during this time, working with individual or small groups of children, commenting, questioning, and guiding. As teachers gain experience with facilitating the children's play, they find that they can also use this time to observe the children carefully. Reflecting on these observations and discussing them with colleagues is the best way for teachers to learn to see the possibilities inherent in play. Therefore, we emphasize again that managers must ensure that the teachers have adequate protected time to carry out this important aspect of planning.

SCHEDULING FOR INFANTS AND TODDLERS   The daily schedule for infants and toddlers will be even more flexible than the schedule for 3- to 5-year-olds, tailoring the flow of events to the individual needs of each child in care. Physical care routines for feeding, diapering, toileting, and sleeping occupy much of the time. These should never be rushed through in order to get to more programmed activities, but should be treated as valuable opportunities for pleasurable interactions with rich possibilities for learning and development, and—most important—for nurturing the responsive relationships that are the foundation of a good program for babies. On the other hand, infant–toddler programs are not only about feeding, diapering, and putting to sleep. Even very young infants benefit when adults make interesting experiences available to them during the times they are awake and alert. When adults take the time to plan interesting experiences, they are often surprised by very young children's sustained engagement. It may seem at first that life in an infant–toddler room is a nonstop sequence of attending to individual needs, but as time goes on, those individual schedules tend to coalesce around a group rhythm of eating, sleeping, and playing together.

Figure 12.3 is one possibility for organizing the flow of time in an infant–toddler program. Note that lunch is scheduled earlier in the day because the smaller stomach capacity of the youngest children means that they get hungry more quickly. They also tire more quickly, so the earlier lunchtime avoids both cranky babies and the possibility that one or more will fall asleep face-down in the mashed potatoes.

Note also that there is no formal group time scheduled, although this does not mean that group experiences are not valued. The daily schedule for infants and toddlers is built therefore around responding to their needs and respecting their competence. Group experiences occur in very natural, unobtrusive ways. Meals are pleasurable occasions for enjoying one another's company and conversation within a rich multisensory encounter. Children also form spontaneous groups around particularly interesting play materials, and with adult support they are able to sustain these interactions for a surprising length of time. Adults can serve as catalysts for such experiences by offering something interesting to do. How many times has a teacher started reading a book to one child and wound up with a lapful of eager listeners? And how different is the experience for the child who is drawn by the story from that of the child who is told to sit and listen because it is group time?

As Dr. Ronald Lally has frequently pointed out, infants and toddlers have their own built-in "curriculum"—a tremendous curiosity and drive to make sense of the people and things in their world. Adults who interrupt that process to "teach" particular concepts at a given moment may or may not be successful at teaching the intended concept, but certainly they risk teaching the child that his or her interests and questions are unimportant.

Planning Experiences for Children

Interesting, enriching experiences for children may "just happen" in the course of your lives together, but they are more likely to occur if teachers plan thoughtfully. Planning must be based on both the goals your educational program has established for children and your observations of the interests and abilities of the children for whom you are planning. The form you select for your educational program may be influenced by several factors. Published curricula often include suggested daily schedules and forms for planning and recording children's experiences. Some state licensing regulations set

Time Block I 7:30–9:30 A.M.	**Arrival and Breakfast** Teachers and parent informally share pertinent information as parent helps child settle into classroom; diapering or toileting and handwashing; bottles or breakfast as needed; infants sleep as needed; older children play freely.
Time Block II 9:30–10:00 A.M.	**Morning Snack** Diapering or toileting and handwashing; group snack for children who can sit up; pleasant conversation encouraged; children allowed to leave table, wash hands, and go play when ready.
Time Block III 10:00–11:00 A.M.	**Self-Selected Activity (Indoors or Outdoors)** Mobile children play freely with blocks, manipulatives, dolls, and dramatic play accessories, books, vehicles and push toys; climb on loft; adults invite individuals or small groups to use play dough, clay, paint, or play with water. Adults either bring materials to babies or take babies to interesting experiences (e.g., mirrors, balls, books, music). All go outside for varying length of time depending upon weather.
Time Block IV 11:00–11:45 A.M.	**Lunch; Transition to Nap** Diapering or toileting and handwashing for mobile children; group lunch for those who can sit up; conversation encouraged; children allowed to leave table, wash hands, and go to cots when ready.
Time Block V 11:45–2:30 P.M.	**Nap** Diapering, toileting, handwashing as needed; adults sit next to children and help them settle (read storybooks, rub backs, etc.); children who wake before others are allowed to get up, perhaps be taken outside or to another room to play so they don't wake sleepers.
Time Block VI 2:30–3:00 P.M.	**Snack** Diapering or toileting and handwashing; group snack for children who can sit up; pleasant conversation encouraged; children allowed to leave table, wash hands, and go play when ready.
Time Block VII 3:00–6:00 P.M. (parents begin arriving about 4:00 P.M.	**Self-Selected Activity (Indoors or Outdoors)** Repeat morning sequence of indoor and outdoor activities. Diapering and toileting as needed and before parents arrive.

FIGURE 12.3 Time block plan for an infant–toddler program.

specific requirements for what plans must include as well as when and where they must be posted. Some educators argue that, rather than post plans that may or may not be followed in a program where children's interests are paramount, it is more appropriate to post detailed descriptions of what in fact happened in a program during the previous week.

Figures 12.4 and 12.5 are examples of weekly planning forms that some programs have found useful. They are intended as a starting point. Note that the forms assume that certain materials and supplies are available to the children every day. When additions or changes are planned, children are given time to explore new materials fully over the course of the week (or longer) so that they have opportunities to become comfortable and to discover new and more complex ways of using or com-

Week of *Oct. 3–7*	Observations to follow up on; possibilities: • Children fascinated with "dear one," the "special name" a child was given by the mother in the book *Mama Do You Love Me?* • Begin collecting children's "special names" and story behind each (reading, writing, connections with families, self-image)

Possible Changes/Additions to Interest Areas Available Every Day

Art	Blocks	Dramatic Play	Writing/Reading
Refresh paint jars; have children help mix several shades of one color each day; note their descriptive words for various hues.	Continue sketching children's constructions: offer clipboards and pens if they are interested in doing so themselves.	Watch for "special names" as children enact family roles.	List of names and special names to copy; album to collect and display letters from families along with child's picture and printed name/special name.

Table Toys/Math	Sand/Water	Science/Nature	Music/Movement
Three sets of cards to sort and match: children's names, special names, and pictures.	Add clear tubes and funnels to water table.	Look for changes in garden.	Add scarves and tambourines.

Large Group: Reread *Mama, Do You Love Me?;* make a chart listing each child's name and "special name"; compose a letter to send home to families; read individual letters aloud as received.

Family Participation: Ask family to send letter to school giving child's special name and the story of how it came about.

Reminders: Send letters home with children; post a reminder in entrance.

FIGURE 12.4   Weekly activity plan for 3- to 5-year-old children.

Week of *Oct. 3–7*

Observations to follow up on

- All fascinated by arrival of 10-week-old Sarah in infant area; talking about "baby"; watching through divider
- Jerome and Keisha walking short distance without hanging on to furniture
- Angie and Heidi pulling open storage bins under cribs in infant area

Possible Changes/Additions to Materials Available Every Day

Books	Blocks	Art Materials	Manipulatives
Books with pictures of babies; invite children to look at their own albums and talk about when they were "babies."	Cardboard "bricks"	Finger paint	Replace items stored in bins with things children can safely explore; household utensils?

Gross Motor Equipment	Dramatic Play	Music/Movement	Sand/Water
Push carts to support independent walking; encourage moving cartloads of toys from one area to another?	Add baby bottles and small blankets to dolls	CD: *Lullabies from around the world*	Baby basin with soapy water and towels for bathing "babies" **Science/Nature** Take "babies" outdoors; dress for weather; support A & H's exploration of space and containment

Family Participation: Ask families for wooden or plastic cooking utensils to put in storage bins; request baby pictures for children who enrolled as toddlers (as center does not have earlier images in our documentation files).

Reminders: Take pictures to document Jerome and Keisha's new walking skills; collect examples of what toddlers know about babies.

FIGURE 12.5   Weekly activity plan for mixed-age infant–toddler room.

bining materials. Teachers record pertinent observations that they intend to follow up on and then write in only the changes or additions that they will make to the various interest centers that week. Note that the topic proposed for investigation is not reflected in every single interest area because it is assumed that play will go on as usual and children will continue to explore many interests in addition to the one the teachers have selected.

Plans for a large group in the 3- to 5-year-old classroom are somewhat open-ended because it is assumed that every large group includes discussion of what the children plan to do or have done, interesting things that have happened, and (in this classroom) reenactment of stories the children have dictated to the teacher during the time block for self-selected activity. The teachers have noted their intention to compose a letter with the children, and this will probably occur on Monday unless other events overshadow their plans that day. They have also indicated their intention to read aloud the letters that families send to school, but because they cannot predict when or how many letters will come in, they have left this as an option for the remainder of the week—and probably for several weeks to come. Because the group is smaller and because very young children are more likely to be pursuing their own developmental challenges, the plan for that room begins with more detailed observations of individual children rather than what teachers have noticed about the group's interests.

Your state or funding body may mandate that you use a planning form with specific requirements for what it must contain. Whatever planning form you adopt, it is likely that you and your teachers will find ways to modify it to suit your own needs and style. Ideally, planning experiences for children is a joyful process, one that taps teachers' deep thinking and creativity, not a tedious ritual that must be repeated for its own sake every week.

FAMILIES' ROLE IN THE EDUCATIONAL PROGRAM

Some parents may reluctantly enroll their children in your center, feeling forced by the demands of earning a livelihood to forego precious moments with their children during their formative early years. Others are eager to give their children the advantage of early educational opportunities and social experiences with peers. All parents expect you to treat their children kindly, to protect them from harm, and to help them develop to their fullest potential.

Many years ago, a study confirmed the value that parents place on good-quality care for their children; it also revealed, however, that parents consistently overrate the quality of care their children are receiving. Nine of ten parents gave their centers "very good" ratings, while professional observers found the same centers to be "poor" or "mediocre" (Cost, Quality, & Child Outcomes Study Team, 1995). The gap between parents' perceptions about quality and reality persists, with parents assuming that government policies hold centers to far more stringent requirements for things like training than is actually the case (National Association of Child Care Resource and Referral Agencies, 2010). It seems that, although parents want the best for their children, they lack the information necessary to help them judge what is best. Perhaps they have not observed enough programs to have a basis for comparison; perhaps they have never seen a high-quality program in operation; perhaps they have been seduced by glossy brochures and an attractive surface appearance, never actually seeing what happens at the center while they are at work.

As manager, you can also contribute to the ongoing education of parents and the public about the components of high-quality early education. Adults who have not studied child development often rely on their own memories of school to form images of what teaching and learning should be like. They may pressure you and your teachers to provide evidence of such "learning" in the form of worksheets, memorized ABCs, rote counting, and a daily "art" project. Depending on the level of their professional backgrounds, your staff members may share these beliefs or feel coerced by parent demands to resort to these stereotyped substitutes for genuine learning experiences.

Many teachers have found, however, that when they provide the parents with evidence that the children are learning, the demands for worksheets and rote skills are replaced by a new enthusiasm for more appropriate experiences. Managers who view this kind of public education as part of their job and plan for it accordingly are less likely to feel burned out at the prospect of facing each year's new group of well-intentioned but uninformed critics.

In addition to informing families about your educational program, you can invite them to participate in meaningful ways. Consider the following example. Rebekah, a teacher in a full-day program, had just finished reading the book *Mama, Do You Love Me?* by Barbara Joosse to her group of 3- to 5-year-olds. At the lunch table that day, she noticed the children giggling over the words with which the mother in the book addressed her child: "dear one." She explained to the children that "dear one" was a special name that the mother gave her child because she loved her. As soon as she suggested that perhaps the children had their own special names that their families called them, the conversation exploded with each child eagerly telling the others about his or her "special name."

Rebekah noted this enthusiasm and, with her colleagues, planned several ways to follow up on it. At group time, she made a large chart listing each child's name and special name, including the child who declared somberly that her given name should be listed in both columns because her family did not have special names. She made three sets of laminated cards—one set with each of the children's names, one set with each of their pictures, and one set with each of their special names—and put them out in an attractive three-drawer desk organizer so children could explore them. Because Valentine's Day was coming soon and she wanted to downplay the commercial aspects of the holiday, she composed a letter with the children asking families to write back whether their child had a special name and, if so, what was its meaning or origin.

The letters began to arrive, one or two per day, over the next several weeks. At large group, Rebekah invited the child who had brought a letter that day to sit in her lap as she read it aloud and the other children listened with rapt attention. Afterward, Rebekah placed the letter (in a plastic sleeve) in an album alongside a page displaying the child's photograph, name, and special name. Many of the letters were so heartfelt that they brought tears to the eyes of visitors to the classroom. Most important, the album became a focal point that children delighted in sharing with their family members during arrival and pickup times. Some insisted on having each page read aloud; others decided to read only the girls' letters one day and the boys' letters the next. Of course, seeing their children's enthusiasm over the "special names book" inspired families who had not yet sent a letter to do so, and eventually the album was complete, including the double entry for the child whose given name was also her special name.

The children often looked at the album alone or with one or two classmates. They used it as a reference when sorting and matching the laminated cards. Soon, many could recognize not only their own and their classmates' names, but the special names as well. They even noted that the special names were always printed with "funny marks" (i.e., quotation marks) in at the beginning and end. The album became part of the classroom culture for many years. As children left the program over the course of each summer, part of the class ritual was to sing the song about new friends and old:

"One is silver and the other, gold." Their pages were then moved to an album appropriately trimmed with gold glitter and titled "Old Friends," while incoming families were invited to add their children's pages to the "New Friends" album.

Table 12.2 provides additional suggestions for fostering families' meaningful involvement in the center's educational program.

TABLE 12.2   Fostering meaningful family involvement in curriculum.

Principle	Examples
Start by keeping families informed about what goes on in the program.	• Post documentation panels with photos and narratives so families can learn about project work during arrival and departure times. • Post documentation on a password-protected web page. • Send a photo and brief email message home to celebrate a child's accomplishment. • Send home lyrics of songs that children enjoy at the center and suggest that they teach their families. • Have children illustrate a booklet of recipes for foods that they enjoy at the center and make copies for each family.
Plan experiences to help build connections between the center and home.	• Have children place notes, drawings, or other "surprises" around the classroom for family members to find when they come to a meeting. • Invite family members to reciprocate by placing similar surprises for their children to find in the morning. • Tell family members their children miss them while at the center and ask that they send a letter telling where they are and what they are doing while the child is at the center. Obtain the same information and record it yourself for those families who may not be able to write the letter. • Provide inexpensive small photo albums to collect photos of family members, pets, or other important people and places for each child to keep at the center. • Invite families and children to a sing-a-long featuring favorite songs suggested by each family, perhaps accompanied by a family member who plays a musical instrument.
Tap into family members' skills and talents.	• Invite someone who gardens to help plan, plant, and tend a small vegetable patch. • Ask for volunteers with carpentry experience and tools to help construct a set of classroom "mailboxes" for children to exchange messages. • Ask family members of an English language learner to come in and teach songs or games in the home language.
Be family-friendly rather than school-like.	• Have children help with sorting, matching, or counting socks. • Ask a child to match the image on a coupon with the cereal or soup on the grocery store shelf. • Let children help with simple parts of meal preparation.
Be cautious about placing demands on families' finances.	• Confine donation requests to found materials (discarded costume jewelry, sewing scraps, milk bottle caps, etc.) that can be used for sorting and creative projects. • Collect magazines, catalogs, grocery coupons.

Technology Toolkit

✓ Make a virtual trip to Reggio Emilia with this CNN story at http://www.youtube.com/watch?v=XVv5ZL9nlgs about a teacher from the United States who, inspired by what she learns on her study trip, makes a change in her practice at her own school.

✓ Read descriptions of project work with children of all ages in the bilingual Internet journal *Early Childhood Research and Practice* at http://ecrp.uiuc.edu/.

✓ Visit the website for Connect: The Center to Mobilize Early Childhood Knowledge at http://community.fpg.unc.edu/. Access a short video providing an overview of inclusion in early education, including a definition and explanation of its legal and policy foundations as well as a discussion of what it looks like in practice.

✓ Download a PowerPoint presentation at http://csefel.vanderbilt.edu/powerpoints/southern-stories.html, the website of the Center on the Social and Emotional Foundations for Early Learning. Southern Stories: Literacy Traditions for Young Children explains the connections between children's social–emotional development and early literacy.

? DECISIONS, DECISIONS . . .

What do you think the children learned through the special names project? How do you think the children and their families felt about their participation? Can you think of other examples where teachers have noticed children's interests and involved families in exploring those interests? Discuss with your classmates.

Conclusion

Serving children and families is the primary reason for a child development program's existence. The manager plays a key role in determining the quality of that service. The educational program must be based on sound developmental principles and must address the needs of *all* children, including those in need of early intervention and English language learners. The manager's job is to hire staff members who are well grounded in those principles, and then to support them as they plan and implement the program. Support includes providing paid planning time, adequate auxiliary staff, sufficient materials and equipment, regular feedback and encouragement, and ongoing opportunities for professional development. The manager also serves as a go-between, interpreting the program for parents and other stakeholders and defending it when necessary.

Questions for Review

1. Review your state's licensing standards pertaining to curriculum. How do they compare with your state's early learning standards? Which standards would be met with a project such as the one about robots described in the chapter-opening vignette?

2. Describe the manager's responsibility for the educational program. How does it differ from that of the teacher?

3. List the basic requirements of a good educational program and give examples of each.

4. Think about a child development program where you have worked or observed. Try to identify the curriculum model that was used and the primary focus (individual child's skills; physical and social context supporting overall development; content or concepts). Give examples to support your conclusion.

5. Compare the daily schedule and weekly activity plans at a child development program you know with the examples provided in this chapter. What changes (if any) would you suggest? Why?

6. Give examples of ways that a center you know has involved families in its educational program. Did they appear to be successful? Explain.

Professional Portfolio

1. Plan a PowerPoint (or other digital imaging technique) presentation on curriculum innovations for a center's staff members. Practice giving the presentation to your class, encouraging suggestions for improvement. Improve the presentation for a larger audience, and propose that it be given at a meeting of a local early childhood professional organization or at a conference of teachers.

2. Develop an annotated list of at least 10 resources (print, video, or Internet) addressing some aspect of developmentally appropriate programs for children. Give the title, author, publisher, publication date, cost, and purchasing information for each resource. Under each entry, summarize and evaluate the content and describe how you might use it in a center.

Resources for Further Study

PRINT

Curtis, D., & Carter, M. (2008). *Learning together with young children*. St. Paul, MN: Redleaf Press.

Epstein, A. S. (2007). *The intentional teacher: Choosing the best strategies for young children's learning*. Washington,

DC: National Association for the Education of Young Children.

Harris, K. I., & Gleim, L. (2008). The light fantastic: Making learning visible for all children through the project approach. *Young Exceptional Children, 11*(3), 27–40.

Websites

NAEYC PROFESSIONAL DEVELOPMENT

www.naeyc.org/

A continuum of activities designed to improve the knowledge, skills, practices, and dispositions of individuals who work with and on behalf of young children and their families. Options include online training programs and DVDs for individual or group self-study.

NATIONAL EARLY CHILDHOOD TECHNICAL ASSISTANCE CENTER

www.nectac.org/

Supported by the U.S. Department of Education's Office of Special Education Programs, the National Early Childhood

Technical Assistance Center's (NECTAC's) mission is "to strengthen service systems to insure that children with disabilities (birth through 5 years) and their families receive and benefit from high quality, culturally appropriate and family-centered supports and services." The website includes links to agency contacts in each state as well as information on topics ranging from specific disabilities to broad social issues and program administration.

CHAPTER

Family Engagement

LEARNING OUTCOMES

After studying this chapter you should be able to

- Explain how regulations and professional standards address the concept of family engagement.
- Discuss the ways in which program directors might apply knowledge of family systems and parenting styles.
- Explain the importance of family-friendly practice and cultural responsiveness for building relationships with families.
- Give examples of several strategies for building and maintaining partnerships with families.

Jeralyn wants Rainbow Center to feel less like school and more like home for families as well as children. She wants family members and teachers to share information about the children on a regular basis, but in a more relaxed manner than the typical formal parent-teacher conference. As a result, families of infants and toddlers are invited to schedule times to sit with a teacher and observe their babies in action through a one-way mirror, discussing what they saw or any questions they had. Families of the older children schedule an appointment for "muffin day" every 6 months or so. Each family selects a date in consultation with the teacher, who records it on the classroom calendar. Appointments are limited to afternoons when the classroom is quiet because children are outside playing and to days when there are enough adults on hand to allow the teacher to spend this one-on-one time with the family. The children, who can recognize their names, know the significance of the calendar notation and keep track of the progression of days with great anticipation. They send notes to Sophie, the cook, requesting that she buy a particular flavor of muffin mix, and on the morning of the appointed day, they help to mix and bake the muffins. When they wake from their naps, they help spread a pretty cloth over an art table where they set out the pitcher of juice and basket of muffins for their families to enjoy as they look at the child's portfolio.

A child development center is an organization designed to provide a service to families. It is part of the human ecological system's social–cultural environment. One way to look at the social–cultural environment is to envision a vast network of interconnected parts. The center has a connection with each family whose child is enrolled. Those families have connections to one another, partly as a consequence of their involvement with the center. The center and the families have specific connections with agencies and institutions outside the center, as well as general connections with society as a whole.

Maintaining these connections is essential to the survival of individuals, families, and institutions. One of your major functions as manager is to facilitate the communication among your center, the families you serve, and the rest of the community. To do this, you must use the managerial processes discussed throughout this book: planning, organizing, leading, staffing, and monitoring and controlling for quality. Your success benefits the children in your care, their families, your center, and your community. This chapter examines the ways in which child development programs partner with and support families.

REGULATIONS AND PROFESSIONAL STANDARDS

Licensing regulations typically require that child development programs provide families with written policies regarding admission, withdrawal, fees, schedule of operation, health requirements, and discipline or guidance upon enrollment of their child. Once children are in care, centers are expected to keep parents informed via posted menus and written records of accidents or injuries. Centers caring for infants and toddlers must provide records of children's food intake, bowel patterns, and developmental milestones.

The Early Childhood and Infant/Toddler Environment Rating Scales address these issues in the indicators for minimal quality in the provisions for parents. Also at the minimal level, programs are expected to offer "some possibilities" for family involvement. Programs must exceed this standard and encourage family involvement in multiple ways at the "good" level. At the "excellent" level, parents participate in decision making along with staff members (Harms, Cryer, & Clifford, 2006, p. 54). A comparable evaluation tool, the Program Administration Scale (Talan & Bloom, 2004), distinguishes among inadequate, minimal, good, and excellent provisions for family support and involvement based in part on the number of ways the center responds to family needs: for example, providing a toy or resource library, extended hours, transportation, scholarships, and/or referral services (pp. 42–43).

National Association for the Education of Young Children Guidelines

The National Association for the Education of Young Children (NAEYC) uses the term family engagement to convey the complex dynamics of an approach, defined as an "on-going, reciprocal, strengths-based partnership between families and their children's early childhood education program" (Halgunseth, Peterson, Stark, & Moodie, 2009). It may be helpful to think of the term *engage* in the sense of mechanical gears engaging with one another to produce some outcome. Unless the gears in your car are engaged, with each element doing its part, the car will not move forward, no matter how much you press on the gas pedal. (See Figure 13.1.) Unless the center and family are

FIGURE 13.1   Family engagement as an ongoing, reciprocal process.

LEADERSHIP LENS

The concept of servant leadership aligns closely with the ideals underlying the family engagement approach described here. **Servant leadership** contrasts with more traditional views of the leader as holding power over others and directing their actions to meet predetermined goals or standards. Servant leaders are characterized by a passion to serve and to view their work as a calling rather than just a livelihood or career. These ideas add a spiritual and ethical dimension to the concept of leadership, as is evident in these questions posed by Robert Greenleaf:

> Do those served grow as persons? Do they, while being served, become healthier, wiser, freer, more autonomous, more likely themselves to become servants? And what is the effect on the least privileged in society; will they benefit, or, at least, not be further deprived? (Greenleaf, 1998, p. 19)

Servant leaders are skilled listeners; they have empathy, awareness, and a strong sense of community. They see themselves as stewards, preparing their organizations to make a positive difference in the world. Some qualities of the servant leader are dispositions, built into the individual's personality and temperament. Others are skills that can be acquired and improved upon with practice. A hallmark of the servant leader is a commitment to a lifelong journey of learning and improving practice (Barbuto, 2007). You can learn more about servant leadership at the website of the Center for Servant Leadership (www.greenleaf.org).

fully engaged with each other, children will not reap the full potential of their participation in the program.

In other words, family engagement is not limited to traditional notions of parent involvement such as attendance at a workshop or teacher conference. Rather, it is something that occurs throughout the time a child is enrolled in a center. It is not one-sided, with centers prescribing menial volunteer tasks or dispensing advice and information; it involves sharing information and decision making. Family engagement means recognizing that all families (often including extended family members as well as parents) are involved in their children's learning and development and that it is up to programs to partner with them to create the best outcomes for children. Family engagement means starting with a vision and policies that support this type of relationship and then providing ongoing professional development and support for program staff members to sustain engagement efforts.

The NAEYC views establishing reciprocal relationships with families as an essential component of developmentally appropriate practices and lists seven characteristics of such relationships:

1. They are reciprocal, built on mutual respect, cooperation, and shared responsibility.

2. They encourage collaboration through regular, frequent, two-way communication with all families.

3. In addition to opportunities for observation and classroom participation, families have a voice in decisions regarding their children's care.

4. Teachers strive for balance, honoring what the families want and hope for their children with what they know about learning and development.

5. Families and teachers have frequent opportunities—both planned and informal—to share information about children.

6. Teachers realize that they have only part of the picture and ask families to share what they know about their children's development and help plan appropriate programs.

7. Program staff members help families build on their existing strengths and support networks as well as access appropriate services, taking into account what the families say they need or want (Copple & Bredekamp, 2009, p. 23).

In other words, child development professionals must realize that, in order to serve children well, they need the families as much as families need them. A director or teachers may disagree with particular families on some matters, but if they remember that the goal they have in common is the good of the child, they can respect each other and work to resolve any difficulties. Families always have the final say in decisions involving their children. The program's job is to provide information to support families as they make those decisions.

Families' involvement is the most important factor for a child's success in school.

Division for Early Childhood Guidelines

While the NAEYC guidelines are intended to apply to programs serving *all* children, the Division for Early Childhood (DEC) of the Council for Exceptional Children focuses specifically on children with or at risk for developing disabilities. This organization has identified 17 recommended practices, organized around four major themes:

1. *Families and professionals share responsibility and work collaboratively*   Family members and professionals work together to establish goals and work toward their accomplishment. Professionals support the families' ability to make informed choices by providing information, and they are sensitive and respectful of each family's unique culture, language, and identity.

2. *Practices strengthen family functioning*   The aim is for families to make choices and access resources in order to reach the goals they set for themselves. Professionals support this process by providing information and opportunities for experience in the least disruptive way.

3. *Practices are individualized and flexible*   Services are not provided in a one-size-fits-all format; rather, they are tuned to the priorities and preferences of individual family members. Professionals recognize and respect the families' unique characteristics stemming from their cultural, ethnic, and socioeconomic background, as well as the community context, and they take into account the families' beliefs and values.

4. *Practices are strengths- and assets-based*   Rather than seeking to "fix" families' deficits or shortcomings, professionals look for strengths and assets that can be mobilized. They foster family competence and confidence by building on existing strengths and offering the families opportunities to acquire new knowledge and skills (Sandall, Hemmeter, Smith, & McLean, 2005, pp. 110–111).

A careful review of these themes and practices reveals close parallels with the NAEYC guidelines, suggesting the extent to which these two organizations have communicated and collaborated.

As facility manager, you have many opportunities to put these guidelines into practice and move beyond the traditional "parent education" approach that has often characterized the interactions between child development programs and families toward a model of family engagement. Start by employing teachers who understand and believe in the concept of partnering with families, teachers who are sensitive to cultural, social, and linguistic diversity. Then help staff members build on these these attitudes and skills through a professional development program.

UNDERSTANDING FAMILY SYSTEMS

Children do not exist in a vacuum. Serving children means serving families, which requires both an understanding of how family systems work and an appreciation for many types of diversity: family composition, culture, parenting styles, and life situations. It means forming partnerships with parents and knowing enough about your community to help the families access resources necessary to promote family wellness.

Uri Bronfenbrenner's ecological model of human development and the family ecosystems framework suggested that, just as families provide the context for the individual child's development, they also exist within a network of formal and informal support systems. These systems provide the resources that enable families to nurture their children, physically and psychologically. The child development facility is one such system. In recent decades, families' awareness of the skills and knowledge needed for school success have risen along with their expectations that early education programs will provide those benefits (Belfield & Garcia, 2011). Still, it is important to remember that the role of the child development center is to supplement and support—not substitute or supplant—the families as the primary context for the children's development. The NAEYC guidelines and the DEC's recommended practices are clearly grounded in this ecological view of families and children.

Family Members as Human Resources for the Center

The family engagement approach requires recognition that communication and relationships in ecosystems are complex affairs. The center is a resource for the families whose children are enrolled, and those family members are a rich source of

One way that family members provide important human resources for centers is to volunteer in the classroom.

human capital for the center. Programs such as Head Start have long made a practice of hiring staff members from within the population they serve. What better way of ensuring that your center's policies and practices are in tune with the cultural backgrounds of the children? In some centers, such as parent cooperatives, the staff consists almost entirely of unpaid parent volunteers who take turns assisting the paid teacher.

Even when they are not regular staff members, parents provide valuable information and support for the teachers and caregivers. Child development staff may know about children in general, but the family knows more about its own particular child. Furthermore, the burden of being the all-knowing "expert" can be a heavy one. When center staff members value the contributions that family members make, everyone gains.

In addition to the expertise they bring about their own children, families provide a center with a rich pool of professional expertise from which to draw. Someone with advanced computer skills might help you set up a system for maintaining the center's health and financial records and train a staff member to use the system. Carpenters, plumbers, electricians, landscape gardeners, or carpet cleaners might contribute a few hours to a special improvement project. People who do not work outside their home might agree to sew new curtains or make a slipcover for the easy chair in your reading corner. A corporate executive might agree to consult on some aspect of the center's management. The list of possibilities is limited only by your imagination.

Besides contributing directly to your center's day-to-day operation, family members can serve the center as leaders and policy makers. This type of family involvement is recognized as an indication of very high quality in the environmental and program rating scales discussed earlier in this chapter. In addition to all of the professional skills they might bring, parents can help you see things from the perspective of your customers, which is a key element of today's quality management.

Community Resources to Support Families

Creating links with agencies in your community is another aspect of family engagement. It helps the families and children you serve and creates opportunities for them to expand their connections within the ecosystem. Many centers keep a file of community agencies and resources for referrals. Such referrals are more productive if you have established contacts in the various agencies and can suggest that families ask for a particular person by name. Your agency contacts might also bring specific resources to the center where they are more accessible to the families. Some centers have health department representatives offer immunization clinics on-site at certain times during the year. Others might invite a parenting expert from the community mental health clinic to conduct workshops for interested family members. A public library, community college, or local church might partner with your center to provide adult literacy or English as a second language classes. Your local child-care resource and referral agency is a good place to begin looking for what is available in your community.

Characteristics of Family Systems

In addition to understanding the broader ecosystems perspective, it is important to understand the many ways that families function and their members relate to each other. Christian (2007) suggests that early childhood professionals will find it useful to think of six characteristics of family systems (boundaries, roles, rules, hierarchy, climate, and equilibrium), each lying on a continuum. Although few families can be placed at either extreme, most do tend toward one direction or the other. Taken together, these characteristics comprise a unique profile for each family. Your awareness of that profile will help you avoid a one-size-fits-all approach in your interactions.

Boundaries refer to the degree to which a family is open to outside influences. At one end of the spectrum, the enmeshed family places a high priority on togetherness and restricts the activities of its members. At the opposite extreme, a disengaged family values independence and respects the individual identity of each member. It is important for caregivers to avoid viewing either extreme as right or wrong and to adjust their practice to meet the families' needs and preferences.

Roles are the parts each member plays within the family (e.g., helper, victim). Children or adults who play a particular role at home are likely to do so in other settings as well, with positive or negative consequences. It is important for teachers to help children who seem stuck in a role to expand their possibilities.

Rules spell out the ways family members live in relation to one another. They may be spoken or unspoken, and they have deep roots in past experience. Your rules at the center may be different from—or even transgress—family rules (e.g., that boys don't play with dolls). Open discussion with families is key to resolving conflicts.

Hierarchy refers to the distribution of power and control within a family. Influenced by culture, it may be based on age, gender, or family position and can shift with the loss or addition of a family member. Ignorance of hierarchy can result in inadvertently insulting a family and can rupture relationships. Therefore it is important to observe the ways family members interact and perhaps even ask direct questions.

Climate refers to the emotional and physical qualities of the child's home life. Can it be characterized as safe, secure, and loving, or threatening and unhappy? Early childhood programs can provide information and support to help families create a more nurturing climate, and they can provide a safe haven for children who must endure a harsh one.

Equilibrium is tied to consistency. Families establish a comfortable balance in their lives that can be upset by sudden change, such as illness or a job loss, that disrupts their ability to function. Early childhood programs can provide an oasis of consistency for children who are experiencing upheaval, perhaps due to a new baby, military deployment of a parent, or homelessness.

Parenting Styles

Another framework for understanding individual families is provided by the work of psychologist Diana Baumrind (1973, 1977), who examined differences in parents' expectation levels for mature behavior, degree of control, amount of communication, and emotional nurturance. She found three distinct profiles, which she labeled authoritarian, permissive, and authoritative. According to Baumrind's scheme, **authoritarian** parents expect very high levels of mature behavior from their children and exert strict control methods, including physical punishment for infractions. They offer little in the way of emotional support, however, and do not spend much time explaining the reasons for their rules. At the opposite extreme, **permissive** parents have low expectations, make few demands, and offer little information to their children about why they should behave in particular ways. They do express high levels of caring and concern, and may use this as their only tool for encouraging the children to obey—"I won't like you if you do. . . ."

According to Baumrind's research, neither of these styles is associated with increased social responsibility in children. Both produce children who rely on external controls for their own behavior and often suffer low self-esteem. The happy medium seems to be the **authoritative** parenting style. These parents balance high expectations and firm limits with clear explanations of the reasons for those limits and the consequences for transgression, together with an attitude of caring and support. Children of authoritative parents tend to enjoy high self-esteem and the ability to control their own behavior and act responsibly.

Based on this description, it is easy to see why early childhood professionals are often taught to adopt the authoritative style of interacting with children, and why many parent education programs attempt to teach it to parents. There is an important caveat, however: Each of the dimensions examined by Baumrind (control, maturity demands, communication, and nurturance) is highly influenced by many factors, including cultural and individual characteristics and values. What appear as harsh, controlling demands to one person might be perceived as emphatic expressions of care and concern by another. One person's effort to foster independence by letting a toddler feed himself might be seen by another as uncaring or missing an opportunity to teach the toddler the importance of nurturing tenderness. A child accustomed to a sharp tone and brusque demands might experience a teacher's softer voice and milder requests as lacking control and caring.

It seems, then, that the three basic parenting styles described by Baumrind can manifest themselves in as many ways as there are parents. What is the child development professional to make of this information? Recall the NAEYC and DEC recommendation that programs work in partnership with the families to establish and achieve goals. One use of this information might be to share with families about the ways in which their behaviors might affect the outcomes they want for their children. Remember always, however, that teachers can also learn from families about effective ways to communicate with their particular children.

> ### ❓ DECISIONS, DECISIONS . . .
>
> #### Using an Ethical Framework
>
> A 4-year-old girl enrolled in your program lives with her grandmother because her mother is currently residing in a rehabilitation facility for drug users. The girl has been having tantrums in the classroom, which the teacher says are sometimes so violent she fears for her own safety as well as that of the other children. When you and the teacher meet with the child's grandmother to discuss the situation, she responds that the problem stems from the teacher's "soft" approach to discipline and reports that spanking has eliminated similar behavior at home. Of course, you explain that your program's policies and licensing regulations regarding discipline prohibit spanking, but the grandmother remains convinced that a firmer approach will solve the problem. The meeting ends with you wondering whether you should ask that the child be withdrawn. You believe that attending your program will help this child build a sense of security, which will eventually enable her to manage her strong feelings more appropriately, but you are worried that you cannot balance her needs with those of the teacher and other children in the classroom. What should you do? Using the NAEYC code, try to determine what core values are involved. What ideals and principles regarding responsibilities to children, families, and employees apply? What course of action seems most right?

RELATIONSHIPS WITH FAMILIES

Once parents enroll their children in your center, they become consumers of your service. The most obvious example of the service is the direct care and education you provide for the children, supplementing the parents' time, energy, and know-how. In a deeper sense, however, parents are much more than consumers. The service you provide is a human service, qualitatively different from tuning a car engine or dry-cleaning a family's clothing. It is a long-term commitment of time and energy—in other words, an enduring relationship with children and with their families.

Relationship-based care is a term usually used in connection with programs for infants and toddlers that build on the infant's earliest relationships with parents and make supporting that relationship one of their most important goals. They view the child's entry into child care as an expansion of that relationship and use it as a model for a primary caregiving system where every child (and his or her family) has the opportunity to form a strong connection with one teacher and maintain that connection as long as possible. Such programs use documentation (e.g., diaries and portfolios) to communicate and build bonds with families as well as to support individualized planning. They also support children's relationships with each other by caring for them in small groups that stay together as long as 3 years in spaces designed to be adaptable to their changing abilities (Raikes & Edwards, 2009, pp. 73–74). Listen to the director in this video describe how her program strives to build strong relationships with families. Which of the strategies that she mentions have been tried by programs where you have worked or observed?

Clearly these characteristics of a relationship-based approach can or should apply equally well to programs for children of all ages. Only as partners with families can you and your staff members fulfill the important task of nurturing children and supporting their development. Building strong relationships with families requires that your overall practices are family-friendly and that you and your staff members are able to communicate and work well with people whose culture, ethnicity, religious beliefs, and/or lifestyle choices are different from yours.

Family-Friendly Practice

Family-friendly practice is the term commonly applied to professional practices based on conscious efforts to acknowledge the central role of families in their children's development and to accommodate the particular needs of today's diverse families. Today's diverse families might include parents who are much younger or older than the typical childbearing age of past times; single-parent- or grandparent-headed households; blended families, with children in widely disparate age ranges; adoptive or foster parents; gay or lesbian parents; families coping with stress created by military deployment; and families struggling with job loss, mortgage foreclosure, and/or homelessness.

Copeland and McCreedy (1998, pp. 311–313) called for a "paradigm shift"—a radical change in the way child development programs view their obligations to meet family needs. They offered several suggestions for making child development programs more family-friendly:

1. *With your teachers, take a hard look at your attitudes and beliefs*   Do you assume that parents who don't read your newsletter or who come late to pick up their children simply don't care? Is that assumption communicated in a look or gesture that makes the parents feel judged or put down? The first step toward a more helpful attitude is talking to the parents to learn what they are really thinking and experiencing. It is likely that your empathy will grow as you acquire accurate information. From that new stance, you can begin the kind of dialogue that leads to collaboration and mutual support.

2. *Rethink your policies*   Do your enrollment forms seem to deny the existence of blended families, single-parent families, families with gay or lesbian parents? If you have a pay-in-advance policy, do you make allowances for the families whose care is subsidized by public funds that are paid after the services are delivered? Do you work with families who experience a financial crisis and must postpone payments? How do you support mothers who wish to breast-feed their babies?

3. *Bend a little*   Find win-win solutions when your program's usual practices conflict with the families' needs and wishes. Suppose your custom is to schedule parent conferences during nap time. Many parents' work schedules make it impossible for them to attend, yet it seems unfair to ask teachers to schedule conferences outside their already long workday. Perhaps you can work with the families to find a way to pay the teachers for this overtime work or to hire substitutes so teachers can hold evening conferences and take compensatory time off at some later date.

4. *Find ways to include the families in decisions that affect their children*   Schedule meetings when most family representatives are able to attend and find ways for the other families to voice their opinions—provide written ballots or put suggestion boxes near the entryway. Let the families know that they have been heard by following up on their ideas and telling them about any adjustments in your newsletter.

5. *Create an environment that welcomes families as well as children*   Comfortable, adult-size furnishings invite family members to linger a few moments with their children before dashing off to work. Some centers make a variety of time-saving services available to busy parents—for example, assistance with tax preparation or voter registration, or access to the center's copy machine and computer.

6. *Keep families informed*   Display staff photos and names in the entryway so that family members know who's who. Provide name tags for substitutes or visitors. Use newsletters, email, websites, and displays in the classroom to give families a glimpse of the life that goes on in your program.

7. *Help families do their job*   Provide lists of community resources; interesting and timely articles; a place to post carpool requests; and class rosters with names, phone numbers, and birthdays. Create a resource library with books and videos on parenting topics—even a collection of high-quality entertainment videos that families can enjoy together.

Many of Copeland and McCreedy's suggestions for program directors echo the NAEYC and DEC guidelines discussed earlier.

Cultural Responsiveness

Given the changing demographics of the U.S. population, it is likely that, as a center manager, you will interact with many people who are different from you in some way. Consider these examples:

- About 40 percent of children today are born to unmarried women, an eightfold increase since 1960 (Olson, 2011).

- Children of immigrants made up nearly 25 percent of the child population in 2010 (New American Children, 2012).

- Nearly one in four school-age children speaks a language other than English at home. The actual percentages range from 13 percent in the Midwest to 34 percent in the West. Five percent of children have difficulty speaking English, again with higher percentages in the West (Federal Interagency Forum on Child and Family Statistics, 2013).

- According to the 2010 census, Hispanics accounted for more than 34 percent of all children from birth to age 5, but only a little more than 10 percent of all preK and kindergarten teachers (Frede, 2011).

- Approximately 2 million children in the United States are being raised by at least one parent who is lesbian, gay, bisexual, or transgender (Child Trends, 2013).

This means that the families you serve may have different ethnic backgrounds; they may not speak the same language you do. Their lifestyle or religious faith might differ from yours. They might have significantly less—or significantly more—education and income than you. Your success as a manager depends on your ability to communicate across these cultural lines and to collaborate effectively with different people.

Cultural responsiveness is the term for this ability, and it is an important hallmark of the early childhood professional (Hernandez, 2011). Cultural responsiveness, sometimes called cross-cultural competence, refers to "ways of thinking and behaving that enable members of one cultural, ethnic, or linguistic group to work effectively with members of another" (Lynch & Hanson, 1998, p. 492). How, you might wonder, can you be expected to acquire this ability if you are likely to work with so many different groups during your career? On the other hand, if you work in a program where everyone seems to share the same ethnic, cultural, and linguistic background, you might think this is something that doesn't apply to you. Either of these views—that cultural responsiveness is impossible or that it is irrelevant—will hinder your efforts to provide the best possible program for young children and their families.

As an early childhood administrator promoting cultural responsiveness, you must address both interpersonal and structural issues. Interpersonal issues concern your own attitudes and the ways you relate to others, as well as your efforts to support culturally responsive attitudes, skills, and dispositions in your staff members. Structural issues include environment, staffing patterns, group sizes, and all of the other ways you set the stage for cultural responsiveness to flourish.

INTERPERSONAL ASPECTS OF CULTURAL RESPONSIVENESS   Cultural responsiveness begins with knowledge—knowledge of your own cultural background and the many ways it has shaped your beliefs. If you happen to be a member of the dominant culture in any community, your culture may be as invisible to you as the air you breathe. All of the notions that you take for granted—how children should behave, what they should learn and when, and how adults should treat them—are products of your cultural upbringing. Someone from another culture might have very different ideas about the same things. Unless you realize how your culture has shaped your ideas, you might dismiss the other person's ideas as simply wrong. The risk of doing this is increased if your culture is strongly reflected in your professional training. Middle-class Anglo-European values, for example, coincide with much of what early childhood professionals learn as "best practice" in the United States (Lubeck, 1994). Uncovering your own cultural heritage is part of the self-reflective knowledge discussed in a previous chapter and is an important first step for you and your staff members. Several of the resources listed at the end of this chapter suggest exercises that you can do to begin this process.

Cultural responsiveness also requires another kind of knowledge—knowledge of the cultures represented by the families you serve. You can acquire this knowledge by reading, viewing video recordings, or any of the ways you might study any academic subject (see, e.g., Hildebrand, Phenice, Gray, & Hines, 2007). No matter how much you learn about any particular group in this way, however, it is important to remember that the members of any particular group are as different from one another as they are from you. It is also possible that individual members of two different racial or ethnic groups have more in common with each other than they do with any set of characteristics associated with their respective groups. While race and language are two of the most obvious indicators of culture, many cultural differences are more subtle. In addition to speaking a particular language, families have particular ways of expressing needs or feelings such as dissatisfaction or distress. They may have reservations about seeking help or dealing with professionals (Bradley & Kibera, 2007). The best way to avoid the pitfall of lumping all members of a group into one stereotype is to take the risk and ask questions. Instead of making assumptions, you can say, "I've read that. . . . What do you think about that?" If you ask respectfully, conveying your sincere openness and desire to learn, most people are happy to share information about their culture with you.

Knowledge, then, is a necessary component of cultural responsiveness, but it is not sufficient by itself. Being willing to ask questions and being open to and respectful of different ideas are also matters of attitude or disposition. If you open yourself to this way of learning about other people, you will inevitably make mistakes. The key is to foster, in yourself and in your staff members, a willingness to apologize frankly for those mistakes and learn from them for the future. When people from different cultures make a sincere effort to work together, whether these discussions occur in one-on-one situations or in group settings, mistakes are forgiven and may even be found amusing. One of the authors of this textbook once lived in an African culture where all references to eating were considered unfit for polite company. In her ignorance, she invited some African colleagues to dinner and was both surprised and grateful when they gently informed her of her faux pas. When conflicts do occur, the parties involved should listen to each other, resolve to think about what they heard, and agree to discuss it again later (Gonzalez-Mena, 2005).

STRUCTURAL ASPECTS OF CULTURAL RESPONSIVENESS   Although the face-to-face interactions among you, your staff members, and the families you serve certainly influence your program's level of cultural responsiveness, there is a great deal that administrators can do to set the stage for those interactions. First, the physical environment can reflect and welcome the cultures represented in a program. This involves more than simply tacking up a few commercial images of people in "native costume." It might mean reflecting the program's community by displaying photographs of family members and people, buildings, or places that play an important role in the families' lives. It might mean creating arrangements of beautiful or meaningful objects from each family that represent some aspect of their heritage or the hopes and dreams they have for their children. It can mean including in your CD or digital audio player samples of music that the families enjoy at home.

Administrators structure the social environment to support cultural responsiveness when they employ staff members who share the cultural and linguistic heritage of the families they serve. This strategy makes it easier to provide cultural consistency between home and school, which facilitates the children's identity formation and communication with the families. It is also just as important to have representation of the diverse groups at the management level and on governing boards. Finally, administrators can limit the total number of children in any one classroom group, thus reducing the potential number of cultures included and making teachers' task of relating to those cultures less daunting (Mangione, 1993).

BUILDING PARTNERSHIPS WITH FAMILIES

Paola Cagliari, a *pedagogista* ("education coordinator") for the municipal early childhood programs of Reggio Emilia, Italy, described a new way to conceptualize the relationships between families and schools. "One essential challenge is that of modifying the idea of the teacher, who is no longer the holder of certain knowledge that is simply taught to children and parents, enclosed in the security of an unchangeable and incontestable institution and context." But, she added, "[a]t the same time we try to avoid moving toward the idea of a teacher and a school that merely offer a service modeled on the individual needs of families" (Gambetti & Kaminsky, 2001, p. 3). In other words, neither teachers nor families dictate program content; instead, they collaborate to create something that neither could have created alone.

A growing body of research in the United States has demonstrated that parents' involvement, regardless of their wealth or education, is the most important factor for a child's success in school (e.g., Harvard Family Research Project, 2006; Gelber & Isen, 2011). This involvement begins with the family's first encounter with the educational system. For many of today's children, that means when they are carried into the infant room at their child development center. The way that the first encounter between parent and educator is handled can color the entire educational career—and thus, the entire life—of that child.

Unfortunately, few early childhood teacher education programs include adequate preparation for working with diverse families (Frede, 2011). This places a heavy responsibility on the center's manager to help staff members develop these skills. Care must be taken to avoid several pitfalls. Some parents may have had bad experiences during their own schooling and, as a result, may feel intimidated or hostile toward representatives of "the system." Others might have the opposite reaction and, relinquishing their own role, depend on you to make all of the decisions as the omniscient expert. Still others might feel that they must compete with center staff for their child's affection and respect. Staff members may exacerbate parents' feelings of ambivalence about placing their child in care by criticizing or talking down to parents (McGrath, 2007). They may show favoritism, let friendships cloud their judgment, or develop a savior complex and stray into areas outside their expertise in an effort to be helpful (Stonehouse & Gonzalez-Mena, 2006).

All of these pitfalls hamper the creation of the kind of partnership that works best for all parties involved. However, there are concrete steps that you can take, from the beginning of your relationship with each family, to help establish that partnership.

We have already discussed the NAEYC's general guidelines for establishing reciprocal relationships with families. NAEYC accreditation criteria require that centers establish provisions for learning from families about their backgrounds and wishes for their children, for sharing information with families in a variety of ways (orientation visits, conferences, daily reports—in languages that families understand), and for promoting families' capacity to advocate for their children. In fact, the NAEYC's assessment of how well your center performs these functions includes input from the parents. As part of your self-study for the accreditation process, you must survey the parents to get their evaluation of your center's parental involvement component (NAEYC, 2007a).

Pre-enrollment Visits

Before enrollment, parents seeking child-care services should be encouraged to come to the center without the child for a conference and a tour of the facility. They should be invited to sit comfortably and observe the children and teachers in action for several hours if possible. This allows them to see more clearly how the children are treated and how problems are handled. As manager, you should be open to such a visit, even suggest it, especially if parents come without their child. They may simply drop by, or they may call to schedule an appointment. Because an open-door policy builds families' confidence in your center, you should be prepared to be cordial on a moment's notice.

An observation period can dispel families' anxieties or raise questions they might like to ask. You must have a procedure in place so families receive answers to questions without disrupting ongoing work. Clearly, the teachers cannot leave their children unattended to talk with the parents of prospective enrollees. Therefore, it must be made clear that any discussion with the child's potential teacher must be scheduled, unless a qualified substitute is available for the teacher's class. Most visiting parents are happy to cooperate if you explain the reason for your policy.

Some parents bring their child along. Depending on the activities under way, it may be unwise to take a visiting child into an ongoing group of children. The children may resent a visitor disrupting their activity and make negative or teasing comments that could be taken as unfriendly by the visitors. If possible, wait until the children have gone outdoors so that the visiting child and parent can explore the classroom without interference or the need to adjust socially to many unfamiliar children. Alternatively, arrange another time for the child's visit—after hours or on a weekend. Such exploration generally leaves a favorable impression, and the child and parent become eager to enroll.

Handbook for Families

One of your primary tools for communicating with families is the center's handbook. (The term *handbook* may soon become obsolete as more families gain access to computers and the internet, and paper handbooks are displaced by digital versions on center websites.) Whatever its format, the handbook provides parents with all of the basic information about your center in one convenient package. Some programs include a statement to be signed by the parents, affirming their understanding and agreement to abide by the policies and procedures described in the handbook. Parents return one copy to the center and keep one for their records.

As noted in a previous chapter, state licensing regulations or funding requirements frequently spell out what must be included in the handbook. Examples include the program's schedule and hours of operation, and its policies regarding admission and withdrawal criteria, immunization and other health issues, discipline, meals, and fees (including late payment penalties). You will probably want to include more than the minimum required information, however. The handbook gives you a chance to highlight the qualities that make your center unique. Many handbooks include a brief history of the program's origin and its development over time, a statement of the program's philosophy, a description of the curriculum and sample daily schedule, and a flowchart or other illustration of the administrative structure. The handbook can also address opportunities for family involvement, and program traditions and rituals such as birthday or seasonal celebrations (including the reasons for those traditions).

Computer word-processing or desktop publishing programs make it easy to create an attractive, professional-looking handbook. With the digital-imaging techniques available, you can make your handbook more appealing to your readers by incorporating photographs and children's drawings. A table of contents, tabs to identify separate sections, and information presented in concise bullet format will make it easier for your readers to find what they need. Because your philosophy and your policies are likely to evolve over time, you may want to print only a limited supply of handbooks, perhaps enough for one year's enrollment. You can then revise the content, or at least review it closely, every year to keep your handbook up to date.

No matter how elegant or comprehensive your handbook is, it will be little more than a dust collector unless families use it. One way to encourage the use of your handbook by families is to provide every classroom with its own copy. When parents have questions, teachers can say, "Let's check the handbook," and search for the answer with the parent. Both teachers and parents may learn things they didn't know in the process, including an idea of what else they might find in the handbook. They can also inform you when particular questions are not covered or information seems unclear—feedback that can guide your next revision.

Figure 13.2 lists possible contents of a center's handbook for families. If your center has a website—and if all your families have access to the internet—you may want to put much of the information there instead of on paper.

1. A welcome to parents and families
2. A statement of the program's mission and philosophy
3. Brief history of the center, including accreditation
4. Flowchart of the program's administrative structure
5. Floor plan of the center showing location of classrooms, office, parent resource room
6. Overview of the general curriculum (e.g., goals, methods, rationale)
7. Admission and withdrawal policies
8. Calendar and schedule of operations (e.g., hours, days closed, inclement weather procedure)
9. Sample daily schedule
10. Fee policy, including policies regarding surcharges for late payment and late pickup
11. Food service policy (e.g., meals and times offered, sample menu)
    - Meals served; times offered
    - Sample menu
    - Policy regarding food from home (e.g., birthday treats)
12. Health policies and practices:
    - Children's initial immunization records and updates, physical examination requirements
    - Staff health requirements (TB tests, physical examinations)
    - Communicable diseases among children and/or staff (exclusion from school, requirements for readmission)
    - Diapering and toileting
    - Resting and sleep (individual cots, cribs, bedding, laundry)
13. Discipline or guidance policy
14. Emergency procedures (fire, tornado, or other emergency; serious accident or injury; required family emergency contact information)
15. What to bring and what to leave at home (transition objects)
16. Communication with families and opportunities for involvement
    - Authorization to visit and/or pick up child
    - Visits and interviews before enrollment
    - Transition period during first week(s) of enrollment
    - Documentation of children's daily experiences
    - Newsletters
    - Conferences
    - Special events, birthday or holiday celebrations
17. Policy for reporting suspected child abuse or neglect
18. Community resources for families
19. Instructions for accessing center web site (URL, password)
20. Statement of understanding and intent to comply with policies

FIGURE 13.2 Possible contents of a center's handbook for families.

Orientation

Orientation is the get-acquainted period for your center and the new family. Ideally, parents have already visited the center to observe the program, and they have received a copy of the center's handbook to read at their leisure. If your center enrolls several families at one time (e.g., the beginning of the school year), you can hold an orientation meeting for the group. If you enroll new families whenever a vacancy occurs (which is typical of most full-day, year-round programs), you must set aside time for an orientation meeting with each family. This is your opportunity to explain the content and purpose of the various application and permission forms that parents are asked to sign, to review your program's philosophy, and to discuss your policies to ensure they are clearly understood. Even though you have provided a written copy of the center's policies and asked the parents to sign statements affirming that they understand and will abide by those policies, the fact is that many families are simply too busy or distracted to read those policies thoroughly. Investing time in a face-to-face discussion at the beginning puts your relationship with a family on a firm footing and prevents unpleasant surprises later on.

Phased Enrollment

If your center operates on a school-year schedule, you can phase in the start-up by having a few children arrive with their parents each day until the maximum capacity is achieved, perhaps by the end of the week. Phasing in makes it easier for staff members to deal with problems than it would be if large groups of children arrive at once. With this approach, children can receive more individual attention. Parents can observe their child playing with other children and interacting with the teachers until the child feels comfortable enough to be left at the center.

Programs that operate on a year-round, full-day schedule can practice phased enrollment as well. First, they can encourage parents to spend as much time as possible at the center with their child during the first week. They can also ask that parents plan for their child to attend only part-time for the first few days. For example, for a few days, a new 3- or 4-year-old child might come for the morning and go home with a family member right after lunch. Frequently, these new children initiate the move to a longer day themselves by announcing that they want to stay for a nap with their friends. During this phase-in period, family members can gradually decrease their time at the center, perhaps stepping out for a cup of coffee or running an errand after the child is settled into play—always with the reassurance that they will be back shortly. Gradually, the "errand time" grows longer until the family can bring the child to the door, say good-bye, and leave secure in the knowledge that the child is playing happily. They know that a member of the staff will call if the child seems to need her or his family.

The benefits of this phasing-in process are numerous. Children feel more secure with a familiar adult present and thus feel free to explore the materials and activities your program offers. The more they explore and engage themselves, the easier it becomes for them to separate from their families later on. Children who are forced to adapt to a new environment without this supportive transition period often spend so much time and energy missing their absent families that they cannot focus on anything else. Families and teachers benefit because they become acquainted and comfortable with one another over the course of the week. Because the families get to see the program in operation, they have a mental image to call on when they find themselves wondering what their child is doing or feeling. Often, the family members themselves have some anxiety that should be recognized. Teachers benefit because they learn from families the particular, subtle ways they relate to their children. How does this baby like to be held for feeding? What does this child mean by a particular word or phrase? Parents and teachers both get a chance to ask questions that neither may have thought of during the initial interview. In short, the family, the child, and the teacher begin to develop trust, an essential ingredient of a productive relationship. Although such procedures may require effort and coordination, the children are better adjusted and the center receives good publicity when the parents tell others that you are a person-oriented manager who really has the child's and parents' interests at heart.

Of course, a gradual initiation to full-day care presents challenges. Many parents do not have the luxury of taking a week off from work, even if they want to do so. Others find it hard to see the value of this investment of their time. As the administrator, you must be flexible as you plan with families. One thing is certain, however—you should make your expectations known before enrollment and ask the families for their commitment to the best possible beginning for their child.

> **? DECISIONS, DECISIONS . . .**
>
> Discuss with your classmates or the manager of a child development center the idea of having parents spend the first week or month with their child at the center. Would you be comfortable doing your job with parents present? How would you make them feel welcome? How would you structure a gradual transition to the point where the child attends the center alone?

Home Visits

A home visit can be the foundation for developing your center's harmonious relationship with the children and their families. Arranging a visit to the child's home before (or soon after) the child begins attending helps strengthen the home–school bond and boosts families' confidence in their interactions with you (Logan & Feiler, 2006). Visits should always be scheduled at the family's convenience. Offer a choice of days and times rather than simply arriving unannounced. A short visit is all that is required to give the child a more secure feeling and provide the teachers with information (e.g., about siblings, pets, family lifestyle, and preferred modes of communication). This visit helps the child adjust to being without the family in the new environment. A picture of the child taken during the visit can be displayed in the child's locker, on the bulletin board, or in a book about the children.

Home visits are a common practice for many programs that operate on a school-year calendar, including more and more schools serving older children. In one study, kindergarten through second-grade teachers who participated in home visits credited those visits with improving their relationships with children and families and with enhancing their understanding of the child and the influence of the home environment (Meyer, & Mann, 2006). In spite of these benefits, some administrators hesitate to require their staff members to make home visits, citing the risks associated with going into unsafe neighborhoods and the added burden on the time and energy of overworked teachers (Mathews, 2011).

Home visits may be especially challenging for full-day, year-round programs with budgets typically based on what parents can pay. Those centers seldom have the extra staff members to supervise the children while directors or lead teachers make

home visits during regular hours of operation. The alternative of asking teachers
to make such visits on their own time,
after long days at school, is both unfair
and unwise because it risks overtaxing
teachers' energy and creating burnout.
One option is to hire a person whose specific role is to visit the home of each new
child to get acquainted with the child, the
family, and the neighborhood. This same
staff member should visit the child's
classroom at the center a few times, providing a familiar face to help bridge home
and center.

A manager's efforts to make home
visits possible pay off in enhanced family
engagement over the long term. They are a
worthwhile investment of time and energy.

Communication with families can occur informally during drop-off and pickup times.

Families Visit the Center

Just as your home visits help to forge relationships with families, welcoming them in
the center reciprocates their hospitality and helps to nourish and maintain those
relationships. Informal visits during which the families can observe the program in
action should be encouraged—with no prior notice required—as long as everyone
understands that the teacher's first priority is with the children. If questions or concerns arise that require the teacher's input, it may be necessary to ask family members to schedule an appointment at a more convenient time to address those concerns
and questions. Another alternative is to have a teacher call the parents during nap
time or later that evening.

In addition to impromptu visits, centers may also plan specific times for family members to come to school—perhaps for a special lunch or to help with a project such as putting in a garden. Centers often host potluck meals—parents bring a
dish to share and have an opportunity to meet other parents and their children.
The children can proudly show off their school to their parents and siblings during
these times.

SAFETY CONCERNS   One caveat in regard to family visits concerns the center's responsibility for the safety of all children. As program manager, you must be aware at all times
and have control over who comes and goes from the center. In a larger facility, that can
mean having a lock system that allows entry only to individuals who have the code.
Even without such a system, you and your staff should feel comfortable asking any
visitors you don't know on sight to identify themselves and state their business. Family
members will be reassured by your vigilance.

Some children are in child-care facilities because they have been abused in their
families. Spending time in the program can be a valuable way for those family members
to learn more appropriate ways of dealing with children. Centers will have to exert
extra precautions to balance that benefit with the need to keep all children safe. At the
most basic level, child-care centers have to ensure that no person with a history of abuse
or neglect is ever left alone with children.

It is not uncommon for a divorced or separated parent to obtain court orders prohibiting the noncustodial parent from contact with the child. As program manager,

you need evidence of the court order in order to comply with the prohibition. Without the court order, you normally have no legal right to restrict a parent's contact with his or her child.

Conferences

In addition to planning group events for family members, you should arrange frequent opportunities for individual encounters between the teachers and the families. Many people think of parent conferences as those hurried, somewhat formal events that are scheduled at the end of each semester, when teachers go over children's grades and point out areas needing improvement. Too often, conferences that occur at other times are precipitated by some misbehavior or serious difficulty the child is having. But how can conferences be used more positively? It helps to think of conferences in a broader context and realize that every contact that you or staff members have with a family can be a mini-conference, an opportunity to exchange information that helps you both do a better job of nurturing and educating the child.

Of course, such exchanges cannot occur unless family members and staff members speak the same language, literally as well as figuratively. If you are unable to hire staff members who share a language with the families you serve, perhaps you can find volunteers from the community to serve as interpreters. These same volunteers might be willing to perform the same service with any written materials you send home. Teachers and caregivers also must refrain from using jargon when they communicate with family members.

As manager, you set an example for your staff members by making it a point to know each child's family members well enough to greet them by name and make pertinent comments or inquiries: "How do you like your new job?" or "Is Melinda's grandmother feeling better?" This type of exchange makes the family feel welcome and provides you with valuable information—it may explain why Melinda has seemed so fretful lately.

By ensuring that enough staff members are scheduled to cover the tasks involved and informing staff members that the relationships with the families are part of their job and not just idle chatter, you can ensure that the primary caregivers have a moment or two to share information informally at drop-off and pickup times. Encourage staff members to call the families or send notes home to share bits of the child's daily life at the center. And, of course, you can provide paid time for staff members to plan and conduct regular, more formal conferences at times when parents are available.

Comfortable, adult-size seating, a quiet corner, and perhaps some coffee or fruit juice set the stage for a relaxed, friendly conversation. Some teachers find it helpful to send a note to the families that explains what they hope to discuss in the conference and asks the families to write down any particular questions they might have. When both parties have given thought to the conference beforehand, precious time is not wasted. See Seplocha (2004) for an example of a chart that could be sent home to families to set the stage for a productive conference.

Many teachers and parents find it useful to have actual examples that illustrate the child's growth. For infants, this might be an album or diary that includes photographs taken at the center and written anecdotes about specific incidents. For slightly older children, these materials can be augmented by drawings and writing samples, photographs of block constructions or dramatic play episodes, or lists of favorite books. These concrete examples are more meaningful to parents than abstract developmental checklists, which can be unconvincing if teachers fail to notice a child doing something that her family knows she does quite well at home. This portfolio method of assessing and recording the children's development is described in the following chapter.

As the chapter-opening vignette described, you could also make the conference a family affair, including one or both parents, and perhaps a grandparent and sibling or two. The child's portfolio can provide a focus for the get-together, often with the child narrating particular sections. Usually, the child moves away from the table after a short time, either to play or to give a guided tour of the classroom to a family member, so the teacher has an opportunity for a more detailed conversation with the parent. If either the teacher or parent has a serious concern to discuss, she or he can arrange a more private time to get together.

> **? DECISIONS, DECISIONS . . .**
>
> Imagine you are the manager of a child development program where one of the toddler teachers has come to share with you her concern that a child in her classroom seems far behind the others in language development. What further information would you want from the teacher? What suggestion(s) would you make for a course of action? Discuss your ideas with your classmates.

Parent Meetings

The manager should establish a policy for parent meetings, give the teachers guidance and support as they plan for the meetings, and assign support staff to provide logistical services—arrange the seating, prepare snacks and beverages, and clean up afterward. A manager wisely stays in the background, encouraging the teachers and caregivers to strengthen their ties with parents. Providing child care during parent conferences and meetings makes it possible for more families to participate.

Parent meetings have a number of functions in the child development center. Because they involve a substantial commitment of time on the part of families and staff members, it is important to use them for purposes that cannot be achieved more efficiently in other ways. Routine announcements about policies and practices can be put in writing or on a center's website, reserving precious meeting time for families to get to know the teachers as well as one another. An outgrowth of this objective is that many parents begin to support one another—for example, babysitting, carpooling, or teaching a skill—thereby forging social networks that build family strengths and foster resiliency.

Some meetings are specifically designed to give parents information about parenting and child development. Others might include classes on English as a second language, nutrition and cooperative food buying, driver's education, and cultural renewal or the history of the parents' culture. Meetings may serve to update parents about recent center activities, show the children's art exhibits, or provide an enjoyable opportunity to share and pass on family traditions, perhaps singing along to favorite songs from their childhoods. If families are involved in planning for educational meetings, the topics are far more likely to fit their needs.

Beyond helping to select topics for the meetings, family members should be encouraged to take an active part in the meetings by asking questions, offering opinions and ideas, raising concerns. Ideally, family members will take part in leadership and decision-making roles. This aspect of family involvement is built into Head Start governing policies and in parent cooperative programs in which family members actually operate the school. Some centers may have parent representatives on their policy board, while others establish ad hoc committees to provide a formal avenue for expressing parental concerns, planning programs, and advising the manager or policy board. Participating in a parent group has opened new career vistas for many parents, especially as parents began to see the breadth and depth of the early childhood education field. Well-organized parent groups have helped more than one program threatened with reduced or discontinued funding. Head Start actually survived during one presidential administration thanks to the countrywide outcry by parents who rallied to its support. Parent groups are organized for various reasons, and political strength is one of them.

Newsletters, Email, and Web Pages

A newsletter is a useful communication device that can be produced weekly, biweekly, or monthly. In a page or two, you can give short accounts of class activities and can update parents on future plans and events. A page of the children's favorite songs and poems helps get parents involved reading and singing with their children. Hints can be given for holiday activities or places that families can take their children to visit, such as a dairy or cider mill. Of course, secretarial help and some expenses are necessary for this activity and must be arranged by the manager. Desktop publishing programs make it easier to produce eye-catching, professional-looking newsletters.

Given the growing number of families with computers and internet access, some centers are moving from paper-based communication to electronic forms. If you know that every family has access to email, you can distribute your newsletter via email. Many teachers send a daily or weekly email to families, sometimes including photographs, to let them know what went on in their classrooms. Often, the children themselves can be involved in producing these messages, selecting photos and dictating content so that communicating with families becomes part of the literacy curriculum, a help for busy teachers rather than just another task competing for their time. Other centers post such information on their web pages and protect the confidentiality of children and families by establishing password access for those enrolled in the program. (Web pages as a tool for marketing and public relations are addressed in the following chapter.)

No matter how creative and well-planned your newsletter or webpage, your efforts will be wasted if families cannot read them. This means providing translated versions of all communications for families who may not read English and paper copies for those without internet access. The initial intake interview is the time to ask families for their preferences and needs regarding language and mode of delivery.

Documentation and Display

Most families are eager to learn about what their children are doing while in your care all day. Many child development programs in the United States have a tradition of using photographs and displays of children's work to share information with families. The early childhood programs of Reggio Emilia, Italy, have inspired even more powerful and effective uses of such displays. Documentation panels (displays of photographs and descriptions of what goes on in the classrooms) draw family members into the life of the school and give them something to talk about with their children beyond the usual "What did you do in school today?" Documentation panels are aesthetically appealing and profoundly reflective products of an ongoing process in which teachers observe children, collect and analyze data, and add their own reflections about the meaning of what they observe (Rinaldi, 2001). Family members enjoy seeing the evidence of their children's thinking captured in the photographs and transcriptions of conversations. The children themselves often serve as guides, escorting families around the displays and explaining the details (see, e.g., Gennarelli, 2004).

Family Resource Corner

Many programs set aside a room or part of a room where materials of interest to parents are made available. A collection of books or videos about child development, early education, discipline, healthy nutrition, and other topics make useful information readily available. Organizations such as Zero to Three and the NAEYC offer a number of inexpensive books, pamphlets, and other media that child development programs can share with families. Many can be downloaded at no cost from the organizations' websites. For example, *Little Kids, Big Questions: A ZERO TO THREE Podcast Series* addresses issues of interest to parents of infants and toddlers, such as sleeping, crying, feeding, and development of self-control, and can be accessed at www.zerotothree.org/.

Family members also appreciate information not directly related to parenting and child development. You could provide information about families' rights to child-care tax credits or subsidy payments. You might post notices of important community events or put out a basket to collect grocery store coupons for products that one family might not use while another does. In short, this is a space that invites family members to spend a few extra moments at the center and begin to see the program not just as a drop-off point for their children, but also as support for the entire family.

Home Activities

Home activities have long been prescribed by child development centers, often as a way of influencing parents to spend more time and energy with their children or teaching them what child development professionals consider more effective or appropriate ways of interacting with children. Some families may be unaware of the need to read to their children, for example, or they may simply feel they are too busy. A workshop on effective ways to read to children, along with a book-lending program, might be helpful, as well as information about the benefits of the public library and the activities it sponsors. Note, however, that 14 percent of adults in the United States lack the ability to read basic prose, and the percentages are much higher for African American and Hispanic populations (Baer, Kutner, Sabatini, & White, 2009, p. 30). Centers serving these families must move beyond the idea of parent involvement as sending books or activities home and instead adopt a family literacy approach of helping children and their parents learn together. The National Center for Family Literacy provides several resources for both parents and teachers at its website, http://www.famlit.org.

Care must be taken to avoid creating undue stress for the children or parents by asking families to spend precious time on activities that are, at best, trivial and, at worst, so much like school that parents resort to the methods they remember being used with them as young children in school. Parents might feel pressured to demand that their children take part in activities that hold no interest for either the children or themselves so that they can send back completed "homework." It is more helpful to provide tactful suggestions of ways that families can enhance learning by including their young children in their daily lives (Dunst, Hamby, Trivette, Raab, & Bruder, 2000). You might suggest that parents of a 4-year-old ask the child to find the items that match cost-saving coupons when they go to the grocery store, for example, or that toddlers be given a collection of clean empty margarine or yogurt containers to stack while the older family members prepare a meal. You and your staff members could brainstorm such a list simply by thinking about every room in a house and imagining the kinds of learning experiences a child can have there. Water play in the bathtub, for example, is a sound way of learning about objects that float and sink. Dorothy Rich (2008) compiled an extensive array of activities that are both age-appropriate and related to important life skills.

Make sure that your efforts to involve families extend to all families:

- Encourage fathers to be involved by making sure to include them in home visits and enrollment procedures, including their names on enrollment forms, sending them all written announcements and newsletters even if they happen to live apart from the child, and inviting them to participate in activities at the center (Fagan, 2007; Green, 2003).

- Help parents stationed in the armed forces stay connected to their children's lives through emailed newsletters or documentation with photos and descriptions of center activities. Let them know what you are doing to provide a safe and caring environment for their children and to support the family members caring for them at home (Allen & Staley, 2007).

- Make lesbian or gay parents feel welcome by proclaiming your center's commitment to diversity in your handbook and providing spaces on your enrollment form for both parents and guardians to list their names rather than designating them as "mother" and "father." Assure them that your center environment and curriculum include images and examples of many types of families and that you will not allow their children to be singled out or treated differently by the others. Avoid treating them as though gender orientation is their only identity and let them decide the degree to which they want to step forward or blend in with other families (Clay, 2007).

All of the suggestions for building reciprocal relationships apply to every family, however families may be configured. Several articles and books on the reading list at the end of this chapter contain suggestions for other ways to share appropriate activities with families.

Resolving Conflicts

Everything you do to build partnerships with families contributes toward preventing conflicts, but it is not realistic to expect that they will never arise. Sometimes, families may want to discuss some concern or complaint with you, and you must make it clear that you are available for this discussion. Although you may find it challenging, it is essential that you convey an openness to listen to the parents' concerns without becoming defensive or prejudging the situation. Assure the parents that you will investigate and take action if necessary. Follow through as quickly as possible, and report back to the parents promptly. If the concern involves staff members, take care to express the same openness and willingness to listen to them as well. It may be helpful to schedule a meeting with the parent and staff member together where you can facilitate communication.

The same advice holds if the complaint originates from a staff member regarding something a family member has done. Consider the following scenario:

Just as the manager arrives at the center one morning, Janelle, one of the teachers, enters her office fuming. She announces that Mrs. Jones was 20 minutes late picking up Olivia the previous night and that she had been late several times already in recent weeks. She says that when this happens, she is late getting home, which upsets the evening routine for her entire family. The situation is becoming so stressful for her that it is affecting her ability to be patient and positive with the children in her room.

What can the manager do? The steps for conflict mediation presented in the chapter on human relations apply here as well:

Step 1: *Name the problem and decide to address it*   In the situation just described, let's assume that the problem is not occurring in more than one classroom, so rather than bringing it up at a parent meeting, the manager schedules an appointment to meet with Olivia's mother and the teacher together. She says, "Mrs. Jones, our sign-out sheet shows that you have been 15 or 20 minutes late picking up Olivia three times this month. This is a problem for Janelle (Olivia's teacher) and for our center because we want to take good care of Olivia and all our children, but we can't do that if we don't also take care of our staff. I'm hoping you will be able to help us think of a solution."

Step 2: *Listen to both sides*   Mrs. Jones might say that the 6:00 deadline for pickup is simply unrealistic. "I'm supposed to get out of work at 5:00, but often my boss has last-minute requests. As a new employee, I just don't feel I can refuse to put in a little extra time. And then I have the drive across town at the height of rush-hour traffic. I really try, but sometimes I just can't make it on time. I'm really worried that you'll ask me to withdraw Olivia from the center and then I'll have to give up my job because I have no child care." Janelle explains that she loves her job and cares a lot about Olivia. She says, "I feel sad for her when she is the last one waiting to be picked up. I don't mean to let my feelings show so obviously, but I'm exhausted at the end of the day and looking forward to getting home to my own family. I need to get supper on the table and then try to squeeze in all my housework along with helping kids with homework and studying for my own classes."

Step 3: *Recap*   Summarize each person's point of view: "Both of you are feeling stressed because of this issue. Mrs. Jones, you are caught between the demands of your job and our expectation that you pick up Olivia by 6:00. Janelle, you also feel stretched beyond your limits when your work hours spill over into time that you need for your family and yourself."

Step 4: *Brainstorm several possible alternatives*   As one party offers a suggestion, the other should be given a chance to react frankly and constructively. In our example, Mrs. Jones might suggest that the center move the deadline for pickup time from 6:00 to 6:30. Janelle could counter that this would mean she gets home late every night instead of just occasionally. Janelle might propose that Mrs. Jones arrange with a parent of another child at the center to pick up Olivia on nights when Mrs. Jones must work late. An objection to this idea could be that Mrs. Jones doesn't feel she knows any of the other parents well enough to ask (or trust) them to do this. If neither can develop potential solutions, the manager might make some tentative suggestions. The same idea might be presented more than once before it is agreed on. No one should leave the conversation feeling coerced into an unacceptable solution.

Step 5: *Agree on a workable solution and plan methods to carry it out*   In this situation, the three participants might arrive at a plan that involves paying overtime to one center staff member who voluntarily agrees to work until 6:30. (This can be one person who works this schedule regularly, or the teachers could agree to rotate the duty among themselves, with one person staying late on Monday, one on Tuesday, and so forth.) The designated staff member will care for the child whose parent is late in that child's classroom, or in the event that more than one parent is late, she will bring the children together in a designated classroom. The stipulation is that parents who are late must call to let the center know and they must pay an agreed-on late fee to cover the overtime pay for the staff member. Under this arrangement, all the other teachers are free to leave at their scheduled times.

Step 6: *Acknowledge the work that each individual contributed to the problem-solving process* The manager thanks both Mrs. Jones and Janelle for listening to each other and for persevering to map out a solution.

Step 7: *Follow up* In this example, the manager puts the plan into place after checking with teachers and finding that the idea of working an extra half-hour one regularly scheduled night per week for overtime pay was acceptable even to Janelle. The manager also explains the new policy to families, in writing and at a parent meeting. At the next month's staff meeting, the manager learns that the plan is working well. Teachers are pleased to know that their workday will end as scheduled. The manager also includes a short survey in the monthly newsletter to solicit families' perceptions of the new system.

Of course, not every conflict will end so peacefully. Most managers of any business have experienced difficult encounters with customers, and child development programs are no exception. Failure to pay fees, behaving in a disrespectful manner toward staff members, constantly criticizing the program, and spreading malicious gossip among other parents are just a few examples of things parents can do to make a manager's life difficult. Confronting the individual calmly and courteously may enable you to discover the root of the problem and work toward a solution. If that doesn't work, it may be time to explain that your program may not be the best fit for the family's needs and to suggest some other alternatives.

Sometimes managers have to do things that parents might perceive as making their life difficult. Certainly, reporting suspected abuse or neglect would be high on that list. Consider, also, the following scenarios:

1. A teacher reports that 2-year-old Jeremy has just not been himself all day. He seems listless and pale, and he did not eat lunch or snack. You agree that they should call his mother at work. She comes to pick him up, but she protests that the child is not sick. Later she calls you to report that the pediatrician found nothing wrong. She is very upset because she missed work and feels that the staff at the center believes she is not a good mother.

2. A woman you have never seen arrives at the center. She tells you that she is a neighbor who has been asked to pick up 3-year-old Brittany because her mother is out of town and her father has had to work late. When you check Brittany's file, you find that the parents have given no authorization for anyone other than themselves to pick up their child.

In each of these situations, your job as manager will be easier if you have made your program's policies very clear in advance. Families need to know in advance that you will report suspected abuse or neglect. They need to know your policies on exclusion of sick children, and what you expect of them should their child become ill while in your care. They need to know that you will not release a child to anyone without their written authorization. If you put these policies in writing and explain them during the orientation, you can remind families that they heard about and agreed to them when an occasion to invoke them arises. During orientation, you can acknowledge frankly that they might be inconvenienced or upset by the policies at some point, and you can emphasize that your primary goal is to protect their child.

Technology Toolkit

To ease a new child's transition into your program and begin to build a reciprocal relationship with families:

- Send a new preschooler a digital photo of her new classmates, including a letter of welcome dictated by them.

- Ask for an audio recording of a child's family members to keep at the center and play during nap or other times the child might be missing them. Lend the recording device if needed and suggest that they sing favorite songs or read a familiar story (in the home language, if applicable).

- Capture an image or brief video clip of the child interacting with a teacher and/or other children on the first day. Send it via cell phone or email, or show it to the family members when they come to pick up the child.

To sustain ongoing relationships with families:

- Create a blog (a web log) to provide information updates or share highlights of daily life at the center. Include photos or video clips as well as narrative. Service is available free at http://www.blogger.com.

- Create a password-protected account, accessible by invitation only, to share photos of children's projects at a site such as http://www.flickr.com.

- Use Twitter (http://www.twitter.com) as a way to send brief reminders or Tweets, such as "Remember our fall get-together this Friday at 7:00."

Conclusion

Child development centers, as organizations designed to provide a service to families, comprise part of the social–cultural environment of the human ecological system. To provide high-quality programs, center managers must engage families of the children they serve as partners in an ongoing, reciprocal relationship. They must form linkages with the people and institutions in the larger community who serve as resources for those families. To accomplish these aims, administrators and staff members must have an understanding of family functions and diverse parenting styles. They must cultivate cultural responsiveness and family-friendly practices. Professional standards for high-quality child development centers, including NAEYC accreditation criteria, place a priority on the parents' involvement. Programs build relationships with families through initial contacts, family visits to the center, home visits, enrollment procedures, conferences, and parent meetings. Policies that are clearly stated in advance, frank discussion of difficulties before they fester, and the use of conflict mediation strategies can resolve disagreements when they occur. It is important for centers to recognize the potential that families offer as human resources for the program and to help link families with community resources.

Questions for Review

1. Compare licensing regulations in your state with NAEYC guidelines for partnering with families. Do the regulations support the concept of family engagement as defined in this chapter?

2. List the six characteristics of families identified by Christian (2007) and give contrasting examples of families at either end of each continuum. How might a child development program where you have

observed or worked relate to each of the families in your examples?

3. Evaluate whether (or how well) a child development program where you have worked or observed employs the family-friendly practices described in this chapter. What examples of cultural responsiveness can you cite?

4. Think again about a program where you have worked or observed. List the strategies it uses for building and maintaining partnerships with families. How many of the strategies described in this chapter are in place? How effectively does the center implement each strategy? What improvements might you suggest?

Professional Portfolio

1. Accompany a child and family member on a trip to the grocery store, to the library, or on some other household errand. With permission, use a digital camera to record the sequence of events. Add a narrative that describes what happened and explains its significance to the child's learning. Create a booklet or display panel that shows other families how learning is embedded in everyday activities. (If you choose the display panel option, you can include the components separately in your portfolio.)

2. Create a plan to promote meaningful family involvement in a child development program. Describe at least three specific strategies, and explain why you think they would be effective.

3. Use a desktop publishing program to develop a brochure for family members on some aspect of child development or early education, such as art for preschool children, biting, or toilet learning. Study several professional articles on your topic and summarize what you have learned; add suggestions that families can use at home. Have your classmates review the brochure and offer suggestions. Revise and polish it so that it is both appealing to readers and easy to understand.

Resources for Further Study

PRINT

Beginnings Workshop: Today's families. (2013). *Exchange, 209*(January/February), 48–68.

Fagan, J., & Palm, G. (2004) *Fathers and early childhood programs.* Albany, NY: Delmar.

Gonzalez-Mena, J. (2008). *Diversity in early care and education*: Honoring differences (5th ed.). New York: McGraw-Hill.

Matthews, H. (2008, September). *Support a diverse and culturally competent workforce.* Available online at http://www.clasp.org/admin/site/babies/make_the_case/files/cp_rationale5.pdf

Mitchell, S., Foulger, T. S., & Wetzel, K. (2009, September). Ten tips for involving families through internet-based communication. *Young Children, 64*(5), 46–49.

National Center on Parent, Family and Community Engagement. (2011). Head Start and Early Head Start relationship-based competencies for staff and supervisors who work with families. Available on line at http://eclkc.ohs.acf.hhs.gov/hslc/tta-system/family/Family%20and%20Community%20Partnerships/Family%20Services/Professional%20Development/ohs-rbc.pdf

Stephens, K. (2004, July/August). Sometimes the customer *isn't* always right: Problem solving with parents. *Exchange, 158*, 68–74.

Websites

ENGAGING PARENTS IN SCHOOL

http://engagingparentsinschool.edublogs.org/

A compendium of resources for enhancing parent engagement in schools, e.g., a collection of multilingual preschool learning guides; a few potentially useful tech tools for parent-teacher communication; and a great video on teachers making home visits.

NATIONAL ASSOCIATION FOR THE EDUCATION OF YOUNG CHILDREN

www.naeyc.org/

Link to family section on home page for information geared to families' interests: choosing a preschool, questions about development, ways to promote learning at home, a parent blog and a collection of children's songs. Enter "engaging diverse families project" in the search box on the home page for links to information about the project and tools and resources such as a program self-assessment, family checklist, and ideas for conducting a family survey.

NATIONAL CENTER ON PARENT, FAMILY, AND COMMUNITY ENGAGEMENT

www.hfrp.org/family-involvement/projects/office-of-head-start-national-center-on-parent-family-and-community-engagement

The Office of Head Start National Center on Parent, Family, and Community Engagement identifies and disseminates evidence-based best practices to Head Start programs across the country.

SPECIALQUEST

www.specialquest.org/

SpecialQuest Birth–Five: Head Start/Hilton Training Program is a special project of the Napa County Office of Education and is funded by the U.S. Department of Health and Human Services, Administration for Children and Families, Office of Head Start. Its multimedia training library includes print and video resources that can be downloaded at the website or ordered in CD/DVD edition at no charge. The focus is children with disabilities, but the concepts and principles are applicable to all families.

ZERO TO THREE

www.zerotothree.org

The Zero to Three website is available in English and Spanish. The parent resource section offers tools to help parents "be aware of what they bring to parenting—the beliefs, values and goals they have for their children, and their own personal style and approach to child-rearing; tune in to who their individual child is—his temperament, strengths, needs, and development; and apply this knowledge to their everyday parenting decisions."

CHAPTER

Marketing and Public Relations

LEARNING OUTCOMES

After studying this chapter you should be able to

- Explain the difference between marketing and public relations.
- Describe examples of effective marketing strategies.
- Describe examples of effective public relations strategies.

With the support and encouragement of the center's policy board, Jeralyn, Tanya, and the entire staff of Rainbow Center worked hard to meet the requirements for a 5-star license. When their new license came in the mail, they posted it prominently for the families to see and put an announcement in their newsletter. They also made sure that their website, brochure, advertisements, and listings with referral agencies identified them as a 5-star center. Having achieved this recognition at the state level, Jeralyn and Tanya decided to reach for a nationally recognized benchmark of quality—accreditation from the National Association for the Education of Young Children (NAEYC). They knew that the process of working toward accreditation would involve surveying families, thereby raising their awareness of what constitutes high quality in early care and education. And they knew that being able to say that Rainbow Center was nationally accredited not only would be a selling point with current and future customers, it would help create a broader public awareness of the importance of high-quality early childhood programs. In this way, they could generate positive effects for children, families, and child-care professionals far beyond those directly involved in Rainbow Center.

No matter how wonderful your program is, it cannot survive without children to serve, and families are unlikely to bring their children to you unless they are aware of two things: that your program exists and that your program offers something that meets their needs. Getting that information out to families is what marketing is all about. Although this may seem obvious if you are the manager of a for-profit program that depends on parent fees for its existence, it is no less true for nonprofit and publicly funded programs that must market their programs to attract and keep potential funders. A child development program is a service, but it is also a business. No business can survive without a steady supply of customers.

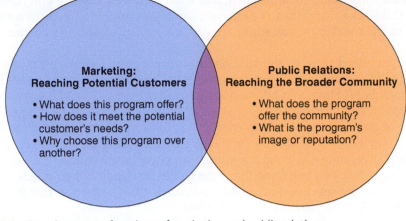

**Marketing:
Reaching Potential Customers**

• What does this program offer?
• How does it meet the potential
  customer's needs?
• Why choose this program over
  another?

**Public Relations:
Reaching the Broader Community**

• What does the program
  offer the community?
• What is the program's
  image or reputation?

FIGURE 14.1 Complementary functions of marketing and public relations.

Marketing, then, is the process by which you make your presence known and inform potential customers about the benefits of your services. Once potential customers inquire about the program, you must apply all of the techniques described in the previous chapter to create and sustain a relationship with the families. Some marketing experts assert that these activities are a continuation of your marketing process—once you attract a customer, you work to satisfy and retain that customer and, ultimately, to enhance the quality of your relationship (Bitner, 2000, p. 38). Attracting new customers is only one purpose of marketing; other purposes might be to convince a corporation to purchase your services for its employees or to persuade a charitable agency to fund a scholarship program so that homeless children can attend your center.

Public relations is a broader concept than marketing, but it is related. Although the target audience for marketing is potential customers, public relations efforts attempt to reach the wider community to build a positive image of the program in the public mind (Clarke, 2000, p. 143). Businesses cultivate good public relations the way farmers cultivate the soil—they create conditions for the seeds of marketing to take root and flourish. The two functions are complementary and can overlap in many ways. Potential customers may be more receptive to your marketing efforts because they have been made aware of your program through news articles about accredited centers in your community or because they have heard you speak at a Rotary or Kiwanis Club meeting. Satisfied customers become public relations spokespersons on your behalf when they carry their positive image of your program with them as they go about their daily business. Figure 14.1 illustrates this complementary relationship between the two concepts. Marketing and public relations both entail all of the management processes you have studied: planning, organizing, staffing, leading, and monitoring for effectiveness.

MARKETING: ATTRACTING AND RETAINING CUSTOMERS

As noted, marketing involves specific activities designed to bring your program's unique service to the attention of those people most likely to want that service. Before you can design marketing activities, you must know—and be able to communicate clearly and concisely—exactly what makes your service unique. This means knowing something about your competition—that is, the programs that offer similar services. In addition, you must know something about your potential customers—who they are, where they are likely to be reached, and what they value. Once you have a clear picture of this background information, you can begin to devise steps to connect the two sides of the marketing equation: the service you offer and the customers who want it.

Begin your marketing by thinking about your program's strongest assets. Is your program NAEYC accredited? Can you highlight the education and experience levels of your staff members? Have you adopted an innovative curriculum? Have you found a way to keep the children with a specific teacher for all or most of their years at your program? Consider asking currently enrolled families for their perspectives on these questions. A key element of effective marketing is addressing the potential customer's point of view. Remember, if people are going to enroll their children in your center, they must know that you exist and that your facility can match their needs regarding location, price, hours, services, and quality indicators. To be effective, that information must be stated briefly, accurately, and positively.

Next, take a look at the other programs and services for families and children in your area. Bush (2001, p. 81) distinguishes between direct and indirect competitors: Direct competitors are all of the other centers serving the same population; indirect competitors include facilities such as family child-care homes, public school preschool and after-school programs, and individual babysitters. What makes your program stand out from all of these alternatives? Why should a parent seeking child care choose you?

The answers to these questions, when boiled down to a few key phrases, comprise the kernel of the public image you want to develop for your program—something you emphasize in all of your advertising and promotional materials. Using a consistent design to convey this information builds program recognition and maximizes marketing effectiveness. If you have the funds, invest in professional help to design your publicity materials. Even if your budget does not allow this, you can tap other resources. A local advertising agency might be looking for a worthy cause to support as part of its own public relations effort. A student—or an entire class—in a college business or communications program might adopt your program for an assignment and design an entire public relations campaign.

Communicating Your Message

Marketing expert Harry Beckwith recommends that all of your promotional materials convey, immediately and clearly, your "key claim" and your "key proof" (Beckwith, 2000, p. 207). In other words, a prospective client or customer should be able to determine at once what your program does and what evidence you have to support that assertion:

> **Key claim**: Rainbow Child Development Center provides peace of mind for the working parents of children ages 6 weeks to 6 years.

> **Key proof**: Our program, accredited by the National Association for the Education of Young Children (NAEYC), features home-cooked, nutritious meals; small group sizes; and individualized care and education from experienced teachers whose education exceeds the norm for child-care programs in this community.

You should consider all of the avenues available as you plan this phase of your marketing strategy: the internet, printed material, mass media, and person-to-person oral communication. You might ask your staff members to brainstorm ideas for a logo and the content to be covered by publicity efforts. Be sure to have your staff and policy board help with the final editing of anything you make public.

? DECISIONS, DECISIONS . . .

Divide into groups of three or four students. Each group should be assigned a different type of child development program, for example, infant–toddler, part-day preschool, after-school program, summer day camp for elementary school children, program for hospitalized children. As a group, write a key claim and key proof for your particular service. Share your group's results with the other groups in your class.

WEBSITES According to the U.S. Census Bureau (File, 2013), the percentage of U.S. households with computers has increased from 61.8 in 2003 to 75.6 in 2011, and it is safe to assume that this upward trend is continuing. Access to the internet more than tripled in the same period, going from just 18 percent of households in 1997 to 71.7 percent in 2011. When shopping for goods or services, people may still follow the old Yellow Pages slogan, "Let your fingers do the walking," but they are likely to be holding a computer mouse in those fingers and to be using an internet search engine instead of a paper telephone directory. Married couples and families with children—groups very likely to be in need of child-care services—are also more likely to use computers and the internet. If your program does not have a presence on the internet, you are missing an important opportunity.

You probably already have such a presence at the most basic level if your program is included in the online directories of licensing and resource and referral agencies. Although these listings let prospective clients know you exist, they will probably give only minimum information about your program, such as licensing status, ages of the children served, and contact information. To really take advantage of the internet's potential, you need to create a website, a virtual "place" with an address, or uniform resource locator (URL), that people can visit to learn more about your program.

Typically, websites have a home page, with links to additional pages, created in HyperText Markup Language (HTML). Each page consists of text, graphics, and often links to other websites. The cost of developing a website varies. If you have the skills or are willing and have the time to learn, you can create your own pages. If you have the funds, you can hire a professional to do the job. If, like most child-care managers, you are strapped for both time and funds, you may be able to tap some volunteer resource: a parent, board member, or local college student majoring in computer technology. In addition to the costs associated with developing the site, you will have to pay for registering your domain name (or URL) and for making your site available through an internet service provider (ISP). Tap your network with community businesses or your local chamber of commerce to get recommendations for reputable providers that are reliable and reasonably priced. When you have created a website, make it visible: Ask to have a link put on the website of your local chamber of commerce, resource and referral agency, and other sites that parents might visit. The more sites or people linked to your website, the more likely it is to show up on a search engine. Put the address (URL) on your brochure, newsletter, and any printed material you produce.

A good way to decide what you want your website to look like is to visit those of other child development programs or comparable services. You will probably get lots of good ideas as well as learn what you definitely want to avoid. Because your website is likely to be a family's all-important first impression of your program, create one that looks professional and is easy to navigate. Too much print to fit easily on one screen, hard-to-read typefaces, and inconsistent format from one page to the next get in the way of your message. "Cute" clip art or other graphics, clashing colors, misspelled words, or inaccurate information can cast doubt on your program's quality. The goal is to attract visitors to your website, to make it easy for them to find what they want when they get there, and to encourage them to take some action (e.g., contact you, schedule a visit) before leaving the site. Once you have done all the work of creating a website, keep the content fresh with regular updates so that people have a reason to visit it frequently.

Many of the suggestions given below for writing brochure content apply to composing text for your website. Include the following:

- Your mission statement and program philosophy
- Your location and travel directions (with a map)
- Photographs or a video tour of your facility
- A description of your curriculum
- Your schedule of operation and fees
- Information about enrollment policies, available openings, and waiting lists
- A page for frequently asked questions (FAQs), organized by subject or intended audience (e.g., prospective and currently enrolled families)
- Photographs, brief biographies, and résumés of staff members
- Galleries of images and descriptions or videos of projects and children's art (with written permission of families obtained when they enroll their children)
- Link to contact you via email
- Links to your handbook and registration forms
- A link to current and past issues of your newsletter, with an invitation to subscribe to future editions
- A calendar of coming events
- Links to information or resources that families might find helpful
- Testimonials from satisfied customers

As the number of people using mobile devices (smart phones, tablets) increases, wise managers make sure their websites are mobile-friendly. Loading speed and ease of navigation with fingers (instead of a cursor) are important. Tailor content to the most likely reasons people will visit the site, with buttons for locating your center, connecting with you by telephone, or using promotional incentives such as coupons they can click on to receive a discount on the initial enrollment fee.

Figure 14.2 is an example of a website for a small program serving 10 children, ages 1 through 3. For an example of a website for a large program with a university-affiliated teacher education component serving 200 infants, toddlers, and preschool children, see www.boulderjourneyschool.com. The navigation bars or menus at the top of the page help visitors locate information they want. While the center's website must be accessible to the public in order to serve as a marketing tool, sections linked to the main page should be reserved for access by families or staff members with passwords. Websites are usually a work in progress. Updating them regularly so that they fulfill their purpose requires a substantial investment of time and energy, albeit one that most successful businesses find very worthwhile.

SOCIAL MEDIA   Social media are internet services that let you engage in two-way communication with an online community. In addition to their obvious social uses, social media offer opportunities for businesses to increase public awareness of their existence

FIGURE 14.2 Example of a website for a small program serving 1-, 2-, and 3-year-olds.

Source: Estes Children's Cottage, Chapel Hill, North Carolina. http://www.esteschildrenscottage.com/Site/Our_Program.html. Used with permission.

and services, find out what customers think of them, strengthen ties with current customers, and attract new customers. Social media offer fast, easy, and free or low-cost ways to reach a broad audience, target those you particularly want to reach, and personalize interactions with individual customers. Examples include Facebook, Twitter, LinkedIn, blogs, YouTube, Google+, Pinterest, photo-sharing sites (e.g., Instagram), forums, geo-location (e.g., Foursquare), podcasting, daily deals (e.g., Groupon), Q&A sites (e.g., Quora), location-based marketing sites, and customer review sites.

A 2012 survey of 3,000 marketing professionals found that nearly all (97 percent) used one or more forms of social media to market their business. A slightly smaller percentage (86 percent) believed that social media use was important for their business, but less than one in four said that they could measure the effect of their efforts. The perceived major benefits of using social media included increased exposure for the business, gaining marketplace intelligence, and developing a loyal fan base; greater returns were seen in these areas for those who spent more time per week and had been using social media longer. Facebook was the top choice for 49 percent, followed by LinkedIn (16 percent), blogging (14 percent), and Twitter (12 percent). YouTube was cited most frequently as the platform where marketers planned to increase their efforts in the coming years. More women marketers than men said that they were likely to increase use of Pinterest, and marketers aged 20 to 29 years were more likely to use photo-sharing sites than those over the age of 40 (Stelzner, 2013).

Using social media to market your child-care program requires a commitment of time on your part. The amount of time that the marketers in the survey cited in the previous paragraph spent on social media ranged from fewer than 5 hours per week to more than 20. Younger marketers, as well as those who had more years of experience using social media, tended to spend more time on it.

When families "like" your program on Facebook or follow it on Twitter, they are contributing to a form of advertising that is second only to word of mouth as a trusted source of information (Nielsen, 2012). A downside, of course, is that complaints from a dissatisfied customer can be broadcast to that wide audience just as quickly and may be viewed as trustworthy too. But even in that case, you can nip the problem in the bud if you respond quickly and forthrightly in your social media outlets.

Privacy is a concern for all social media users, and it is a particular concern for child-care programs. Learn how to set controls to distinguish between information that you want to make public and information that you want shared with only a specific group of people on sites like Facebook, Twitter, and YouTube. Make sure that you have families' written permission to post photos or videos of their children. When families enroll their children, ask them which social media they use or prefer.

Using a social media dashboard or management system (e.g., www.hootsuite. com or www.tweetdeck.com) helps you keep track of all your networks, track mentions of your center, and analyze traffic patterns on your sites. For free, step-by-step tutorials on how to build a presence on the platform of your choice, visit www. socialquickstarter.com.

? DECISIONS, DECISIONS . . .

Using an Ethical Framework

One of your board members introduces you to a producer of computer-based learning games for children. The producer wants to add links to all local child-care centers to the company's website as a service to the community. Allowing the link will generate more traffic for your website, but you question the developmental appropriateness of the games. You also worry that people visiting your site will think that you endorse the games and perhaps gain the impression that screen time in general is an acceptable activity for children. Checking with other centers in your community, you learn that most have accepted the offer. If you decline, it could place your center at a disadvantage by reducing its visibility in the public eye. What should you do? Using the NAEYC code, try to determine what core values are involved. What ideals and principles regarding responsibilities to children, families, and employees apply? What course of action seems most right?

BROCHURES   Although computer and internet use is growing nationwide, a completely paperless marketing strategy would be unwise. Many people simply prefer to get their information in paper-and-print format. And there is still a substantial population with limited access to the internet—a situation referred to as the digital divide. Percentages of computer and internet users among Black and Hispanic families, those with lower incomes and less education, and those living either in rural or inner-city areas are far lower than the percentage of White, upper-income, college-educated, metropolitan residents (File, 2013). Thus you will need to get your message across on paper as well as electronically.

Printed brochures can convey much of the information you include in your website. Like web pages, they must be carefully planned with up-to-date and accurate information. The writing must be clear and interesting to convey the message that your program is a stimulating place for children. Computer software packages often include templates for two- or three-column brochures that can be printed on both sides of standard letter- or legal-size paper. Pictures from the center add visual appeal and augment the information in the text. Remember to give specific, concrete information and avoid using professional jargon.

The brochure should state the center's name, address, telephone number, and web address, along with a brief description of the age groups served, prices of the service, hours of operation, philosophy, typical activities, and additional services such as meals or transportation. Driving directions or nearby bus routes for parents without private means of transportation are helpful. Brochures can be given to a community Welcome Wagon or placed in the chamber of commerce, pediatricians' offices, businesses, churches, libraries, labor union offices, schools, and other places of public access.

Desktop publishing programs and digital photography make it easy and economical to produce an attractive, professional-looking brochure.

ADVERTISEMENTS In an era when people increasingly turn to internet search engines to find the products and services they need, your center's web page will probably serve as your most effective advertisement. To capture the attention of potential customers who may not have internet access, the most basic form of print advertisement is a listing in the local telephone company's Yellow Pages. Listing the center under several headings is helpful because families may be looking for day care, nursery school, preschool, child care, or some other term. You can supplement the telephone directory listing by advertising in your local newspaper on a regular basis. The least expensive ad consists of a few lines in the classified section. You can make both the classified ad and the telephone listing stand out by paying for extras (e.g., bold print) or by including a slogan or motto that captures your program's best qualities.

Here is an example of a center's advertisement that is brief and to the point:

The Edgewater Little People's Child Development Center, a nationally accredited program with a 5-star license, is enrolling 3- and 4-year-old children for the fall term. Call 555-1111 or visit our website at www.littlepeoplecdc.com.

This type of notice may appear in a newspaper classified advertisement, on a television or newspaper community calendar, or on a laundry room bulletin board. It informs parents of an available service and it tells them where to get more information. Using the terms *nationally accredited* and *5-star license* conveys the message that the facility has achieved recognition for quality.

A more expensive form of advertising is the print display ad. Display ads (like web pages) must strike a balance between formats that catch the reader's eye and those that appear cheap because they are overdone. A successful layout and headline should hold readers' attention for about 3 seconds, long enough to get them to spend another 20 seconds reading the rest of the ad (Schon, 1998). Put yourself in the reader's place when composing your ad, and try to address his or her interests. Your ad in the Yellow Pages remains in place for a year, but your newspaper ads last only as long as the particular edition of the paper in which they appear. Because families might be scanning the paper for child-care leads at any time, it is important to repeat your ads and to place them in the publications most likely to reach your target audience.

Electronic billboards, pop-up ads, and automated phone calls are more sophisticated ways of reaching your target audience in the twenty-first century. You have probably witnessed firsthand the attention-grabbing power of a brightly lighted electronic billboard while driving along a major thoroughfare in your community. While such billboards do make a strong visual impression, most of the vendors are located in Asia, which can increase the time and cost involved should you decide to use that medium. It is also important to make sure that the size and placement of the billboard meets local regulations and zoning laws. Pop-up ads are just what they sound like— little panels of images and print, sometimes animated, that pop up when you visit various websites on your computer. Many people find them more annoying than helpful. You can find instructions for making pop-up ads by searching on the internet, but the fact that you will get a far greater number of results telling you how to block such ads on your computer suggests that this might not be the most effective addition to your advertising strategy. Automated phone calls, like pop-up ads, might serve more to irritate rather than entice your prospective customers. And they may be a strategy that works for political candidates but seems counterproductive in connection with a service like child care. Such calls can be effective, however, for getting a message out quickly to all your current customers. For example, a sudden severe snowstorm might make it wise to close the program before the roads become hazardous, so you use the automated call system to notify all the families and ask them to come pick up their children. Phonevite.com is a free online tool for creating automated calls.

Advertising costs money and requires an investment of time by you or a member of your staff. Make sure you are using those resources efficiently by checking to see which forms of advertisement bring the greatest returns for your center. Ask families how they learned about your center when they call for information and when they enroll a child. Keeping a tally of their responses will help you decide whether it is worthwhile to continue paying for a particular type of advertisement. Word of mouth is the form of information most trusted by consumers, so your most important advertising investment is probably the time and energy you put into your program quality and family engagement efforts.

Identifying and Reaching Potential Customers

In addition to thinking about what you have to offer and how to package that information, you must think about the audience you are trying to reach—who they are, where to reach them most effectively, and how to enlarge that audience. The answer to the first question involves creating a customer profile: "a description of a typical customer . . . [including] age, income level, education, profession, geographic area, lifestyle, or interests" (Bush, 2001, p. 82). You compile this information by asking your current customers as well as people calling to inquire about your program. What are they looking for in a child-care program? Have they had prior experience with early care and education? How did they find out about your center? The answers to these questions provide a psychographic profile of your potential customer base to complement demographic characteristics such as age, income, and occupation (Wassom, 2006).

Schon and Neugebauer (1998, pp. 324–325) suggested that programs analyze their potential customer base by considering four angles: the characteristics of the parents

---

🔍 **LEADERSHIP LENS**

From a management perspective, your marketing and public relations efforts are intended to benefit your center: keeping enrollment high to generate revenue, cultivating a positive image and community goodwill. Viewing these functions through a leadership lens, you might begin to see how your efforts can also have an impact for the better in a larger context. Posting new content on your website, for example, is an effective way of generating increased traffic and creating "buzz" about your center, but the content you choose to post can also help ensure that the "buzz" contributes toward a greater good. Use the following examples as a starting point to inspire your own creative ideas:

- Families will delight in seeing images and stories of their children's experiences and accomplishments on your password-protected site. The thoughtful interpretation added by you or your teachers will help them see the learning that is happening and contribute to a richer understanding of what learning in early childhood is all about.

- Post announcements about staff member accomplishments. Letting the world know when one of your teachers has completed an associate's, bachelor's, or master's degree not only boosts your center's image, it also sends a message about the value of higher education for teacher preparation. You help raise public appreciation for the child-care workforce and ultimately support the argument for appropriate compensation.

- Posting the center's lunch menu each week generates traffic for your website and helps families keep abreast of their children's daily nutrition. Adding a recipe for a healthful dish that the children enjoy at the center might contribute toward more healthy eating habits for the entire family, or at least it can broaden their perception of what children like to eat.

---

who want or need the service, the characteristics of the children you are prepared to serve, the type of program you offer, and the way your program operates. A program designed to provide a low-cost, partial-day educational experience for 3- and 4-year-old children with stay-at-home mothers has a different customer profile than one serving dual-career, upper-income families seeking a full-day as well as after-school care for children from infancy through the early school years.

The fit between a potential customer and a service provider can also involve personal characteristics or "natural affinity" (Beckwith, 2000, pp. 170–180). Suppose you are a free-spirited, highly creative, and artistic person with a flair for the dramatic, and your program reflects those qualities with its loose schedule and emphasis on messy activities. The button-down, success-oriented parents who want their child to "learn discipline" are not likely to be happy with you, nor are you likely to be happy with them. Being clear about who you are and communicating this at the outset will avoid many future difficulties. The concept of natural affinity leads to a corollary—that no one can satisfy everyone. Your unique characteristics determine your customer profile as much as the wants and needs of your potential clients.

Once you have identified your customer profile, the next step is to determine the best way to reach that particular group. As we will discuss a little later, you need to reach the entire community for public relations purposes. For marketing purposes, however, you must target your efforts more precisely. One way to do this is through generational marketing, an approach that takes into account crucial differences between today's generation X and the baby boomer generation that preceded them. Because they have grown up in an era characterized by political scandal, environmental disasters, and economic challenges, Generation X parents tend to be skeptical and take more time to comparison-shop before committing themselves. They are willing to pay more for a service if given convincing concrete evidence of quality. They are technologically savvy and expect to get information and pay bills electronically. To appeal to this group, your marketing message needs to be couched in clear, concise bullets, communicating what the prospective customer will get from your service (Wassom, 2004).

Most communities have a child-care resource and referral (CCR&R) agency that provides families with information about existing programs and guidelines for choosing among them. You can locate your community's CCR&R agency at the website of the National Association of Child Care Resource and Referral Agencies, at http://www.naccrra.org. These CCR&R agencies are likely to advertise themselves in the community in a number of ways, and you can take advantage of that groundwork by ensuring that your program is listed with them. The NAEYC, in addition to setting the criteria and administering the accreditation process, has also worked to inform the public about the components of high-quality children's programs and the significance of accreditation as a mark of excellence. If your center is accredited, the name of your center appears on the list of accredited programs in your community.

Making the Most of First Contacts

Marketing does not end with getting your name in front of potential customers. If they have been sufficiently intrigued by your advertisements, web page, brochures, and/or recommendations from satisfied customers, the families will take the next step and call about your program. Not every family who calls follows up by enrolling a child, but you can increase the chance of that happening. Ideally, you have a sufficient number of staff members to ensure that all callers are greeted in a friendly, professional manner by someone who can either answer their questions or connect them with the person who can.

If your program does not have secretarial support, you might want to use a telephone answering machine or voice-mail system to take incoming messages. You must weigh the relative advantages and disadvantages carefully. On the plus side, you and your staff gain control of your time and energy. Instead of being interrupted throughout the day, you can plan to return calls at particular times. On the negative side, callers who reach a machine when they want an immediate response are likely to be frustrated. You might lose potential customers. It may soften the irritation if the message suggests that callers may find quick answers to their questions at the center website and explains that staff members cannot come to the phone because they are busy with the children. Add that messages are checked regularly (perhaps every hour) and that calls are returned at a specific time. Of course, the system works only if you do check messages at regular intervals and return calls promptly. As you watch this video, notice how the director describes the highlights of her program (emphasis on nutrition, highly educated staff) while also being

A cheerful greeting on the telephone can go a long way toward turning a simple inquiry into an enrollment in your program.

very forthright about aspects that families might perceive as potential drawbacks (cost, center closing for professional development). How did directing the caller to the program's website build on this first contact?

Neugebauer (1998a) has provided numerous suggestions for handling phone calls. First, ensure that callers are greeted in a professional manner. "ABC Child Development Center. How may I help you?" said in a pleasant, professional tone lets the caller know who you are and that you welcome the call. A harsh or whining tone, interruptions in conversation, or nervous speech habits (e.g., "um," "you know") all convey the opposite impression. Speaking softly and smiling as you speak are recommended techniques to improve the effectiveness of your telephone communication.

The next few minutes provide a marketing opportunity: Find out what the caller needs and explain how your service fulfills those needs. Being able to state, in capsule form, your program's strongest points and most attractive qualities is part of the payoff for all your work preparing marketing materials. If you delegate the task of answering the telephone, prepare that person by reviewing the points in advance and post a list of key points near the telephone. If person answering the phone cannot answer a question, make sure he or she gets callback information so you can follow up.

Just as the headline and format of the display ad must entice the reader to continue reading the ad, one of your goals when handling a telephone inquiry is to get the caller to spend more time learning about your program. Parents seeking child development services may be unskilled in requesting the information they need. You can help by asking questions about the type of service they are seeking. Avoid discussing fees until after you have determined what the caller is looking for and talked about what your program offers—information that they might not hear if they have already decided the price is too high. Suggest that they visit your website and offer specific options for dates when they might visit the center. Scheduling that visit during the first telephone contact is more likely to result in follow-up than leaving the matter vague. Be sure to ask callers how they found out about your center (so you know which of your advertising efforts is effective) and thank them for calling (Vicars, 2009).

Not every call is going to lead to an enrollment or even to an appointment to visit the center. Nevertheless, the way you handle the call gives the callers a lasting impression about your center's helpfulness. A good marketing strategy is to take the names and addresses of all callers and routinely mail them a copy of your program's brochure. This is additional evidence of your professionalism and friendly interest. It is also an efficient use of your resources because it puts your marketing material in the hands of a self-identified target audience. Your postage and printing costs might be repaid by a new enrollment, or you might simply reap the benefits of a heightened public awareness of your program's positive image.

? DECISIONS, DECISIONS . . .

Divide into teams of two and role-play a telephone conversation between a center manager and a parent seeking child care. One person in the team tries using the techniques described in this section, and the other person deliberately violates these concepts. A volunteer team demonstrates for the entire class. Discuss the demonstration as a class.

By carefully displaying framed photos of each child's family, this center hopes to create a servicescape that emphasizes awareness of the importance of families in their children's lives.

Service Environment as Marketing Tool

Marketing theorists have coined the term service-scape to include the physical, or built, environment, as well as the social environment, where a particular service takes place (Bitner, 2000, p. 37). As you recall from the discussion of the human ecological system, the human-built environment comprises everything that human beings have constructed or altered to fit their needs; in this case, it is the center's building, grounds, and furnishings. The social–cultural environment includes other people—the teachers, support staff members, parents, and children who interact within the center. Earlier chapters examined these elements from the perspective of their connection to program goals and quality of care. Now, we turn our attention to the role of the servicescape in marketing.

Bitner (2000, pp. 40–41) suggested that the servicescape fills at least four important marketing functions:

1. It *packages* the service you provide, conveying a particular image and evoking certain emotional or intellectual responses, just as the wrappings associated with more tangible products do. Imagine yourself as a parent in search of child care. You walk up a beautifully landscaped, curving walkway to the center's entryway. As you open the door, you are greeted by the aroma of fresh-baked bread and the pleasant hum of active children, punctuated by giggles. The staff members are wearing neatly pressed slacks and attractive smocks. One of them welcomes you with a smile and invites you to be seated on a wicker settee in a foyer decorated with healthy green plants and carefully framed children's artwork. Contrast this experience with another: You approach a dilapidated modular unit from a barren asphalt parking lot. As you open the door, your nostrils are assailed by the unmistakable odor of dirty diapers, which penetrates the mask of disinfectant spray. You hear children crying and adults speaking in loud, harsh tones. There is no place to sit and you feel that you are in the way; no one approaches to greet you. Which "package" appears to contain the quality of program you want for your child?

2. The servicescape *facilitates* the delivery of the service you provide. In other words, it makes it easier for employees to do their jobs and for customers to get what they need. As a consequence, staff members and families are more likely to experience pleasure and satisfaction. This means that their interactions with one another will be more positive, leading to still greater levels of pleasure and satisfaction. Consider this example: In one center, the teachers noticed that the children had an easier time saying good-bye to their parents in the morning if they could wave and blow kisses to them through the window. The windows, however, were too high for the children to reach, and the center's location made it impossible to lower them. The program evolved a custom of letting individual children stand on a countertop just below the window, watching until their parents were out of sight. Because a staff member stood next to them for safety reasons, this meant one less adult to help greet the children at the busy start of the morning. When the center had the opportunity to purchase a new loft, the staff decided to remove the

wall cabinets under the window so the loft could be installed in front of it. Because the loft and stairway leading up to it were enclosed, the children could independently position themselves to wave good-bye, and the teachers were free to do other tasks. This simple change in the servicescape reduced the stress and increased the satisfaction for parents, children, and teachers.

3. The servicescape *socializes* both customers and employees, sending a message about how they are expected to act and relate to each other in that space. An infant–toddler classroom equipped with a comfortable adult-size sofa invites staff members as well as parents to take time to snuggle with the children. It also says that adults are respected and that their need for comfort is as important as that of the children. Walls adorned with striking photographs of children and teachers engaged in playful activities speak volumes about what happens in a space. The room arrangement lets the children know whether to run and jump or to sit quietly with a puzzle. Thoughtfully placed, adequate storage space encourages staff members to maintain an orderly, harmonious environment. Steps leading up to the diapering surface suggest that children are participants in their own caregiving routines, as well as showing a concern for the caregivers' back muscles.

4. The servicescape *differentiates* your program from others offering similar services. The look and feel of the servicescape tells people whether to expect a fast-food menu of hamburger, fries, and soft drink or a gourmet five-course repast. Even in fast-food outlets, the décor and color scheme of one chain distinguish it from all of the others. In the world of child care, some large chains purposely cultivate a uniform corporate image so that potential customers recognize the logo on signs or even the particular type of architecture. When this is done purposefully, it serves the marketing purpose of promoting brand recognition and consumer comfort. When a particular center looks like every other one simply because all equipment is purchased from the same catalogs and all are decorated with items from the same teacher-supply store, it fails to tap the servicescape's potential. Making a center stand out from the crowd and thus give potential customers reasons to choose it over competitors need not cost a fortune. In fact, it could be less expensive to build equipment tailored to your particular needs and to decorate with homelike objects that reflect the lives of the families who use the center than to purchase commercial materials.

An important aspect of the servicescape is its aesthetic quality or the general attractiveness of its design. Wagner (2000, pp. 69–70) argued that a well-designed service environment communicates information about the quality of the service and increases the pleasure and satisfaction that customers derive from their experience in that environment. Thus, attention to form, shape, light, color, and texture is an investment that pays doubly. Not only does it contribute to a higher-quality experience for the children and caregivers, it also helps you "sell" your program.

?   DECISIONS, DECISIONS . . .

Think of a store where you like to shop or a restaurant where you like to eat. Describe the servicescape of the place(s) you select. How do the stores and/or restaurants work to attract customers and enhance their satisfaction with the service?

INCREASING CUSTOMER SATISFACTION

Probably one of your best referral sources for new customers is word-of-mouth advertising done by enrolled families who are satisfied with your services. Many centers ask new parents how they heard about the center, and the most common answer is that they have a friend, neighbor, or coworker who uses the center and is highly satisfied with its service. Some programs capitalize on this marketing resource by offering a discount on 1 month's tuition to families who refer someone who enrolls a new child. A good way to ensure that your current customers sing your praises is to apply basic principles of customer service.

Principles of Customer Service

Small-business expert William Franklin (1998) listed eight principles that we have adapted and applied to the business of child development programs. Each principle is discussed in detail in the following subsections.

UNDERSTAND WHAT YOU ARE SELLING   Child development programs struggle with the public's perception that they are selling a babysitting service where incidental learning takes place; all too often, the teachers buy into that perception as well. Actually, high-quality, developmentally appropriate programs are providing an educational service that also happens to fill the function of keeping children safe and happy while their parents work. Consider the example of a company that produces high-quality fountain pens (Clarke, 2000, pp. 48–49). When the company markets its product as simply a writing implement, it competes with mass-produced, disposable ballpoint pens. On the other hand, when it sells a luxury gift item that happens to double as a writing implement, it appeals to an entirely different market, one likely to be willing to pay much higher prices.

ASK WHAT THE CUSTOMERS WANT   Asking what the customers want shows your concern and pinpoints what they actually need. A single parent faced with getting to work on time or losing her job may want to know more about your program's hours of operation and proximity to public transportation than its Piaget-based curriculum. This doesn't mean that program quality is unimportant, just that it might not be uppermost in the parent's mind at the moment. You can always find ways to communicate the quality of your service later.

FOCUS ON RELATIONSHIPS   When you accept a child for care in your program, you are embarking on a relationship with that child's family that will last, ideally, for years. Think of the trust that the families must have to leave their children in your care, and think of how much that trust will grow as you and the families get to know each other—as your relationship strengthens. The previous chapter described a number of strategies that programs can use to build a strong foundation for that relationship. Those strategies not only help you serve the families better, they also make good business sense.

FOCUS ON WHAT YOU CAN DO TO HELP   You may not be able to solve every problem, but you can take some steps to help. For example, your concern for the teachers who want to get home to their own families may mean that you are unwilling to bend your program's rule about picking children up on time. But you can help the families work out buddy systems so that parents who are unavoidably detained can make emergency arrangements easier.

DON'T PASS THE BUCK   Ensure that the customer connects with the person who can help with a problem. For program managers, this might mean personally following through to find out what happened to a child's lost mittens and reporting back immediately to the irritated parent on the telephone, rather than putting the caller on hold until a busy teacher can come to the phone.

LOOK FOR THE REASON FOR ANGER AND DEAL WITH THAT INSTEAD OF BECOMING DEFENSIVE Parents who are angry that their child has come home with a case of head lice don't want to hear that such occurrences are "part of being in child care." They want to know that you understand their concern and share their determination that it does not happen again.

WORK TOWARD AGREEING ON A PLAN FOR ACTION   Suppose some parents are upset and believe their toddler has regressed in his toilet training progress since entering your program. Simply telling them that you will instruct staff members to invite the child to sit on the toilet at regular times during the day is not likely to appease them. Suggesting a particular strategy and asking for the parents' opinion before embarking on it is more likely to make them feel part of the decision making.

GO THE EXTRA MILE AND LET THE FAMILIES KNOW ABOUT IT   This advice applies to businesses that absorb the cost when a mistake by one of their employees creates an inconvenience or dissatisfaction. Most child development programs operate on a tight budget that does not allow such an option. Nevertheless, there are many ways that the programs and their employees can provide service above and beyond the customers' expectation. The teacher who brings her own guitar and shares her musical gifts with the children is an example. So is the manager who shops for better food prices in order to provide more nutritious meals, or the cook whose ingenuity adds gourmet touches to make those meals more attractive. None of these extra measures of quality are readily apparent to the families—you have to tell them.

PUBLIC RELATIONS: HAVING AN IMPACT ON PERCEPTIONS AND OPINIONS

Forward-thinking managers are concerned with more than enlarging their customer base. They also strive to become—and to be recognized as—important members of the community at large. A building contractor might contribute lumber for a playground structure. A financial institution's president might serve on an arts council board. A manufacturing firm might give employees paid leave to volunteer in schools or hospitals, or it might match any monetary contributions those employees make to specific community organizations. They do these things, not simply for an immediate or direct payoff in increased sales, but because they view themselves as corporate citizens, contributing money, employee time, and expertise to enhance the quality of life in their communities. In other words, they cultivate good public relations. Of course, those corporate

Documentation of projects completed with children can become marketing and public relations tools that convey important information about a program's curriculum and basic philosophy.

citizens hope to reap the benefits of their good works in the form of increased business or some other desirable outcome, so the line between public relations and marketing can become blurred. In fact, what we are calling public relations is sometimes termed community marketing (e.g., Wassom, 2001).

Public relations has been defined as "the shaping of the broader context within which the public in general—or, more likely, specific target publics, forms opinions and makes decisions" (Saffir, 2000, p. 7). Like all communication, public relations is a two-way street. Skillful opinion shapers do not work in a vacuum; they attempt to gauge current public perceptions and to predict how those perceptions might change in various circumstances. Understanding how this works—and how important it is—is what Saffir called **public relations literacy**. His term for the ability to apply that knowledge skillfully is **public relations competency** (Saffir, 2000, pp. xii–xiii). The practice of public relations, then, is "the art and science of analyzing trends, predicting their consequences, counseling organization leaders, and implementing planned programs of action which will serve both the organization's and the public's interest" (Newsom & Haynes, 2008, p. 3).

Saffir predicted that public relations will emerge in the 21st century "as the dominant force in what is fundamental to success in business and politics" (2000, p. xiii). With this in mind, early childhood administrators are wise to follow the lead of their counterparts in the business world. Consider the many "publics" whose opinions directly influence child development programs. At the most local level, more than one manager has been faced with disgruntled individuals who would like to see the center shut down or moved. They might be neighbors who object to the noise from the playground or church members who resent messy Sunday school rooms left behind by the child-care center that uses the space during the week.

Corporate executives, looking for ways to contribute to their community for their own public relations purposes, can become program benefactors only if they know about the work the programs do. Members of the governing bodies that make decisions about subsidy rates are likely to question proposals for increases if they are unaware of the true costs and benefits of high-quality child care. Everything that you do to promote public awareness of your program also contributes to public awareness of the benefits of high-quality programs and the risks of poor-quality care.

This awareness benefits the children, the families, and the early childhood professionals because people become more willing to invest personal and government resources in paying for high-quality care. One of the findings of the four-state study called *Cost, Quality, and Child Outcomes in Child Care Centers* was that "inadequate consumer knowledge . . . reduces incentives for some centers to provide good-quality care" (Cost, Quality, & Child Outcomes Study Team, 1995, p. 9). In other words, parents, although they value good-quality care, do not have sufficient information about what constitutes high quality. The NAEYC accreditation system and the tiered licensing systems in many states represent two attempts to help families identify higher-quality programs.

According to a study, accredited centers charge up to 30 percent more for their services than other centers (National Association of Child Care Resource and Referral Agencies, 2009a, p. 14). States with tiered (or rated) licensing systems pay higher reimbursement rates to centers and family child-care homes that achieve higher ratings. Still, as a manager striving to provide high-quality care and fair compensation for your staff members, you will have a harder time making ends meet than the manager who settles for meeting minimum licensing standards. Stronger licensing regulations could reduce this financial advantage for mediocre centers, but it takes an informed public to demand those stronger standards and to invest the resources necessary for their consistent enforcement. A public that perceives child care as menial work will not support licensing standards requiring higher levels of teacher education or salaries commensurate with those qualifications.

Clearly, wise managers see to it that as many people as possible have been informed of all the good that their program accomplishes. Does this mean that you must factor the cost of an expensive public relations representative into your already strapped budget? We think not. Much public relations work is simply an extension of what you already do to forge relationships with the families and the community and to foster professional development in yourself and your staff members. It requires only that you make a conscious effort to make the most of your efforts. Once you have done that, you can take additional steps to make your program more visible and more highly regarded in your community. Ultimately you will be contributing to a growing recognition on the part of civic planners and business leaders that child care is a "critical infrastructure for family-friendly communities," helping to ensure "the overall health of a community and the broader regional economy" (Warner, Anderson, & Haddow, 2007, p. 19).

Family Members as Public Relations Representatives

View every family you serve as a potential ambassador for your program. We have already mentioned the role that families play in marketing through word-of-mouth advertising. When they are informed, these same families can also carry your message about the value of highly qualified staff, better adult–child ratios, and other elements of quality to the community at large. They can help prospective customers understand why the lower rates at another center are not necessarily a bargain. They can become advocates, for example, when a building owner moves to evict a center or when funding and licensing safeguards are threatened by government cutbacks.

Note that the key to tapping this resource is education. The more clearly you communicate what you do and why you do it to the families you serve, the more prepared they are to take that message to the entire community. This suggests that all of the strategies discussed in the previous chapter for building strong relationships with the families are public relations strategies as well. You do not have to reinvent the wheel to educate. You have powerful allies in the NAEYC and your community's CCR&R agency. Both of these organizations can provide you with a wealth of materials in attractive, readable formats that present information about high-quality child care and its importance. You need only serve as the conduit to get these materials into the hands of the families served by your program.

Expanding the Audience

Of course, you cannot rely entirely on families to carry your message to the community. You must carry your message directly. Again, begin with what you are already doing instead of adding a huge new undertaking to your busy schedule. Think of all the ways you currently communicate with family members. Then think of how these same efforts can be extended to the community at large.

SPREAD THE NEWS(LETTER) You have already invested time and energy to create an attractive, professional-looking newsletter, chock full of substantive information about your curriculum and other program aspects. For a few pennies each, you can print several (or several dozen) extra copies and distribute them to key individuals or organizations in your community. For even less cost, you can distribute your newsletter via email, either within the body of the message or as an attachment. Potential email

TALK ON PARENTING: On April 15 at 8 p.m. at the Edgewater Little People's Child Development Center, Dr. James Service, noted child development specialist, will discuss "Problem-Solving Techniques to Use with Your Young Child." All community parents are invited. Edgewater Child Development Center, 123 Child Way, Watertown. Child care for young children is available during the meeting. Call 555-1111 for more information.

FIGURE 14.3   Sample public meeting announcement.

subscribers include the chief executive officer of the company where many of your parents work, your local CCR&R agency, the loan officer or president of the bank that holds the mortgage on your building, or parents of program alumni who may hold influential positions in the community. You can probably think of several others. Create a database of names and addresses and add to it as you meet other people who might be encouraged to develop an interest in your center. Remember to delete the names of those individuals who have moved, changed jobs, or indicated that they do not wish to receive your newsletter.

OPEN UP YOUR FAMILY MEETINGS   Again, you and your staff members invest considerable time and energy planning and preparing for family meetings. Some of those meetings will be of concern only to currently enrolled families. Other meetings might appeal to a broader audience. Advertising that meeting lets people know your program exists, enhances your program's prestige by establishing a connection with a professional organization, and broadens the scope of services identified with your program from "just" child care to parenting education for the larger community. Of course, this ad also fills a marketing function by putting your name and telephone number into the hands of potential customers who may save it for future reference. Figure 14.3 is an example of a public service announcement that you could use to advertise with the local newspaper or radio or television station. Most of these media outlets have community calendar features that carry such announcements at no charge.

Agency Links

Cultivating links with the agencies in your community can benefit your center in numerous ways. Licensing representatives can often offer advice and information to help you meet or exceed regulatory requirements. Instead of dreading the annual inspection visit and becoming defensive when problems are noted, assume that you and the licensing agent are both working toward the same goal—protecting the health and well-being of the children in your care. Licensing representatives are human and, like you, enjoy getting a friendly reception. They are likely to view sincere requests for advice as a welcome change from tedious checklists and reports.

Centers that have established good contacts with their community health services have experts to call when, for example, an outbreak of head lice occurs. Public health agencies can provide literature on this and other topics that you can distribute to families. They might also have experts on staff who can speak at your professional development meetings or visit your center to help you evaluate its health and safety practices. As noted in Chapter 10, you should work with a health professional to review your program's health policies and procedures.

Your local CCR&R agency is your link to a large pool of prospective customers, as well as a possible resource for staff training. Many CCR&R programs sponsor workshops for child development staff on topics such as room arrangement or behavior guidance. Some have specialists on staff who can provide on-site technical assistance and consultation.

Maintaining close ties with the public and private schools in your service area benefits all concerned. Families appreciate the smooth transition when their children move from child care to kindergarten, and the children thrive when the teachers from both levels communicate with each other (with the permission and participation of families, of course). Teachers find it helpful to know something about the children they will have in their class, and the children and their families will be more comfortable entering the new school environment if you have helped them learn about it in advance. Schools can also be a source of referrals for your program. Families new to a community may turn to school personnel for information about available options for after-school care or the care of younger siblings. The more the school personnel know about your program and its quality, the more likely they are to mention its name.

If all of these reasons are not sufficiently convincing, networking with other agencies in your community can ultimately have a financial payoff. It puts you in a position to hear about new funding sources or requests for proposals offered by corporate or charitable foundations. Representatives of those agencies may be able to provide letters of support when you do submit grant proposals. Finally, the representatives of those agencies might serve on committees formed to evaluate the proposal merits.

Publicizing Events and Accomplishments

Every high-quality child development program has countless stories that deserve a wider audience. Telling your program's stories to that wider audience can be accomplished in several ways. You might get acquainted with a reporter who likes to do stories about children and give a standing invitation to her to visit your center. Or you can write a press release and submit it to the local paper when the children in your program undertake an interesting project or field trip. A press release is most effective when it is typed, double-spaced, and brief. It should answer the journalist's questions—who, what, when, where, why—within the first paragraph. Clearly indicate the date of intended release, and include a name, email address, and telephone number of someone to contact for further information.

The paper might print your release as written, or the editor might send a photographer or reporter to develop a more extensive human interest piece. If the paper does print your release, it may be shortened to fit available space. Because editors may accomplish this by deleting sentences or paragraphs at the end of the story, it is important to get all essential information as close to the beginning as possible.

Remember to thank the people who help put your story before the public. A letter to the editor, or directly to the reporter (with a copy to her supervisor), builds goodwill and paves the way for future event coverage. On the other hand, calling or writing to complain when your story is not published is likely to have the opposite effect (Stephens, 1998).

Staff Development as a Public Relations Vehicle

You are engaging in public relations work whenever you or your staff members participate with or appear before other groups. For example, you may be invited to speak to a church group about child care. Depending on how well you do your homework and how clearly you communicate, your audience forms an impression about you, about your center, and about the early childhood profession. Be sure to share opportunities to represent your center with staff members. This approach encourages them to learn new things and become more reflective about their practice. It makes them feel good and shows the public that you value your teachers' abilities.

These benefits also are realized when you and your staff members are active in local, state, and national professional associations. Presenting at conferences or writing articles for their journals are ways for you and staff members to reflect on what you do and to clarify your thinking. National organizations usually publish a call for presentation proposals in their journals and on their websites about a year before their annual meetings. Your state and local associations may work in the same way, perhaps within a shorter time frame. Because the competition for slots on the program is greater at the national level, first-time presenters may be wise to start with a local or state venue and use that experience to polish their presentation before moving to the next level. Thoughtful use of presentation software (e.g., PowerPoint or Apple Keynote) enables you to use charts, graphs, and digital photographs or video clips to communicate your message in a compelling way.

You can further capitalize on your efforts in researching and organizing a presentation by using it as a springboard for writing an article. Check publication guidelines on the organization's website and study issues of the journal to determine the nature, style, and length of articles. Prepare your article: Write and rewrite until it is clear, interesting, and error-free. Follow instructions for submissions: Some publications prefer manuscripts in digital format; others may want two or three hard copies of each article along with a self-addressed return envelope and postage to facilitate the article's return should the editors find it not suitable for their publication. If the article is returned, look it over for errors or outdated material, improve wording where possible, and submit it to another magazine or journal. Persistence pays off, so never give up after the first rejection slip. Your byline should include information about your center, which adds to public recognition of your center. Thus, your center gains professional recognition at the same time you and your staff members grow professionally.

Networking

Even if you do not choose to present a topic at a professional conference, you and your staff can take advantage of opportunities to meet with people with similar interests and problems. Successful managers actively cultivate a wide network of professional contacts—people you can turn to (or who can turn to you) for advice, information, recommendations, referrals, or other types of assistance. Thus, it is important not only to attend conferences sponsored by professional organizations, but to join those organizations and become actively involved in their projects and governance. The NAEYC, with its various local, state, and regional affiliates, is a good starting point for all child development professionals. Administrators are also likely to benefit from organizations more particularly tailored to their role, such as a local director's support group or the National Association for Early Learning Leaders (http://www.naccp.org).

A simple tool to help make the most of your networking efforts is the business card. Like your brochure and print advertisements, a business card should have an identifiable look that conveys an image of quality. In addition to essential information (e.g., the program's name and web address, your name and title, address, telephone, fax, and email), the card might also contain a logo or very brief phrase that communicates something about your program's mission. Exchanging cards with people you meet at professional gatherings is one way to help both of you remember each other's names after the event. The next step is to organize the contacts so they are accessible when you need them. This might mean scanning or otherwise entering the information on the card into a database, organized by category as well as alphabetically by the name of the company or individual.

THE WORLD BEYOND CHILD CARE

So far, we have examined ways that your public relations efforts can piggyback your ongoing efforts to communicate with families and to develop professional capabilities in yourself and your staff members. Once you have these initiatives in place and begin to see their advantages, you are ready to move into the world beyond child care.

Making Connections

Remember that the word *public* in public relations actually has a broad connotation—every organization has many publics, each with a different perspective on what the organization does. Corporations gain a competitive edge in recruiting highly qualified employees if they can point to excellent child-care facilities in the community—but they may need your help to realize this potential benefit. Think of all the other seemingly unrelated entities that stand to benefit from the existence of your program—real estate agents and others with an interest in selling a neighborhood or community, or taxpayers with an interest in welfare-to-work programs. Your goal is to reach each of those publics in a way that addresses their interest.

TAKE STOCK OF YOUR COMMUNITY   Bagin and Gallagher (2001, pp. 137–138) suggested compiling a list of key contacts who can serve as liaisons with community organizations. These key contacts can provide feedback about the opinions held by their members and help convey your message. Bagin and Gallagher also suggested considering the following group categories: civic (e.g., Rotary, Lions Club), cultural (e.g., arts or humanities councils), economic (e.g., labor unions, retail merchants' associations), fraternal (e.g., Knights of Columbus), governmental (e.g., health and/or recreation departments), patriotic (e.g., American Legion, veterans' groups), political (e.g., League of Women Voters), professional (e.g., doctors' or lawyers' associations), religious, retirees, and youth (e.g., YMCA, YWCA, 4-H Clubs).

REACH OUT   In addition to joining organizations with a focus on children or child care, consider joining organizations that bring you into contact with people with other interests, skills, and connections. Your community's chamber of commerce and the League of Women Voters are two examples. Use the listed categories to think about all the groups that exist in your community. By participating in these groups, you learn a great deal about issues affecting your center, and you can bring your unique perspective as a child development professional to the discussions. As you become more comfortable and take a more active role in these organizations, you gain respect for yourself as well as for your program and the profession in general.

JOIN HANDS   Work with community partners to do things that benefit you both. Wassom (2001) suggested providing copies of articles on parenting topics (stamped with your program's name, web address, and phone number) to businesses where parents are likely to spend time waiting (e.g., hair salons). Once that relationship is established, she suggested that the center and salon could collaborate further by arranging on-site haircuts during center hours for the children of busy parents. On a broader scale, child development programs can partner with a number of community agencies or businesses to hold events that draw in a larger number of families than any single program could attract. For example, children's fairs celebrate the Week of the Young Child in many communities. In one town, child development programs set up booths with simple activities for the children, the public health department offers immunizations, other helping agencies provide information about their programs, and businesses sponsor refreshments or provide small gifts for those attending.

> **? DECISIONS, DECISIONS . . .**
>
> With your classmates, brainstorm a list of organizations in your community with which a child development program manager might make networking contacts.

"DOUBLE DUTY" IN PUBLIC RELATIONS

Developing a sound public relations strategy pays off in numerous ways. The preparation of one type of information may be useful as you develop other types of public information. For example, carefully prepared talks to parents can form the nucleus for professional articles, or vice versa. Carefully stated objectives can enhance your written reports to the policy board, as well as serve as key statements on a public information brochure. Pictures taken to document children's project work can, with families' permission, be used in brochures or other publicity materials. Because many materials serve several purposes, you must develop a system for managing the storage and retrieval of the items you develop. Investing the time to do this allows you to locate a previous piece that might serve a present need.

COUNTERING NEGATIVE PUBLICITY

A common lament among child development professionals is that negative stories about child care always receive more extensive and prominent coverage than all of their positive efforts. News of a child-care provider who has been convicted of molesting a child overshadows the fact that countless others provide safe, loving care day in and day out. It is small comfort that this seems to be true in every arena. Sensational news sells newspapers and attracts viewers, and sensational news is, more often than not, bad news. (See, for example, the article by Jonathan Cohn that appeared in the April 15, 2013, issue of *The New Republic*: The hell of American day care: An investigation into the barely regulated, unsafe business of looking after our children. Accessible on line at http://www.newrepublic.com/article/112892/hell-american-day-care#.)

Sometimes the effects of negative publicity can spill over even when your program is not directly involved. In the mid-1980s, when a prominent researcher was quoted in the national press comparing sanitation conditions in child care to life in the Middle Ages, the follow-up by local television crews in one city could have put directors on the defensive. Because they had good health practices in place, however, and because they could keep cool under pressure, the directors could explain what they did to prevent the spread of infection and to keep the children healthy. As a consequence, the news that night showed children washing their hands and staff members cleaning tables with a bleach solution.

Of course, your first defense against negative publicity is the prevention of incidents that might trigger it—in other words, good management. From the initial planning to monitoring and controlling for quality, the manager's first goal is to protect the children's health and well-being. No amount of "spin" can make up for negligence, and it is unethical to suggest otherwise. But negative incidents happen in the best of programs, and when they do occur, wise managers have a plan in place to minimize the damage.

That plan should clearly designate the spokesperson for the program who is responsible for handling all contacts with media representatives. In most cases, this duty falls on your shoulders. Although staff members should be kept informed of the situation, they should not communicate their version of events, which may be incomplete or inaccurate, to reporters. Rather, they should be instructed to decline all comment and to refer any questions to you. This is not an effort at secrecy; it is merely a precaution to help eliminate confusion and ensure the clear communication of complete information.

By communicating all of the facts as clearly and quickly as possible, you can avoid the appearance of having something to hide or defend. Often, this strategy helps defuse a story before it is blown out of proportion. Dorothy Hewes (1998, p. 346) related a story of a director confronted with questions about a suspected child molester who had, at one time, been a volunteer at the center. The director was able to inform the reporter that the individual in question had done only maintenance work and that had occurred many years earlier. The director also took the proactive measure of informing her employer and staff members in anticipation of further questions. As the result of her quick action, the story mentioned the center only in passing and other news coverage focused on the center's policies for protecting children.

When presenting information to the news media, the *how* is often as important as the *who* and the *what*. All of your preparation for positive publicity will stand you in good stead here. Your printed materials give reporters accurate information about the name of your program and its essential features. Your practice writing press releases that lead with the essentials reminds you to concentrate on getting the facts stated at the outset because your interview is likely to be edited down to only a sentence or two. Speak slowly and distinctly, look at the reporter, and focus as much on the positive as possible. If it turns out that your program was in the wrong, a sincere apology will probably do more to repair your image than a barrage of excuses.

Technology Toolkit

✓ Use a free online code generator (e.g., http://goqr.me/) to create a quick response (QR) code that links to your center's webpage when a smartphone user clicks on it. Incorporate the QR code in your printed advertisements and brochures.

✓ Use a free resource for creating a website, for example, Google sites (http://sites.google.com); webs (www.webs.com); or wikispaces (www.wikispaces.com).

✓ Use a presentation software program (e.g., PowerPoint or Apple Keynote) to create Learning Stories—short slide shows—depicting the discoveries and accomplishments that occur in your center. Learning Stories were devised by early educators in New Zealand (Margaret Carr and Wendy Lee) and the United States (Tom Drummond) as a naturalistic, authentic approach to assessing young children's learning and development. Although they do serve that purpose, when shared with parents and others, they convey powerful messages about your program and about the ways children learn. See examples at http://earlylearningstories.com or http://earlylearningstories.info.

You may agree in your heart with the joke that equates an executive's definition of a bad day as any day in which a secretary announces that the *60 Minutes* camera crew is waiting outside. And, in fact, you may never achieve a high level of comfort handling negative publicity. Still, it does not make sense to pretend that it cannot happen to you. Accepting and planning for the possibility are part of the manager's job.

Conclusion

Child development programs occupy a particular niche of the business landscape because their "product" is an intangible service. Program administrators are learning that, just like the managers of other service businesses, they must cultivate effective communication and positive relationships with people and institutions in the larger community, as well as with the families they serve. For their programs to survive and thrive, they must learn the skills of marketing and public relations to broaden their customer base, attract funding sources, and develop a pool of potential advocates. They must form links with community agencies to help the program operate smoothly and effectively, as well as to create a network of resources to which the families can turn for assistance. Child development programs can promote public awareness of the hallmarks and advantages of high-quality care, as well as the liabilities of mediocre care. Such promotion helps create a demand for excellence in all services for young children.

Questions for Review

1. Define the term *marketing* and explain how it differs from public relations.

2. Collect examples of marketing materials used by child development programs in your community. Compare each to the descriptions and guidelines offered in this chapter. What changes (if any) would you recommend?

3. Think about a child development center where you have observed or worked. Imagine you are hired as a public relations representative for the center and, using the examples provided in this chapter, create a list of specific strategies you would recommend.

Professional Portfolio

1. Explore the websites of child development programs such as those presented in Figures 14.2 and 14.3 (or other types of small businesses). Then collaborate with a small group of your classmates to design a website for a hypothetical child development program. Decide what information you should include and how it should be organized so that the site is easy to navigate. Consider adding links to sites that provide other types of information your prospective clients might want or need. Pay attention to the aesthetic aspects of layout, background, and design. Print out a hard copy of your home page for inclusion in your portfolio.

2. Design a brochure or create a sample newsletter for a child development program. Include information about the program that is of interest to parents as well as informative to people who may not have firsthand knowledge of your program. Make sure that your publication is attractive and reader-friendly and that it can be reproduced easily and inexpensively.

3. Plan an event for a child development program to which key public officials and community leaders are invited. Describe the event and explain what you hope to accomplish with it. When and where will the event be held? Write a letter of invitation and list those to whom you will send it. Explain your rationale for each decision.

Resources for Further Study

PRINT

Arnold, M. (2005). *Effective communication techniques for child care.* Clifton Park, NY: Delmar.

Hunt, T. (2009). *The whuffie factor: Using the power of social networks to build your business.* New York: Crown Publishing (Random House).

Websites

BUILDING A SCHOOL WEBSITE: A HANDS-ON PROJECT FOR TEACHERS AND KIDS

http://www.wigglebits.com

A beginner's guide to creating a website; includes definitions of terms and directions for using HyperText Markup Language (HTML), formatting, and adding pictures or links.

HTML GOODIES

http://www.htmlgoodies.com/introduction/intro/

A "nontechnical" introduction to website design, including discussion of content, style, function, and ease of maintenance.

CHAPTER

Assessment and Evaluation

LEARNING OUTCOMES

After studying this chapter you should be able to

• Describe the manager's role in monitoring and controlling for quality.

• Explain the elements of program evaluation: who is involved and what is evaluated.

• Discuss the advantages and drawbacks of methods for assessing children's learning.

Rainbow Center adopted the use of portfolios to assess children's progress and communicate with families as an essential element of its program. Part of Tanya's job as assistant director is to monitor and control the implementation of this policy. Every teacher is expected to maintain a portfolio for each child with anecdotal records of observations, dated samples of drawing or writing, photographs of block or clay creations, or other examples of the child's thinking.

Tanya knows that collecting these materials at regular intervals dramatically captures the unfolding of development over time in ways that checklists or tests cannot. She also knows how much families appreciate seeing this concrete evidence, not only that their children are learning, but that their teachers really are paying attention. She wants to help the teachers make the job of collecting images and work samples easier and to show them how to get maximum payoff from their efforts. At the next staff meeting, she makes sure everyone knows how to take digital photos, save them in files, and insert them into Word documents. The teachers are delighted to eliminate the problem of storing bulky collections of drawings and to realize that the same photo can be part of an illustrated anecdote for a child's portfolio, an article for the class newsletter, and documentation of project work for classroom display or the center website.

The fifth major management function is to monitor and control for quality. The manager is charged with knowing the standards; establishing systems to meet those standards; evaluating the program against the accepted standards; and when performance falls short, taking action to correct the problem.

THE MANAGER'S ROLE

Monitoring and controlling are the evaluative and action functions of maintaining high quality in the promised services. **Monitoring** requires being alert to and continuously observing for compliance with applicable standards. **Controlling** requires that you state the standards you expect each program component to achieve, measure the performance against the standards, and either correct any deviations from the established standards and plans or modify any standards that prove unrealistic or inappropriate (DuBrin, 2000, p. 332). Monitoring and controlling for quality are functions that each staff member must be concerned about daily, hourly, and moment to moment. In short, after a manager has developed a plan and put that plan into action, she or he must check regularly to determine whether the plan is being implemented properly and is meeting its intended aims.

Monitoring and controlling are already part of your life. Consider this example: When you are driving your car, you continually monitor speed, road conditions, time, and dozens of other factors. You have standards to meet in the form of traffic regulations, common courtesy, a schedule, and personal ideas about efficiency or the beauty of the selected route. As you drive, you measure your performance against those standards and correct any deviations: adjusting your speed, turning the steering wheel when the road curves, or deciding to take another route if there is too much traffic. A child-care center manager makes similar observations and adjustments to maintain efficiency and quality.

Managers establish personal standards that are based on professional knowledge and individual experience; they also observe the standards established by outside sources. Wise managers understand that the rules are minimum standards, the results of a collaborative effort of many people just like themselves. They ensure that their centers adhere to the rules and do not try to get around them. They also understand that they have a voice in improving the rules as new needs arise or new information develops. In other words, a center manager works in partnership with the licensing agency to establish a baseline of quality.

Having determined which standards apply to your center and why, your ability to maintain high quality depends, in part, on encouraging each staff member to take responsibility for his or her performance and to make adjustments whenever inadequacies occur. It is easier to encourage this type of responsibility if you select your staff members carefully, orient and train them thoroughly, and provide feedback on their performance.

You must make it easy, however, for staff members to comply by structuring the environment, providing needed supplies, and ensuring that other supports are in place. A staff member left alone with too many crying infants, for example, may be tempted to take shortcuts when it comes to sanitizing a diapering table between changes. Similarly, if there is no running water nearby or no hand lotion to soothe chapped hands, busy caregivers are less likely to be conscientious about handwashing.

All of the center's units must be the focus of the manager's monitoring and controlling functions. That is, you must set minimum standards for each and make corrections when deviations are observed. For example, it is appropriate to evaluate the policy board's decision-making process, the method used to present items to the board, how professionalism is increased, how to serve more children and families, and ways to increase the board's effectiveness. If any item does not measure up to the predetermined standards, you must initiate corrective action.

Any deviations from standards on the part of staff members should be brought to their attention immediately, especially when it concerns matters having an effect on the children. Because the process of hiring and training new staff members is very expensive, it is sensible to focus on improving the performance of those who have been hired. It is reasonable to expect people to be punctual and to carry out the job as explained by the job description. Following the standards set by the profession or service is also to be assumed. Like teachers, food service, maintenance, and clerical personnel are expected to comply with professional standards. Staff members can help set the criteria or standards by which they will be judged. To be fair, the criteria for pay raises, promotions, or

Spending a little time with children at breakfast gives family members an opportunity to evaluate many aspects of the program. Is the food served nutritious and appetizing? Is the atmosphere at the table relaxed and enjoyable?

dismissal should be set early and communicated to staff members at that time, rather than when it is time to make a judgment at the end of a year.

Finances

Money management must be evaluated continuously. You are responsible for careful, accurate, and honest accounting in collecting fees and paying expenses. Both profit and nonprofit organizations should stick to their budgets. In profit-making centers, figuring in a reasonable percentage for profit is necessary. Establishing an accounting system with the assistance of a competent accountant is essential.

The Physical Plant

The safety, sanitation, security, and aesthetics of the entire physical plant might be your responsibility, or you may have only a portion of a building as your concern. We discussed specific requirements for establishing facilities that are safe and inviting in previous chapters. Monitoring and controlling for quality in these areas means that the manager establishes a regular schedule for completing specific tasks as well as a regular schedule for verifying that standards are being maintained. When deficiencies are noted, the manager must work with staff members to correct them. For example, when staff members focus on children's needs (as they should), they may lapse into habits of leaving items out instead of putting them away. If you notice this occurring, you might evaluate the situation to see whether a change in the storage arrangements or additional storage space is needed.

The security of your facility during nights, weekends, and vacations must be planned and controlled. Many centers have difficulty preventing the older neighborhood children from coming into the playground after hours to play on, and possibly damage, the equipment. This may dictate choosing heavier or more substantial equipment than the size and age of the center's enrollees requires. Security locks are also essential. Some of the "visitors" might be of the four-legged variety, so you should cover outdoor sandboxes when they are not in use to prevent them from becoming unsanitary litter boxes.

Food Service

Items to evaluate in the food service area include the following:

1. Do meals and snacks offer sufficient quantity, variety, and nutritional content to meet the recommended daily allowances?
2. Are mealtimes pleasant and relaxing for children and adults? Are children's attitudes toward meals, manners, and nutrition education positive?
3. Are good sanitation procedures strictly adhered to?
4. Are the kitchen and dining areas arranged efficiently?
5. Are noise levels moderated?

6. Is the space adequate to attend to an individual child's needs?

7. Are all food workers healthy, clean, and dressed appropriately for the job?

8. Is information about children's food allergies, preferences, and food intake shared between the center and families?

9. Do teachers and food service staff members collaborate about the appropriate use of food in classroom learning activities?

10. Is the food shopping monitored with regard to cost, waste, and leftovers?

As you watch this video, notice how many of these items the director addresses as she checks with the center cook on her morning rounds.

Children's Health and Safety

Items requiring evaluation in this category include the following:

1. Are child health records, including immunizations, up to date?

2. Are center records clear about how families may be contacted if a child becomes ill during the day? Do all staff members know where these records are filed?

3. Do staff members monitor the children's health continually to be aware of the signs of illness?

4. Does the center have a relationship with a child-care health consultant who can provide information and guidance regarding health issues? Is that person's contact information readily available to staff members?

5. Is there a comfortable, quiet place for a sick child to rest apart from the others until she or he can be taken home? Is medical clearance required to readmit a child following an absence?

6. Are medications stored safely and appropriately? Are they administered only according to written instructions with parental permission and medical authorization as needed?

7. Are evacuation plans known and practiced so that each staff member knows his or her role in an emergency evacuation—for example, taking the children's emergency information and an attendance list; calling for help and giving directions to the center?

8. Is the nap room space adequate, free of drafts, and accessible to exits in case of fire? Are sufficient staff members available during nap time to evacuate the building in case of fire?

9. Are provisions adequate for those children who will not sleep?

10. Is the temperature of the building correct for active children?

11. Do children have ample time for vigorous play outdoors? Are they dressed appropriately and protected from overexposure to sun by shade and the use of sunscreen?

12. Do children have adequate access to drinking water?

13. Are diapering and toilet facilities child-size, readily accessible, and adequately supplied?

14. Have all appropriate precautions been taken to prevent child abuse, including screening and supervising staff members?

15. Are procedures in place to verify the identity of persons picking up children and to ensure that children are released only to authorized individuals?

Public Relations

There is some overlap in evaluating those actions that affect parents and evaluating those that affect the general public. Careful attention to the following areas is necessary:

1. Are telephone calls answered politely and returned promptly?
2. Are letters, email messages, and other queries answered politely and promptly?
3. Are advertisements, brochures, newsletters, and the website adequate and up to date?
4. Does to the center make sure that new families feel welcome and understand all policies and procedures (e.g., for dealing with a sick child, food service, emergency evacuation)?
5. Are families invited to provide feedback to the center? Do they indicate that their needs are being met?
6. Does the center support families in their roles as decision maker and advocate for their child?
7. Are publications or other resources available to help families with parenting questions?
8. Do all staff members have a clear understanding of who should speak with the parents, the public, or media representatives when complaints or criticisms arise?
9. Are staff members who fill leadership roles in the community well prepared to represent the center?

STEPS IN THE MONITORING AND CONTROLLING PROCESS

The monitoring and controlling process consists of five steps. The manager's first step in the monitoring and controlling process, then, is to *understand the requirements thoroughly.* Managers who lack this in-depth understanding are likely to be so consumed with the petty details of meeting the letter of the law that they quickly become candidates for burnout.

Next, the manager must *communicate the standards clearly* so that every staff member understands the importance of the standards and her or his responsibility for meeting them.

Third, the manager must *monitor compliance with the standards and act to maintain high performance standards in every center unit.* As mentioned in a previous chapter, one strategy for achieving this is a technique called managing by walking around (MBWA). MBWA is the practice of making informal visits to work areas and listening to employees in order to collect information, listen to suggestions and complaints, and generally keep a finger on the pulse of the organization. This should not be construed as casually meandering through the facility when the whim strikes. To be effective, you must have a purpose in mind, make notes of what you see, and follow through by sharing your observations of problem areas with the people who can do something to correct the situation (Reiling, 2008).

Fourth, the manager must *listen to and understand others' views.* When leading staff members toward high-quality performance, it is essential to practice good communication skills. It is not enough to realize that some employees are failing to comply with established standards—you should also know why. In other words, until you understand the problems they experience, you cannot begin to solve them. The most direct—and effective—way to accomplish this is to ask. Staff members who believe that their views are respected are more likely to become partners in the program's quality enhancement effort (Senge, 2006). When this happens, everyone's stress is reduced—yours and your staff members'.

Fifth, the manager must *strive to maintain objectivity when evaluating problems and issues*. It is certainly a challenge to confront problems in a cool, calm manner, but it helps if a manager develops the habit of seeking information before leaping into action. Covey (1992, p. 139) recommended asking four questions: "(1) Where are we? (2) Where do we want to go? (3) How do we get there? (4) How will we know when we have arrived?" He cautioned that strong emotions can often color one's perceptions regarding the first two questions, which can lead to premature and energy-draining battles over the third. Consider the following example:

> In a small center, a teacher in the infant–toddler classroom became upset with the teacher of the 3- to-5-year-old group over sharing the playground. "For the past several days," she fumed, "she has brought the older kids outside within a few minutes of the time I have arrived with the babies. That means that, after all of the time we have spent bundling our children up for outdoor play, we have to turn around and go back inside—or run the risk of having the babies trampled by the big kids. I thought we had agreed on a schedule!" Instead of solving the problem by decree, the director asked the two teachers to discuss it with her at the weekly staff meeting devoted to administrative issues. The discussion became heated almost immediately, as one teacher defended herself from what felt like an attack. "We can't always stick to a precise schedule for coming outside," she said. "Sometimes we finish our group time early, or the children just seem more restless than usual." The other teacher reacted by emphasizing her point even more strongly, and both voices rose in volume. The director intervened, reminding them that the goal was to find a solution that worked for everyone. After much discussion, they decided that what they really needed was a fence to create a protected space for the babies so that both age groups could be outside at the same time. The director agreed to apply for a grant to provide the needed funds, and the two teachers found a way to coordinate their schedules in the meantime. The older children were fascinated with the construction of the fence, calling it the "baby cage!" and the subsequent interactions between older and younger children through the fence have been a joy for the adults and children on both sides.

In this example, the answers to the questions "Where are we?" and "Where do we want to go?" were somewhat distorted by the teachers' strong feelings. One was exasperated at working so hard to get outside, only to have to come right back in; the other was equally frustrated at the prospect of being chained to a rigid time schedule. Both leapt to the conclusion that the only answer to "where do we want to go" was the enforcement of that rigid schedule, and the conversation turned to confrontation as they argued about how to get to that point. Once they understood that they both agreed on the importance of outdoor play *and* a flexible schedule, they could begin to work toward a win-win solution.

❓ DECISIONS, DECISIONS . . .

Your center has a policy of sending a brief note home when children get scrapes and bumps on the playground. You have noticed that these are occurring more frequently of late and worry that a more serious accident could occur. How can you monitor the quality of the care children receive on the playground? List the factors you want to consider.

STANDARDS

Standards are defined as the designated level or degree of quality that is proper and adequate for a specific purpose. They are the measuring sticks used to determine how well the center is accomplishing its aims. As discussed in previous chapters, standards for child development programs are set by a number of different bodies, each with a particular focus. Some standards apply to the program as a whole, others apply to some particular aspect such as health and safety, and still others address qualifications required for individuals working in the program, such as teacher licensure in public school programs or a child development associate (CDA) credential in Head Start. Many states have established standards for child outcomes, that is, commonly held expectations for what children should know and be able to do by the end of the program (Scott-Little, Kagan, & Frelow, 2005). (See Table 15.1.)

Standards vary with regard to the level of quality they mandate. State governments, for example, establish licensing agencies to act on behalf of the public and enforce rules that protect children's safety and welfare. These rules are considered minimum standards and govern the amount of space and equipment a program must provide, the number of staff members and their qualifications, health practices, fire safety, and many other areas. Some states have established a tiered system, awarding higher levels of licensing to programs that meet more stringent standards, such as the indicators of quality set forth in environmental rating scales for early childhood, infant–toddler, school-age, and family child-care settings (Harms, Clifford, & Cryer, 2005; Harms, Cryer, & Clifford, 1989, 2006; Harms, Jacobs, & White, 1995).

Professional organizations have also developed standards for child development programs. Some represent allied fields of health, sanitation, and fire safety. Others come from prominent early childhood professional groups, for example, *Developmentally*

TABLE 15.1 Sources and focus of standards applied to early childhood programs.

	Program	Staff	Child Outcome
State and Federal Government	State licensing regulations Tiered licensing Head Start performance standards	Caregiver certification Child development associate (CDA) Public school teacher licensure	Early learning standards
Allied Professional Organizations	American Public Health Association and the American Academy of Pediatrics (APHA/AAP): National standards for health and safety in child-care programs American Consumer Product Safety Commission: Guidelines for playground equipment and surfacing National Life Safety Fire Code	American Public Health Association and the American Academy of Pediatrics (APHA/AAP): National standards for health and safety in child-care programs	
Early Childhood Professional Organizations	National Association for the Education of Young Children (NAEYC) Guidelines for Developmentally Appropriate Practice NAEYC accreditation criteria DEC Recommended Practices in Early Intervention/Early Childhood Special Education	NAEYC Guidelines for Developmentally Appropriate Practice NAEYC Accreditation Criteria	

Appropriate Practice in Early Childhood Programs Serving Children from Birth through Age 8 (Copple & Bredekamp, 2009) from the National Association for the Education of Young Children; and DEC Recommended Practices in Early Intervention/Early Childhood Education (Sandall, Hemmeter, Smith, & McLean, 2005) from the Division for Early Childhood (DEC) of the Council for Exceptional Children.

Accreditation

Although programs may strive to adhere to the highest professional standards because it is the right thing to do, they may also decide to take the next step. Accreditation is the process of obtaining recognition or credit for achieving quality. The National Association for the Education of Young Children (NAEYC) instituted a system for early childhood programs to obtain such recognition in 1985. Since that time, other organizations, targeting more narrow population segments, have followed suit. Examples include the National Association for Family Child Care, the National AfterSchool Association, the American Montessori Society, the Association of Christian Schools International, and the Evangelical Lutheran Education Association. Currently, more than 8,000 programs have earned NAEYC accreditation.

The NAEYC Academy for Early Childhood Program Accreditation is responsible for the NAEYC program and provides various forms of technical assistance to help programs as they go through the process. The standards were revised in 2005 and may be found at the NAEYC website: http://www.naeyc.org/academy/primary/standardsintro. Both the original and the revised standards were reviewed and debated by early childhood professionals and other stakeholders across the nation. The criteria are related to 10 program standards: relationships, curriculum, teaching, assessment of child progress, health, teachers, families, community relationships, physical environment, and leadership and management.

Steps in the accreditation process include a self-study and self-assessment, submitting documentation of compliance with criteria, and participation in a site visit conducted by trained NAEYC assessors. Programs produce evidence of their compliance with criteria in five forms: classroom portfolios, a family survey, teaching staff survey, program portfolio, and observation of practices. Some argue that the revised standards have become so stringent and the accreditation process so costly that only an elite few will be able to achieve accreditation. They suggest that simpler, less costly, state-level quality rating systems may become an intermediate step toward accreditation for many. But standards vary from state to state, and NAEYC accreditation, the closest thing to national standards in the United States, is still regarded as the "gold standard" for many in the profession (Neugebauer, 2009). NAEYC offers online technical assistance to help programs meet the criteria (http://www.naeyc.org/academy/) as well as scholarships to help programs pay the fee associated with each step of the process. This video gives an overview of the benefits of accreditation for children, families, and child development programs.

EVALUATING PROGRAM QUALITY

To evaluate something is to find the value of it. According to the U.S. Child Care Bureau,

> program evaluation is a systematic process of clearly articulating the services and desired outcomes of an intervention or program. Data tied to the program goals documents the quality and effectiveness of the program over time. Program evaluation can incorporate many methods of data collection, such as child assessment, observations of practice, measures of the environment, and surveys or interviews of teachers or parents. (National Child Care Information and Technical Assistance Center, 2008)

You may have heard of two other terms in connection with evaluation. Programs use **formative evaluation** throughout their operation to obtain the feedback they need to improve their performance; **summative evaluation** occurs after the fact and summarizes what the program accomplished, perhaps in a final report to a funding body.

As we have seen, child development programs are part of the social–cultural environment. A widely publicized study in the mid-1990s clearly demonstrated how a governmental system, as part of that environment, affects center quality. It found that the quality of care at most centers in the United States is poor to mediocre—even lower for infants and toddlers—and that higher-quality care was associated with more stringent licensing standards as well as the availability of outside funding through donations, employer sponsorship, or public subsidies (Cost, Quality, and Child Outcomes Study Team, 1995, pp. 2–5). In addition to regulations and financial support, other elements of the social–cultural environment that either establish or affect center standards include professional organizations, market forces, and public opinion. All of these elements interact to raise or lower the level of quality deemed acceptable for out-of-home child care.

LEADERSHIP LENS

Conceptual leadership—taking the big picture into account—is required to deal with the complex issue of raising standards. According to Kagan and Neuman (1997), conceptual leadership transcends even visionary leadership. Visionary leaders focus on their own organizations, while conceptual leaders are concerned about broad issues of social justice and human betterment. Kagan and Neuman identify five key characteristics of conceptual leaders: "They (1) think in terms of the whole field; (2) are responsive to diverse perspectives; (3) think long term; (4) push the what-is to the what-might-be—thinking possibility, invention, and vision; and (5) seek to impact the social good." The many individuals who participated in the original as well as subsequent revisions of NAEYC's accreditation criteria and position statement on developmentally appropriate practice were practicing conceptual leadership.

Early childhood education leaders might advocate for more stringent standards regarding the educational qualifications of child-care workers, but if the public does not understand or concur with the importance of such qualifications, parents are likely to object to the higher rates that centers must charge in order to attract and retain highly qualified staff members with adequate salaries. Nor will governmental bodies be likely to subsidize such centers. If rules are perceived as unfair or too stringent, regulatory agencies will be unable to secure the support they need from the judicial system to deal with violators. When quality is viewed from the perspective of the ecological systems framework, it becomes clear that monitoring in the child development center must go hand in hand with establishing good relations with parents and with public and professional advocacy on behalf of the children and families.

Instead of becoming discouraged at this complex interplay of factors, leaders in the early childhood profession make the case for investment in such programs. They take every opportunity to point out that high-quality early childhood education raises the lifetime productivity of children and saves public expenditures on special education enrollment, juvenile delinquency, imprisonment, and welfare. They publicize facts about its immediate as well as long-term economic effects: child-care facilities employee large numbers of people, they generate taxable income in every state, and they make employment or the pursuit of higher education possible for hundreds of thousands of parents whose earnings contribute billions of dollars to the economy. In other words, conceptual leaders use their knowledge to help others to see issues from the broader perspective of promoting a common good.

TABLE 15.2 Examples of tools for measuring the quality of early childhood programs.	
Focus	**Examples**
Global assessment of program environment	Harms, T., Clifford, R. M., & Cryer, D. (2005). *Early childhood environment rating scale* (rev. ed.). New York: Teachers College Press.
	Harms, T., Cryer, D., & Clifford, R. M. (2006). *Infant/toddler environment rating scale* (rev. ed.). New York: Teachers College Press.
	Harms, T., Jacobs, E. V., & White, D. R. (1995). *School-age care environment rating scale*. New York: Teachers College Press.
	High/Scope Educational Research Foundation. (2003). *Preschool program quality assessment* (2nd ed.). Ypsilanti, MI: High/Scope Press.
Focus on teaching strategies and adult–child interactions	Goodson, B. D., Layzer, J. I., & Layzer, C. J. (2005). *Quality of early childhood care settings: Caregiver rating scale*. Cambridge, MA: Abt Associates.
	Pianta, R. C., LaParo, K. M., & Hamre, B. K. (2008). *Classroom assessment scoring system (CLASS)*. Baltimore, MD: Paul H. Brookes.
	Smith, M. W., Brady, J. P., & Anastasopoulos, L. (2008). *Early language and literacy classroom observation tool (ELLCO)*. Baltimore, MD: Paul H. Brookes.
Focus on program administration and management systems	Talan, T. N., & Bloom, P. J. (2004). *Program administration scale: Measuring early childhood leadership and management*. New York: Teachers College Press.
	Talan, T. N., & Bloom, P. J. (2009). *Business administration scale for family child care*. New York: Teachers College Press.

Since the release of the Cost, Quality, and Child Outcomes Study in 1995, media attention on the discoveries of neuroscience has generated great public awareness of early childhood as a critical period for brain development. Other research has highlighted the persistence of an "achievement gap" between middle-class children and their less-advantaged peers (Copple & Bredekamp, 2009). Awareness of these facts has proven to be a double-edged sword: contributing to growing public investment in early childhood education (e.g., the Universal PreK movement) on the one hand, while on the other hand putting pressure on programs for young children not only to meet standards, but to provide evidence of their effectiveness. In short, parents (or funding bodies) expect early childhood programs—in the private sector as well as in public schools—to be accountable, and to take responsibility for preparing young children to succeed in school. In response to this interest, and perhaps fueling it, there has been a proliferation of instruments for measuring everything from global quality to individual child performance (Macmillan & Neugebauer, 2006). Some examples are listed in Table 15.2.

Who Evaluates?

Monitoring and controlling the program for children is a central concern of administrators. All the other components (e.g., food service, safety and sanitation, health practices) exist in order to support that program. In addition to the manager's self-evaluation, at least five groups of people may provide helpful information regarding the center's program quality: children, teachers and other staff members, families, the community members, and professional organizations.

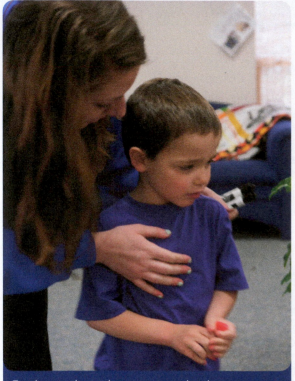

Teachers evaluate the program and make adjustments to meet the needs of individual children. Sometimes that means helping a child cope with the frustration of waiting for a turn with a popular toy.

CHILDREN EVALUATE A child development program has many customers: Parents who enroll their children are purchasing a service; society at large expects the programs to keep children safe and prepare them for later life. Certainly, one of the customers is the person who experiences the service firsthand—the child. One way that children provide feedback on how your center is doing is through their own development, as reflected in the types of assessments discussed earlier. But if the aim of quality management is customer satisfaction, then managers must be concerned with the way their young customers *experience* the program. Are they happy to come to school in the morning? Are they clean, rested, and well fed? Do the adults and children seem to enjoy each other's company? Do adults converse with children rather than telling them what to do and reprimanding them when they fail to comply? Are children greeted pleasantly on arrival and not left to find their own way to enter the play of other children? Does the pace of activity suit them so that they are not hurrying to keep up with others or waiting for others to catch up with them? Are they generally constructively engaged rather than wandering aimlessly? All are signs of satisfied customers that managers can observe as they walk around the center each day.

Of course, a few children here or there does not give you a picture of what the program is like for all the children or what it is like for one particular child over a longer span of time. You should augment this informal check with some systematic data collection. For example, you could choose one or more children to shadow for a day or a week, noting things such as the child's activity, mood, and partners in play or conversation at regular, predetermined intervals. Are the classrooms filled with the pleasant hum of busy children constructively engaged in a variety of intriguing activities? How much time is devoted to teacher-directed crafts or games and how much to projects that you and the other children instigate? This approach, which Katz (1998) referred to as a bottom-up view of program quality, puts you in the children's shoes and helps you see the program through their eyes.

? DECISIONS, DECISIONS . . .

Looking over the notes of your day's observation of 4-year-old Mia, you see that at least four times during the day, she cried for several minutes—when another child took something she was using, when she could not get her boots on, when she fell on the playground, and when she was told to lie on her cot at nap time. No adult approached her during any of these incidents, and each time she gradually stopped crying and went on to some other activity. What does this behavior suggest to you? As center manager, what should you do? Discuss your ideas with your classmates.

TEACHERS EVALUATE The teachers evaluate their planning, organizing, and interacting with the children, measuring their actions against professional standards. They make adjustments to correct shortcomings. They are wise to monitor, evaluate, and control from moment to moment. For example, if they offer an experience to the children and notice that some are unable to participate, they may conclude that the task is too difficult. That is an evaluation. The standard of performance is in the teacher's mind, based on prior knowledge and experience with children of this age. Using an instant evaluation, the teacher has at least two alternatives. The activity can be postponed until a later date when the children are more mature, or the teacher can make adjustments to scaffold the children's participation.

Educators assess young children to find out where they are developmentally and how much they have changed over time.

Teachers monitor, evaluate, and control their practices over longer time spans as well. For example, if they review their observational records and notice that children are not using a particular interest center in the classroom or not using the materials constructively, they can explore options to manage this. They might change the location of the interest center, rearrange or add new materials, or discuss the situation at group time to involve the children in problem solving.

As discussed earlier, teachers assess children's learning and development as part of program evaluation. More important from the teacher's standpoint, appropriate assessment serves as a guide to curriculum planning as well as a tool for building partnerships with parents. Teachers must set up systems to ensure that they collect the needed information (anecdotal records, checklists, photographs, video recordings, and work samples) for each child. They can collect these samples in a digital file for each child; each file can be organized into sections on physical, social, emotional, and cognitive development, with a list of developmental goals at the start of each section. Or teachers can collect paper artifacts and observation notes in a three-ring binder for each child. Whichever method they use, every few weeks, as they sort and add new items to the files, they can double-check to make sure they are observing and documenting the growth of the whole child and that no one is being overlooked. Obviously, teachers need time and support to organize, interpret, and share this information with families. One possibility is to plan to focus on two or three children one day, another two or three the next, and so on, until the entire class roster has been covered; then begin again at the top of the list and repeat the process. Another way of organizing this task is to focus on a particular developmental domain each week.

Teachers evaluate the effectiveness of the program and manager as evidenced by their motivation, job satisfaction, and feeling that they are supported and treated fairly. Managers can gauge how well they are doing by observing the teachers' enthusiasm and participation on one hand or absenteeism, complaints, and lethargy on the other. They can solicit verbal or written feedback at any time as well as through a regularly scheduled, formal evaluation, conducted via anonymous survey. Figure 15.1 is an example of such a tool.

Please respond to the following questions as carefully and objectively as possible. Return the survey in the envelope provided. Do not put your name on it. Your answers will remain completely confidential.

	Agree	Disagree	Not Sure
I understand the mission and goals of Rainbow Child Development Center. **Comment**	o	o	o
I have a clear understanding of my job duties and expectations for my performance. **Comment**	o	o	o
The center provides me with the resources (time, materials, training, and support) to do my job well. **Comment**	o	o	o
In comparison with others doing similar work in this community the compensation I receive is fair. **Comment**	o	o	o
My work is evaluated fairly and I receive timely feedback about the quality of my performance. **Comment**	o	o	o
I am given clear explanations and an opportunity to correct any deficiencies. **Comment**	o	o	o
I am encouraged to pursue professional development and have opportunities for advancement. **Comment**	o	o	o
The manager of the center is fair. **Comment**	o	o	o
The manager listens to employees' concerns and responds in a timely manner. **Comment**	o	o	o

FIGURE 15.1   Staff evaluation of program and manager.

The manager respects confidentiality and models professional behavior in dealings with employees. Comment	o	o	o
The manager facilitates positive relationships between staff and families. Comment	o	o	o
The manager is an effective advocate for employees and for the center with the board and the larger community. Comment	o	o	o

FIGURE 15.1 *(Continued)*

? DECISIONS, DECISIONS . . .

Michael, a 3-year-old with Down syndrome, had been coming to Rainbow Child Development Center for 2 months. The lead teacher in his classroom has observed that Michael has never joined large-group songs and games. Instead, he sits somewhat listlessly a little behind the others, his gaze wandering toward the ceiling. Discuss what the teacher should do. What should the manager do?

FAMILIES EVALUATE Families evaluate your program from the moment they step in the door. They may tell you directly what they think, or they may do so indirectly, communicating their satisfaction by referring friends and acquaintances to you, their dissatisfaction by withdrawing their children. Monitoring admissions, withdrawals, and the reasons for both can help you gain clues about the parents' evaluation of your center's program and service.

? DECISIONS, DECISIONS . . .

Two families abruptly withdrew their children from your center last week. They did not say anything to you, but another parent with whom you have a long-standing relationship has suggested that they were unhappy because it seemed their children had a different teacher every week. Your center *has* undergone several staff changes recently: One teacher had a baby and decided to stay at home, another found a higher-paying job in the public school system, and one of the new teachers you hired just did not work out. What should you do as manager?

In addition to these informal appraisals of families' attitudes toward your program, it is important to solicit their feedback systematically. The NAEYC guidelines

Families evaluate the program when they see their children enjoying activities or when they have an opportunity to review a portfolio of the child's work with the teacher.

for developmentally appropriate practice require that centers build reciprocal relationships with families (Copple & Bredekamp, 2009, p. 22–23), and this means communication has to go both ways. Many questions can be answered during a private conference, which may bring out more elaborate responses than a written questionnaire. You can ask questions such as "Do the center's hours fit your family's needs?" "Are your needs for consulting with the teacher being met?" "What changes would you suggest?"

Interviewing every family this way is time consuming and probably impractical in a large center. Therefore, you might develop a questionnaire such as the one in Figure 15.2 to get helpful feedback as well as draw the parents' attention to the high-quality features of your service. Ready-made survey instruments are available from many sources. (See Resources for Further Study at the end of this chapter.) Note that busy family members are more likely to respond to a survey that they can complete quickly, but the results may leave you to puzzle out exactly what they mean by certain responses. An alternative would be to ask a few open-ended questions, such as "What do you like best about . . . ?" or "What concerns do you have?" Although some may take the time to provide detailed, helpful responses, there is also the risk that others will give hasty, superficial answers or, worse yet, put the survey aside, never to be completed.

As mentioned earlier, a family survey is one component of the NAEYC accreditation process. DEC recommended practices go a step further, with a provision that family members participate in an annual program evaluation that "take[s] into account differing cultural, contextual, demographic, and experiential perspectives including those of parents and individuals with disabilities" (this is one of seven strands addressed by the standards) (Sandall et al., 2005, p. 179). Although the standard is intended to apply to programs serving children with disabilities, any program can aspire to the ideals it represents. It seems just good marketing practice to ask families to participate in designing your survey instrument and to translate it into other languages as needed. Because not all families will be comfortable with written communication, programs might supplement a survey with focus group discussions, perhaps moderated by a community representative with whom families feel they can speak freely.

THE COMMUNITY AND PROFESSION EVALUATE   Recall that some outside evaluations take place because they are required by law or a center's funding source (e.g., state licensure or public school approval). Others are solicited voluntarily, such as the final evaluation of a center's application for NAEYC accreditation. Still others are not really formal evaluations at all, but rather general impressions of your program in the minds of other child-care providers and members of the community at large.

Dear Families,

We want Rainbow Child Development Center to be the best it can be, and we need your help to make it so. Please let us know how we are doing in each of the following areas by checking the appropriate rating. You may add comments on the back and drop the completed form in the box inside the main entrance. Thanks for your participation!

	Agree	Disagree	Not Sure
My child enjoys coming to the center.	o	o	o
The center is clean and well maintained.	o	o	o
The outdoor play area is inviting, safe, and well maintained.	o	o	o
The center's fees are affordable.	o	o	o
The center's fees are comparable to other centers in the area.	o	o	o
The center's fees seem fair for the quality of care delivered.	o	o	o
Staff are friendly and courteous.	o	o	o
I received enough information, in person and in writing, to know what to expect regarding the centers policies and practices.	o	o	o
The services provided by the center measure up to what was promised.	o	o	o
I know who to ask if I have questions or concerns.	o	o	o
I know who my child's teacher is.	o	o	o
My child's teacher seems interested in my child.	o	o	o
I have regular opportunities to meet with my child's teacher to discuss progress and concerns.	o	o	o
The center does a good job keeping my child safe and healthy.	o	o	o
The center helps my child develop healthy habits (good nutrition, plenty of fresh air, vigorous activity, and rest).	o	o	o
The center helps my child learn to get along well with others.	o	o	o
The center is helping to prepare my child for success in school.	o	o	o
I am satisfied with the quality of care my child receives.	o	o	o
I would recommend the center to a friend.	o	o	o

FIGURE 15.2 Family evaluation of program.

The public relations strategies discussed in the previous chapter contribute to making these general impressions positive. It is also wise to think of other child-care providers as part of your professional community rather than just your competition. You may find it valuable to exchange evaluation services with other centers so you can gain new perspectives and learn from each other. Cultivating these relationships could lead to mutually beneficial collaboration and ultimately create a united voice for the profession in your community.

Managers evaluate the program by—and are themselves evaluated for—evidence of children's joyful engagement with each other and the materials offered.

THE MANAGER EVALUATES   As manager, you must monitor the program to compare its performance to your stated goals and with current professional standards. Informal spot checks can be done daily. More formalized periodic procedures—checking lesson plans, taking detailed notes in each group, or using checklists—are necessary.

The evaluations, standards, and feedback systems must be established with teacher input and carried out in an agreeable, supportive way to increase the teacher's confidence, motivation, and ability. An example of a teacher performance appraisal was provided in a previous chapter. (See Figure 8.4, p. 172.) Other possibilities can be found in the resources listed in the Technology Toolkit later in this chapter. Regardless of what instrument you use, staff members should be able to review it in advance to know what is expected of them and how they will be evaluated. It is unfair to add new items to the evaluation without notice.

Ideally, the elements of quality to be evaluated are established together with teachers and other center stakeholders. Recall from the discussion of management techniques in a previous chapter that staff members are more likely to follow through on goals for which they feel some ownership. When they do, the manager can evaluate by serving more as a mirror than as a judge.

Evaluations should be stated objectively and clearly. Instead of saying that a staff member does a "good job" providing a variety of art experiences for the children, the manager might indicate that this is observed only occasionally, adding that the same watercolors and manila paper have been put out on the art table every day for the last several weeks. This type of remark gives the teacher an opportunity to explain that he was trying to make sure that every child had an opportunity to paint with watercolors or that he wanted the children to explore additional possibilities with the same media. Another explanation might be that the teacher lacked other materials and did not know how to request them. Of course, a teacher may simply have no other ideas about what art experiences to offer the children. In a conference discussing the evaluation, the manager might learn something about the wisdom of offering the children repeated opportunities to experience materials, or the manager might take action to provide different materials and ensure that the teachers know how to get what they need. In the scenario about the art experiences, the evaluation becomes a training tool if the manager and teacher collaborate to establish a goal for the next evaluation and a plan of action for meeting that goal.

The possibility remains that a teacher's performance simply is not acceptable, in which case it is the manager's job to make this clear and state any expectations for improvement, as well as any consequences for the failure to do so. Ongoing professional development activities help the teachers become more effective partners in this aspect of their evaluation. The manager must document the results of all evaluations as well as warnings and steps taken to help an employee improve. When a teacher fails to improve in spite of these efforts, dismissal is the only option.

> ## ? DECISIONS, DECISIONS . . .
>
> ### Using an Ethical Framework
>
> Over the course of the past few months, you've noticed that the performance of one of your teachers has noticeably declined. She has missed several days of work and come in late on other days. Her coteacher mentioned to you that she seems distant and withdrawn, seldom smiling or engaging in the cheerful, playful interactions with children that had been her custom. Family members have begun to notice the change; a few have complained to you and even suggested that she be removed from the classroom. When you meet with the teacher for her annual evaluation, you learn what her colleagues and family members do not know: that she has recently been diagnosed with a serious, though not communicable, chronic disease. The physical effects of the disease may eventually make it impossible for her to do her job, but no one knows how far in the future that will happen, perhaps many years. Meanwhile, her family will not be able to make ends meet without the income from her job. She does not want her colleagues or the families of children in her room to know about her situation. What should you do? Which principles regarding responsibilities to children, families, and employees apply here?

THE MANAGER IS EVALUATED   As manager, you must regularly seek an evaluation of your own performance from the policy board and staff members so that you have the chance to improve your management and operation of the enterprise. You can work with the board and staff members to set up the evaluation process. You should learn much from it in a friendly, cooperative, and harmonious fashion, just as you expect your staff members to learn from their evaluations. Figure 15.3 is a suggested form for a manager's evaluation by the board.

By now it should be clear that maintaining high quality at the classroom level depends on the overall quality of a program's administrative practices. The Program Administration Scale (PAS) (Talan & Bloom, 2004) is a tool for assessing that quality. It is analogous to the environment rating scales that we have mentioned several times throughout this book, but it is broader in scope. The authors state that they were specifically interested in tapping "organizational practices that foster collaboration, diversity, cultural sensitivity, and social justice" (p. 1). Like the Early Childhood Environment Rating Scale, Revised Edition (ECERS-R) (Harms et al., 2005), the PAS uses a 7-point scale, from inadequate to excellent, to rate 25 items in 10 areas called subscales. The subscales are human resources development (including supervision and performance appraisal), personnel cost and allocation, center operations, child assessment, fiscal management, program planning and evaluation, family partnerships, marketing and public relations, technology, and staff qualifications.

Making Appropriate Use of Evaluation Results

The primary purpose of any evaluation should be to enhance program quality. That means an appropriate instrument must be used, the evaluation must be conducted objectively, and the results must be clearly understood so that they can inform decisions about possible changes in practice. It is the manager's job to model this process for staff members, helping them make constructive use of feedback (Guss et al., 2013).

Dear Board Member,

Please provide your feedback on _____'s performance of each essential function expected of the manager of Rainbow Child Development Center. You may add comments on the back and return the completed form in enclosed envelope. Thanks for your participation!

	Not Evident	Acceptable	Strong
The manager demonstrates knowledge of best practice and all applicable regulations and standards. **Comment:**	o	o	o
The manager recruits and hires qualified personnel and institutes an effective professional development program. **Comment:**	o	o	o
The manager delegates responsibility appropriately and insures that employees have adequate resources to perform effectively: e.g., appropriate group sizes, sufficient support staff, planning time, supplies and materials. **Comment:**	o	o	o
The manager supervises and mentors employees effectively with clearly stated expectations, regular performance evaluations, and feedback. **Comment:**	o	o	o
The manager handles the center's finances appropriately. **Comment:**	o	o	o
The manager communicates effectively with families and facilitates positive relationships between families and teachers. **Comment:**	o	o	o
The manager communicates effectively with board members, serves as a liaison between board and center staff, and carries out board directives efficiently. **Comment:**	o	o	o

FIGURE 15.3 Board evaluation of manager.

The manager deals effectively with licensing or other public agencies. **Comment:**	o	o	o
The manager promotes the center's public image through effective marketing and public relations strategies. **Comment:**	o	o	o

FIGURE 15.3 *(Continued)*

Monitoring and controlling for quality is an ongoing process. There are inevitably times when a program fails to meet one or more particular standards, whether its own or those established by an outside agency. In general, such occasions should be handled as an opportunity to correct the problem and improve services. Becoming defensive may be tempting, particularly if the deficiency affects the program's licensing status or funding, but it usually just wastes precious energy. It may help to step back and put the particular deficiency into perspective. Failing to meet one criterion does not necessarily mean the program is "bad." NAEYC accreditation standards, for example, identify criteria that all centers must meet (e.g., minimum adult–child ratios, prohibition of corporal punishment), but beyond that the expectation is that centers will achieve compliance with 80 percent of the criteria associated with program standards. It is also possible to achieve a "good" or "excellent" overall score on the environmental rating scales with less than perfect scores on each individual item. Notice how the director in this video helps the teacher to see that even requirements that seem "picky" are important and to use evaluation results to make needed corrections.

On the other hand, failure to meet some standards can have serious consequences for children, as well as legal or funding implications for the program. Unless a problem presents an immediate danger for children, licensing agencies generally give programs a period of time to correct the situation. Your job is to make the correction and submit documentation that you have done so to your licensing representative.

Because evaluators are human, they can sometimes be in error. If you feel that this has happened to your program, it is important to approach the situation calmly and professionally. Present evidence that your program does in fact meet the criteria in question and request a reevaluation. If you are unsuccessful, find out what options you have for appeal or mediation and follow through.

ASSESSING OUTCOMES FOR CHILDREN

To assess something is to measure its quantity or weight. Assessment is part of the evaluation process. Educators assess young children to find out where they are developmentally and perhaps how much they have changed since the last time they were assessed. The information contributes to an impression of how well a program is doing—an evaluation. We evaluate the program's effectiveness, not the children. It is important to note that assessment is not the same as testing; it involves gathering information from many sources that may or may not include a formal test. An assessment of an individual child should be used only to inform decisions about that child. Information from assessments of a group of children should also be used to help teachers tailor curriculum. For purposes of evaluating a program, assessment results for all the children, or for a representative sample, should be aggregated (combined) to give an idea of how the group as a whole is doing.

Efforts to evaluate early childhood programs have traditionally emphasized "inputs," or the degree to which programs provided the conditions required for children to thrive. These conditions can be categorized as **structural variables** (e.g., class size, materials available, teacher qualifications) or **process variables** (e.g., teaching strategies and quality of adult–child interactions). With the increasing demand for accountability, the emphasis has shifted somewhat toward outcomes, or measures of change in children's knowledge, skills, and abilities. The good news is that this type of evidence can bring greater credibility and economic support for the early childhood field and may, in fact, be a catalyst for meaningful conversations about appropriate assessment among teachers, family members, and public stakeholders (Israel, 2004). The risk, in the minds of some early childhood professionals, is that this shift can push programs to resort to developmentally inappropriate practices in order to meet arbitrary performance expectations. They worry that a focus on academics will overshadow the importance of social, emotional, and physical development; require costly investments in staff training; and introduce bias when applied to children with disabilities or those who are learning English (National Early Childhood Accountability Task Force, 2007).

Assessment approaches include **direct assessments**, sometimes called on demand, in which a teacher asks a child to answer questions or perform a specific task; **observational assessments**, which are made during a designated activity, with performance measured according to a rubric or checklist; and **authentic assessments**, which are based on observations of children in naturally occurring activities that are then analyzed or catalogued in terms of the program's goals or learning standards for children (Bornfreund, 2013). One example of this type of assessment is **portfolio assessment**, which is the systematic collection of examples of children's work and teacher's observation notes to provide evidence of children's growth in knowledge, skills, and abilities over time. Teachers who enlist children's participation in selecting the examples help them to think about their own thinking. This is another way of fulfilling the ultimate goal of assessment to support children's learning (Laski, 2013).

All types of assessment require training to ensure that they are administered appropriately, and each has its strengths and limitations. Because the first two approaches are **standardized assessments**, i.e., based on a set of standard questions or tasks that children either get right or not, they are thought to be more objective and less susceptible to errors of interpretation. For example, a teacher might pull children aside one at a time and ask them to identify or copy specific shapes, point to particular alphabet letters, or count various quantities of small items. Results for one child or group of children can be compared with established norms for each task. However, such assessments can disrupt classroom routines when children are pulled out, and they sometimes incur expenses for substitute teachers who can keep the rest of the class activities on schedule. Furthermore, such assessments cannot gauge social or emotional development, and they may fail to reflect a child's true cognitive ability if the child is uncomfortable or distracted or because of language or cultural barriers.

Authentic assessments avoid many of these drawbacks because they are unobtrusive and occur over time, providing maximum opportunity for assessors to capture what a child can do in all domains. A teacher interested in whether children understand number concepts, for example, can observe them as they play board games requiring that they move pieces a particular number of spaces or argue that someone took more crackers than another. This **video** provides a brief glimpse of a teacher sitting near and carefully observing two children who are playing with blocks. Try to think of what she might be noticing about the boy's behaviors and then watch this **video** to hear what she has to say.

Because there are no predetermined questions for authentic assessments, teachers cannot teach to the test. Still, teachers' interpretations of what they observe can result in inaccurate judgments due to language or cultural barriers or some other personal bias (National Early Childhood Accountability Task Force, 2007, pp. 83–84).

Regardless of the approach adopted, that approach it must be used appropriately for it to have any value, and that requires training for staff members. This is particularly crucial because some research indicates that many early childhood teachers are either using inappropriate assessment strategies with young children, or they are using appropriate instruments in an inappropriate way (Brewer, 2006). Table 15.3 lists several examples of each type of assessment instrument.

Authentic assessments are valued in early childhood education because they capture what the child is able to do in real-life situations rather than how the child performs on isolated tasks in artificial situations (Bagnato & Simeonsson, 2007). Observations can take place in the classroom as described above, or family members can be interviewed regarding what the child does at home. Engaging families in this type of collaborative assessment promotes more two-way communication with many benefits for children, their families, and the programs that serve them. Families provide valuable information to round out the overall picture of the child's competencies

TABLE 15.3   Examples of instruments for assessing children's abilities.

Type	Examples
Observation in regular classroom activities	Dodge, D. T., Colker, L., & Heroman, C. (2006). *Creative curriculum developmental continuum assessment toolkit for infants, toddlers and twos*. Washington, DC: Teaching Strategies; and Dodge, D. T., Colker, L., & Heroman, C. (2002) *Creative curriculum developmental continuum assessment toolkit ages 3–5*. Washington, DC: Teaching Strategies. www.teachingstrategies.com
	High/Scope Educational Research Foundation. (2005). *Infant and toddler child observation record*, Ypsilanti, MI: High/Scope Press; and High/Scope Educational Research Foundation. (2003) *Preschool child observation record* (2nd ed.). Ypsilanti, MI: High/Scope Press. www.highscope.org
	Meisels, S. J., Marsden, D. B., Dichtelmiller, M. K., & Jablon, J. R. (2001). *Work sampling system*. San Antonio, TX: Pearson. http://pearsonassess.com
Observation in other settings	Bricker, D. (Ed.). (2002). *Assessment, evaluation, and programming system (AEPS®) for infants and children*. Baltimore, MD: Paul H. Brookes. Interactive version at http://www.aepsinteractive.com/
	Linder, T. (2008). *Transdisciplinary play-based assessment* (2nd ed.). Baltimore, MD: Paul H. Brookes. http://brookespublishing.com/store/books/linder-tpbai2/index.htm
Parent/caregiver interview	Squires, J., & Bricker, D. (2009). *Ages and stages questionnaire (ASQ-3)*. Baltimore, MD: Paul H. Brookes. http://www.brookespublishing.com/
Individually administered	Brigance, A. H. (2009). *Brigance early childhood screens (ages 0–35 months, 3–5 years, K–1); Developmental inventory 0–7 years*. North Billerica, MA: Curriculum Associates.
	Mardell, C., & Goldenberg, D. S. (1998). *Developmental indicators for the assessment of learning (DIAL-3)*. San Antonio, TX: Pearson. http://pearsonassess.com
	Sanford, A. R., Zelman, J. G., Hardin, B. J., & Peisner-Feinberg, E. (2004). *Learning accomplishments profile (LAP-3)*. Lewisville, NC: Kaplan Early Learning Company. http://www.kaplanco.com/curriculum/LAP3_index.asp

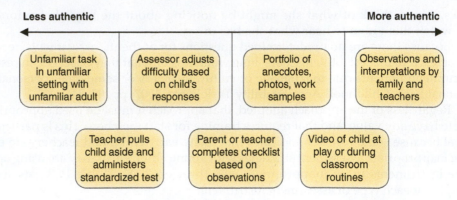

FIGURE 15.4   Continuum of authenticity in assessment approaches.

because they see that child in many settings and situations and under many conditions. They learn more about developmental expectations for children and become part of a team with the center's staff (Caspe et al., 2013).

The concern about authentic assessment has particular importance in intervention and early childhood special education, but the principles have been applied by the broader, early childhood field as well as education in general. Authenticity or the ability to capture a "true" picture of the child can be thought of occurring along a continuum, with the least authentic or most artificial approaches at one end and the most authentic approaches, those most indicative of the child's actual functioning at home as well as in school, at the other.

As illustrated in Figure 15.4, the least authentic assessment involves an unfamiliar situation, perhaps with an unfamiliar adult, asking the child to perform unfamiliar tasks. Moving along the continuum, a familiar teacher may be able to elicit a performance that more accurately reflects a child's ability. Adjusting the level of difficulty as the assessment proceeds is likely to yield a truer picture because it avoids the possibility that a child will stop trying if she or he is bored or frustrated by tasks that are too easy or too difficult. Checklists, questionnaires, or parent interviews represent a midpoint because they focus on what children do in the typical settings of their daily lives. The resulting products, however, are made up of the assessor's judgment about whether or not a child has demonstrated a particular type of task, rather than actual evidence of the child's performance, such as the anecdotes, photographs, and work samples included in portfolios. Video clips of children actually engaged in play or classroom routines allow any observer to make an independent judgment about their developmental significance, providing what George Forman (2009), a pioneer in the use of technology for such purposes, calls the democratization of documentation. Finally, what is captured in videos or other forms of documentation will be understood more fully and yield a truer, more authentic assessment of a child if it is considered alongside family observations and interpretations.

To avoid these pitfalls, managers must retain a strong focus on the "inputs" that will produce desired "outcomes." Although more study is needed to determine exactly which components of quality are most crucial, research has shown that higher quality in early child-care and education programs is positively correlated with higher academic and language outcomes and better social skills (Burchinal et al., 2009). The *assessment* of child outcomes, then, is just one part of a cyclical process of program *evaluation,* as illustrated in Figure 15.5.

The manager begins by recruiting well-qualified staff members and then provides the support, resources, and ongoing professional development they need in order to do their jobs well. Those staff members, in turn, collaborate with the manager to create and maintain the physical and social environment; design and implement curriculum; and

An effective manager...

recruits and supports well-qualified staff...

who collaborate to create developmentally appropriate physical and social environments;...

design and implement developmentally appropriate curriculum; and...

cultivate respectful, reciprocal relationships with families...

leading to positive child outcomes and family satisfaction-evidence of...

High Quality Programs for Young Children

FIGURE 15.5 Evaluation and assessment cycle in high-quality programs for young children.

cultivate respectful, reciprocal relationships with families. All of these inputs can be measured with a variety of program evaluation tools, using results to guide improvements. Ultimately, they contribute to the outcomes: developmental gains for children and high levels of family satisfaction, the assessments of which become part of the evidence that the manager is functioning effectively.

Technology Toolkit

- Locate and print reproducible forms for evaluating aspects of program quality in the *Exchange* CD Book, *Taking Stock: Tools for Evaluating Programs, Directors, Teachers and Children* (www.ccie.com).

- Use an early childhood curriculum that includes a companion system for digitally recording and coding observations and generating reports. Examples include High/Scope and The Creative Curriculum; each has both an infant–toddler and a preschool version. (See Table 15.2.)

- Visit the website for the PreK–K Teachers' Performance Appraisal Instrument (PKKTPAI) at http://education.uncc.edu/pkktpai/ to access an instrument for evaluating teacher performance that can be used as a basis for ongoing professional development planning. The instrument is part of a training project created by the North Carolina Office of School Readiness and the University of North Carolina at Charlotte.

Conclusion

Monitoring and controlling for quality are major concerns for a manager. Both involve evaluation of overall program quality and staff performance as well as assessment of children's learning and family satisfaction. Every aspect of the center must come under regular scrutiny, and the resulting information must be put to use to improve program quality. Various publics share in the monitoring or evaluating function: the board; the teachers; the manager; other staff members; families; the community; professional organizations; and, most of all, the children, whose ready participation and enjoyment of the experiences offered signals their satisfaction.

Evaluation may be used as a step toward improvement (formative) or as a final statement of accomplishment (summative). By setting standards, measuring performance, and leading staff members to correct problems, the manager performs essential monitoring and controlling functions. Minimum standards are embodied in local and state licensing regulations, with quality rating systems and NAEYC accreditation criteria establishing higher benchmarks.

Assessment of children's learning and development is one aspect of overall program evaluation. Assessment approaches range from formal standardized instruments to observation-based. Authentic assessment taps real-life examples as opposed to artificial approximations.

Questions for Review

1. Describe the manager's role in monitoring and controlling for quality.

2. Explain the elements of program evaluation: Who is involved and what is evaluated?

3. Discuss the advantages and drawbacks of two types of assessment of children's learning.

Professional Portfolio

1. Locate one of the instruments listed in Table 15.1 for evaluating overall program quality. Describe how you might use the instrument and give specific examples of what you should do with your findings.

2. Assume that you are the manager of a child development center that has received a "poor" rating from the licensing consultant because staff members failed to wash their hands at required times—before preparing and serving food, after diapering, or after helping children wipe their noses. Develop a plan to correct this problem. Describe who will take what action when and how.

3. Develop a questionnaire to evaluate parent satisfaction with a child development program. Describe when and how often you will administer the questionnaire, how to encourage responses, and what you should do with the findings.

Resources for Further Study

PRINT

Bloom, P. J. (2010). *A great place to work: Creating a healthy organizational climate.* Lake Forest, IL: New Horizons.

Cryer, D., Harms, T., & Riley, C. (2004). *All about the ITERS-R: A detailed guide in words and pictures to be used with the ITERS-R* and *All about the ECERS-R: A detailed guide in words and pictures to be used with the ECERS-R.* Lewisville, NC: PACT House Publishing.

Freeman, N. K., & Brown, M. H. (2000, September). Evaluating the child care director: The collaborative professional assessment process. *Young Children, 55*(5), 20–28.

Saxton, R. R., Dombro, A. L., Bingham, G. E. & Kelly, W. (2013, July). The Piramide Approach: A conversation about deepening children's learning. *Young Children, 68*(3), pp. 80–86.

Websites

DEC RECOMMENDED PRACTICES: PARENT CHECKLIST

http://www.dec-sped.org/uploads/docs/about_dec/recommended_practices_tools/Parent%20Checklist.pdf

A checklist created by the Council for Exceptional Children, Division for Early Childhood, based on DEC Recommended Practices in Early Intervention/Early Childhood Education. Although primarily designed for use by parents of children with special needs, it could easily be adapted for use with all families.

EARLY CHILDHOOD JOB SATISFACTION SURVEY TOOL

http://mccormickcenter.nl.edu/early-childhood-job-satisfaction-survey-tool/

A career guidance tool that early childhood directors can use with staff members. The resulting profile helps staff members reflect on those aspects of their work that contribute most to job fulfillment. Developed by the McCormick Center for Early Childhood Leadership. The home page includes a link to subscribe to a free monthly e-bulletin.

MAKING LEARNING VISIBLE

http://www.makinglearningvisibleresources.org/

Website for a collaborative effort of Project Zero at the Harvard Graduate School of Education and the Municipal Preschools and Infant–Toddler Centers of Reggio Emilia, Italy. The website includes detailed examples of documentation to aid teachers' reflection, to be shared with learners, and to be shared with a wider audience.

NAEYC ACCREDITATION OF PROGRAMS FOR YOUNG CHILDREN

http://www.naeyc.org/academy/

Information and resources about the NAEYC accreditation criteria and the process to become NAEYC accredited.

RESULTS MATTER VIDEO LIBRARY

http://www.cde.state.co.us/resultsmatter/RMVideoSeries.htm

Collection of video clips provided at no cost by the Colorado Department of Education to provide early child-care and education providers opportunities to practice observation, documentation, and assessment skills. See especially the section titled Clips for Practicing Observation, Documentation and Assessment Skills.

GLOSSARY

accreditation The process of obtaining recognition or credit for achieving quality.

active listening Using facial expression, gestures, and body language to indicate attention and rephrasing statements to indicate understanding.

active reflection Thinking about what is happening, possible courses of action, and probable outcomes while in the midst of challenging experiences.

advisory board A group of individuals, usually representing various areas of expertise, recruited for the purpose of providing advice to management. The group may be formally or informally organized.

advocacy Speaking or acting on behalf of an individual, group, or cause.

assessment The process of measuring the quantity or weight of something, for example, measurement of children's knowledge, skills, and abilities.

authentic assessment Process of measuring a child's knowledge, skills, and abilities by observing them in naturally occurring activities and analyzing findings in terms of the program's goals or learning standards for children.

authoritarian A parenting style characterized by high expectations for mature behavior, strict control methods, and little emotional support or explanation for rules.

authoritative A parenting style that balances high expectations and firm limits with clear explanations of the reasons for those limits and the consequences for transgression, together with an attitude of caring and support.

autocratic leader One who holds most of the authority in an organization and focuses on getting the job done rather than on people's feelings.

behavioral paradigm A characteristic of organization theory that focuses on the group rather than the individual. It views social connections and job satisfaction as more powerful than economic motivators; social change rather than profit is seen as the goal.

behaviorist *See* environmentalist.

boundaries Degree to which a family is open to outside influences; ranges from enmeshed to disengaged.

budget A plan, expressed in dollar amounts, for how an organization will use its resources to meet its goals. A *start-up budget* is a plan for starting a new program from scratch, an *operational budget* plans for the upcoming year, and a *narrative budget* is a written explanation of what is included in each category and why.

cash-flow analysis A tool that tracks the rate at which money is coming in and going out. It shows how much cash your program has on hand and compares expected receipts and expenses with the actual figures for each month.

central concept A statement that describes the program's ultimate goal in general terms. Also known as *vision* and *mission statement*.

central-satellite A pattern of decision making in which a central decision is followed by several satellite decisions, each of which depends on the central decision

chain pattern A series of decisions characterized by a straight line, each decision being dependent on the preceding choice.

child abuse Any recent act or failure to act on the part of a parent or caretaker that results in death, serious physical or emotional harm, sexual abuse, or exploitation.

child development center A facility that provides out-of-home education and care for young children in groups, a service that supplements the education and care parents give their children. The term encompasses programs that are full- or part-day; profit or nonprofit; and those known as preschools, child-care centers, kindergarten, prekindergarten, cooperative, Head Start, or variations of any of these.

child-care trilemma Reference to the challenge faced by child-care programs in achieving program quality, fair compensation, and affordability.

classical paradigm A characteristic of organization theory that views the individual worker as the unit of analysis; assumes that monetary rewards will be effective motivators because workers are rational beings.

climate Emotional and physical qualities of the child's home life.

community reflection A particular type of proactive reflection in which a group of managers approaches similar questions under the guidance of a facilitator.

consensus leader *See* participative leader.

consultative leader *See* participative leader.

consumer An economic term referring to an individual or organization that acquires goods or services, usually in return for payment.

continuity of care The practice of ensuring that children remain with the same primary caregiver for a sufficient period of time (ideally for the first three years of life) to form a healthy attachment that supports overall development.

controlling Stating the standards, measuring performance against standards, and either correcting any deviations or modifying any standards that prove unrealistic or inappropriate.

cultural responsiveness The ability to communicate across these cultural lines and to collaborate effectively with different people. Also known as *cross-cultural competence.*

curriculum coordinator An individual assigned to help plan programs for children and advise teachers about curriculum choices and children's behaviors.

cycle menu A 15- or 20-day sequence of menus repeated throughout a season with minimal changes.

decentralized authority Sharing responsibility and decision-making power among employees rather than concentrating it in the hands of management.

democratic leader *See* participative leader.

density The number and size of the people who use a space at one time.

direct assessment Process of measuring a child's knowledge, skills, or abilities in which a teacher asks a child to answer questions or perform a specific task. Also known as *on-demand assessment.*

disinfectant A product that destroys germs on hard, non-porous surfaces such as diaper change tables, countertops, door and cabinet handles, and toilets and other bathroom surfaces.

early intervention Services for children from birth to age 3 with or at risk for developmental delays or disabilities. Some examples of early intervention services are speech therapy, occupational therapy, and physical therapy.

early learning guidelines *See* early learning standards.

early learning standards Statements of what young children should know or be able to do by the end of their participation in a preschool program. Similar standards for children under 3 are called early learning guidelines.

ecological model of human development Theory of Uri Bronfenbrenner that defines development as the child's growing competence within, and understanding of, a series of concentric systems, beginning with the family (microsystem) and culminating with the society at large (macrosystem).

ecological Descriptor applied to development theory that considers the individual within the context of all the systems comprising his or her environment

economic rationalism The view that parents bear sole responsibility for their children and thus for providing substitute care when they are unavailable.

emotional abuse A pattern of behavior that impairs a child's emotional development or sense of self-worth. This may include constant criticism, threats, or rejection, as well

as withholding love, support, or guidance. Also known as *psychological abuse.*

emotional intelligence The ability to recognize, express, and manage one's feelings and to apply these skills to relationships with others.

emotional labor The psychological effort involved in controlling the expression of one's emotions on the job.

environmentalist Descriptor applied to development theory that focuses on the ways that growth and development can be influenced from the outside. Also known as *behaviorist.*

equilibrium Consistency achieved when families establish a comfortable balance in their lives. It may be upset by sudden change, such as illness or a job loss, that disrupts the family's ability to function.

ethical decision Choosing what is right or wrong according to the accepted principles of a profession.

ethical dilemma Situation in which two or more basic principles are in conflict so that any course of action seems to violate one or the other.

extrinsic motivation Actions driven by external rewards or punishments.

facilities management The competency required to create and maintain space that supports human interactions.

family ecosystem framework An approach to understanding families by examining interactions within and across the physical–biological, human-built, and social–cultural environments.

family engagement An ongoing, reciprocal, strengths-based partnership between families and their children's early childhood education program.

family-friendly practice Professional practices based on conscious efforts to acknowledge the central role of families in their children's development and to accommodate the particular needs of diverse families.

fertility rate The number of children the average woman is predicted to have in her lifetime.

food insecurity A household condition of limited or uncertain access to adequate food.

foodborne illness Any illness resulting from consumption of contaminated food. Also known as *food poisoning.*

formative evaluation Process of gathering and analyzing feedback during an activity or operation in order to improve performance.

free-rein leader Manager who relinquishes authority to the group and expects its members to figure out the best way to accomplish a given task.

goals General statements of what a program hopes to achieve in the long term.

hierarchy   Distribution of power and control within a family. It is influenced by culture; it may be based on age, gender, or family position; and it can shift with the loss or addition of a family member.

human capital   The skills, talents, knowledge, and abilities that an individual can use to create economic value.

human capital   The sum of the traits such as knowledge, skills, abilities, and other personal characteristics that constitute an individual's ability to be a productive member of society.

human ratio   Mathematical ratio adjusted to account for the fact that each adult in a classroom actually interacts with all the children.

human-built environment   Constructions or alterations to the natural world, such as factories, roads, farms, and pollution, to fit human needs.

indirect guidance   Arranging a classroom environment to give children cues regarding expected behaviors.

instrumentalism   The view that a society acts in its own best interest when it funds child-care programs to counter the likelihood that abused or poor children will grow up to become burdens on society.

interactionist   Descriptor applied to development theory that examines the ways that internal and external forces interact to propel development.

intrinsic motivation   Deriving internal satisfaction in accomplishment without expectation of reward.

job analysis   The process of identifying the specific tasks associated with an existing job, the competencies (knowledge, skills, and abilities) directly related to performing those tasks, and the factors that are important for evaluating candidates for the position.

job classification   A means of comparing jobs within an organization and assigning a specific level to each based on degree of difficulty, responsibility, preparation required, and the amount of supervision necessary.

job description   A written statement describing the duties, hours, and specific responsibilities associated with a particular position.

job design   The process of laying out responsibilities and duties for a proposed job and describing how they are to be performed.

job enrichment   Adding challenge and responsibility to a job to increase its appeal to employees.

job specification   A detailed statement spelling out the type and level of education and previous experience required, essential personal characteristics and skills, responsibilities of the position, compensation, procedure for applying, a deadline, and contact information.

key claim   In marketing, a statement of what a business does or what it offers its clients.

key proof   Evidence offered in support of an organization's key claim.

leadership   The process of helping an organization clarify and affirm values, set broad goals, articulate a vision, and chart a course of action to achieve that vision.

leading   A process of directing and influencing others through example, talent, information, and personal interaction skills.

Learning Stories   A naturalistic, authentic approach to documenting and assessing young children's learning and development using images, descriptive narrative, and the teacher's interpretative remarks.

licensing   The mechanism by which the state prohibits a particular activity or enterprise and then selectively lifts that prohibition for individuals or organizations who meet specific requirements.

management by objectives (MBO)   A system designed to increase employee involvement and motivation by involving them in setting clearly defined objectives and measuring performance according to those objectives.

management by walking around   Management method emphasizing importance of frequent, informal, face-to-face contact with employees to build comfortable relationships.

management   The day-to-day work required to fulfill an organization's mission and make the vision a reality through processes of (1) setting specific goals, (2) allocating human and material resources judiciously for achieving the goals, (3) carrying out the work or action required to achieve the goals, (4) monitoring the outcome or product of the work or action based on established standards, and (5) making necessary adjustments or improvements to ensure that performance reaches or exceeds goals.

mandatory reporter   Individual belonging to one of the professions required by law to report to the appropriate authorities any evidence of a child's having been abused.

marketing   The process of promoting and selling a product or service. Marketing makes the presence of a business known and informs potential customers about the benefits of its services.

mathematical ratio   Numerical representation of the relationship between two numbers; in a classroom, the total number of adults compared with the total number of children.

maturationist   Descriptor applied to development theory holding that growth and development come largely from within the child and follow a predictable timetable.

medical home An approach to providing health-care services that are accessible, continuous, comprehensive, family-centered, coordinated, compassionate, and culturally effective.

mentor Individual who provides information, guidance, and emotional support for a person with less experience.

MESH An acronym that stands for the four categories of resources required for a child development center: materials, equipment, space, and human energy.

monitoring Being alert to and continuously observing for compliance with applicable standards.

multiple intelligences According to Howard Gardner, humans are capable of at least seven ways of knowing the world: language, logical–mathematical analysis, spatial representation, musical thinking, the use of the body to solve problems or to make things, an understanding of other individuals, and an understanding of themselves.

narrative budget *See* budget.

needs assessment A systematic process to acquire an accurate picture of the potential demand for a particular service or commodity in a given community.

neglect Failure of a parent, guardian, or other caregiver to provide for a child's basic needs. Neglect may be physical, medical, educational, or emotional.

nonprogrammed decisions *See* programmed decisions.

obesity Weight greater than what is generally considered healthy for a given height. It is associated with an increased likelihood of certain diseases and other health problems.

objectives Specific statements outlining the strategies or steps the program will take to reach its stated goals.

observational assessment Process of measuring a child's knowledge, skills, or abilities in which a teacher watches a child complete a designated activity and measures performance according to a rubric or checklist.

operational budget *See* budget.

operational planning *See* planning.

organization A group of people intentionally coordinated to achieve a common goal.

organizing Arranging elements (e.g., people, supplies, and equipment) and coordinating joint activities so that all of the interdependent parts contribute effectively to the desired goal.

participative leader One who involves group members in decision making. Includes *consultative leader,* who seeks the group's opinions but maintains final authority; *consensus leader,* who facilitate discussion until some level of agreement or consensus is achieved; and *democratic leader,* who bases decisions on majority vote.

Patient Protection and Affordable Care Act Legislation passed in 2010 aimed at increasing the affordability and accessibility of health-care insurance and reducing health-care costs through a system of mandates, subsidies, and tax credits. Also known as the *Affordable Care Act (ACA)* and *Obamacare.*

pedagogical leadership The state of being knowledgeable about, and able to apply, current theories and research findings in early childhood education, and being able to explain the reasons for particular teaching practices to other teachers, parents, and the public.

pedagogista Italian term for a staff member who works collaboratively with teachers from several centers to analyze and interpret observations, develop curriculum, and facilitate parent-teacher relations.

pedagogy The science of teaching.

permissive A parenting style characterized by low expectations, few demands, little information about reasons for expectations, and high levels of expressed caring and concern.

personal space A cubby, cot, or other space provided for a child's individual use and protected from infringement by others.

personnel management Process of deciding what jobs must be done, what skills or training are required, and how those jobs relate to one another (organizing) and then developing procedures for recruiting, selecting, and retaining employees to do the various jobs (staffing).

physical abuse Nonaccidental physical injury (ranging from minor bruises to severe fractures or death) as a result of punching, beating, kicking, biting, shaking, throwing, stabbing, choking, hitting (with a hand, stick, strap, or other object), burning, or otherwise harming a child that is inflicted by a parent, caregiver, or other person who has responsibility for the child.

physical–biological environment The natural world, including soil, climate, animals, vegetation, and mineral resources.

planning Management process of creating a mental image of an organization's goals and the methods for achieving those goals; three levels include *strategic planning* or identifying the overall master plan; *tactical planning,* identifying specific goals within the master plan and delegating responsibility for accomplishing them; and *operational planning,* spelling out steps for meeting goals.

policy board Group of individuals holding ultimate authority in an organization, making plans for services, hiring the individuals to carry out the plans, and monitoring the provision of the services.

policy   A general guideline that an organization follows in making decisions or taking action. It is developed by a policy board and stated in writing, in sufficiently broad terms to allow flexibility.

portfolio assessment   Systematic collection of examples of children's work and teacher's observation notes, organized to show children's growth in knowledge, skills, and abilities over time.

postmodern perspective   Critical rejection of belief that science can discover "reality" or "truth" because there is no such thing apart from our beliefs and perceptions, which are dominated by those in power at particular times and places.

prepared environment   A classroom arrangement with appropriate-size furniture and organized display of materials promoting children's ability to locate materials, use them independently, and replace them when finished.

proactive reflection   Thinking back after completing a particular task or project to review what happened, compare it to other experiences, formulate explanations, and make plans for what might be done differently another time.

procedure   A statement of steps required to accomplish a goal.

process variables   Fluid aspects of inputs, or the degree to which programs provide the conditions required for children to thrive (e.g., teaching strategies and quality of adult–child interactions).

program administrator   An individual responsible for planning, implementing, and evaluating a child-care, preschool or kindergarten program.

program evaluation   A systematic process of clearly articulating the services and desired outcomes of an intervention or program.

program type   Classification of child-care programs based on the central mission or purpose of the organization, often reflecting the program's historical roots.

programmed decisions   Those decisions made so frequently that they become routine and involve simply following prescribed procedures; contrasted with *nonprogrammed decisions,* which are made when new or more complicated situations arise.

project approach   Type of curriculum planning in which teachers identify a topic based on children's interests, then help the children organize an investigation of that topic, beginning with a discussion to elicit the children's current knowledge of the topic as well as their questions and curiosity. This investigation can consist of field trips, special

visitors, or other activities designed to gather information, and small-group work., and a culminating event to show what was learned.

proposal   A documented request that shows an organization's expertise and ability to fulfill the proposed project, including a timetable, budget, and procedures.

psychological type   Category ascribed to the human personality based on individual preferences in approaching and understanding the world (for example, extroverted versus introverted, thinking versus feeling).

public relations competency   Ability to apply knowledge to influence public perceptions of an organization.

public relations literacy   Understanding the importance of influencing public perceptions and strategies for doing so.

public relations   The process of promoting positive impressions and goodwill toward an individual or an organization in the community at large. It also includes the resulting public image or reputation of an individual or organization.

Quality Rating Improvement System (QRIS)   A method used by states to raise the quality of child care beyond minimal licensing requirements by establishing graduated standards, accountability processes, training and technical assistance for providers, financial incentives, and information for parents and consumers.

reflection   The process of looking back and making sense of one's experience.

reflective supervision   Collaborative process of holding regularly scheduled meetings with individual staff members to help them reflect on their experiences, thoughts, and feelings about their work with families, and to develop new insights or skills.

Reggio Emilia approach   An approach to early education developed in a town of northern Italy. It is based on an image of children as competent, capable protagonists of their own learning, and it features carefully planned environments; collaboration among children, teachers, and families; nurturing multiple "languages" or modes of expression; and documentation as a means of making learning visible.

request for proposals (RFP)   An announcement issued by a funding body outlining specific goals and inviting applications from individuals or agencies whose projects align with those goals.

resource   A means (a person or item) through or by which an end or goal is attained.

risk management   The continuing process of identifying, analyzing, and evaluating potential exposure to damage or loss and taking steps to reduce the effects.

risk Exposure to the possibility of damage or loss.

role The part that each member plays within the family (e.g., helper, victim).

rule Detailed statement of criteria and methods for procedures to be carried out.

rules The ways that family members live in relation to one another. The rules may be spoken or unspoken.

sanitizer A product that reduces germs on inanimate surfaces to levels considered safe by public health codes or regulations; for use on food contact surfaces and toys or other objects that children may place in their mouths.

scaffolding Process by which an adult or more experienced individual provides just the amount of help a child needs to perform a task or understand a concept that is just beyond the child's current abilities.

self-reflective knowledge An understanding of one's purpose or mission and of one's strengths and weaknesses in relation to that purpose.

self-regulation Ability to act intentionally rather than merely react to external force, and to inhibit particular behaviors and purposefully focus attention on a task.

servant leadership A leadership philosophy and set of practices based on sharing power, putting the needs of others first, and supporting their performance and continual development.

servicescape The physical, or built, environment as well as the social environment where a particular service is obtained.

sexual abuse Activities by a parent or caregiver such as fondling a child's genitals, penetration, incest, rape, sodomy, indecent exposure, and exploitation through prostitution or the production of pornographic materials.

social construction of knowledge Process by which adults and older children in a culture communicate with a child who is learning, thus aiding the child's thinking and learning.

social enrichment perspective The approach to funding child care that recognizes children as citizens with rights in the present. It is characteristic of policies in Europe, Australia, and New Zealand.

social media Internet services that provide opportunities for two-way communication with an online community. Some example of social media include Facebook, Twitter, LinkedIn, blogs, and YouTube.

social–cultural environment People and the abstract results of interactions between people, such as cultural values and institutions.

span of control The number of subordinates that a manager can handle effectively.

sponsorship Financial resources and associated governance structure for a child-care program.

staffing The process of recruiting and dealing with the human resources (human capital) required to perform an organization's functions.

staffing The process of recruiting, developing, and deploying the human resources (human capital) required to perform the functions of the center.

stakeholder A person or group who stands to benefit (or suffer) in some way as a result of an organization's success (or failure).

standardized assessment A test that is administered and scored in a consistent manner so that results for an individual can be compared with that of others.

standards The designated level or degree of quality that is proper and adequate for a specific purpose.

start-up budget *See* budget.

strategic planning *See* planning.

structural variables Fixed aspects of inputs, or the degree to which programs provide the conditions required for children to thrive (e.g., class size, materials available, teacher qualifications).

summative evaluation Review of what has been accomplished after completion of an activity or operation.

sustainability Practicing conservation of resources and reducing waste to protect the environment for future generations.

systems paradigm Type of organization theory based on cybernetics; it holds that any system must continuously adapt in response to feedback from its environment and to maintain equilibrium or to survive.

tactical planning *See* planning.

territoriality People's use of space to communicate ownership of areas they are occupying.

thematic approach Type of curriculum planning in which teachers select a topic (such as farm animals or community helpers) and organize activities or infuse materials related to that topic throughout the classroom.

theory An organized set of related ideas, concepts, and principles that describes and attempts to explain a particular phenomenon.

time block plan Method of planning a daily schedule by designating ample periods for each particular type of activity, allowing for flexibility within each block of time.

total quality management An approach to management based on the belief that organizations must strive for continuous improvement in order to survive; power and responsibility are shared among all levels of the organization, with a primary focus on customer satisfaction.

universal design Characterizes products and environments designed to be usable by people of all ages and/or abilities, without the need for adaptation.

Universal PreK An initiative aimed at making publicly funded preschool services available to all 3- and 4-year-olds on a voluntary basis.

zone of proximal development (ZPD) Cutting edge of child's cognitive development; those concepts or skills beyond the child's current ability but that the child can tackle with help.

REFERENCES

Adams, G., Tout, K., & Zaslow, M. (2007, May). *Early care and education for children in low-income families: Patterns of use, quality, and potential policy implications.* Paper 4 prepared for the Urban Institute and Child Trends Roundtable on Children in Low-Income Families. Retrieved May 29, 2009, from http://www.urban.org/UploadedPDF/411482_early_care.pdf.

Albrecht, K. (1998). Managing teacher performance while walking around. In B. Neugebauer & R. Neugebauer (Eds.), *The art of leadership: Managing an early childhood organization* (pp. 266–267). Redmond, WA: Exchange Press.

Albrecht, K. M., & Plantz, M. C. (Eds.). (1991). *Developmentally appropriate practice in school-age child care programs.* Alexandria, VA: Project Home Safe, American Home Economics Association.

Allen, M., & Staley, L. (2007, January). Helping children cope when a loved one is on military deployment. *Young Children, 62*(1), 82–86.

American Academy of Pediatrics. (2002a). Caring for children within a medical home. *Healthy Child Care America: Promoting optimal health for America's children.* Summary Report 1997–2001, p. 9. Retrieved July 21, 2005, from http://www.healthychildcare.org/pdf/summaryreport.pdf.

American Academy of Pediatrics. (2002b). *Television—How it affects children.* Retrieved August 5, 2005, from http://www.aap.org/healthtopics/mediause.cfm.

American Academy of Pediatrics, American Public Health Association, National Resource Center for Health and Safety in Child Care and Early Education. (2011). *Caring for our children: National health and safety performance standards; Guidelines for early care and education programs* (3rd ed.). Elk Grove Village, IL: American Academy of Pediatrics; Washington, DC: American Public Health Association. Also available at http://nrckids.org.

American Heritage Dictionary of the English Language (5th ed.). (2011). Boston, MA: Houghton Mifflin.

Anderson, D. R., & Evans, M. K. (2001, October/November). Peril and potential of media for infants and toddlers. *Zero to Three, 22*(2), 10–16.

Baer, J., Kutner, M., Sabatini, J., & White, S. (2009). *Basic reading skills and the literacy of America's least literate adults: Results from the 2003 National Assessment of Adult Literacy.* Washington, DC: U.S. Department of Education, National Center for Education Statistics.

Bagin, D., & Gallagher, D. R. (2001). *School and community relations* (7th ed.). Boston, MA: Allyn & Bacon.

Bagnato, S. J., & Simeonsson, R. J. (2007). *Authentic assessment for early childhood intervention.* New York, NY: Guilford.

Bailey, D. B., & Wolery, M. (1992). *Teaching infants and preschoolers with disabilities* (2nd ed.). Upper Saddle River, NJ: Merrill/Prentice Hall.

Barbuto, J. E. (2007). *Becoming a servant leader: Do you have what it takes?* University of Nebraska-Lincoln Extension, Institute of Agriculture and Natural Resources. Available online at http://www.ianrpubs.unl.edu/live/g1481/build/g1481.pdf.

Barnett, S., Brown, K., & Shore, R. (2004, April). The universal vs. targeted debate: Should the United States have preschool for all? *Preschool Policy Matters.* Available online at http://www.nieer.org.

Barnett, W. S., Carolan, M. E., Fitzgerald, J. & Squires, J. H. (2013). *The state of preschool 2012: State preschool yearbook.* National Institute for Early Education Research. Retrieved June 19, 2013, from http://nieer.org/publications/state-preschool-2012.

Baumrind, D. (1973). Current patterns of parental authority. *Developmental Psychology Monographs, 4*(1, Pt. 2) 1–103.

Baumrind, D. (1977). Some thoughts about childrearing. In S. Cohen & T. J. Comiskey (Eds.), *Child development: Contemporary perspectives.* Itasca, IL: F. E. Peacock.

Belfield, C. & Garcia, E. (2011, February). *Parental notions of school readiness: How have they changed and has preschool made a difference?* NIEER Working Paper. Available online at www.nieer.org

Beckwith, H. (2000). *The invisible touch: Four keys to modern marketing.* New York, NY: Warner Books.

Bellm, D., Gnezda, T., Whitebook, M., & Breunig, G. S. (1994). Policy initiatives to enhance child care staff compensation. In J. Johnson & J. B. McCracken (Eds.), *The early childhood career lattice: Perspectives on professional development* (pp. 161–169). Washington, DC: National Association for the Education of Young Children.

Benfari, Robert C. (1999). *Understanding and changing your management style.* San Francisco, CA: Jossey-Bass.

Birch, L., Johnson, S. L., & Fisher, J. (1995, January). Children's eating: The development of food acceptance patterns. *Young Children, 50*(2), 71–78.

Bishop-Josef, S. J. (2005). *The Edward Zigler Center in Child Development and Social Policy Yale University: Annual Progress Report 2004–2005*. Retrieved June 10, 2009, from http://ziglercenter.yale.edu/publications/documents/ZiglerCenter2004-2005annualreport.pdf.

Bitner, M. J. (2000). The servicescape. In T. A. Swartz & D. Iacobucci (Eds.), *Handbook of services marketing and management* (pp. 37–50). Thousand Oaks, CA: Sage Publications.

Blank, H. K. (1998). Advocacy leadership. In S. L. Kagan & B. T. Bowman (Eds.), *Leadership in early care and education* (pp. 39–45). Washington, DC: National Association for the Education of Young Children.

Bloom, P. J. (1998). Commentary. In S. L. Kagan & B. T. Bowman (Eds.), *Leadership in early care and education* (pp. 34–37). Washington, DC: National Association for the Education of Young Children.

Bloom, P. J. (1999). Building director competence: Credentialing and education. *Journal of Early Childhood Teacher Education, 20*(2), 207–214.

Bloom, P. J. (2008, Spring). Dedication doesn't have to mean deadication. *The Director's Link,* 1–3, 6. Available online at http://mccormickcenter.nl.edu/wp-content/uploads/2013/04/dlsp08.pdf.

Bloom, P. J., Jackson, S., Talan, T. N. & Kelton, R. (2013). *Taking charge of change: A 20-year review of empowering early childhood administrators through leadership training*. Retrieved June 26, 2013, from http://mccormickcenter.nl.edu/wp-content/uploads/2013/06/tcc20report.pdf.

Bodrova, E., & Leong, D. J. (2008, March). Developing self regulation in kindergarten: Can we keep all the crickets in the basket? *Young Children, 63*(2), 56–58.

Bolman, L., & Deal, T. (2008). *Reframing organizations: Artistry, choice and leadership* (4th ed.). San Francisco, CA: Jossey-Bass.

Boots, S. W. (2010). *Improving access to public benefits: Helping eligible individuals and families get the income supports they need*. Annie E. Casey Foundation. Retrieved June 14, 2013, from http://www.aecf.org/~/media/Pubs/Topics/Economic%20Security/Family%20Economic%20Supports/ImprovingAccesstoPublicBenefitsHelpingEligibl/BenefitsAccess41410.pdf.

Bornfreund, L. A. (2013). *An ocean of unknowns: Risks and opportunities in using student achievement data to evaluate prek-3rd grade teachers*. New America Foundation. Accessed August 1, 2013, at http://earlyed.newamerica.net/sites/newamerica.net/files/policydocs/OceanofUnknowns-LBornfreund.PDF.

Bowman, B. T., Donovan, M. S., & Burns, M. S. (Eds.). (2001). *Eager to learn: Educating our preschoolers*. Washington, DC: National Academies Press.

Bradley, J., & Kibera, P. (2007). Closing the gap: Culture and the promotion of inclusion in child care. In D. Koralek (Ed.), *Spotlight on young children and families* (pp. 38–43). Washington, DC: National Association for the Education of Young Children.

Branscombe, N. A., Castle, K., Dorsey, A. G., Surbeck, E., & Taylor, J. B. (2003). *Early childhood curriculum: A constructivist perspective*. Boston, MA: Houghton Mifflin.

Brault, M. (2012). *Americans with disabilities: 2010. Current population reports*. U.S. Census Bureau. Retrieved June 29, 2013, from http://www.census.gov/prod/2012pubs/p70-131.pdf.

Brauner, J., Gordic, B., & Zigler, E. (2004). Putting the child back into child care: Combining care and education for children ages 3–5. *Social Policy Report,* XVIII:III. Retrieved June 16, 2005, from http://www.srcd.org/Documents/Publications/SPR/SPR183.pdf.

Bredekamp, S., & Copple, C. (Eds.). (1997). *Developmentally appropriate practice in early childhood programs* (rev. ed.). Washington, DC: National Association for the Education of Young Children.

Brewer, D. M. (2006). *The association between the occupational stress of early childhood teachers and their beliefs and practices concerning the assessment of young children*. UMI Microform 3207807. Unpublished doctoral dissertation, University of Michigan, Ann Arbor.

Bricker, D. (Ed.). (2002). *Assessment, evaluation, and programming system (AEPS®) for infants and children*. Baltimore, MD: Paul H. Brookes.

Brigance, A. H. (2009). *Brigance early childhood screens (ages 0–35 months, 3–5 years, K–1); Developmental inventory 0–7 years*. North Billerica, MA: Curriculum Associates.

Bronfenbrenner, U. (1997). *The ecology of human development: Experiments by nature and design*. Cambridge, MA: Harvard University Press.

Bronfenbrenner, U. (2005). *Making human beings human: Bioecological perspectives on human development*. Thousand Oaks, CA: Sage.

Brown, N. H., & Manning, J. P. (2000). Core knowledge for directors. In M. L. Culkin (Ed.), *Managing quality in young children's programs: The leader's role* (pp. 78–96). New York, NY: Teachers College Press.

Brown, W. H., Googe, H. S., McIver, K. L., & Rathel, J. M. (2009). Effects of teacher-encouraged physical activity on preschool playgrounds. *Journal of Early Intervention, 31*(2), 126–145.

Bubolz, M. M., & Sontag, M. S. (1993). Human ecology theory. In P. G. Boss, W. J. Doherty, R. LaRossa, W. R. Schumm, & S. K. Steinmetz (Eds.), *Sourcebook of family theories and methods: A contextual approach* (pp. 419–448). New York, NY: Plenum.

Buckleitner, W. (2008, January/February). The state of children's interactive media. *Exchange, 179,* 62–66.

Burchinal, P., Kainz, K., Cai, K., Tout, K., Zaslow, M., Martinez-Beck, I., et al. (2009). *Early care and education quality and child outcomes.* Child Trends OPRE Research-to-Policy Brief No. 1. Retrieved August 10, 2009, from http://www.childtrends.org/Files/Child_Trends-2009_5_21_RB_earlycare.pdf.

Burdette, H. L., & Whitaker, R. C. (2005). *Resurrecting free play in young children: Looking beyond fitness and fatness to attention, affiliation and affect.* American Medical Association. Retrieved August 3, 2009, from http://www.childrenandnature.org/uploads/Burdette_LookingBeyond.pdf.

Bureau of Labor Statistics. (2012a). May 2012 national employment and wage estimates United States. Retrieved June 29, 2013, from http://www.bls.gov/oes/current/oes_nat.htm#00-0000.

Bureau of Labor Statistics. (2012b). *Occupational outlook handbook.* Retrieved June 16, 2013, from http://www.bls.gov/ooh/occupation-finder.htm.

Bush, D., Nell, M. L. & Drew, W. F. (2013). *From play to practice: Connecting teacher's play to children's learning.* Washington, DC: National Association for the Education of Young Children.

Bush, J. (2001). *Dollars and sense: Planning for profit in your child care business.* Albany, NY: Delmar.

Buysse, V., Wesley, P. W., Snyder, P., & Winton, P. (2006, Summer). Evidence-based practice: What does it really mean for the early childhood field? *Young Exceptional Children, 9*(4), 2–11.

Carter, M. (2008a, November/December). Assessing quality: What are we doing? Where are we going? *Exchange, 184,* 32–36.

Carter, M. (2008b, January/February). What could you be thinking? *Exchange, 179,* 26–29.

Carter, M., & Curtis, D. (1998). *The visionary director: A handbook for dreaming, organizing, and improvising in your center.* St. Paul, MN: Redleaf.

Caspe, M., Seltzer, A., Kennedy, J.L., Cappio, M. & DeLorenzo, C. (2013, July). Engaging families in the child assessment process. *Young Children, 68*(3), 8–14.

Cassidy, D. J., Lower, J. K., & Kintner, V. L. (2008). Early childhood professional development: How it matters to child care quality. Presentation at the North Carolina Early Childhood Professional Development Research Forum, Greensboro, NC, May 6, 2008.

Center for Law and Social Policy. (2009). *CCDBG: What's in the law?* Retrieved June 10, 2009, from http://www.clasp.org/publications/ccdbginbrief.pdf.

Center for the Child Care Workforce. (1998). *Creating better child care jobs: Model work standards for teaching staff in center-based child care.* Washington, DC: Author.

Center for the Study of Child Care Employment. (2008). *Early childhood educator competencies: A literature review of current best practices, and a public input process on next steps for California.* Berkeley, CA: Center for the Study of Child Care Employment, Institute for Research on Labor and Employment, University of California at Berkeley.

Center for Universal Design. (1997). *Principles of universal design.* Retrieved July 19, 2005, from http://www.design.ncsu.edu:8120/cud/univ_design/princ_overview.htm.

Centers for Disease Control and Prevention. (2012). Trends in the prevalence of extreme obesity among US preschool-aged children living in low-income families, 1998–2010. *JAMA, 308*(24), 2563–2565.

Centers for Disease Control and Prevention. (2013). *Blood lead levels in children aged 1–5 years—United States, 1999–2010.* Retrieved July 7, 2013, from http://www.cdc.gov/mmwr/preview/mmwrhtml/mm6213a3.htm?s_cid=mm6213a3_e.

Ceppi, G., & Zini, M. (Eds.). (1998). *Children, spaces, relations: Metaproject for an environment for young children.* Reggio Emilia, Italy: Reggio Children and Comune di Reggio Emilia –Nidi e Scuole dell Infanzia.

Chen, X., Sekine, M., Hamanishi, S., Yamagami, T., & Kagamimori S. (2005, July). Associations of lifestyle factors with quality of life (QOL) in Japanese children: A 3-year follow-up of the Toyama Birth Cohort Study. *Child: Care, Health and Development, 31*(4), 433–440.

Child Care Action Campaign. (2001). *Business outreach. Some facts about business and child care.* Retrieved from www.childcareaction.org.

Child Care Aware of America. (2012). *Parents and the high cost of child care: 2012 report.* Retrieved June 28, 2013, from http://www.naccrra.org/sites/default/files/default_site_pages/2012/cost_report_2012_final_081012.

Child Care Bureau. (n.d.). *What congregations should know about federal funding for child care.* http://www.acf.hhs.gov/programs/ccb/providers/faithbased.htm.

Child Care Services Association. (2012). *College completion for the early education workforce: A focus on student success.* National annual program report. Retrieved June 30, 2013, from http://www.childcareservices.org/_downloads/TEACH_AnnualReport_2012.pdf.

Child Life Council, Committee on Hospital Care. (2006). From the American Academy of Pediatrics: Child Life Services. *Pediatrics, 118*(4), 1757–1763. Retrieved November 11, 2013, from http://pediatrics.aappublications.org/content/118/4/1757.full

Child Mental Health Foundations and Agencies Network. (2000, September 6). *A good beginning: sending America's children to school with the social and emotional competence they need to succeed.* Retrieved from www.naeyc.org/childrens_champions/reports_research/good_beginning.

Children's Defense Fund. (2012). *The state of America's children 2012.* Washington, DC: Author. Retrieved June 18, 2013, from http://www.childrensdefense.org/child-research-data-publications/data/soac-2012-handbook.pdf.

Child Trends. (2013, June 25). *Why it's time to learn more about the children of LGBT parents.* Retrieved July 18, 2013, from http://www.childtrends.org/why-it-is-time-to-learn-more-about-the-children-of-lgbt-parents/?utm_source=Civic+Participation+is+Down&utm_campaign=E-News+7+10+13&utm_medium=email.

Child Trends. (2013, July 22). *Home front alert: The risks facing young children in military families.* Retrieved July 22, 2013, from http://www.childtrends.org/wp-content/uploads/2013/07/2013-31MilitaryFamilies1.pdf?utm_source=Child+Trends+5%3A+5+Risks+Facing+Young+Children+in+our+Military+Families&utm_campaign=5+risks+facing+young+children+in+our+military+families&utm_medium=email.

Christian, L. G. (2007). Understanding families: Applying family systems theory to early childhood practice. In Koralek, D. (Ed.) *Spotlight on young children and families* (pp. 4–11). Washington, DC: National Association for the Education of Young Children.

Christie, J. F., & Wardle, F. (1992, March). How much time is needed for play? *Young Children, 47,* 28–32.

Clarke, G. (2000). *Marketing a service for profit: A practical guide to key service marketing concepts.* London: Kogan Page Limited.

Clay, J. W. (2007). Creating safe, just places to learn for children of lesbian and gay parents. In D. Koralek (Ed.), *Spotlight on young children and families* (pp. 24–27). Washington, DC: National Association for the Education of Young Children.

Clements, R. (2004). An investigation of the state of outdoor play. *Contemporary issues in early childhood, 5*(1), 68–80.

Copeland, M. L., & McCreedy, B. S. (1998). Creating family-friendly policies. In B. Neugebauer & R. Neugebauer (Eds.), *The art of leadership: Managing early childhood organizations* (pp. 311–313). Redmond, WA: Exchange Press.

Copple, C., & Bredekamp, S. (2009). *Developmentally appropriate practice in early childhood programs serving children from birth through age 8.* Washington, DC: National Association for the Education of Young Children.

Cost, Quality, & Child Outcomes Study Team. (1995). *Cost, quality, and child outcomes in child care centers.* Public Report (2nd ed.). Denver, CO: Economics Department, University of Colorado at Denver.

Council for Professional Recognition. (2001, October). Helping children cope with disaster. *Council News and Views,* 8–9.

Covey, S. R. (1989). *The seven habits of highly effective people.* New York, NY: Simon & Schuster.

Covey, S. R. (1992). *Principle-centered leadership.* New York, NY: Fireside.

Covey, S. M. R. (2006). *The SPEED of trust: The one thing that changes everything.* New York, NY: Free Press.

Cox, M. (2009, June). *What's love got to do with it? The role emotions play in burnout and provider mental health.* Presentation at Professional Development Institute of the National Association for the Education of Young Children, Charlotte, NC.

Curtis, D., & Carter, M. (1996). *Reflecting children's lives: A handbook for planning child-centered curriculum.* St. Paul, MN: Redleaf.

Curtis, D., & Carter, M. (2008). *Learning together with young children: A curriculum for reflective teachers.* St. Paul, MN: Redleaf.

Curtis, K. F. (1995). On entering and staying in the teaching profession. *Childhood Education, 71*(5), 288-F.

Dahlberg, G., Moss, P., & Pence, A. (1999). *Beyond quality in early childhood education and care: Postmodern perspectives.* London: Falmer Press.

Daly, D. L., & Dowd, T. P. (1992, November/December). Characteristics of effective, harm-free environments for children in out-of-home care. *Child Welfare, 71*(6), 487–496.

Delaney, E. M. (2001, September). The administrator's role in making inclusion work. *Young Children, 56*(5), 66–70.

Dickens, W. T., & Baschnagel, C. (2009, April). *The fiscal effects of investing in high-quality preschool programs.* CCF Brief No. 42. Center on Children and Families. Available online at www.brookings.edu/ccf.

Dodge, D. T., Colker, L., & Heroman, C. (2002). *Creative curriculum developmental continuum assessment toolkit ages 3–5.* Washington, DC: Teaching Strategies.

Dodge, D. T., Colker, L., & Heroman, C. (2006). *Creative curriculum developmental continuum assessment toolkit for infants, toddlers and twos.* Washington, DC: Teaching Strategies.

DuBrin, A. J. (2000). *The active manager: How to plan, organize, lead and control your way to success.* London: International Thompson Publishing.

Dunst, C., Hamby, D., Trivette, C. M., Raab, M., & Bruder, M. B. (2000). Everyday family and community life and children's naturally occurring learning opportunities. *Journal of Early Intervention, 23*(3), 151–164.

Dunst, C., Trivette, C. M., Hamby, D. & Simkus, A. (2013). *Systematic review of studies promoting the use of assistive technology devices by young children with disabilities.* Research Brief *8*(1). Available on line at http://tnt.asu.edu/files/ResearchBriefVolume8-1.pdf.

Durrett, C., & Torelli, L. (2009, May/June). Deconstructing "green": A holistic approach to designing sustainable child development centers. *Exchange, 187,* 20–25.

Early, D. M., Maxwell, K. M., & Burchinal, M. (2007). Teachers' education, classroom quality, and young children's academic skills: Results from seven studies of preschool programs. *Child Development, 78*(2), 558–580.

Easter Seals Child Development Center Network. (2003). National Director. Chicago, IL. Cited in White, R., & Stoecklin, V. (2003). The great 35 square foot myth. Kansas City, MO: White Hutchinson Leasure & Learning Group. Retrieved from http://www.whitehutchinson.com/children/articles/35footmyth.shtml.

Elkind, D. (1994). *Ties that stress: The new family imbalance.* Cambridge, MA: Harvard University Press.

Elkind, D. (2008, March/April). Some misunderstandings of school readiness. *Exchange, 180,* 49–52.

Evans, B. (2009). *You're not my friend anymore! Illustrated answers to questions about young children's challenging behaviors.* Ypsilanti, MI: HighScope Press.

Fagan, J. (2007). Research on children's environmental program efforts. *Applied Developmental Science, 11*(4), 260–265.

Falk, G. (2013, May). *The Temporary Assistance for Needy Families (TANF) Block Grant: Responses to frequently asked questions.* Congressional Research Service. Retrieved August 5, 2013, from http://www.fas.org/sgp/crs/misc/RL32760.pdf.

Federal Interagency Forum on Child and Family Statistics. (2013). *America's children: Key national indicators of well-being.* Washington, DC: U.S. Government Printing Office. Retrieved August 16, 2013, from http://www.childstats.gov/pdf/ac2013/ac_13.pdf.

Fenichel, E. (Ed.). (1992). *Learning through supervision and mentorship to support development of infants, toddlers, and their families: A source book.* Washington, DC: Zero to Three.

Fiene, R. (2002). *13 indicators of quality child care: Research update.* Report to Office of the Assistant Secretary for Planning and Evaluation and Health Resources and Services Administration/Maternal and Child Health Bureau, U.S. Department of Health and Human Services. Retrieved August 11, 2005, from http://aspe.hhs.gov/hsp/ccquality-ind02/#Child.

File, T. (2013, May 13). *Computer and internet use in the United States: Population characteristics.* Retrieved July 23, 2013, from http://www.census.gov/prod/2013pubs/p20-569.pdf.

Filippini, T. (1994). The role of the *pedagogista.* In C. Edwards, L. Gandini, & G. Forman (Eds.), *The hundred languages of children: The Reggio Emilia approach—advanced reflections* (pp. 127–137). Norwood, NJ: Ablex.

Finkelhor, D., Williams, L. M., Kalinowski, M., & Burns, N. (1988). *Sexual abuse in day care: A national study.* Durham, NH: Family Research Laboratory, University of New Hampshire.

Forman, G. E. (2009, June). *The power of digital video to reveal the power of children's play.* Presentation at the NAEYC 18th National Institute for Early Childhood Professional Development, Charlotte, NC.

Fortune Magazine. (2012, February). 100 best companies to work for. Retrieved June 18, 2013, from http://money.cnn.com/magazines/fortune/best-companies/2012/benefits/child_care.html.

Fox, L., Hanline, M. F., Vail, C. O., & Gallant, K. R. (1994, Summer). Developmentally appropriate practice: Applications for young children with disabilities. *Journal of Early Intervention, 18*(3), 243–257.

Franklin, W. H. (1998). Who cares? Eight principles for dealing with customers. In B. Neugebauer & R. Neugebauer (Eds.), *The art of leadership: Managing early childhood organizations* (pp. 329–331). Redmond, WA: Exchange Press.

Frede, E. (2011). *Key workforce issues around diversity. The early childhood care and education workforce: A workshop.* National Institute for Early Childhood Education Research. Available online at http://www.iom.edu/~/media/Files/Activity%20Files/Children/EarlyChildCareEducation/Frede_ECCE_2-28-11.pdf.

Freeman, N. K., & Brown, M. H. (1999). How soon can you close the center? A story of survival. *Journal of Early Childhood Teacher Education, 20*(1), 49–58.

Frost, J. L., Brown, P-S, Sutterby, J. A., and Thornton, C. D. (2004). *The developmental benefits of playgrounds.* Olney, MD: Association for Childhood Education International.

Gadzikowski, A., & Lipton, L. (2004, September/October). An opportunity for board development. *Exchange, 159,* 8–11.

Galinsky, E., Aumann, K., & Bond, J. T. (2008). *Times are changing: Gender and generation at work and at home.*

Families and Work Institute. Retrieved July 21, 2009, from www.familiesandwork.org.

Gambetti, A., & Kaminsky, J. A. (2001, Spring/Summer). The fundamental role of participation in the experience of the Reggio Emilia municipal infant–toddler centers and preschools: An interview with Paola Cagliari. *Innovations in Early Education: The International Reggio Exchange, 8*(3), 1–6.

Gandini, L. (1984, Summer). Not just anywhere: Making child care centers into "particular" places. *Beginnings, 00*(00), 17–20.

Gardner, H. (2006). *Multiple intelligences: New horizons.* New York, NY: Basic Books.

Gebhard, B. (2010). *States' use of early learning guidelines for infants and toddlers.* Zero to Three. Retrieved July 17, 2013, from http://main.zerotothree.org/site/DocServer/States__Use_of_ELG_for_IT_FINAL.pdf?docID=11861.

Gelber, A. M., & Isen, A. (2011, December). Children's schooling and parents' investment in children: Evidence from the Head Start Impact Study. Cambridge, MA: National Bureau of Economic Research. Available online at http://www.nber.org/papers/w17704.

Gennarelli, C. (2004, January). Communicating with families: Children lead the way. *Young Children, 59*(1), 98–100.

Gilliam, W. S. (2005, May). *Prekindergarteners left behind: Expulsion rates in state prekindergarten programs.* FDC Policy Brief Series No. 3. New York, NY: Foundation for Child Development. Available online at http://www.challengingbehavior.org/explore/policy_docs/prek_expulsion.pdf.

Gilliam, W. S., & Marchesseault, C. M. (2005, March 30). *From capitols to classrooms, policies to practice: State-funded prekindergarten at the classroom level.* The National Prekindergarten Study. Yale University Child Study Center. Retrieved July 5, 2005, from http://nieer.org/resources/files/NPSteachers.pdf.

Goffin, S. G., & Wilson, C. (2001). *Curriculum models and early childhood education: Appraising the relationship* (2nd ed.). Upper Saddle River, NJ: Merrill/Prentice Hall.

Goleman, D. (1995). *Emotional intelligence: Why it can matter more than IQ.* New York, NY: Bantam Books.

Goleman, D. (2000, March/April). Leadership that gets results. *Harvard Business Review,* 78–90. Retrieved August 17, 2009, from http://0-web.ebscohost.com.wncln.wncln.org/ehost/results?vid=2&hid=106&sid=e46b8bdd-0d55-4c2e-8ffc-135ab3b5a7a8%40sessionmgr104&bquery=(JN+%22Harvard+Business+Review%22+and+DT+20000301)&bdata=JmRiPWJ0aCZoeXBlPTAmc2l0ZT1laG9zdC1saXZl.

Gonzalez-Mena, J. (2005). *Diversity in early care and education: Honoring differences.* New York, NY: McGraw-Hill.

Goodson, B. D., Layzer, J. I., & Layzer, C. J. (2005). *Quality of early childhood care settings: Caregiver rating scale.* Cambridge, MA: Abt Associates.

Gordon, T. (1970). *P.E.T.: Parent effectiveness training.* New York, NY: Wyden.

Gordon, T. (1974). *T.E.T.: Teacher effectiveness training.* New York, NY: Wyden.

Green, S. (2003). Reaching out to fathers: An examination of staff efforts that lead to greater father involvement in early childhood programs. *Early Childhood Research and Practice, 5*(2). Retrieved August 1, 2007, from http://ecrp.uiuc.edu/v5n2/green.html.

Greenleaf, R. K. (1998). Servant-leadership. In L. C. Spears (Ed.), *Insights on leadership: Service, stewardship, spirit, and servant-leadership* (pp. 15–20). New York, NY: Wiley.

Greenspan, S. I., & Wieder, S. (1998). *The child with special needs.* Reading, MA: Addison-Wesley.

Guss, S. S., Horm, D. M., Lang, E., Krehbiel, S. M., Petty, J. A., Austin, K., Bergren, C., Brown, A., & Holloway, S. (2013, July). Using classroom quality assessments to inform teacher decisions. *Young Children, 68*(3), 16–20.

Hale-Jinks, C., Knopf, H., & Kemple, K. (2006, Summer). Tackling teacher turnover in child care: Understanding causes and consequences, identifying solutions. *Childhood Education, 82*(4), 219–226.

Halgunseth, L. C., Peterson, A., Stark, D. R. & Moodie, S. (2009). *Family engagement, diverse families, and early childhood education programs: An integrated review of the literature.* National Association for the Education of Young Children. Available online at http://www.naeyc.org/files/naeyc/file/ecprofessional/EDF_Literature%20Review.pdf.

Harms, T., Clifford, R. M., & Cryer, D. (2005). *Early childhood environment rating scale* (rev. ed.). New York, NY: Teachers College Press.

Harms, T., Cryer, D., & Clifford, R. (1989). *Family child care environment rating scale, revised. (FCCRS-R) (2007).* New York, NY: Teachers College Press.

Harms, T., Cryer, D., & Clifford, R. M. (2006). *Infant/toddler environment rating scale* (rev. ed.). New York, NY: Teachers College Press.

Harms, T., Jacobs, E. V., & White, D. R. (1995). *School-age care environment rating scale.* New York, NY: Teachers College Press.

Harms, T., & Tracy, R. (2006, July). Linking research to best practice: University laboratory schools in early childhood education. *Young Children, 61*(4), 89–93.

Harvard Family Research Project. (2006, Spring). Family involvement in early childhood education. Cambridge, MA: Harvard Graduate School of Education. Available online at http://www.hfrp.org/family-involvement/publications-resources/family-involvement-in-early-childhood-education.

Hatch, M. J. (1997). *Organization theory: Modern, symbolic, and postmodern perspectives*. New York, NY: Oxford University Press.

Haugen, Kirsten (n.d.). *Steps for adapting materials for use by all children*. Retrieved July 19, 2005, from http://www.childcareexchange.com/library/5016101.pdf.

Hayden, J. (1995, July/August). Applying early childhood principles in extraordinary circumstances. *Child Care Information Exchange, 104*, 64–66.

Haynes, M. (2009). *Promoting quality in preK–grade 3 classrooms: Findings and results from NASBE's early childhood education network*. National Association of State Boards of Education. Retrieved June 10, 2009, from http://nasbe.org/index.php/file-repository?func=startdown&id=884.

Hearron, P., & Hildebrand, V. (2013). *Guiding young children* (9th ed.). Upper Saddle River, NJ: Merrill/Prentice Hall.

Hernandez, R. P. (2011, Summer). Transforming for diversity. *Director's Link*. McCormick Center for Early Childhood Leadership. Retrieved July 1, 2013, from http://mccormickcenter.nl.edu/wp-content/uploads/2013/03/dlsu11.pdf.

Hewes, D. W. (1994, July/August). TQ what? Applying total quality management in child care. *Child Care Information Exchange, 98*, 20–24.

Hewes, D. (1998). When shaming fingers point: Dealing with negative publicity. In B. Neugebauer & R. Neugebauer (Eds.), *The art of leadership: Managing early childhood organizations* (pp. 345–347). Redmond, WA: Exchange Press.

HighScope Educational Research Foundation. (2003). *Preschool program quality assessment* (2nd ed.). Ypsilanti, MI: HighScope Press.

HighScope Educational Research Foundation. (2005). *Infant and toddler child observation record*, Ypsilanti, MI: HighScope Press.

Hildebrand, V. (1993). *Management of child development centers* (3rd ed.). Upper Saddle River, NJ: Merrill/Prentice Hall.

Hildebrand, V., Phenice, L., Gray, M., & Hines, R. P. (2007). *Knowing and serving diverse families* (2nd ed.). Upper Saddle River, NJ: Merrill/Prentice Hall.

Hill-Scott, K. (2000). Leadership in child development programs: Prospects for the future. In M. L. Culkin (Ed.), *Managing quality in young children's programs: The leader's role* (pp. 203–220). New York, NY: Teachers College Press.

Hiss, T. (1987, June 22 and 29). Experiencing places. *New Yorker*, 45–68, 73–86. Cited in J. Greenman. (1988). *Caring spaces, learning places: Children's environments that work*. Redmond, WA: Exchange Press.

Hitz, R., & Driscoll, A. (1994, Spring). Give encouragement, not praise. *Texas Child Care, 17*(4), 2–11.

Hochschild, A. R. (1983). *The managed heart: Commercialization of human feeling*. Berkeley, CA: University of California Press.

Hogan, N., & Graham, M. (2001, Winter). Helping children cope with disaster. *A.C.E.I. Focus on Pre-K & K, 14*(2), 1–6, 8.

Howden, L. M. & Meyer, J. A. (2011, May). *Age and Sex Composition: 2010* Census Brief. U.S. Census Bureau. Retrieved June 13, 2012, from http://www.census.gov/prod/cen2010/briefs/c2010br-03.pdf.

Howes, C. 1997. Children's experiences in center-based child care as a function of teacher background and adult:child ratio. *Merrill-Palmer Quarterly 43*, 404–425.

Huettig, C. I., Sanborn, C. F., DiMarco, N., Popejoy, A., & Rich, S. (2005, March). The O generation: Our youngest children are at risk for obesity. *Young Children, 59*(2), 50–55.

Humphrey, R. H., Pollack, J. M., & Hawver, T. (2008). Leading with emotional labor. *Journal of Managerial Psychology, 23*(2), 151–168.

Israel, M. S. (2004, November). Ethical dilemmas for early childhood educators: The ethics of being accountable. *Young Children 59*(6), 24–32.

Kagan, S. L., & Neuman, M. J. (1997). Conceptual leadership. In S. L. Kagan & B. T. Bowman (Eds.), *Leadership in early care and education* (pp. 59–64). Washington, DC: National Association for the Education of Young Children.

Kamii, C. (1982). *Number in preschool and kindergarten*. Washington, DC: National Association for the Education of Young Children.

Katz, L. (1994). Pedagogical leadership. In S. L. Kagan & B. T. Bowman (Eds.), *Leadership in early care and education* (pp. 17–20). Washington, DC: National Association for the Education of Young Children.

Katz, L. (1998). Looking at the quality of early childhood programs. In B. Neugebauer & R. Neugebauer (Eds.), *The art of leadership: Managing early childhood organizations* (p. 287). Redmond, WA: Exchange Press.

Katz, L. G. (1984). Developmental stages of preschool teachers. In M. Kaplan-Sanoff & R. Yablans-Magid

(Eds.), *Exploring early childhood* (pp. 478–482). Upper Saddle River, NJ: Prentice Hall.

Katz, L. G., & Chard, S. C. (2000). *Engaging children's minds: The project approach* (2nd ed.). Stamford, CT: Ablex.

Khanagov, D. (2007, January/February). Working effectively with different personality types. *Exchange, 173*, 66–68.

Kilbourne, S. (2007, March/April). Performance appraisals: One step in a comprehensive staff supervision model. *Exchange, 174*, 34–38.

Kilburn, M. R., & Karoly, L. A. (2008). *The economics of early childhood policy: What the dismal science has to say about investing in children.* Santa Monica, CA: RAND Corporation. Available online at http://rand.org/pubs/occasional_papers/2008/RAND_OP227.pdf.

Kohn, A. (1994, December). *The risks of rewards.* ERIC Digest, EDO-PS-94-14. Urbana, IL: ERIC Clearinghouse on Elementary and Early Childhood Education.

Kostelnik, M., Gregory, K., Soderman, A. & Whiren, A. (2012). *Guiding children's social development and learning* (7th ed.). Stamford, CT: Cengage.

Kreader, J. L., Ferguson, D., & Lawrence, S. (2005, August). *Infant and toddler child care arrangements.* Research-to-policy connections, No. 1. Child care and early education research connections. Retrieved June 4, 2009, from www.childcareresearch.org.

Lally, J. R. (1999). Brain research, infant learning, and child care curriculum. In *Child Care Information Exchange, Inside child care: Trend report 2000* (pp. 105–108). Redmond, WA: Exchange Press.

Lally, J. R. (2005, January). The human rights of infants and toddlers: A comparison of child-care philosophies in Europe, Australia, New Zealand, and the United States. *Zero to Three, 25*(3), 43–46.

Laski, E. V. (2013, July). Portfolio picks: An approach for developing children's metacognition. *Young Children, 68*(3), 38–43.

Laughlin, L. (2013). *Who's minding the kid: Child care arrangements spring 2011.* U.S. Department of Commerce, Economics and Statistics Administration, U.S. Census Bureau. Retrieved June 17, 2013, from http://www.census.gov/prod/2013pubs/p70-135.pdf.

Legendre, A. (2003, July). Environmental features influencing toddlers' bioemotional reactions in day care centers, *Environment and Behavior, 35*, 523–549.

Lemak, D. J. (2004). Leading students through the management theory jungle by following the path of the seminal theorists: A paradigmatic approach. *Management Decision, 42*(10), 1309–1325. Retrieved December 13, 2013, from http://www.emeraldinsight.com/journals.htm?articleid=865548.

Levitt, P. (2009, May). Keynote address. Presented at 2009 National Smart Start Conference, Greensboro, NC. Available online at http://www.youtube.com/watch?v=nQAqeQnCh7o&NR=1.

Linder, T. (2008). *Transdisciplinary play-based assessment* (2nd ed.). Baltimore, MD: Paul H. Brookes.

Livingston, G., & Cohn, D. (2012, November 29). *U.S. birth rate falls to a record low; decline is greatest among immigrants.* Pew Research Social & Demographic Trends. Retrieved June 13, 2013, from http://www.pewsocialtrends.org/2012/11/29/u-s-birth-rate-falls-to-a-record-low-decline-is-greatest-among-immigrants/.

Logan E., & Feiler, A. (2006). Forging links between parents and schools: A new role for Teaching Assistants? *Support for Learning, 21*(3), 115–120.

Louv, R. (2006). *The last child in the woods: Saving our children from nature-deficit disorder.* Chapel Hill, NC: Algonquin Books.

Lowry, F. (2010, February 16). Prevalence of chronic illness in US kids has increased. Medscape today. Retrieved July 7, 2013 from http://www.medscape.com/viewarticle/717030.

Lubeck, S. (1994). The politics of developmentally appropriate practice: Exploring issues of culture, class, and curriculum. In B. L. Mallory & R. S. New (Eds.), *Diversity and developmentally appropriate practices: Challenges for early childhood education.* New York, NY: Teachers College Press.

Lumeng, J. (2005, January). What can we do to prevent childhood obesity? *Zero to Three, 25*(3), 13–19.

Lynch, E. W., & Hanson, M. J. (1998). *Developing crosscultural competence: A guide for working with children and their families* (2nd ed.). Baltimore, MD: Paul H. Brookes.

Macartney, S. (2011). *Child poverty in the United States 2009 and 2010: Selected race groups and Hispanic origin.* U.S. Census Bureau. Retrieved June 13, 2013, from http://www.census.gov/prod/2011pubs/acsbr10-05.pdf.

Macartney, S., & Laughlin, L. (2011). *Child care costs in the current population survey's annual social and economic supplement (CPS ASED): A comparison to SIPP.* Retrieved June 19, 2013, from http://www.census.gov/hhes/povmeas/methodology/supplemental/research/ChildCareCPS.pdf.

Macmillan, L., & Neugebauer, R. (2006, January). *Rush to assessment: The role private early childhood service providers play in assessing child and program outcomes.* Paper prepared for the National Task Force on Early Childhood Accountability. Retrieved August 10, 2009, from http://www.pewtrusts.org/our_work_report_detail.aspx?id=31168.

Maher, E. J., Li, G., Carter, L., & Johnson, D. B. (2008). Preschool child care participation and obesity at the start of kindergarten. *Pediatrics, 122*(2), 322–330.

Mallory, B. L. (1994). Inclusive policy, practice, and theory for young children with developmental differences. In B. L. Mallory & R. S. New (Eds.), *Diversity and developmentally appropriate practices: Challenges for early childhood education.* New York, NY: Teachers College Press.

Mallory, B. L., & New, R. S. (Eds.). (1994). *Diversity and developmentally appropriate practices: Challenges for early childhood education.* New York, NY: Teachers College Press.

Mangione, P. L. (1993). Child care video magazine. *Essential connections: Ten keys to culturally sensitive child care.* Sacramento, CA: Far West Laboratory/California Department of Education.

March of Dimes. (2013). Illicit drug use during pregnancy. Retrieved July 7, 2013, from http://www.marchofdimes.com/pregnancy/illicit-drug-use-during-pregnancy.aspx.

Mardell, C., & Goldenberg, D. S. (1998). *Developmental indicators for the assessment of learning (DIAL-3).* San Antonio, TX: Pearson.

Marsili, A., & Hughes, M. (2009). Finding Kirk's words: An infant mental health approach to preschool intervention. *Young Exceptional Children, 12*(2), 2–15.

Maslow, A. H. (1954). *Motivation and personality.* New York, NY: Harper & Row.

Mathews, J. (2011, August 18). Should teachers visit student homes? *Washington Post.* Retrieved July 19, 2013, from http://m.washingtonpost.com/blogs/class-struggle/post/should-teachers-visit-student-homes/2011/08/17/gIQApbzoMJ_blog.html.

Matos, K. & Galinsky, E. (2012). 2012 National Study of Employers. Families and Work Institute. Retrieved June 18, 2013, from http://familiesandwork.org/site/research/reports/NSE_2012_.pdf.

Maxwell, L. E. (2007). Competency in child care settings: The role of the physical environment. *Environment and Behavior, 39*(2), 229–245.

McBride, B. A., & Hicks, T. (1999). Teacher training and research: Does it make a difference in lab school program quality? *Journal of Early Childhood Teacher Education, 20*(1), 19–27.

McCormick Center for Early Childhood Leadership. (2012). *Director qualifications in state professional development and quality rating and improvement systems.* Retrieved June 14, 2013, from http://mccormickcenter.nl.edu/wp-content/uploads/2013/03/credentials_qris.pdf.

McGinnis, J. R. (2000). *Children's outdoor environments: A guide to play and learning.* Raleigh, NC: North Carolina Partnership for Children.

McGrath, W. H. (2007). Ambivalent partners: Power, trust, and partnership in relationships between mothers and teachers in a full-time child care center. *Teachers College Record, 109*(6), 1401–1422. Retrieved June 3, 2009, from http://www.tcrecord.org.

Meisels, S. J., Marsden, D. B., Dichtelmiller, M. K., & Jablon, J. R. (2001). *Work sampling system.* San Antonio, TX: Pearson.

Meyer, J. A., & Mann, M. B. (2006). Teachers' perceptions of the benefits of home visits for early elementary children. *Early Childhood Education Journal, 34*(1), 93–97.

Miles, D. (2008, July 21). *Defense Department to deliver more, improved child care.* U.S. Department of Defense. Retrieved June 10, 2009, from http://www.defense.gov/news/newsarticle.aspx?id=50552.

Mitchell, A. (2012). Quality rating and improvement systems: A state by state listing of QRIS websites. QRIS National Learning Network. Retrieved June 25, 2013, from http://www.qrisnetwork.org/sites/all/files/resources/gscobb/2012-05-28%2008:04/WebsitesforQRIS.pdf.

Mitchell, A., & David, J. (Eds.). (1992). *Explorations with young children: A curriculum guide from the Bank Street College of Education.* Mt. Rainier, MD: Gryphon House.

Morgan, G. G. (2000). The director as a key to quality. In M. L. Culkin (Ed.), *Managing quality in young children's programs: The leader's role* (pp. 40–58). New York, NY: Teachers College Press.

National Association for Family Child Care. (2007, August). *NAFCC's vision for family child care.* Retrieved June 9, 2009, from http://www.nafcc.org/documents/NAFCC%20vision%20statement.pdf.

National Association for Regulatory Administration. (2007). The 2007 Child Care Licensing Study. Retrieved July 8, 2009, from http://www.naralicensing.org/displaycommon.cfm?an=1&subarticlenbr=160.

National Association for Sick Child Daycare. (2009, June 9). *About NASCD.* Retrieved June 9, 2009, from http://www.nascd.com/.

National Association for the Education of Young Children (2006, July). *Code of ethical conduct: Supplement for administrators.* Washington, DC: Author. Available online at http://www.naeyc.org/positionstatements.

National Association for the Education of Young Children. (2007a). *NAEYC Early Childhood Program Standards and Accreditation Criteria: The mark of quality in early childhood education.* Washington, DC: NAEYC.

National Association for the Education of Young Children. (2007b). *Program administrator definition and competencies.* Retrieved April 13, 2009, from http://www.naeyc.org/academy/criteira/core_competencies.html.

National Association for the Education of Young Children and National Association of Early Childhood Specialists in State Departments of Education. (2004, November). *Where we stand on early learning standards.* Washington, DC: Author. Available online at http://208.118.177.216/about/positions/pdf/elstandardsstand.pdf.

National Association of Child Care Resource and Referral Agencies. (2009a). *Parents and the high price of child care: 2009 update.* Retrieved July 2, 2009, from http://issuu.com/naccrra/docs/parents-and-the-high-price-of-child-care-2009?mode=embed&layout=white.

National Association of Child Care Resource and Referral Agencies. (2009b). *We CAN do better: 2009 update.* Retrieved June 26, 2009, from http://issuu.com/naccrra/docs/we-can-do-better-2009-update?mode=mbed&layout=white.

National Association of Child Care Resource and Referral Agencies. (2009c). *What child care providers earn.* Retrieved June 8, 2009, from http://www.naccrra.org/andd/child-care-workforce/what-providers-earn.

National Association of Child Care Resource and Referral Agencies. (2010). *The economic impact on parents' choices and perceptions about child care.* Retrieved July 18, 2013, from http://www.naccrra.org/sites/default/files/default_site_pages/2011/final_2010_economic_impact_poll_report_dec_2010.pdf.

National Center on Family Homelessness. (2011). *America's youngest outcasts: State report card on child homelessness.* Retrieved June 13, 2013, from http://www.scribd.com/doc/75506633/Report-Americas-Youngest-Outcasts.

National Center on Parent, Family, and Community Engagement. (n.d.). *Head Start and Early Head Start relationship-based competencies for staff and supervisors who work with families.* Retrieved July 29, 2013, from http://eclkc.ohs.acf.hhs.gov/hslc/tta-system/family/Family%20and%20Community%20Partnerships/Family%20Services/Professional%20Development/ohs-rbc.pdf.

National Child Care Information and Technical Assistance Center. (2008). *Program assessment tools for early childhood programs.* Child Care Bureau, Department of Health and Human Services. Retrieved August 11, 2009, from http://nccic.acf.hhs.gov/pubs/goodstart/assess-eval2.html.

National Coalition for Campus Children's Centers. (2008). *Child care and laboratory schools on campus.* Retrieved June 9, 2009, from http://www.campuschildren.org/pubs/cclab/cclab1.html.

National Early Childhood Accountability Task Force. (2007). *Taking stock: Assessing and improving early childhood learning and program quality.* Foundation for Child Development; the Joyce Foundation, and PEW Charitable Trusts. Available online at http://www.pewtrusts.org/uploadedFiles/www.pewtrustsorg/Reports/Pre-k_education/task_force_report1.pdf.

National Early Childhood Technical Assistance Center. (2011). *The importance of early intervention for infants and toddlers with disabilities and their families.* Retrieved June 13, 2013, from http://www.nectac.org/~pdfs/pubs/importanceofearlyintervention.pdf.

National Governors' Association Center for Best Practices. (n.d.). *Early childhood advisory councils.* Retrieved June 18, 2013, from http://www.nga.org/cms/home/nga-center-for-best-practices/center-issues/page-edu-issues/col2-content/main-content-list/early-childhood-advisory-council.html.

National Institute for Early Education Research. (2009). *Facts and figures: What states offer preschool to all children.* Available online at http://nieer.org.

National Research Council and Institute of Medicine. (2000). *From neurons to neighborhoods: The science of early childhood development.* Committee on Integrating the Science of Early Childhood Development. Jack P. Shonkoff & Deborah A. Phillips (Eds.). Board on Children, Youth, and Families, Commission on Behavioral and Social Sciences and Education. Washington, DC: National Academies Press.

National Women's Law Center. (2013). *Impact of sequestration cuts on Head Start, child care and early education: State and local examples.* Retrieved July 22, 2013, from http://www.nwlc.org/resource/impact-sequestration-cuts-head-start-child-care-and-early-education-state-and-local-example.

Neugebauer, B., & Neugebauer, R. (Eds.). (1998). *The art of leadership: Managing early childhood organizations* (Vols. 1 and 2). Redmond, WA: Exchange Press.

Neugebauer, R. (1998a). Ma Bell and child care: Handling telephone inquiries. In B. Neugebauer & R. Neugebauer (Eds.), *The art of leadership: Managing early childhood organizations* (pp. 332–335). Redmond, WA: Exchange Press.

Neugebauer, R. (1998b). Step-by-step guide to team building. In B. Neugebauer & R. Neugebauer (Eds.), *The art of leadership: Managing an early childhood organization* (pp. 250–254). Redmond, WA: Exchange Press.

Neugebauer, R. (2000, May/June). Religious organizations taking proactive role in child care. *Child Care Information Exchange, 133,* 18–20.

Neugebauer, R. (2008, November/December). Trends in religious-affiliated child care. Status report no. 6. *Exchange, 165,* 79–80.

Neugebauer, R. (2009, March/April). Trends in quality assurance: Where are we headed with center accreditation? *Exchange, 186,* 14–17.

Neugebauer, R. (2010, March/April). Employer child care surviving and thriving: Employer child care trend report #17. *Exchange, 192,* 26–28.

Neuman, S., & Roskos, K. (2005, July). Whatever happened to developmentally appropriate practice in early literacy? *Young Children, 60*(4), 22–26.

New American Children. (2012). New York, NY: Foundation for Child Development. Retrieved August 16, 2013, from www.fcd-us.org/our-work/new-american-children.

Newsom, D., & Haynes, J. (2008). *Public relations writing: Form and style* (8th ed.). Belmont, CA: Thompson Higher Education.

Nicholson, S. (2009, June 4). Losers are winners: Childcare providers square off in weight-loss competition. *The Mountain Times,* pp. 2, 21.

Nickols, S. Y. (2003). Human eco-system theory: A tool for working with families. *Journal of Family and Consumer Sciences, 95*(2), 15–18.

Nielsen (2012, April 10). *Consumer trust in online, social and mobile advertising grows.* Retrieved July 24, 2013, from http://www.nielsen.com/us/en/newswire/2012/consumer-trust-in-online-social-and-mobile-advertising-grows.html.

Olds, A. R. (2001). *Child care design guide.* New York, NY: McGraw-Hill.

Olson, S. (Ed.). (2011). Demographic perspectives on family change. In *Toward an integrated science of research on families. Workshop report.* U.S. National Research Council Committee on the Science of Research on Families. Washington, DC: National Academies Press. Retrieved August 16, 2013, from http://www.ncbi.nlm.nih.gov/books/NBK56255.

Paolucci, B., Hall, O. A., & Axinn, N. (1977). *Family decision making: An ecosystem approach.* New York, NY: Wiley.

Passel, J., Livingston, G. & Cohn, D. (2012). *Explaining why minority births now outnumber white births.* Pew Research and Social Demographic Trends. Retrieved June 13, 2013, from http://www.pewsocialtrends.org/2012/05/17/explaining-why-minority-births-now-outnumber-white-births/.

Pastalan, L. (1971, December). *How the elderly negotiate their environment.* Paper prepared for Environment for the Aged: A Working Conference on Behavioral Research, Utilization, and Environmental Policy. San Juan, Puerto Rico.

Pate, R. R., Pfeiffer, K. A., Trost, S. G., Ziegler, P., & Dowda, M. (2004). Physical activity in children attending preschools. *Pediatrics, 114,* 1258–1263.

Patten, E. (2012). *Statistical portrait of the foreign-born population in the United States, 2010.* Pew Research Hispanic Center. Retrieved June 13, 2013, from http://www.pewhispanic.org/2012/02/21/statistical-portrait-of-the-foreign-born-population-in-the-united-states-2010/#sub-menu.

Phillipsen, L. C., Burchinal, M. R., Howes, C., & Cryer, D. (1997). The prediction of process quality from structural features of child care. *Early Childhood Research Quarterly, 12,* 281–303.

Pianta, R. C., LaParo, K. M., & Hamre, B. K. (2008). *Classroom assessment scoring system (CLASS).* Baltimore, MD: Paul H. Brookes.

Poelle, L. (1993). I'll visit your class, you visit mine: Experienced teachers as mentors. In E. Jones (Ed.), *Growing teachers: Partnerships in staff development* (pp. 118–134). Washington, DC: National Association for the Education of Young Children.

Pugach, M. C. (2001, Summer). The stories we choose to tell: Fulfilling the promise of qualitative research for special education. *Exceptional Children, 67*(4), 439–453.

Raikes, H. H., & Edwards, C. P. (2009). *Extending the dance in infant and toddler caregiving: Enhancing attachment and relationships.* Baltimore, MD: Paul H. Brookes, and Washington, DC: National Association for the Education of Young Children.

Rampersad, H. K. (2001). *Total quality management: An executive guide to continuous improvement.* Berlin: Springer-Verlag.

Ratekin, C., & Bess, G. (1998). Making the partnership stronger—Working with a board of directors. In B. Neugebauer & R. Neugebauer (Eds.). *The art of leadership: Managing early childhood organizations, Volume 1* (pp. 111–114). Redmond, WA: Exchange Press.

Reiling, J. (2008, February 15). *MBWA: Managing by walking around (what it is and what it is not). Project management insights and exchange.* Retrieved August 12, 2009, from http://pmcrunch.com/project_management_process/mbwa-managing-by-walking-around-what-it-is-and-what-it-is-not/.

Reynolds, A. J., Temple, J. A., Suh-Ruu, O., Robertson, D. L., Mersky, J., Topitzes, J. W. & Niles, M. D. (2007, March 30). *Effects of a preschool and school-age intervention on adult health and well being: Evidence from the Chicago Longitudinal Study.* Paper presented at the biennial meeting of the Society for Research in Child Development, Boston, MA. Retrieved November 21, 2013, from http://fcd-us.org/sites/default/files/EffectsOfAPreschoolAndSchoolAgeInterventionReynolds.pdf.

Rich, D. (2008). *Megaskills: Building our children's character and achievement for school and life.* Chicago, IL: Sourcebooks.

Rinaldi, C. (1994). Staff development in Reggio Emilia. In L. Katz & B. Cesarone (Eds.), *Reflections on the Reggio Emilia approach* (pp. 55–60). Urbana, IL: ERIC Clearinghouse on Elementary and Early Childhood Education.

Rinaldi, C. (2001), Documentation and assessment: What is the relationship? In C. Giudici, C. Rinaldi, & M. Krechevsky (Editorial Coordinators), *Making learning visible: Children as individual and group learners* (pp. 78–89). Cambridge, MA: Project Zero, Harvard Graduate School of Education, and Reggio Emilia, Italy: Reggio Children.

Rose, E. (1999). *A mother's job: The history of day care 1890–1960.* New York, NY: Oxford University Press.

Rous, B. (1994). Perspectives of teachers about instructional supervision and behaviors that influence preschool instruction. *Journal of Early Intervention, 26*(4), 266–283.

Ruopp, R., Travers, J., Glantz, F., & Coelen, C. (1979). *Children at the center: Final report of the National Day Care Study* (Vol. 1). Washington, DC: Department of Health, Education, and Welfare.

Russell, S., & Rogers, J. (2005 March/April). T.E.A.C.H. Early Childhood: Providing strategies and solutions for the early childhood workforce. *Child Care Information Exchange, 162,* 69–73.

Saffir, L. (2000). *Power public relations: How to master the new PR* (2nd ed.). Lincolnwood, IL: NTC Business Books.

Sandall, S., Hemmeter, M. L., Smith, B. J., & McLean, M. E. (Eds.). (2005). *DEC recommended practices: A comprehensive guide.* Longmont, CA: Sopris, and Missoula, MT: DEC.

Sandberg, S. (2013). *Lean in: Women, work, and the will to lead.* New York, NY: Alfred A. Knopf.

Sanders, R. (2008, December 2). EEGs show brain differences between poor and rich kids. *UCBerkeley News.* Retrieved June 5, 2009, from http://berkeley.edu/news/media/releases/2008/12/02_cortex.shtml.

Sanford, A. R., Zelman, J. G., Hardin, B. J., & Peisner-Feinberg, E. (2004). *Learning accomplishments profile (LAP-3).* Lewisville, NC: Kaplan Early Learning Company.

Scheinfeld, D. R., Haigh, K. M., & Scheinfeld, J. P. (2008). *We are all explorers: Learning and teaching with Reggio principles in urban settings.* New York, NY: Teachers College Press.

Schickedanz, J. A. (2008). *Increasing the power of instruction: Integration of language, literacy, and math across the preschool day.* Washington, DC: National Association for the Education of Young Children.

Schon, B. (1998). Promoting your center with advertisements. In B. Neugebauer & R. Neugebauer (Eds.), *The art of leadership: Managing early childhood organizations* (pp. 336–337). Redmond, WA: Exchange Press.

Schon, B., & Neugebauer, R. (1998). Marketing strategies that work in child care. In B. Neugebauer & R. Neugebauer (Eds.), *The art of leadership: Managing early childhood organizations* (pp. 324–328). Redmond, WA: Exchange Press.

Schumacher, R. B., & Carlson, R. S. (1999). Variables and risk factors associated with child abuse in day care settings. *Child Abuse & Neglect, 23*(9), 891–898.

Scott-Little, C., Kagan, S. L., & Frelow, V. S. (2005, March). *Inside the content: The breadth and depth of early learning standards.* Greensboro, NC: SERVE. Available online at http://www.serve.org/downloads/publications/insidecontentfr.pdf.

Seibert, K. W., & Daudelin, M. W. (1999). *The role of reflection in managerial learning: Theory, research, and practice.* Westport, CT: Quorum Books.

Senge, P. M. (2006). *The fifth discipline: The art and practice of the learning organization* (rev. ed.). New York, NY: Doubleday.

Seplocha, H. (2004, September). "We": The most important feature of a parent-teacher conference. *Young Children, 59*(5), 98.

Shareef, I., & Gonzalez-Mena, J. (1997, May/June). Training and staff development in early childhood education: Beneath the veneers of resistance and professionalism. *Child Care Information Exchange, 115,* 6–8.

Shellenbarger, S. (2001, September 26). Quality child care protected kids caught in terrorist attacks. *New York Times,* p. B1.

Shonkoff, J. P., & Phillips, D. A. (2000, April/May). From neurons to neighborhoods: The science of early childhood development—an introduction. *Zero to Three, 21*(5), 4–8.

Smith, K. (2000). *Who's minding the kids? Child care arrangements: Fall 1995.* U.S. Census Bureau, Current Population Reports, Series P70-70. Washington, DC: U.S. Government Printing Office.

Smith, M. W., Brady, J. P., & Anastasopoulos, L. (2008). *Early language and literacy classroom observation tool (ELLCO).* Baltimore, MD: Paul H. Brookes.

Sosinsky, L. S., Lord, H., & Zigler, E. (2007). For-profit/nonprofit differences in center-based child care quality: Results from the national institute of child health and human development study of early child care and youth development. *Journal of Applied Developmental Psychology, 28*(5–6), 390–410.

Squires, J., & Bricker, D. (2009). *Ages and stages questionnaire (ASQ-3).* Baltimore, MD: Paul H. Brookes.

Staley, C. C., Ranck, E. R., Perrault, J., & Neugebauer, R. (1986, January). Guidelines for effective staff selection. *Child Care Information Exchange, 47,* 23.

Stelzner, M. A. (2013). *2013 social media marketing industry report: How marketers are using social media to grow their businesses.* Social Media Examiner. Available online at http://www.socialmediaexaminer.com/report/.

Stephens, K. (1998). Courting the media with special events. In B. Neugebauer & R. Neugebauer (Eds.), *The art of leadership: Managing early childhood organizations* (pp. 340–344). Redmond, WA: Exchange Press.

Stonehouse, A., & Gonzalez-Mena, J. (2006, March/April). Crossing lines in parent relationships: Perception, reality, ethics, and need. *Exchange, 168,* 10–12.

Talan, T. N., & Bloom, P. J. (2004). *Program administration scale: Measuring early childhood leadership and management.* New York, NY: Teachers College Press.

Talan, T. N., & Bloom, P. J. (2009). *Business administration scale for family child care.* New York, NY: Teachers College Press.

Taylor, A. F., & Kuo, F. E. (2009). Children with attention deficits concentrate better after walk in the park. *Journal of Attention Disorders, 12*(5), 402–409.

Tobin, J., Hsueh, Y. & Karasawa, M. (2009). *Preschool in three cultures.* Chicago, IL: University of Chicago Press.

Topal, C. W., & Gandini, L. (1999). *Beautiful stuff: Learning with found materials.* Worcester, MA: Davis Publications.

Travis, N. E., & Perreault, J. (1981). *The effective day care director: A discussion of the role and its responsibilities.* Atlanta, GA: Save the Children, Inc.

U.S. Census Bureau (2005). *Who's minding the kids? Child care arrangements Spring 2005.* http://www.census.gov/population/www/socdemo/childcare.html.

U.S. Census Bureau. (2013). *Who's minding the kids? Child care arrangements: Spring 2011.* Retrieved June 29, 2013, from http://www.census.gov/prod/2013pubs/p70-135.pdf.

U.S. Consumer Product Safety Commission. (2008). *Public playground safety handbook.* Bethesda, MD: Author. Available online at http://www.cpsc.gov/cpscpub/pubs/325.pdf.

U.S. Department of Agriculture Food Safety and Inspection Service. (2013). *Salmonella questions and answers.* Retrieved December 1, 2013, from http://www.fsis.usda.gov/wps/portal/fsis/topics/food-safety-education/get-answers/food-safety-fact-sheets/foodborne-illness-and-disease/salmonella-questions-and-answers/CT_Index.

U.S. Department of Education, National Center for Education Statistics. (2007). *The condition of education 2007.* Retrieved June 4, 2009, from http://nces.ed.gov/fastfacts/display.asp?id=78.

U.S. Department of Health and Human Services. (2011). *Connecting kids to coverage: Steady growth, new innovation. 2011 CHIPRA annual report.* Retrieved July 7, 2013, from http://insurekidsnow.gov/chipraannualreport.pdf.

U.S. Department of Health and Human Services, Administration for Children and Families. (2008). *About TANF.* Retrieved June 10, 2009, from http://www.acf.hhs.gov/programs/ofa/tanf/about.html.

U.S. Department of Labor, Bureau of Labor Statistics. (2011). *Employment characteristics of families—2011.* Retrieved June 13, 2013, from http://www.bls.gov/news.release/famee.nr0.htm.

U.S. Department of Labor, Bureau of Labor Statistics. (2012). *Women in the labor force: A databook.* Retrieved June 13, 2013, from http://www.bls.gov/cps/wlf-databook-2011.pdf.

U.S. Global Change Research Program. (2009). *Global climate change: Impacts in the United States.* Retrieved June 22, 2009, from http://www.globalchange.gov.

U.S. Green Building Council. (2007). *LEED for schools.* Retrieved July 20, 2009, from http://www.usgbc.org/DisplayPage.aspx?CMSPageID=1586.

U.S. Office of Personnel Management. (2007). *Delegated examining operations handbook: A guide for the federal agency examining offices.* Retrieved July 8, 2009, from http://www.opm.gov/deu/Handbook_2007/DEO_Handbook.pdf.

VanderVen, K. (1999). The dual functions of director competencies and leadership: A model for early childhood teacher education. *Journal of Early Childhood Teacher Education, 20*(2), 193–199.

Vicars, D. (2007, November/December). Always recruiting, always interviewing, and always prepared to hire! *Exchange, 178,* 84.

Vicars, D. (2009, July/August). The $17 investment. *Exchange, 188,* 18–19.

Vu, J. A., Jeon, H-J., Howes, C. (2008). Formal education, credential, or both: Early childhood program practices. *Early Education and Development, 19*(3), 479–504.

Wagner, J. (2000). A model of aesthetic value in the servicescape. In T. A. Swartz & D. Iacobucci (Eds.), *Handbook of services marketing and management* (pp. 69–85). Thousand Oaks, CA: Sage Publications.

Walker, T., & Donohue, C. (2005, January/February). Decoding technology: Program management tools. *Child Care Information Exchange, 161,* 33–36.

Warner, M., Anderson, K., & Haddow, G. (2007). Putting child care in the picture: Why this service is a critical part of community infrastructure. *Planning, 73*(6), 16–19.

Wassom, J. (2001, May/June). Community marketing made easy. *Child Care Information Exchange, 139*, 18–20.

Wassom, J. (2004, March/April). Do they see what you see? *Exchange, 158*, 6–9.

Wassom, J. (2006, March/April). Know me or no me—Finding your best prospects for enrollment. *Exchange, 168*, 14–16.

Wenner, M. (2009, February). The serious need for play. *Scientific American Mind, 20*(1), 22–29. Retrieved July 28, 2009, from http://www.scientificamerican.com/article.cfm?id=the-serious-need-for-play.

West, N. T., & Albrecht, K. (2007, May/June). Building emotional competence: A strategy for disaster preparation and recovery. *Exchange, 175*, 20–27.

White, R. & Stoecklin, V. (2003). The great 35 square foot myth. Kansas City, MO: White Hutchinson Leasure & Learning Group. Retrieved from http://www.white-hutchinson.com/children/articles/35footmyth.shtml.

Whitebook, M., & Bellm, D. (1999) *Taking on turnover: An action guide for child care center teachers and directors.* Washington, DC: Center for the Child Care Workforce.

Whitebook, M., Gomby, D., Bellm, D., Sakai, L., & Kipnis, F. (2009). *Preparing teachers of young children: The current state of knowledge, and a blueprint for the future. Executive Summary.* Berkeley, CA: Center for the Study of Child Care Employment, Institute for Research on Labor and Employment, University of California at Berkeley. Retrieved July 29, 2009, from http://www.irle.berkeley.edu/cscce/pdf/teacher_prep_summary.pdf.

Willer, B. (Ed.) (1990). *Reaching the full cost of quality in early childhood programs.* Washington, DC: National Association for the Education of Young Children.

Xavier, S. (2005). Are you at the top of your game? Checklist for effective leaders [Electronic Version]. *Journal of Business Strategy, 26*(3), 35–42.

Yaven, L. (2005). *Documentation, assessment, and the digital: Teaching interpretation in design education.* Retrieved August 17, 2005, from http://futurehistory.aiga.org/resources/content/2/2/6/8/documents/l_yaven.pdf.

Zeece, P. D. (1998). Power lines—The use and abuse of power in child care programming. In B. Neugebauer & R. Neugebauer (Eds.), *The art of leadership: Managing early childhood organizations* (pp. 29–33). Redmond, WA: Exchange Press.

Zigler, E. F., & Lang, M. E. (1991). *Child care choices: Balancing the needs of children, families, and society.* New York, NY: The Free Press.

INDEX